Butterflies & Barbarians
Swiss Missionaries & Systems of Knowledge in South-East Africa

Books on Southern Africa
published by James Currey, Weaver Press
& Ohio University Press

Jocelyn Alexander
The Unsettled Land
State-making &
the Politics of Land
in Zimbabwe
1893–2003

David Maxwell
*African Gifts
of the Spirit*
Pentecostalism
& the Rise of a Zimbabwean
Transnational Religious Movement

Patrick Harries
Butterflies & Barbarians
Swiss Missionaries
& Systems of Knowledge
in South-East Africa

Overleaf: *Henri-Alexandre Junod hunting butterflies on the escarpment near Shiluvane (© Swiss Mission Archive, Lausanne)*

Butterflies & Barbarians
Swiss Missionaries & Systems of Knowledge in South-East Africa

PATRICK HARRIES
Professor of History
University of Basel

James Currey
OXFORD

Weaver Press
HARARE

Wits University Press
JOHANNESBURG

Ohio University Press
ATHENS

James Currey Ltd
73 Botley Road
Oxford OX2 0BS

Ohio University Press
19 Circle Drive, The Ridges
Athens, Ohio 45701

Weaver Press
Box A1922
Avondale, Harare

Wits University Press
University of the Witwatersrand
1 Jan Smuts Avenue
Johannesburg 2001

Copyright © Patrick Harries 2007
First published 2007

1 2 3 4 5 11 10 09 08 07

British Library Cataloguing in Publication Data

Harries, Patrick
Butterflies & barbarians: Swiss missionaries & systems of knowledge in South-East Africa
1. Junod, Henri-Alexandre, 1863–1934 2. Missionaries – Africa, Southern 3. Missionaries – Switzerland 4. Africa, Southern – Discovery and exploration
I. Title
266'.023494068

ISBN 978-0-85255-984-0 (James Currey cloth)
ISBN 978-0-85255-983-3 (James Currey paper)

**Library of Congress Cataloging-in-Publication Data
available upon request**

ISBN 978-0-8214-1776-8 (Ohio University Press cloth)
ISBN 0-8214-1776-2 (Ohio University Press cloth)
ISBN 978-0-8214-1777-5 (Ohio University Press paper)
ISBN 0-8214-1777-0 (Ohio University Press paper)

ISBN 978-1-77922-064-6 (Weaver Press paper)

ISBN 978-1-86814-448-8 (Wits University Press paper)

Typeset in 10.5/11.5 Monotype Ehrhardt
by Frances Marks, Harare
Printed in Malaysia

*In memory of
Carlo Schlettwein
Sylvestre Vautier
Albert Wirz*

Contents

List of Maps and Figures	xi
Chapter Openings	xii
Acknowledgements	xiii
Colour Plates between	xvi and xvii

Introduction — 1

1
Switzerland — 10
Evangelism and Identity	11
Political Revolution and Religious Change	16
The Independent Church of Neuchâtel	22
Missionary Origins	27

2
African Itineraries & Swiss Identities — 35
Africa Comes to Switzerland	35
African Images and Swiss Identities	39
Europe's Past in Africa's Present	44
Africa in Switzerland	50

3
Christianity — 67
Native Christianity or the Limits of Tolerance	68
Mission Christianity	80
Economic Development and Evangelical Expansion	86

4
Landscape — 96
Landscape and Identity: Switzerland	97
The African Landscape	101
Landscape and Society	109
Creating a Sense of Place: Cartography	113

5
Natural Sciences — 123
Collecting in Switzerland — 124
Science in Support of Religion — 125
African Adventures in Taxonomy — 131
Social Evolution and Natural Imperialism — 140

6
Language — 155
Defining a Written Language — 157
Adapting Borders: Classification — 162
Language and Structures of Power — 165
Adapting Borders: the Ronga Language — 169

7
Literacy — 182
Reading in western Switzerland — 182
The Transformative Powers of the Word — 184
Literacy as a Local Skill — 189
Ways of Reading — 193
Literacy and Politics — 200

8
Anthropology — 206
New Knowledge — 206
Anthropology and the Scientific Method — 216
Salvage Anthropology — 219
Evolutionism — 228
Race and Politics — 234

9
Politics — 246
Anthropology and Social Change — 249
Bantu Heritage and History — 254

Conclusion — 261

Bibliography — 266
Index — 280

List of Maps & Figures

Maps

1	Western Switzerland	xiv
2	Delagoa Bay and Hinterland	xv

Figures

2.1 (a) A popular image in missionary literature portrayed Africans as victims of the slave trade. (b) Several generations of Sunday school children followed Fritz Ramseyer's account, written in the early 1870s, of his captivity in the Asante kingdom. This illustration of the king's executioners was published in a wide range of missionary periodicals. — 41

2.2 Fund-raising was a crucial aspect of missionary activity: the 'thank you' box was redesigned to take the shape of an African hut and the '*tirelire à nègre*' is still to be found in a few parishes. — 43

2.3 The Swiss missionaries took pride in the size of their mission field. This map, published in 1893, showed their field of operations to be far larger than Switzerland. — 56

2.4 Mission propaganda often featured 'before' and 'after' images. One flyer contrasts a 'witchdoctor' with a 'native pastor' (Calvin Matsivi Mapopé), another contrasts a young man 'still pagan!' with a group of industrious 'future primary school teachers'. — 59

3.1 Yosefa Mhalamhala and Zebedee Mbenyane, early converts. — 72

4.1 Swiss missionaries started to photograph the environment in 1884. In this picture, taken north of Pretoria, human figures are lost in an empty veld and dwarfed by an engulfing sky. — 108

5.1 Henri-Alexandre Junod hunting butterflies on the escarpment near Shiluvane. — 134

5.2 African collectors provided Junod with a range of plants and insects. — 136

5.3 Butterfly and insect trays. — 139

6.1 Henri-Alexandre Junod and Henri Berthoud. — 174

7.1 Jim, Paulus and Philemon Ximungana. — 199

8.1 Left out of this illustration of 'Thonga weapons' is the most common weapon of all by the 1890s: the second-hand or remaindered European gun. — 226

8.2 (a) The diviner Hokoza and his assistants. (b) The diviner and his Swiss visitors. — 227

8.3 (a) Photograph of Ntchoungi, a Khosa sub-chief, leaning against a chair of European manufacture. In the illustration (b) taken from the photograph, the chair has been removed. — 229

9.1 Calvin Matsivi Mapopé and Henri-Alexandre Junod. — 248

Chapter Openings

Henri-Alexander Junod's beetles, used as chapter openings,
are from the Transvaal Museum, Coleoptera collection.
Specimens were selected by its curator Mr James du Guesclin Harrison,
and the digital images were taken and processed by Mr Dries Marais
(20 February 2006):

Chapter 1
File PA5720, Fam. Cerambycidae, Genus Oxyprosopus, Spec. junodi

Chapter 2
File PA5721, Fam. Cerambycidae, Genus Hypsideroides, Spec. junodi

Chapter 3
File PA5722, Fam. Cerambycidae, Genus Peleconus, Spec. junodi

Chapter 4
File PA5723, Fam. Cerambycidae, Genus Phantasis, Spec. carinatus

Chapter 5
File PA5725, Fam. Cerambycidae, Genus Monochamus, Spec. leuconotus

Chapter 6
File PA5727, Fam. Cerambycidae, Genus Prosopocera, Spec. lactator

Chapter 7
File PA5728, Fam. Staphylinidae, Genus Paederus, Spec. junodi

Chapter 8
File PA5730, Fam. Cerambycidae, Genus Tetralux, Spec. junodi

Chapter 9
File PA 5731, Fam. Cerambycidae, Genus Saphronica, Spec. junodi

Acknowledgements

Swiss history has had a bad press. Flaubert thought Switzerland had no real history and that the country was only good for 'botanists, geologists and honeymooners'. Harry Lime commented famously, in Graham Greene's film version of *The Third Man*, that 500 years of democracy and peace in Switzerland had produced only the cuckoo clock. And with some irony, Jonathan Steinberg entitled his classic work on the subject *Why Switzerland?* (Cambridge, 1976, 1996). My own encounter with the history of western Switzerland started thirty years ago when, as a young South African, I began to work in the superb archives of the Swiss Mission in Lausanne. At that stage I was interested in missionaries merely as observers of the changes brought to life in southern Mozambique by the mining revolution. However, my interest soon spread to the ways in which missionaries made sense of their African world – and this inevitably drew me into their lives in Switzerland.

Along the way I gathered debts to various institutions and individuals. These started with a fellowship from the Federal Commission for Scholarships for Foreign Students in Bern (FCS). In Lausanne my father-in-law's library (built on that of his father and grandfather) gave me access to the mysterious history of the canton of Vaud. In Basel I found homes in both the archives of the Basel Mission and in the library of the Basler Afrika Bibliographien (BAB). I started the research for this book in the History department of the University of Cape Town and finished it in the History department of the University of Basel. En route I spent a semester at the University of Wisconsin, Madison. I owe a debt of gratitude to the members of all these departments but especially to Nigel Penn, Florence Bernault, Georg Kreis and Regina Wecker. Dag Henrichsen and Giorgio Miescher turned the BAB into an intellectual home in Basel, while Paul Jenkins and Guy Thomas generously introduced me to the literary treasures of the Basel Mission. Terence Ranger, Jean and John Comaroff inspired much of what is best in this book. David Birmingham initiated and inspired a two-way traffic of ideas between Switzerland and Africa. Nor would this book have been possible without the help of a younger generation of scholars in Switzerland, particularly Veit Arlt, Didier Péclard, Eric Morier-Genoud and Nicolas Monnier. Susan Newton-King and Patricia Davison kept me aware of my roots in Cape Town. Hugh Robertson at the Iziko South African Museum, John Manning at Kirstenbosch, James Harrison at the Transvaal Museum, Pat Lorber at the Bolus Herbarium and Christian Dufour of the Natural History Museum in Neuchâtel all did their best to conduct me through the intricacies of the natural sciences. Theo Schneider and Mary Bill helped with the linguistics and Roland Kaehr opened the collections of the Ethnographic Museum in Neuchâtel. Many years ago Robert Thornton drew my attention to the historical aspects of the field of Anthropology. My most tenacious guide to the geography and culture of western Switzerland remains Isabelle Vautier.

Finally, I gratefully acknowledge the financial support of the Schlettwein Foundation in Basel and the Société academique vaudoise in Lausanne, together with the universities of Cape Town and Basel. I hope the transcontinental approach of this book will receive the approbation of these friends, colleagues and institutions. Its faults remain the responsibility of the author.

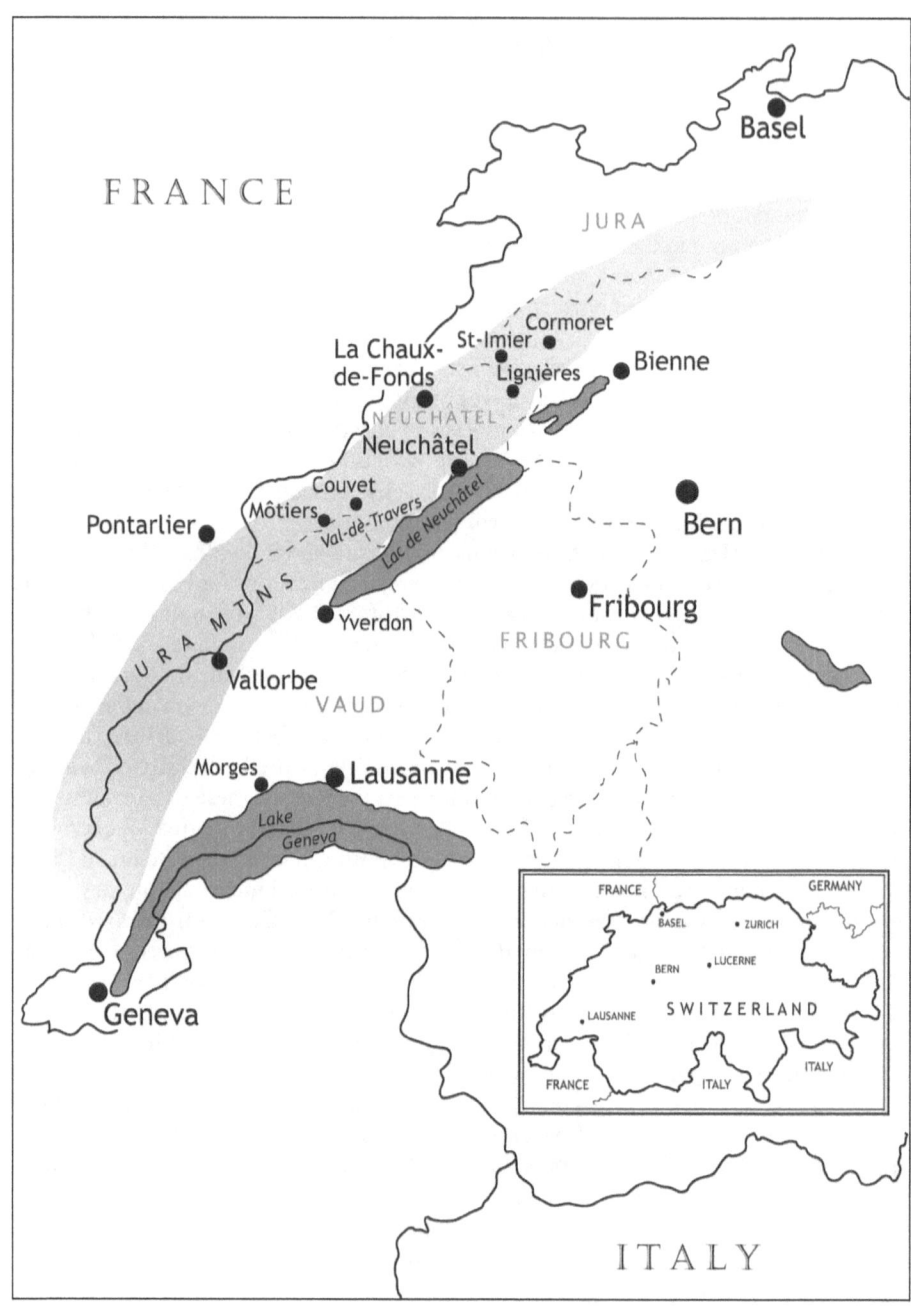

Map 1 Western Switzerland

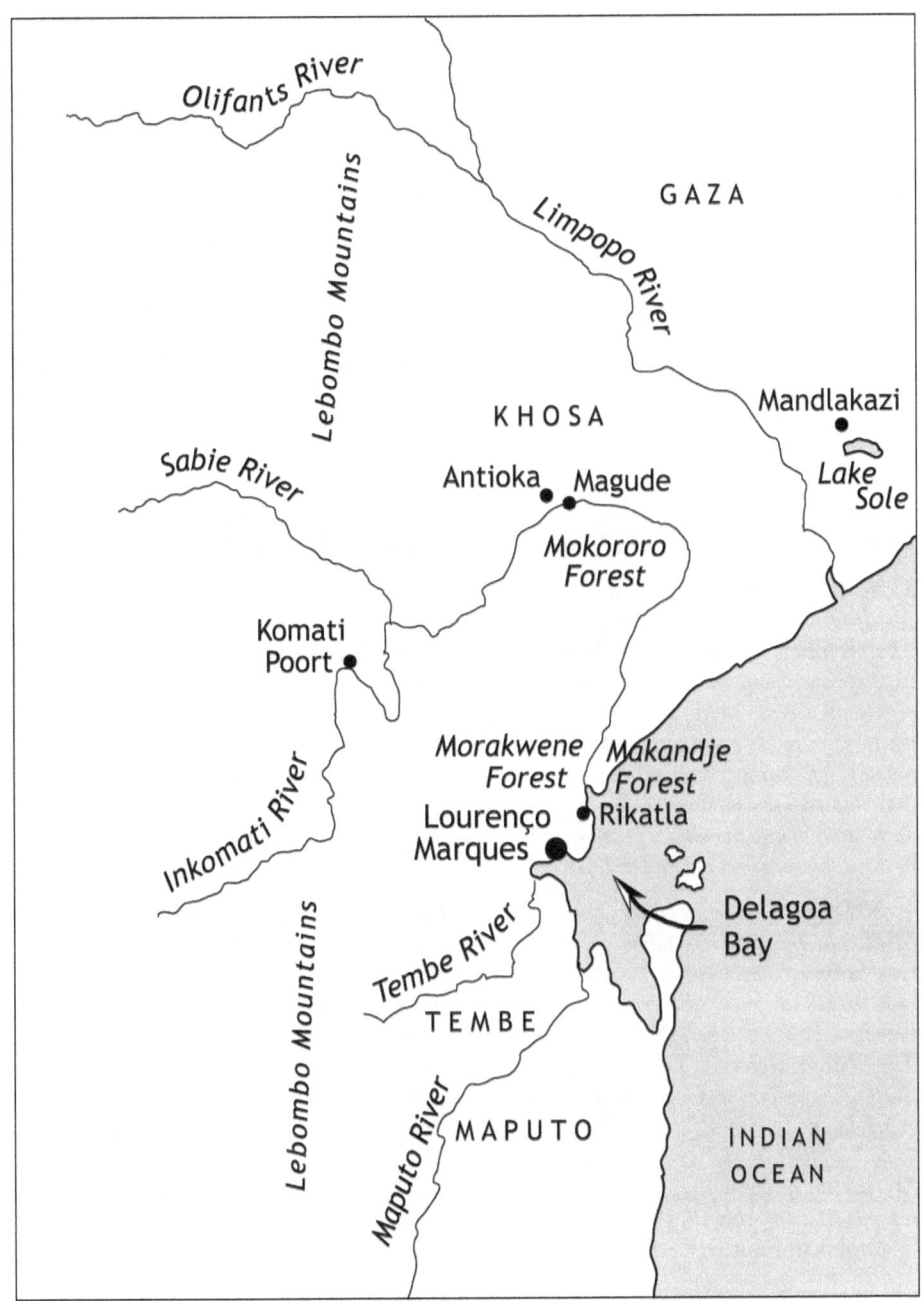

Map 2 Delagoa Bay and Hinterland

Colour Plates

1. *The Mission employed various media to publicize its message and to raise funds for its endeavours. This postcard brought the mission in Africa and Europe into a single, visible space in which the supporters of the mission fête at Morges on Lake Geneva in 1909 were linked to the community at Valdezia in the northern Transvaal. Swiss Mission Archive, Lausanne.*

2. *Henri-Alexandre Junod, 'Map of the Thonga tribe showing the different groups of clans'. Cartographers become the classifiers of the geographical world when, as in this map, they draw sharp lines where none existed previously. Borders between languages or ethnic groups, like those dividing species and genera of plants and animals, depend on the scientific authority of the person who defines them. Yet the vivid categories they create are often a pragmatic response to given situations. Unlike species and genera in the natural world, once linguistic or ethnic groups are created they may take on a life of their own as people come to see them as resources on which to build new social communities. (Junod,* The Life of a South African Tribe *(London, 1927) I, p.17). See p. 218 below.*

3. *Henri Berthoud's map of the Zoutpansberg, 1903. Maps such as this one condensed an engulfing landscape into the manageable proportions of a single representation on paper. The profusion of red lines on the map reinforces Berthoud's authority as a cartographer as they document the routes he has taken between 1881 and 1898. Parallel black lines represent wagon routes that meet and diverge at mission stations and at the homes of white settlers. Blue rivers and shaded brown mountains reduce 'unexplored ranges' to the top left-hand corner of the map. Clear lines of longitude and latitude divide space into ordered proportions. The busy European presence fills the land with energy and animation, while the names given to geographical features and human settlements contribute to the domestication of the land. See p. 115.*

4. *In 1893 Henri-Alexandre Junod discovered a new gladiolus at Howick in the Natal Midlands. By this time missionaries in Mozambique habitually spent the deadly summer months in upland areas in Lesotho and Natal. Junod saw these occasions as opportunities to botanize unexplored terrains. He sent a specimen of this plant to the Royal Botanical Gardens at Kew where John Gilbert Baker described it as Gladiolus junodii in 1901. The British collector Thomas Cooper had found a similar plant in the Orange Free State that, after he sent it to Kew in 1862, was named Gladiolus crassifolius fourteen years later. The small differences between the two species of gladiolus eventually caused Junod's plant to be synonymized within the earlier category: Gladiolus crassifolius. My thanks to the artist, Auriol Batten, and the author, John Manning, for allowing the reproduction of this illustration first published in Pieter Goldblatt and John Manning,* Gladiolus in Southern Africa *(Vlaeberg, South Africa, 1998). See p. 133 below.*

(Captions for Colour Plates 5 to 8 on page xvii)

Souvenir de la Fête Vaudoise de la Mission romande
à Morges le 14 Septembre 1909

Chapelle de Valdézia

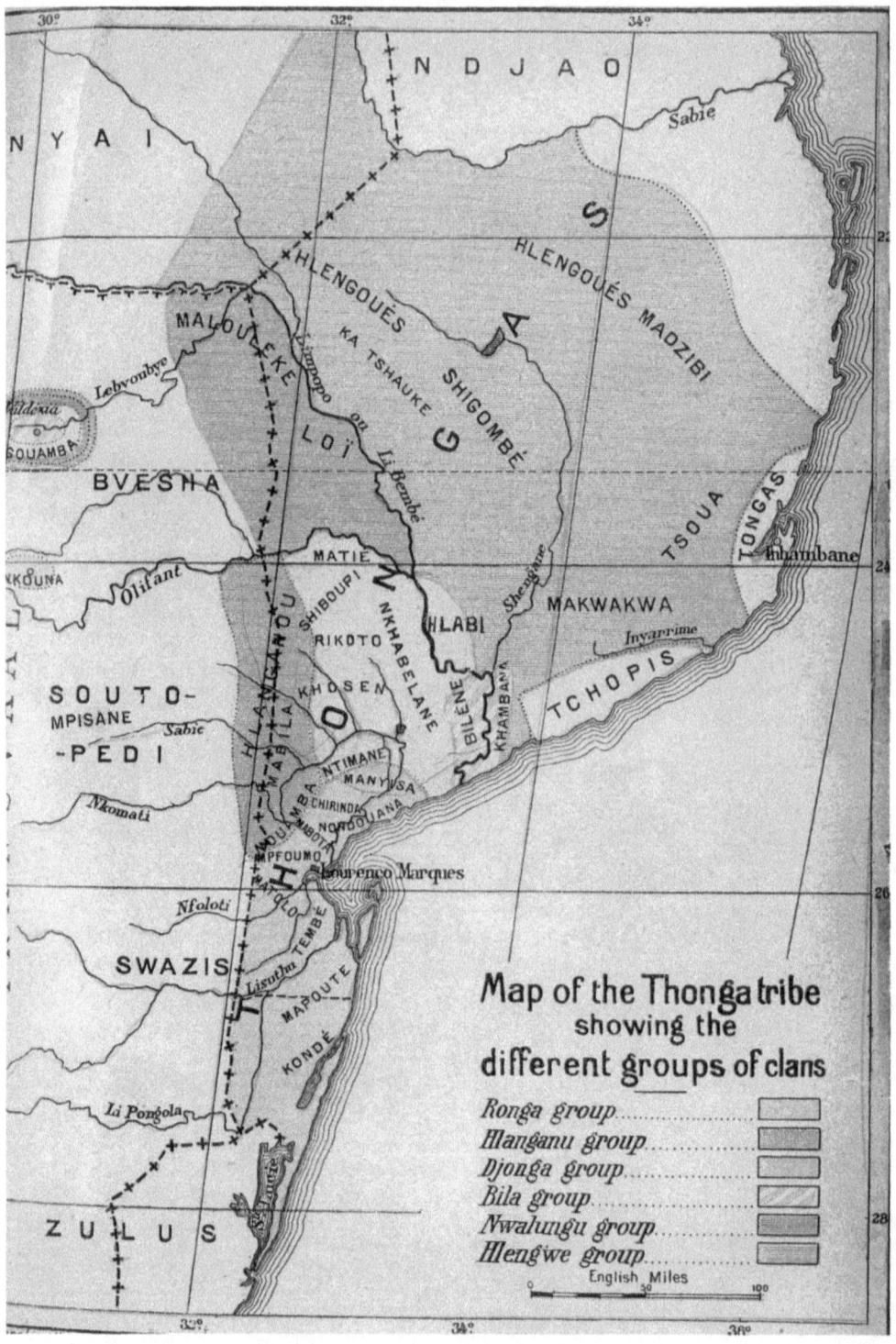

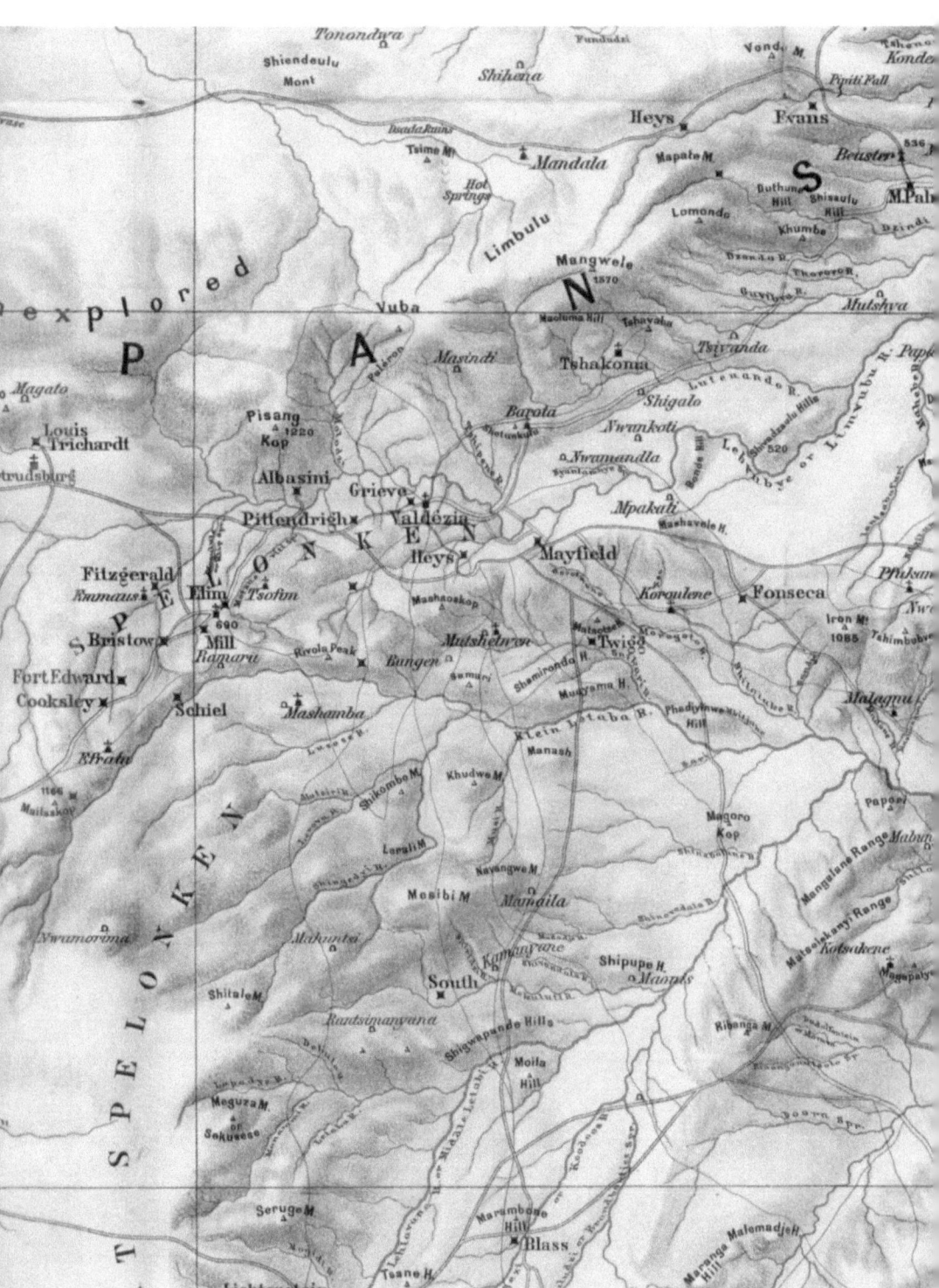

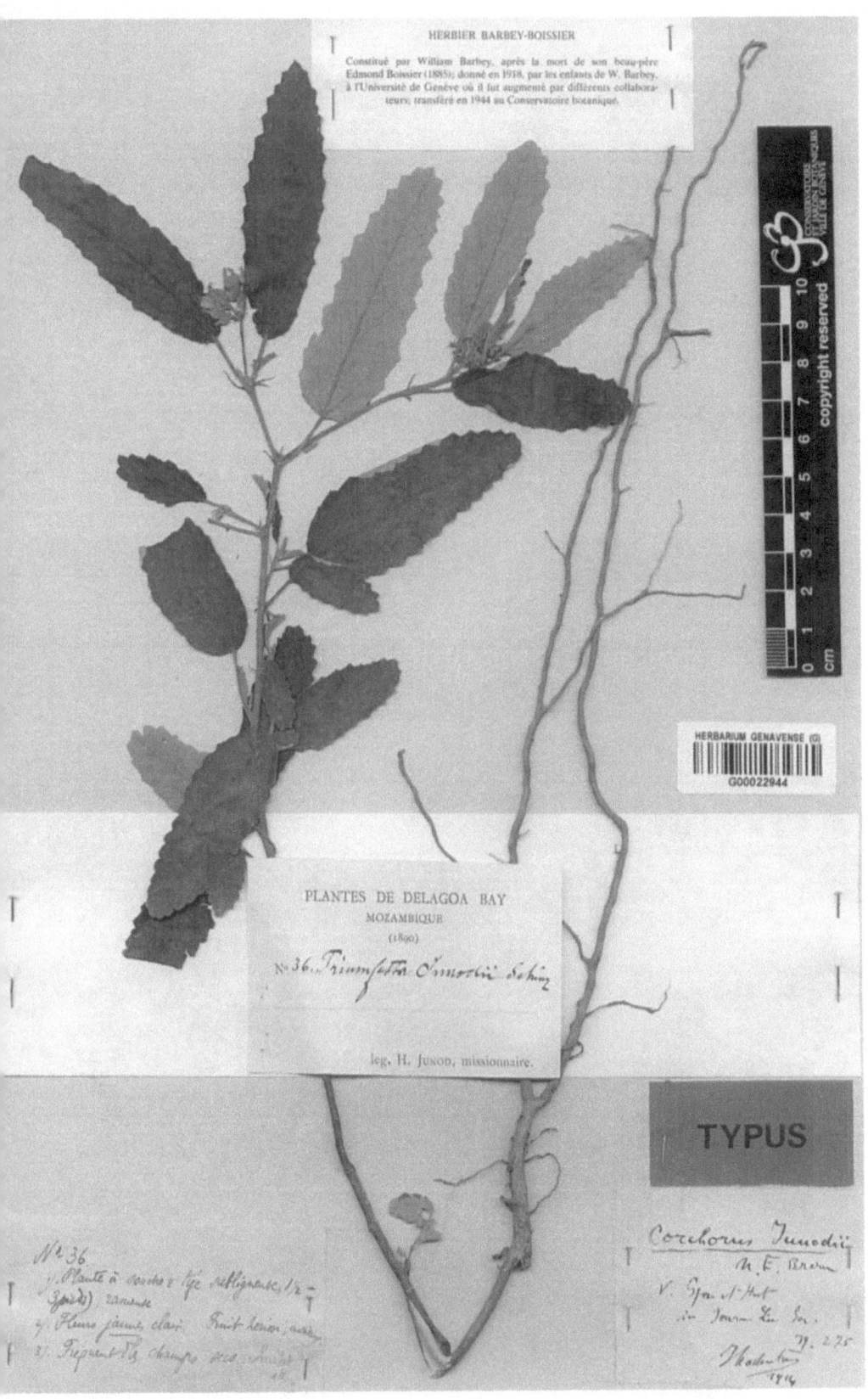

6a 6b

INS. TRANSVAALIENSIA. TAB. XVI.

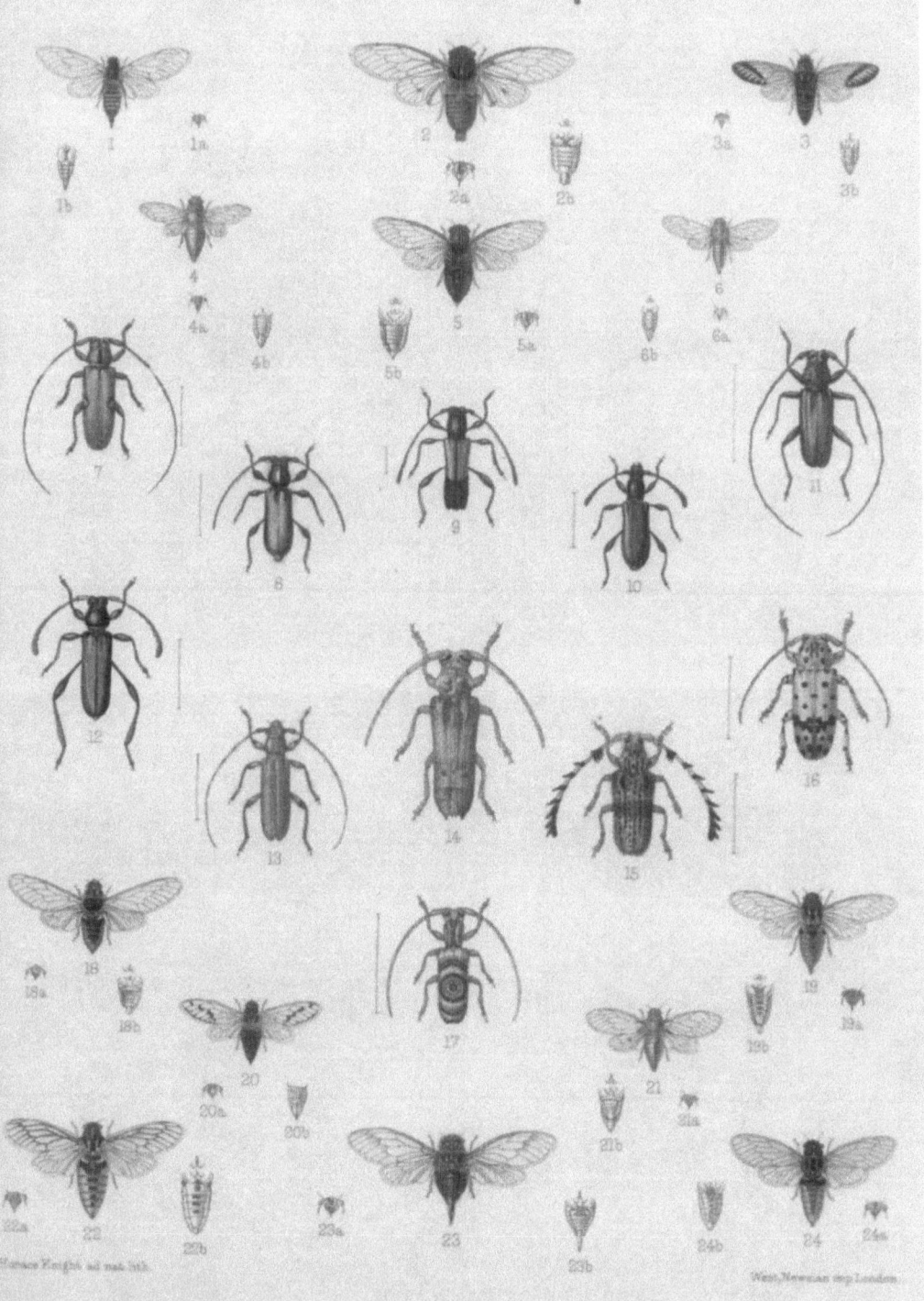

5. Triumfetta junodii *Schinz, Boissier Herbarium, Geneva. Henri-Alexandre Junod discovered this plant in 1890, shortly after his arrival in the Delagoa Bay area. He sent it to William Barbey at the Boissier Herbarium in Geneva who had it determined by the botanist Hans Schinz. It is plant no. 36 in the Herbarium's collection of Junod's dried and pressed plants. The red ticket indicates that this example of the plant stands as the type for the species. The card on the lower left-hand side describes the plant as a small bush with a light-yellow flower and reddish fruit that is frequently found in dry areas. The card on the lower right-hand side indicates that the plant was synonymized with a similar species,* Corchorus junodii *N. E. Brown and described in an article in the* Journal of the Linnean Society 39, 1914, p. 275. *See p. 132 below.*

6. (a) *Junod's Swordtail. In 1891 one of Junod's assistants brought him a large, fast-flying butterfly. The man had caught the insect in the Morakwene forest on the Nkomati River and Junod quickly sent the magnificent specimen to Roland Trimen, the entomologist who served as director of the South African Museum in Cape Town. In 1893 Trimen described the butterfly as a new species and gave it the name* Papilio junodi *(a 'Swallowtail'). The butterfly was later reclassified in the genus* Graphium *and is today known as* Graphium junodi *(Trimen, 1893). Its common name is 'Junod's Swordtail'. This photograph shows the original specimen sent by Junod to Trimen. Iziko South African Museum, Cape Town.*
(b) Paralethe dendrophilis junodi *(Van Son). See pp. 134–5.*

7. *Henri-Alexandre Junod's beetles. Junod collected these coleoptera in the eastern and northern Transvaal and sold them to Walter Rothschild's Tring Museum. They include several beetles classified at the time as flat-faced longhorns (*Lamiinae*):* Peloconus junodi *(fig. 14),* Freadelpha junodi *(fig. 16) and* Hypsideres junodi *(fig. 17). (W. L. Distant,* Insecta Transvaaliensia: A Contribution to the Entomology of South Africa *(London, 1924) pp. 161-3, 229). See p. 135 below.*

8. (a) Augacephalus junodii. *Junod found this 'baboon' spider or tarantula near Shiluvane at the start of the twentieth century. It remains a prized specimen for any arachnophile.*
(b) *Panther devouring an Englishman. Many Europeans came to admire African art in the last decades of the nineteenth century. Henri-Alexandre Junod particularly admired this wooden sculpture of a panther devouring an Englishman made in the Lourenço Marques area by Mouhlati in about 1896. Junod considered it 'absolutely original ... the most beautiful object of native art I have ever seen' and sent it to the Ethnographic Museum in Neuchâtel. This opinion seems exaggerated today as the sculpture was almost certainly inspired by the famous Tippu's Tiger in the Victoria and Albert Museum, London. The original belonged to sultan Tippoo of Mysore and represented a tiger devouring an English soldier. It was carried to London after the English East India Company seized his capital in 1799. It was originally housed in the museum of the East India Company where it became a firm favourite with the public. Over the years the sculpture was reproduced in many forms for the growing tourist market, including the version shown here. See Junod, 'Les Ba-Ronga: étude ethnographique sur les indigènes de la baie de Delagoa',* Bulletin de la société neuchâteloise de geographie *X, 1898, pp. 236-7; Roland Kaehr, 'Léopard dévorant un Anglais',* Bibliothèques et Musées *1990 (Neuchâtel), pp. 105-7. Museum of Ethnography, Neuchâtel. Photo: Alain Germond. (a) See p. 135; (b) see pp. 52–3 below.*

Introduction

In 1936 the anthropologist Max Gluckman reached the top of the low range of mountains separating the north-western edge of KwaZulu-Natal from southern Mozambique. As he looked down from the Lebombos onto the coastal plain, Gluckman raised his hat in tribute to a Swiss missionary whose anthropological work in the region had laid the foundations of the discipline in South Africa.[1] Henri-Alexandre Junod had died two years earlier in Geneva and his ashes were interred at Rikatla near the graves of his infant son Henri-Alexis, his second wife, Hélène Kern and Paul Berthoud, one of the founders of his Mission. At Shiluvane, in the Lowveld to the west of the Lebombos, lay the graves of Junod's first wife, Emily Biolley and the remains of their unborn child, as well as that of Helen Kern's infant daughter Eveline. In fact the graves of Junod's colleagues and their companions marked his entire area of fieldwork, from the foothills of the Zoutpansberg down to the coastal plain south of the Limpopo river.

The young Gluckman was unaware of these grim reminders of the high price of early missionary anthropology, nor was he aware of the collective intellectual enterprise that had supported Junod's anthropological work. Gluckman's teachers had established anthropology as a professional discipline in South Africa and were increasingly critical of the methodology employed by amateurs like Junod. By the mid-1930s, the importance of missionaries had declined in the field, and they had lost their foothold in the universities. The new university professionals believed that the missionary was unable to look at African societies in an objective and scientific way because of his vocation. Missionaries like Junod had seen themselves as friends of the native; the professional anthropologists increasingly viewed them as part of the problem of change besetting the native and his world. Anthropologists criticized the theory and method employed by missionaries who were unwilling to leave the safety of the verandah; their evolutionist ideas were outdated, unhelpful and increasingly racist in inspiration and effect. In many ways, anthropologists had defined the professional borders of their discipline in opposition to the amateur missionary-in-the field. Although it went unsaid, this figure often challenged the anthropologist, partly because of the missionary's linguistic skills and his knowledge of deep rural communities and partly because he was a real or potential competitor for funds and professional posts.[2]

Although Junod's work inevitably fell out of fashion, it retained the respect of the anthropological profession. In 1951 Evans-Pritchard called his *The Life of a South African Tribe* 'one of the best anthropological monographs ever written'.[3] Fourteen years later Gluckman would still regard this work as 'a classic . . . one of the best books that we have on a single tribe'.[4] In the 1970s-80s, French-speaking structuralists examined Junod's ethnography with a new eye, just as British anthropology sank into a fog of embarrassment over the outdated approaches used by authors like Junod.[5] But even during these difficult years for the British school, Adam Kuper could refer to Junod's monograph as one of its 'magisterial ethnographies'.[6] In 1994 Adrian Hastings called it a 'masterpiece', the finest work produced in Africa before the arrival of professional anthropology.[7] More recently, in perhaps the greatest tribute to the missionary-anthropologist, W.D. Hammond-Tooke used Junod's picture as the frontispiece to his reflection on the history of modern anthropology in South Africa, a place from which the missionary-anthropologist casts a patriarchal gaze on the professional work of subsequent generations.[8]

One of the major themes I pursue in this book is an examination of the factors that predisposed a young theological student from Neuchâtel in Switzerland, the author of an 1885 thesis on 'The Perfect Holiness of Jesus Christ', to become an internationally renowned anthropologist.[9] But this book is not a biography of Junod nor is it a study of his missionary society, a theme that has received the attention of several generations of worthy scholarship.[10] My main concern is to undertake a microstudy of one small missionary society as a site for the construction of knowledge about Africa. In the process I focus on the interaction between the Swiss missionaries and the people who, at least partly under their influence, would come to see themselves as members of the Thonga or Tsonga ethnic group. In this book I am less concerned with capturing subaltern experience than I am with showing how a small group of European intellectuals came to portray Africa and, in the process, to construct an 'African voice'.[11] I look at how their ideas were shaped and ordered by their social origins and interests in Europe and by the context of the times in which they lived; how these ideas changed through contact with a richly eclectic variety of traditions in the growing fields of missiology, the natural sciences, linguistics and anthropology. I am particularly concerned to examine the way in which their partial immersion in the field led them, and later their congregants and others, to construct systems of knowledge that gave meaning to their changing world. In the process, I look at the various narrative practices employed by the missionaries, as well as the institutions that legitimated and spread their representation of Africans and their environment, and how disputes and differences within the mission changed their perspectives.

The *Kulturträger* of the Swiss Romande Mission were resolutely middle-class and generally highly educated. They carried to Africa a series of experiences and values forged during a period of social and political upheaval in French-speaking, western Switzerland. In the late nineteenth and early twentieth centuries they applied to Africa a series of scientific practices, rooted in the Enlightenment, that quickly cast them, once in Africa, as experts on 'the native question'. Their representation of tribal life had a strong influence on various leaders of public opinion in southern Africa, stretching from lawmakers to jurists and politicians to those who adopted a Thonga ethnic consciousness.[12] This book emphasizes how these European intellectuals, who were brought by their vocation from a country without colonies to deep rural areas of Africa, formulated and debated, ordered and arranged, knowledge about Africa.

In the early part of the nineteenth century, scientific and secular ideas associated with the Enlightenment were altering the way in which the Swiss related to their environment and to each other. Romanticism and waves of religious revival added to the chaos of comprehension as people and communities attempted to provide their tumultuous world with order and understanding. Their notion of space was transformed as much by the telescope and microscope as by new geographical discoveries. At the same time, advances made in geology, glaciology and palaeontology hurtled the age of the world backwards. As the Swiss struggled to orientate themselves in space and time, their views of everything from religion to landscape and politics underwent a rapid and shifting transformation.

The missionaries took this experience of rapid change to Africa where they used a number of established practices to give meaning to their new world. Their propaganda described Africa as a continent of darkness to which missionaries carried the light of spiritual and secular salvation. Through a mixture of religion and science and with the help of their supporters at home, they promised to raise a population of enigmatic pagans from a state of intellectual childhood to a responsible maturity. But in another genre of literature, aimed at a more secular readership and carried by the journals of scientific and geographical societies, as well as by specialized religious magazines, the missionaries described a very different Africa. In the picture of the world carried by this literature, Africans contributed to the vision of the missionary *Aufklärer* in various ways. African evangelists, guides, collectors, translators and specialists in anything from medicine to music, plant life to linguistics, supplied the missionaries with the knowledge needed to make sense of the environment and its inhabitants. Most missionaries were only interested in the raw data provided by their informants. Henri-Alexandre Junod stands out, however, because his curiosity extended to the ways in which his informants organized and regulated their knowledge and, in so doing, infused their world with meaning. He was particularly impressed by the grammatical structures of the languages he studied and by the patterns of music, folklore and kinship he observed. Although he viewed the ways people arranged their knowledge of plant- and animal-life as archaic and outmoded, and advocated more 'modern' and 'universal' ways of understanding nature, he took seriously native systems of framing data and making sense of it. Like Junod, Africans adopted and adapted foreign ways of seeing and doing things and rapidly made them their own.[13] This book is a history of the swirling interaction of ideas, beliefs and practices in one part of Africa before and during the early years of colonialism. But it is equally a history of ordinary people and of their ability to challenge, adapt, change and subvert those ideas.

The book starts with an examination of the Christian revival that swept across western Switzerland in the early nineteenth century. This gave birth to various Free Churches, an important missionary society, and an intellectual milieu that produced individuals such as Adolphe Mabille, Frédéric Ellenberger, Henri-Alexandre Junod, Henri Berthoud, Edouard Jacottet, Héli Chatelain and Henri Perregaux, who would make pioneering contributions to the field of African Studies. The chapter draws attention to the turbulent nature of a church produced by the dramatic politics and religious changes of mid-nineteenth-century Switzerland. The consequences for the mission of the struggle to create a church independent of government controls, but responsive to the ideals of the Christian revival, are traced in later chapters. These include the emergence of a new and dynamic church equipped with a particularly tolerant theology but unsure of its position and place in Switzerland and the world.

This caused the church to grow into an especially intellectual institution for which missionary work was associated with revival and with the establishment, in Africa, of a world it had lost in Switzerland.

In the second chapter, I turn to the reverberations of mission work in Africa on the home community in Switzerland. Here I emphasize the way in which missionary work, and with it an image of Africa, filtered into and influenced many aspects of life in the metropole. Transnational missionary societies provide a good field of study for this form of global experience that C.A. Bayly has recently called 'lateral history'.[14] The widespread support for missionary activity during the second half of the nineteenth century may be attributed partly to the influence on the cultural life of French-speaking Switzerland of images and experiences produced in Africa. The mission played an important role in shaping the way in which the Swiss – a people severely divided by language, religion, region and class – came to see themselves as a single community. The mission also introduced the Swiss to Africa as a world in which they could at once recover their own lost values, situate themselves in geological time and discover a range of new creative energies. The mission introduced Switzerland to forms of art, music and storytelling that were not confined by the conventions of the age. Missionary propaganda brought Africa directly into the intimate recesses of Swiss homes. In both private and public spaces, the picture of the dark continent served as a foil against which the Swiss could measure the evolution of their own society; a repository for a range of resources that would help revitalize that society and revivify its institutions and practices. Institutions such as the Sunday school, the museum and the botanical garden introduced the Swiss – a people without colonies or a population of slave-descent – to this exciting new world. I stress in this chapter that they also created the cultural conditions for the normalization of imperialism.[15]

The first French-speaking Swiss missionaries arrived in Lesotho in the 1850s where they worked for the Paris Evangelical Missionary Society. Twenty years later, the Free Church of the canton of Vaud established its own Society and sent missionaries to the northern Transvaal. From their base in the foothills of the Zoutpansberg, native converts extended the work of the mission to the coastal plain of Mozambique. The establishment of a native church, free of missionary control, underlines the important role of black converts in the spread of Christianity. It also stresses the significant part played by Africans in the construction of Christian beliefs and practices, especially in areas where white missionaries exercised little control. In chapter three I examine this Christian movement, the success of which depended on a notion of revealed religion that was initially shared by both white missionaries and black congregants. But when the Swiss missionaries sought to contain and control the movement, they subjected their society to soul-searching debates over the limits of religious toleration. This was a divisive and emotional issue for a mission born of a church that was itself the product of intolerance at home. In the event, the discipline imposed on the native church had to take account of the competing forms of Christianity on offer in southern Mozambique. The final part of the chapter traces the appeal of new forms of Christianity that arrived in the coastal areas of southern Mozambique, often without the direction and supervision of missionaries. I stress here, as in the first and last chapters and the conclusion, that Christianity was a moving force open to high levels of contestation in both Switzerland and Africa. Migrant workers returning from South Africa with a knowledge of Christianity or with a Christian wife, or merely with a vague ability to read or a cash wage, initiated a movement of change that the missionaries could do little to restrain. This view of a dynamic and indigenized Christianity, the issue of a religion born in the Levant and nurtured in North Africa, questions the degree to which the central missions in South Africa, and particularly their numerous out-stations, can be seen as colonial institutions or as sites for the colonization of consciousness.

In the following chapter I examine the ways in which the missionaries looked at an unfamiliar landscape.[16] I suggest that their view of the land in Africa was produced by conventions of seeing that were, like their practice of Christianity, the result of a long history in Switzerland. The missionaries' inability to see the African landscape was a product of a visual estrangement that partly explains how they saw, or failed to see, the occupants of that land. However, as they explored the country and subjected it to a new gaze, these *Aufklärer* reduced it to the manageable proportions and familiar outlines of a map. At the same time, they carefully collected and classified animals and plants and engaged in meticulous meteorological studies. Once they had established a cognitive control over the land, the missionaries were able to view the African population in new and more empathetic ways.

In chapter five I expand on the methods used by the Swiss missionaries to establish a cognitive control over their environment. While cartography reduced the land to the proportions of a map, their research in the natural sciences helped fit them into a global network that brought the chaos of nature into well-ordered collections. In this chapter I particularly focus on Henri-Alexandre Junod, who arrived in Mozambique in 1889 with a passion for the natural sciences and a thorough training in philology and theology. In Africa he became a pioneering collector in the fields of entomology and botany.[17] Through the scientific method that he applied to the study of nature, Junod created regularity, order, patterns, uniformities and recurrences. By sending plants and animals to Europe to be arranged and classified, he constructed the discrete, named categories that made nature, like landscape, perceptible to Europeans.

This scientific approach also provided Junod with a more dispassionate gaze when he turned later to 'discover' laws and systems in the cultural practices of the people he came to call the 'Thonga'. His experience in the field in Africa and his interaction with professional scientists also led him to reinforce his belief in God and divine providence with an acquired faith in the laws of nature and natural selection.[18] Junod believed that this combination of God and science would bring about both the religious and secular conversion of unbelievers and in the process would fill the dark corners of his world with progress and improvement. At the same time, Junod's understanding of nature and its powers of conversion supported contemporary ideas about Europe's civilizing mission. However, unlike some modern historians of this process, he recognized both the different ways indigenous people comprehended and gave meaning to nature and the ways in which they contributed to his knowledge of the subject.[19] But at the same time, Junod insisted on the gulf between local and universal knowledge systems that in the African context contributed to the racialization of 'science' as a European construct.

The scientific method also influenced how the Swiss missionaries transcribed oral languages.[20] When they arrived in the northern Transvaal, the missionaries outlined the borders and content of a written, standard language they called Gwamba. In chapter six I investigate the ways in which they defined and delineated this mission language, or 'discovered' it, in much the same way as they 'discovered' (rather than assembled and invented) various species of plants and animals. The chapter looks at the debate within the mission over the division of Gwamba into two separate languages: Ronga and Thonga. It also broaches the history of the Tswa language, transcribed by American Board missionaries and later grouped along with Ronga and Thonga in the Tsonga cluster. The chapter pays particular attention to the role of African intermediaries in the construction of these written languages and underlines the political pragmatism behind the scientific work in the field of Bantu philology.

The transcription of a language has multiple consequences for its speakers. In chapter seven I look at the task of social engineering undertaken by the missionaries through their control of a standard, written Thonga language. Literacy was the basic tool through which the laws of God and science would bring about a strictly controlled transformation of African society. However, the missionaries lacked the resources needed to turn Africans into the avid readers and writers found in Switzerland. In a vibrantly oral society, the power of literacy was often yoked to the interests of the established political order. Far from taming the savage mind, literacy in the Thonga language often reinforced the power of the old order.[21] Yet at the same time, a fragile new elite adopted and harnessed the missionaries' meaning of literacy. Thirty years after the Swiss missionaries arrived in southern Africa, some of these converts started to identify themselves as 'Thongas', the people to whom the missionaries had been called by their vocation. Through their control of the skills of reading and writing, these Christians were able to establish themselves as modernizers and progressives who would one day seize the political crown abandoned by colonialism.

In chapter eight I look at the anthropology produced by the Swiss Mission and particularly concentrate on Junod's emergence as the dominant figure in this field.[22] The chapter attempts to explain how Junod came to write the highly influential *Life of a South African Tribe* in three successive stages between 1898 and 1927. As I suggest in this and the following chapter, many of Junod's ideas served to build the intellectual foundations of segregation. Yet just as politicians came to see the separation of the races as an answer to 'the native question', a new generation of professional anthropologists questioned the intellectual foundations of this new political policy.

By the 1930s, African society had little in common with the tribal communities first studied by Junod some forty years earlier. For many of the new anthropologists and their liberal political cousins, his work was unable to explain the rapid transformation of society in industrializing South Africa. Yet, as I attempt to show in chapter nine, they were unable to free themselves of many of the basic ideas about Africa contained in Junod's classic work. This intellectual inheritance not only had important political consequences for South Africa; it also reflected and reinforced many of the ideas on which a general understanding of Africa has been built.

A Note on Terminology

In the South African political climate, the meaning attached to words has undergone extensive change. I use the word 'native' throughout this book to mean indigenous people. As the Cape Colony annexed new territories, the 'native question' became increasingly important. During the early decades of union the term acted as a shorthand for the 'problem' posed by the administration, control and political representation of the indigenous population. I use the term without inverted commas. I have also used anglicized terms for Bantu languages, e.g. South Sotho rather than SeSotho or Ronga rather than Xi-Ronga. I have left proper names in the languages used in the original texts, e.g. Henri or Edouard instead of Henry or Edward; Yosefa and Yonas instead of Joseph and Jonas. In the same vein, I use the term Swiss Romande to refer to French-speaking western Switzerland.

Notes

1. Max Gluckman, *Politics, Law and Ritual in Tribal Society* (Chicago, 1965), p. 21.
2. I look at the rise and fall of missionary anthropology in Harries, 'Anthropology' in N. Etherington (ed.), *Missions and Empire*, The Oxford History of the British Empire, Companion series (Oxford, 2005).
3. E. Evans-Pritchard, *Social Anthropology* (London, 1951), p. 142.
4. Gluckman, *Politics, Law and Ritual*, p. 20–21. See also Gluckman, *Essays in the Ritual of Social Relations* (Manchester, 1962), pp. 8–9.
5. Luc de Heusch, 'The Debt of the Maternal Uncle: Contribution to the Study of Complex Structures of Kinship', *Man* (1974) 9, 4; de Heusch, 'Heat, Physiology and Cosmogony: rites de passage among the Thonga' in I. Karp and C. S. Bird (eds), *Explorations in African Systems of Thought* (Bloomington IN, 1979); de Heusch, *Sacrifice in Africa: a structuralist approach* (Manchester, 1985); Dominique Zahan, P. Erny, M.-L. Witt, *Le feu en Afrique et thèmes annexes: variations autour de l'oeuvre du H. A. Junod* (Paris, 1995).
6. A. Kuper, *Anthopologists and Anthropology. The British School 1922–72* (London, 1973), p. 18.
7. A. Hastings, *The Church in Africa, 1450–1950* (Oxford, 1994), pp. 304–5.
8. W. D. Hammond-Tooke, *Imperfect Interpreters: South Africa's Anthropologists 1920–1990* (Johannesburg, 1997). See also Hammond-Tooke, *The Roots of Black South Africa* (Johannesburg, 1993), p. 7.
9. A question first posed by Luc de Heusch, 'Heat, Physiology and Cosmogony', p. 29.
10. The historiography of the Mission stretches from in–house accounts of missionary achievements to more recent texts laying stress on African initiative. For the former, see Paul Berthoud, *La Mission romande à la Baie de Delagoa* (Lausanne, 1888); P. Berthoud, *Les Nègres gouamba ou les vingt premières années de la mission romande* (Lausanne, 1896); A. Grandjean, *La Mission romande: Ses racines dans le sol Suisse romande: Son épanouissement dans la race thonga* (Lausanne, 1917). For the latter, see especially Jan van Butselaar, *Africains, missionnaires et colonialistes: les origines de l'église presbytérienne du Mozambique, 1880–1896* (Leiden, 1984) and Nicolas Monnier's extended essay, 'Stratégie missionnaire et tactiques d'appropriation indigènes: La Mission romande au Mozambique 1888–1896' in *Le Fait Missionnaire* (Lausanne, December 1995) no. 2; B. Sundkler and C. Steed, *A History of the Church in Africa* (Cambridge, 2000), pp. 438–47.
11. My approach is closer to Pierre Bourdieu than to James Clifford and George Marcus. See Bourdieu, 'Participant Objectivation', *Journal of the Royal Anthropological Institute* (2003) 9; J. Clifford and G. Marcus (eds), *Writing Culture: the poetics and politics of ethnography* (Berkeley, CA, 1986).
12. I look at the emergence of a Thonga identity, particularly from the perspective of unschooled migrant workers, in my *Work, Culture and Identity: Migrant Labourers in Mozambique and South Africa, c. 1860–1910* (Portsmouth, NH, London and Johannesburg, 1994).
13. Cf. the adoption by the Marxist government of Mozambique of many of the ideas on literacy advocated by the mission and treated in chapter seven. Harries, 'Missionaries, Marxists and Magic: Power and the Politics of Literacy in South-East Africa', *Journal of Southern African Studies* (2001) 3: 27.
14. C. A. Bayly, *The Birth of the Modern World 1780–1914* (Oxford, 2004), p. 4. The importance of empire to the history of the metropole has become axiomatic in British history, cf. David Cannadine, *Ornamentalism: How the British saw their Empire* (London, 2001); Linda Colley, 'Britishness and otherness: an argument', *Journal of British Studies* (1992) 31. On its application to the history of Christian missions, see Kathleen Wilson, *The Island Race: Englishness, Empire and Gender in the Eighteenth Century* (London, 2003), pp. 80–84; Catherine Hall, *Civilising Subjects: Metropole and Colony in the English Imagination 1830–1867* (Cambridge, 2002); Susan Thorne, *Congregational Missions and the Making of an Imperial Culture in nineteenth-century England* (Stanford, CA, 1999); John L. Comaroff and Jean Comaroff, *Ethnography and the Historical Imagination* (Boulder, CO, 1992), p. 293; Jean and John Comaroff, *Of Revelation and Revolution*, I, *Christianity, Colonialism, and Consciousness in South Africa* (Chicago, 1991) chapter three. See also Isabel Hofmeyr, *The Portable Bunyan: a transnational history of The Pilgrim's Progress* (Johannesburg, Princeton, NJ, 2004). Many of these ideas originated in the context of Imperial History, cf. J. M. MacKenzie, *Propaganda and Empire: the Manipulation of British Public Opinion, 1880–1960* (Manchester, 1984); 'Introduction' by John M. Mackenzie (ed.), *Imperialism and Popular Culture* (Manchester, 1986); Shula Marks, 'Sniping from the sidelines: History, the nation and empire', *History Workshop Journal* (1990) 29, pp. 111–19; Annie Coombes, *Reinventing Africa:*

Museums, Material Culture and Popular Imagination (New Haven, CT, 1994); Frederick Cooper and Anne Stoler (eds), *Tensions of Empire: Colonial Cultures in a Bourgeois World* (Berkeley, CA, 1997). They were first mentioned, as far as I am aware, by Max Gluckman, *Order and Rebellion in Tribal Africa* (London, 1963), p. 215.

[15] It is often overlooked that the great age of Sunday schools coincided with the age of imperialism. The role of Sunday schools and other religious institutions in the propagation of racism and imperialism is not mentioned in Eric Hobsbawm's classic *The Age of Empire: 1875–1914* (London, 1987) or Andrew Porter's review of the literature on '"Cultural Imperialism" and Protestant Missionary Enterprise, 1780–1914', *Journal of Imperial and Commonwealth History* (1997) 25: 3. Nor does it find a place in Andrew Porter's *Religion versus Empire? British Protestant missionaries and overseas expansion, 1700–1914* (Manchester, 2004) or John M. MacKenzie, 'Empire and Metropolitan Cultures' in Andrew Porter (ed.), *The Oxford History of the British Empire*, III, *The Nineteenth Century* (Oxford, 1999). The relationship between race, imperialism and evangelical literature is mentioned in passing in F. K. Prochaska, *Women and Philanthropy in Nineteenth Century England* (Oxford, 1980), pp. 92–3.

[16] Some of the following themes have been raised by Sandra E. Greene, *Sacred Sites and the Colonial Encounter: a history of meaning and memory in Ghana* (Bloomington, IN, 2002); Terence Ranger, 'African views of the land: a research agenda', *Transformation* (2000) 44; Johannes Fabian, 'Hindsight: Thoughts on Anthropology upon reading Francis Galton's Narrative of an Explorer in tropical South Africa (1853)', *Critique of Anthropology* (1987) 7: 2.

[17] Few scholars have worked on the role of missionaries in the expansion of western scientific knowledge. Exceptions are Neil Gunson, 'British missionaries and their contribution to science in the Pacific islands' in Roy MacLeod and Philip F. Rehbock (eds), *Darwin's Laboratory: Evolutionary Theory and Natural History in the Pacific* (Honolulu, 1994) and David N. Livingstone, 'Scientific inquiry and the missionary enterprise' in Ruth Finnegan (ed.), *Participating in the Knowledge Society: Researchers beyond University Walls* (Basingstoke, 2005) and John Stenhouse, 'Missionary Science' in David N. Livingstone and Ronald Nimbers (eds), *The Cambridge History of Science* (New York, forthcoming) vol. 8. Abolitionists' attempts to take both science and religion to Africa are examined in Howard Temperley, *White Dreams, Black Africa: the Antislavery Expedition to the River Niger, 1841–1842* (New Haven, CT, and London, 1991) and D. Liebowitz, *The Physician and the Slave Trade: John Kirk, the Livingstone expeditions and the crusade against slavery in East Africa* (New York, 1999). The scientific work of travellers and explorers is well served by Johannes Fabian, *Out of Our Minds: Reason and Madness in the Exploration of Central Africa* (Berkeley, Los Angeles and London, 2000), pp. 180–3, 299n3; Beatrix Heintze, *Ethnographische Aneignungen: Deutsche Forschungsreisende in Angola* (Frankfurt am Main, 1999), pp. 21, 26, 102, 126, 180, 202, 233, 362.

[18] On similar processes elsewhere in the world see Ron Numbers and John Stenhouse (eds), *Disseminating Darwin: The Role of Place, Race, Religion, and Gender* (Cambridge, 1999); D. N. Livingstone et al., *Evangelicals and Science in Historical Perspective* (New York, 1999). It is now common to stress the similarities rather than disagreements between these two systems of belief. Cf. Livingstone, 'Scientific enquiry' in Finnegan (ed.), *Participating in the Knowledge Society* and Edward Said, *Orientalism* (London, [1978] 1985), pp. 134–5.

[19] Historians who have done pioneering work from a critical perspective on the relationship between the natural sciences and the extension of empire seldom take into account native ways of looking at and understanding nature. Ironically, this produces a picture of European scientific practices as the only ones worthy of study. Cf. Roy MacLeod, 'Embryology and Empire: The Balfour students and the quest for intermediate forms in the laboratory of the Pacific' in Macleod and Rehbock (eds), *Darwin's Laboratory*, pp. 141–4; David Philip Miller and Peter Hanns Reill (eds), *Visions of Empire: Voyages, botany and representations of Nature* (Cambridge, 1996); Nicolaas A. Rupke, *Richard Owen: Victorian Naturalist* (New Haven, CT, and London, 1994), pp. 80–83.

[20] Richard Drayton starts to fuse indigenous and imported forms of knowledge in Drayton, 'Knowledge and Empire' in P. J. Marshall (ed.), *Oxford History of the British Empire. II, The Eighteenth Century* (Oxford, 2001). The history of the transcription of African languages has become an important theme in African history. Classic works include Terence Ranger, 'Missionaries, migrants and the Manyika: the invention of ethnicity in Zimbabwe' in Leroy Vail (ed.), *The Creation of Tribalism in Southern Africa* (Berkeley, CA, 1989); Johannes Fabian, *Language and Colonial Power: The appropriation of Swahili in the former Belgian Congo, 1880–1938* (Cambridge, [1986] 1991). Adrian Hastings, in his *The Construction of Nationhood: Ethnicity, Religion and Nationalism* (Cambridge, 1997), chapter six, criticizes constructivist views on the history of the transcription of language and, from a perspective I question in this work, the ties between modernity and identity. The Swiss missionaries that I follow in this chapter were able to control the process of language standardization more effectively than the groups working on the Kikuyu language. See Derek Peterson, *Creative Writing: Translation, Bookkeeping, and the Work of Imagination in Colonial Kenya* (Portsmouth, NH, 2004). In South Africa, G. P. Lestrade wrote on this theme in his 'European influences upon the development of Bantu language and literature' in I. Schapera (ed.), *Western Civilization and the Natives of South Africa: Studies in Culture Contact* (London, 1934). More recently it is pursued by Jean and John Comaroff (eds), *Of Revelation and Revolution*, I, pp. 213–30. Although Johan du Bruyn and Nicholas Southey remarked in 1995 that the

study of the transcription of African languages in South Africa 'awaits systematic research', this perspective is not reflected in more recent collections on mission history in South Africa, cf. R. Elphick and R. Davenport (eds), *Christianity in South Africa: A Political, Social and Cultural History* (Cape Town and London, 1997); John De Gruchy (ed.), *The London Missionary Society in Southern Africa* (Cape Town, 1999). De Bruyn and Southey, 'The treatment of Christianity and Protestant missionaries in South African historiography' in Robert Ross and Henry Bredekamp (eds), *Missions and Christianity in South African History* (Johannesburg, 1995), p. 42.

[21] On literacy and different ways of reading in Africa, see Derek R. Peterson, *Creative Writing*; Hofmeyr, *The Portable Bunyan*; Gesine Krüger, 'Die Verbreitung der Schrift in Südafrika: Zur praxis des Schreibens in alltags- und sozialgeschichtlicher Perspektive, 1830–1930' (unpublished Habilitation, University of Hanover, 2002).

[22] For the contribution of missionaries to the development of anthropology, cf. S. Sohmer, 'The Melanesian Mission and Victorian anthropology: a study in symbiosis' in R. MacLeod and P. E. Rehbock (eds), *Darwin's Laboratory*; R. E. Reid, 'John Henry Holmes in Papua', *Journal of Pacific History* (1978) 13; W. John Young, *The Quiet Wise Spirit: Edwin W Smith 1876–1957 and Africa* (Peterborough, 2002); Henk J. van Rinsum, 'Edwin W. Smith and his "Raw Material": Texts of a missionary and ethnographer in context', *Anthropos* (1999) 94; Paul Cocks, '*Musemunuzhi*: Edwin Smith and the Restoration and Fulfilment of African Society and Religion' in *Patterns of Prejudice* (2001) 36, 2; Harries, 'Anthropology' in Etherington (ed.), *Missions and Empire*.

1
Switzerland

And Jesus came and spake unto them, saying, All power is given unto me in heaven and earth. Go ye therefore, and teach all nations, baptizing them in the name of the Father, and of the Son, and of the Holy Ghost. (Matthew 28:18-19)

In 1823 a young Swiss missionary named Félix Neff wrote despairingly of the 'wild' and 'ignorant' people to whom he had been called by his vocation. Their 'architecture, agriculture, education, of every sort', he complained, was 'still in its earliest infancy.' His compatriot and successor, Ami Bost, was equally critical of congregants who, 'plunged in the deepest ignorance', shared their dark, smoke-filled huts with cows, sheep and goats and their beds with one another. The dress and food of these 'primitives' were coarse and unwholesome, their hygiene non-existent, and their treatment of women 'barbarous'. They marked the passage of time in the manner of 'savages' and few could speak French, let alone read or write.[1]

Neff and Bost believed their work amongst the uncivilized people of the High Alps resembled that of missionaries in Africa and other corners of their world. Neff considered 'the work of an evangelist in the [Freyssinières] valley' to be 'greatly similar to that of a missionary in uncivilized countries' and Bost wrote that 'the work of an evangelist in the High Alps, generally resembles that of a missionary among the savages'.[2] These men were drawn to exotic locations where the sentiments of Christian revivalism and Romanticism overlapped. Individualism, mystery, emotion, zeal, dark spiritual torment and a defiance of social convention could be expressed in areas untouched by the contrived and frivolous materialism of the towns. The uncorrupted simplicity of obliging blacks, as popularized in novels like Bernardin de Saint-Pierre's *Paul et Virginie*, the tracts of the anti-slavery movement, and soon a tidal wave of Sunday school literature, portrayed Africa as a continent ready for the Gospel, a place in which courageous missionaries could draw up a new civilization unfettered by urban and industrial corruption.[3] Neff and Bost drew inspiration from these ideas and laboured in the hope of generating a revival, 'a repetition, among the High Alps, of the mission to Sierra Leone and Tahiti'.[4]

Evangelism and Identity

During the eighteenth century, Geneva had developed as a centre of enlightened thought marked by a flexible and tolerant Calvinist Church. The liberal approach of the Company of Pastors and the town's Faculty of Theology had allowed the reincorporation into the church of sects excluded at the time of the Reformation. These ranged from Arians who denied the consubstantiality of the Trinity (a heresy for which Calvin had burned Michael Servetus) to Socians who disputed the divinity of Christ. It particularly kept within the church those who were concerned to expose and extirpate the superstition, irrationality and hypocrisy in Christian doctrine and who looked for reason rather than revelation in the Bible. The liberalism of this broad church had defused the appeal of the anticlericalism and materialism practised in neighbouring France. When Geneva was incorporated into revolutionary France as the department of Léman in 1798, divergent cantonal interests found a unifying institution and identity in their church. The church's tolerance of difference had produced a remarkable absence of sectarian strife, but it had been achieved under the guidance of a political oligarchy and at the cost of avoiding any potentially disruptive, open discussion on questions of faith.[5]

German pietists had planted the seeds of revival in Geneva, but it was only after the canton had freed itself of French rule and rejoined the Swiss Confederation in 1814 that Scottish and English dissenters arrived to raise the fruits of the movement. These turbulent spirits stressed the need for a recognition of personal sin not just as a vice or problem to be resolved through confession or a simple act of contrition, but as the implacable cause of humankind's fall from grace. This was of overwhelming importance, as without God's help and assistance men and women were condemned to eternal damnation. Prayer, hymns and Bible study provided direct, emotional contact with God; as did a form of Natural Theology, through which individuals could admire God through the splendour of His environment.[6] This introspective, unique experience provided the spiritual rebirth or conversion needed for the individual to acquire the strength to overcome the malevolent influence of society. For many, the profound corruption inflicted on humankind by original sin was only too visible in the violent upheavals accompanying revolution and war. But God's grace had once provided the world with a saviour whose suffering had served to expiate the sins of humankind. Few now believed in the predestination that would save only the elected from eternal damnation, as the Reformed Church had once argued. 'For God so loved the world,' Calvinists were now reminded in sermons, tracts and Bible readings, 'that he gave his only begotten Son, that whosoever believeth in him shall not perish, but have everlasting life' (John 3:16). However, salvation could not be won through the performance of good works alone, and for this reason conversion had to be accompanied by a thorough moral renovation, what in French was called a *réveil* or 'awakening' and in English, a revival.

Revivalists in Geneva increasingly advertised their message through blunt and uncompromising confrontations that highlighted the prevarication and silence of the church on doctrinal issues. The revivalists' religious certainties appealed to a narrow constituency, but their disdain for ritual and hierarchy and their uncompromising attitude inevitably undermined the authority of the clergy. This quickly brought them into conflict with the Genevan Company of Pastors. In May 1817, church ministers were prohibited from preaching on such topics as original sin, the nature of Christ, predestination or salvation. This interdiction destroyed the inclusive nature of religious life in Geneva as it obliged many followers of the revival to leave the Reformed Church. These independent spirits initially assembled at the church of the Bourg-de-Four, where Neff converted, and in Carouge under Ami Bost. A less conciliatory tendency emerged later at the Chapelle du Témoignage where César Malan transmitted a more traditional Calvinist message to his congregants.[7] Strong evangelical convictions persuaded these tight communities to form a Society of Evangelical Missions in 1821 and to send hard men like Neff and Bost to pursue mission work in France and the neighbouring cantons of Vaud and Neuchâtel.[8]

Most churchmen and politicians looked with displeasure on the conventicles formed by those 'awakened' by the Revival. For these critics, the religious enthusiasm of the *réveillés* was marked by an unsavoury emotionalism, a self-reliance that contradicted traditional forms of deference and a passionate and unbending conviction in the power of faith and Biblical revelation that negated the spirit of reason. The revival was accompanied by an unwelcome absence of pastoral supervision and it threatened the cohesion of both church and society.

In the canton of Vaud, the church founded by Pierre Viret, like that of Calvin in Geneva and Guillaume Farel in the canton of Neuchâtel, was at the heart of social as well as spiritual life. Its rituals marked an individual's passage through life with dignity and respect, entertainment and consolation. The church assisted those afflicted by indigence or ill-health and, at a time when theological science was considered the key to knowledge, clergymen played an important role in all aspects of education. With a mixture of vigilance and paternal care, pastors and elders patrolled the material and moral well-being of parishioners from conception to the grave. For nearly three hundred years clergymen had been in every sense of the word solicitous 'shepherds' anxious to guide their 'flocks' through life according to the established traditions of their church.[9]

Part of the power held by this caste of pastors came from an accommodating relationship with a state that had undergone a dizzying transformation. In 1798 the troops of revolutionary France had brought an end to three hundred years of Bernese rule over the canton of Vaud. A Jacobin republic briefly replaced the Bernese bailiffs before Vaud rejoined the Swiss Confederation in 1803 as one of nineteen sovereign cantons. Church bells rang throughout the canton when the first elected *Grand Conseil*, or cantonal legislature, met in Lausanne. This event was blessed by services held in every church in the territory. In Lausanne the members of the new government celebrated the canton's change of status with a colourful ceremony held in the thirteenth-century Gothic cathedral built on the summit of the Jorat buttress overlooking the town. During all this activity, clergymen wrote songs celebrating the patriotism and independence of their canton. The fall of Napoleon brought a new, more conservative government to power but did little to stall the growing relationship between church and state. A new constitution both confirmed the religious rights of Catholics, who made up an important part of the Swiss population, and recognized Evangelical Reformed Christianity as the religion of the canton. In 1820 the government officially confirmed pastors in their role as auxiliary state officials.[10]

The revival provoked a strong response from those in western Switzerland who, after years of revolution and war, saw it as a source of renewed political instability. In Geneva the establishment of an independent church prompted street demonstrations and violent denunciations of their foreign, 'Moravian' members.[11] In Vaud the conventicles established by the revivalists were condemned as socially divisive and alien in origin and were prohibited in May 1824 by legislation declaring them a 'sect formed by people foreign to the family'.[12]

This authoritarian suppression of religious difference made the question of religious freedom an important issue in both political and religious circles almost overnight. It also led to the establishment of the first dissident churches in the canton of Vaud.[13] At the same time, people influenced by the revival founded a range of evangelical institutions that complemented, paralleled and challenged the work of the established church. These included Evangelical Societies that brought together Christians wishing to explore aspects of their religion in a space free of the formal control of the Reformed Church. It also included Bible and Tract Societies, modelled on and supported financially by counterparts in Britain, that aimed to give readers direct access to the word of God without having to pass through a caste of pastors or rationalizing theologians.[14]

A growing network of Sunday schools also spread the revivalist message. Religious dissidents in Geneva established the first of these with their Independent Church in 1817. Three years later a Sunday school was formed in Lausanne and, over the next decade, several small schools opened in various parts of Vaud and Neuchâtel. In some isolated hamlets, the only education received by young children was that given by the minister before or after the Sunday service. Sunday schools displayed the private initiative, individual zeal and lively independence of ecclesiastical control that were marks of the revival. They also provided a space for women, many of whom were drawn from the local gentry and immigrant aristocracy, to cobble together an evangelical culture and related social network.[15] Perhaps because the early Sunday school movement was dominated by women who challenged the patriarchal structure of the evangelical organizations, it was only in the mid-1830s that these bodies turned their attention to the small gatherings held in private homes, students' rooms, or the large houses of local notables.[16] When the Vaudois Sunday schools were incorporated into the broader evangelical movement, they started to occupy more formal premises and, by the 1840s, succeeded in attracting several hundred pupils.[17]

One of the defining characteristics of the revival was the notion that Christians should take seriously Christ's invocation (in Matthew 28:19) to 'go and teach all nations'. The missionary zeal of the revivalists also sprang from a fervent belief in the need for individual rebirth and a constant, driving desire for religious and moral reform. This focused implicitly, and at times explicitly, on the energy of primitive communities that had been protected from the corrosive forces of materialism, disbelief and immorality and thus had not fallen from grace in the manner of urban populations. Evangelical work in areas of the world untouched by the vices of modernity had the potential to rebuild the primitive Church and to revitalize and renew the parent body in Europe in the same way as the monasticism of the early Christian Church in Egypt.[18] At the same time, the act of mission could serve as a process of self-improvement as the missionary withdrew from a corrupt world and entered into an encounter with the authentic values and virtues of primitive society. Hence missionary activity formed an integral part of the movement for Christian revival. Members of the earliest conventicles not only prayed and read the Bible together; they also produced their own missionary literature and supported evangelical endeavours at home and abroad through their prayers and donations. While Geneva concentrated on the evangelization of primitive France, Vaud and Neuchâtel looked to more exotic parts of the world.[19]

In 1821 missionary societies were established in Geneva and in Yverdon in northern Vaud. But the Vaudois government immediately prohibited this form of evangelical activity because of its telescopic philanthropy. In pursuance of the widely supported conviction that charity starts at home, the government believed that 'an inconsiderate zeal for far-off enterprises' would deflect pastors from the parish work to which they had been called by their 'patrie'. Vaudois politicians considered mission work 'beyond the reach and means of a small country' whose clergymen should be more concerned with the plight of the parish poor than with the fate of inscrutable, foreign pagans. Even within the church, missionary activity was frequently condemned as a foreign import that served to spread sectarian divisions.[20]

The economic recovery of the post-war years and a growing evangelical enthusiasm eventually led the Vaudois government to reconsider its opposition to mission work. The establishment of the Evangelical Missionary Society of Lausanne in 1826 elicited both widespread interest and public condemnation. The first meeting of the society attracted three hundred eager participants, as well as a large crowd which, gathered in the street, exhibited its disapproval of the proceedings in a loud and disorderly manner. Despite this and later boisterous surges of opposition, local enthusiasm for missionary activity generated sufficient excitement for the society to spread to the major towns of the canton. From these urban centres it fed the public hunger to participate in mission work through open, summertime assemblies and a number of publications. It also established ties with a recently formed interdenominational Missionary Society in Paris busy raising funds and recruiting personnel in the French provinces and neighbouring countries. The Vaudois were fully prepared to engage in efforts that, within six years, would send the first wave of missionaries from Paris to Lesotho. But unlike many other auxiliaries of the Paris Evangelical Missionary Society (PEMS), they refused to abandon a separate identity and opened their own institute for the training of missionaries in Lausanne in 1829.[21]

Problems arose immediately when the institute succeeded in recruiting only young men of reduced means, such as colporteurs, carpenters and primary school teachers. It was thought that the modest origins of these individuals deprived the student body of the natural leadership of the 'educated classes'. Almost from its inception, the Institute was racked by religious disputes and organizational problems. In the event, it sent only a handful of graduates and missionaries to evangelize the Sioux before closing its doors in 1839. The institute's director, Samuel Thomas, became pastor of the Oratory in Yverdon, and its last student, Joseph Maitin, was entrusted to the Paris Mission and a future career in Lesotho.[22] A few years later the Lausanne Missionary Society halted its work in North America and restricted its activities to fund-raising for interdenominational mission societies.

This collapse of the missionary movement was largely the product of a widening split within the church at home. The multitude of evangelical organizations founded in western Switzerland had provided followers of the revival with a space in which to meet and exchange ideas without contravening the law. It also allowed them to develop an organizational base, language, and set of common practices and beliefs without having to leave the established church. But the proliferation of evangelical groups created an institutional diversity that grew stronger as insistent voices propagated the need to separate church from state.

Alexandre Vinet quickly became the champion of this cause, particularly after he moved from the University of Basel in 1837 to become Professor of Theology at the Lausanne Academy. The views of Vinet and his supporters on the importance of a personal religion coincided with those of many liberal Vaudois politicians. These men, brought to power by street demonstrations in 1830, wanted a stronger and more united Switzerland but remained distrustful of all institutions, including those of church and state, capable of curbing individual freedoms.[23] This wave of liberal opinion confirmed and conformed to the growing religious tolerance practised in many parts of Europe. Although the liberal constitution of 1831 guaranteed the established position of the 'National Evangelical, Reformed Church' in Vaud, the liberals took no action against the growing number of revivalist assemblies, or *oratoires*. Because of their respect for individual freedoms, the liberal politicians soon allowed the act prohibiting conventicles to pass into desuetude. They also sought to protect religious dissidents who were unable to marry in the established church by instituting civil marriages in 1835. The nature of the Lausanne Academy, which had served essentially as a theological seminary, was transformed at this time by the establishment of secular disciplines and the hold of the church over education was loosened by the founding of an *école normale*, or teacher's training college, run by the state.

This creeping secularization and a growing cantonal patriotism culminated in the passage of a new ecclesiastical law in 1839. This abolished the *Confession de foi helvétique*, the common doctrinal core that had bound the Vaudois Church to the other Reformed churches of Switzerland since 1566. By replacing the old articles of faith with a vague reference to revelation by Holy Scripture, the new ecclesiastical law served to hold people of diverse religious beliefs within an inclusive Reformed Church. At the same time, it infused the 'National church' with a degree of public control when it gave the legislature in Lausanne the ultimate right to determine doctrine, liturgy and catechism. The politicians underlined this new intervention in church-state relations when they erected a stained glass window in the Lausanne cathedral to Major Davel later that year. This tribute to the Vaudois patriot executed by the Bernese a century earlier symbolized the new, narrowly cantonal direction taken by the church in the wake of the ecclesiastical law. For those who believed their church had become little more than a spoke in the wheel of state, the new law was a source of despair. Indignation and ill-feeling quickly precipitated the resignation of Vinet and others.[24]

Tensions rose as government supporters saw in growing communities of Plymouth Brethren or Darbyites, Methodists and Baptists, proof that the revival, far from renewing the Church, was the source of its disintegration. They saw sectarian and foreign religious ideas undermining the cohesion of the canton as a community and they expressed their opposition to these ideas in a new language of exclusion that denigrated followers of the revival as alien 'methodists' or bigoted and hypocritical *mômiers*.[25] Opponents of the 1839 ecclesiastical law came together in a new society aimed at defending their religious beliefs and they circulated their ideas with renewed vigour in journals and tracts. Their adversaries condemned them as 'individualists' with little concern for wider society; they were a narrow and exclusive elite, undermining the egalitarian nature and unity of a society held together by the 'national' church.[26] At times this opposition to religious dissent could become violent. In 1833 plebeian participants in the vine-growers' festival in Vevey sacked numerous *oratoires* and temporarily halted the monthly meetings of the Missionary Society in Lausanne. A year later, the inhabitants of Vallorbe mounted a boisterous charivari as a way of displaying their opposition to the religious dissidents in their midst.[27] Religious difference and political identity had become irrevocably linked.

Political Revolution and Religious Change

Twenty-five years after the loose federal pact of 1815 the French-speaking, western section of the Swiss nation was a fissiparous, often fractious, patchwork of interests haunted by a colonial past and held together by little more than a fear of Catholic, monarchical France. Each canton had its own tariffs and tolls, laws, currency, army and historical myths. But as the Protestant cantons industrialized and grew rich, radicals called for closer federal ties, more popular access to government and an increased role for the state in daily life. In the canton of Vaud, where radicals had quit the Liberal Party in 1832, the government initially placated their demands through the secularization that culminated in the ecclesiastical law of 1839. But a crisis arose five years later when Catholic Lucerne handed education in the canton to the Jesuit order. Many Protestants and free thinkers viewed this as a provocation, for they saw in the Jesuits the shadow of an authoritarian, reactionary papacy. The liberals, in their turn, interpreted the developing crisis in Lucerne as yet another challenge to the principles of religious and political freedom and refused to intervene in the affairs of another canton. When the Catholics suppressed an uprising supported by Protestant volunteers in Lucerne, Vaudois radicals melted Jesuits and *mômiers* into a broad reactionary front. 'Jesuit Protestants', they claimed, threatened to divide the Confederation and overturn the forces of progress and reason. In a largely bloodless *coup d'état* in February 1845, the radicals seized the legislature in Lausanne, overturned the Liberal government and later threw their weight behind the federal government's armed suppression of Lucerne and its Catholic allies in the Sonderbund.[28]

These events had a direct impact on the church in the canton of Vaud where the new radical regime reactivated the old law restricting freedom of religion. Relations between the radicals and those pastors influenced by the revival developed into a crisis in August 1845 when the government required ministers to read from the pulpit a circular supporting their proposed constitution. Forty-three pastors refused to comply with this proclamation, partly because it required them to accept and even propagate the subordination of the church to a barely legitimate government and partly because the constitution made no mention of freedom of religion. But many other churchmen, such as pastor Henri Berthoud at Vallorbe, hesitated to enter into a confrontation that would divide the church and isolate its evangelical wing.[29] The radicals' demand that clergymen take an oath of allegiance to the secular state was a direct descendant of the Civil Constitution of the Clergy, passed little more than fifty years earlier by revolutionary France. Their trees of liberty, triumphal arches, festivals of fraternity, revolutionary slogans and castigation of 'refractory' ministers were prominent signs of a local secularism that could easily spill into anti-clericalism. The refusal of the radical government to condemn attacks on *mômiers* merely heightened these fears and encouraged evangelicals to look to Scotland where, three years earlier, conflicts in the Kirk had led to the formation of a Free Church.[30] But matters came to a head when the government's suspension of the forty-three dissident ministers provoked their colleagues to resign *en masse*.

A year later, delegates from dissident communities formed a constituent synod that established the Free Evangelical Church of the canton of Vaud, in March 1847. Anxious not to be relegated to the position of a sect, the Free Church founded a Faculty of Theology in November 1847. Numerous professors and students left the town academy to join this institution and soon it became a centre of theological innovation and excellence. This gave the Free Church a cerebral reputation that contrasted markedly with that of the National Church that, in an attempt to replace the lost clergy, was obliged to lower standards of entry into the ministry.[31] While pastors who stayed with the National Church retained their state salaries and status, Free Church ministers and their families had to leave their churches and quit presbyteries that some had occupied for several decades. As they were no longer recognized as state functionaries, they lost their government salaries. In some districts they faced popular, even violent, criticism from the radical members of their congregations. Each Free Church pastor was reduced to living off the voluntary contributions provided by what remained of his parishioners. Several found themselves without a viable congregation and had to find work in Reformed parishes elsewhere in the world. Even their assemblies had to be held in secret, for it was only in 1859 that the government lifted the ban on unofficial religious gatherings. Even then, it took a further two years before the government officially recognized their church. Meanwhile there were bread riots in Lausanne and Yverdon when the potato crop failed in 1845-47. The pastors of the Free Church of the canton of Vaud quickly developed a separate identity and sense of sacrifice out of a frugal lifestyle; they forged a long memory of persecution that would separate the two churches for the next one hundred and twenty years.[32]

Opponents of the Free Church quickly denounced its members as a narrow elite alienated from the people by their moral superiority, refined education and monopolistic hold on the truth. The radicals accused the Free Church clergy of being part of a vague conspiracy of professors, pastors and professionals that had maintained the old liberal oligarchy in power.[33] This collaboration between the patriciate and a pastorate possessing 'the authority of divine right' was contrasted with the democratic, sturdy simplicity of the peasant farmers who supported the radicals. For the radicals the Free Church pastors were at once *mômiers* and 'aristocrats'; they were alternatively *messieurs* with private means or servants of the wealthy *bonnes familles* responsible for their salaries.[34] Once he had retracted his resignation, Pastor Samson Vuilleumier thought the Free Church pastors 'a very aristocratic small coterie' of *belles Dames et beaux Messieurs*, an 'elite flock' that held its religious meetings in smart drawingrooms. His sister was also of the unsolicited opinion that the supporters of the Free Church constituted a fashionable *beau monde* easily distinguishable from the popular, milling crowds supporting the radicals.[35] More ominously Henri Druey, the radical leader, raised the threat of anti-clericalism when he accused this 'aristocracy' of treason by dividing the canton at a time when *la patrie est en danger*.[36] The anomalous image of a Free Church supported by a 'republican aristocracy' would last well into the twentieth century.[37]

Mission work was an early casualty of the schism in the church. The monthly meetings of the Missionary Society of Lausanne, along with those of the Bible and Evangelical Societies, were cancelled for over four years. When they reassembled discretely in 1850, only Free Church pastors remained on the board of the ostensibly interdenominational Mission Society. But there was little money for mission work during these years of upheaval. The Free Church of Vaud had attracted fewer than 4000 adherents, and these were obliged to pay the wages of their ministers and shoulder the costs of constructing new chapels and presbyteries. What little money could be spared for evangelical work in distant parts of the world was sent to the Moravian, Basel or Paris missionary societies.[38]

Despite the political and economic uncertainties of the time, a new sense of mission invigorated the Free Church. Before the schism in the National Church, evangelicals had been marginalized and their energies channeled into a Mission Society separated from the established church. Under the influence of Henri Berthoud and others, the Free Church created an Evangelical Commission that took over the activities of the old Missionary Society in 1857.[39] Although the Synod blocked requests for the Evangelical Commission to take on the responsibilities of an active missionary society, enthusiasm for evangelical work in foreign lands grew naturally after the formation of the Free Church. By severing their ties with the state, the evangelicals shook off the control of politicians concerned to further the welfare of local parishioners rather than that of distant, voteless sinners. As the National Church left support for evangelical work overseas to individual conscience, missionary activity became a marker of identity for the Free Church and a sign of devotion for its members. For many it became 'a primary obligation of the [Free] Church'.[40] Missionary work was also an alternative to the expatriation of pastors and students caused by the lack of Free Church parishes and the difficult conditions under which the new church had to operate. But growing support for mission work was also the product of an attitudinal sea change that, as shown in the next chapter, was not unconnected to movements in the political climate in Switzerland.

As the Free Church started to funnel its energies and resources directly into evangelical work, the Theological Faculty in Lausanne began to attract students. Samuel Thomas' congregants in northern Vaud were particularly willing to enter the mission field under the aegis of the Paris Evangelical Missionary Society (PEMS).[41] In 1859 one of their graduates, Paul Germond, left to join the PEMS and his compatriot Joseph Maitin in Lesotho, and Louis Duvoisin followed him three years later. Four other young Vaudois left to become missionaries at this time: Auguste Glardon embarked for India and Henri Gonin for the Transvaal. Adolphe Mabille and Frédéric Ellenberger, both from Yverdon, studied at the mission school in Paris before leaving for Lesotho in 1859-60. The influence of the Swiss Romande was also felt indirectly by the arrival in Lesotho in 1858 of François Coillard whose decision to join the PEMS had been inspired by Ami Bost's work in central France.[42] These men would make an indelible mark on the mission field, and several would achieve renown by modernizing the study of humanity in Africa.[43] Most of these missionaries were the sons of clergymen or church elders whose ties to the pastorate were frequently reinforced by bonds of marriage.[44] They were drawn from the *classes cultivées* of evangelical society or were products of the new educational opportunities open to men of energy and talent. Brought up during the hard years following the church schism, several had an intimate experience of material deprivation and personal sacrifice and a firm notion of devotion; few would ever return to Switzerland.

As the Free Church grew in strength, it was supported by a range of institutions, rituals and beliefs that confirmed and asserted the urgency of evangelical work. Religious and charitable organizations proliferated as industrialization killed domestic industries; workshops, factories and public schools displaced the patriarchal home as a site of training, socialization and fellowship. The enlightened elite heading the Free Church played an important role in the establishment and maintenance of these institutions. They saw humankind's fall from grace in the growing problems facing society: the breakup of the family, disrespect for authority, alcoholism, crime, sexual promiscuity, social uprootedness and disbelief. Evangelicals traced this social degeneration less to poverty than to the immorality of the working class as the community most shaken by the forces of industrialization. Young Christians in western Switzerland sought to guide and tutor their fallen kinsmen through a combination of evangelical zeal and moral reform.

Probably the most renowned group formed by these citizens of the world was the *Réunion de jeudi* (the Thursday meeting), a collection of young people awakened by the *réveil* who met in Geneva for the first time in 1847 to combine Bible study with prayer and philanthropic work. Five years later, under the leadership of Henri Dunant, they combined with colleagues in Lausanne to form the *Union chrétienne de jeunes gens* (the Young People's Christian Union). In 1855, this organization provided the impulse for the establishment of the World Alliance of Young Men's Christian Associations in Geneva.[45] The same urge to propagate a form of universal welfare marked by evangelical Christianity led Dunant and his friends to establish a Geographical Society in Geneva in 1858. A year later, Dunant and the military surgeon Louis Appia witnessed the Battle of Solferino in Italy. Being exposed to such suffering led the two men to draw up the First Geneva Convention for the Treatment of Wounded Soldiers and to establish the International Red Cross in 1864.[46] The Geographical Society of Geneva particularly drew attention to Africa through its journal, *Le Globe*, founded in 1860. After the Geographical Conference held in Brussels in 1876 initiated a new level of African exploration, the same circles in Geneva established a more specialized monthly magazine, *l'Afrique explorée et civilisée*.[47] The founding of new geographical societies in Bern (1873), St. Gallen (1878) and Neuchâtel (1885), added to the exposure given to the evils of the slave trade in Africa, and gave new emphasis to the work of exploration and evangelization in the continent.[48] The same cocktail of Christianity and cosmopolitan care underscored various anti-slavery movements in western Switzerland and stimulated the creation of the *Croix bleu*, an international temperance society, and the formation of a popular Sunday Observance movement. It also found expression in the vigorous industrial paternalism that marked labour relations in western Switzerland.[49]

Children were early beneficiaries of this new social responsibility. Deprived of the old patterns of sociability based on the family, they looked to religious associations to organize their leisure time. Parents separated from their children by a new work regime found the schools a particularly useful site of education and training for their offspring. In July 1852, five years after the schism in the Vaudois church, a Sunday School Society was founded in the canton. Its object was to coordinate and reinforce the scattered, often ephemeral work of Sunday schools in the canton and to reinforce religious training in the face of the growing secularization of public schools. The Vaudois Sunday School Society quickly produced a manual for monitors and (in 1855) an inexpensive collection of fifty hymns for children.[50] It sent out edifying pamphlets, sold religious books and maps, took subscriptions to the Paris Mission's *Petit messager des missions évangéliques*, established a circulating library and laid the foundations of a Sunday school culture by encouraging the exchange of ideas and experiences. In 1860 its activities were further strengthened by the appointment of a full-time agent.

Enrolments soared. Between 1852 and 1858 the number of Sunday schools doubled and almost doubled again over the next four years, when 10,000 Vaudois children attended 250 Sunday schools. The 440 monitors and 60 pastors who served these schools were motivated by proselytizing ideals and supported financially by evangelical movements in Britain and America.[51] Although ostensibly interdenominational, the schools tended to be dominated by non-conformists. Indeed, in some National Church quarters they were associated with *mômiers* bringing into the canton 'imported merchandise ... smelling strongly of odours coming from across the Channel, or even from across the Atlantic'.[52]

Cantonal patriotism emerged as another force underscoring the evangelical impulse of the Free Church. As early as 1828 Vinet had refuted critics' claims that missionary work overseas was unpatriotic. 'Will he ever see that dear land again,' he wrote of the departing missionary, 'this messenger we see leaving?'[53] The *démissionnaires* of 1845 had been quick to call their church 'the Church of the nation' and had stressed that their differences lay with politicians and their 'government church', rather than with the people of the canton.[54] The Free Church's claims to be the true religious representatives of the canton grew with the attempts of radical politicians to centralize and 'modernize' the loose collection of sovereign states called Switzerland. The constitution of 1848 had turned the Confederation into a common space by dismantling punitive tariffs and tolls; this process had been hastened by the construction of roads, railways, postal communications, a telegraph system and a common currency. But each canton continued to use its own coins and banknotes, weights and measures and retained its own army. Little attempt had been made to standardize the legal system or the social legislation needed to control the exploitative aspects of an uneven, spasmodic industrialization. Despite the introduction of universal male suffrage in 1848, some of the humbler sectors of the population were still unable to vote or alter this situation by sending their children to school. The rise of a militant nationalism on the borders of Switzerland, particularly following Prussia's victories over Denmark, Austria and France, and the establishment of the German Empire in 1871, caused many radicals to demand a revision of the constitution. But their vision of a more centralized, if defensible, country was opposed by liberals who saw in it a threat to the political sovereignty of the individual cantons and a danger to their vibrant, traditional cultures. For many, the destructive nature of nationalism was self-evident as thousands of wounded, sick and dying refugees poured into western Switzerland during the Franco-Prussian war. While the radicals saw the centralization of the economy and its unfettered expansion as a sign of progress, liberals tended to view this process with apprehension. As the growth of industry was accelerated by an unrelenting search for profit and a sterile materialism, it seemed to initiate a cultural crisis. This threatened to dehumanize society, cripple the individual's powers of creativity and destroy the cultural diversity of Switzerland. In the canton of Vaud, the uprooting of rural populations was accompanied by the introduction of foreign values and alien customs as cheaply printed books, huge numbers of tourists and (generally Catholic) immigrant workers flooded across the borders.

The old issue of religious freedom, responsible for the war of the Sonderbund, flared up again as the *Kulturkampf*, provoked by Bismarck's attempt to curb the influence of the Roman Catholic Church in Germany, was felt in Switzerland. When the Catholic Syllabus of Errors and the doctrine of papal infallibility were promulgated in 1864 and 1870, the radical governments of various Swiss cantons vigorously suppressed the implementation of these decrees and instead launched campaigns aimed at bringing the established churches more fully into line with the values and beliefs of the Enlightenment. To the Free Church and its allies in the Liberal Party, state-sponsored 'Liberal Christianity', and the religious intolerance of the *Kulturkampf* provided particularly vivid evidence of the dangers posed to individual freedoms by an interventionist state.

By the late 1860s the Free Church was able to combat the threat of state interference by stressing its role as the protector of local liberties. It underplayed the voluntarism of Vinet and his colleagues, who had supported the principled separation of church and state and, instead, blamed the schism in the cantonal community on the national church and its political allies. It portrayed missionary activity as a 'national' duty that, far from undermining local interests, would strengthen the base of the Free Church as a pivotal institution in the maintenance of cantonal identity. At a more general level, evangelical Christianity and universal compassion had become crucial elements in the mosaic of images that allowed the Swiss to think of themselves as a distinctive community. The spirit of neutrality and human concern driving institutions like the International Red Cross and the World Alliance of YMCAs bound the Swiss as a people and a nation. In this new social and political climate, the missionary movement promised to carry this same unique and uplifting message into the dark corners of Switzerland's world.

As the Swiss found a common sense of purpose and a new unity in this mission of compassion and care, the tide of popular opinion came to support missionary activity. By May 1869, it had moved sufficiently for two young students of the Free Church faculty, Ernest Creux and Paul Berthoud, to address their Synod on the 'pressing need' and 'serious obligation' of the church to establish an evangelical branch overseas. They were careful to distinguish themselves as 'sons of the Church', 'sons of the faith' or simply 'your sons'. This metaphor of biological kinship developed further as they couched their appeal in patriotic terms distinguishing 'we' Vaudois from foreign 'others', including even the interdenominational PEMS. 'Why send us away to others whose principles are not our own, whose customs are foreign to us?' they asked rhetorically. 'Others', they continued, 'to whom we are not attached by ties of blood?' The two students, one from Vaud and the other from Neuchâtel, were also careful to stress that Christians at home would find the mission field a testing ground for their faith and a source of strength for their church.[55]

Here was a clear expression, coming from two young members of the evangelical establishment, of the ties between blood and religion, nation and church, and the revitalizing role of missionary work.[56] The Berthouds had particularly grown into a pillar of the Free Church of the canton of Vaud. Paul was the fourth son of Henri Berthoud, by this stage a Free Church pastor in the fashionable town of Morges on Lake Geneva and a strong advocate of missionary activity. Paul's maternal grandfather was the notary Auguste Bonnard, a fervent revivalist, supporter of missionary work and member of the federal parliament. His three elder brothers were Free Church ministers who supported mission work in various ways. Paul's younger brother Henri would become a leading member of the mission in South Africa.[57]

The church was divided between those in favour of establishing a Vaudois Mission and a minority who wanted to continue channeling funds to the historic, interdenominational and international missionary societies in Paris and Basel. Some also feared that an expensive missionary programme in foreign lands might draw the disapproval of government at a time of resurgent state interference in religious matters. A Missionary Commission was hesitantly created in September 1869 and, three years later, Creux and Berthoud were 'apprenticed' or 'lent' to the PEMS in Lesotho.[58] This policy of caution and compromise was dropped, however, when the new Swiss constitution of 1874 both ended the demands on pastors to serve as administrative officers of the state and accepted freedom of religion as a practice. At the same time, the new constitution further entrenched local rights when it introduced a popular referendum aimed at curbing the powers of the central state and the political classes in general. Ten days after the passage of the new constitution the Synod voted to establish a mission in pagan lands.

Meanwhile, Berthoud and Mabille had left Lesotho for the Transvaal where, in 1873, they located a group of refugees living without a missionary in the Spelonken, a range of hills at the foot of the Zoutpansberg. Berthoud returned with Creux to the area in 1875 and, in the name of the *Mission vaudoise*, established a mission on a farm they called Valdezia.[59] The missionaries soon realized that the homeland of their congregants lay on the coastal plain of Mozambique. To fund the expansion of their activities into this new area, the Vaudois Mission looked for support to the other Free Churches in the Swiss Romande.

The Independent Church of Neuchâtel

The Free Church of Neuchâtel brought to the mission an experience of Christianity that at once reinforced and challenged the Vaudois influence. In the early part of the century, the established church in Neuchâtel had been governed by a Venerable Class of Pastors whose power and authority had not changed since the early sixteenth century. The Venerable Class, led by their annually elected Dean, effectively constituted a caste responsible for the nomination of all pastors. Like their cousins in the canton of Vaud, pastors exercised a strict control over the lives of church members. They controlled all religious education in the canton and exercised a monopoly over social functions, such as baptism, schooling, communion, marriage and funerals, that marked individuals as members of both the church and canton. Church records provided the state with basic statistics and the pulpit, particularly in rural areas, served to announce government decrees, decisions and news. Church elders looked after the poor and reported parishioners' improprieties to their pastor. Some consistories had the right to fine or even imprison recalcitrant parish members. Pastors could reduce recidivists to an effective internal exile by refusing to include them in the civic functions performed by the church. The Venerable Class also exercised an important hold over intellectual life in the town by creating a Theological College in the early 1830s, choosing all its professors and controlling the examination of their students. A harmonious relationship existed between church and state. The church was dependent for a major part of its funding on the state and, in return, sought its blessing when nominating pastors to their posts. A crack emerged in this relationship, however, when in 1838 the church refused to incorporate its theological college into the secular town academy established by the state.[60]

Although a Swiss canton, Neuchâtel had also been a Prussian principality since 1707. It had been incorporated into France in 1806 but was handed back to the

Prussian king in 1814 when it became the twenty-first canton of the republican Swiss Confederation. This unique situation brought Neuchâtelois students to Berlin where they came into contact with Moravians and pietists, and were confronted by the liberal Protestantism of Immanuel Kant, Friederich Schleiermacher and others. Their religious views were particularly influenced in the post-Napoleonic years by German advances in the fields of science and philosophy. The students brought these ideas back to Neuchâtel where they introduced a slow ferment into the church and challenged its structures with their conventicles and Bible-study groups. They often sympathized with proselytizing revivalists from Geneva and frequently supported the work of missionary societies based in Basel, Paris and Lausanne. They formed their own Missionary Society in the mid-1820s and sent Alphonse-François Lacrois from Lignières and Samuel Gobat from the Bernese Jura to the soon-to-become renowned training college for missionaries in Basel.[61] The Venerable Class criticized these separatist tendencies and in 1826 prohibited the Society's attempts to undertake its own mission work in foreign lands. In the long run, the pastorate managed to contain much of this religious enthusiasm and diversity within the church. This was partly because it had never signed the *Confession helvétique*, and the basis of church membership was national rather than dogmatic, and partly because, in accordance with the Prussian education of many of its élite members, most church leaders saw no fundamental barrier between reason and religion, or science and faith. The Venerable Class also discouraged its members from expressing their opposition to the revival in violent ways and, in general, it managed to include various religious tendencies within the national fold.[62]

The church had dominated social life in Neuchâtel for over three hundred years. In 1831 the failure of a republican rebellion against the Prussians accentuated the political importance of the church. In a climate of distrust, the clergy worked hard to heal the rift in the body politic and to prevent Neuchâtel's relationship with Switzerland from degenerating into that of a simple ally. But in 1848 the church's comfortable relationship with the state came to a sudden and abrupt end when radicals seized the government, expelled the Prussian governor, and dissolved one of the pillars of support for the old régime, the Venerable Class, or Company, of Pastors. The radical government then exerted its control over the church by passing a new ecclesiastical law on 1st January 1849. This shifted power in the church away from the pastors, many of whom looked back nostalgically to the lead once given by the Prussian king, and gave parishioners the right to elect both their councils of elders and ministers. Perhaps most importantly, the new law created an overarching Synod dominated by laymen and transformed pastors into salaried officials paid by the state. Unlike the situation in Vaud, the loss of clerical independence did not spill into a formal split between church and state. Although the Synod governed the church in place of the Company of Pastors, it was effectively led by clergymen, and dissidents were free to follow their religious conscience.

A remarkable group of theologians saw the church through this difficult period. James Du Pasquier, who had studied in Berlin under Schleiermacher and von Neander, served as the last Dean of the Company of Pastors and as the president of the Synod for almost twenty years. Frédéric Godet (1812-1900) also studied at the new university in Berlin and in 1835 became preceptor to the future Frederick III of Prussia. On his return to Neuchâtel he joined the theological college and played an important role, along with Du Pasquier and others, in negotiating the post-revolutionary relationship between church and state. The benefits to the state of a single, national church were underlined in 1857 when an abortive royalist *coup d'état* threatened to explode into violence and divide the canton. In the constitution drawn up the following year, the national basis of the church was reaffirmed when neither politicians nor pastors were allowed to dominate the institution. In 1859 the old Class of Pastors was even reconstituted, although without its former powers, as the Society of Pastors and Ministers of Neuchâtel. 'Our Church is national', DuPasquier announced confidently in 1865, 'it has its own life, perfectly distinct from that of the state.'[63]

After a decade of peace, the church in Neuchâtel found itself threatened from a new direction when its loose conformity of doctrine was subjected to a sudden challenge. In 1859 the publication of *The Origin of Species* focused critical attention in the English-speaking world on the Biblical narrative of creation and introduced a new wave of rational enquiry into religious life. In Switzerland, a German émigré scientist and political radical, Carl Vogt, who had translated Robert Chambers' *Vestiges of the Natural History of Creation*, found support for his materialist ideas in Darwin's work. When *The Origin of Species* appeared in French in 1862, Vogt embarked on an extensive lecture tour of Neuchâtel where his message was well received in working-class towns such as La Chaux-de-Fonds. Moving from town to town, Vogt drew large audiences to talks in which Darwin's ideas were used to explain the evolution of humankind for the first time. His starkly scientific approach to life, brawling anti-clericalism and confrontational approach alienated even Darwin, but Vogt's materialism questioned the very basis of religious morality in the canton of Neuchâtel, and challenged the church's domination of intellectual life. It provoked some Christians to reassess their religious ideas in the light of scientific discoveries.[64]

In western Switzerland, secular approaches to the history of the church and the Bible had deep roots in the work of Voltaire and Edward Gibbon. But in other parts of the Confederation, pietists had opposed these new tendencies with vigour, most famously in Zurich in 1835 when David Strauss' historical life of Christ provoked extensive rioting. By the early 1860s, the Germanic tradition of higher criticism, which applied the critical tools and methodology of secular literature to the Scriptures, had started to find an international readership.[65] At the same time that Carl Vogt left Neuchâtel, the literary critic, Ernest Renan, published his *Life of Jesus* in neighbouring France. Like Strauss, Renan subjected the New Testament to a thoroughly modern analysis of sources and a patient examination of details and dates. This attempt to present Christ as an historical figure led to a clash with those in the French-speaking world who believed the Second Person of the Holy Trinity could not be understood in human terms.[66] It also brought a new disequilibrium to Christian teachings as higher criticism seemed, for many, to enter into an unholy alliance with Darwinian evolutionism. This new tension in the relationship between science and religion was made particularly visible through a series of sometimes vicious disputes that occurred in places as far removed as South Africa and New Zealand in the early 1860s.[67]

In Neuchâtel, the publication of Vogt's lectures was welcomed by radicals who sought to challenge the hold over intellectual life in the canton exercised by liberal politicians and evangelical pastors.[68] The radicals launched a local *Kulturkampf* in 1866 when they challenged the carefully balanced *status quo* by attempting to wrest control of the old town academy from the liberals. After the revolution and the loss of the patronage of the Prussian king, this institution had lost its independence and had become little more than a tertiary extension of the school system. When the radicals re-established the academy as an independent body, they tried to reduce the influence of the church by engineering the resignation of two distinguished, evangelical professors. At the same time, they appointed Ferdinand Buisson, a republican refugee from Louis Napoleon's France, to the Chair of Philosophy and Comparative Literature. Buisson was a proponent of 'Liberal Christianity' who, two years after his appointment, called for primary schools to stop using the Old Testament as a reader and work of history. He condemned the turpitude and immorality in the Old Testament and qualified the laws propagated by Leviticus as 'disgusting'. Buisson stood for a church without dogma, a religion stripped of mystery and a personal morality tied to the concept of duty. He particularly called for complete religious freedom and, as a means of ensuring this, advocated the separation of church and state.[69]

Buisson's lectures in the winter of 1868-69 won a strong popular following but provoked a wide backlash from the clergy.[70] Frédéric Godet initially opposed the radicals' attempt to harness the academy and rationalize religion by joining the theological college on a full-time basis in 1867 as Professor of Exegesis and Criticism. Godet and others actively opposed Buisson's views in lectures to packed halls throughout the canton. After four years of protracted campaigning, the liberal Christians suffered a setback when their leader returned home after Louis Napoleon's fall from power. In France, Buisson quickly became a moving force behind the radical reforms brought to education by Jules Ferry in 1881–82. Director of Primary Education under the Third Republic, and editor of the teaching manual, the *Dictionnaire de pédagogie*, he came to exercise a major influence over several generations of *instituteurs*.[71] In 1905 Buisson would play a central role in drafting a law governing the separation of church and state that remains a pillar of French republicanism to this day. But in 1870, his retreat from Neuchâtel created a gap that was more than filled when the Vatican provoked new levels of outrage by promulgating the doctrine of Papal infallibility. Voters in Neuchâtel showed their appreciation for those who protected them from this narrow religiosity by voting in greater numbers for the radicals. This resulted in Numa Droz, the radical leader, taking over the portfolio of Public Education and Religion in May 1871. Later that year Droz called for the Ecclesiastical law of 1848 to be redrawn in such a way as to accommodate the tenets of Liberal Christianity. The draft law drawn up in February 1873 aimed to strip the Synod of its power to ordinate pastors and oversee their examination. These functions would be transferred to the Faculty of Theology that was to be incorporated into the Academy, an institution dominated by a radical government that ultimately would even choose the theology professors. While the draft law sought to place the structure of the church under state control, it also included a paragraph giving pastors the right to complete freedom of religious belief.[72]

Evangelicals and their allies vigorously resisted the passage of a law they believed would lead to dogmatic chaos and religious anarchy. While the Godets led the fight in Neuchâtel, they received unexpected support from Franz Overbeck, the free-thinking Professor of Theology in Basel, who denounced both liberal theology and the attempts of politicians to turn religion into a pillar of the state and its social order.[73] In March, the Synod, together with fifty-five members of the Society of Pastors, described the legislation as 'ruinous for the Church'. Despite this opposition, the law was adopted by a narrow margin in the legislature. It came into operation in September, but only after evangelicals and liberals lost a cantonal plebiscite on the issue, in which there were over a hundred spoiled ballots, by sixteen votes. To prevent the control of the church passing into the hands of radicals and atheists, representatives of twenty-one congregations met two months later to form a constituent synod. At its first meeting, held at the Collégiale, this body decided to form the Independent Church of Neuchâtel.[74]

Unlike the religious schism in Vaud some thirty years earlier, the establishment of the new church in Neuchâtel was the product of a drawn out, almost negotiated, separation of church and state. Although the entire theological college joined the Independent Church, just under half of the forty-three pastors decided to take this path. The government was careful not to inflame animosities when it chose to fill empty presbyteries with moderate pastors whose views were not calculated to provoke congregants into defecting to the Independent Church. It was also careful not to expel *démissionnaires* and their families from their homes or to prevent them from using church buildings. Yet at the same time, the government replied to the demands of the liberal Christians when it added a Professor of Hygiene to the five Professors of Theology appointed to the academy. For in this way, it recognized both the material, and moral, causes of social degeneration.[75]

The new church rested on its network of parishes, the theological college and the Sunday schools. Its printing was done by the Attinger family, just as that of the Free Church of Vaud was done by the Bridels. This close world was held together by a strong disdain for drink, dancing and gambling that found issue in active temperance and Sunday observance societies, and in a flourishing Sunday school movement. The leaders of the new church included Frédéric Godet, advocate Henri Jacottet, a professor of Law at the academy, and pastors Frédéric de Rougemont and Henri Junod, men who have some bearing on the course of this book.[76] When Du Pasquier died in 1867, Junod inherited both his job and his presbytery, a house first occupied by Guillaume Farel. From this urban vantage point on the slopes of the Jura, Junod looked eastwards over the lake and the fertile plains of northern Vaud and Fribourg to the Bernese Alps.[77] The building was a stone's throw from the Collégiale, the theological college, and the chateau housing the cantonal government. Junod was a staunch supporter of church independence and ran a newspaper supporting this cause during the crisis.

Henri Junod's start in life was unpromising. He was born in Saint-Imier in 1825 as the eleventh child of a farmer who had left the sunny pastures overlooking Lake Bienne and the Alps, to enter the dark, watch-making valley. When Henri was nine years old, the family moved back, across the Chasseral, to its place of origin at Lignières, a village in eastern Neuchâtel known principally for its cattle and cheese. Henry's scholastic abilities and social grace secured him the patronage of the village teacher and a local *grande dame* of deep piety. In 1842, when Junod moved to Neuchâtel to study theology, the same qualities won him the support of a relative prepared to house his impecunious kinsman. At a time when the front pews of the Collégiale were still closed to men of Junod's class, the young student financed his studies and acquired new social skills, grace and patronage, by working as the preceptor to a patrician family in Neuchâtel. He further inserted himself into the local bourgeoisie when in 1851 he became a minister in the local church and an important figure in the town's emerging Sunday school movement.

Able and articulate, Junod employed his cultural and social capital to marry into the industrial and political elite of the canton. His wife, Marie Dubied, was strongly influenced by the pietism of the Moravians and spoke highly of their missionary spirit. Her mother's father was Louis Courvoisier, an important watchmaker and local politician in La Chaux-de-Fonds. Louis' brother, Fritz Courvoisier, had played a leading role in the cantonal rebellions against the Prussians in 1831 and 1848.[78] The Dubieds lived at Couvet in the Val-de-Travers where the family had built its fortune on the manufacture and sale of absinthe. But mid-century the women in the family converted to the new evangelical Christianity sweeping the valley. Marie then married the young temperance activist Henri Junod in 1857 and, on the death of her father, her mother sold the family's share in a successful absinthe distillery. Her younger brother, Gustave (1827-99), then started a cement factory at Saint-Sulpice and her elder brother, Edouard Dubied (1823-78), established a prosperous knitting-machine factory at Couvet. Edouard's son Edouard (1854-1911) would build the House of Dubied into a major industrial enterprise.[79] In 1861 Henri Junod was posted to Chezard-Saint-Martin near the town of Neuchâtel where, two years later, Marie gave birth to their first son, Henri-Alexandre Junod. The Junods used this occasion to tie their fortunes more tightly to the successful Dubieds when Gustave became the godfather and his sister Rose the godmother of the infant. Henri-Alexandre's mother's brothers would play a dominant role in a world tightly held by the bonds of kinship. In a way that reinforced and strengthened the importance of blood and place, Gustave Dubied later moved to Couvet where another of his sisters married Alexis Biolley. Their daughter Emilie would marry the missionary Henri-Alexandre Junod in 1889. In the meantime these families set about applying the modern principles of science to a series of concerns ranging from religion to botany to industrial equipment.[80]

Missionary Origins

'The fathers founded the Church,' the secretary-general of the mission, Arthur Grandjean, would write from Lausanne in 1917, while 'the sons would found the Mission.'[81] This was true of the eminent evangelical families, such as the Berthouds and Junods, drawn from the comfortably patrician lakeside towns of Vaud and Neuchâtel. But it said little about the young men of strained circumstances who found in the mission an avenue for social advancement. Several of these young missionaries came from the small farms or the isolated hamlets and towns scattered along the cold, rocky valleys of the Jura mountains. Discouraged by the thin soil and long winters in these areas, many people supplemented a threadbare livelihood by spinning and weaving ribbons, cloth and lace, and, especially, by turning to the manufacture of pocket watches and clocks. The long, harsh winters also encouraged people to gather in the living room where they sang, talked and read by candlelight. These *veillées*, sometimes frequented by a pastor or a revivalist orator, often encouraged a reflective, philosophical religiosity amongst the three generations seated in the single heated room.

Arthur Grandjean came from the upper reaches of the Val-de-Travers where he was apprenticed to a watchmaker in 1874, at the age of fourteen, by his father, a peasant farmer turned village factotum. The boy experienced an emotional conversion at this time, partly caused by the death of his religious mother and partly due to a revival sweeping through the canton. The Sunday school, the Christian Union and the weekly evangelical assemblies held in the home of a village notable nurtured his faith. In 1877 Grandjean, inspired by a talk given by the missionary to the Ashanti, Fritz Ramseyer, and perhaps pushed by one of the cyclical downturns in the watchmaking industry, decided to become a missionary. As the young man was armed with only a primary school diploma, the Independent Church took charge of his education for the following nine years. This drew Grandjean into the centre of the evangelical community in Neuchâtel where he met a stream of missionaries returning home on furlough from Africa. In 1882 he joined the theological college in Neuchâtel, spent a year studying in Berlin and Tübingen and graduated four years later. In 1887 he was in Edinburgh, picking up English and some medical knowledge and preparing himself for his departure as a missionary to Africa.[82]

Membership of the missionary society afforded Georges Liengme a similarly steep social ascent. Liengme was born in March 1859 in the small village of Cormoret in the Saint-Imier valley. His family was poor. In his later life Georges remembered an uncomfortable period that saw the entire family billeted in one room at the top of his grandmother's house. He slept on a mattress filled with beech leaves and fetched coffee-grounds and leftovers from the miller, the richest individual in the village. As one of the eldest of seven children, Georges was obliged to take work as the village postman at the age of twelve. The following year he, too, entered a three-year apprenticeship as a watchmaker. The fortunes of the family improved when Georges' father drowned in a roadside ditch in a drunken stupor and several of the children reached an age when they could be employed in the booming watchmaking industry. At the same time, Liengme was caught up in the religious passion unleashed by the revival sweeping through the dark valleys of the Jura in the mid-1870s. After a turbulent conversion, he joined the local Christian Union and became a Sunday school monitor, activities that introduced him to a Christian fellowship and took him beyond the borders of Cormoret for the first time. He later signed a temperance pledge, largely because of unsavoury memories of his alcoholic father. Despite these manifestations of Christian zeal, Liengme's attempts to join the Basel Mission and the missionary Institut de Glay in France met with little success, largely because of the responsibility he was obliged to accept for his deceased father's debts.[83] At this time he undertook his military service in the medical corps and on his demobilization ended his watchmaking career in order to work as a nurse in the Saint-Imier hospital near his home village. But he still hankered after a career with the Basel Mission and as a means of learning German sought a position as a valet in Alsace, where a sister was in domestic service.[84]

Liengme's life took a new turn, however, when the Independent Church of Neuchâtel recognized his potential as a scholar and enrolled him in a school from which he succeeded in graduating, after almost four years, with passes in Latin and Greek.[85] Meanwhile he had decided, after talking to Paul Berthoud, to train as a medical missionary. This path was supported by the Mission which sent him to the University of Bern for three years before enrolling him, in April 1888, in the medical faculty of the University of Geneva. Liengme graduated two years later with a thesis on hypnosis and suggestive therapy. He spent the next few months at hospitals in Neuchâtel and Scotland before he married and, eventually, embarked with his wife for Lourenço Marques in July 1891.

During the 1870s, when the Independent Church of Neuchâtel held fewer than 5,500 adult members and had to scramble to find the funds to build its own churches and presbyteries and pay its pastors, it had little time for mission work. The investment in the careers of men like Grandjean and Liengme only came to fruition in 1883 when the Independent Church combined with the French-speaking Free Churches of Vaud and Geneva to form the Swiss Romande Mission. Through the concerted efforts of the three churches, nine Swiss made their way to the Transvaal in 1884 where their labours helped extend the mission into the coastal areas claimed by the Portuguese.[86] Almost a decade later, only two Neuchâtelois were left in the Transvaal, while ten others, including Henri-Alexandre Junod, Arthur Grandjean and Georges Liengme, were engaged in mission work in the Delagoa Bay hinterland. Henri Jacottet's son, Edouard, and four others worked for the PEMS in Lesotho. Another four Neuchâtelois missionaries were engaged in evangelical work on the Zambezi for the PEMS, while four others worked for the same institution in the French Congo. On the Gold Coast the Basel Mission employed Edmond Perregaux, his aunt and her husband, Fritz Ramseyer.[87] In Angola, Héli Chatelain worked for the Mission Philafricaine. Many of these men were university-trained intellectuals who found themselves in deep, rural areas of Africa. Imbued with a natural curiosity, a literary training and a great respect for science, several would produce pioneering, indeed classic, works of ethnography on the people to whom they had been drawn by their vocation.

The French-speaking Swiss missionaries in Africa came from a closely-knit community of believers. They were united by careful marriage alliances and by a memory of hardship and even persecution. Their history, values and ideals were ably caught in the publications of the Bridel family in Lausanne and the Attinger brothers in Neuchâtel. Their experience had produced an individualistic, emotional and flexible form of Christianity reflected in the democratic structure of their religious community. This community was the product of a recent history of struggle, even revolution; and the missionaries carried the dynamic tension produced by their Church into the mission field. Although the Church could no longer contain the diversity within its ranks in Europe, it was able to look to Africa for a new, homogenous, 'national' congregation.

While the church emerged as a deeply democratic institution in both structure and belief, it should not be forgotten that this development was a sudden, unwelcome reversal of the long, historical relationship between church and state. The Free and Independent churches retained vestiges of the political dominance they had once exercised. They refused to allow female members of the church to vote in ecclesiastical matters, despite their numerical superiority and their importance to the fields of fund-raising and Sunday education. They were financially dependent on the goodwill of the landed gentry and urban professionals as well as on the new class of industrialists who, like the Dubieds in Couvet, treated their workshops and factories as family enterprises. The deep-seated paternalism produced in this milieu had been one of the provocations leading to the radicals' seizure of power in mid-century. But paternalism continued to govern social relations in many parts of the canton where the Free Church's allies in the Liberal Party considered it the best way of defusing class antagonisms and the threat of social violence.[88]

The strains within the church growing out of the opposition between the individual and the community, freedom and duty, secularism and religion, democracy and paternalism, even the artisanal and the industrial, would play themselves out in the mission field in Africa. In this sense Africa served as an experimental field in which courageous missionaries could (re)constitute a civilization untrammelled by tawdry politicians and industrial corruption. But before turning to these points, I want to draw your attention to the widespread interest, enthusiasm and energy that fired the missionary movement in western Switzerland. Without the financial and social support of a large part of the population, the Swiss missionary enterprise could not have succeeded. The fascination engendered by the missionary cause and the deep commitment needed to support its logistics, brought Africa directly into the homes of the Swiss. Through this everyday encounter with Africa, the Swiss built and reinforced their sense of personal and social identity. Africa was on the periphery of their geographical world but it was a central component in the set of images through which the French-speaking Swiss constructed a picture of themselves and others.

Notes

1. Ami Bost, *Letters and Biography of Félix Neff, Protestant Missionary in Switzerland, the department of Isère and the High Alps* (trans. M. Wyatt, London, 1843), pp. 145–7. See also pp. 134, 142, 145–6, 178; Bost, *Visite dans la portion des Hautes-Alpes de France qui fut le champ des travaux de Félix Neff* (Geneva, 1841), pp. 66–7
2. Bost, *Letters and Biography of Félix Neff*, p. 145. Bost, *Visite dans la portion des Hautes-Alpes*, pp. 71, 81.
3. Daniel Robert, *Les églises réformées en France 1800–1830* (Paris, 1961), p. 358; Gonzague de Reynold, 'Notre Romantisme' in Daniel Baud-Bovy et al. (eds), *La vie romantique au pays romand* (Lausanne, 1930), p. 12. See also Philippe Bridel, 'Théologiens, moralistes et philosophes' in Baud-Bovy et al. (eds), *La vie romantique*, pp. 147–8. Also Henri Perrochin, 'La vie de la société au pays de Vaud' in Baud-Bovy et al. (eds), *La vie romantique*, pp. 33–4.
4. Bost, *Letters and Biography of Félix Neff*, pp. 145, 204, 178. The publication of Denis Diderot's *Supplément au Voyage de Bougainville* in 1796 had placed the archetypal noble savage in the Pacific, particularly Tahiti.
5. Samuel S. B. Taylor, 'The Enlightenment in Switzerland' in Roy Porter and Mikulas Teich (eds), *The Enlightenement in National Context* (Cambridge, 1981). See also M. d'Alembert's article, strongly influenced by Voltaire (who lived at Ferney near Geneva) on 'Geneva' in the *Encyclopédie* of 1757 where he represented the pastors – or at least several of them – as an ideal clerical community rejecting dogma and 'mysteries' (such as the divinity of Christ or the existence of Hell) that were opposed to 'reason'. See Voltaire, *Lettre à M. d'Alembert sur les spectacles* ([1758], n. d. : 1957?) introduction and notes by L. Brunel.
6. M. I. Klauber, 'The Eclipse of Reformed Scholasticism in Eighteenth-century Geneva: Natural theology from Jean-Alphonse Turretin to Jacob Venet' in J. B. Roney and M. I. Klause (eds), *The Identity of Geneva: the Christian Commonwealth, 1564–1864* (London, 1998).
7. Charles Marc Bost, *Mémoires de mes fantômes I: Ami et ses dix fils* (Ruffec, 1981), pp. 73–7; Robert, *Les églises réformées en France*, ch. 7; J. B. Roney, 'Notre Bonheureuse Réformation: the meaning of the Reformation in nineteenth-century Geneva' in Roney and Klause (eds), *The Identity of Geneva*; Timothy C. F. Stunt, *From Awakening to Secession: Radical Evangelicals in Switzerland and Britain, 1815–35* (Edinburgh, 2000).
8. C. M. Bost, *Mémoires de mes fantômes*, p. 76. Malan's grandson, Major Charles Malan, would play an important role in the South African missionary movement.
9. J. Cart, *Histoire du mouvement religieux et ecclésiastique dans le canton de Vaud pendant la première moitié du XIXième siècle* (Lausanne, 1870) vol. I, pp. 2–3.
10. Ibid.: pp. 10–11, 27.
11. C. M. Bost, *Mémoires de mes fantômes*, p. 18; Cart, *Histoire du mouvement religieux* I, p. 164.
12. E. Vautier (ed.), *Alexandre Vinet: Questions Ecclésiastiques* (Lausanne, 1945) I, pp. xv–xvi. Evangelicals were condemned on the same grounds in Geneva, see Roney, 'Notre Bienheureuse Réformation', p. 177.
13. P. Perret, *Nos églises dissidentes* (Nyon, 1966). Alexandre Vinet, *Mémoire en faveur de la liberté des cultes* (Lausanne, 1826).
14. Cart, *Histoire du mouvement religieux*, II, pp. 171–74, 205–6. The first Bible Societies were established in Vaud and Neuchâtel in 1814–15. H. Vuilleumier, 'Les origines de la société de Bible du canton de Vaud et son fondateur', *Revue de théologie et de philosophie*, Lausanne, 1915; A. Bost, *Letters and Biography of Félix Neff*, p. 209. The Religious Tract Society of Great Britain was established in 1799 and the British and Foreign Bible Society in 1804.
15. See, for instance, the Sunday school started by Valérie Boissier at Vallèyres in the 1830s, and later run by the de Gasparins and Barbeys, who were leading Vaudois families in the fields of education, science, politics, religion and missiology.
16. E. Bridel, *Résumé de l'histoire des écoles du dimanche dans le canton de Vaud* (Lausanne, 1927), pp. 6–15
17. J. Joseph, *Les écoles du dimanche de la Suisse romande* (Lausanne, 1896), pp. 8–10.
18. Bost, *Visite dans la portion des Hautes-Alpes*, pp. 31, 37, 59, 81; Bost, *Letters and Biography of Félix Neff*, pp.

    34, 77, 139, 218, 235.
19 Robert, *Les églises réformées en France*, chs 8 and 9. The *Magazine évangelique*, founded in Geneva in 1819, spread news about mission work. In 1821 Pastor L. Gausseu published his *Exposé de l'état des missions chez les Païens* in Geneva and Pastor Vallouy published *Coup d'oeil sur les missions* in Vaud.
20 Cart, *Histoire du mouvement religieux I*, pp. 189–95. For similar sentiments in Britain, see Jean and John Comaroff, *Of Revelation and Revolution: Christianity, Colonialism and Consciousness in South Africa*, I, (Chicago, 1991), pp. 49–52.
21 A. Grandjean, *La Mission romande* (Lausanne, 1917), p. 10.
22 Joseph Maitin (1816–1903) arrived in Lesotho in 1843. *Livre d'or de la Mission de Lessouto* (Paris, 1912), p. 184.
23 P. Bridel, 'Théologiens, moralistes et philosophes', p. 165.
24 Cart, *Histoire du mouvement religieux III*, pp. 281–82; Cart, *Histoire du mouvement religieux IV*, p. 54; R. Centlivres and H. Meylan (eds), *L'église vaudoise dans la tempête: lettres choisies de Samson Vuilleumier 1843–1846* (Lausanne, 1947), pp. 19, 67–8. E. Vautier, *La maison des Cèdres: la faculté de théologie de l'église libre vaudoise* (Lausanne, 1935), p. 15n1.
25 *Mômier* served as a term of denigration applied to religious dissidents. It was derived from *momie* (mummy), *momerie* (bigotry) and *môme* (child).
26 L. Vischer et al. (eds), *Histoire du christianisme en Suisse* (Genève, Fribourg, 1995), pp. 200, 204; Centlivres and Meylan, *L'église vaudoise dans la tempête*, 71; Cart, *Histoire du mouvement religieux* V, pp. 58–9, 114–18.
27 Grandjean, *Mission romande*, p. 18; Cart, *Histoire du mouvement religieux VI*, p. 522.
28 Vischer et al. (eds), *Histoire du christianisme en Suisse*, p. 210; Centlivres and Meylan, *L'église vaudoise dans la tempête*, p. 116; P. Centlivres and M. Fleury, *De l'église d'état à l'église nationale* (1839–1863) (Lausanne, 1963), p. 37; Pierre du Bois, *La guerre du Sonderbund: la Suisse de 1847* (Paris, 2002).
29 H. Berthoud, *La question ecclésiastique du canton de Vaud* (Lausanne, 1845).
30 Centlivres and Meylan, *L'église vaudoise dans la tempête* pp. 118, 124, 130, 139–40, 167, 179, 190; Cart, *Histoire du mouvement religieux*, V, p. 498. Stewart J. Brown and Michael Fry (eds), *Scotland in the Age of Disruption* (Edinburgh, 1993).
31 Centlivres and Meylan, *L'église vaudoise dans la tempête*, pp. 241, 247–8.
32 The two churches were finally reunited in 1967. On the memory of persecution, cf. Grandjean, *Mission Romande*, p. 287; C. Clerc, *Portrait de Philippe Bridel* (Lausanne, 1938), pp. 16–17. On the economic situation, Emile Buxcel, *Aspects de la structure économique vaudoise, 1803–1850* (Lausanne, 1981), pp. 53–56.
33 Vuilleumier in Centlivres and Meylan, *L'église vaudoise dans la tempête*, pp. 121, 241; Centlivres and Fleury, *De l'église d'état à l'église nationale*, p. 37; Clerc, *Portrait de Philippe Bridel*, p. 16.
34 Centlivres and Fleury, *De l'église d'état à l'église nationale*, p. 36; Vischer et al. (eds), *Histoire du Christianisme en Suisse*, p. 204; Centlivres and Meylan, *L'église vaudoise dans la tempête*, p. 247.
35 Centlivres and Meylan, *L'église vaudoise dans la tempête*, pp. 117, 237, 240–1.
36 Ernest Deriaz, *Un Homme d'état vaudois: Henri Druey, 1799–1855* (Lausanne, 1920), p. 232.
37 Auguste Forel referred to them as 'aristocrats' in his *Mémoires* (Neuchâtel, 1941), p. 26. A 'republican aristocracy' was Ernst Troeltsch's term for the Basel elite. Troeltsch, *The Social Teaching of the Christian Churches* (translated by O. Wyon, London, [1912] 1981) II, p. 687.
38 Contributions of SF18,000 in a good year had dwindled to SF700. Grandjean, *Mission romande*, pp. 30–31.
39 In 1844 Henri Berthoud advocated mission work as a responsibility of the (National) church. The following year he published his correspondence with the Conseil d'État on the separation of church and state in *La question ecclésiastique dans le canton de Vaud expliquée dans une correspondance officielle* (Lausanne, 1845). See also the role of Samuel Thomas, the former director of the defunct Mission Institute in Lausanne, in Yverdon where he rallied support for the mission cause. J.-F. Zorn, *Le grand siècle d'une mission protestante: la mission de Paris de 1822 à 1914* (Paris, 1993), p. 404. Centlivres and Meylan, *L'église vaudoise dans la tempête*, pp. 266, 292; Grandjean, *La Mission romande*, p. 36.
40 H.-A. Junod, *Ernest Creux et Paul Berthoud: Les fondateurs de la mission suisse dans l'Afrique du Sud* (Lausanne, 1933), p. 43; A. Grandjean, *Labours, semailles et moissons dans le champ de la mission romande* (Lausanne, 1898), p. 7. On the mission activities of the National Church at this time, see Centlivres and Fleury, *De l'église d'état à l'église nationale*, pp. 61–2; Grandjean, *Mission romande*, p. 36.
41 Edwin W. Smith, *The Mabilles of Basutoland* (1936, Morija, 1996), pp. 74, 78.
42 E. Favre, *François Coillard: Enfance et Jeunesse* (Paris, 1908), pp. 18–32.
43 Mabille (1836–94), the son of an elementary school teacher in Baulmes, northern Vaud, was educated in Yverdon and Basel (in German), Kendal (in English) and under Eugène Casalis at the PEMS' Mission House (in French). In 1859 he married Adèle, Casalis' eldest daughter. Mabille authored numerous translations and grammatical and lexicographical studies in South Sotho and he edited the first Bantu–language newspaper in Southern Africa, *Leselinyana* (1863). On Mabille's upbringing in Switzerland, see Smith, *The Mabilles of Basutoland*, pp. 69–87; *Dictionary of South African Biography* (*DSAB*) vol. I. Orphaned at the age of fourteen, Ellenberger (1835–1920) qualified as a printer and wrote the classic *History of the Basotho, ancient and modern* (1912). *DSAB* vol. III.

44 Duvoisin (1835–1891) was the son of a pastor and son–in–law of Maitin. The Germond and Duvoisin families were linked by marriage. Henri Gonin (1837–1910) was related to both the Duvoisins and more distantly the Moravian Count Zinzendorf. He was educated in Basel, Lausanne and the Oratoire in Geneva. While in Scotland, he was recruited for the Dutch Reformed Church. See *Livre d'or de la Mission du Lessouto* (Paris, 1912), p. 264; Grandjean, *Mission romande*, p. 40; *DSAB* vol. I.

45 C. Prouty Shedd, *History of the World's Alliance of Young Men's Christian Associations* (London, 1955), pp. 11–14, 32–3, 82–101; John Jaques, *Histoire des Unions Chrétiennes de jeunes gens de la Suisse romande* (Genève, 1902); T. Geisendorf, *Soixante ans de souvenirs de l'Union Chrétienne de jeunes gens de Genève* (Geneva, 1913).

46 C. Moorhead, *Dunant's Dream: War, Switzerland and the History of the Red Cross* (London, 1998), pp. 12–13.

47 H. Boutillier de Beaumont, 'Introduction', *Le Globe: journal géographique, organe de la société de géographie de Genève*, 1860, pp. v–xi; Anon., 'A nos lecteurs', *l'Afrique explorée et civilisée* 1879–80, pp. 3–4; A de Claparède, 'Coup d'oeil sur la société de géographie de Genève depuis sa fondation (1858–1896)', *Le Globe* (1896), 35, pp. 1–34.

48 A Swiss Topographical Society was also founded in Geneva in 1880. Dominique Lejeune, *Les sociétés de géographies en France* (Paris, 1993). The role of Swiss Geographical Societies in the construction of knowledge about overseas territories has yet to be investigated. For a start, see A. Barampama, 'L'Afrique vue à travers les publications du *Globe* entre les années 1860 et 1910' in the special issue on 'Cent ans d'exploration à Genève: L'Afrique au tournant des siècles.' *Le Globe*, (2000) 14. This has become an important theme in the imperial history of Britain and France. Cf. J. M. MacKenzie, 'Provincial Geographical Societies in Britain' in M. Bell, R. Butkin and M. Hefferman (eds), *Geography and Imperialism, 1820–1940* (Manchester, 1995); M. S. Staum, 'The Paris Geographical Society constructs the Other, 1821–1850', *Journal of Historical Geography*, (2000) 26:2.

49 Janick Schaufelbuehl, 'L'anti-esclavagisme Suisse sous l'emprise du Réveil' in O. Pétré–Grenouilleau (ed.), *Abolitionnisme et Société: France, Portugal et Suisse, XVIIIe–XIXe siècles* (Paris, 2005); B. Girardin, 'Le mouvement anti-esclavagiste genevois de 1860 à 1900 et son echo en Suisse', *Genève-Afrique* (1984) 22:2; Vischer et. al. (eds), *Histoire du Christianisme en Suisse*, pp. 225–27; Quartier-la-Tente, *Le district de Neuchâtel* (Neuchâtel, 1898), pp. 118–24. On industrial paternalism, see notes 79 and 88 below.

50 *Petit manuel des écoles du dimanche*; *Choix de cantiques à l'usage des écoles du dimanche*.

51 Joseph, *Ecoles du dimanche*, p. 12; Bridel, *Résumé de l'histoire*, pp. 16–19.

52 Bridel, *Résumé de l'histoire*, p. 21

53 Grandjean, *Mission romande*, p. 8.

54 Centlivres and Meylan, *L'église vaudoise dans la tempête*, pp. 189–90; Vautier, *Maison des Cèdres*, p. 14; Cart, *Histoire du mouvement religieux* VI, p. 187.

55 'Lettre de Mme. Creux et P. Berthoud au Synode des Eglises évangéliques libres du canton de Vaud', in Grandjean, *Mission romande*, pp. 285–89.

56 Grandjean, *Mission romande*, p. 43; Junod, *Creux et Berthoud*, pp. 12–14.

57 Henri Berthoud was pastor at Morges from 1849 to 1875. His eldest son, Aloys, was pastor at Lausanne 1877–87 after which he became professor at the School of Evangelical Theology in Geneva. He received an honorary doctorate from the University of Lausanne in 1912.

58 On the painful withdrawal of Vaudois support for the PEMS, see Zorn, *Le grand siècle*, pp. 405–13.

59 Smith, *The Mabilles of Basutoland*, pp. 213–18. On the early years of the mission, see J. van Butselaar, *Africains, missionnaires et colonialistes: les origines de l'église presbytérienne du Mozambique (Mission Suisse) 1880–96* (Leiden, 1984); N. Monnier, 'Strategie missionnaire et tactiques d'appropriation indigènes: La Mission romande au Mozambique 1888–1896', *Le Fait Missionnaire* (Lausanne, 1995) Décembre, no. 2.

60 C. Monvert, *Histoire de la fondation de l'église évangélique neuchâteloise indépendente de l'état* (Neuchâtel, 1896), pp. 1–20. Gottfried Hammannn, 'L'église réformée et les communautés protestantes' in Jean-Marc Barrelet (ed.), *Histoire du Pays de Neuchâtel*, Vol III: *de 1815 à nos jours* (Hauterive, 1993), pp. 220–33.

61 Lacroix (1799–1859) worked for 28 years in Bengal for the Dutch Reformed Church and the London Missionary Society. Bost, *Letters and Biography of Félix Neff*, p. 176; Grandjean, *Mission romande*, pp. 7, 10. Gobat became an important missionary ethnographer who played a central role in religious affairs and politics in both Ethiopia and Palestine. D. Crummey, *Priests and Politicians: Protestant and Catholic Missions in Orthodox Ethiopia, 1830–1868* (Oxford, 1972), pp. 29–49, 116–22.

62 This did not include a few groups of Plymouth Brethren or Darbyites and isolated communities of Mennonites that had existed in the region since the 16th century, or the small Free Church established in 1833. Monvert, *Histoire de la fondation de l'église évangélique neuchâteloise*, p. 72; Hammann, 'L'église réformée', pp. 238–40.

63 Cited in Philippe H. Menoud, 'L'église réformée neuchâteloise il y a cent ans', *Musée neuchâtelois* (1973) 10: 56–7.

64 Frédéric de Rougemont, *L'homme et le singe, ou le matérialisme moderne* (Neuchâtel, 1863). On Vogt, see Aidrian Desmond and James Moore, *Darwin* (London, 1991), pp. 543, 573.

65 Most famously in the *Essays and Reviews* published by nine clerics in England in 1860. Cf. John Rogerson, *Old Testament Criticism in the Nineteenth Century: England and Germany* (London, 1984).

66 Pressure from the Catholic Church led to the removal of Renan from his Chair at the prestigious Collège de France. See M. Rebérioux, 'L'heritage révolutionnaire' in A. Burgière and J. Revel (eds), *Histoire de la France: Choix culturels et mémoire* (Paris, [1993] 2000), pp. 154, 164–66. Alan Pitt, 'The cultural impact of science in France: Ernest Renan and the vie de Jésus', *The Historical Journal* (2000) 43:1.

67 Cf. Jeff Guy, 'Class, Imperialism and Literary Criticism: William Ngidi, John Colenso and Matthew Arnold', *Journal of Southern African Studies* (1997) 23:2; J. Guy, *The Heretic: A study of the life of John William Colenso, 1814–1883* (Pietermaritzburg, 1983); J. Stenhouse, 'Darwinism in New Zealand, 1859–1900' in R. L. Numbers and J. Stenhouse (eds), *Disseminating Darwinism: The Role of Place, Race, Religion, and Gender* (Cambridge, 1999). Scholars now tend to stress the continuing accommodation between science and religion in the period following the publication of *The Origin of Species*. Cf. F. Gregory, 'The Impact of Darwininan Evolution on Protestant Theology in the Nineteenth Century' in D. C. Lindberg and Ronald L. Numbers (eds), *God and Nature: Historical essays on the encounter between Christianity and science* (Berkeley and Los Angeles, 1984), esp. pp. 374, 379–81.

68 The lectures had appeared in German in 1863 and were translated into French in 1865 as *Leçons sur l'homme, sa place dans la création et dans l'histoire de la terre* (Paris).

69 Cf. F. Buisson, *Le Christianisme libéral* (Paris, 1865); Buisson, *Une réforme urgente dans l'instruction primaire* (Neuchâtel, 1868). Yves Bridel and Roger Francillon, *La 'Bibliothèque universelle' (1815–1924): Miroir de la sensibilité romande au XIXe siècle* (Lausanne, 1998), pp. 140–44.

70 Monvert, *Histoire de la fondation de l'église évangélique neuchâteloise*, pp. 86–120; Menoud, 'L'église réformée neuchâteloise', pp. 58–61; Philippe Godet, *Frédéric Godet – 1812–1900* (Neuchâtel, 1913), pp. 355–64. Marc-Antoine Kaeser, *L'Univers du préhistorien: science, foi et la vie d'Edouard Desor (1811–1882)* (Paris, 2004), pp. 336–74; Frédéric de Rougemont, *La divinité et l'infirmité de l'Ancien Testament: nouveau dialogue neuchâtelois sur le manifeste du christianisme libéral* (Neuchâtel, Paris, 1869).

71 Buisson wrote effusively of the 'living democracy' found in Neuchâtel and praised the canton's pedagogical institutions. President of the League of the Rights of Man, he received the Nobel Peace Prize in 1927. Theodore Zeldin, *France 1848–1945: Intellect and Pride* (Oxford, 1980), pp. 155–56; Pierre Nora, 'Le "Dictionnaire de pédagogie" de Ferdinand Buisson' in Nora (ed.), *Les Lieux de Mémoire* (Paris, 1997) I. For Frédéric Godet's reply, see *En réponse à la seconde lettre de M. le Professor Buisson* (Neuchâtel, 1869).

72 Hammann, 'L'église réformée', pp. 244ff.

73 Overbeck, an intimate friend of his colleagues Nietzche and Burckhardt, published *On the Christian Character of our Present-Day Theology* in 1873. L. Gossman, *Basel in the Age of Burckhardt: A Study in Unseasonable Ideas* (Chicago, 2000), p. 421.

74 Monvert, *Histoire de la fondation de l'église évangélique neuchâteloise*, pp. 157–225; Philippe H. Menoud 'L'église réformée neuchâteloise', pp. 61–70; Godet, *Frédéric Godet*, pp. 407–17.

75 Menoud, 'L'église réformée neuchâteloise', p. 72; Kaeser, *L'Univers de la préhistoire*, pp. 374–5.

76 Henri Jacottet (1829–73) was also a well–known poet. See Charles Secrétan, 'Henri Jacottet' in *Bibliothèque universelle* (1873) XLVIII: 526–35; D. Maggetti, 'La bibliothèque universelle à Genève' in Y. Bridel and R. Francillon (eds), *La 'Bibliothèque universelle' 1815–1924: Miroir de la sensibilité romande au XIXe siècle* (Lausanne, 1998), pp. 44, 50, 53.

77 *Société de Belles-Lettres de Neuchâtel: Livre d'or 1832–1962* (Neuchâtel, 1962), p. 59. Henri Junod, *Sermons* (Neuchâtel, 1884); *Le Messager boiteux de Neuchâtel* 1884.

78 Alfred Chapuis, *Fritz Courvoisier 1799–1854, chef de la révolution neuchâteloise* (Neuchâtel, Paris, 1947); Mario Jorio (ed.), *Historisches Lexikon der Schweiz* (Basel, 2004), III, pp. 522–3.

79 H. Junod and A. Bourchadat (eds), *L'eau–de–vie, ses dangers* (Paris, 1863). On the Dubieds, cf. E. Quartier-la-Tente, *Le Val de Travers* (Neuchâtel, 1893), p. 505; Jules Baillods, *La maison Dubied à Couvet, 1867–1947. Petite histoire d'une grande entreprise* (Neuchâtel, 1947); Georges Roulet, 'De la communauté d'entreprise à la communauté professionnelle', *Pouvoir et travail* (1944):133–49; Marcel North, *La maille et ce qui s'ensuit* (Neuchâtel, 1967). François Jequier, *Une Entreprise Horlogère du Val-de-Travers: Fleurier Watch Co AS* (Neuchâtel, 1972), pp. 94–5.

80 H.-A. Junod, 'Fritz Courvoisier et sa famille en 1831', *Musée neuchâtelois* (1912); University of South Africa (UNISA), Junod Collection, 1. 1 biographical notes on H.-A. Junod; Swiss Mission Archive, Lausanne (SMA) 303/11C, P. Loze on H.-A. Junod, 5 June 1934.

81 Grandjean, *Mission romande*, p. 41.

82 Jean Rambert, *Arthur Grandjean* (Lausanne, n. d. , 1931?), pp. 1–14.

83 Fondation pour l'histoire des Suisses à l'étranger, Geneva, Switzerland: Papers of Georges Liengme. Secretary of the Basel Mission to Georges Liengme, 7 November 1878.

84 This account is based on 'Dr Georges-Louis Liengme: notice biographique suivie d'extraits de ses lettres' (in SMA 180/1641/A) and on papers and extracts from his private diary kept in the archives of the Fondation pour l'histoire des Suisses à l'étranger, Geneva, Switzerland: Papers of Georges Liengme.

85 SMA 805/D, Secretary of the Evangelical and Mission Commission of the Independent Church of Neuchâtel to council of the Romand Mission, 1 May 1885.

86 Grandjean, *Labours, semailles*, pp. 15–17, 19.
87 *Nouvelles de nos missionnaires* (1893) 16, 1. P. Favre, 'Neuchâtel et la Mission protestante du Gabon à la fin du XIXe siècle', *Musée Neuchâtelois* (2004) 4. See especially Tim Couzens' biography of Edouard Jacottet, *Murder at Morija* (Johannesburg, 2003).
88 François Jequier, *Une Entreprise Horlogère*; Jequier, 'Fondements éthiques et réalisations pratiques de patrons paternalistes en Suisse romande, xixe–xxe siècles' in E. Aerts (ed.), *Liberalism and Paternalism in the 19th Century* (Brussels, 1990); Jean-Bernard Vuillème, *Suchard: la fin des pères* (Neuchâtel, 1993); M. Perrenoud, 'Economie et société' in *Histoire du Pays de Neuchâtel* III, pp. 162–3.

2
African Itineraries & Swiss Identities

> And God blessed them, and God said unto them, Be fruitful, and multiply, and replenish the earth, and subdue it: and have dominion over the fish of the sea, and over the fowl of the air, and over every living thing that moveth upon the earth. (Genesis 1:28)

Switzerland was a nation without colonies, but its very sense of nationhood emerged just as Swiss evangelists, traders, scientists and soldiers spread into the peripheries of their world. These adventurers were propelled by the search for profit and souls, but equally by an indefatigable curiosity and an organizing spirit. Through a wide range of lectures, sermons, exhibitions and popular writings, stretching from the spiritual to the scientific, these men brought an exotic world into the cultural heartland of Switzerland, and in so doing they extended the history of the country beyond its political borders.

Africa was a central element in the web of evangelical signs that captured the imagination of many Swiss in the nineteenth century. They found in the imagery of Africa tools with which to criticize their own society, but more importantly, they found in this imagery a means of self-definition. Evangelical propaganda helped portray Africa as a continent in need of the guiding hand and protection of Christian Europe.[1] But in the process the same views helped shape and create aspects of quotidian culture at home in Switzerland. The Swiss, a people deeply divided by differences of language, religion, region and class, saw themselves reflected as a group in opposition to what they saw in Africa, and they found a unity of purpose in the Dark Continent that would bind them both at home and abroad.[2]

Africa comes to Switzerland

In the previous chapter I remarked on the surge of support for the expansion of the Mission in the 1880s, a time of economic hardship in Switzerland. Although economic depression and unemployment caused emigration to quadruple at this time, support for mission work in far-off 'pagan lands' grew unabated. Between 1880 and 1890 the Swiss Romande Mission started to occupy an important place in the minds and pockets of many believers at home. During this period the amount of money collected for the mission doubled from 15 per cent to 30 per cent of the SF230,000 (£9,200) gathered by the Free Churches for mission work overseas. Following the recovery of the Swiss economy in the 1890s, collections for mission work soared to a peak of SF580,000 (£23,200) in 1901, of which one third went to the Swiss Romande Mission.[3]

This effort and enthusiasm rested on a capillary of energetic, popular organizations devoted to raising funds and generating propaganda for missionary activity. Fund-raising was considered an important means of spreading and developing interest in evangelical activity, particularly as it implicated donors directly in the development of the mission. Individuals were encouraged to support the mission through financial grants, by subscribing to make regular donations, by contributing to special collections, or by donating to the mission the profits from selling wild flowers, stamps or pewter paper.[4] Women played a central role in generating the financial and social capital needed to advance the mission. Women's sewing clubs adopted the names of individual mission stations; and they met regularly to provide clothing for public sale or to send to Africa. The large sums of money raised by the church indicate that the popularity of the missionary cause extended far beyond evangelical militants or even the formal members of the Free Churches. Fund-raising drew the backing of a wide community of supporters because, as this chapter suggests, the mission overseas came to reflect a broad Swiss ethos.

The widespread popular support for missionary activity was also manifested when members of the church left for Africa. These were occasions for celebrating and reinforcing the new, all-embracing evangelical community that cut across divisions of gender, age, denomination and class to even claim the support of those of little faith. In 1884 the Temple Neuf in Neuchâtel was filled to capacity when Ruth Junod and her husband, Paul Berthoud, left with Jeanne Jacot for the Transvaal and Edouard Jacottet departed for Lesotho. After these 'grandes et imposantes réunions des adieux', the Berthouds proceeded to Lausanne, where they joined other missionaries preparing to leave for Africa. In the Vaudois capital the Marterey chapel was too small to accommodate the well-wishers crowding into its narrow confines and a second meeting had to be held at the Tonhalle to celebrate this alliance between two of the leading evangelical families in the Swiss Romande.[5]

Five years later, when the recently married Henri-Alexandre Junod prepared to leave for Lourenço Marques with his wife, Emily Biolley, the couple was fêted at a number of churches in the French-speaking cantons. This long farewell culminated in a colourful ceremony in the large, official lecture hall in the chateau, overlooking Neuchâtel, that was occupied by the cantonal administration. The audience packed the hall and overflowed into the lobby and corridors. At this ceremony, church leaders from throughout the Swiss Romande led the celebrations and prayers. Singing raised the emotion of the occasion and united those present in a religious communion fastened by the cords of a shared patriotism.[6] Together with the large number of mission fêtes and bazaars held every year in different parts of the canton, these assemblies helped forge a dynamic community of faith. The Christian kinship forged in these assemblies secured and sustained the confidence of the church in its mission. Through this sense of evangelical duty, the Free Church convinced a wide range of people to encounter areas of the world such as Africa.[7]

The immense popularity of mission work stretched beyond physical communities to reach people linked only by their ability to follow the written word. This wide community of readers was kept abreast of events in Africa by the publications of individual missionaries.[8] The news-sheets produced by local evangelical societies, and the large number of sturdy, illustrated bulletins issued by the missionary societies, also informed readers of affairs in Africa.

In Vaud the *Feuille religieuse*, established in 1826, contained articles on Africa as a field of missionary activity. After the religious schism in Vaud, these articles were carried by the National Church's *L'Ami de l'Evangile* (1854) and the Free Church's *Chrétien évangélique* (1858). Subscribers were sent the Paris Evangelical Missionary Society's *Journal des Missions évangéliques* (1830) and the Moravians' *L'Ami des Missions* and *Journal de l'Unité des frères* (1836). The Basel Missionary Society directed the *Magazine évangelique* (1819) at Geneva, the *Feuille de Sou bâlois* and, from 1843, published *La Voix des Missions adressée à tous les chrétiens*. This society attempted to reach a more popular readership by selling *Le Missionnaire* in public bookshops. In 1862 pastor Nagel in Neuchâtel started to publish *Les Missions évangéliques au XIXe siècle* for the Basel Missionary Society. The work of the Neuchâtel Missionary Society, undertaken on the Gold Coast of West Africa in conjunction with the Basel Mission, was publicized in the *Bulletin de la mission achantie*. As the scope of Neuchâtelois activity in the mission field grew, this journal was replaced in 1878 by the bi-monthly *Les nouvelles de nos missionnaires*.[9] The bulletin of the Missionary Commission of the Free Church of Vaud started in 1872 as a quarterly review with a run of 5500 copies. Within a decade it had risen to 8000 copies published every two months; and by 1894 it was published monthly as the *Bulletin de la mission romande*. In 1917 distribution would reach 15,000 copies.[10] The Mission also engineered the publication of the private letters of missionaries and their wives and the printing of pamphlets on various subjects of topical importance to Africa.[11] Between 1870 and 1885, the Religious Tract Society of Lausanne managed to distribute some 120-130,000 copies of its publications every year, several of which related to Africa or what a later generation would call 'race relations'.[12]

Adults supported missionary activity and turned their thoughts to Africa, through their prayers and reading matter, and by joining various religious organizations. Parishioners were particularly made aware of this world in the lectures given by missionaries at home on furlough. In the 1830s-40s, Lacroix and Gobat returned from India and Ethiopia to address large audiences on the nature of mission work in those lands. The lectures were generally given in winter and provided a source of entertainment for auditors kept from their fields by long nights and harsh weather.[13] The popularity of these meetings grew as lecturers added to their talks on the achievements of the mission, information on African ethnography, geography and various branches of natural history. The folklore and songs of pagan peoples, often accompanied by music played on exotic instruments, spiced many lectures and brought the missionary cause and with it, Africa, to the attention of an audience well beyond that of the small Free Churches.[14]

Knowledge of Africa was also spread through church sermons and magic lantern shows, as well as through a series of photographs sold in commemorative albums, or singly in a manner suitable for framing.[15] In the late 1920s–30s missionaries advertised the problems facing communities in south-east Africa by staging short plays on African topics and by producing a series of pamphlets on topical subjects such as the race problem in Africa and the future of native education.[16] In 1900 the mission produced its first calendar, an important source of publicity and revenue that brought Africa directly into Swiss living rooms. Postcards also became an important means of advertising the mission. These were often produced to commemorate special events, such as anniversaries, or were sold as souvenirs, in towns and villages, at the annual mission fêtes that became important social occasions in many parts of western Switzerland (see plate 1).[17] A sketch by Ida Creux of the early settlement at Valdezia was strategically altered to serve as the central image in the iconography of the mission. In the reproduction, the founding mission station, bathed in a light absent from the original, looked onto the dark and threatening Zoutpansberg mountains. For the Swiss, this picture, displayed in their homes and carried in their books, was a constant reminder of their participation in the struggle against darkness in a faraway land.

Probably the most influential medium for the propagation of evangelical Christianity in Africa was aimed at children. A large part of the appeal of the highly successful Sunday school movement in the canton of Vaud turned around the image of the heroic missionary. The Sunday school movement had begun as an evangelical mission aimed at assisting parents in providing their children with a knowledge of Christian teaching and it had grown with the secularization of state schools. But it had also developed as a philanthropic mission, initially supplying children with an elementary secular education and continuously with a reverence for such virtues as probity and punctuality, responsibility and respect, benevolence and charity and above all, hard work. The Sunday schools were careful to ensure that the 'vertical charity' associated with the missionary movement fed into and reinforced the 'horizontal charity' of the self-help groups at home. The Sunday schools also took care to develop a popular, cantonal patriotism in opposition to critics who emphasized the foreign origins of their movement. When asked to sing *Les Capitales de l'Europe*, Vaudois Sunday school children thundered the lines *Lausanne surpasse Bruxelles et Paris!*[18] They listened respectfully to stories of 'our glorious Helvetic faisceaux' and of 'the humble martyr' Davel, the patriot executed by the Bernese overlords of Vaud.[19] The class monitor spread this philosophy to the children in her (more frequently than his) care. The broad appeal of the schools, run largely by monitors who served as social and spiritual guides, grew sufficiently to attract children attached to the National Church. By the end of the century Sunday schools had become such an established local institution as to host even the children of irregular churchgoers. Enrolments grew from 10,000 pupils in 1862 to 18,000 in 1883 and 30,000 at the turn of the century. By this stage, there was one Sunday school for every 600 Protestants in the canton and one monitor for every thirteen children; and nearly five-sixths of all Vaudois children were exposed to some degree of formal Sunday school teaching. In Neuchâtel each Sunday school served, on average, 580 Protestants, and a monitor was, in general, in charge of fourteen students.[20]

The influence of the Sunday schools spread beyond the formal instruction extended to children. A growing range of publications spread the Sunday school message, and with it a knowledge of Africa to children's parents and even into the homes of obdurate anti-clericals. In 1862 the small, monthly *Lecture pour les enfants*, founded thirty years previously by the Religious Tract Society, was replaced by the Sunday School Society's *Lectures illustrées*, a magazine attracting up to 14,000 subscribers. Two years later a weekly magazine, the *Messager de l'école du dimanche*, was established to supply families with edifying stories and Bible readings. In the same year, Neuchâtel introduced a twelve-page monthly magazine for children, *La Messagère du monde païen: feuille de missions pour la jeunesse*. With the support of the Basel Mission, this magazine was able to secure over 8,000 subscriptions. From 1865 illustrated religious cards (the *vignette biblique*) were distributed in an attempt to draw those unable to read into the ambit of the Sunday school movement.

The Society attempted to move in a new direction when, in 1872, it established a 48-page monthly journal for monitors and parents, *L'Education chrétienne*. Filled with illustrations and quick-reads, this journal was also a source of information on life in Africa and particularly on ways to spread support for the missionary cause in parishes and Sunday schools.[21] About 25,000 *Messagers* and *vignettes* were distributed every year and *L'Education chrétienne* reached some 1,500 subscribers.[22] Sunday school pupils' knowledge of Africa developed further when they entered into direct correspondence with young scholars in Mozambique and sometimes paid their fees. There was also a long history, going back to 1870, of adolescents in various parts of Vaud banding together to support the work of a specific mission station.[23]

African Images and Swiss Identities

So far I have attempted to trace how the growth of various institutions and practices brought a knowledge of missionary activity into most Vaudois homes and with it an image of Africa. I now want to examine the content of this knowledge and follow its entry into the mainstream of local culture. The object is to show how the missionary experience in Africa influenced the perception of the self held by the Vaudois and by extension other French-speaking Swiss.

A multitude of religious publications informed the Swiss public about Africa. *L'Education chrétienne* cautioned teachers to introduce the story of a mission to their pupils by starting with

> A topographical description of the place, then the interesting plants and animals to be found there, the people who inhabit the area, their nature and habits; this would be followed by a history of the mission.[24]

Auguste Glardon advised Sunday school monitors to transport their charges into the exotic world of the missions on the first Sunday of every month as this attracted their interest and won converts.[25] Information purveyed about the dark continent and its inhabitants tended to take a particular form. Missionaries writing home were well aware of the sensibilities of their readers; they were equally aware of the importance of their writings to the fund-raising efforts of their Society.[26] These different demands resulted in confusing imagery in which Africans were portrayed at once as obdurate obstacles to the spread of civilization and innocent victims in need of protection from foreign greed. In articles illustrated with pictures of human sacrifice, emaciated casualties of the slave trade and the local despots who ruled over these unholy practices, brave abolitionists were portrayed as the saviours of the African population. As the slave trade diminished and colonialism curbed the chiefs' autocracy, missionaries exposed a new and vicious product of Europe's search for wealth: the alcoholism accompanying the trade in pernicious whiskeys, gins and brandies and particularly in Mozambique, *vinho para os pretos* (wine for blacks). In this way Africans were portrayed as innocent victims who, like the poor at home, had to be protected from the malicious aspects of the pursuit of profit.

Missionary writings frequently emphasized the romantic virtues of freedom, discovery and strangeness; this contributed to the cult of feeling by employing powerful Gothic imagery. But the missionaries' writings also conformed to the literary conventions of realism and naturalism when they documented human conditions with the intention of exposing injustice. The slave trade was a popular topic in this genre. A wave of articles encouraged young readers to empathize with African children torn from their parents, sold into slavery and driven to the coast.[27] Vivid engravings, copied from photographs or drawn from the imagination, showed emaciated slaves making their way to the coast under the terrible gaze of their Arab captors; or presented the horrible conditions under which slaves were transported in the bowels of Arab dhows. The cruelty, death and destructiveness of the slave trade focused the minds of Swiss children on immorality and sin, yet implicitly offered a solution that at once blended earthly liberation with spiritual salvation.

The experiences of individual missionaries accentuated these messages. Readers shuddered in horror as they followed the adventures of Fritz Ramseyer and his wife at the hands of the Asante. From 1869 to 1874 these Neuchâtelois missionaries were held to ransom in the West African kingdom. Their station had been burned and they watched helplessly as well-organized armies left Kumasi to return with long caravans of slaves. The missionary couple recorded the large-scale practice of human sacrifice and recounted with dread how, following the death of an Asante prince, six hundred slaves and prisoners had their throats cut and three of his wives were strangled. The Ramsayers waited daily for the drum of death to call them before hideous executioners who 'in the guise of music, knocked together skulls, and threatened to skewer their cheeks with the dagger that would later cause their heads to roll on the "field of the vultures"'.[28] The terror aroused by these nightmarish characters with their accoutrements of human tibia and skulls was captured in photographs and dramatic engravings that adorned both the pages of Fritz Ramseyer's memoirs of captivity and a wide range of evangelical publications.[29] This picture of evil, against which the missionary couple pitted their heroism and faith, became an enduring evangelical icon that inspired a long string of popular commemorative works for almost a century.[30]

The missionaries and their readers came across, in south-east Africa, other shocking transgressions of practices considered normal by their society. In a way that confirmed the Ramsayers' picture of bloated evil, many missionaries presented an impassioned picture of the despotism, human sacrifice, slavery, and general cruelty of local politics. They denounced the infanticide, ritual murder, witchcraft and cannibalism practised by the natives; readers recoiled in horror before the incest, adultery and polygamy that marked sexual life in Africa.[31] Dark forces and unspeakable rites kept the natives in a state of immorality that cried out for both missionary intervention and the funds needed to support that intervention. At the same time, these bloodthirsty superstitions were signs of backwardness against which the Swiss could test their masculine character and measure their own level of evolution and civilization.

The success of the missionaries in protecting and transforming pagan peoples was recounted in various ways to generations of Sunday school pupils and their parents. Colourful tales recounted how African children, born into heathendom or slavery, were delivered from bondage by Christian missionaries. Such children ranged from Ogouyomi, a young slave girl found in an orphanage in Ibadan, to Mosodioa, a girl captured by the Swazi and freed by the Berlin Mission.[32] Several articles explained to readers that Africa was known as 'the dark continent' not because of the colour of its population, but because of 'the dark acts that are committed there'. Human sacrifice was an enduring aspect of these 'sores for which there is no remedy other than "the Gospel of Christ"'.[33] In one particularly ghoulish article of this genre in *La*

2.1 (a) *A wide range of missionary literature publicized the need to evangelize Africa. A popular image in missionary literature portrayed Africans as victims of the slave trade. In other images they were portrayed as victims of their own dark practices, or their despotic chiefs or, later, of imported alcohol and firearms. These images constituted genres of seeing that would have a lasting effect on the way Europeans imagined Africa.* Evangelisches Missionsmagazin, *1876, pp. 128-9.*

2.1 (b) *By exposing the horrors of the 'Dark Continent' to their readers, missionaries advertised the urgency of their task. Several generations of Sunday school children followed Fritz Ramseyer's account, written in the early 1870s, of his captivity in the Asante kingdom. This illustration of the king's executioners was published in a wide range of missionary periodicals.* Paul Steiner, Quatre ans de captivité chez les Ashantis. Récit abrégé, d'après les notes journalières des missionaires Ramseyer et Kühne *(Lausanne, 1876) p. 43.*

Messagère, an author recounted how, following the death of a chief 'in Angola', three children were captured by his followers, who then broke their victims' arms and legs before burying them alive with the corpse of the chief.³⁴ In another article in the same journal, tucked away in a footnote, an author informed his young readers in 1882 of having 'just learned that the king of Coumassie has had the throats of 200 young girls slit', in order to spray the foundations of his palace with their blood.³⁵ 'Every year tens of thousands of human lives are sacrificed in Africa to these cruel superstitions', an anonymous author informed his young readers in 1895. Five years later an article on human sacrifice in *La Messagère* was accompanied by a thirty-year-old photograph by Ramsayer of one of the Ashanti king's executioners, a man who 'estimated the number of victims to have died at his hand at seven hundred!' In neighbouring Dahomey, the article continued, 'five hundred victims were burned in one day, and they sprayed the former king's tomb with their blood'. The appeal of these images to youthful readers proved such that, as late as 1916, the magazine could carry the same old article on human sacrifice that it had run some twenty-one years earlier, word for word.³⁶

Cannibalism also proved an enduring topic in *La Messagère*. In 1881 readers could follow the uplifting journey of 'Zébédée Lefoula: the son of the cannibal who became a pastor'. Twelve years later they were treated to the story of 'How I escaped being eaten'. As late as 1900 an article entitled 'Are there still cannibals?' gave a long text providing evidence in the affirmative. A stream of articles aimed at children on subjects such as witchcraft, spirit possession and infanticide confirmed the picture of darkness and terror against which the missionaries struggled in Africa.³⁷ In one particularly grisly story, readers were told of mothers in south-east Africa having to open the graves of their infants who had recently died. By exposing the putrifying remains of their children to the elements, the women would cause the sun to cover itself in clouds that, in time, would bring rain. ³⁸ The editors of *La Messagère* were aware that their concentration on these detailed accounts of dark practices in Africa, at the expense of other less sensational stories, could frighten their young readers and give them nightmares. However, they estimated that this was a chance worth taking, because it was necessary to describe 'the dark acts that take place in the Dark Continent'. Only this knowledge, they claimed, would inspire Christians to engage in the intervention needed to end these cruel and savage practices.³⁹

Young Vaudois readers were captivated by tales of excitement, adventure, and heroic self-sacrifice in Africa.⁴⁰ When in 1883 the thirteen-year-old Paul Ramseyer decided to enter his uncle's profession, he felt compelled to add that 'it doesn't mean a thing to me, if the savages eat me'.⁴¹ The following year the annual play of the local chapter of the Neuchâtel students' *Société de Belles-Lettres*, headed by a young Henri-Alexandre Junod, was a tragedy set in the country of the Nyam-Nyam, a supposedly anthropophagous, tailed people living in the heart of Africa.⁴² Youths separated from their fathers by long hours in workshops and factories found important new role models in the courageous, masculine missionary whose picture (or that of his faithful family) was often displayed in their homes. In Switzerland these youths found a special hero in François Coillard whose exploits on the Zambezi seemed to parallel those of Livingstone.⁴³

Africa provided an unassailable picture of the immorality from which Swiss children were protected by their church and its clergy. Here was a graphic illustration of unambiguous sin, the need for repentance and the role of moral regeneration in the

2.2 *Fund-raising was a crucial aspect of missionary activity. New and innovative fund-raising mechanisms had continually to be developed. The success of the 'thank you' box soared after it was redesigned to take the shape of an African hut. The* 'tirelire à nègre' *is still to be found in a few parishes. Placed in public and private spaces, these and other objects brought an image of Africa into intimate corners of Swiss life. (© Swiss Mission Archive, Lausanne)*

search for salvation. The image of Africa portrayed in religious works also impressed on Vaudois children the need to show compassion, and to protect the 'weak and oppressed'.[44] Sunday school monitors supplied their charges with small cards divided into a hundred squares that were pierced with a pin on the payment of one centime. Later, inflation replaced these squares with a tree whose fruit could be pierced on the payment of five, ten or twenty centimes. Children were also encouraged to raise money by selling anything from wild flowers to pewter paper.[45]

A small 'thank you box' was employed as a receptacle for loose change in the home, Sunday school and meeting place. Placed on the family table on Sundays or birthdays, the revellers were encouraged to share their good fortune with far-off 'poor pagans'. When introduced in 1904, the *boîte merci* was a simple clock box that attracted about SF4000 in donations for the mission each year. Six years later it was transformed into a small African hut and donations rose by fifty per cent. Fund-raisers hoped 'to see a *boîte merci* in all families that are friends of the Mission'.[46] Another successful fund-raising device was a little statue of a black boy (a *tirelire à nègre*) that was placed in church entrances and, later, in shops. To the delight of children, the head of this little African figure bobbed approvingly each time a coin or a mischievous button was dropped into its lap. The *boîte merci* and the *tirelire* became important figures in a Swiss childhood as well as reminders of Africa's place in the world of children.

These fund-raising efforts drew children into the task of bringing salvation to Africa and, perhaps most importantly, brought the mission work to the attention of their parents. But fund-raising was also a pedagogical practice that through small everyday economies taught Vaudois children to be frugal and diligent, to value the virtues of benevolence, fidelity and dedication, and to appreciate community service.[47]

The large sums of money raised by the church indicate that the popularity of the missionary cause extended far beyond evangelical militants or even the formal members of the Free Churches. Fund-raising drew the backing of a wide community of supporters because the mission overseas came to reflect a broad Swiss ethos.

Europe's Past in Africa's Present

In the previous section, I showed how Sunday schools employed a picture of primitive Africa to tame the domestic savages of Swiss parents. The picture of the primitive condition of African society also presented the Swiss with the picture of a living prehistory that filled the 'the breach in cultural time' opened by contemporary geological discoveries.[48] By the mid-nineteenth century, Christians were being confronted by startling new evidence about the nature and age of the act of Creation. Some of these ideas had originated in Geneva, where the work of Charles Bonnet had shown that reproduction in micro-organisms was possible without the participation of two sexes. This kind of work had fuelled diverse questions about the process of creation. These in turn eventually led to Cuvier's discovery of the relationship between the fossilized remains of living organisms and the geological strata or ancient environments in which they were found.

A protegé of Cuvier and Alexander von Humboldt, Louis Agassiz, the son of the pastor at Saint-Imier, brought these ideas to Neuchâtel in 1832 when he arrived in the town to lecture on natural history. Agassiz's work on fossil icthyology and glaciology convinced him that the world was far older than the 6,000 years claimed by Biblical scholars. For many pietists, the origins of humanity were clearly explained in Genesis, or possibly in the works of Fontenelle and Paley who saw the world as the product of divine design.[49] To some public consternation, Agassiz distanced God's guiding hand from the process of creation when he drew a relationship between organisms and their environment. He informed his alarmed readers and spectators that Genesis was not a textbook of geology but simply a reminder of God's omnipotence.[50] The direct descendant of five generations of Neuchâtelois pastors, Louis Agassiz saw the existence of different species of fish in different geological strata as proof of a series of divine creations. His ideas influenced Frédéric Godet and his friends Arnold Guyot and Frédéric de Rougemont to reinterpret the Biblical act of Creation from a scientific perspective.[51] Darwin's discoveries and Vogt's lectures further unsettled this environment by posing new and startling questions about the place and nature of man in the history of the world. If humanity was indeed descended from the apes, then humankind was surely equipped with at least vestiges of the brutal drives and base instincts of animals. For most churchmen this idea was repugnant as it negated the moral basis of human life. But many people outside pietistic circles were attracted by humanity's dark and instinctual past and looked on with growing interest as scientists uncovered the prehistoric origins of their world.

At a time when many Frenchmen believed that Adam had spoken a form of Breton, Adolphe Pictet in Geneva developed a 'linguistic palaeontology' through which he reassembled the Celtic and Indo-European (or Aryan) languages and speculated on the lives of these primitive 'peoples'.[52] Others studied the regional patois to get at 'the most original, the least altered' forms of language spoken in western Switzerland.[53]

For these romantics, the patois formed a bridge between modern French and Celtic; it was a primitive vestige of an earlier, simpler age that represented the true essence of the character of the Swiss. The various linguistic forms spoken in the mountains of Switzerland were particularly considered 'naïve'. They were 'the voice of the valleys and alpine mountains', even 'pastoral' and 'melodious'.[54]

The historian Juste Olivier tightened the knot linking language and identity when he described the 'parents' of his present-day Vaudois as 'a new people' produced by a mixture of degenerate Gauls, provincial Romans and Germanic Burgundians. But when he turned to the dark days before this 'fusion of races', he filled western Switzerland with a jumble of prehistoric peoples who sprang from the most febrile Gothic descriptions of Africa. Olivier pictured the ancestors of the Swiss as an intensely primitive people whose warriors, in one exemplary passage, return home with the heads of their enemies slung across their horses. The primitive Helvet then enters his homestead where, in a phrase worthy of Conrad, 'in the light of the moon sliding under the branches, the human prey nailed above the door hideously saluted the master'. While the master drank from an ancient skull, outside his hut 'the magicians consulted the pot in which boiled the blood of a captive'.[55]

In the mid-1850s the riotous imagination deployed by Olivier and others to construct the history of Switzerland before the Roman invasion was replaced by science. This occurred when a severe drought lowered the water level of some of the major lakes in the country and uncovered extensive lacustrine villages dating back to the Stone Age. As archaeologists reassembled the material culture of this prehistoric world, physical anthropologists busied themselves with digging up and putting together the human remains of its early inhabitants.[56] The discoveries of these new, modern sciences gave people who had been shaken from their existential moorings a new sense of place anchored in both time and space. As the Ramseyers had shown, dark and mysterious places were associated with feeling and emotion. But the penetration of these primitive areas of the world was paralleled by the discovery, or recovery, of an equally dark and mysterious past at home. The romance of exploration could be experienced in both space and time, especially when time-travel involved the thrill of unearthing origins and reconstructing authenticity.

In Switzerland, the inspiration drawn from the past was vividly expressed by the Gothic revival movement that drew inspiration from medieval monuments, particularly the cathedrals that dominated the nation's cities. Until the middle of the nineteenth century, 'gothic' was a term of denigration used to describe these dark edifices as symbols of the ignorance and cruelty that marked the age preceding the Renaissance. But for romantics in search of the authentic, the original, the real, the mystery of these dark buildings had to be 'unveiled' or 'penetrated'. They were shown to be the product of a successive accretion of architectural styles that hid the actual creative essence of their architects and builders. The large-scale restoration of the Collégiale in Neuchâtel to its romano-gothic origins, at a cost of SF250,000, centred around the demolition of the fifteenth-century additions that 'disfigured' the edifice. Workmen spent the years between 1867 and 1870 dismantling the wooden gallery and repairing the pillars and capitals disfigured during the wars of religion.[57] Similar works of restoration were undertaken in Lausanne and other Swiss towns where it now seemed possible to strip away the layers of time and uncover the very source of national art and creativity. The architects of the Gothic revival believed they were restoring ancient times in the same manner as paleontologists, linguists and anthropologists.[58] Much of this reconstitution of the past involved, as we shall see, a good deal of creative energy.

The Swiss also laid great stress on their more recent past. In a country lacking the cultural constituents of nationhood such as a common language and religion, history explained the voluntary pact through which the diverse cantons had created the Swiss confederation. Swiss intellectuals were also under increasing pressure to define the historical character of a nation subjected to the scrutiny of literary tourists. The Swiss defined their identity by turning to the study of local dialects or patois, regional literature, history and folklore. Through colourful carnivals, processions and pageants, they constructed new rites of fellowship and built a new fraternity on a visibly common past. Swiss missionaries and their supporters were raised in the intellectual excitement engendered by the discovery of this shared past; and they played an important role in the establishment of the new disciplines of geology, palaeontology, archaeology, philology and history.[59]

Most missionaries had been members of the student Society of Belles Lettres. The social activities of this institution, created in 1806, and the articles published in its journal, the *Revue de Belles Lettres*, were particularly important in creating a powerful strand of literary nationalism in the Swiss Romande. In Neuchâtel, the local History Society founded the journal *Musée neuchâtelois* in 1864 in which articles were published on cantonal history and archaeology. The *Musée neuchâtelois* attempted to combat 'unhealthy' literature, fortify religious faith, and recover the 'essential truths' and virtues of the past. These would reconcile royalists with republicans, unite and strengthen the state, and contribute to a general moral renaissance. Henri Junod and his son Henri-Alexandre were active members of the Historical Society, contributing articles to *Musée neuchâtelois* from its inception, for over fifty years.[60] They were also active members of the Club Jurassien, the junior branch of the Natural History Society, which turned frivolous rambles through the countryside into instructive and edifying excursions. On these outings, what a later generation would call 'fieldwork', young people were taught to infuse geography, natural history and prehistory with a new sense of utility.[61]

In this context, the Swiss developed a deep concern with the past and imbued themselves with the ability to recover it through documents and the direct observation of its material vestiges. So it is perhaps not surprising to find that the missionaries discovered in Africa further historical evidence that contributed to both the political identity of the Swiss and their own creative energies. For Europeans coming from parts of the world that had been ditched, drained and fenced into submission, the African landscape stood as a relic of an earlier age.[62] The magnificent fauna and flora of Africa also represented a more primitive stage in the development of the world.[63] Visiting Africa was like entering the time capsule or forgotten valley favoured by contemporary writers of science fiction. When Henri-Alexandre Junod arrived in Africa he thought the condition of the people had remained unchanged 'for centuries, perhaps for tens of centuries', and found their civilization to be 'of an extremely ancient date'.[64] By conflating differences of culture and time, he was able to compare the archaeological remnants of Stone-Age communities on the banks of Swiss lakes with those of 'the black in present-day South Africa'.[65] This led him to value African society for the glimpse it gave of the world Europeans had lost. 'When we turn to these primitives to decipher their conception of life and the world, our own ancient history surges up before our eyes', wrote Junod in 1898. 'These societies explain certain problems inflicting our civilized souls, which are merely grown up versions of their primitive ones. We become more conscious of ourselves and of the mysteries of our evolution.'[66] Junod reiterated this opinion twelve years later when he ascribed 'the great interest in the study of these primitives', to the fact that 'they help us to understand ourselves'.[67]

This practice was well established in Europe where the deciphering of ancient scripts, such as hieroglyphic and Demotic Egyptian and Cuneiform, had led to the discovery of lost worlds. The translation of equally ancient religious texts, such as the Zoroastrian *Zend Avesta* and Hindu *Bhagavad Gita*, provided access to very early, non-Christian religious beliefs. The study of language and folklore also brought new light to the understanding of prehistoric times. Through the collection and comparison of the affinities between different languages and their oral literatures, philologists believed they could construct a chronology of development. It was widely believed that, because writing had not contaminated the mentality of pre-literate peoples, the folklore gathered from isolated communities could provide Europeans with a glimpse of the thoughts and practices of their forgotten ancestors.[68] When taken to Africa, these ideas led folklorists to believe they could use their discipline to recover an impression of the very earliest concerns of humanity. It caused some linguists to search for elements of Breton or Welsh in African languages.[69] For the German philologist at the Cape, Wilhelm Bleek, tales and songs could be put together and analyzed in much the same way as the sounds of dying languages that through careful comparison could take philologists back to the beginnings of time.[70]

Through this approach, scientists believed they could reconstitute extinct languages, folklores and religions, or salvage them before they succumbed to the forces of modernity. This task bore many parallels with that of the paleontologist and fossil icthyothogist, who reassembled prehistoric animals from a few scattered bones. Langham Dale, the superintendent-general of education in the Cape Colony, believed that philologists could reassemble the earliest African languages in the same way that 'the great anatomist, from the fragment of a bone, reconstructs the animal, and gives it due position in the world'.[71] Junod also believed that 'linguistic research resembles in more than one sense the work of the palaeontologist'. 'Man's history, his migrations', he continued, 'is revealed to he who investigates the languages and traditions of primitive people.'[72] Africa was a living museum in which to study the evolution of language at first hand. It was possible to see how words were invented, adopted and changed in a continent where languages had not yet been frozen by writing. Directly observing the evolution and growth of oral linguistic forms in Africa, wrote Junod, 'can do much to explain the origin of language'.[73]

According to this vision of things, looking at primitive cultures enabled Europeans to recover a picture of their true, unexpurgated selves. In Conrad's *Heart of Darkness*, Marlow echoes this idea when he finds 'truth stripped of its cloak of time' in Africa. But whereas Conrad saw Africa as a place where civilization seemed only a 'flash of lightning' in the long space of time, Junod saw in the continent a glimmer of the dawn of civilization. While the missionary found in Africa the beginnings of a hesitant but ultimately comforting march towards perfectibility, the novelist found confirmation of humankind's fleeting appearance on earth. 'Contact with pure unmitigated savagery, with primitive nature and primitive man', he wrote elsewhere, brought 'sudden and profound trouble into the heart.' For those of little faith, this was a distressing but exciting reading of a world in which humanity was no longer the fixed endpoint of creation, the physical being closest to the angels, but merely a brief and insignificant phenomenon in the long flow of time. In literature and art, this dark picture coalesced with that of the Calvinists who, labouring under the weight of original sin, looked on the world and people's place within it, with equal anxiety.

Europeans drew different messages from their readings of the dark continent, but most agreed that Africa was a place of fear where, without the trammels of civilization, disquieting and deeply repressed instincts could surge to the surface. Freud located the origins of many aspects of human behaviour in mankind's lost past, and compared the mind to a geological deposit in which primitive and archaic strata lie buried beneath more recent layers. Civilization was indispensable to modern life but it was only achieved by sublimating primitive instincts. Stored in the unconscious, these unacceptable lusts and destructive passions exhibited themselves in forms of human behaviour considered disagreeable or antisocial. Psychoanalysis was a journey into the darkness of the unconscious mind through which people came to terms with, contained or corrected aspects of behaviour considered unacceptable by civilized society. Only once they had recognized the stifling effect of civilization could individuals find a personal liberation and, at the same time, release the creative energy associated with repressed, instinctual urges. For this reason, in *Totem and Taboo* Freud turned to ethnographic works by evolutionist anthropologists such as Frazer and Junod. In their description of primitive humanity, he found a European society stripped of its thin veneer of civilization. In this picture, Freud sought 'the oldest and most powerful of human desires', and the origins of the taboos used to control them. Taking evolutionist thinking to its logical conclusion, Freud believed that anthropology provided psychoanalysis with access to vestiges of ancient cultural practices that could explain the (mis)behaviour of modern humanity.[74]

In the dark and discomforting figure of Kurtz, Conrad wrote in *Heart of Darkness* of the atavistic urges and brutal drives that easily surge to the surface when Europeans are separated from the institutions and values through which they construct their civilization. But not all Europeans saw the disturbing side of the unconscious reflected in their reading of Africa. In his anthropological work, Junod displayed a serious interest, albeit in Latin (as did Boas), in the sexual practices of people whose customs and habits represented a primitive, early stage of mankind's development. Readers scandalized by the actions of Emma Bovary sat goggle-eyed before the sexual transgressions of African tribespeople. Even when the missionaries condemned the natives' unbridled sensuality, their descriptions served to provide a deeply repressed European society with the space in which to discuss various aspects of sex. For those less concerned with sexual drives, Africa's primitiveness seemed a prelude to Europe's modernity. For many, even the Regius Professor of History at Oxford University in 1964, Europe's past was to be found in Africa's present.[75] In a way that had multiple ramifications for their self-confidence and identity, many Europeans placed themselves at the summit of an ineluctable line of progress and perfectibility.

The image of a primitive Africa provided the Swiss with an important means of self-criticism and improvement. In a social context strongly influenced by religious Revival, Romanticism and even a return to Gothic architecture, primitivism was associated with the energy and excitement unleashed by the exotic. For many Swiss, European civilization was stale, moribund and weighed down by custom and tradition. If readers were unaware of this, *L'Education chrétienne* brought it to their attention in 1872 in its first issue. 'Our old Europe', they were informed, was marked by 'routine, habit, prejudices'.[76] Europe was burdened by the dissension and doubt caused by wars of religion, dry rationality, cold logic and sterile materialism, and a civilization built on the moral leadership of the church had been fatally undermined by the rise of the secular state. The result was everywhere to be seen in the absinthe-ravaged and alcohol-dependent populations of Neuchâtel that old Henri Junod and his son Charles-Daniel struggled to save.[77] In the uprooting and breakdown of the family, the threat posed to its reproduction by prostitution, the spread of venereal diseases and even masturbation, European civilization had become 'depraved and unscrupulous', wrote Henri-Alexandre Junod: 'the curses of civilization far exceed its blessings.'[78]

Frédéric Godet advocated the revitalization of society when he taught his students that the Reformation had brought the faith back to its source. By dismantling elaborate rituals and by casting aside the interference of priests and politicians, the Reformation had re-established the tie between the individual and his God.[79] In Africa, the church could almost start again. For some, the primitive beginnings of religion could be found in the social practices of African peoples. Junod stated this clearly when, on frequent occasions, he compared the religious practices of the Thonga with those of the ancient Greeks or when he described their ancestor worship as 'extremely ancient'. In a scholarly paper published in 1910, he went so far as to compare a prehistoric burial in Europe with the funeral rites, performed in December 1908 at Rikatla, of his neighbour Sokis (who had died of TB, a disease associated with industrialization). 'It is extraordinary, but it is a fact', he concluded, that 'the Bantu of today is almost identical to the Mousterian of 20,000 years ago.' He would later state quite categorically 'that the funeral rites of the first races were very similar to those practised by the Bantus of the present day'.[80] Through these comparisons, Junod believed he had uncovered what prehistoric Europeans thought and believed. The musings of 'elderly, intelligent natives' merely reconfirmed his opinion that the Thonga practised one of the earliest, original religions in the world. Viewed in this way, the pristine underpinnings of Thonga religion provided an original contribution to higher criticism, perhaps even a new epistemological foundation for the church.[81] For Junod, the delineation of an 'ancient' Thonga religion also served to confirm the widespread belief in the universal nature of religion; that the practice of religion was an almost natural state of being.

For many missionaries, religion in Africa had suffered a degeneration, and the task of the church was to awaken and revive the vestiges of monotheism on the continent. Using its experience in Europe, the church could build a fresh Christian community, almost a new world, in Africa.[82] Mission work in Africa would also bring the church back to 'apostolic times and pull it from its egoism and torpor', declared a Free Church pamphlet. 'Far from exhausting it, as many imagine, this spiritual exercise constantly revives and fortifies it.'[83] This picture of the mission rejuvenating the mother church in Europe became a popular Free Church image. 'The account of the victories achieved by the Gospel in the pagan world', wrote Arthur Grandjean, by this time secretary-general of the mission, would bring a 'spiritual comfort' to the home church and 'encourage and maintain the revival'.[84] The experience of the Mission in Africa impressed on the church the need for a well-trained clergy and a defined dogmatic base. By the early part of the twentieth century zeal and enthusiasm, those hallmarks of the Revival, were no longer the only keys to membership of the Church.[85]

However, many Europeans believed the picture of Africa presented by missionaries cast a critical reflection on their own civilization. As early as 1859, Eugène Casalis felt it necessary to warn against readings of missionary work that idealized and romanticized Africa, creating 'a golden age in those regions that language rightly calls *the dark places of the earth*'.[86] The missionary writer had to be careful that his words were not seized upon by 'some outraged communist who dreams of a new Arcadia' or by disciples of Rousseau, 'made *blasé* by civilization'. For they would attempt to find in his writings, Casalis continued, 'conclusive proof that the people we call pagans or savages are worth a thousand times more than us'.[87] Over sixty years later, Junod cautioned Sunday school monitors to point out that 'the black is not always as happy as is thought' for 'the African village, which could be a little paradise, is often rendered a hell by the profusion of sin'.[88] Despite these warnings, a nostalgia for a more secure, harmonious world governed by simple values and everyday traditions pervaded much of the missionary literature on Africa.

Africa in Switzerland

Many Swiss watched anxiously as railways, tourism, urbanization and secularism overturned the world they knew. Even the uncorrupted Alpine peaks fell victim to the advance of civilization when, in the summer of 1855 alone, fifteen climbers reached the summit of Mont Blanc. The important Swiss literary critic, poet and essayist, Eugène Rambert, portrayed this process in metaphorical terms when he referred to a struggle for survival in Switzerland between 'two rival races' of plants: the indigenous and the immigrant.[89] He decried the way in which 'civilization hunts down and destroys' these 'plant victims ... persecuted races ... whose fate is no different to that of certain human races'.[90] For the climber Emile Javelle, the Malthusian struggle for survival was most clearly visible in the Alps where the forces of change rising from the plains were transforming village communities.[91] Clustered around the fountain and the fireside *veillées*, the 'spirit that made one single, large family of all the inhabitants' of the village of Salvan was about to fall apart as 'what one calls progress' advanced up the mountain. Javelle decried the decline of 'the real, simple Salvan' and the disappearance of 'the innocent religion of olden times, the old ways, the tradition of simplicity, and all too often of honesty'. This was a serious matter, as the 'simple and unaffected' alpine village, 'unified and happy despite its laborious existence', constituted for many people the essence of what it meant to be Swiss.[92] As this world disappeared, intellectuals locked its spirit within idealized exhibitions and a literature filled with nostalgia for an earlier, more simple age. But the same spirit was captured in the primitive world discovered by Swiss missionaries in Africa.

Africa offered the Swiss an example of a living society uncontaminated by the disenchantment and conflict of an industrial age. This led many missionaries to be critical of aspects of imperialism. Europeans not only brought colonial wars and debilitating liquor to Africa; their civilization was inflicted with 'vices', 'curses', 'debasing influences', wrote Junod, and with 'immoral customs that paganism itself had never known, unbridled luxury, sometimes crying injustices and almost everywhere a selfishness without pity'.[93] His sister Ruth saw this process of degeneration most clearly in the drink, dancing and fighting that characterized life at Lourenço

Marques in the mid-1880s. 'The paganism that has been in contact with a Christianless civilization', she wrote, 'was worse than that found in isolated areas where Whites had not yet penetrated.'[94]

For those missionaries who refused to see the devil's hand behind the natives' cultural practices, Africans had a good deal to teach Europe. Unencumbered by the scepticism of a material age, Africans were able to embrace Christianity in a way no longer possible for most Europeans. 'From various perspectives', wrote Junod in 1898,

> it is easier for them to take at face value various aspects of Christianity, for example the precepts of the Sermon on the Mount, for example, than it is for us, Europeans of the nineteenth century, whose existence is so complicated. To never put yourself into a state about tomorrow, to never refuse to lend to those who want to borrow, to never amass worldly wealth, to live like birds in the sky and flowers in the field, is much easier in the simplicity of the lovely African kraal, with the system of common ownership of the soil and the limited role of money, than in our cities where everything is for sale, everything is valued in terms of money, and where the struggle for existence has become an everyday part of human existence.[95]

Thirty years later, Junod would reassert and develop this observation when he contrasted 'our cities where everything is for sale, everything is valued in money', with African villages where people displayed 'the respect for elders, the sense of family unity, the habit of mutual help, the readiness to share food with others'.[96] The African villager lived in the freedom Rousseau had found in the Val-de-Travers in the canton of Neuchâtel a century earlier. 'At little cost', wrote Junod

> he obtains from nature whatever he requires to satisfy his very restricted material needs. ...He is perhaps happier in the simplicity of his primitive life, with his diet of vegetable foods, his simple costume and his long leisure time than us, his superiors, taken by the impetuous current of our civilization with our industry and our strikes, with our slave-like existence, sometimes, our splendid comfort and our ever growing needs![97]

Europeans not only found in the culture of African peoples aspects of their civilization that had been destroyed by the values associated with unbridled economic growth, materialism and scepticism. In an attempt to escape the conventions of their age, European artists and philosophers found inspiration in the creativity of African tribespeople. They saw Africa as a place untrammelled by the constraints of civilization, as a continent of cultural experimentation where instinct and the soul triumphed over the dull intellect of the mind and creativity burst through the bonds of logic. In Europe, Alphonse de Lamartine had trained a romantic eye on the narrow conformity imposed on the wellspring of creativity by industrial society and mass consumption. How

> One saw with what care these dull-witted beings,
> had all been converted into living machines.[98]

In Basel, where Junod spent a semester at Switzerland's oldest university, Jakob Burckhardt stressed the contribution of individual enterprise to the history of civilization in Europe and warned of the dark consequences associated with the bureaucratization of culture and the rise of mass politics. According to this anti-modernist critique, the individual energies responsible for contemporary modernity had been undermined by the commodification of art and literature and by the rise of a popular market for paintings, novels and scholarship. This threatened to replace the creative independence of the individual with a popular mediocrity that, in combination with the political excesses of democracy and nationalism, threatened European civilization with annihilation.[99]

Junod expressed his own concerns about the century of the Chassepot, the eclipse of the individual, and the commercialization and levelling down of culture in Europe when he wrote with some sarcasm that Africa's creative vitality showed that 'spiritual activity is not only manifested by machines or by commercial speculation'.[100] In Africa he was moved by the 'power and beauty of African music', driven by strong rhythms, choreographed dancing and 'harmonic laws and rhythms unknown to us'. Junod found a subversive originality in the natives' oral literature, in songs and tales that were an almost instinctual, creative expression.[101] However, he opposed the idea that folklore was the primitive expression of unchanging, 'pure' cultural communities and that, unless copied down verbatim, it would be sanitized and drained of its creativity. Folklore was, instead, 'plastic matter unconsciously undergoing constant and extensive modifications in the hands of the story-tellers'. Ingenious and delicate allusions enriched tales in ways that were almost invisible to European writers. Restricted by the conventions of their times, European literary genres seemed calculating and bland. African folklore was a subject in which 'imagination overflows', wrote Junod of this early magical realism. 'It completely submerges all reason ... from this perspective certain tales are stupefying. It beats all moderation.'[102]

The innovation and strength of African narrative traditions were brought together in collections of folklore assembled by Junod, Chatelain, Jacottet and Henri Berthoud, missionaries from Neuchâtel and Vaud working in various parts of southern Africa.[103] A mental 'Cubism' grew out of Junod's foray into anthropology as he discovered totally different meanings for the words 'family' and 'religion' in Africa and uncovered new and subverting ways of looking at figures, such as the 'mother' or 'uncle', through whom people situated themselves in social terms. His picture of the family, or of a specific kinship relationship, served to destabilize existing conventions. Junod recalled a world still governed by enchantment when he described the ointment, mixed with the powdered larynx of a lion and the head of a grallatorial bird, rubbed into the calabash resonators of a xylophone, or the Gothic ingredients, such as the fat from a long-deceased leper, used in a magic philtre employed to catch witches.[104] This unexpected mixture of ingredients, like the incongruous juxtaposition of images in oral literature or musical notes in choreographed performances, helped to undermine conventional, mechanical habits of perception in Europe. It influenced one Swiss, Blaise Cendrars, to regard Africans as primitives living close to nature, and to discern in their folklore the ingenuity and authenticity of the early human spirit. His *Anthologie nègre* drew on the picture of an imaginative alterity created by missionaries like Junod and Jacottet that helped break both literary rules and the insular tradition of the Swiss Romande.[105]

Junod also discovered an artistic enchantment in much of the material culture he found in Africa; he and some of his colleagues sent a steady stream of indigenous artefacts to the ethnographic museum in Neuchâtel. These examples of 'primitive' art contributed to a renewal of artistic appreciation in Switzerland where painting was dominated by the romantic landscapes of Alexandre Calame and the naturalism of Gustave Courbet. In the 1870s, as European artists searched for feeling rather than fidelity in their portrayal of nature, this tradition was challenged by Impressionism. But others soon became critical of the passivity with which artists surrendered to the impressions of nature. These modernists wanted to express in entirely subjective art forms the spirituality, intuition and imagination of the mind, rather than merely capture the visible impressions received by the eye. To break the bonds of conformity that restricted European aesthetic principles, they attempted to find the primal, elementary forces of human creativity. These they located in 'artworks', considered 'primitive', whose lines, colours and perspectives shattered the conventions and controls of the European aesthetic tradition. Ten years before Picasso transformed the 'curiosities' in the Trocadero museum into 'works of art' that would galvanize European painting and sculpture, and Ernst Kirchner found inspiration in the African and Oceanic artifacts displayed in Dresden's ethnographic museum, Junod commented on the originality of African objects. These were produced out of an intensely spiritual, inner need he believed, and were not made merely to supply a mass consumer market generated by money. 'The Ronga are still in the childhood of art', he wrote of the people around Delagoa Bay, but this 'childhood also has its charms…'

> For primitives art is always the product of individual genius. It never becomes a mechanical exploitation as in the factories of the civilized world. That is why it conserves a character of sincerity, simplicity and beauty that we do not always find in the products of nineteenth-century European industry.[106]

Through this biological metaphor, Junod situated African sculpture in a single family of art dominated by the aesthetic values of parental Europe. This was a challenging perspective at a time when intellectuals like the Cambridge anthropologist A. C. Haddon still thought that, as the artworks of primitive people moved from naturalistic to more stylized forms, they reflected a process of degeneration. A radical like Gauguin would go much further, and overturn this hierarchy. Gaugin felt European artwork to be shrivelled, anaemic, small-minded and calculated. In a way that gave substance to Casalis' fears, he thought it inferior to the spontaneous, unconscious, almost instinctual creations of humanity to be found in primitive areas of the world such as Africa.[107] More temperate spirits, like Junod, also found in primitive art an image of ancestral instincts and primal sensuality. The raw simplicity and energy found in the artworks sent by Junod and others to museums in Neuchâtel and elsewhere (see plate 8b) would revitalize stale and cumbersome European aesthetic forms and provide them with sincerity and honesty. As critics from Guillaume Apollinaire to Sally Price have recalled, the appreciation of primitive art in Europe was about self-discovery rather than the discovery of the Other.[108]

Europeans discovered many other aspects of their own predicament as they penetrated the darkness of Africa, unveiled the continent's mystery and harnessed its creative energies. The network of fund-raisers and supporters of the mission at home was joined to the men in the field by a wide commonality of purpose and dedication. Criticism of their own civilization seldom extended into the outright rejection proposed by turbulent spirits such as Gauguin. For members of the Free Churches, the missionary was a heroic figure engaged in liberating Africans not only from the wages of sin, but from superstition, backwardness, despotism, and slavery. Sunday school children caught the essence of this enterprise when they sang

> Of mysterious Africa
> where an ignorant people vegetates
> the voice of the people calls to us
> to deliver them from their irons.[109]

Their elder siblings and parents joined in this celestial chorus at Sunday services, prayer groups and meetings of a range of evangelical societies stretching from the Christian Union to the Temperance Association.

> Glory be to God, the sovereign of the world!
> May the universe submit to His perfect law
> And his name, carried on land and sea,
> cause the irons of the captives of sin to fall.[110]

Delivering a people from bondage and submitting them to the universal morality of Christianity was both a spiritual and a secular task. For Arthur Grandjean, native women were 'slaves' of their husbands until transformed into 'companions' by the liberating powers of Christianity.[111] For Junod, evangelical Christianity introduced an individual consciousness that would free the native from the stranglehold of custom and community, and the autocracy of chiefs and ancestors.[112] All missionaries believed in the 'emancipatory' powers of their church and its civilization.[113]

This notion of liberation easily developed out of the need to atone for personal sin. It lay at the heart of Henri Berthoud's decision to enter the mission church, for he considered his labours in Africa 'a work of reparation' for the evils of the slave trade. Berthoud dedicated his life to the evangelical cause in Africa because of 'the immense debt that the civilized nations, and especially the Christian nations, have contracted towards this unhappy continent whose major rivers have, so to say, carried to the sea the blood of its inhabitants'.[114] Arthur Grandjean also viewed the mission's task to be 'a work of reparation' for the vices brought to Africa by Europeans.[115] Just as an individual could be rejuvenated or reborn through atonement for sin, so too could a nation or race be regenerated socially through the performance of reparative work in Africa. Hence, in the same breath as the Swiss construed it their duty to bring light to the dark continent and uplift its population, they celebrated their membership of the only race capable of achieving this task. 'The awakened soul', wrote Grandjean, 'approves quite naturally the need to share the light it has received with those who are still in darkness.'[116]

The Swiss found further proof of their superiority when they measured their achievements with those of Africa at national and cantonal exhibitions. The mission's collection of African artefacts, housed in a makeshift museum in the theological college in Lausanne, was first displayed at the Swiss National Exhibition in Zurich in 1883. The collection was again on display thirteen years later at the National Exhibition in Geneva, the Vaudois cantonal exhibition in Vevey in 1901 and another National Exhibition in Bern in 1914. In 1903 the mission exhibited a small part of its photograph collection in a Federal and International Exhibition held in Berne.[117]

The organizers of these exhibitions were concerned to present a vivid and life-like picture of various aspects of life in Africa. But the verisimilitude of the displays and their juxtaposition with manufactures of modern European industry served to reinforce Swiss perceptions of Africans as simple and backward.[118] The self-respect and pride of the Swiss as a nation grew when over two million visitors passed through the

Hall of Machines at the Swiss National Exhibition in Geneva in 1896. The admiration with which they gazed on their achievements mounted as they contrasted the power of their turbines, flywheels and presses with the simple industries and manufactures of the visibly 'prehistoric' people occupying the 'negro village'. And while they laughed at the 'bizarre gestures' and 'grotesque contortions' of African dancers and musicians, Swiss visitors to the exhibition discovered a sturdy comfort and unity of purpose in the pure, uncontaminated life presented by the bucolic 'Swiss village'.[119]

The mission celebrated its role in this hymn to progress by displaying its singular achievements in the transcription and translation of African languages.[120] Church members drew pride from their involvement in a mission field larger than France and from maps that showed their terrain of operations in Africa to be larger in extent than the entire Swiss confederation.[121] But the tone of celebration became more chauvinistic when the mission proved, statistically, that its rate of conversion was higher than that of other missions; or when it occluded other cultures when writing of its 'thirty-nine centres of light in the middle of a country of darkness' and its '3000 souls torn from the corruption of paganism'.[122] Swept up in the mood of these exhibitions, the mission asserted, 'in our time the development of missionary activity in pagan country goes hand-in-hand with that of colonialism. In many cases it precedes colonialism and even opens the way for it.'[123] This unequivocal support for imperialism, voiced in 1896, contradicted the cautious approach of individual missionaries. But it sprang from, reflected and gave support to the tenor of exhibitions demonstrating the forward march of humankind. At the same time, it celebrated the industrial and intellectual élite of Switzerland and reinforced the confidence of this class in its ability to guide and shape the evolution of society from savagery to civilization.

The sense of confidence and achievement produced by this frame of mind is also manifest in the missionaries' discoveries in the domain of natural history. For Henri-Alexandre Junod, Africa was a physically primitive continent occupied by animals and plants that had died out in Europe many centuries earlier. Africa was a dark corner of the world in need of light, a place of mystery calling for investigation.[124] The discovery and classification of species gave the ambitious missionary a sentiment of having conquered and domesticated the land. It also provided the Swiss with a sense of international achievement as missionaries published their findings in national and international scientific journals and, partly out of patriotic concern, delivered plants, insects, animals and ethnographic curiosities to museum collections.[125] The colony-less Swiss participated in the intellectual redrawing of the world as their scientists ordered the rare entomological and botanical specimens sent home, and arranged their findings in maps and charts. Scientific articles, museum collections, botanical gardens and herbaria, as well as local, cantonal and national exhibitions provided a constant reminder of the link between individual enterprise and the material achievements of the Swiss people. The exultation felt by missionaries in Africa as they gazed on the strength and power of their nation and their civilization, was reflected at home through these scientific institutions.[126] A product of their exhibitions and publications was the energy and enterprise that, by the turn of the century, had turned Switzerland into one of the wealthiest countries in the world.

Much of this energy had gendered overtones. Although women played an important part in building an evangelical culture in Switzerland, they were excluded from leadership positions within the church and its mission. As women could not serve

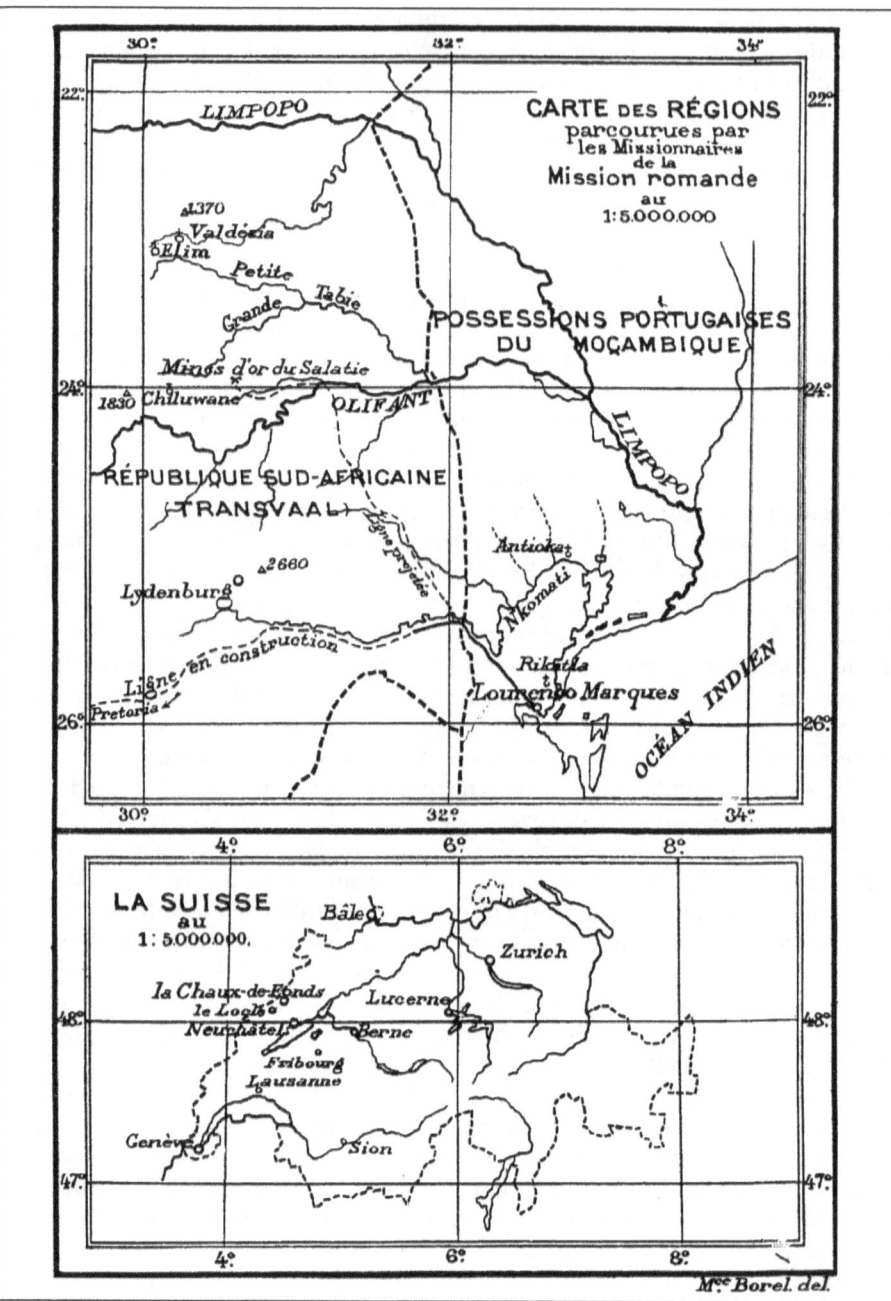

2.3 The Swiss missionaries took pride in the size of their mission field. This map, published in 1893, showed their field of operations to be far larger than Switzerland and, implicitly, advertised the need for supporters at home to help the work of the Mission. E. H. Schlaefli-Glardon, 'De Valdezia à Lourenço Marques', Bulletin de la société neuchâteloise de géographie *7, 1892–93, pp. 180–1.*

as missionaries, their energy tended to be confined to the domestic sphere, sewing and singing lessons, or mundane duties such as visiting the sick. As women rarely wrote reports and were inevitably relegated to the margins of mission biographies and histories, men seemed to dominate the mission field. Nor was there much place for romantic love in an evangelical task considered a duty and 'work of reparation'. Most missionaries married only weeks before leaving for Africa. When Adolphe Mabille courted his wife 'he spoke less about love than the Mission', wrote his biographer: 'he was as much his fiancée's pastor as anything else'.[127] Wives and *demoiselles missionnaires* were crucial helpmates in the field. Yet their role was hidden by a masculine language describing the missionary's task as a 'holy war' undertaken by the 'soldiers of Christ' equipped with 'spiritual arms' in a battle against 'the enemy of the soul'.[128] This martial imagery was particularly prominent in hymns calling out, 'Rise up, valiant army!' and 'Soldiers of Christ, into combat!'[129] 'You must hear us', Paul Berthoud called out to readers at home, 'to want to support an all-out struggle against the enemy of the soul.'[130] Even the discovery, conquest and domestication of the environment was described by missionaries in starkly masculine terms.[131]

Race was also a component of the reflected identity found by the Swiss in their image of Africa. Most Swiss missionaries rejected biological explanations for Europe's material success and Africa's stagnation; they opposed racist theories, including those of leading Swiss intellectuals of the preceding generation, such as Johan von Tschudi, Louis Agassiz and Carl Vogt.[132] But the missionaries' vision of mankind's common humanity was interwoven with a discourse of inequality. The African population was at an 'immature' stage of evolution from which it could only be released by a mixture of Christianity and enlightened knowledge, a brew of reason and religion.[133] The process of intellectual 'emancipation' had to be carefully supervised. Because Africans were a 'primitive, childish ... inferior race ... of weak character', wrote Junod, they fell prey to many of the vices of industrial, European society.[134] 'The Black', he wrote, required 'a sympathetic voice to instruct him and to put him on guard against the dangers of a civilization of which he attempts, all too often, to assimilate only the faults and vices.'[135] The missionaries carefully depicted the degeneration brought to areas of African society through contamination with the dark forces of industrialization.[136] In a wide range of stridently didactic publications, Swiss readers were shown the social ravages brought to Africa by alcoholism, avarice and alienation, nefarious forces that confronted the weak races of the dark continent with the threat of physical extinction.[137]

This starkly materialist view of the Calvinist insistence on man's fall from grace gave an added urgency to the role of the mission in Africa as social guide and tutor.[138] The Mission had to teach blacks to work and to accept the colonizer as their master. But in return for the black's 'unshakable loyalty,' his white rulers should exercise the justice and benevolence preached by Christianity.[139] The success of the mission in protecting and transforming pagan peoples was recounted in various ways to generations of Sunday school pupils and their parents. Colourful stories told of the tragic fate of African children born into heathendom or slavery and recounted their delivery from bondage by Christian missionaries.[140] Other popular stories told of the loyalty and respect with which black servants viewed their employers, and related the stoicism and fortitude with which they faced adversity.[141] This was a world in which good intentions were mixed with adventure and achievement; a world in which courageous missionaries fought the slave trade, unveiled the mysteries of the dark continent, penetrated its gothic gloom and, with the aid of trusty assistants, brought a redeeming morality to its population.

The achievements of the mission were summed up in flyers (selling at SF17 per thousand) comparing the image of a native pastor with a witch-doctor, or a half-naked pagan with scholars at the mission school. A similar image was created by contrasting the photograph of a heathen chief and his numerous wives with that of a Christian counterpart dressed in Victorian finery, or by placing the photograph of an Iron-Age furnace alongside another featuring the skilled handiwork of mission scholars.[142] This dualistic imagery of the African population, before and after conversion, had an obvious propagandistic appeal.[143] But it also had the pernicious effect of portraying Africans as either barbarians or what Arthur Grandjean called the 'ideal little negro of Sunday school children'.[144] While the idealistic picture impressed on readers the benefits brought to the natives by Christian tutelage, the 'before-conversion' image provided an illustration of what European society would be without the guiding hand of the church. In Africa the absence of a Christian clergy had led to the degeneration of religious belief and practice.[145] Without the protective hand of the church, Africa had fallen into darkness. Implicitly, this same fate threatened to engulf European nations that had shrugged off Christian guidance and with it the morality that constituted the cornerstone of European civilization. In perusing these texts and images of a primitive, churchless society, many readers probably saw a reflection of their own religious condition; and saw in Africa the fearful image of the decline into barbarism of a people without Christianity. Woven into the missionaries' representation of Africa was a call for clergy and church to play a leading role in the development of European society, a role that had only recently been suppressed in Switzerland by radical politicians and the forces of secularization.

By drawing frequent comparisons between the culture of 'tribesmen' in Africa and 'the peasantry or less cultivated portion of the town population' in Switzerland, Junod and others emphasized two important aspects of the church's role as tutor and guide.[146] First, the incomplete nature of the civilizing mission undertaken by the church in Europe. In France, Eugène Sue had compared the labouring poor of Paris with James Fennimore Cooper's American savages. These 'barbarians in our midst' had only recently displayed their ferocious disregard for civilized values during the 1871 uprising in Paris.[147] This picture of the Paris poor as almost a race apart was particularly disseminated by Emile Zola when he described their heroic but futile struggle to overcome the forces of heredity, alcohol and milieu.[148] The Swiss missionaries followed in this literary tradition and, by comparing the popular classes in their country with the younger and immature members of the family of man in Africa, gave notice of both their paternal obligations and their position at the summit of progress. This was the image of a church and clergy capable of protecting and redeeming Africans and of lifting them from darkness. But equally importantly it was the image of an enlightened elite that, strengthened and revitalized in the testing-ground of the mission field, had the duty and capacity to lead the Christian population of Switzerland into the twentieth century.

Junod and others believed that Switzerland, as a neutral country untainted by imperial wars and colonial excesses, could play an international role as a mediator in colonial matters. In the wake of the Congo scandals at the beginning of the century, a Swiss League was established in 1908 to fight the exploitation of colonial peoples. Five years later an International Organisation for the Defence of Natives was founded

2.4 Mission propaganda often featured 'before' and 'after' images. The flyer on the left, printed in about 1911, cost SF17 per thousand copies. It contrasts a 'witchdoctor' with a 'native pastor' (Calvin Matsivi Mapopé). The text describes the 750,000 Thonga in Mozambique and South Africa as the Swiss Romande Mission's field of operations. The flyer on the right contrasts a young man 'still pagan!' with a group of industrious 'future primary school teachers'. Both flyers outline the achievements of the Romande Mission but create fixed dichotomies that hide the process of social change linking the 'before' to the 'after'. This imagery was soon compounded by the creation of other discrete categories, such as the 'traditional' and the 'modern', that served to trap Africans in a discursive world stripped of history.
(© Swiss Mission Archive, Lausanne)

in Geneva to coordinate the work of various national associations calling for colonial reform. The same evangelical circles founded this organization as had established the World Alliance of Young Men's Christian Associations, the Geographical Society and the International Red Cross in Geneva. After World War I, the International Organisation for the Defence of Natives grew in importance when Geneva was chosen as the headquarters of the League of Nations and the International Labour Organisation.[149] In retirement, Junod became an active member of the International Organisation for the Defence of Natives, which some advocated calling the 'Black Cross', and its president in 1929. Here again, the mission fed into, and reinforced, the image of the Swiss as a small nation playing a large role on the international stage and as a diverse people united by particularly humane and just practices and values.

The Swiss at home saw in the image of Africa's manifest backwardness the outline of their own development, a visible material progress that could be ascribed to the accomplishments of a vigorous nation, an industrious middle class, a manly race and a true religion. Moreover, through their actions in Africa, the Swiss could claim to be a chosen people carrying God's message, as well as bearing a transcendent morality that distinguished them from other European nations. Through their prayers, financial contributions and personal devotion, the Swiss were able to contribute to the civilizing mission without implicating themselves in its violent, repressive aspects. As I have attempted to show, this positive self-image was reinforced by an absolutist language ranging Switzerland on the side of religion, emancipation and enlightenment in a war with paganism, slavery and superstition.

Out of this unambiguous, Manichean view of the world grew a moral superiority strengthened by photographs and texts displaying the image of hundreds of converts gathered beneath the many colourful flags of the Swiss confederation and its cantons. Far from home, Swiss missionaries expressed an embracing national identity at these rituals of welcome and departure. Converts at these events sang tunes drawn from Swiss hymnals while their children waved the red and white flag of the Confederation. Readers at home saw themselves reflected in gatherings in Africa where missionaries shared 'the lovely vaudois accent, *empeigne* shoes and Vetterlis rifles'; and they swelled with pride as far-off natives sang

> Oh Switzerland! Country of mountains
> You are a land blessed by God
> For it's from you that come those
> Who make God known to us

and

> Ah! you, Switzerland, little country,
> Although small, you are great
> Amongst the nations
> So numerous, through your love.[150]

These words were carried to a wide audience by Sunday schools, evangelical associations, churches and the flood of broadsheets, pamphlets, magazines and journals produced by these institutions. And the same ideas were transmitted by a multitude of images captured in exhibitions, engravings and photographs.

Identity in Switzerland had to rest on an imagery, mythology and history acceptable to people separated by sharp divisions of religion, language, wealth and culture. The Alps provided the Swiss with a powerful imagery of themselves as a sturdy peasant people living in a rustic democracy. This identity distanced and separated the Swiss Romande from the urbane, artificial French who, in the nineteenth century, slithered between revolution and autocracy. The Swiss also carved out of their invidious geographical situation a political neutrality and humanitarian vocation, while simultaneously defining themselves chauvinistically in opposition to working-class, Catholic immigrants, mainly of Italian origin.

This chapter has looked at the importance of missionary writings about Africa to Swiss conceptions of self. Enormous popular support and enthusiasm for mission work united a diverse cross-section of this population and provided it with a mirror in which to view its deep history and strength, and to renew its creativity. Missionaries took to Africa the material and moral support of a large part of this population and sent home a set of perceptions about Africa that helped shape the contours of Swiss identity.

Notes

1. I look at the image of Africa produced by the Sunday school movement in the canton of Vaud in more detail in Harries, 'Dompter les sauvages domestiques: le rôle de l'Afrique dans les écoles du dimanche en Suisse romande, 1860–1920' in Sandra Bott et al. (eds), *Suisse-Afrique (18e–20e siècles): De la traite des Noirs à la fin du régime de l'apartheid* (Berlin, 2005). I treat the same theme, produced by the Ethnographic museum in Neuchâtel, in Harries, 'Primitivisme au musée: la récolte des missionnaires' in Marc-Olivier Gonseth, Jacques Hainard and Roland Kaehr (eds), *Cent ans d'ethnographie sur la colline de Saint-Nicolas, 1904–2004* (Neuchâtel, 2005).
2. The cultural construction of Europe through interaction with colonial peoples is a growing field. See pp. 4, 7n14.
3. Donations to the Swiss Romande Mission only surpassed the other major recipients (the Paris and Basel Missionary Societies) in 1902. A. Grandjean, *La Mission romande* (Lausanne, 1917), pp. 330–31.
4. A. Grandjean, *L'Union chrétienne et la Mission* (Lausanne, 1899), pp. 8–13. In 1911–12 the Mission collected 255 kilos of stamps that it sold for SF2,745 and 280 kilos of pewter and lead worth SF531. *BMR* (1912), p. 403.
5. H. A. Junod, *Ernest Creux et Paul Berthoud: Les fondateurs de la Mission suisse en Afrique du Sud* (Lausanne, 1933), p. 118.
6. *Bulletin de la Mission romande BMR* (1889) April, 7, pp. 83, 212.
7. Missionary fêtes were held for the first time in Neuchâtel in 1852 and in Vaud in 1881. E. Hotz, *Paul Ramseyer missionnaire 1870–1929* (Paris and Geneva, 1930), p. 7; Henri Perregaux, *Edmond Perregaux missionnaire: d'après sa correspondance 1868–1905* (Neuchâtel, 1906), p. 17; E. Favre, *Notice sur la Mission vaudoise chez les Magwamba* (Lausanne, 1883), p. 10; Grandjean, *La Mission romande*, pp. 278–9.
8. Cf. S. Gobat, *Journal d'un séjour en Abyssinie pendant les années 1830–32* (Paris, 1834); F. Ramseyer, *Quatre ans chez les Achanties* (Paris, Neuchâtel, 1876); E. Perregaux and E. Vaucher, *Une visite aux négrillons de la côte d'or* (Neuchâtel, Paris, 1895).
9. P. Centlivres and M. Fleury, *De l'église d'état à l'église nationale (1839–1863)* (Lausanne, 1963), pp. 37,175n5; A. Grandjean, *L'Union chrétienne*, p. 11n1.
10. Grandjean, *La Mission romande*, p. 263n1, 278; Favre, *Notice sur la Mission vaudoise chez les Magwamba au sud-est de l'Afrique – souvenir de l'exposition nationale suisse de Zurich* (Lausanne, 1883), p. 15.
11. See the series *Actualités missionnaires*. See also Paul Berthoud, *Lettres missionnaires: 1873–1879 de M. et Mme P. Berthoud* (Lausanne, 1900) and *Du Transvaal à Lourenço Marques: Lettres de Mme R. Berthoud-Junod* (Lausanne, 1904).
12. Franco Ardia, 'Entre idéalisme et pragmatisme: Georges-Victor Bridel (1818–1889), Editeur-imprimeur', Mémoire d'histoire, Université de Lausanne, (1992) Octobre, p. 121.
13. Botanical Conservatory Geneva (BCG): Boissier Herbarium (BH), Barbey Collection: H.-A. Junod to W. Barbey 27. 1. 97; Favre, *Notice sur la Mission vaudoise* 10; Junod, *Ernest Creux et Paul Berthoud*, pp. 116–17.
14. Junod often played the guitar or the Chopi *timbila* (xylophone), Swiss Mission Archive, Lausanne (*SMA*)

303/11C, P. Loze to mission council, 5 June 1934; Perregaux, *Edmond Perregaux missionnaire*, pp. 184, 236; René Guison, *René Guison: Par ses lettres* (Lausanne, 1940), p. 50.

15 The cards sold for SF1. 50. There is a good collection in the Vaudois Cantonal Archives, Lausanne, Free Church Collection, section Saint–George 886, P. de Mestral. See also Paul Berthoud's photographs in P. Trivier, *Album de la Mission romande: mission des églises libres de la Suisse romande* (Lausanne, [1888], 1889). This work consisted of portraits of the missionaries and their families, views of the stations and various pictures taken along the route.

16 Henri-Alexandre Junod wrote and staged theatrical sketches on African topics in various parts of western Switzerland. Cf. *Théatre africain* (Lausanne, 1928); *Les Perplexités du vieux Nkolélé* (Lausanne, 1910), *L'homme au grand coutelas* (Lausanne, 1910), *La jeteuse de sorts* (Lausanne, 1923), *L'année de la famine* (Lausanne, 1930). The pamphlet series 'Actualités missionnaires' focused on social and political issues.

17 Cf. the postcards produced to celebrate the fiftieth anniversary of the establishment of the Mission. See below, pp. 247–8.

18 One wonders if they sang with equal enthusiasm the many songs beginning with lines such as *Travaillons sans paresse* (Let's work hard and not be lazy): Anon., *Chants pour écoles enfantines et pour les familles* (Lausanne, 1882) nos. 15 and 16.

19 Cf. Ch. Vulliemin, 'Centenaire Vaudois' in *Le Messager de l'école du dimanche*, (1903) April, nos 15–19, pp. 57–8.

20 J. Joseph, *Ecoles du dimanche de la Suisse romande* (Lausanne, 1896), pp. 14, 25–26; Georges E. Bridel, *Résumé de l'histoire des écoles du dimanche dans le canton de Vaud* (Lausanne, 1927), pp. 25, 27.

21 Topics included sketches of the Moravian Brethren and Count Zinzendorf, the colony of Sierra Leone, the Zambezi Mission, the Basel Mission on the Gold Coast, 'how God brought the missionaries to Lesotho', the Bamangwato; 'the Missions at Sunday school', and 'how to interest a parish in mission work'. Cf. *Le Messager de l'école du dimanche* (1883) February, no. 5; *L'Education chrétienne* (1908), nos 5 and 6; *L'Appel du monde païen*, (1920), pp. 4–5.

22 Joseph, *Ecoles du dimanche* 25; *L'Education chrétienne* (1872), November, p. 478.

23 Cf. *Aux écoles du dimanche: sections de l'espoir et autres sociétés qui s'intéressent à l'école d'évangélistes de la Mission romande* (Lausanne), Circulaire 1, September 1905, pp. 1–8; Grandjean, *Mission romande*, pp. 279–80.

24 *L'Education chrétienne*, September 1872.

25 Auguste Glardon, *Jésus sauveur des enfants: lettres sur les écoles du dimanche* (Lausanne 1879), p. 19. See also Junod, *Causeries sur l'Afrique à l'usage des cercles d'études missionnaires pour enfants* (Lausanne, [n. d., 1917] 1922).

26 Grandjean, 14 November 1889 in *Nouvelles de nos missionnaires* (1890) 4, 12; Junod 'Les Ba-Ronga: étude ethnographique sur les indigènes de la baie de Delagoa', *Bulletin de la société neuchâteloise de géographie (BSNG)* (1898), X, p. 12.

27 Cf. *Les Missions évangéliques: appel aux Chrétiens* (Geneva, 1855), pp. 21–3; 'Un élève du dimanche devenu missionnaire' *Le Messager de l'école du dimanche*, (1884) February and March, 9 and 10.

28 Perregaux, *Edmond Perregaux missionnaire*, p. 10.

29 See Ramseyer, *Quatre ans chez les Achanties*. For a critical assessment of their book, see Adam Jones, 'Four Years in Asante', *History in Africa* (1991), p. 18.

30 On the 25th anniversary of the Ramseyers' ordeal, Georges-Victor Bridel published a version of the book, abbreviated by P. Steiner, in the series 'Bibliothèque missionnaire', under the title *Quatre ans de captivité chez les Achantis* (Lausanne, 1894). This was followed seven years later by H. Perregaux (ed.), *Jours d'angoisse à Coumassie* (Neuchâtel, 1901). The Ramseyers' heroism was recalled again, sixty years later, in E. Porret, 'Prisonniers des Achantis: une extraordinaire aventure des temps héroïques de la Mission', *Clartés* (Société des écoles du dimanche, Lausanne) 1962. Arthur Grandjean ascribed his decision to join the mission to a speech given by Ramseyer in Neuchâtel. Jean Rambert, *Arthur Grandjean* (Lausanne, n. d., 1931?), pp. 5–6.

31 Cf. Henri Berthoud, letter of 20 January, 1887 in *BMR* (1887), p. 211; Grandjean, 14 November, 1889 in *Nouvelles de nos missionnaires* (1890) 4, 12, p. 52; P. Berthoud, *Les Nègres gouamba* (Lausanne, 1896), p. 74; Grandjean, *Le vieil évangile a-t-il fait son temps?* (pamphlet written about 1898 and published by the Société de traités religieux, Lausanne, 1907), pp. 8ff; Junod, *BMR* (1906) 19, January, p. 27; Ernest Creux, cited by Grandjean, *La Mission romande*, p. 98. Junod, 'Les Ba-Ronga', p. 390; Junod, *Life of a South African Tribe (LSAT)* (London, 1927) II, p. 413. This image of Africa was particularly strong in mission propaganda, especially in the Sunday school literature, Harries, 'Dompter les sauvages domestiques'.

32 Cf. 'L'esclave racheté', *L'Education chrétienne* (1872) II, February; 'Ogounyomi: la petite négresse' in *La Messagère du monde païen* (MMP) 1870, republished as 'Oguyomi: la petite africaine' (Société de traités religieux, Lausanne, n. d.); 'Véra, la jeune esclave' in *Chez les Gouamba* (Lausanne, c. 1893), pp. 34–40. See also 'Ajaï: le petit esclave devenu évêque', *MMP* (1892), pp. 50–7; 'Histoires d'esclaves au Togo', *MMP* (1908), pp. 197–8.

33 'Les sacrifices humains en Afrique,' *MMP* (1900), p. 17.

34 'Le continent noir,' *MMP* (1895), pp. 36–8.

35 *MMP* (1882), p. 3n1.
36 'Les horreurs du continent noir', *MMP* (1897), p. 180. This story was reprinted in *MMP* (1918), p. 83; 'Les sacrifices humains en Afrique', *MMP* (1900), pp. 17–18.
37 'Le nouveau–né chez les Gouambas', *MMP* (1895), p. 8; 'L'infanticide en Afrique', *MMP* (1893), p. 76.
38 'La pluie chez les Gouambas', *MMP* (1890), pp. 98–9.
39 'Le continent noir', *MMP* (1895), p. 38.
40 Glardon, *Jésus sauveur des enfants*, pp. 19–20. This belief was still alive in the 1950s when E. Porret could include an article on 'Boula Matari: la vie aventureuse de Stanley' in the Sunday school annual *Clartés* (Lausanne, 1956).
41 E. Hotz, *Paul Ramseyer missionnaire 1870–1929* (Paris and Geneva, 1930), p. 15.
42 'Chronique neuchâteloise', *Revue de Belles-Lettres* (1884) 12, 6. By the 1890s stories of tailed Nyam-Nyam (Azande) were no longer fully accepted; but the cannibalistic nature of the people of the region was left largely unchallenged. See *La Grande Encyclopédie: inventaire raisonné des sciences, des lettres et des arts* (Paris, n. d., c. 1890) vol. 12, pp. 413–14.
43 Cf. the biographical sketches in *L'Education chrétienne* of missionaries such as Van der Kemp and Moffat.
44 Joseph, *Les écoles du dimanche*, p. 36; Glardon, *Jésus sauveur des enfants*, p. 19.
45 Grandjean, *L'Union chrétienne et la Mission*, pp. 8–13. The sale of herbal tea was introduced in 1928 when it raised FS1,600 for the Swiss Mission. *Rapport annuel de la Mission suisse romande* 1928 (Lausanne 1929), p. 68.
46 *La messagère du monde païen* 1919, p. 126. *Rapport annuel de la Mission suisse romande* 1919 (Lausanne 1920), pp. 60–1.
47 *Aux écoles du dimanche: ou l'oeuvre des missions faite par des enfants* (Publications pour la Jeunesse, Paris, 1856); Grandjean, *L'Union chrétienne et la Mission*, pp. 12–13; Glardon, *Jésus sauveur des enfants*, p. 19. Grandjean lists some of the strategies used to encourage saving in *La Mission romande*, pp. 274–80.
48 The term is used by George Stocking in *Victorian Anthropology* (New York, 1987).
49 Bernard Le Bovier de Fontenelle, *Entretiens sur la pluralité des mondes* (1686); William Paley, *Natural Theology, or the Evidence of the Existence & Attributes of the Deity collected from the Appearances of Nature* (1802).
50 L. Agassiz, 'The diversity of the human races' in *Christian Examiner* (1850) 49, pp. 135n1, 138.
51 See pp. 128, 149n19.
52 Adolphe Pictet, *Essai sur l'affinité des langues celtiques avec le sanskrit* (1837) and *Les origines indo-européennes ou les Aryans primitifs: essai de paléontologie linguistique* (Paris, 1859–63), 2 vols.
53 L. Favrat, 'Introduction' to Dean Bridel, *Glossaire du patois de la Suisse romande* (1845, Lausanne, 1866), p. v.
54 J. L. M[oratel], *Bibliothèque romane de la Suisse ou recueil de morceaux écrits en langue romane de la Suisse occidentale* (Lausanne, 1855), p. iii.
55 Juste Olivier, *Canton de Vaud*, I, pp. 150–2, 162, 202.
56 See p. 126.
57 E. Quartier-la-Tente, *Le District de Neuchâtel* (Neuchâtel, 1898), p. 134.
58 Bruno Foucar, 'Viollet-le-Duc et la restauration' in P. Nora (ed.), *Les lieux de mémoire* (Paris, 1997) vol. I, p. 47; André Vauchez, 'La cathédrale' in Nora, *Lieux de Mémoire*, III, pp. 31, 34.
59 On the natural sciences, see chapter 5.
60 On the *Musée neuchâtelois* (*MN*), see Louis-Edouard Roulet, preface to E. Buser (ed.), *Musée neuchâtelois: table générale des années 1864–1963* (Neuchâtel, 1965), p. 7. The Junods contibuted articles on the political, religious and literary history of the canton to this journal. Cf. Henri Junod (Sen.) 'Un récit neuchâtelois de la 2ième bataille de Vilmergue', *MN* (1865), pp. 114–16; Henri-Alexandre Junod, 'Un très vieux livre neuchâtelois', *MN* (1889), pp. 53–7; 'Une moralité du XVIième siècle', ibid., pp. 101–12; 'Quelques lettres d'Alphonse Bourquin à Fritz Courvoisier: à propos des événements de 1831', *MN* (1898), pp. 221–30, 256–64, 280; ibid., 'Fritz Courvoisier et sa famille en 1831 (d'après des lettres inédites)', *MN* (1912), pp. 89–121. See also Henri Junod, Guillaume Farel (Tonneins, 1872) and, especially, Henri-Alexandre Junod's essay on the Neuchâtelois bookseller, 'Jules Gerstner' in *Revue de Belles Lettres*, (1884), pp. 7–23. Henri-Alexandre has become a recent subject of study in the journal. See Serge Reubi, 'Aider l'Afrique et servir la science: Henri-Alexandre Junod, missionnaire et ethnographe (1863–1934)', *Revue historique neuchâteloise: musée neuchâtelois* 2004, 4.
61 This is discussed on pp. 126–7.
62 See chapter 4.
63 See chapter 5.
64 Junod, *LSAT* II, pp. 147–8.
65 Junod, 'Les Ba-Ronga' (1898), pp. 7–8, 235, 238, 245, 247; *LSAT* I, pp. 1, 151; *LSAT* II, pp. 104, 133. For the time, this was not an outlandish speculation. The reconstruction of the first Stone Age lacustrian village, discovered at Obermeilen near Zurich in 1853–54, was strongly influenced by contemporary drawings of the modern village of Dorei in 'primitive' New Guinea. Marc-R. Sauter, *Suisse préhistorique: des origines aux helvètes* (Neuchâtel, 1977), pp. 86–7.

66 'Certains problèmes de nos âmes civilisées, filles agrandies de ces âmes primitives, s'expliquent. Nous prenons mieux conscience de nous-mêmes et des mystères de notre évolution', Junod, 'Les Ba-Ronga', p. 8.
67 Junod, 'Sorcellerie d'Afrique et sorcellerie d'Europe: étude d'ethnographie comparée', *Foi et Vie* (1910) 13, pp. 616–17.
68 The faithful transcriptions of folklore undertaken by Jacob and Wilhelm Grimm and in Africa by bishop Callaway, Jacottet and others, should be contrasted with the more fanciful tales written for children by Hans Christian Andersen. On the relationship between folklore, authenticity and identity, cf. A. Thiesse, *La Création des identités nationales: Europe XVIIIe–XXe siècle* (Paris, 1999), chapter 5.
69 John and Jean Comaroff, *Of Revelation and Revolution* (Chicago, 1991) vol. I, pp. 220–21.
70 W. H. I. Bleek, *Ueber den Ursprung der Sprache* (Weimar, 1868) translated as *On the Origin of Language*. David Chidester, *Savage Systems: Colonialism and Comparative Religion in Southern Africa* (Charlottesville, VA, 1996), p. 144.
71 Langham Dale, 'Anthropology – a review of modern theories', *Cape Monthly Magazine* (1874) VIII, June.
72 Junod, *Grammaire ronga suivie d'un manuel de conversation et d'un vocabulaire ronga-portugais-français-anglais pour exposer et illustrer les lois du ronga, langage parlé par les indigènes de district de Lourenço-Marques* (Lausanne, 1896), p. 2; Junod, 'Les Ba-Ronga', p. 278. See also his review of Jacottet's *Contes populaires des Bassoutos* (Paris, 1895) in *Bulletin de la société neuchâteloise de geographie* X 1898, p. 514. For Louis Agassiz on this topic, see Elizabeth Cory Agassiz, *Louis Agassiz: his Life and Correspondence* (Boston, MA, 1885) II, p. 498.
73 He provided the example of the word 'nxoko', invented by an elderly blind man. This word, an expression of satisfaction at finding oneself in good company, had become fashionable and, in its turn, had produced a verb 'ku nxoka', to be happy; and even 'nxokela', to be happy in a certain place. Junod, *LSAT* II, p. 166.
74 *Totem and Taboo and Other Works* was published in 1913–14. The first four chapters, on 'The Horror of Incest' were subtitled 'Some points of Agreement between the Mental Lives of Savages and Neurotics'. Anthropologists in the United States, where evolutionist ideas had shallow roots in the discipline, were particularly critical of *Totem and Taboo*, cf. R. W. Clark, *Freud: The Man and the Cause* (New York, 1980), pp. 352–7.
75 Hugh Trevor-Roper, *The Rise of Christian Europe* (London, 1965), p. 9. In a chapter entitled 'The stages of progress' that included his celebrated remark on the 'unrewarding gyrations of barbarous tribes in picturesque but irrelevant corners of the globe', Trevor-Roper wrote of African 'tribes whose chief function in history, in my opinion, is to show to the present an image of the past from which, by history, it has escaped'.
76 *L'Education chrétienne* (1872) I, January, 24.
77 Henri Junod and Professor Bouchardat, *L'eau-de-vie et ses dangers* (Paris, 1854); Henri Junod (*père*), *Sermons* (Neuchâtel, 1884), p. xvii. Like his father, Charles-Daniel Junod (1865–1941) was the Independent Church's pastor to the parish formed by the Collégiale. He served as president of the Neuchâtel chapter of the Société de la Croix Bleu and in 1926 became international president of this temperance movement. On Charles-Daniel, see the *Société de Belles-Lettres de Neuchâtel. Livre d'or, 1832–1960* (Neuchâtel, 1962); 'Ch-Daniel Junod, 1865–1941', *Le messager de l'église neuchâteloise indépendante de l'état*, 2 December 1941.
78 Junod, *LSAT* I, p. 10; *LSAT* II, p. 629.
79 University of South Africa (UNISA). Junod Collection (JC) 4. 2 Junod, 'Critique du Nouveau Testament, cours de Godet suivi en 1881–82'.
80 Junod, *LSAT* II, p. 447; Junod, 'Deux enterrements à 20,000 ans de distance', *Anthropos*, V. 1910, pp. 964–7.
81 Junod, *LSAT* II, pp. 364, 429, 447; ibid., I, p. 139; David Chidester has shown in some detail how Colenso, Bleek and Callaway created the picture of a primitive and original religion in mid-nineteenth-century Zululand and Natal by developing a discursive practice that compared what they determined to be 'Zulu religion' with that of the Old Testament. See his *Savage Systems*, chapter 4.
82 Junod, 'Les Ba-Ronga', p. 403.
83 Anon., *Evangélisation des Païens au sud-est de l'Afrique par les églises libres de la Suisse romande* (Exposition Nationale Suisse, Geneva, 1896), pp. 3–4; P. Berthoud, *Les Nègres gouamba*, pp. 20, 140.
84 Grandjean, *Mission romande*, pp. 2, 28, 41; Junod, *Ernest Creux and Paul Berthoud*, p. 20. The Mission's role in the revival of metropolitan churches was stressed by many clergymen. Cf. the Anglican bishop of New Zealand at this time. S. Sohmer, 'Melanesian Mission' in Roy MacLeod and Philip F. Rehbock (eds), *Darwin's Laboratory: Evolutionary Theory and Natural History in the Pacific* (Honolulu, 1994), p. 319.
85 Edouard Vautier, *Maison des cèdres* (Lausanne, 1948), pp. 88–9; Grandjean, *Mission romande*, pp. 241ff. The French Protestant missionary-anthropologist, Maurice Leenhardt, made similar statements, see J. Clifford, *Person and Myth: Maurice Leenhardt in the Melanesian World* (Berkeley and Los Angeles, 1982), p. 29.
86 E. Casalis, *Les Bassoutos ou vingt-trois années d'études et d'observations au sud de l'Afrique* (Paris, 1859), p. 385.
87 Ibid., emphasis in the original.
88 Junod, 'La biographie d'Elias Libombo, jadis connu sous le nom de Spoon' in *Causeries sur l'Afrique à l'usage des cercles d'étude missionnaire pour enfants*, pp. 4–5.
89 Eugène Rambert, 'La Flore Suisse – et ses origines' published in 1880 and reprinted in his *Etudes d'histoire naturelle* (Lausanne, 1888), pp. 225–7.

[90] E. Rambert, 'Les plantes alpines' published in 1865 and reprinted in his *Etudes d'histoire naturelle* (Lausanne, 1888), pp. 42–3.
[91] Emile Javelle, *Souvenirs d'un Alpiniste* (Lausanne and Paris, [1886], 1920), pp. 224, 236.
[92] Ibid., pp. 232–5, 243–8.
[93] Junod, 'Les Ba-Ronga', p. 481; Junod, *LSAT* II, p. 541.
[94] R. Berthoud-Junod, letter of 7 July 1887 in *BMR* (1887), 72, p. 323.
[95] Junod, 'Les Ba-Ronga', p. 485.
[96] Junod, *LSAT* I, pp. 9, 539; Junod, *LSAT* II, p. 614.
[97] Junod, 'Les Ba-Ronga', p. 114.
[98] A. de Lamartine, 'The fall of an angel' or 'La chute d'un ange'.
[99] Lionel Gossman, 'Jacob Burckhardt: Cold War Liberal?', *Journal of Modern History* (2002), 74, 3, pp. 541–2; Gossman, *Basel in the Age of Burckhardt: A study in unseasonable ideas* (Chicago, 2000).
[100] Junod, 'Les Ba-Ronga', p. 248.
[101] Junod, 'Quelques contes africains' *Bibliothèque universelle et revue suisse* (1897) VII, p. 515–16; Junod, *Le Noir africain. Comment faut–il le juger?* (Lausanne, 1931), p. 9. These observations would only be absorbed into anthropology thirty years later, E. M. von Hornbostel, 'African Music', *Africa* (1928) 1, 1.
[102] 'Il depasse toute mésure'. Junod, 'Les Ba-Ronga', p. 252. Junod, *LSAT* II, pp. 211, 215, 218–9, 221–2.
[103] Junod's *Les Chants et contes des Ba-Ronga* (Lausanne, 1897) and *Nouveaux contes ronga* (Neuchâtel, 1898) were preceded by similar collections by Neuchâtelois missionary-anthropologists, Heli Châtelain in Angola and Edouard Jacottet in Lesotho.
[104] Junod, *Le Noir africain*, p. 13; Junod, *LSAT II*, pp. 531–3.
[105] B. Cendrars, 'Notice' to *Anthologie nègre* (1921, édition définitive, Paris, 1947); Cendrars, *Petits contes nègres pour les enfants des Blancs* (Paris, 1943). A. Berchtold, *La Suisse romande au cap du vingtième siècle* (Lausanne, 1966), p. 851. For other literary figures who drew on folktales, see D. Fabre, 'Le "Manuel de folklore français" d'Arnold van Gennep' in P. Nora (ed.), *Les Lieux de Mémoire* (Paris, 1997), p. 3587. In South Africa, Jan Smuts wrote with admiration of the cultural freedom to be found in Africa, see p. 245n176.
[106] Junod, 'Les Ba-Ronga', pp. 231–7. This quote was reproduced in full in an anonymous review of this monograph in the important Swiss journal *Bibliothèque universelle* (1898) XII, 4, p. 206. Junod repeated it later in *LSAT* II, p. 125. He recognized the importance of African sculpture long before most anthropologists, cf. E. von Sydow, 'African sculpture', *Africa* (1928) 1, 2.
[107] Peter Gay, *Pleasure Wars* (New York, 1999), p. 215. A. C. Haddon, *Evolution in Art* (London, 1895).
[108] S. Price, *Primitive Art in Civilized Places* (Chicago, 1989).
[109] 'Hymne missionnaire' in *Le Messager de l'école du dimanche* (1867) 48, 1 December.
[110] 'Eglise du Seigneur', hymn number 96 in *Chants évangéliques et nouveaux chants* (Lausanne, [1885], 1912), p. 152.
[111] A. Grandjean, *Labours, semailles*, p. 27.
[112] Junod, 'Les Ba-Ronga', p. 246; Junod, *LSAT* I, pp. 152, 271, 525–7.
[113] P. Berthoud, *Nègres gouamba*, p. 164; H. Dieterlen, *Adolphe Mabille missionnaire* (Paris, 1898), p. 32.
[114] *BMR* (1880), 3, 39, December p. 210.
[115] Grandjean, *Mission romande*, p. 84.
[116] Grandjean, *Mission romande*, p. 2.
[117] *Notice sur la Mission vaudoise chez les Magwamba au sud-est de l'Afrique – souvenir de l'exposition nationale suisse de Zurich 1883*; P. Trivier, *Album de la Mission romande*; *BMR* (1904) 17, pp. 197–8. In his *Drei Sweizerische Landesausstellungen: Zürich 1883, Genf 1896, Bern 1914* (Zurich, 1970) Hermann Büchler omits the African exhibitions.
[118] For Henri Perregaux's critical comments on the 'village nègre' at the 1896 Exhibition, see his *Edmond Perregaux missionnaire*, p. 185.
[119] Gérald Arlettaz et al., *Les Suisses dans le miroir: les expositions nationales suisses* (Lausanne, 1991) especially pp. 16, 58; C. Detraz and B. Crettaz, *Suisse, mon beau village: regards sur l'exposition nationale de 1896* (Geneva, 1983), pp. 39–40.
[120] Favre, *Notice sur la Mission vaudoise chez les Magwamba*, p. 15.
[121] E. H. Schlaefli-Glardon, 'De Valdezia à Lourenço Marques', *BSNG* (1892–93) vii, map between pp. 180–1.
[122] *Souvenir de l'Exposition cantonale vaudoise* (Vevey, 1901).
[123] Anon., *Evangélisation des Païens*, p. 3.
[124] Junod, 'The best means of preserving the traditions and customs of the various South African native races' in *Report of the South African Association for the Advancement of Science* (1907), p. 142.
[125] On this patriotism, cf. Cantonal and University Library, Neuchâtel: Société neuchâteloise de géographie: A. Grandjean to secretary, 7 April 1895; BCG. BH. Barbey Collection: Junod to Barbey, 25 February 1898.
[126] Darwin had once written that 'seeing, when amongst foreigners, the strength and power of one's own nation, gives a feeling of exultation that is not felt at home.' P. Brent, *Charles Darwin* (London, 1983), p. 152, cited in J. M. MacKenzie (ed.), *Imperialism and the Natural World* (Manchester, 1990), p. 6.

127 Dieterlen, *Adolphe Mabille, missionnaire* (Paris, 1898), p. 29.
128 Ibid., pp. 28, 31; P. Berthoud, *Mission romande* 13; SMA 1760 Grandjean 26 January 1895.
129 See particularly the section 'Au combat!' in the hymnal *Chants évangéliques*, pp. 222–37.
130 P. Berthoud, *Mission romande*, p. 13.
131 See p. 107.
132 Junod, 'Quelques contes africaines', p. 547; Junod, 'Les Ba-Ronga', pp. 245–9, 278, 480, 483–4; Junod, *LSAT* II, pp. 148, 154–7, 175, 331. On the racism of von Tschudi, Agassiz and Vogt, cf. R. J. C. Young, *Colonial Desire: Hybridity in Theory, Culture and Race* (London, 1995), pp. 17–18, 175–6.
133 Junod, 'The best means of preserving', p. 143; Junod, 'Le climat de la baie de Delagoa', *Bulletin de la société des sciences naturelles de Neuchâtel* (1896–97) 25, pp. 77ff.
134 'Les Ba-Ronga', pp. 481–2, 486; Junod, 'The best means of preserving', pp. 141. Junod, 'The Magic conception of nature amongst Bantus' in *South African Journal of Science* (1920) xvii, November, pp. 76–7; Junod, *LSAT* I, p. 11; *LSAT* II , pp. 166, 595, 621. These were common views at the time, cf. Archives de la Mission suisse, Lausanne: 514 Grandjean to council, 7 July 1895; P. Berthoud, *Les Nègres gouamba*, p. 163; Dieterlen, *Adolphe Mabille*, pp. 25–6.
135 Junod, 'Correspondences de Rikatla', 23 November 1891, *BSNG* vii, 1892–93, p. 529; Junod, *Chants et Contes*, pp. 11–12; Junod, 'Les Ba-Ronga', pp. 8–9.
136 Cf. Junod, 'Les Ba-Ronga', p. 481; Junod, 'Le climat de la baie de Delagoa', p. 77; Junod, *LSAT* I, p. 10; A. Grandjean, 'Notice relative à la carte du Nkomati inférieur et du district portugais de Lourenço Marques', *BSNG* (1892–93) vii, p. 121.
137 See pp. 145, 214, 222.
138 Just as in South Africa, where the governor of the Cape called for enlightened government as a means of preventing the racial extinction practised in the United States and Australia. See Bartle Frere, 'The Native Races of South Africa' in *Transactions of the South African Philosophical Society* (1877) 1, 1, p. xxiv.
139 Junod, 'Les Ba-Ronga', pp. 432, 483.
140 Cf. 'L'esclave racheté' in *L'Education chrétienne* (1872) II, February; 'Oguyomi: la petite africaine' (Société de traités religieux, Lausanne, n. d.); 'Véra, la jeune esclave' in *Chez les Gouamba* (Lausanne, c. 1893), pp. 34–40.
141 Cf. The Lausanne Religious Tract Society's 'L'Enfant missionnaire' (1882) and 'Le juge et la Négresse' (1903).
142 Compare with Junod, *LSAT* II, pp. 129 and 139.
143 Most clearly expressed in Grandjean, 'Le vieil évangile a-t-il fait son temps?' On mysterious Africa, cf. 'Les champs de diamants de l'Afrique ne seraient-ils pas l'Ophir de la Bible?', *L'Education chrétienne*, (1872) May.
144 Grandjean, 14 November 1889 in *Nouvelles de nos missionnaires* (1890) 4, 12.
145 P. Berthoud, *Les Nègres gouamba* (1907), p. 74; Grandjean, 'Le vieil évangile a–t–il fait son temps?', pp. 18–19; Junod, *LSAT*, II, p. 628.
146 Junod, 'The Magic conception of nature amongst Bantus', *South African Journal of Science* (1920), p. 84; Junod, *Le Noir africain: Comment faut-il le juger?*, p. 8; R. C. Germond, *Chronicles of Basutoland* (Morija, 1967), p. 526 cited in T. Ranger, 'New approaches to African landscape' (unpublished typescript, 1997), p. 1.
147 Eugène Sue, *Les Mystères de Paris* (Paris, 1845); Louis Chevalier, *Classes laborieuses et classes dangereuses à Paris pendant la première moitié du XIe siècle* (Paris, 1958), pp. 162, 510–11; Alice Bullard, *Exile to Paradise: Savagery and Civilization in Paris and the South Pacific, 1790–1900* (Stanford, CA, 2000).
148 Nancy Leys Stepan, 'Race and gender: the role of analogy in science' in David Theo Goldberg (ed.), *Anatomy of Racism* (Minneapolis, 1990), p. 44; Frederick Brown, *Zola: A Life* (London, 1995), pp. 346–57.
149 Edouard Junod, 'Le bureau international pour la défense des indigènes' in *Revue international de la Croix Rouge* (1922) 37, January. See also Henri-Alexandre Junod, 'Le Mécontentement aux colonies', *Christianisme Social* (1928) 3; 'Une Question de morale coloniale', *Stockholm International Review for the Social Activities of the Churches* (1929) 3.
150 Rambert, *Arthur Grandjean*, p. 31. 'Hymne de Mboukazi' *Aux écoles du dimanche: sections de l'espoir et autres sociétés*, pp. 7–8. Grandjean, *Mission romande*, p. 98.

3
Christianity

> Jesus said 'The spirit of the Lord is upon me, because He has chosen me to bring good news to the poor. He has sent me to proclaim liberty to the captives and recovery of sight to the blind; to set free the oppressed and announce that the time has come when the Lord will save his people.' (Luke 4: 18)

The Vaudois Mission arrived in South Africa just as the diamond discoveries in Griqualand West brought a revolution to the economy of the entire region. As the industrial revolution rolled from Kimberley to the gold fields on the Witwatersrand, it carried the Christian message into the most isolated parts of southern Africa. In these areas, the missionaries looked on anxiously as the dark forces of paganism threatened to engulf and extinguish the flickering light produced by small Christian communities. They saw the mission station as a place of refuge for people wishing to escape a narrow and oppressive tribal society, a protected world in which both missionaries and converts combated sin and temptation through the redeeming powers of work, duty and education. This closed 'station system' had reinforced the missionary's confidence in his civilization and kept at bay the values and standards of 'heathen' society.[1] But while the station system had stemmed the backsliding of converts, it had also inhibited the spread of the Christian message beyond the closed environment of the mission.

The mineral revolution revitalized the nature of evangelical Christianity in South Africa. By the mid-1870s, black migrant workers were returning home from Kimberley and other centres of employment in South Africa with a knowledge of Christianity or an ability to read the Christian message. These men spread the gospel far beyond the small knots of Christian worshippers huddled around the mission station. Their knowledge and practice of Christianity was often assembled in new and unexpected ways, but it planted the seed of belief that would later be nurtured by evangelists in many corners of southern Africa. In this chapter I lay stress on the African nature of the Christian message taken by converts from the Transvaal to southern Mozambique and on the limits of toleration practised by the mission.

Native Christianity or the Limits of Tolerance

The discovery of diamonds and gold brought a sudden prosperity to the economy of southern Africa. Within ten years, thousands of men were making their way from the area on the coast claimed by the Portuguese to the diamond fields at Kimberley. Evangelists quickly recognized the potential of this new mission field. For many migrant workers, uprooted from their homes, labouring under atrocious conditions and living in confined spaces, the gospel provided a message of consolation and hope. This often brief experience of Christianity, or the associated skill of reading religious material, spread a knowledge of Christianity throughout southern Africa. Numbers of men were also introduced to the gospel in Natal where they broke their journey on the long walk to Kimberley, sought work on the sugar plantations or laboured in the bustling Durban port. Others encountered Christianity as they travelled further south to work in the ports of the Cape Colony or on the railways and farms in the interior.

The Paris Evangelical Missionary Society regarded the large number of Pedi migrants who returned home via Lesotho as a potential conduit along which Christianity could be carried into the interior. Several of these men, tramping northwards from the Cape, converted to Christianity and three of their number were sufficiently moved by the new religion to study its tenets at Morija. The ease with which these men mastered the Sotho language led Adolphe Mabille to view their homeland as a natural extension of the Lesotho mission and as a stepping-stone to the Sotho-speakers on the Zambezi. The PEMS hoped to expand into these areas where it could spread the gospel in an inexpensive manner through its abundant Sotho literature. Mabille and François Coillard were designated to explore the area in the mid-1860s with a view to establishing a new mission to be managed by the native church of the PEMS. But it was only when Ernest Creux and Paul Berthoud arrived from Switzerland that the mission had the personnel needed to undertake this task.

Mabille and Berthoud finally travelled to Sekukuniland in the winter of 1873. The hostile reception they received from the Pedi king persuaded the two Vaudois missionaries to continue their voyage northwards to the Zambezi, where a large number of South Sotho-speakers lived without a missionary. As they approached the Zoutpansberg, the Swiss were advised by Dutch Reformed and Lutheran missionaries to concentrate their energies on a cluster of immigrant refugee communities living in a series of foothills that the Boers called the Spelonken. Because these people lived without a missionary, and because they spoke a derivation of Sotho, Mabille considered them a potential field for the PEMS. When he and Berthoud returned to Lesotho, three Sotho evangelists stayed on to run the fledgling mission in the Spelonken. But the PEMS was prevented from directing resources to this new venture when, in 1873, the Free Church Synod in Yverdon established a separate Vaudois Mission. The loss of Vaudois financial support and the inevitable future redeployment of Creux and Berthoud led the PEMS to hand responsibility for the new mission to the Swiss. The French were also wary of working in an area claimed by the Boers and feared that the hostility generated by the Franco-Prussian war would make collaboration with the Berlin Mission difficult.[2] In 1875, as winter settled on South Africa, the two Swiss missionaries left Lesotho for the Spelonken. They reached the Sotho evangelists near the headwaters of the Levubu and Small Letaba rivers in July and quickly bought a stretch of land, called Klipfontein, on which to start their mission. This 'farm' was several square kilometres in extent and was occupied by several thousand people. This was a captive audience for the missionaries who renamed the land Valdezia in honour of their canton in Switzerland and began to work on the transcription of the local language.[3]

The Swiss were not the first missionaries to work in the region. Representatives of the Berlin Missionary Society and the missionary branch of the Dutch Reformed Church laboured in isolated outposts to the north, west and south of the Spelonken. Migrant workers had also carried Christianity into the area. Just north of the Levubu river, in the community ministered to by the Berlin Mission, a 'Knobnose' was teaching children to read from a heavy English Bible.[4] To the south, at Rhenoster Poort, the Swiss came across a man known to us only as Daniel, who had spent fifteen years working in the Cape Colony. On his return home, he had started to school his compatriots in catechism and the skills of literacy. In the community targeted by the Swiss, the Sotho evangelists had achieved about fifteen conversions. Several men saw the establishment of the mission as an opportunity to formalize a conversion started earlier in Kimberley, Pretoria or Natal. Yacob and Yosefa Mhalamhala, John Songele and his brother-in-law Zambiki had all worked on the diamond fields. Hlakamela Tlakula had learned to read at Kimberley and Jacob Mbizana, who had lived in Pretoria for three years, served as a Sotho interpreter.[5]

Creux and Berthoud gathered these adherents around a chapel, school and small clinic and their preaching attracted individuals such as the thirteen-year-old Matsivi and his elder brother Chihoçi, to settle at Valdezia. Native evangelists were soon placed in charge of three out-stations established around the mission. All went well until 1879 when, in the space of fourteen harrowing months, Eugènie Berthoud and five missionary children died. Ernest and Ida Creux and their single remaining child moved to a new station called Elim. Paul Berthoud, broken by the loss of his wife and three children, returned home to Switzerland; Matsivi and Chihoçi, who had worked in his home, were sent with Samuel Malalé to study at Morija in Lesotho. In June 1881 the abandoned Valdezia was reoccupied when Paul's younger brother, Henri, arrived from Lausanne. Filled with enthusiasm for his calling, Henri Berthoud soon revived the community at Valdezia and looked for ways in which to expand the mission.

A year earlier, Yosefa Mhalamhala had made his way to the coast to re-establish contact with his family. On his return to the Transvaal he spoke enthusiastically of the welcome he had received in the east and placed his sister's daughter, Ruth Holene, in the new school at Valdezia. Henri Berthoud readily supported Mhalamhala's desire to take Christianity along the corridor of language and kinship that led to the east. In July 1881 Mhalamhala eventually succeeded in returning to the coast with Hlakamela Tlakula and two other converts. As they made their way across the long coastal plain, the men were warmly received on the bend in the Nkomati river by Magude, the ruler of the important Khosa chiefdom. Mhalamhala then struck out in a south-easterly direction to visit his sister and her husband, the parents of Ruth Holene. Lois Xintomane and Eliachib Mandlakusasa lived in a small village near Lourenço Marques, the ramshackle Portuguese settlement on the northern edge of Delagoa Bay, and they listened attentively to the Christian message carried by their relative. Towards the end of the year they agreed to return with him to Valdezia for instruction in this new religion. Together with their daughter Ruth, they would play an important role in the spread of Christianity from the Spelonken to the coast.

At Lourenço Marques the Protestant converts were less well received. Migrants who had worked in Natal and the Cape showed interest in welcoming missionaries who would further their knowledge of reading and Christianity.[6] But the governor of the settlement greeted foreign, black Calvinists with suspicion. This was partly because the Portuguese colonial outpost was passing through lean times. The growth of the settlement had been built on the ivory and fur trade, but the animals responsible for this lucrative commerce had been decimated. By the early 1880s, the profitability of the settlement rested on a modest trade in buckskin and horns and the export of small quantities of fruits and seeds used in the fabrication of vegetable lubricants and soaps. Even the repatriation of the wages of migrant workers had ground to a halt as Kimberley experienced a severe depression, and political upheavals in the wake of the Anglo-Zulu war closed the routes taken by migrants tramping home from the sugar plantations in Natal. In this uncertain climate, the governor of Lourenço Marques refused to allow the establishment of a Protestant mission in his territory. This meant that the spread of the Vaudois Mission into the coastal plain had to be centred on the Khosa who lived beyond the effective control of the Portuguese. As the climate on the bend in the Nkomati river was unsuitable for white missionaries, Yosefa Mhalamhala was hastily ordained in April 1882 and charged with this task.

Funding for this new evangelical mission came from an unexpected quarter when Ndjakandjaka, the major chief living on the sprawling Elim mission domain, showed a sudden interest in Christianity. With his support, the 180 Christians at Valdezia and Elim rapidly assembled £40 for Yosefa Mhalamhala's new mission.[7] The newly ordained minister then established himself at the Khosa king's homestead at Mugude, while Lois Xintomane and Eliachib Mandlakusasa made their way down to Rikatla, a small hilltop village near the coast. One of Eliachib's relatives served as councillor to a son of the local chief, Mapounga, and with his support the couple gained permission to settle in the village. Little more than twenty-five kilometres north of Lourenço Marques, Rikatla lay just beyond the area of Portuguese control. Like Yosefa Mhalamhala's following at Magude's, the small Christian community at Rikatla would develop entirely independently of European control.

While the mission sank new roots on the coast, two new missionary families arrived in the Spelonken to reinforce the home community. The Vaudois Mission was further strengthened when in 1883 the Free Churches of western Switzerland combined to form the Swiss Romande Mission, and the following year several new missionaries arrived in the Spelonken. These new arrivals gave support to the idea of an African-driven mission and encouraged the Spelonken Church to raise another £30 for the work of Yosefa Mahlamhala at Magude's.[8] With this support, Yacob Mhalamhala, who had been ordained in the same year as his brother, left the Spelonken to visit his brother on the Nkomati bend. In the winter of 1885 he proceeded to the coast where the work of Eliachib Mandlakusasa and Lois Xintomane was showing signs of success. Paul Berthoud would later praise this family as a 'light in this dark country'.[9] Their daughter Ruth Holene had been particularly important in spreading the Christian message as her ability to read, together with her evangelical zeal, had taken the gospel beyond the small village at Rikatla.

Ruth fanned the embers of belief through her visits to the small Christian communities around Rikatla. These included several women who met to read the Gospel in Mahazule's village north of Rikatla and another group of 25 Christians at Nouamohluène's village on the route to Lourenço Marques.¹⁰ One of her assistants, known to us only as Martha, travelled as far south as her home in Tembeland where she came into contact with a sizeable group of Christians. This congregation was considered sufficiently important for Yacob Mhalamhala to visit it before returning home. On his arrival he discovered a community directed by Jim Ximungana, a nephew of the Tembe king, Mabaï, who worked for a Dutch trader named Franken. Ximungana topped his imposing six-foot six-inch frame with a large sombrero, was well dressed and of noble bearing. Most importantly, he was fluent in Portuguese and after a spell working in Natal could speak, read and write in English. In the space of a few years he had acquired a small fortune by selling liquor, imported by his employer through Lourenço Marques, to Banyan retailers in the interior. These men had responded to a local consumer boom as migrant workers returned from the plantations and mines of South Africa in growing numbers and paid for their wares in gold coin. Ximungana owned a wagon drawn by eight oxen and was rumoured to sell goods worth £10,000 every month. He had further secured his position as a local notable by purchasing male and female slaves, by acquiring several wives and by arranging for his sister to marry Franken. Ximungana's interest in Christianity had been sparked when he stumbled across a copy of the first book published in the Gwamba language by the Vaudois Mission, in Lourenço Marques.¹¹ For the missionaries, the interest in Christianity shown by Ximungana's small community marked the beginnings of a timorous religious revival on the coast.¹²

Further inland the fortunes of the mission at Mugude fluctuated with the changing political situation. In 1884, the death of the Gaza king, Umzila, reverberated in the lands north of the Limpopo. Twenty years earlier, a vicious civil war had forced Umzila's brother Mawewe into exile in Swaziland. Now, with Umzila out of the way, Mawewe's son Hanyane and his followers sought to return to their homes on the coastal plain. They were particularly drawn to the southern marches of the Gaza empire south of the Limpopo, which were occupied by the Khosa people.

Magude was strong enough to prevent any encroachment on his territory, but when he died unexpectedly in 1885, the Khosa feared they would be drawn into a war between Hanyane and Gungunyana, the new Gaza king. The little mission 'at Magude's' was shaken when four men were smelled out as witches and killed for causing the death of Magude. But the Christians were initially protected because the Khosa regent, Mavabaze, found Yosefa Mhalamhala a useful ally. However, once the new Gaza king had secured his hold over the throne, he tried to block the ambitions of his cousin Hanyane by reasserting his control over the foreign affairs of the Khosa. In the process, Gungunyana prohibited them from entering into negotiations with outside forces, including missionaries. Mavabaze quickly fell under the influence of his powerful northern neighbour and in deference to Gungunyane displayed an increasingly hostile attitude towards Yosefa.¹³

The plight of the Christians in Khosaland led Henri Berthoud and Eugène Thomas, a newly-arrived missionary, to travel to the area to investigate its value as an on-going field of evangelical activity. After an exploratory voyage of three months they confirmed the presence of several Gwamba communities in the lowveld to the east of the Spelonken. Most importantly, they found that 'the real homeland of our Ma-Gwamba' in the Transvaal was to be found along the coast, stretching from the Zulu border to perhaps as far north as the Zambezi river.¹⁴ In 1886 Henri Berthoud produced a fold-out map that vividly marked in splendid colour the western edge of

3.1 *Yosefa Mhalamhala and Zebedee Mbenyane. In the late 1880s the Swiss missionaries still saw a reflection of the virtues of modesty and humility in the bare feet of their converts. Mhalamhala, an ordained minister, is holding a copy of the first book published in Gwamba (later called Thonga), a collection of Bible readings called the* buku. *On the signification of this image, see pp. 196, 199.*
(© Swiss Mission Archive, Lausanne)

the Gwamba as a people and circled their communities in the Transvaal.[15] Berthoud and Thomas believed the mission had been divinely ordained through the medium of the language transcribed in the Spelonken, to take the gospel to the entire Gwamba 'nation'. Although Yosefa Mahlamhala had achieved little formal success, they considered his work especially important as it was situated in the Gwamba heartland, what Henri Berthoud called the 'place of origin' of the immigrants in the Spelonken.[16]

On the coast the young church had achieved some notable successes. Life in the small Christian communities stretching from Tembeland, just south of Lourenço Marques, to Rikatla in the north, had been marked by more than thirty conversions. Berthoud particularly stressed his confidence in the religious vigour and conviction with which his black colleagues had carried and spread the Christian message. He especially commented on the 'remarkable effort' that had led to the conversions supervised by Jim Ximungana. Franken had ordered a batch of Gwamba *bukus* for the edification of his employees and this, too, would help spread the Gospel. In general, the 'depth of the movement' on the coast impressed Henri Berthoud.[17] Several converts left the Spelonken at this time to visit Yosefa's mission on the Nkomati bend, now called Antioka, as well as Rikatla and Tembe on the coast. They, too, presented highly favourable reports on the 'magnificent work' undertaken in these areas and even offered to work on the coast.[18] Berthoud admired the way in which African evangelists had taken the gospel into new areas, particularly those considered unfit for Europeans because of high levels of malaria. His positive report led the mission in the Spelonken, in November 1886, to advise the Council in Lausanne to commit the work on the coast to a 'purely Native Church'.[19]

These events were accompanied by news that the political turbulence in Khosaland had calmed and that Yosefa Mahlamhala's small community was experiencing a religious revival. As the spiritual movement spread inland from the coast, the Free Church missionaries viewed its progress with great optimism. Southern Africa had experienced several religious awakenings and this new revival, however delicate, gave every impression of duplicating in Africa the missionaries' very special experience of Christianity in Switzerland.[20] The revival not only provided immediate evidence of the redeeming powers of the Holy Spirit; because it was led by people living close to nature, it promised to take the mission, and perhaps even the church, back to its primitive, authentic origins. At Rikatla the Christian community had not been exposed to stale church rituals, hierarchy and dogma. The growth of the church depended entirely on local initiative and enterprise. Rikatla was like an 'animated beehive', wrote an otherwise critical Paul Berthoud, a place 'where everything is held in common, as in the primitive church'.[21] Lois supervised communal work on the fields that fed the visitors to Rikatla. Jim Ximungana had visited the village on several occasions, and had sent his three wives, slaves and his sister to this small centre of pilgrimage. Others came to Rikatla for short periods and then returned home to spread the message preached by Lois and Eliachib or sent their children to this site of learning.[22] The followers of the revival expressed a 'lively ... joyous piety', wrote the elder Berthoud, when they addressed each other as 'children of the Lord', 'children of the father,' or 'beloved of God'. They regarded Rikatla as 'the source', spoke of their 'hunger' to know God, and of their need to be 'beaten by God' before effecting a true conversion.[23] This language drew together those touched by the revival and seemed to bring them closer to God.

For the missionaries, the spiritual movement on the Mozambican coast offered the prospect of both large numbers of conversions and, equally importantly, the development of a dynamic, living church.[24] Congregants at Rikatla experienced Christianity as an intensely personal, emotional revelation born of an intimate relationship with God or with his word. They were shaken by powerful visions and dreams that produced emotional, spontaneous conversions. Lay members of the church gave long speeches in which they denounced sin and extolled the need for guilt and remorse. 'It is the tears of repentance and love', wrote Henri Berthoud, 'that create the astonishing strength of the women and girls who serve as evangelists'.[25] The resultant spiritual rebirth was accompanied by the likelihood of moral renovation as Christians formed tight communities around places like Rikatla, the centre of the movement. People read the Bible at Rikatla and proselytized the surrounding villages in a way that confirmed the missionaries' ideal of a self-governing, self-supporting and self-propagating native church. But the very success of the spiritual movement on the coast, together with its ecclesiastical and dogmatic independence, soon raised anguished and divisive debates over the degree of independence to be extended to the native clergy and church.

For the missionaries in the Spelonken, particularly Henri Berthoud, the revival on the coast seemed the natural product of a Free Church mission. The movement was largely self-generating, it was run in an intensely democratic manner, defied the formalistic rituals and tired religiosity of the old continent and had no ties with government. The emotion displayed by the revivalists was a sign of the raw energy needed to revitalize the Christian message and rejuvenate the entire church. However, not all members of the mission held this view, for, as an institution, the mission was made up of individuals whose beliefs and practices reflected the unresolved tensions within the church at home. The missionaries inevitably brought to Africa the old, unfinished experiences of the church in western Switzerland and played out these differences on African soil. Henri Berthoud's elder brother Paul, whose energy and courage had marked the mission since its beginning, represented an older generation that had grown up in the years after the church schism. The 1845 revolution had brought a formal end to the paternalistic role of the pastor within Vaudois society. But it had not killed the memory of paternalism within the church and had little more than dented the strength of this social relationship in the cantons of western Switzerland.[26] Paul Berthoud brought this view of the pastor's role in the church to Africa, a view that in the long run would prove particularly tenacious. Furthermore, while Henri Berthoud saw Christianity as a system of belief driven by crises and dramatic decisions, his elder brother invoked the need for a continuity of belief that required a greater degree of intervention in congregants' lives.

These sharp differences of opinion were played out in the growing impasse facing the church on the coast, for, as it grew in strength and numbers, troubling news about the nature and direction of the church's development filtered back to the Spelonken in letters and reports. From our distance in time and space it is easy to see the 'revival' on the coast as a bricolage of beliefs and rituals, an indigenous way of making the world more comprehensible and controllable by reworking foreign and local sources of power into a battery of Christian ideas and practices. We might classify the 'revival' as a version of the pentacostalism that Sundkler called 'Zionism'; and from this perspective, we might view it as one of the first independent church movements in southern Africa.[27]

The missionaries in the Spelonken, however, very quickly became divided over whether to support the independence of the congregations on the coast, or whether to subject them to the control of a white missionary. Part of the division stemmed from Paul Berthoud's invidious position at Valdezia where he had been appointed mission doctor on his return to the Transvaal in 1884. This was effectively a subordinate role to that of his younger brother Henri who occupied the post of missionary, and Paul looked anxiously for a chance to return to mission work. The growing religious disorder on the coast gave him this opportunity and, in the winter of 1886, he asked the mission council in Lausanne to send him to the coast to take charge of the fledgling native church.[28]

A degree of tension had, almost unavoidably, arisen between the Berthoud brothers at Valdezia. This burst dramatically to the surface in November 1886, when Henri and the other missionaries in the Spelonken formally opposed Paul's request to take charge of the mission stations on the coast. They considered the coastal area too unhealthy for a white missionary and recommended that it remain in the charge of the mission converts. In January 1887 Henri Berthoud reported that a group of Christians had returned from the coast with 'overall excellent news' about the spread of the gospel in that area, particularly in Tembeland. In the interior, at Antioka, the school established by Yosefa Mhalamhala was attracting young Christians from both Rikatla and Tembeland.[29] Despite this encouraging news, the governing body of the mission threw its weight behind the elder Berthoud when it decided two months later that the running of the church on the coast could not be left in 'the hands of young and untested native Christians who have little education or experience'.[30] Paul Berthoud's move to the coast would reinforce the expansion of the mission eastwards that had started, a few months earlier, with the establishment of a new post at Shiluvane by Eugène Thomas.

In May 1887 Paul Berthoud left for the coast with his family and a party of evangelists. He was aware that many aspects of the revival on the coast appealed to the Christianity practised by the Free Churches in Switzerland. 'From far away,' he wrote soon after his arrival, 'only the bright colours attract the attention; close up, one has to advance carefully for fear of injuring or even crinkling the petals.'[31] Nevertheless, he quickly laid the blame for the problems he found at Rikatla on the poor training of the native clergy in both dogma and ecclesiastics and on their inability to run a large organization. Eliashib Mandlakusasa had spent only one month under the guidance of the missionaries in the Spelonken.[32] Jim Ximungana was adding to his adherents in Tembeland a growing following in Lourenço Marques where he had bought a house for the mission. Yet, although he had learned to read and write while working in Natal, Ximungana had received no formal religious instruction or training and was totally ignorant of church liturgy. He was unbaptized, had three wives, several concubines, a large number of slaves and lived off the profits of selling liquor. Equally seriously, when obliged by his commercial activities to absent himself from his congregation, Ximungana frequently placed his church in the hands of an unbaptized slave girl, a literate agnostic or, perhaps most insidiously, in the charge of a Roman Catholic notable.[33]

Paul Berthoud discovered a form of Christianity on the coast in which the first stages of conversion were often marked by powerful messages revealed through visions and dreams. This idea was not totally foreign to members of the Free Churches who read in the Bible that dreams served to bring people into direct contact with God or as a means through which they could receive his advice. But in a society where the ancestors habitually contacted the living through the medium of dreams, this tenet of revivalist Christianity took on a subversive meaning.[34] Some people learned of the existence of Christianity in their dreams. Long before Poungana, a female diviner, had heard of Christianity, she had seen Christ in the middle of the sea, supported by an angel on either side. The Son of God had told her to abandon her divining, and when she refused lightning had entered her home and overturned her charms and amulets. A few days later, when her husband was visiting Lourenço Marques, he heard of Christianity for the first time. This led him to identify the figure of Christ in her dream and in this way contributed to his wife's conversion. In Tembeland God spoke directly to a woman working in the fields, ordering her to recognize her sins and convert, or face eternal damnation. In another area, a woman converted after she had a vision of Jesus holding up the sky.[35] Jesus approached yet another woman in a dream, telling her to go to Rikatla because he had need of her services. When she arrived in the village she confessed her sins and a severe nervous tick, with which the woman was afflicted, disappeared. Elsewhere a young man attended a Christian meeting after dreaming that Jesus had intervened directly in his life to rescue him from Satan.[36]

Although dreams and visions brought individuals into direct contact with God, Berthoud was critical of the emotions they released and of the pragmatic conversions they inspired. He feared that many people failed to understand the true nature of Christianity when their conversion was the product of a wish to gain access to the power associated with dreams. But he was even more critical of the dominant role played by women within the church. They not only constituted eight out of ten congregants and occupied almost all leadership posts; women were also overly assertive and spoke loudly and in public in a manner that men found unbecoming. Berthoud believed the emotional instincts of the women pushed the church in unwarranted directions. He thought their 'exaggerated imagination and sensitivity' contradicted the modesty and internal reflection required of converts.[37] Furthermore, women exercised little control over who spoke and placed no restriction on the length of speeches. Church services would go on for hours; in Tembeland they were sometimes even held in the middle of the night. The general exuberance of these services passed into intemperance as thunderous sermons, often filled with rabid denunciations of sin, provoked congregants to sob, cry and experience hysterical convulsions. Moreover, congregants measured the depth of this second stage of conversion in terms of the vigour of these emotional outbursts; those unable to express themselves in this manner were denied membership of the church. One old man, for instance, was excluded from the congregation until he was able to shed tears, and another was kept out of the church, complained Berthoud, until he could produce 'a scene capable of attracting everyone's attention'.[38]

In the third and final stage of the conversion demanded by the members of the coastal church, God had to reveal himself to initiates. Those who were unable to see God were advised to work themselves into a physical state capable of drawing the attention of the Holy Spirit. For Paul Berthoud, the visions experienced in this manner were easily embroidered into revelations that, as in one prominent example, had led a slave woman to proclaim herself to be the Virgin Mary. The missionary's deep concern over this case was fully justified, for in various parts of the world, stretching from Ethiopia to the Congo and China, charismatic individuals had used Christian revelations to mobilize a violent, millenarian following. Berthoud's anxiety rose as the convert at Rikatla attracted a number of supporters, and it was with an equal degree of relief that he observed the interest in the movement die away.[39]

Paul Berthoud regarded this form of revelation as an affront to his Christianity. But for people who had grown to adulthood with a deep respect for the ability with which skilled experts uncovered the meaning of messages from the spiritual world, these revelations were entirely convincing. They were both a vigorous indication of the depth of an individual's religious conviction and a fitting end to a long process of conversion. Berthoud recognized the sincerity of this spiritual transformation but he was worried that the physical convulsions and noise with which it was achieved and the exaggerated emphasis on the role of the Holy Spirit bore the hallmarks of local possession cults. For instance, several women who had joined the revival movement had been brought to the new religion by one of the spirits by whom they were possessed.[40] Berthoud's distress might have risen further had he realized that the revivalist ideas and practices of reborn Christians were entirely familiar to people who cleansed and revitalized their society by eradicating evil, in the form of witchcraft, from its ranks. Instead, the missionary merely criticized the formulaic language or 'dialect of Canaan' used by converts to express their religious ideas. Through this clichéd phraseology, Christians touched by the revival merely imitated and repeated what they had learned. Berthoud believed that this caused their practice of Christianity to be marked by stale and unthinking ritual rather than dynamic revelation. Furthermore, through a pious language that church members barely understood, they forged a self-elected elite that banned the neighbouring heathen from its moral world. In Lourenço Marques, this sanctimonious attitude had even led Christians to criticize the tunes produced by a small brass band in the town square as 'Satan's music'. It seemed to escape Berthoud that Swiss radicals had criticized his own church, only a few decades earlier, for a similar 'aristocratic' bearing and exclusive attitude.

Berthoud was particularly anxious that the profound spirituality of local religious experience should not draw attention away from the flesh and from the all-important process linking sin to guilt, contrition, judgment and salvation.[41] His church in Switzerland did not lay much emphasis on the Holy Spirit and, indeed, included in its ranks members who denied the tripartite nature of God. Perhaps most seriously, Paul Berthoud believed the native clergy to be ill-prepared or unwilling to direct and channel the spiritual enthusiasm displayed by novice converts. He was dismayed when Yosefa Mahlamhala, a pastor ordained by his mission, ascribed to the will of the Holy Spirit both the disorderly nature of church services and the undisciplined conduct of their participants. Paul Berthoud thought that Mahlamhala, through his belief in the omnipotence of the Third Person of the Trinity, effectively hoped to absolve himself of responsibility for the actions of his congregants. Most seriously, this meant the native minister was unable to provide pastoral guidance in matters ranging from moral comportment to the all-important interpretation of revelations.

Paul Berthoud believed that much of the force of the religious movement on the coast came from Yosefa's willingness to interpret, as Christian messages, revelations that were an integral part of pagan spirituality.[42] Berthoud was suspicious of the frequency of the revelations, the familiarity with which they were received and the pragmatic responses they evoked. Essentially, the *massinguita* contradicted his own religious experience, which held that sightings of God or his Son were miraculous, sacred moments that could not be integrated into everyday life; nor could the messages received at these moments be interpreted as signs sent to guide and direct individuals in their daily journey through life. Yosefa claimed that the revelations called *massinguita* by his congregants were the product of the Holy Spirit, but Berthoud remarked that the ancestors or the devil could just as easily have inspired them. In many ways, Yosefa had merely appropriated the job of local professionals, called *gobela*, who were trained to enter into a dialogue with possessing spirits and expel them or harness their power. This explained the frequency with which spirits spoke about Christianity to the individuals they possessed, for through this action they succeeded in curbing the spirits' hostile intentions. The *gobela* might also be called upon to interpret the dreams through which spirits spoke to the people they possessed. Because these dreams were normally the channel through which ancestors communicated with individuals, people habitually turned to professional diviners for their interpretation.[43]

Berthoud feared that Yosefa had shouldered these traditional functions and that as a consequence the conversions he achieved were not synonymous with religious rebirth. Instead, in the eyes of the native minister and his congregants, conversion merely required new, Christian interpretations of old, pagan messages, ultimately an almost seamless shift from one cosmology to another. From this perspective the so-called revival of Christianity on the coast, received so enthusiastically by Henri Berthoud and the missionaries in the Spelonken, had not provoked the fundamental transformation of belief and practice required by the Free Church. It had not even laid a solid basis for the spread of Christianity for it depended on continuous revelations that could be (re)interpreted in non-Christian ways at any moment. For Berthoud, Yosefa had encouraged these *massinguita* to such an extent that they had become a 'doctrine of revelations' rather than a religion based on Christian belief and practice.[44]

In Berthoud's judgement, far from re-awakening the dormant belief in a Supreme Being, the revelations driving the 'revival' on the coast would halt the development of Christianity in that region. If novices were not carefully directed, pagan customs drawn from the practices of spirit possession and divination would contaminate the church and undermine its strength and cohesion. These were serious allegations, for Berthoud saw 'superstition' and fear at the heart of a native religion that had 'degenerated' from its monotheistic origin. 'It is not an *awakening* of the negro soul that is provoked by Christianity,' he wrote, 'it really is a *revival*, where the soul emerges from a bad dream, where consciousness *reassumes* control of the rights it has lost.'[45] Berthoud believed the locals had completely lost their original belief in a Supreme Being. W. C. H. Peters, a German naturalist travelling in the area some thirty years earlier, had been mistaken when he took the word *Tilo* to mean 'God'. *Tilo* only meant 'sky', wrote the premier Swiss linguist, and made no allusion to a supernatural power. The only gods worshipped by the locals were their dead, senior, male ancestors who, for fear of their powers, had constantly to be propitiated.[46] Religious belief in Africa had degenerated because of the natives' weak morality. Because their lives were dominated by communal values, they were unable, as individuals, to recognize personal sin; nor were they capable of exercising the discipline and restraint required to control primitive, often diabolical urges. Paul Berthoud no longer thought the native clergy capable of spreading the light of Christianity. They had 'deviated from the correct path' and were filled with 'erroneous tendencies'. Their 'emerging Church' reflected 'an inconceivable moral disorder, an extraordinary ignorance'.[47]

Many of these criticisms were rooted in the long series of debates that had defined the church as an institution in Europe. Church policy, if such a term can be applied to the turbulent politics that drove it, had for centuries outlawed to the devil's realm various pagan gods, spirits and other lesser deities. A major debate within the early church had turned around the moment of the Last Judgment and the role of the church in facilitating the departure of the souls of the dead, as well as their reception in the afterlife. Many believed that when God chose not to allocate souls immediately to heaven or hell, or even purgatory, they became wandering spirits or ghosts seeking to possess unwary individuals. Following St Augustine, the early church had considered these souls demonic rather than human. At the time of the Reformation, Luther disputed their existence as he thought all souls 'slept' until the final Day of Judgment. In Geneva Calvin characteristically abolished any ambiguity over the indeterminacy of life by assigning Judgment to the moment of death. However, it was difficult for the reformed churches in Europe to quash popular beliefs about the ambiguity of death or the place of the soul on the spectrum of existence stretching from damnation to salvation.[48]

Berthoud's criticisms of the coastal church echoed many of these and other issues on which the wider church had built its theology. But his critique also incorporated a racist element when he condemned the 'childish' perspective of Christianity held by black converts and when he stressed their need for a lengthy period of missionary tutelage in order to bring their church to adulthood.[49] Berthoud believed that the mission could not introduce the 'pure Presbyterianism' of the mother church in Switzerland, with its consistories and synods, into Africa without spreading 'disorder and confusion'. At the same time he was convinced that the spread of Christianity on the coast could only be achieved under the guidance of a white missionary.[50]

From Rikatla, Berthoud attempted to impose on the small bands of believers along the coast a dogmatic and liturgical conformity that was foreign to his church in Switzerland. He combated the stress on spirituality in their Christianity by preaching on the importance of the flesh, including the recognition of both personal sin and the redeeming powers initiated by Christ's sacrifice. He stressed that becoming a Christian had to be accompanied by a spiritual rebirth rather than a visual sighting of God.[51] This attempt to standardize and contain the evangelical message was carried to the small knots of Christians along the coast by Matsivi, recently returned from Morija where he had taken the name Calvin Mapopé, and by converts trained in the Spelonken. Relations between these outsiders and local Christians deteriorated rapidly as they attempted to 'correct' the dynamic form of Christianity practised on the coast.[52] The tension between the two communities caused the number of Christians at Rikatla and Tembe to drop sharply. Paul Berthoud responded to this deteriorating situation by prohibiting Lois Xintomane, her daughter Ruth, and other women, from holding leadership positions in the church. Although they were permitted to lead Bible-study classes, women could no longer preach. At the same time, Berthoud called on congregations to replace their displays of emotion during church services with a new composure.

The arrival of Arthur Grandjean at Rikatla in July 1888 consolidated the European missionary's control over the coastal church. With the help of this new missionary, Paul Berthoud was able to move to Lourenço Marques where he took charge of that fledgling congregation. A year later Jim Ximungana was baptized and he entered into a monogamous union, blessed by the church, with one of his several wives.[53] When Henri-Alexandre Junod arrived at Rikatla a few weeks later, Grandjean moved to Antioka on the bend in the Nkomati River. By placing the three major Christian communities on the coast under the supervision of European missionaries, this new development formally ended the short reign of the native pastorate. For the next decade missionaries would choose church elders, and untrained laymen, such as Jim Ximungana in Lourenço Marques, would be replaced by members of the church, for example, Calvin Matsivi Mapopé, who had received a Christian education.[54] Equally importantly, the end of the native church initiated the separation of the mission into two physically distinct branches: one in the Spelonken and one on the coast. This turn of events would deeply mark the direction taken by the mission in southern Africa.

Mission Christianity

Junod and Grandjean believed, like Berthoud, that the mission had to be run by men with a firm grasp of the 'full meaning' of Christianity.[55] These two Neuchâtelois missionaries agreed that immoral cultural practices had swamped individual reflection, and that a swell of mindless sensuality had caused local society to experience a regression in its level of evolution. This was most clearly seen in the sphere of religion, for Africans seemed unable to recognize the elevated forms of social evolution associated with Christianity. Ultimately their sluggish response to the Gospel could only be explained by the tenacity of Satan's hold over the African people and by the implacable gloom into which the prince of darkness had thrown them.[56] The coastal missionaries feared that this visible degeneration would undermine the coherence of the Christian message if the mission incorporated or condoned the pagan customs practised by the local population. In adopting this new, interventionist approach to the local population, the mission had to familiarize itself with the habits and customs of the people occupying its field of operations.[57]

Junod liked to refer to the missionary's task in stark metaphors. 'The consciousness and moral life of the Primitive vegetates in a dark cave' in which, he would say, the mission had 'discovered some trembling rays of light'.[58] This meant that positive aspects could be found in local cultural practices. Grandjean, for instance, believed that the passage of bridewealth, or *lobolo*, 'assures the validity and solidarity of marriage, the basis of the social order'. But he also regarded the practice as a means of turning women into interest-bearing commodities that could be exchanged or inherited. The dissolution of a marriage held together by *lobolo* both threatened to undo a string of marriages, as the wife's kinsmen recalled her brideprice and to destroy the family as the husband's kin retained the children. Polygamy encouraged the Gaza to mount razzias against the Chopi, in which men were killed and women and children seized and enslaved. Polygamy also contradicted the (nuclear) family and allowed men to vent their sensuality in a way that undermined and dissipated moral consciousness.[59] Junod considered polygamy 'immoral and savage' and felt it should be 'extirpated'.[60] His opinion on this issue would mellow with time, but he would continue to regard *lobolo* and polygamy as the linchpins in a communal mentality that curbed individual expression and restricted the spiritual and secular development of African society. *Lobolo* should be prohibited, he would write many years later, as it was 'a practice which is the negation of the moral character of the human being'.[61]

The missionary was tasked with liberating Africans from practices and beliefs that held back the development of the continent. A Christian marriage, for Arthur Grandjean, meant that a native woman 'ceases to be the slave of her husband and becomes his companion'. By ending polygamy, the missionaries would bring to a close the ceaseless disputes over bridewealth and at the same time discourage the practice of slavery. The end of polygamy would also free the individual's creative energies from the inertia induced by a despotic communalism.[62] It would serve to break the chief's grip on the notion of justice, and would infuse individuals with a much wider sense of right and wrong.[63] The mission station acted as a place of safety and emancipation, particularly for freed slaves who, Junod hoped, would eventually be accommodated in specially constructed villages.[64]

The missionaries believed that the vices of industrial Europe threatened to snuff out the 'trembling rays of light' to be found in the natives' culture. Wage labour increased the individual's ability to acquire, or 'purchase', numerous wives, and imported alcohol encouraged the new level of sensuality required of the polygamist. The natives had unlimited access to liquor and prostitutes in Lourenço Marques, 'Satan's citadel', from where they carried venereal diseases into the countryside. The missionaries looked on anxiously as large numbers of men also returned from South Africa with a frightening range of new diseases and with the money and stolen diamonds needed to purchase liquor, brides and guns.[65] In the Transvaal a new threat to the native population emerged when the Boers, who had secured their hold over the Spelonken in the mid-1880s, threatened to expel Christian and other communities labeled as 'squatters' from their farms. As the strength of the Transvaal state grew on the revenue from the Witwatersrand goldmines, the process of land alienation threatened to take new and tragic proportions.[66] For the missionaries, this contact with modern civilization threatened to drag an already fallen race even further down the path to perdition.[67]

The experience of the missionaries in Europe made this a familiar trail, and they applied the same paternal care to the African population that they extended to the people of the towns and valleys of western Switzerland. But in Africa the familial metaphors were made stronger by the presence of race and the isolated nature of mission communities. Converts frequently addressed missionaries and their wives as 'father' and 'mother', and ascribed to themselves the role of 'children'.[68] This everyday discourse forged close social ties within the mission community, but also created a 'natural', biological hierarchy of power. 'This child, this younger brother, the black', wrote Junod, 'needs a sympathetic voice to instruct him and to put him on guard against the dangers of a civilization of which he attempts, all too often, to assimilate only the faults and the vices.'[69]

The missionaries sought to advance the cause of the gospel by supplying the indigenous people with human rights and personal freedoms. 'The native,' wrote Grandjean, 'liberated from his servitude to the chief, feeling his consciousness and individuality reawaken, will be ready to jump into the arms of the missionary.'[70] Under the tutelage of the missionary a 'new society' would emerge as Africans dropped those aspects of their culture found repugnant to Christian morality and civilization. Africans 'should not be transformed into our image and made pale copies of educated European Christians', wrote Junod. 'We deplore the system adopted by certain Anglo-Saxons, although filled with the best ideals, who aspire to create in South Africa black English Christians who speak the language of Shakespeare and live exactly like typical subjects of Her Britannic Majesty.'[71] Junod called for 'an ordered and free regime under which [Africans] would carefully learn to use the perfumed but often unhealthy fruit of civilization'.[72]

New forms of identity were inculcated in Christian converts. Parents and children were encouraged to occupy a single dwelling, and eat together in a way that created and reinforced the nuclear family. Square houses fostered individualism as, ideally, each member of the family was provided with a separate room. The missionaries attempted to generate a wider sense of community by ranging the houses on both sides of a long street instead of building them in the traditional, circular manner that caused the village to look inwards.[73] The Christian village constituted a voluntary community that freed members of the church from the despotism of the chief and released them from the restrictions of kinship and custom. This facilitated monogamy and reflected a new morality based on a universal religion rather than the narrow confines of local politics or kinship.[74] The church stood at the centre of the mission community and its bell dominated the rhythms of life. The church bell was rung in such a way as to divide the day into manageable portions devoted to the regular performance of specific tasks. Its sound marked the flow of life from birth until death and it punctuated the passage of time by celebrating arrivals, departures and other rituals of social life.[75] The missionaries laid great emphasis on the 'gospel of work' as a means of rendering an otherwise 'capricious existence' into an 'orderly life'.[76]

Part of this reordering of life extended to notions of gender. Through their sewing classes, missionary women attempted to introduce a new domesticity that took native women out of the fields and placed them in the home. But sewing was a practice traditionally performed by men and Christian women were at first unwilling to enter into an activity that seemed to suppress their femininity.[77] However, this attitude changed as clothing became both a sign of Christian respectability and a source of income. Within a few years large numbers of women, particularly young schoolgirls, were attending sewing classes.[78]

It is easy for the historian to see Christianity on the mission station purely from the perspective of those who brought the new religion and described its progress in their reports and correspondence. Indeed, mission archives and printed texts naturally draw the reader to this view. The complex forms of Christianity practised on the mission and its outstations only become fully visible in these records at times of crisis, such as during the revival on the coast in the mid-1880s or following the expulsion of individuals from the mission for social misdemeanors ranging from inveterate inebriation to taking a second wife. Missionary correspondence does, however, provide brief, unexpected and occasional glimpses of how people received Christianity and reshaped its message.

Many migrant workers almost inadvertently spread the Christian gospel in their home areas after acquiring a knowledge of the religion, perhaps merely from listening to evangelists in the compounds or from learning to read. Some men returned home with Christian wives who carried the message of their religion to their new communities.[79] For others, like Jim Ximungana, Christian beliefs lay dormant until they were activated by the circulation of Christian literature or by the exhortations of visiting evangelists. Some migrants came home to represent the churches to which they had attached themselves in South Africa and left a thin documentary record. But we know little of more independent spirits; men like Andreas Hongwana, who built a small chapel-school near the mouth of the Tembe river, or Isaac Mavilo, who attempted to bring Christianity to the capital of the young Maputo king.[80] Many of these shadowy figures established their own schools on returning home, taught catechism and held church services in their villages. When these men looked to the Swiss for help, the missionaries attached their establishments as annexes to the central mission stations. Many of these outstations prospered and grew in strength but some developed their own, isolated versions of Christianity and had to be disciplined by the central mission. This was particularly the case when in 1907 the Portuguese attempted to contain the proliferation of schools teaching in English and Zulu in southern Mozambique. Two new laws forced evangelists to teach in Portuguese, and when they left for Lourenço Marques to study the language, the mission experienced a crisis as the outstations fell into the hands of those with little or no religious training.[81]

It was not only on the outstations that Christianity took new and uncertain directions. Rainmaking was a familiar local practice that converts expected their religious leaders to perform on both the central mission and its outstations. At Valdezia relations with the newly arrived missionaries improved markedly in late 1877 when the prayers of Berthoud and Creux, like those of the prophet Elijah in the Old Testament, brought an end to an extended and severe drought.[82] Fifteen years later Arthur Grandjean's appeals for rain at Antioka ended another drought and brought a new trickle of converts to the mission.[83] However, the trickle grew into a stream of visitors when Grandjean rewarded church attendance with pots of non-alcoholic beer on some Sundays.[84] He also drew on local sentiments when he explained misfortune as the product of God's judgement rather than a failure to propitiate the ancestors. This increased his standing in the local community on one occasion when, like a diviner, he predicted that God would punish members of his mission if they went fishing on Sunday - and two of the offenders suffered snakebites and the others failed to catch a fish.[85]

Conversion seemed to make little dent in older beliefs that accompanied the new faith in Christ. Christians frequently turned to specialists like the diviner to discover the cause of their misfortune, or they looked to the *nanga* to supply them with protective medicines in a time of need.[86] The tenacity of the old beliefs became particularly clear at the annual synod held on the coast in 1904, when only about six of the fifty-five church leaders stated unambiguously that they did not believe in witchcraft. Most witchcraft accusations were confined to mission outstations. On one occasion, Christians accused their evangelist of getting help from zombies when he reaped a rich harvest from his maize fields although he had persuaded people not to work on Sundays. On another occasion the *baloyi* were blamed for attracting small buck to eat the sweet potatoes planted by a Christian community. Even church leaders were suspected of involvement in the practice of witchcraft. On one mission station life was severely disturbed when an evangelist accused two women of witchcraft and chased them from his outstation. Another commotion occurred when a church elder accused an evangelist's wife of witchcraft after she had imprudently compared his baby to a pumpkin. Another elder fomented yet another scandal at Rikatla in 1907 when he accused Junod's cook of witchcraft.[87] For the Swiss, witchcraft remained an unacceptable practice that had to be eradicated from their missions with the utmost discipline.[88] We have only these scattered reports on the Christianity emerging on the early mission stations, but they provide every indication that the religion was more contested and diverse than the missionaries' reports would lead us to believe. While the reports provide a picture, albeit indistinct, of what Junod sometimes called 'Kaffir Christianity', they also indicate the willingness of the mission to incorporate some local beliefs into its set of everyday, accepted practices.

The evangelical message carried by the missionaries turned around the image of hell's fires and the path to salvation offered by the mission.[89] This individualistic form of Christianity initially had little success in a world governed by communitarian values. Conversion required individuals to distance themselves from many of the social practices that bound their community as a unit. It was also difficult for people to move from a system of explanation that ascribed misfortune to the malfeasance of others to one in which ill fortune was seen as the product of personal responsibility and sin. Missionary teachings often fell on deaf ears when they referred to the need for indigenous peoples to submit to colonial authorities, abandon the alcoholic beverages that outlined the contours of community, or condemn widows to a lonely and insecure old age.[90] On several occasions parents and their chiefs refused to send their children to schools on the outstations when evangelists or students fell unexpectedly ill or died. Despite the missionaries' protestations that the deaths were due to dysentery or other recognizable diseases, the distressed parents found comfort in the belief that witches operated in these places or that they even gathered under the protection of the missionaries.[91] Resistance to Christianity sometimes took a muted form, as when young girls 'strangely' refused to marry converts who had not been initiated, or when a chief prohibited the construction of square houses.[92] It also produced theological reflections from people importuned in their home villages by itinerant missionaries. One village chief told Grandjean that he had heard of Christianity in Port Elizabeth and was quite prepared to go to hell and burn. A young woman waited patiently for him to finish exhorting her to recognize her sins and then, disarmingly, put out her hand and asked him for thruppence! Elsewhere an old man informed Junod that he could not understand the story of the resurrection, as all living things must die and rot.[93]

At times an individual might express opposition to the principles of Christianity more forcefully, for instance, when a woman refused to allow her newly-converted husband to abandon her by undoing his polygamous marriages, or when a convert rejected missionary demands that she free her slaves.[94] Grandjean was dismayed at the tenacity of local custom in the area around Antioka where converting to Christianity was considered a 'disgrace' and 'near madness'. To illustrate this problem, he recounted the story of a 'demented woman' who had arrived at the mission accusing him of having 'stolen' her son because, having converted to Christianity, he would not bring wives into his mother's homestead. People were wedded to their ways and found it difficult to abandon such customs as *lobolo* and polygamy, explained Grandjean, because these formed the basis of their economic and affective lives. Heavy drinking, he recognized, was also a locus of social intercourse.[95] 'We cannot accept to live in poverty', one man had explained to the missionary, 'to have only one wife and to no longer drink beer.'[96] On another occasion in 1891, when the missionaries persuaded a group of Christian boys at Shiluvane to refuse to undergo initiation, one of their distraught mothers almost strangled Mrs Thomas whom she accused of stealing her son.[97]

A more immediate obstacle to the spread of the church on the coast emerged as several of the church elders exhibited a muted truculence in their relations with the mission hierarchy. As we have seen, when Paul Berthoud arrived at Rikatla, friction quickly developed between the evangelists who accompanied him from the Transvaal and the local Christians inspired by the revival. When differences of approach to Christianity became personalized, Berthoud had felt obliged to stamp his authority on the local congregation.⁹⁸ In so doing, he introduced a far more hierarchical approach to the running of the mission on the coast. Paul Berthoud further widened this division in the mission field when he refused the services of an evangelist sent to him by the mission in the Spelonken. At the same time, he introduced a system of payment in kind to evangelists on the coast that differed radically from the annual wages of twelve pounds paid to their colleagues in the interior.

Paul Berthoud, Grandjean and Junod saw this form of payment in kind as a sign of providence. As Africans became 'haughty and lazy' when they received high wages on the mines, it was important to stress the virtues of providence and frugality.⁹⁹ At first these low and inconsistent wages seemed little more than an inconvenience to the coastal evangelists. But when Yacob Mhalamhala and Yonas Makhunye arrived from the Spelonken in 1890 they encouraged their colleagues on the coast to demand the salaried conditions of employment operating in the Transvaal. This led to heated discussions that finally resulted in the coastal evangelists being granted up to eighteen pounds a year. No sooner had this dispute died down than another took its place when Henri-Alexandre Junod tried to get the evangelists to undertake manual labour. This introduced a sharp division between black evangelists and white missionaries, for the Swiss were not expected to engage in heavy physical work. Over time, the mission had developed a policy of bringing Swiss masons and carpenters to Africa whose skills released the missionaries to engage more fully in their evangelical and linguistic work. This led the black evangelists vehemently to oppose the idea that they should add manual labour to their duties as teachers and translators, and when the threat of a strike failed to move the missionaries, Yonas Makhunye tendered his resignation. It was only after a good deal of convincing that the remaining evangelists eventually agreed to take part in the maintenance and building operations on the different mission stations.¹⁰⁰

A new dispute arose in 1892 when the missionaries ordered Yosefa Mhalamhala to accompany an expedition to Gazaland. For the pioneering black missionary, this was the latest in a series of unwelcome orders received from Paul Berthoud. When Berthoud took control of the coastal church he had reduced Mhalamhala to the status of an evangelist. He was at that stage an ordained pastor with the right to administer the sacraments of baptism, confirmation, communion, and marriage. Then in 1890 the mission on the Nkomati bend had been demoted to an out-station of the mission established by Grandjean. To make matters worse, the name Antioka was transferred to Grandjean's post and Yosefa's outstation was simply renamed 'at Magude's'. Naturally enough, Yosefa was disturbed by this series of demotions and felt disinclined to embark on a long and hazardous journey to Mandlakazi. But when he openly refused to leave for Gazaland he was placed under disciplinary orders. This caused his brother Yacob to resign from the church and move to Magude's. When Lois Xintomane died, her husband Eliachib Mandlakusasa, another founding figure in the coastal mission, also left Rikatla to join the Mhalamhalas at Magude's. During these conflicts, the church council in the Spelonken had consistently cautioned the white missionaries on the coast to treat their black evangelists with care and consideration. In the event, the dispute with the Mhalamhalas was only settled in 1895 when the two evangelists returned to the Spelonken and were reintegrated into the church. But in the meantime the mission field had undergone a marked transformation.

Economic Development and Evangelical Expansion

In 1892 the mining industry on the Witwatersrand started to exploit the gold deposits at deep levels. The fabulous wealth of these mines drew new waves of men from Mozambique and transformed Lourenço Marques into the principal commercial entrepot for the Witwatersrand. In 1893 the Anglicans established a mission in the town to minister to converts who had returned home from the Witwatersrand. The initial interest for this new mission had come from the Anglican church in Natal where the northern limits of the bishopric, created in 1853 to serve both settlers and Africans, had been as uncertain as those of the colony.[101] At this time the British in Natal communicated freely with the independent chiefs living behind Lourenço Marques and Inhambane and, until 1875, formally claimed the southern shore of Delagoa Bay.[102] Bishop Colenso's home outside Pietermaritzburg hosted several embassies from the Gaza who spoke a language closely related to that of the Zulu, and who traced their historical roots back to his diocese.[103] British interests in the area claimed by the Portuguese were reinforced in 1870 when a dispute in the Anglican community in Natal led Colenso's High Church opponents to create a separate bishopric for the independent territory of Zululand. This new diocese nominally included the vast country stretching 'towards the Zambezi River'.[104]

The formal establishment of a separate Anglican diocese in southern Mozambique was first mooted in 1875 and was again raised in 1879, the year the British defeated the Zulu and gained partial control of Lourenço Marques.[105] But the will to create a new bishopric evaporated with Britain's desire for a South African confederation, and it was only with the development of Lourenço Marques as a strategic port for the Witwatersrand that the plan was resuscitated. In 1891 the whole of Mozambique south of the Zambezi River was incorporated into the Anglican mission field when the Sabie River was delineated as the border between the dioceses of Lebombo and Mashonaland. Two years later Edmund Smyth was consecrated bishop of Lebombo and Anglican mission stations were established at Lourenço Marques, Inhambane and, a decade later, in Chopiland.[106]

Much of the Anglican drive into the interior of Africa had been spearheaded by Mozambicans who had joined the church while working in the Cape Colony. As early as 1861 four interpreters drawn from the large community of Mozambican freed slaves in Cape Town had been included in Bishop Mackenzie's fateful expedition to the Shire Highlands. Others had helped explore east central Africa. In the early 1890s Bernard Mizeki, who had migrated from Inhambane to Cape Town in search of work twenty years earlier, became a pivotal figure in the founding of the Mashonaland Mission.[107] Other Mozambicans returned home from South Africa with a less formal evangelical enthusiasm. When Bishop Douglas McKenzie surveyed the Lourenço Marques area in 1889, he feared that the many 'natives who had known Christian influence or teaching in the mines' would lose their faith without the support of an active and organized diocese.[108] The desire to 'follow up' these men, particularly as Lourenço Marques turned its back on a history of neglect and decay, became a major reason for the extension into southern Mozambique of Anglican and other churches.

When the Anglicans established their mission at Lourenço Marques they chose to proselytize a group of Chopi refugees living on the edge of the town. These men had fled south to escape the constant razzias launched by the Gaza against their kinsmen living on the coast between the Limpopo and Inhambane. By turning to these foreigners in the district, the Anglicans sought to avoid duplicating the work of the Swiss Presbyterians. In their search for a lay member of their church capable of interpreting and undertaking linguistic work in the Chopi language, the Anglicans turned to their communities on the Witwatersrand. There they located a group of Chopi attached to the St. Cyprian native church in Johannesburg, and persuaded one of their number, a churchwarden named John Matthews Nyoko, to undertake this mission work on the coast. Funded by Chopis in the Johannesburg area, Nyoko gave up his job in a jeweller's shop and moved to the Hlamankulu location occupied by the Chopi refugees. He and Bishop Smyth soon produced the first grammar, vocabulary and reader in the Chopi language.[109]

Around Inhambane the Anglicans came across American missionaries who had settled near the bay at roughly the same time that the Swiss had started their operations in the south. The American Board of Commissioners for Foreign Missions had been active in Zululand and Natal since 1835. But after forty years of evangelical effort the mission-field in that colony had become overcrowded. In 1878 Major Charles Malan, the representative of British missionary societies (and grandson of the Genevan evangelist César Malan) raised this issue with the American Board in Boston and soon after the Americans sought to extend their pioneering form of Christianity into new areas. They were particularly anxious to employ their Zulu-speaking converts to open a new mission-field and, in this way, to realize the ideal of the self-propagating mission. The Gaza empire was a 'natural' extension of their work in Natal, mainly for linguistic reasons, but also because, like Colenso, the American missionaries had received visiting Gaza embassies.[110] Gazaland also appealed to the pioneering spirit of the Americans as it had not been 'contaminated' by European missionaries or settlers. Through the conversion of the Gaza king, the missionaries hoped to bring about the salvation of the entire population between the Limpopo and the Zambezi rivers.[111]

The Swiss missionaries had encouraged the Americans to push into 'Umzila's kingdom', for they frequently met men in the Spelonken returning home to this region after working in the Cape. Many of these men had heard of God at the diamond fields and were anxious to attract missionaries to their homes in Gazaland.[112] The development of a busy coastal trade based on the shipping of ivory and furs and, increasingly, skins, horns and labourers, further assisted the Americans' plans to move north. But their first envoy to the region died of fever, and it was only in October 1881 that Erwin Richards succeeded in getting to the Gaza capital on the upper Sabi river. Having extracted a commitment from Richards to make gunpowder, Umzila agreed to allow five missionary couples to settle in his country.[113] But the Americans had difficulty finding the funds needed to open this new mission-field and, instead, limited their endeavours to the Inhambane area where, in July 1883, William Wilcox started preaching on a tract of land purchased by the mission.

In the next eighteen months Wilcox was joined by Richards and Benjamin Ousley. Ousley was a former slave (belonging to Jefferson Davis' brother Joseph) who had managed to acquire an education at Fiske and Oberlin colleges in the years after the civil war. He and Wilcox established new stations to the west of Inhambane where, with the help of John Pohleni and Cetewayo Goba, a Lovedale graduate, they worked on a linguistic form that they called Tswa and that would later be classified as the northernmost language in the Tsonga cluster. Richards stayed at Mongwe on Inhambane Bay where he worked on the transcription of Tonga, a language first put to paper by Sigismund Koelle some forty years earlier in Freetown, West Africa, on the basis of information acquired from slaves liberated by the Royal Navy's anti-slavery squadron.[114] Over the next few years several revivalist tremors passed through the three mission stations around Inhambane, and the American Board regarded the progress of its East Central African Mission with pride.[115]

The spread of Christianity in the Inhambane region seemed assured when in 1886 several American Free Methodists established themselves about 80 kilometres south of Inhambane where people spoke both Tswa and Chopi. Two years later the American Board resumed its attempt to establish a mission at the Gaza capital. In the winter of 1888 two of its missionaries made their way up the Buzi river to seek an interview with the Gaza king, but the political situation had changed considerably over the previous few years. Umzila had died in 1883 and three years later, following the discovery of gold on the Witwatersrand, European adventurers invaded his kingdom in the hope of winning mining concessions from his son, Gungunyana. In October 1885 Gungunyana had strengthened his position within Gazaland by concluding a 'treaty of vassalage' with the Portuguese who, the following year, established a Residency at Mossurize, the Gaza capital near the headwaters of the Buzi river.[116] Thenceforth, the Portuguese considered Gazaland a protectorate, the so-called 'province of Gaza', under the direct administration of Lisbon. Under the terms of the vassalage agreement, Gungunyana agreed to pay an annual tribute or *sagwati* to the Portuguese. But while the Portuguese viewed this arrangement as a sign of his formal subordination, the Gaza monarch merely regarded it as a means of establishing and making public a relationship of friendship and respect.[117]

This working misunderstanding collapsed when the Portuguese attempted to expand their control over the lands around Inhambane by demanding taxes from local chiefs. Gungunyana was affronted by this challenge to his power and in October 1886 sent an army into the territory nominally claimed by Portugal. Several chiefs who had agreed to pay taxes to the Portuguese were killed and a colonial force, although armed with modern rifles, was resoundingly defeated.[118] On top of this setback, the Portuguese Resident found himself powerless to prevent the Gaza king from launching bloody raids against the Chopi for slaves and food.[119] But he was able to influence the Gaza king's relations with concession seekers and other wandering adventurers. Much to the chagrin of the American emissary sent to visit Gungunyana, in July 1888 the Gaza king revoked his father's earlier decree on the advice of the Portuguese Resident and refused to allow their mission to establish a presence in his territory.[120]

The punitive raid launched by the Gaza into the Inhambane area in 1886 proved a turning point for the American Board's East Central African Mission. One of their stations was severely damaged during the incursion and the mission-field was disrupted yet again when Gungunyana moved south to Bilene on the lower Limpopo with about 80,000 followers in late 1889. As neglectful and distant as ever, the Portuguese government seemed incapable of stabilizing the political situation. Matters worsened when the missionaries and their wives started to fall sick. The disputes between these natural dissenters eventually culminated in the resignation of Wilcox and the expulsion from the church of Erwin Richards. As the coastal mission faltered, the Americans turned their gaze to the healthy uplands in which the Buzi river found its source. Moreover, the British South Africa Company unilaterally annexed the territory after

Gungunyana abandoned it in September 1889. The prospect of stable government and the establishment of an economic infrastructure made the highlands particularly attractive to the Americans. The area was also blessed with good sources of water and timber, a clement climate, and access to river transport on the Buzi.[121] But the Americans hesitated to transfer their mission to the interior. This was partly because most of the population around the old Gaza capital had tramped south with Gungunyana, but also because various missionaries, together with their Zulu-speaking assistants from Natal, had developed strong ties of loyalty to the Christian communities around Inhambane. They had also invested heavily in the transcription of Tswa and Tonga, and had overseen the printing of religious and other works in these languages.[122]

When the border between the British and Portuguese territories was finally decided, and the BSA Company offered the Americans extensive tracts of land, the missionaries felt 'the Lord ha[d] thrown the door open for us which was closed by Gungunyana'.[123] With this inducement and the promise of a large land grant, the American Board of Commissioners for Foreign Missions closed its operations at Inhambane and towards the end of 1893 relocated to the Mount Selinda area in what would become south-eastern Rhodesia.[124]

The departure of the mission left the small Congregationalist communities around Inhambane dependent for their knowledge of Christianity on migrant workers returning from the Witwatersrand for the next twenty-five years.[125] Erwin Richards remained at the Bay, despite his expulsion from the American Board, and attracted numerous Congregationalists to the church of his new employers, the Methodist Episcopal Mission. The new arrivals included Tizora Neves, a printer-turned-charismatic preacher, and Muti Sikobele, one of a growing number of graduates returning from American Board colleges in Natal.[126]

A more immediate source of competition for the Swiss around Delagoa Bay came from the Catholics. For over half a century, anti-clerical sentiments in Portugal had prevented the country's religious orders from operating in Mozambique. But when Portuguese patriotism was challenged by British encroachments on the sovereignty of Mozambique, a realignment of political forces came to see Catholicism as a potential arm of the state. In 1888 the Catholics established a mission at Lourenço Marques that soon started to attract interest. This was partly because the rules for entry into the Catholic church were more flexible than those of the Swiss, and partly because they opened a school in which black pupils were taught Portuguese.[127] For the dynamic imperialist António Ennes, as well as for the newly-appointed Bishop of Mozambique, António Barroso, the Catholic church had become an important means of bringing about the effective occupation of the colony.[128]

This was a difficult period for the Swiss. When Paul Berthoud arrived on the coast, many Africans had viewed him with deep suspicion as yet another European slaver in search of their children.[129] Christians on the coast initially greeted his arrival with pleasure but, as we have seen, the energy they contributed to the mission dissipated as Berthoud and his colleagues tightened their hold on dogma and ecclesiastics. In the Transvaal the slow pace of progress and the 'material preoccupations' of the evangelists led Honoré Schlaefli to resign from the mission in 1893.[130] The mission had made few converts and seemed unable to protect its members from a Boer government that was tightening its hold over the African population, strengthened by revenues from the mines.

In the early 1890s the position of African men in the Zoutpansberg changed dramatically when they were required to pay hut and dog taxes, buy permits to hunt and supply unpaid labour for the construction of roads. As the Transvaal imposed its rule on the area, farmers demanded higher rents in money and labour from their tenants. Most seriously, the Kruger government threatened to implement an anti-squatter law aimed at chasing Africans from white-owned land, or to so change their conditions of residence as to render them virtual serfs.[131] This caused many followers of the mission to leave the farms on which they lived and to look to the independent areas of Mozambique for a better life. As the Swiss missionaries feared their converts would move back to their original homes on the coast *en masse*, and because Antioka had been included in the Gaza empire by this stage, they hastily negotiated a presence at Gungunyana's new capital at Mandlakazi on the north bank of the lower Limpopo river.[132]

The medical missionary Georges Liengme filled this post in June 1892. He worked assiduously at his clinic but converted only a few slave girls and grateful patients. His task was rather to prepare Gazaland as an area of refuge for members of the mission emigrating from the Transvaal. It was only in Lourenço Marques, the white man's town (*Xilungwini*), that large numbers of people were sufficiently separated from the grip of kin and custom to adopt Christianity. While the membership of rural missions like Rikatla and Antioka had stagnated since the late 1880s, that of Lourenço Marques had almost doubled. In 1894 fully 815 of the 938 members of the Swiss Mission were to be found in *Xilungwini* and neighbouring Tembeland.[133]

A new source of competition for the Swiss on the coast came from a migrant labourer named Robert Ndevu Mashaba. After working in Natal and the Eastern Cape, Mashaba had spent three years at Lovedale, followed by a spell in the Kimberley Telegraph Office. In 1885 he returned home determined to spread the gospel in the Delagoa Bay area. His Christianity was closely tied to the civilizing mission. 'Africa is a dark continent', he wrote to his old headmaster at Lovedale, 'the greater part of her children are brooding on darkness as if on white fresh eggs.' And to achieve a cultural renaissance he believed it his duty to 'fight with darkness in the name of Christ … till darkness gives way to light.'[134] In pursuit of this mission he opened a school near Lourenço Marques and started to study Portuguese. But as a Protestant trained by British missionaries, he received little support from the Portuguese and was obliged to find the funds for his church by working for a Swiss trader named Frey at Komati Poort. Like Jim Ximungana in Tembeland, Mashaba was fluent in English and read the Gwamba *buku* with ease.[135] With his savings he established a day school in May 1888 and quickly attracted sixty-six children on a regular basis. Preaching in his own language, Mashaba was able to draw a large following. Within three years he had built a church at Nkasana and nine out-stations along the Tembe River, four of which included day schools. In this task he was assisted by four local preachers and five class leaders; and some two hundred people were on trial for communion.

In 1890 the Methodists officially recognized Mashaba as a minister, his church was incorporated into their Transvaal District, and his converts were baptized.[136] During this time he produced two reading primers, a collection of hymns and helped draw up a thirty-one-page dictionary in the local language form, to which he affixed the label 'Ronga'.[137] The familiarity of Mashaba's Ronga literature appealed to local sentiments and won converts in much the same way as the Swiss missionaries' *buku* had, only a few years earlier. The popularity of religious works printed in Ronga almost certainly accounts for much of the success with which Thomas Gebuza, another remarkable Methodist migrant worker-turned-evangelist, spread the gospel in the southern part of the Maputo kingdom.[138]

Written in the Gwamba dialect drawn up by the missionaries in the Spelonken, the language of the *buku* had more in common with the Thonga or Tsonga language form employed in the area between the Nkomati and Limpopo rivers. For this reason Mashaba's Ronga literature was more favourably received than the 'foreign' Gwamba or Thonga reading material. The Swiss Presbyterians, with their experience of the ties between nation and church, were opposed to this intrusion into what they considered 'their' linguistically defined mission-field. When their attempts to combine with Mashaba failed, and they realized they were placed at a competitive disadvantage by their inability to publish in the local language form, Henri-Alexandre Junod published his own grammar, dictionary and, later, a New Testament in Ronga.[139] This linguistic activity, the subject of chapters six and seven, led Junod into the subject of anthropology. But to understand this shift in his thinking, and that of many of his colleagues, I want to move back to the beginnings of the Swiss Mission in Africa and to focus attention on the question of landscape and ways of seeing.

Notes

[1] On the station system, cf. J. Whiteside, *History of the Wesleyan Methodist Church of South Africa* (London, 1906), pp. 275–76. On reverse colonization, see p. 10 above.

[2] *Rapport adressé au Synode par la commission des missions de L'église évangélique libre du canton de Vaud, 1869–70*, pp. 32–3; Paul Berthoud, *Lettres missionnaires: 1873–1879 de M. et Mme Paul Berthoud* (Lausanne, 1900) pp. 76–8, 103; Arthur Grandjean, *La Mission romande: ses racines dans le sol Suisse romand: son épanouissement dans la race thonga* (Lausanne, 1917), pp. 45–9; J. F. Zorn, *Le Grand siècle d'une mission protestante* (Paris, 1993), pp. 410–12.

[3] P. Berthoud, 'Les Spelonken' in *L'Afrique explorée et civilisée* (1880–1881), p. 163. For this and much of the background to the following paragraphs, see Jan van Butselaar, *Africains, Missionnaires et Colonialistes: les origines de l'église presbytérienne du Mozambique, 1880–1896* (Leiden, 1984) chapters two and three. The work of Nicolas Monnier, which draws on social constructivism, is an excellent complement to van Butselaar's pioneering work on African initiative. See Nicolas Monnier, 'Stratégie missionnaire et tactiques d'appropriation indigènes: La Mission romande au Mozambique 1888–1896' in *Le Fait Missionnaire* (Lausanne, 1995) December, no. 2.

[4] *Berliner Missions-berichte* (1876) 23, 24, p. 400. My thanks to Alan Kirkaldy for this source.

[5] P. Berthoud to J. Favre, 21 July 1875 in *Lettres missionnaires de M & Mme Paul Berthoud*, pp. 249–50; *Bulletin de la Mission vaudoise* (*BMV*) (1876), pp. 46, 65; *BMV* (1876) 30 September, p. 30; *BMV* (1877), p. 120; Grandjean, *La Mission romande*, p. 48.

[6] *Missionary Herald*, (1880) November, p. 465.

[7] Grandjean, *La Mission romande*, p. 131.

[8] Another £10 was promised by the mission: P. Berthoud, *Les Nègres gouamba ou les vingt premières années de la Mission romande* (Lausanne, 1896), p. 103

[9] P. Berthoud, *La Mission romande à la baie de Delagoa* (Lausanne, 1888), pp. 17ff.

[10] Berthoud, *Nègres gouamba*, p. 160; Ruth Berthoud-Junod, *Du Transvaal à Lourenço Marques: lettres de Mme R. Berthoud-Junod* (Lausanne, 1904), p. 25.

[11] This was a collection of hymns and readings from Genesis and the New Testament, called the *buku*, assembled and printed by Paul Berthoud in Lausanne. On Jim Ximungana, see Swiss Mission Archive, Lausanne (SMA) 8. 10. B, Henri Berthoud to mission secretary, 28 October 1886; H. Berthoud, letter of 20 January 1887 in *Bulletin de la mission romande* (*BMR*) (1887) 71, pp. 210–11; R. Berthoud-Junod, 4 July 1887 in *BMR* (1887) 72, p. 321; *BMR* (1889) 83, 7, p. 228; P. Berthoud, *La Mission romande*, pp. 19, 138; A. Grandjean, letter of 1 April 1890 in *Nouvelles de nos missionnaires* (1890) 5, p. 90; Junod, 'Une course au Tembé', *Bulletin de la société neuchâteloise de géographie* (*BSNG*) (1894), p. 191.

[12] Henri Berthoud, letter of 28 October 1886 in *BMR* (1887) 71, pp. 172–5.

[13] On the political disputes in the Khosa territory, see SMA 483 A. Grandjean to mission secretary, 17 October 1891. Most of this letter is reproduced in the *BMR* (1891) 10 December. See also P. Berthoud, 20 December 1884 in *l'Afrique explorée et civilisée* (1885), pp. 98–100; SMA 8.10.B. H. Berthoud to mission secretary, 20

January 1887 (reprinted in *BMR* (1887) 71, pp. 212–13); SMA 497D. P. Berthoud to mission secretary, 4 February 1888; SMA 497/E. P. Berthoud to Conseil, 11 October 1888.
14 Berthoud, *Les Nègres gouamba*, pp. 102, 107, 109.
15 The map was reproduced in *l'Afrique explorée et civilisée* (1886), p. 317. See p. 114.
16 Berthoud, *Les Nègres gouamba*, p. 110. For the original, see SMA 1255B. H. Berthoud, 'Rapport sur l'expedition chez Magude', 6 October 1885.
17 H. Berthoud, 28 October 1886 in *BMR* (1887) 70, 6, p. 172; Ibid, 20 January 1887 in *BMR* (1887) 71, p. 206; R. Berthoud-Junod, 3 July 1887 in *BMR* (1887) 72, p. 319.
18 R. Berthoud-Junod to her parents, 14 September 1886 in *NM* (1886) 1, 9, pp. 40, 43.
19 SMA 511C5, Conférence des Spelonken, 16–19 November 1886. See also *BMR* (1887) 'Rapport du conseil pour 1886', p. 235. A. Grandjean, *Labours, semailles, et moissons dans le champ de la Mission romande* (Lausanne, 1898), p. 18.
20 Southern Africa had experienced revivals in 1860 (following similar movements in America and Britain in 1858–59) and 1866 (after the trauma of the lungsickness epidemic). Another revival spread to southern Africa from Europe and America in 1874. Whiteside, *History of the Wesleyan Methodist Church*, pp. 262–78; Edouard Favre, *François Coillard: Missionnaire au Lessouto* (Paris, 1912), pp. 146–8. For an extensive examination of the 1859 revival, see J. Edwin Orr, *The Second Evangelical Awakening in Britain* (London, 1949).
21 Berthoud, *La Mission romande*, p. 16. Berthoud drew up this report on 'the state of work on the coast' in September 1887, three months after his arrival at Rikatla.
22 Berthoud, *Les Nègres gouamba*, p. 138; Berthoud, *La Mission romande*, p. 16.
23 Berthoud, *La Mission romande*, p. 15.
24 Ibid., pp. 13, 16.
25 H. Berthoud, 'Un réveil au littoral', 28 October 1886, *BMR* (1887) 71, p. 173.
26 Cf. chapter one, p. 19.
27 It was contemporaneous with Nehemiah Tile's Thembu National Church formed in the Eastern Cape in October 1884, the Native Independent Congregational Church in Taung, Bechuanaland (1885) and the Lutheran Bapedi Church (1889). Much later, Junod would compare the revival with the pentacostal Christian movements that attracted a large following in the early twentieth century. By this time he had come to see the revival as an example of 'evolution' towards monotheism. See chapter 8, p. 232.
28 H.-A. Junod, *Ernest Creux et Paul Berthoud* (Lausanne, 1933), pp. 129–30.
29 H. Berthoud, letter of 20 January 1887 in *BMR* (1887) 71, pp. 206–10.
30 'Rapport du conseil, 1886' in *BMR* (1887) June, 72, pp. 234–6; SMA 1031 P.V. du conseil (Minutes of council meeting), 1887, p. 144.
31 Berthoud, *La Mission romande*, pp. 13, 17.
32 Ibid., p. 17.
33 *Lettres missionnaires de M & Mme Paul Berthoud*, p. 169; Berthoud, *La Mission romande*, p. 19. See chapter 7, pp. 194–5.
34 Berthoud, *Les Nègres gouamba*, p. 59; Junod, *Life of a South African Tribe (LSAT)* (London, 1927) II, pp. 382–5.
35 Berthoud, *La Mission romande*, pp. 23–4; Berthoud, *Les Nègres gouamba*, pp. 23, 115; R. Berthoud-Junod, *Du Transvaal à Lourenço Marques*, pp. 155–7 and pp. 94–5, 192, 208.
36 Berthoud, *La Mission romande*, pp. 22–3.
37 Ibid., pp. 16–17; Berthoud-Junod, *Du Transvaal à Lourenço Marques*, p. 199.
38 Ibid., pp. 175, 239, 242; Berthoud, *La Mission romande* p. 17; Berthoud, *Les Nègres gouamba* pp. 114, 142.
39 Berthoud, *La Mission romande*, p. 22; Berthoud, *Les Nègres gouamba* pp. 115, 138; R. Berthoud-Junod, *Du Transvaal à Lourenço Marques*, pp. 143, 240–2; H. Berthoud, 20 January 1887 in *BMR* (1887) 71, p. 207. In Ethiopia Za-Krestos claimed to be the new Christ and in the Congo Beatrice Kimpa Vita proclaimed herself to be St Anthony. See G. Haile, 'A Christ for the Gentiles' in *Journal of Religion in Africa* (1985) 15; John Thornton, *The Kongolese Saint Anthony: Donna Beatrix Kimpa Vita and the Antonian Movement (1684–1706)* (Cambridge, 1998). In mid-nineteenth century China, the leader of the Taiping rebellion, Hong Xuiquan, declared himself to be the younger brother of Christ. C. A. Bayly, *The Birth of the Modern World 1780–1914* (Oxford, 2004), pp. 148, 153.
40 Junod, 'Deux cas de possession', *BSNG* (1909–10) XX, pp. 393–4; Junod, *Ernest Creux et Paul Berthoud*, pp. 144–5.
41 Berthoud, *Les Nègres gouamba*, pp. 134–38; Berthoud, *La Mission romande*, pp. 19–20. See also Junod on this question, *Ernest Creux et Paul Berthoud*, p. 145.
42 On revelations as a key to Christian conversion, see John Thornton, *Africans and the Atlantic World, 1400–1800* (Cambridge, 1998), pp. 253–62; James Sweet, *Recreating Africa: Culture, kinship, and religion in the African-Portuguese World, 1441–1770* (Chapel Hill, NC, 2003), pp. 109–115.
43 Berthoud, *Les Nègres gouamba*, p. 50. Junod would later stress the importance of dreams, and their interpretation, to the cosmology of the natives. *LSAT* II, pp. 384, 481.
44 Berthoud, *Les Nègres gouamba*, pp. 133–4; Berthoud, *La Mission romande*, p. 19; R. Berthoud-Junod, *Du*

Transvaal à Lourenço Marques, pp. 243–4.
45 Berthoud, *Les Nègres gouamba*, p. 76. His italics.
46 Berthoud, *La Mission romande*, pp. 54, 56–60.
47 Berthoud, *Les Nègres gouamba*, pp. 47, 117, 132, 136. On the idea that religious belief had degenerated in Africa, see pp. 75–6, 117; Junod, 'Les Ba-Ronga: étude ethnographique sur les indigènes de la baie de delagoa', *Bulletin de la Société des Sciences Naturelles de Neuchâtel* (*BSNN*) (1898) X, p. 403; Junod, *LSAT*, II, p. 628.
48 Diarmid MacCulloch, *Reformation: Europe's House Divided 1490–1700* (London, 2003), pp. 576–80; Kaspar von Greyerz, *Religion und Kultur: Europa 1500–1800* (Gottingen, 2000), pp. 65–110.
49 Berthoud, *La Mission romande*, p. 25; Berthoud, *Les Nègres gouamba*, p. 135. On the consequences to missionary circles of the rise of racist ideas at this time, see most famously J. F. Ade Ajayi, *Christian Missions in Nigeria, 1841–1891: the Making of a New Elite* (Evanston, IL, 1965) and E. A. Ayandele, *The Missionary Impact on Modern Nigeria, 1842–1914* (London, 1966).
50 Berthoud, *Les Nègres gouamba*, pp. 47, 164.
51 Berthoud-Junod, *Du Transvaal à Lourenço Marques*, pp. 174, 239, 242.
52 Berthoud, *La Mission romande*, p. 32.
53 A. Grandjean from Rikatla, 2 June 1889, in *Nouvelles de nos missionnaires* (1889), p. 16.
54 Although Jim Ximungana was marginalized within the mission, he maintained a cordial relationship with the missionaries. See *BMR* (1912) 25, pp. 47, 147–8.
55 A term still used by Junod in 1920; see his 'The Magic conception of nature amongst Bantus' in *South African Journal of Science* (1920) 17, November, p. 76.
56 Junod, 'Les Ba-Ronga', pp. 403, 377; Berthoud, *Les Nègres gouamba*, pp. 60, 74–6. Junod, *LSAT* II, p. 628.
57 Junod, 'Les Ba-Ronga', p. 403; Junod, *LSAT* II, p. 628.
58 Junod, 'Les Ba-Ronga', p. 377.
59 Grandjean, *La Mission romande*, pp. 77–83.
60 Junod, 'Les Ba-Ronga', p. 485
61 Junod, *LSAT* I, pp. 526, 528, 532. See also chapter 8, pp. 230-1.
62 SMA 8.10.C. Creux to council, 5 June 1880; SMA 8.10.B. H. Berthoud to A. Grandjean, 5 July 1886. Creux before the South African Native Races Committee, *The South African Natives* (London, 1908), p. 142.
63 Grandjean, *La Mission romande*, pp. 96, 108–9.
64 This perspective was common in much of the missionary correspondence. Cf. R. Berthoud-Junod, *Du Transvaal à Lourenço Marques*, p. 120; Berthoud, *Mission romande*, pp. 11–14, 32.
65 Yosepha Mhalamhala in *BMR* (1888) 7, 78, pp. 77–8; *BMR* (1889) 7, 87, p. 358; R. Berthoud-Junod, *Du Transvaal à Lourenço Marques*, pp. 28, 49.
66 Junod, 'Les Ba-Ronga', pp. 8–9. See also Junod, *LSAT* I, pp. 609–11, 633.
67 Grandjean, *Labours, semailles*, p. 27; Berthoud, *Nègres gouamba*, p. 45.
68 Junod, *LSAT*, II, pp. 581 n1, 582–83.
69 SMA 516A, Junod to Swiss anti-slavery society, 26 April 1893. See also R. Berthoud-Junod, 'Véra, la jeune esclave' in Anon., *Chez les Gouamba* (Lausanne, n. d. , 1893), pp. 34–40, and R. Berthoud-Junod, *Du Transvaal à Lourenço Marques*, pp. 230–2.
71 Junod, 'Les Ba-Ronga', p. 485. For similar statements, see Berthoud, *Les Nègres gouamba*, p. 164; *Nouvelles de nos missionnaires* (1892) 15, 1, p. 6. See also Junod, *LSAT* I, pp. 1, 11, 526, 539, 546–7.
72 Junod, 'Les Ba-Ronga', pp. 485–6.
73 Cf. P. Loze's description of Jim Ximungana's village in 'Séjour à Tembé', November 1893, in *Nouvelles de nos missionnaires* (1894) 16, 5, p. 74. On the new sense of commensality, see Junod, *LSAT* I, p. 537.
74 Junod, 'Les Ba-Ronga', p. 104; Junod, *LSAT*, I, p. 549; *LSAT*, II, pp. 535–7, 540.
75 The first mission bell was installed at Valdezia on Sunday 8 July 1877. See also Junod, *LSAT*, II, p. 298; B. Jaques–Garin, 'Inauguration de la cloche d'Elim', *BMR* (1912) 321, December, pp. 399–403.
76 SMA 517/B Junod to Renevier, 10 October 1895; Junod, 29 August 1891 in *Nouvelles de nos missionnaires* (1891) 3, 14, p. 38; Junod, 'Les Ba-Ronga', p. 116; Junod, *LSAT*, II, p. 630. Grandjean 14 November 1889 in *Nouvelles de nos missionnaires* (1890) 4, 12, p. 54.
77 P. Berthoud, letter of 2 April 1873; Eugènie Berthoud, letter of 14 September 1875 in *Lettres missionnaires*, pp. 60, 260, 265; Ida Grandjean in *Nouvelles de nos missionnaires* (1890) 4, 12, p. 55.
78 Berthoud-Junod, *Du Transvaal à Lourenço Marques*, pp. 246–7, letter of 17 October 1887.
79 SMA 497/E. P. Berthoud to mission council, 11 October 1888; SMA 513/Arthur Grandjean to Leresche, 21 August 1893; Henry O'Neill, 'Journeys in the district of Delagoa Bay, December 1886–January 1887', *Proceedings of the Royal Geographical Society*, IX, (1887), pp. 502–3; Archives of the Society for the Propagation of the Gospel, Oxford (SPG), Bishop MacKenzie, letter of 31 July 1889.
80 SPG, Bishop MacKenzie's journal for July, 1889; SPG. , Charles Johnson's 'Amatongaland trip', part I, 1895; *The Net*, November 1889. See also Berthoud-Junod, *Du Transvaal à Lourenço Marques*, pp. 228–9.
81 Grandjean, *La Mission romande*, pp. 177–8. See also pp. 246–7 below.

[82] P. Berthoud to mission council, 22 December 1877 and Creux to mission council, 28 December 1877 in *BMV* (1877) 24, pp. 129–30.
[83] SMA 872, Grandjean to mission council, 31 October 1892.
[84] SMA 513, Grandjean to mission council, 25 September 1893.
[85] Grandjean at Antioka, 18 September 1892 in *Nouvelles de nos missionnaires* (1892) 15, 3, p. 39.
[86] Calvin Mapopé, 'Comment les peuples africains pourront-ils trouver le salut?', *Revue missionnaire* (1925) 5, April, p. 2.
[87] *BMR* (1904) 17, 216, March, pp. 73, 224; *BMR* (1904) 17, 222, August, p. 207; *BMR* (1904) 17, 224, November, pp. 298–9. Junod, *Domesticité africaine* (Lausanne, 1923), pp. 12–13; *LSAT*, II, pp. 511–12, 525, n1, n2.
[88] Junod, 'The Theory of witchcraft amongst South African natives', *Report of the South African Association for the Advancement of Science* 1905/6, p. 240.
[89] Cf. SMA 503b, Grandjean to mission council, 9 September 1889; *BMR* (1889) 7, 87, p. 339; R. Berthoud-Junod, *Du Transvaal à Lourenço Marques*, pp. 174, 258.
[90] On the Bible preaching submission to 'constituted authority,' see Junod to mission council, 3 February 1891 in *Nouvelles de nos missionnaires* (1890) 5, 13, p. 77.
[91] Grandjean, *La Mission romande*, p. 180–3; T. M. Masuluke, *N'wanghovela Khujane* (Pretoria, 1966), p. 53, cited in Tinyiko Maluleke, 'A Morula Tree Between Two Fields. The Commentary of Selected Tsonga Writers on Mission Christianity', (unpublished PhD. , University of South Africa, 1995), p. 73n. 33.
[92] Junod, *LSAT* I, p. 524; ibid., II, p. 150.
[93] SMA 1760, Grandjean diary, 8 December 1889; ibid., Grandjean diary, 1890, p. 112; Grandjean to mission council, 1 February 1890; Junod, 'Les Ba-Ronga,' p. 403; Junod, *LSAT*, II, p. 364.
[94] Berthoud, *La Mission romande*, p. 19; Berthoud-Junod, *Du Transvaal à Lourenço Marques*, p. 221.
[95] SMA 503b, Grandjean to council, 9 September 1889; SMA 1256/A Grandjean, 'Rapport sur l'oeuvre missionnaire', 1890; SMA 513, Grandjean to mission council, 8 March and 30 July 1894.
[96] SMA 872, Grandjean to mission council, 24 August 1892.
[97] Grandjean, *La Mission romande*, p. 109.
[98] SMA 497B, Berthoud to council, 26 October 1887; Berthoud, *La Mission romande*, p. 28.
[99] Junod, 'Les Ba-Ronga', p. 244.
[100] This and the following paragraph are based on van Butselaar, *Africains, missionnaires et colonialistes*, pp. 79–91. See also Junod at Rikatla, 29 August 1891 in *Nouvelles de nos missionnaires* (1891) 3, 14, p. 38. Clara Jacot, *Nouvelles de nos missionnaires* (1892) 4, 14, p. 60.
[101] J. J. Guy, *The Heretic* (Pietermaritzburg, 1983), pp. 56, 86–9.
[102] The southern border of Mozambique was based on an anti-slavery treaty of 1817 recognizing Portugal's suzerainty from Cape Delgado to Delagoa Bay. The border dispute flared up intermittently and was submitted in 1872 for adjudication to President MacMahon of France.
[103] Cf. Natal Archives (NA), Secretary for Native Affairs (SNA) 1/6/2 Statement of Umkunhlana, 5 October 1859; SNA 1/1/10 Statement of Mabulawa, 12 January 1860; SNA 1/1/96 no. 73, Statement of Umzungulu and Dubule, messengers from Umzila, 16 August 1870; Colonial Office 179/90 no. 101/12269, Keate to Buckingham, 24 September 1868. Anon., *The Mission to Umzila's Kingdom* (Boston, MA, 1882), p. 10. The last of these embassies arrived in October 1883, some four months after Colenso's death. *Missionary Herald*, January 1884, p. 4; Alf Helgesson, *Church, State and People in Mozambique: an historical study with special emphasis on Methodist developments in the Inhambane Region* (Uppsala, 1994), p. 41.
[104] W. C. H. Malton, *The Story of the Diocese of Lebombo* (London, 1912), p. 9.
[105] The MacMahon award had given the southern shore of Delagoa Bay to Portugal in July 1875. The British then employed economic and diplomatic pressure to push through the Lourenço Marques treaty that gave them a direct involvement in the running of the town. P. Harries, *Work, Culture and Identity: Migrant Labourers in Mozambique and South Africa* (London, 1994), pp. 24, 84, 100.
[106] Malton, *The Diocese of Lebombo*, pp. 10–11; P. Hinchliff, *The Anglican Church in South Africa* (London, 1963), pp. 174–5.
[107] P. Harries, 'Culture and classification: a history of the Mozbieker community at the Cape', *Social Dynamics* (2000) 26, 2.
[108] C. Lewis and G. E. Edwards, *Historical Records of the Church of the Province of South Africa* (London, 1934), p. 742.
[109] This was published in 1902 as *A Vocabulary with a Short Grammar of Xilenge: the Language of the People commonly Called Chopi, spoken on the East Coast of Africa between the Limpopo River and Inhambane* and *A Short Grammar of the Shilenge Language (Xilenge)*. In 1896 the Anglicans installed a printing press at Inhambane and published a Service Book in Tonga. Malton, *The Diocese of Lebombo*, pp. 18–19, 25, 32; Lewis and Edwards, *Historical Records*, p. 744.
[110] SMA 6007D., David P. Prideaux, 'E. Richards: A biography – and an account of his explorations in Gaza, his school, the Gungunyana attack at Inhambane ... and other related stories', *Missionary Herald* (1884) January, p. 4; Norman Etherington notes that, by 1880, Natal had the heaviest concentration of missionaries in the

world. See his *Preachers, Peasants and Politics in Southeast Africa, 1835–80* (London, 1978), pp. 5, 25, 275.

111 *Missionary Herald* (1875) March, p. 130; John O. Means, *Umzila's Kingdom: A Field for Christian Missions* (Boston, MA, 1880), pp. 1–16. *Missionary Herald* (1880) July 'Umzila's Kingdom,' pp. 260–63. Richard Sales, 'The Work of the American Board Mission in Inhambane' in Steve de Gruchy (ed.), *Changing Frontiers. The Mission Story of the UCCSA* (Gaberone, 1999), pp. 93–106.

112 *Missionary Herald* (1877), pp. 147–8.

113 Witwatersrand University Library, Johannesburg. A. 170. American Zulu Mission. Our Lamented Pinkerton's Story. Diary of an expedition from Durban up the East Coast (July–November 1880).

114 Sigismund Koelle, *Polyglotta Africana* ((London, 1854), p. 16. The first literature in these languages started to emerge in 1885. Alf Helgesson, *Church, State and People in Mozambique*, p. 55. See also SMA 6007D, E. Richards – a short biography, p. 18.

115 *Missionary Herald* (1883) July, p. 260; *Missionary Herald* (1885) October, p. 397; *Missionary Herald* (1886) May, pp. 181–2; *Missionary Herald* (1886) September, pp. 172, 444.

116 M. Caetano (ed.), *As Campanhas em 1895, segundo os contemporaneos* (Lisbon, 1947), p. 37.

117 Fondation pour l'histoire des Suisses à l'étranger, diary of Georges Liengme, 19 August 1893. SMA 840 Liengme to Rossel, 3 January 1896.

118 Harvard University, American Board Mission (ABM): ABC:15.4, vol. 12. Ousley to Smith, 25 October, 15 November 1886. Sections of this letter are reproduced in *Missionary Herald* (1887) February, pp. 58–9; Anon., 'Affairs in East Africa,' *Missionary Herald* (1887) March, pp. 92–3. SMA 6007D, David Prideaux, 'A short biography of E. Richards', pp. 28–31; René Pelissier, *Naissance du Mozambique* (Orgeval, 1984), pp. 567–9.

119 J. T. Botelho, *Historia Militar e Politica dos Portugueses em Moçambique* (Lisbon, 1936), p. 425.

120 *Missionary Herald* (1889) February, pp. 55–7.

121 *Missionary Herald* (1891) July, pp. 274–6.

122 See chapter 6, pp. 167, 181n114.

123 *Missionary Herald* (1892) October, pp. 402–3. See also *Missionary Herald* (1892) June, p. 234; *Missionary Herald* (1892) November, p. 459.

124 *Missionary Herald* (1894) April, p. 158; Francis W. Bates, 'The East Central African Mission, Gazaland', *Missionary Herald* (1895) May, pp. 189–91. By April 1894 the American missionaries had succeeded in surveying and beaconing 24,000 acres of land in this new area.

125 The Congregationalists returned to Inhambane in 1917 when Revd Zakeu Likumbe arrived to coordinate the running of these small communities. Helgesson, *Church, State and People in Mozambique*, p. 115n272.

126 The efforts of Richards and those of the newly-arrived Anglicans were, however, counterbalanced by the departure for the Witwatersrand of Harry Agnew, the single remaining Free Methodist at Inhambane. W. T. Hogue, *Harry Agnew: a Pioneer Missionary* (Chicago, 1905).

127 P. Berthoud to council, 20 August 1889 in *BMR* (1889) 7, 87, p. 347; P. Berthoud, *Les Nègres gouamba*, p. 149.

128 Antonio Ennes, *Moçambique: Relatório apresentado ao Governo* (Lisbon, 1893) chapter 21; A. Brásio, *António Barroso, Missionário, Cientista, Missiologo* (Lisbon, 1961). See also Severino Ngoenha, *Estatuto e Axiologia da Educaçao* (Maputo, 2000), pp. 65–71.

129 Junod, 'La biographie d'Elias Libombo' in *Causeries sur l'Afrique* (Lausanne, 1922), p. 11. See also Harries, *Work, Culture and Identity*, pp. 32, 241n88.

130 Schlaëfli-Glardon, letter of 13 February 1893 in *Nouvelles de nos missionnaires* (1893) 15, 6, p. 95.

131 Schlaëfli-Glardon, letter of 16 March 1891, in *Nouvelles de nos missionnaires (NM)* (1891) 6, 13, pp. 86–9.

132 Schlaëfli-Glardon, letter of 18 March 1892 in *NM* (1892) 14, 6, p. 85; Berthoud, *Nègres gouamba*, p. 182; Grandjean, *La Mission romande*, pp. 96, 107–9.

133 A. Grandjean, *Labours, semailles et moissons*, p. 18.

134 University of Cape Town (UCT), Stewart Papers (SP), BC 106: Mashaba to Stewart, 22 October 1892.

135 R. Berthoud-Junod, letter of 3 July 1887 in *BMR* (1887) 72, p. 320.

136 UCT.SP.BC 106, Mashaba to Stewart, 18 May 1902; Whiteside, *History of the Wesleyan Methodist Church of South Africa*, pp. 447–8.

137 E. W. Smith–Delacour, *Shironga Vocabulary* (London, 1893). On Mashaba, see Harries, *Work, Culture and Identity*, pp. 34, 105–6, 160. See also chapter six, pp. 171–2, 187–8 below.

138 By the turn of the century Gebuza was assisted by seven evangelists servicing sixteen churches and a community of 400 full and on-trial members. Gordon Mears, 'Thomas Gebuza of Tongaland' in his *Methodist Torchbearers* (Cape Town, 1955), pp. 25–6. The southern half of the Maputo chiefdom had been allocated to the British under the MacMahon award of 1875. An Anglo-Portuguese treaty defined the border in 1891 and, four years later, 'British Amatongaland' was proclaimed a Protectorate. In 1897 it was incorporated into Zululand. See P. Harries, 'History, Ethnicity and the Ingwavuma Land Deal: The Zulu Northern Frontier in the Nineteenth Century', *Journal of Natal and Zulu History* (1983) VI, pp. 14–26.

139 This is examined in chapter 6, pp. 169ff. below.

4
Landscape

Go and make a survey of the land and write a description of it.
(Joshua 18:8)

Soon after Henri-Alexandre Junod finished his long training in theology he took up the position of pastor of the Independent Church of Môtiers in the Val-de-Travers. In January 1887 he mounted the pulpit that stood at the centre of his church and, in his farewell sermon, before leaving for Edinburgh, spoke to his congregation about the dark side of human nature. 'At the bottom of the heart of man, and consequently of states,' he told his listeners, 'there lie the vestiges of savage brutality, of untamed pride.'[1] He believed these remnants of humankind's primitive condition, only partially locked within the unconscious in Europe, were still an element of everyday life in Africa. These conditions provided fertile soil for Satan, wrote an anonymous poet (perhaps Junod himself), in the *Mission Bulletin* just as the apprentice missionary and his wife Emilie prepared to embark for Africa:

> Over there, where, made drunk by his victories,
> Satan, in the dark shadows,
> Commits his odious crimes.
> Over there, where dark misery
> is broken, by no ray of light.[2]

The early dispatches sent by Henri-Alexandre Junod from Rikatla reflected this same concern with the power of diabolical agency in a primitive land. 'It is night', he wrote in August 1889, a month after his arrival in Africa:

> In the pagan village neighbouring the station one hears horrible noises. These are outbursts of strident, savage, breathtaking laughter, sometimes dominated by a strange cry, like the wailing of a child. Then the whooping, howling, all the most hideous noises of which the human throat is capable. When the shouting calms a little, the voices of young boys or women intone a sort of song without melody in which violent inhalations and gutteral sounds abound. What a concert! I think of the descriptions of Goethe and others of witches' Sabbaths. ... these sinister outcries are marvelous expressions of sensual passion, warlike defiance, boastful pride.

Like Marlow, who discovered 'monstrous passions' up the Congo river and refused to leave the steamer for 'a howl and a dance', Junod found the mission to be surrounded by 'the sound of war songs and the echoing clamour of unchained passions'. The art of singing practised by these 'big children', he believed, was still at the 'noisy phase'. Fortunately, a ray of light broke the darkness as Christian hymns rose from the mission station to compete with 'the echo of the Sabbaths of hell'.[3]

Junod assembled these and other, similar, lines just after his arrival. They are redolent with late-nineteenth-century racism and, you might think with some justification, unworthy of recollection. Yet they represent an important train of thought within the mission and an early stage in the thinking of a pioneer anthropologist. Although Junod would later come to reject most of these ideas, several other missionaries would continue to discern the devil's hand behind many African cultural practices. In this chapter I attempt to account for the tenacity of these ideas by examining the ways of seeing brought to Africa by the missionaries. I want to suggest that when they arrived in Africa, the missionaries lacked the visual conventions needed to 'see' either the landscape or its inhabitants. To put this another way, when Junod and his colleagues looked at the land, their gaze was shaped by a very particular, European aesthetic experience. It was only through their cognitive (re)organization of the land that the missionaries gradually took charge of their environment.

This chapter first considers the Swiss context in which the missionaries' attitudes towards landscape emerged. It then examines the ways in which this practice of viewing influenced the missionaries' perception and representation of landscape in Africa. By investigating how these representatives of the Enlightenment saw the physical world, or infused it with meaning, we may come to a closer understanding of the ways in which Europeans saw – or failed to see – the local population.

At the same time, looking at the ways in which landscape was constructed helps explain how colonization was normalized. The missionaries' imprint on the land was part of a wider genre, reflected in the Victorian novel, medical manual, Sunday school text, or handbook of natural history, that portrayed imperialism as a natural process, and colonialism as a civilizing mission.[4] As they redrew the ways in which they saw the land, particularly through their cartographic work and their intellectual domestication of the environment, the missionaries reorganized the ways in which they saw its occupants. Maps of the land, supported by zoological and botanical collections, turned (empty) space into (recognizable) place. Once the environment had been brought under control, the missionaries could turn to the ordering of society by means of ethnographic collections and anthropological monographs.

Landscape and Identity: Switzerland

For the missionaries of the Free Church of Vaud who arrived in Southern Africa in the 1870s and for their colleagues from Neuchâtel who joined them a decade later, landscape constituted a particularly evocative imagery. For their generation, the Alps had come to personify the character and unity of the Swiss, a people rent by deep divisions of religion, language, class and locality.[5]

The Swiss had once seen the Alps as a fearful place from which violent storms, boulders and murderous avalanches of snow and mud descended into the inhabited valleys. Rock, ice and a thin crust of soil, together with a long list of insalubrious monsters and ghosts, allowed only the most hardy to exploit the High Alps. However, as early as the sixteenth century a hardy band of explorers started to examine the plant and animal life of the mountains. Epitomized by Konrad Gessner (1516–65), one of the pioneers of modern zoology and botany, these men searched out, named and classified rare mountain species. As this new way of seeing extended from the physical to the spiritual world, many came to see the infinite diversity of nature as the result of God's handiwork and, thus, as proof of his existence.[6]

A major victory for the cognitive domestication of the Alps was achieved in 1729 when Albrecht von Haller, the eminent botanist and anatomist, published a long epic poem in which he celebrated the beauty of the mountains and extolled their moral and ethical qualities. In opposition to those who feared the Alps and rooted civilization in the towns, von Haller and his followers found in the mountains a refreshing physical and spiritual freedom and a means by which to criticize urban corruption. As an untouched vestige of the world created by God, the Alps served as a symbolic antidote to the growing immorality and disbelief of the towns. While the towns were filled with noise, raw smells, movement, anxiety and infection, the mountains provided a quiet space in which to reflect on life. The immediate popular success of *The Alps* initiated grand tours to the mountains where travellers aimed to complement their education by exploring von Haller's exhortation that 'man only knows happiness in the order of nature'.[7] Jean-Jacques Rousseau and his contemporaries added to this vision of the Alps a transcendent swell of emotion when they emphasized the savage, uncontrolled aspect of nature; the fear generated in the viewer by plunging precipices, the deep solitude evoked by harsh, uninhabited mountains, and the terror of uncharted spaces.[8] The Romantics found an unsettling excitement and profound challenge in the dark disorder of the land.

As Rousseau's international readership made their way into the Alps, Christianity conquered the mountains. Crucifixes and religious statues replaced the dragons and winged serpents guarding the passes; churches and chapels were built in the villages and, as literacy spread, individuals took less notice of the gnomes, demons and witches inhabiting the mountains. At the same time, the curious continued to scale the alpine peaks in search of edification, to give them names and measure their height, atmospheric pressure, temperature and rainfall at various altitudes; and to present their findings in statistical tables and maps. They accounted for the geological features of the Alps, dated and described their formation, and developed hypotheses to explain the long historical action of glaciers. With growing attention to detail they classified and catalogued the plants, minerals and animals of the alpine world. But the men of science who tamed the cognitive chaos of the mountains and reduced the terror of the unknown were frequently also men of art and letters who cultivated the new sensibility brought to Switzerland by Romantics such as Byron, Shelley, Goethe, Schiller and Turner.

The invasion of Switzerland in the late eighteenth century by the literary elite of Europe generated a wave of patriotic reaction from a new generation of Swiss who laid claim to the image of their country.[9] Over time, Swiss intellectuals transformed their world-renowned landscape into an organic source of national identity that cut across deep historical divisions of language, religion, region, class and culture. Through their efforts, the shallow and precarious unity of western Switzerland was counterbalanced by a shared pride in the magnificence of the region's mountains, lakes and pastures. The Romantics attached a strong emotional appeal to the landscape of Switzerland

and they spread this sentiment in the form of poetry, prose and landscape painting. In the middle of the nineteenth century the Alps were invaded by a wave of middle-class tourists who returned home with representations of the mountain wilderness that were as strictly framed and controlled as the views on their postcards.

The Swiss drew a patriotic pride from the awe with which visitors gazed at their mountain peaks and shuddered with fear at the sight of their alpine precipices, avalanches and storms. Their extensive lakes engendered poetic reflection and a fashionable, spiritual melancholy. The idea that people were formed by their historical interaction with the environment was a basic tenet of the Romantics' criticism of the universalism preached by the Enlightenment. In the Swiss Romande the appeal of this message was heightened by the magnificence of the landscape and the need to found local patriotism in a set of grandiose symbols that was not shared with the pompous, contrived French. Travellers found in the Alps a primitive population that bore many of the traits later found in the peoples of Africa. Simple, sturdy and respectful of tradition, the Swiss *montagnards* seemed to represent an earlier, less complicated stage in the evolution of humanity. In the 1830s the historian Juste Olivier popularized the idea that a *génie de lieu*, a sense of place or *genius loci*, shaped the character and creative spirit of the Vaudois people. The common culture and identity of the people of western Switzerland was the product of a shared language; and the 'vigour' of the population could be traced to its outdoor existence. But it was the locally specific 'sense of place' that determined both the unique 'racial temperament' of the population and its collective sense of attachment to the soil.[10]

Olivier believed that 'our nature, agricultural and pastoral, its magnificent scenery,' provided Swiss poets with the experience and inspiration distinguishing them from the French. While national consciousness in France was the product of a form of reasoning that was as artificial as it was unconvincing, in Switzerland it was deeply rooted in the striking physical reality of the landscape. Behind this image of natural Swiss constancy was the counterfoil of a corrupt and degenerate France. French poetry lacked nothing so much as 'primitive life, life in the open air, life in the fields'.[11] This exaltation of the outdoors and a life close to nature, was combined with an emphasis on the passion and emotion evoked by the Alps. The mountains were 'sublime and echoing' in a way that contradicted the straight lines and calculations of more controlled ways of seeing. Mountains that were 'dark and mysterious' were filled with the adventure, danger and excitement of discovery.[12]

The desire of the fiercely independent cantons of western Switzerland to distance themselves from their Gallic neighbour increased as the nineteenth century progressed and France slithered between authoritarian rule and bloody revolution. 'French literature has become the most urban of European literatures' wrote Eugène Rambert in 1868, while 'we have remained attached to the soil'.[13]

The politicization of landscape continued in other ways. Albrecht von Haller and his colleagues had found a physical freedom in the mountains where they could walk without coming across human habitation, and had easily extended this idea into a spiritual freedom based on the ability to think in a manner uninhibited by the conventions of society. But, for the new generation, the 'freedom of the soul' found in the mountains slid into a 'political freedom' that was sufficiently ambiguous to transcend many of the social divisions in the country.[14] It could, after all, be interpreted to mean freedom from the dictates of the patrician class, the expanding bourgeoisie, the tyranny of the towns, clerical dogma and state interference in religious matters, or merely freedom to speak the local patois. But above all, by sinking the image of political freedom in a solidly stable natural environment, the Swiss invested themselves with a durable, democratic character very different from that of the alternatively despotic or violently turbulent French. At the heart of what it meant to be Swiss lay the alpine villager, noted for his spontaneous, candid and cordial character and the democratic traditions of his *landsgemeinde*.[15] By 1885 a student could remark that 'there are few countries the size of western Switzerland that can claim such a clearly defined national literature' based on 'the picturesque lifestyle of our *montagnards*, the interesting characteristics of our peasants, even the particularities of our towns.'[16] Within a few years, two major critical guides would capture much of the richness and originality in a literature celebrating the physical distinctiveness of the Swiss Romande.[17]

In a time of rapid social and economic change, many drew a moral lesson from the peaceful contemplation of nature's constancy and found a virtue in the disinterested study of natural history. Increasingly, intellectuals saw a reassuring reflection of society in the harmony and regenerative power of nature's laws. While the evangelical traced these to the hand of the Creator, evolutionists saw them as the product of a system of natural laws. The Alps were not only associated with patriotism, democracy, freedom, morality and a pervading religious spirituality: they were viewed as a wilderness where the purity of nature was beyond the contagion of modernizing farmers and invading foreign plants.[18] At the same time their peaks held a special appeal for those who saw their conquest as a testing ground for masculinity, a symbol of man's domination over the land, and a place to commune with the Almighty.[19]

However, viewers could read the imagery of the mountains in very different ways. The frequent personification of nature and the use of environmental metaphors to explain society fused the natural and the social into one sphere. Both writers and artists consciously and unconsciously employed images of the land to provide their views of society with natural explanations. At different times or from different viewpoints, the noble values of constancy and continuity could be perceived as brakes on the forces of change and modernization, or the closeness to nature of the herdsman could be interpreted as the source of both his innocence and his ignorance, his beauty and his brutality.[20] Others could find in the Alpine wilderness both freedom from the conventions and controls of civilization and the undisturbed, primitive origins of the world. Travelling into the Alps was the equivalent of a voyage back through time. Olivier saw the Alps as a world in which 'the fatal combat between man and nature takes place just as in the primitive days of the world'.[21] In his essays on the Alps, Rambert equated altitude with time in the same way that Descartes or Talleyrand saw travelling as a means of talking with men of past centuries. 'The higher we climb', he wrote in 1865, 'the more we believe we are moving back into the past; we are persuaded that we are accomplishing a voyage through time, and that in approaching the summits we are approaching its origins.'[22] As social and economic forces everywhere altered the natural environment created by God, individuals felt closer to their Maker in the mountain wilderness. This religious sentiment inspired the climber Emile Javelle to find in the undisturbed Alpine environment 'something of the peace and happiness of earliest times'.[23] For Rambert, it was a place where people 'lived as they had since time immemorial'.[24]

Under the combined influence of Romanticism and the modern concern with the geological origins of the world, the Alps seemed to provide a corridor back to the dark beginnings of time. When Rambert looked at the Alps he saw not just the mountains, but the metamorphic character of a land created by millennia of geological movement. A detached boulder reminded him of the immense pressure generated when water gathered in the cracks in the rockface and, at night, dislodged great boulders as it froze and grew in volume. A bucolic mountain stream spoke to him of the destruction it wrought when transformed by torrential rains into a roaring monster choked with mud and debris. The silence of a deep Alpine valley reminded him of a prehistoric world untroubled by the destruction accompanying human settlement. The mountain wilderness spoke to Javelle in a similar way when it evoked a picture of 'the brutal upheavals of nature in the perpetual process of giving birth or destroying'.[25] The Alps were a monument to the power of nature, the product of towering forces that dwarfed the capacities and very existence of humanity. At the same time, their pristine peaks represented a final vestige in Europe of the world in its original state, a place in which to commune with the Creator. This earnest religiosity was captured by many poets and painters who felt able to enter into direct contact with God in areas of the world that remained as he had created them. Far from the grime and routine of industry, this was a world 'invested with a religious function', wrote Javelle, 'almost something sacred'.[26]

The African Landscape

The geomorphology of Africa, like that of the Alps, seemed to date back to some petrified, primeval origin. Charles Darwin had sufficient confidence in Africa's great age to situate the origins of humanity in the continent. Sir Roderick Murchison, the influential president of the Royal Geographical Society, held the ancient, unchanging physical structure of Africa responsible for the docile and unresponsive nature of its population and, ultimately, for the undeveloped condition of the continent.[27] This image was well captured by James Bryce who, like Rambert in the Alps, discovered in the pristine African landscape the fragility and powerlessness of humanity. When he gazed on 'a boundless wilderness which seems to have known no change since the remote ages when hill and plain and valley were moulded into the forms we see today', Bryce was brought to 'more fully realize and more deeply feel ... the self-sufficingness of nature, the insignificance of man, the mystery of the universe which does not exist, as our ancestors fondly thought, for the sake of man, but for other purposes hidden from us and forever undiscoverable'.[28]

Europeans were accustomed to reading the landscape through the myths, legends and stories associated with specific geographical formations. But in Africa, their only way of associating the unfamiliar environment with time was through the 'memory' of prehistory. Geology provided the landscape with a history of imagination and meaning encapsulated in each stratum of rock. These geological formations were the 'archives of Creation' read by Arnold Guyot as a chronicle of the planet's past.[29] The Swiss painter Ferdinand Hodler, a student of Carl Vogt, saw in the landscape the immutable laws of nature and he attempted to capture the profound movement they initiated by scrambling and liquifying the rocky surfaces of the Alps in his paintings. Henri Berthoud had the same impression of deep change when he gazed at the Lebombos for the first time in the winter of 1885. He saw them not as an unimpressive range of hills separating Mozambique from South Africa, but as a means of measuring the new, boundless time in which his generation was attempting to situate itself. As he looked over the coastal plain, Berthoud pictured the Lebombos, in prehistoric times, as a rampart against the Indian Ocean and he imagined the peaks of these hills, in an even earlier age, to have formed a series of islands in a sea reaching to the base of the Drakensberg.[30] Later, when he explored the coastal plain, Berthoud found evidence 'everywhere' of the prolonged action on the land of a sea that had once stretched to the foot of the inland High Plateaux.[31] By looking at the environment in this way, Berthoud situated himself in the deep time uncovered by geology and, in the process, he portrayed Africa as an ancient continent in which Europeans could encounter lost, primitive worlds.

Novelists capitalized on this imagery to build Africa into a device through which they could sound the profound geological history of the world. Perhaps most famously this takes place in Conrad's *Heart of Darkness,* when Marlow enters the upper reaches of the Congo river and finds himself as far as possible from the movement that he associates with Europe. From this vantage point he conjures up a picture of Africa as an ancient continent against which the existence of humanity seems but a brief instant in time. 'Going up that river was like travelling back to the earliest beginnings of the world', he recalls, and at the Central Station he imagines an icthyosaurus taking a bath. A year after his arrival at Rikatla, Junod experienced the same voyage into the unbounded past when he visited a grove of palm trees, 'a pre-Flood palace whose silence we alone trouble'.

> The marriage of these black palm trees with the deliciously green, transparent ferns is striking and, for a moment, I believed myself in the middle of one of those antediluvian landscapes that Oswald Herr [sic. Heer] resurrected in his *Primeval World of Switzerland.* These are the same early plants, the same surprising dimensions, the same abundant growth that is unknown in our climes. One would not be surprised to see a few plesiosaurus or icthyosaurus, hanging about across the centuries, spring into the fetid marshland.[32]

By the end of the nineteenth century, just as this kind of time travel died away in the Alps, it became a common image in European writing on Africa.[33]

The picture of Africa's physical quiescence led Bryce to write that the geology of the continent was without 'the power and ceaseless activity of nature' that he had seen in the tropical forests of India or the Pacific islands. For Bryce, the charm of the monotonous, parched and colourless African landscape lay in its primeval solitude and silence. There was 'something specially solemn and impressive in the untouched and primitive simplicity of a country which stands now just as it came from the hands of the Creator'.[34] This perspective was also reflected by Junod when he referred to Africa as an 'ancient land,' whose people 'for centuries, perhaps for tens of centuries, have remained in the same primitive condition…at the most, progressing almost imperceptibly'.[35]

The ways in which the Swiss missionaries saw the landscape conformed and contributed to this primordial picture. They saw the land in a very different way from that of the indigenous population. Local people had a sense of place through which they categorized land according to its utility. Young boys called uncultivated land 'monkeyland', and their elders referred to barren, sandy bushland as *nhoba*. In contrast, they called dark patches of fertile soil in the coastal areas *nyaka* and termed the reddish earth in the interior *hundjusi*.[36] Indigenous people also infused the environment with spiritual meaning. Large trees or rocks, often inhabited by spirits, marked the landscape. So, too, did sites of memory, such as the sacred forest housing the ancestors of the politically dominant family, the graves of deceased ancestors or the simple cairns alongside footpaths to which travellers added a stone as they passed on their way.[37] Spirits inhabited dangerous places like forests, rivers and waterless tracts of land. These were the shades of people killed in battle or by animals, or who had drowned or committed suicide; or they were the spirits issuing from pregnant women who had died and been buried without being cut open. Near Lake Sule, a noisy 'dragon-like aquatic monster', the *ntsanda-vahloti*, preyed on unwary bathers.[38] Travellers in these areas propitiated the spirits and sought to protect themselves with potions and talismans.

Local people had a system of knowledge that explained the environment, assisted its exploitation and invested it with historical significance. They had knowledgeable experts, like the *nanga* (medicine-man) and *ngoma* (magician) who were familiar with the powers of specific plants, animals and stones.[39] Missionaries sometimes succeeded in Christianizing indigenous sites of memory when they pressed shade trees into serving as meeting places or used water sources in baptismal rites. But they felt far removed from local notions of landscape. Like unschooled Swiss peasants, the people to whom the missionaries had been brought by their vocation had no concept of landscape as an aesthetic principle.[40] Adolphe Mabille wrote from Lesotho that 'the Basotho ... are thoroughly utilitarian (and) insensitive to the beauties of nature; the search for lovely landscapes, for natural grandeur, never haunts their minds.'[41] His colleague Paul Germond felt that Sotho tribesmen, like Swiss peasants, could not share the missionaries' feeling for a landscape that was at once romantic, picturesque and sublime.[42] Edouard Jacottet also bemoaned the locals' limited ability to express any 'sentiment for the beauties of nature'. The Sotho took little care to name the features of their environment, complained Jacottet, and when they did, they made little attempt to distinguish between the many Black Mountains (Thaba-Ntsu), White Mountains (Thaba-Tsuen) or High Mountains (Thaba-Telle).[43]

Landscape as an aesthetic notion seems only to have emerged in Europe in the late sixteenth century as the civilization of the towns prized open the stranglehold of nature.[44] By the late nineteenth century, educated Europeans had developed three broad traditions through which they perceived and represented landscape. The first required nature to be organized in such a way as to present a picture of ordered beauty following a set of established, classical rules. The second was a schema of representation based on the picturesque ideal of clear fore-, middle- and backgrounds broken by objects such as trees, rivers, mountains or ruins. This was the way that many Swiss had been taught to appreciate the joys of landscape. The third way in which cognition ordered the environment into landscape was through the conventions of the sublime. These placed special value on the individual feelings and deep emotion conjured up by wild and untamed nature, open untrammelled spaces and the promise of dark, unexplored areas. The picturesque and the sublime often overlapped in ways that disdained the untroubled order and control exercised by earlier ways of perceiving landscape. Europeans could employ the sublime to make sense of the African wilderness, but for it to be employed successfully, as J. M. Coetzee has pointed out, the landscape had to conform to other criteria found in Europe.[45] These included different combinations of light and shade dependent on atmospheric conditions and shifting cloud cover; familiar shades and hues of green accompanying spring's promise; water as a reflective and transparent medium that encourages contemplation; and a population to provide both perspective and a reassuring inscription on the land. Ways of seeing were shaped by topography, vegetation and atmospheric conditions; by visual genres stressing the beautiful, the picturesque and the sublime; and by the sight of familiar plants or smells and sounds.

When Ernest Creux and Paul Berthoud arrived in Lesotho, they were struck by the familiar scenery of the mountainous kingdom. But they were also dismayed by the listless, anaemic shades of green, the small, odourless flowers and the dry, barren and empty veld. The absence of trees and ordered gardens seemed to increase the nakedness of the dry, brown surroundings. This was well-expressed by Eugènie Berthoud in a letter to one of her former Sunday school pupils in the village of Perroy, overlooking Lake Geneva.[46]

> You know how much I have travelled since leaving you, but I have nowhere seen woods as beautiful as those of Perroy. Our dear Switzerland is still the most beautiful country in the world; in any case, if you want to see nature at its best, you shouldn't come to the place where I am living. In this country there is not a single wild tree; the land is everywhere arid and naked; it's only in the missionaries' gardens that one can find flowers and greenery ... [the flowers] do not give off the lovely odour we know from home. We only find one or two little flowers here and there, lost in grass withered by the sun and the wind, and no flower has any scent.

The topography was not entirely foreign. In Lesotho, Paul Berthoud could find himself 'in a very picturesque valley, completely in the alpine genre, with its great walls of rock, its steep grassy slopes, its gracious contours, its little stream of sky-blue water, its narrow gorges and open meadows'. But he felt the light was abrasive and the perspective wrong; and for someone who took the crowded valleys of Switzerland as his norm, the land was empty.[47]

> It's not the light that is missing. There is just not a single tree to provide the landscape with grace by subtly playing with light and shadow; and for our sins, they have just burned the grass, with the result that all the slopes are as if draped in a pall, which gives them a mournful and ghastly aspect. The carbon spread everywhere greatly diminishes the light and completely destroys the perspective. Not a village, not a dwelling, the valley seems deserted.

Even the snow at Thaba Bossiou, despite the cheerful aspect it gave to the landscape, was 'painful to see' because the local population was not equipped to withstand the cold.[48] On the edge of the escarpment in the eastern Transvaal, Junod was charmed by the peaks of the Drakensberg mountains. But he found the many flat mountains in the area 'dense, unfeeling and without ideals, as though crushed by a giant compressor'. 'This is Africa', wrote the weary missionary and, laying stress on the relationship between environment and national character, he continued, 'such is the land, and so are the people.'[49]

On their arrival in Africa in 1872, the Berthouds were attracted by Cape Town's scenery. The town was 'verdant and wooded', the houses in the 'charming village' of Rondebosch were surrounded by hedges of jasmin, myrtle and pomegranate, and on Table Mountain they had found a 'fairytale spot' near the source of a cascading stream.[50] They also considered Lovedale in the Eastern Cape a 'charming', well-wooded 'nest of green'.[51] On her way to Africa *demoiselle missionnaire* Jeanne Jacot had been warned of 'the aridity of the mountains and the plains, the treeless perspectives'.

For those leaving the green fields and imposing oaks of the south of England, she had been told, it was not a good thing suddenly to arrive in Africa. Not surprisingly, this had led her to believe that everything in Africa would be of 'a sombre character'. Yet in Durban she had been pleasantly surprised to find that 'the sea, the sky, the earth are here as beautiful as in Europe and the daylight is more radiant'.[52]

The missionaries were initially delighted with the location of their first station in the Northern Transvaal, as the Spelonken hills resembled the northern part of the canton of Vaud. From this situation they looked northwards onto the wooded slopes of the Zoutpansberg, where streams and summer flowers recalled the Jura or even some of the mountains in the upper Rhone valley.[53] They expressed 'real pleasure' when they stumbled upon plants such as ferns, ivy, primulas and daisies that were familiar to them from home.[54] And they were particularly delighted to find 'real jasmine' with its 'wonderful smell' growing among the rocks. In an attempt to recall the sight and odour of home, they filled their residences with these flowers and even dressed their picket fences with jasmine.[55]

Wherever the missionaries ventured they were 'charmed' by the combination of water, mountains and trees.[56] Edouard Jacottet wrote ecstatically from Lesotho that in the Malutis 'one would imagine oneself somewhere among the loveliest nooks of the Gruyère ... This is the pasture of the High Alps at its best; and above all that, a blue sky, brilliant sunshine, the like of which is unknown in Switzerland.'[57] Even on the hot Mozambican coast, the Swiss could be delighted by the pure air, pleasant shade and blue sky of late winter, a period that recalled 'a lovely summer's morning at home in the countryside'.[58]

But these were isolated moments in a dauntingly alien landscape. In 1873 Eugènie Berthoud found Port Elizabeth situated in 'an arid and rocky landscape, no greenery, no trees'.[59] Her husband found the plains of the Southern Transvaal to be 'uniform, monotonous without end. Not even a few trees as a source of diversion.' Only a small range of hills called the Witwatersrand was 'a little less ugly than the rest'.[60] A decade later his second wife, Henri Junod's sister Ruth, when on her way to the Zoutpansberg, thought the route north of Pretoria 'lovely' because of the thick bush, scattered trees and charming streams. But she was startled by the overpowering emptiness of a country marked by 'real solitude; not a farm, not a native village, not a soul for leagues around'.[61] A few years later, when passing through the Drakensberg near Lydenberg, she was struck by a landscape made up of 'only naked mountains, with piles of rocks'. 'Not a tree, not a bush,' and, although the veld had only recently been burned, 'not a living soul'. She found the landscape 'mournful' and, as she moved further from the Spelonken, it inspired in her a 'deep sadness'.[62] Honoré Schlaefli had the same impression of the country between Ladysmith and Pretoria. Shortly after his arrival he wrote that it 'is as naked as the back of the hand; one hardly finds, from time to time, a small, stunted tree'.[63] A compatriot from Neuchâtel in the employ of the PEMS had a similar experience, crossing the Orange Free State on his way to the Zambezi. He found the veld

> monotonous: no mountains, no flowers, no trees; a few undulations of earth are the only things to break the uniformity of the landscape. The farms seem lost in this solitude ... Those who see Africa as a country of dreams are fooling themselves. It can't compare with our homeland. I am talking about what I have seen ... we end up calling whatever is not arid beautiful; our ambition goes no further.

He conceded that there were some attractive places in the Transvaal but declared that, without the life needed to animate nature, these could never rival the plateaux of Switzerland.[64]

When Henri-Alexandre Junod arrived in Africa in the winter of 1889 he used the same sort of negative imagery to describe the landscape. Yet as a young man in Neuchâtel he had displayed a strong appreciation of nature and its social messages. His essays published in the journal of the student Société de Belles-Lettres show the strong influence of Romanticism which, refracted through the writings of Lamartine and Lafontaine, as well as local poets like Jules Gerster and Jules de Pury, tied landscape indefatigably to identity, morality and religious spirituality.[65] As a student he wrote nationalistic essays on the history and literature of the canton of Neuchâtel and saw landscape as an important feature distinguishing his homeland from that of Prussia, its former political suzerain.[66] The young Junod admired the pastoral poetry of Racan who praised the peace and contentment of peasants living in the 'simple countryside' and who, in the process, presented an implicit critique of the materialism and corruption of the great cities and the intrigues of court life.[67] In his student essays on natural history, strongly derivative of Lamartine and Rambert, the young Junod frequently anthropomorphized the environment and combined sentimentality indiscriminately with information and moral philosophy.

Despite the literary and scientific empathy with which he viewed landscape, when Junod arrived in Southern Mozambique he found himself without the means to describe it. With regret, he found it difficult to express in words the flat and monotonous countryside and he fell back on either exoticizing the plants or describing them by means of analogy with those he knew at home. The hill above Lourenço Marques was arid, tiring to the eye and, because of the thick fine sand, equally tiring to the legs. There were few flowers, the vegetation was meagre and the drab bush presented a sad appearance.[68] Junod was unable to describe the landscape as it lacked the grass, trees, mountains and reflective water needed to fill it.

Bryce provided an interesting insight into the conscious way in which some European viewers constructed their vision of the veld. He realized that a lack of rainfall and cloud cover made the scenery of South Africa wholly unlike that of Europe or of most parts of America. It was a land 'where no clear brooks murmur through the meadow, no cascade sparkles from the cliff, where mountain and plain alike are brown and dusty except during the short season of the rains'. He attributed the absence of forests and contrasting shades of green to the lack of rain. The trees were thin and stunted, or evergreens whose leaves bore little variety of colour. Hence in comparison with Europe where 'the presence of water in lakes and running streams, and, above all, foliage and verdure, are the main elements of beauty', the veld displayed little 'variety of form [or] boldness of outline'.[69] Bryce acknowledged the presence of the local population but felt they left few marks on the landscape; their fields returned to bush when left fallow and their huts disintegrated under the hot sun and driving rain. He believed that

> Here in South Africa the native races seem to have made no progress for centuries, if, indeed, they have not actually gone backward; and the feebleness of savage man intensifies one's sense of the overmastering strength of nature. The elephant and the buffalo are as much the masters of the soil as is the Kafir, and man has no more right to claim that the land was made for him than have the wild beasts of the forest who roar after their prey and seek their meat from God.[70]

For this servant of empire the implications were clear. Europeans would make the land useful by subjecting it to their knowledge and enterprise. They would fill its emptiness with points of reference, erect landmarks to create perspective, cut the coruscating light and relieve the monotony with clear lines and divisions. They would bring distinctive hues, shades and even odours to the landscape.

Honoré Schlaefli also participated in this moral geography. He was struck by the unexploited potential of the land and by its poverty.

> The products of the soil are nothing compared with what they could be. And, when one considers these immense stretches of land covered in grass, without a single man to cultivate the soil, one has the impression that the country is waiting to be inhabited.[71]

Others expressed in less conscious ways the opinion that the African landscape was a blank slate to be written upon by industrious European men. As a passionate entomologist and botanist, Junod took great pleasure in finding himself in 'a completely new natural environment, full of surprises and still virgin'.[72] His colleagues Paul and Henri Berthoud, and Arthur Grandjean, used the same expression at various times when they described the Manununu Forest on the Nkomati as 'virgin', or 'virgin of humanity'.[73] They consciously used this term to present the dense woodland as a primeval, pure landscape untouched by human activity.[74] More generally, Junod believed it was the 'mysterious charm of the unknown' that constantly attracted scientific expeditions to Africa.[75]

Underlying these descriptions were the unconscious fantasies of domination produced by the idea of Africa in the mind of European romantics. For this 'virgin' bush or forest was 'penetrated' by travellers in the same way that civilization 'penetrated' an area, or that 'virgin' nature had to be 'conquered by intelligent man'.[76] In one particularly striking phrase, that speaks of Africa as the female partner in the sex act, Junod referred to the need for the continent's 'intellectual energies and inventive faculties' to be 'fertilized' by 'outside influences'.[77] This portrayal of Africa as a virgin, feminine, passive continent conquered by a virile, masculine Europe is a long way from the rational economic and political decisions behind imperialism. But it highlights the ways in which overseas expansion was unconsciously construed as a 'natural', masculine, even regenerative task and yet, at the same time, as both seductive and threatening.[78]

By placing the forest in the visual category of the exotic the missionaries could praise as 'splendid' and 'fabulous' its thick underbush, dense foliage and colossal trees hung with creepers and moss. It was at once imposing and frightening. Impenetrable, unoccupied, and feared by locals who saw only snakes or hostile spirits in its dark interior, the forest was a symbol of the challenge and adventure that 'mysterious' Africa presented to men such as Junod: a place to be opened to both the sun's rays and the light of reason and religion. The image of virgin bush and primeval forest was so powerful in the missionaries' texts as to dominate and hide the extensive policy of deforestation and land-clearing undertaken by the local population. Even when tens of thousands of Gaza immigrants moved south in 1889–90 to settle along the lower Limpopo, where they cleared and cultivated new fields, Junod and his colleagues continued to portray the environment as inanimate and unchanging. So it should come as little surprise that, in 1898, surrounded by this pre-historic environment, Junod could write 'that the state of civilization in which the Europeans found the Bantu tribes of South Africa is extremely ancient'.[79]

4.1 Swiss missionaries started to photograph the environment in 1884.
Their photographs often caught the sense of estrangement felt by Europeans in an unfamiliar landscape. In this picture, taken north of Pretoria, human figures are lost in an empty veld and dwarfed by an engulfing sky.
(© Swiss Mission Archive, Lausanne)

One of the most striking aspects of these early descriptions of landscape drawn by the young Junod and his colleagues is that they were frequently an assemblage of negations of an idealized European standard. When the environmental features did not speak in a language understood by the viewers, they merely invented a new vocabulary by inverting the composite elements of their own, familiar landscape. The land was empty, monotonous, colourless, treeless, silent, naked, devoid of perspective and unmarked by human enterprise. Once Paul Berthoud started to use a camera for the first time in 1884, they had photographs to prove it: perspectives that highlighted the vast nothingness of the veld by swamping tiny human figures, buildings or wagons in great seas of land and sky. White South African writers and artists would employ the sublime to organize this vision of the landscape and they would funnel its excitement into a new, national consciousness.[80] A writer like Olive Schreiner or a painter like Jacob Pierneef would stand in awe and reverence before the silence, find a freedom of movement and thought in its boundlessness, and a reassuring sense of place in its sharp luminosity. But where they would discern a slumbering behemoth, alternatively menacing or regenerative beneath Africa's geological quiescence, and an oppressive beauty in her dusty browns, many Europeans found a feeling of agoraphobia and bleak melancholy that lapsed into sadness.

Landscape and society

One of the premises of this chapter has been that the Swiss, and Europeans more generally, were nurtured and trained to read or visually organize the landscape according to established conventions, and that they drew a social message from these readings. This conscious or unconscious link between landscape and society can be extended further to account at least partially for the negative way in which the Swiss missionaries initially described the local population. It is noteworthy that it was only when seated on the banks of a wide river that Junod drew a positive picture of an autochthon for the first time. This was a framed, domesticated space, a medium commonly employed by poets and painters to provide their work with introspection. Junod described

> A big chap travelling on the Nkomati in a tiny dugout. He comes and goes, and returns, with consummate skill. What a beautiful body and how his black-brown colour enhances the dark swells and the green forest of orange trees! M. de Pury's Neapolitan fishermen do not have better muscles than this savage handling his only oar.[81]

The reference to Italy allowed Junod's readers to tame Africa's foreignness by incorporating it into a scene made familiar to Europeans by romantic writers and painters. In this unthreatening context the native could be assimilated into the harmony of nature. But in unfamiliar settings the description of the population was less generous, demonstrated by Junod's discomfiture, mentioned at the beginning of this chapter, when he was confronted by the hideous hullabaloo in the village next to the mission at night. This was a 'mysterious' world, and the 'primitive savages' who occupied it were immoral, lazy and ignorant; at best 'grown-up children'.[82] He was particularly appalled by the drunkenness induced by local and imported alcohol. Soon after his arrival he wrote that 'generally the negro is quiet, dull. One finds him crouched before his hut preparing his food without saying a word, stupid and as though half asleep.' But under the influence of alcohol he was seized by a dementia comparable to 'satanic possession'.[83] 'A scene from [a witch's] Sabbath of the middle-ages could not bear a more infernal character' than the picture produced by the natives' violent, drink-inspired dances.[84]

For strict Calvinist missionaries, this drunken dancing and singing was a vivid instance of the body rebelling against reason and instinct defying the prescriptions of culture. In the process, individual morality slipped beneath a sharp swell of raw, primordial drives. The native's barely-repressed cruel, brutal and destructive instincts surged to the surface as his inhibitions were swamped by alcohol and his individuality lost in collective performances. Arthur Grandjean was appalled by the 'savage and inhuman cries' emitted on these occasions, just as Paul Berthoud recoiled with 'disgust and horror' before an 'abominable rite' performed by a group of women. For readers at home, the unspeakable nature of the 'uproar and improper dances' performed by these 'pagans' was made more horrible by leaving its content to their imagination.[85] 'Poor country!' Georges Liengme exclaimed on a later occasion, 'in what gloom it is plunged: ignorance, sin, moral inertia, darkness everywhere.'[86] Ruth Berthoud-Junod wrote that it was a place where 'one feels the influence of evil more than at home'.[87]

This dark picture seemed to be confirmed by the 'reverse colonization' affecting isolated Boer communities in the northern Transvaal. After the fall of Schoemansdal in 1867 the frontier became particularly porous as many Boers left the region and those who remained came to depend for their survival on African allies and assistants. With disturbing frequency the missionaries came across Europeans who, isolated from their institutions and beliefs, employed slaves and traded in 'black ivory'.[88] European immigrants like Coenrad de Buys and João Albasini had married Africans or taken local concubines and, together with other people of European descent, they consulted rainmakers, diviners and healers, or personally threw the bones.[89] The mode of production practised on this impoverished frontier seemed to have regressed from a form of settled farming to a shiftless, itinerant hunting. Whites trekked after migrating game, lived from their rifles, and squatted in the same primitive conditions as the natives. The sight of a black servant teaching his master to read appalled Honoré Schlaefli; it was an image that encapsulated for him the 'astonishing' ignorance to which the Boers had reverted in the wilderness.[90]

For fervent Calvinists, current notions of social degeneration reinforced this tangible evidence of man's fall from grace. The missionaries were in Africa to bring about the spiritual and secular redemption of primitive man. But in the process of their evangelical work, they became aware of the precariousness of their own hold on civilization. For the actions of the primitive peoples who surrounded them indicated the extent to which their own European civilization had only barely repressed the base instincts and brutal drives of humanity. Africa was not only 'dark' because of the absence of light; it was also a continent where 'dark things' and 'dark forces' could rush to the surface.

Sickness seemed to incarnate the obscure fears and inchoate anguish experienced by many Europeans in Africa. In December 1875, six months after arriving in the Spelonken, the Creux family lost their youngest daughter Jeanne to croup. Less than five years later, fever and diptheria took the lives of two of their three remaining children, Jean and Valdo, as well as those of Eugènie Berthoud and her three children:

Anna, Emile and Adèle.[91] When the mission extended its activities to the coast, it entered a malarial area colloquially termed 'the white man's grave'. In this area every missionary contracted malaria; their letters were haunted by diphtheria and dysentery and the enigmatic fevers that seemed to rise from the mephitic landscape or to descend with the rays of the tropical sun.[92] Their major fear was for their children; as Junod wrote in the conversation manual attached to his *Grammaire ronga*, 'the heat of this country kills the children of the whites.'[93] But it was not just the children who died. Even after the missionaries started to take quinine and spend the fever season in the highlands of Natal or Lesotho, a change in the ecological balance could bring epidemic diseases in its wake. During the South African War overcrowded living conditions and poor supplies of water and food initiated a general decline in physical welfare that, when combined with dysentery and typhoid, caused the death of five Swiss missionaries, including Junod's sister Ruth, his wife Emilie, and their stillborn child.[94]

This was not a world for which the missionaries were prepared. When they arrived in Africa, many expected to find only victims of the slave trade, noble savages or the Sunday school's innocent *petit Nègre*. Their first problem was to accustom themselves to the natives' physiognomy which they initially regarded as ugly because of its foreign character.[95] Although they quickly familiarized themselves with physical difference and came to see the locals as handsome, the missionaries stared into the dark side of primitive society when confronted by cultural practices that contradicted the norms of their own civilization. Young missionaries were shocked to find that local people could sacrifice human beings in an attempt to win the favour of the ancestors. Further, in their search for rain or victory in war, local communities sometimes abandoned young victims in sacred forests where they would be 'eaten by the gods', or dug up decomposing corpses.[96] It was also rumoured that iron-smiths strengthened their hoes and weapons by dipping them in the blood of murdered strangers and that they disinterred the dead so as to mix their bones with the coals in their furnaces.[97] The missionaries were also shocked by the practice of infanticide. If the incisors of a young infant emerged next to the palate rather than from the lower jaw, the child had to be killed to prevent the misfortune that would inevitably arise. In many communities, twins were also put to death as they were a sign of suspiciously good fortune that aroused the jealousy of the ancestors. If they were not killed and misfortune overtook the community, the father would be executed, his goods confiscated and homestead destroyed.[98] On one particularly grisly occasion at the height of a drought, mothers were obliged to open the graves of their recently deceased infants and, by exposing their putrifying remains to the elements, bring rain to the fields.[99]

In a way that compounded this picture of primitive savagery, the missionaries believed the locals had once been cannibals. Less than half a century earlier, Eugène Thomas told the readers of the missionary bulletin in 1889, 'they hunted down men on a large scale'.[100] Swiss republicans were appalled by chiefs who were clearly murderous despots. On several occasions missionaries or their evangelists were confronted by the blood-stained assegais of executioners who had just slaughtered opponents of their chief.[101] In Gazaland the missionaries were met by the sight of war parties returning home with large numbers of slaves. These expeditions stormed Chopi villages, killed the adult male population and enslaved the women and children. Slaves were treated as commodities and were to be found in most of the areas occupied by the mission.[102] Perhaps most seriously, the natives seemed incapable of accounting for their world. Missionaries imbued with a deep respect for scientific explanation regarded witchcraft and spirit possession with horror; they roundly condemned people who turned for protection to a variety of amulets, claws, bones and horns rather than to the one, true God.[103]

The missionaries at first made little attempt to understand these customs. Indeed, they were often attributed to the agency of the devil whose handiwork required their presence in Africa. The dark world beyond the mission station, and the menacing inner turmoil with which it was associated, was compounded by the missionaries' view of the uncontrolled sensuality of the natives. Just as their view of the landscape was moulded by their preconceptions and projections, so too was their understanding of local society. Hence the pagan world was a morally, deeply threatening place where wives were bought and sold, adolescents practised a form of free love and husbands were encouraged to commit adultery. It was a place where men entered into publicly incestuous relations with their sisters-in-law and where, on the death of a husband, a woman was condemned to marry her brother-in-law or even a nephew, a sister-in-law's son.[104]

For the new missionary, Ernest Creux wrote, 'the black race ... seems so simple, so new, so pleasant!' But it took just two months for him to be disabused of this view and to realize the extent of 'the barbarity, the dirt, the negligence, the desperate nonchalance of this black race'.[105] After a long investigative tour in 1885, Henri Berthoud wrote, 'The Gwamba people are still plunged in the deepest darkness and the most coarse paganism.'[106] Africa provided a living example of the extent of the fall from grace suffered by a population cut off from the word of God, and the degraded condition in which savages lived in Africa gave but a brief glimpse of the eternal damnation to which they were condemned in the afterlife. In 1890, for Henri Junod and Paul Berthoud, this was the 'hard reality' of Africa to which the supporters of the mission, and the thousands of readers of its journal, had to become accustomed.[107] It was this view of Africa, in turn, as a continent to be redeemed from perdition that was widely circulated in authoritative missionary publications, photographs and ethnographic exhibitions.

Photography conserved and diffused the mixture of apprehension and excitement with which the missionaries viewed Africa. These sentiments were transferred onto heavy glassplate images of the executioners employed by the Gaza king, frightening witchdoctors, the physical deformities of natives savaged by wild animals or disease, chiefs surrounded by their numerous wives, or nearly-naked tribespeople whose images contrasted sharply with that of well-dressed converts. The missionaries also expressed this feeling through depictions of the land that contrasted the Valdezia mission station, bathed in light, with the dark Zoutpansberg in the background, or through the popular image of the ox-drawn wagon taking its missionary occupants across a stream and into a new land. Their subliminal fears emerged in letters home in which they wrote of a country infested with not just crocodiles, lions and hyenas, but tigers, and the wolves that had only recently been exterminated in western Switzerland.[108] This was 'a desert', 'an arid and savage land', wrote an anonymous poet in the mission bulletin, where 'the rose never flowers'.[109] More generally they read what they saw as the 'depravity,' 'immorality' and spiritual emptiness of the local people into their negative depiction of the land. And in turn the empty, naked and silent land spoke to them about the wretched spiritual and moral condition of its inhabitants. This was a frightening world in which to embrace the domain of instincts and emotion, the cultural liberation associated with the sublime. Without the institutions needed to harness the sublime to an expansive colonial culture, as in America, lonely European settlers could only find security in the controls and strictures of more formulaic ways of seeing.

Creating a Sense of Place: Cartography

Isolated from the institutions and practices that provided life with security at home, the missionaries fell back on their families and each other for company. They celebrated special occasions and read the Bible together, talked of their homeland and sang hymns to the accompaniment of Ruth Berthoud-Junod's piano or the guitar and violin of her brother Henri-Alexandre.[110] From this secure position they sought actively to create a familiar sense of place by imprinting themselves on the landscape.

The missionaries normally erected their houses on hills from where they cast an organizing gaze on the land below.[111] From this vantage point they conceived cleanliness as their major defence in the battle against the dark forces attached to the land; they obsessively washed themselves and particularly their children. Although washing was directed against disease, it also served to remove dirt as 'matter out of place' and it regulated and ordered the body and the home as markers of identity and morality. Ruth Berthoud-Junod believed that domestics and evangelists washed themselves on Saturdays so as to be 'clean and joyous' on Sundays.[112] Dirt brought with it a fear of contagion that caused the missionaries to distance themselves from the local population. 'You can love him in your heart', Junod cautioned employers to address the servants working with their children, 'but don't kiss him.'

The missionaries sought to tame their unruly environment with the tools of science. They used aneroid barometers to measure atmospheric pressure and altitude and gauges and thermometers to establish mean variables of rainfall, temperature and wind velocity. With these instruments, missionaries at Valdezia, Rikatla and Lourenço Marques drew up charts and provided the state with some of its earliest meteorological statistics. In the process they erected a range of probability and an element of cognitive control on the vagaries of climate.[113] Compasses, sextants, quadrants and even pedometers allowed them to measure and divide the land into containable space. In the next chapter we will see how, at the same time, they reduced the chaos of nature by collecting insects, animals and plants. They sent these environmental and spatial markers to Europe to be classified and placed in herbaria, botanical gardens, hothouses, natural history museums and zoos. Through this categorization and conservation of nature the missionaries imposed on Africa the familiar practices and perspectives through which they had made sense of the Alpine wilderness.[114]

Most importantly, the missionaries invested long hours in cartographic work through which they condensed the otherwise engulfing landscape into the manageable proportions of a simple representation on paper. Swiss missionaries produced many of the earliest maps of the northern Transvaal and southern Mozambique. When Paul Berthoud left for Africa, he carried with him a good aneroid barometer capable of reading altitudes of up to 13,000 feet. During his trip in 1873 to the Zoutpansberg, via Sekhukhuniland, he noticed that earlier maps of the South African Republic had placed the northern border of the country, and many of its landmarks, half a degree too far north. Berthoud was right about the landmarks, which he situated correctly on his map published in 1874, but was mistaken about the northern border of the territory, which he placed too far south.[115] Six years later, during his furlough in Switzerland, he published the first reliable maps of the Spelonken in the bulletin of the Vaudois Missionary Society and in the geographical journal, *L'Afrique explorée et civilisée*.[116] The Mission Council in Lausanne then used this map, together with the earlier works of Friedrich Jeppe and St Vincent Erskine, to compile a thorough picture of their entire mission field. This map provided a detailed overview of the Zoutpansberg, together with parts of the eastern Transvaal and southern Mozambique.[117]

Meanwhile, Henri Berthoud emerged as the mission's premier explorer. In 1881, soon after his arrival at Valdezia, the younger Berthoud followed the course of the Levubu river down to chief Xikundu's territory, and two years later, he undertook a trip to the Xingwedzi area east of the Spelonken. Armed with pocket and surveyor's compasses and an aneroid barometer, Berthoud was able to draw up detailed sketch maps of the Levubu and its tributaries as far north as its confluence with the Limpopo.[118] In 1885 he left Valdezia with Eugène Thomas to survey the lowlands separating the Spelonken from the sea. The American missionary, Erwin Richards, had taken measurements of distance and temperature along the lower Limpopo, and had engaged in a little cartographic work, but the lower reaches of the river remained largely uncharted.[119] At the end of his three-month trip, Henri Berthod was able to produce a map of south-east Africa that filled in some of the empty spaces on the coast and that corrected and updated his brother's earlier work in the Transvaal.[120] In June the following year he spent three weeks travelling along unfamiliar paths to Shiluvane, about 150 kilometres south-south-east of Valdezia. In this region, on the edge of the Drakensberg, he climbed several peaks from which he took the basic readings for a trigonometrical survey.[121]

In 1889 Henri Berthoud and Honoré Schlaefli-Glardon embarked on a major expedition along the Olifants and Limpopo rivers to ascertain whether mission stations could be established in these areas. They were particularly concerned to find a route for their donkeys on the Nkomati from Valdezia to Antioka, unhindered by difficult drifts and patches of tsetse fly. On their way to the coast the two missionaries took precise readings of altitude, temperature and location with the help of two aneroid barometers, a centigrade thermometer, a surveyor's compass and a pair of binoculars. They also compiled careful notes on the climate and demography of the country, and drew up the first detailed maps of the Olifants to its confluence with the Limpopo, as well as the right bank of the Limpopo to its opening on the coast. Berthoud and Schlaefli-Glardon produced another significant achievement when they sketched the mouth of the Limpopo. The two missionaries subjected a fourth uncharted area to their cartographic gaze when they surveyed the coastal route leading from the mouth of the Limpopo, via the mouth of the Nkomati, to Lourenço Marques.[122] Henri Berthoud's discoveries were included in 1892 and 1899 in Jeppe's standard maps of the South African Republic.

Arthur Grandjean also emerged as a major cartographer who made several corrections to maps of the coastal plain south of the Inkomati river, using only a watch and compass.[123] In 1893 he completed a map of the lower Nkomati and Lourenço Marques district that was reproduced by *The Press* in Pretoria a year later.[124] Joachim Machado used this map to erect the exact location of the border separating Mozambique from the Transvaal Republic. In 1895, the Portuguese army relied on its detail to find the route to the Gaza capital at Mandlakazi.[125] Together with a more precise map drawn up seven years later, Grandjean's 1893 map served as the basis for later surveys of the region between the Nkomati and Limpopo rivers.[126] From the Transvaal Henri Berthoud criticized the altitudinal readings of Machado and his colleagues: during his travels he had taken 10-15 barometric readings per day.[127] In 1903 Berthoud completed a large coloured map in English of the northern parts of the Transvaal and the adjoining Portuguese territory. This sturdy, fold-out map, produced in Switzerland, quickly became the standard cartographic guide to the region.[128]

Berthoud and Grandjean used their knowledge of hydrography to explain the seasonality of lakes and rivers in the Portuguese colony and to speculate on the navigable nature of these waterways. Although both men respected local informants' knowledge about the country, they were critical of the natives' ability to explain phenomena or systematically name geographical features. 'Diviners and wizards', wrote Henri Berthoud, had used gimcrack arguments based on nothing more than bone-throwing and excited dancing, to explain hydrographic features such as the formation of Lake Sule.[129]

Through their scientific exploration, the missionaries ordered and explained nature in a way that domesticated the environment and provided a strategy for its conquest and exploitation. The missionary cartographers took symbolic possession of the land through their practice of unsolicited naming. Their principal mission station in the Transvaal was called Valdezia after the the Latin word for Vaud; the nearby secondary school (established in 1906) was given the name Lemana from *lac Leman* (Lake Geneva) and the out-station of Barcelona was named after its Protestant supporters in Catalonia. The Bible provided another important source of names through which the missionaries appropriated and Christianized the land. The leading mission station of Elim was called after the well-watered site where the Israelites rested after crossing the Red Sea (Exodus 15:27); and the first mission established outside the Spelonken, on the bend in the Nkomati river, was called Antioka in memory of Antioch, the first Christian colony established outside Palestine (Acts 11:19-25).[130]

The missionaries' maps distinguished wagon routes and paths as unbroken single or parallel black lines that met and diverged at the homesteads of white settlers and at the busy stations of the Swiss and German missionaries. These markers filled the quiescent land with animation as they drew attention to the knots of white settlement and the attendant enterprise carried along the multiple axes of communication. Blue rivers and shaded brown mountains reduced 'unexplored ranges' to a corner of Berthoud's 1903 map; and clear lines of longitude and latitude divided space into manageable, ordered portions (see plate 3). The 'native kraals' were also displayed, but less prominently than the single homesteads of the settlers. Their sense and meaning were subverted when villages were inscribed on paper, for Nivotingolube (the pig man) or Nivatunbuti (the goat man) were lived places that retained their names only as long as they were occupied by the individual after whom they were named. Europeans also had difficulty in transcribing these names because of the foreignness of their sounds and because of the absence of a uniform system of orthography. But they also infused the names with a new historicity and foreign utility when describing them as 'important markers along the route'.[131]

Even a large settlement such as the one on the bend in the Nkomati river named after Magude, lost its colloquial meaning after the chief's death. To solve the problem caused by the ephemeral nature of local names, Paul Berthoud recommended that cartographers adopt the local clan name to denote a geographical district. Berthoud noted that after Magude died, his Khosa clan remained, and that the locative declension of the clan name could be used to designate the region on the Nkomati bend as

'Khosen', using Lepsius' system.[132] Although commonly adopted by Europeans in the area, Berthoud's system of naming was based on nothing more solid than the need to mark the land in familiar ways. First, the people of the coastal area had experienced a long history of in- and out-migration due to famine, war and disease and many who recognized Magude as chief were immigrants drawn from kin groups unrelated to the dominant Khosa clan. Second, in his search for a stable and historic marker of identity, Berthoud transformed the word Khosa, from that of a shared marker of descent into the equivalent of a (Christian) surname. In common usage, Khosa was merely one of Magude's ancestors whose name was employed on occasions to recognize common agnatic descent. It was not always and everywhere used as the clan name. In everyday life members of the extended family recognized the senior male figure of their clan, in this case Magude, as the predominant local marker of kinship. But Magude was also a chief whose followers, irrespective of their kin ties, referred to themselves as 'people of the land of Magude' (*wakaMagude*). So, while local people inscribed the environment with terms that spoke to them of their sense of belonging, European cartographers transformed the meaning of these terms by turning them into permanent markers of space.

The missionaries' ways of seeing the land were certainly new to its inhabitants. But it would be wrong to overlook the many ways in which Africans helped to direct the gaze of these Europeans. Individuals like Henri Berthoud were guided in their exploration of the land by information gathered from locals or by merely following the pedestrian paths established by native hunters, traders and travellers.[133] As the missionaries were the first to admit, it was their knowledge of the local language and that of their African assistants that allowed them to capture and transcribe the names of geographical markers supplied by informants.[134]

Another strategy employed by the missionaries in their attempt to domesticate the land was to plant their gardens with shade and fruit trees, geraniums, laurel, verbena, carnations, pansies and other flowering plants, grown from local seeds and cuttings.[135] The missionaries on the coast attempted to maintain a European diet by growing potatoes, lettuce, carrots, beans and spinach; but it was soon recognized that the tropical sun and dry soil made it difficult to grow these plants. Local vegetables, 'prepared in a civilized way', could be eaten with pleasure.[136] They mixed the foreign and the familiar in many other ways. It was common, for example, for converts to take Biblical names, so that Ndlopfou became Eva, Ndjoumo became Yosefa, Kossine Lydia, Moukandi Naomi or Tondjyane Sara. But they often twisted their local names into European-style surnames, as long as the church deemed these respectable. In this way, Matsivi became Calvin Mapope, Mbizana became Gideon Mpapele, and Zambiki became Timothee Mandlati.[137]

Rituals of welcome, departure and celebration formed an important part of life on the mission stations. At these times the colourful flags of the Swiss Confederation and its many cantons were hoisted and converts assembled in large numbers to wave more flags and sing from the Free Church's hymnal. In July 1891, six hundred members of the church met the Liengmes on their arrival at Lourenço Marques. 'During these lovely festivities', wrote Ida Grandjean, as speeches and songs filled the air, 'the Swiss flag floated above our heads and a joyful recognition filled our hearts.'[138] New arrivals were often greeted with a local version of 'The Alps belong to us' or the well-known 'The Swiss Rhine', that struck deep chords in a Swiss listener. So, too, did the rousing Hallelujah chorus from Handel's *Messiah* which rang in the ears of departing missionaries. Inevitably, newcomers were filled with surprise and emotion to hear such 'joyful music' in Africa.[139] But these rituals of welcome and departure were never exclusively Swiss. The tonality of the songs was marked by the local appreciation of music and even the flagpoles were made of the nerve of a long palm found in the region.[140]

At the mission station, converts were expected to eat in a manner considered salubrious by the missionaries.[141] Their new clothing served as a marker of identity and sewing introduced new concepts of gender and respectability. On Sundays the missionaries waxed and shined their shoes and brushed their clothes, 'as though we were in Switzerland', and they expected the same *endimanché* concerns of their converts.[142] Yet they refrained from imposing formal dress codes and were constantly surprised by the novel ways in which their congregants assembled their clothes. Several missionaries would later even associate tuberculosis and syphilis with European clothing.[143]

Housing and furniture were other important signs of cultural change. With its rows of neat huts, the mission station seemed to defy what the missionaries saw as the dirt and chaos of the pagan village. Square houses that let in light and air replaced dark, smokey and unhealthy huts.[144] Furnishing habitations seemed to reinforce the image of the house as a cradle of civilization. 'Little by little we are recivilizing ourselves and we delight in this, not having been born in a state of barbarousness', Ruth Berthoud-Junod reported after installing a stove, beds and mattresses in her new house.[145] Nevertheless the missionaries never called on their converts to construct replicas of European dwellings, partly because these had to be adapted to the climate and local building materials, and partly because they should reflect the distinctiveness of local culture. The missionaries themselves constructed wide verandahs to protect the pole and dagga walls of their houses against the sun, thatched the roofs according to local practice and fashioned beams, rafters and timber supports out of the nerves of the local, giant palm.[146]

The Swiss looked out onto the land from the safety of the mission station they portrayed as 'a black and white colony'. With the help of the *homo novus* created by evangelical Christianity, they subjected the landscape to their cognitive control and, as they did so, they started to order and domesticate, or modernize, their vision of the population living beyond the mental and physical confines of the mission station.

When Henri-Alexandre Junod arrived in Africa in 1889, as mentioned at the start of this chapter, he heard the echo of witches' Sabbaths in the songs rising out of the pagan village next to Rikatla. Eight years later, in one of his first, tentative ethnographic essays, Junod discerned innovative harmonic laws and excitingly unfamiliar rhythmic patterns in the same songs. And the language that had once presented the 'most hideous noises of which the human throat is capable', he then described as 'rich, melodious, capable of expressing all thoughts, even the most nuanced ideas'.[147] As we shall see, discerning the features of the local culture was closely tied to discerning the features of the landscape. But for someone trained to stress the impact of environment on national characteristics, Junod remained concerned that the people on the coast, whom he now called the Ronga, had little feeling for the beauty of nature. To correct this shortcoming, he composed a 'sort of national anthem' for them in 1898 in which environment was linked to identity.

We love you, oh country of the Rongas
Country of wide rivers and large forests!

> Others may mock us and say that we
> have no mountains
> But they themselves do not have the fertile *nyaka*![148]

It had taken Junod almost a decade to come to see the local population as 'children of nature' rather than merely objects of Satan's attentions.[149] I have tried to show in this chapter how this transformation in his thinking was preceded and accompanied by the subjugation of nature to new ways of seeing. But an environment initially viewed as wild and untamed was also subjected to a number of other strategies of control. The next chapter is concerned with one of these: the order brought to the land by the natural sciences.

Notes

1. University of South Africa (UNISA). Junod Collection (JC) 1. Sermons. Môtiers 1 January 1887.
2. *Bulletin de la mission romande* (*BMR*) (1889) 7, 83, April, p. 212.
3. Junod, *BMR* (1889) 7, p. 86. He expressed similar views in *Nouvelles de nos missionnaires* (*NM*) (1889), pp. 38, 73, 76; Junod, *Nouvelles de nos missionnaires* (1890), p. 44.
4. Elizabeth Delmont and Jessica Dubow, 'Thinking through landscape: colonial spaces and legacies' in *Panorama of Passage: Changing landscapes of South Africa* (Johannesburg and Washington, DC, 1995), p. 11; W. T. J. Mitchell, *Landscape and Power* (Chicago, 1994).
5. Clarissa Campbell Orr, 'Romanticism in Switzerland' in Roy Porter and Mikulas Teich (eds), *Romanticism in National Context* (Cambridge, 1998); Oliver Zimmer, *A Contested Nation: History, Memory and Nationalism in Switzerland, 1761–1891* (Cambridge, 2003).
6. P. Guichonnet (ed.), *Histoire et Civilisation des Alpes*, II, *Destin Humain* (Toulouse and Lausanne, 1980), pp. 198–9.
7. Ibid., pp. 200–1.
8. Cf. Jean-Jacques Rousseau, *Les rêveries du promeneur solitaire* (1782, Paris, 1933), pp. 724–5. A. Murith, *Le guide du botaniste qui voyage dans le Valais* (Lausanne, 1810), pp. iv, 13.
9. L. Vulliemin, *Le Doyen Bridel* (Lausanne, 1854), pp. 79, 130.
10. Juste Olivier, *Le Canton de Vaud* (Lausanne, 1837), I, pp. 24, 50, 209, 216. This work, in two volumes, is uncannily Braudelian in its division into three parts – the (almost immobile structure of the) environment; the (slow-moving) history of the customs and traditions of the people; and the (fast-moving) history of events.
11. Ibid., I, p. 510.
12. Ibid., I, pp. 34, 38.
13. E. Rambert, 'Schiller, Goethe et les Alpes' in his *Les Alpes suisses: études de littérature alpestre* (Lausanne, [1868] 1889), p. 3.
14. Ibid., p. 31.
15. H. Perregaux, *Edmond Perregaux missionnaire: d'après sa correspondence 1868–1905* (Neuchâtel, 1906), p. 75; E. Rambert 'Les plantes alpines'in his *Etudes d'histoire naturelle* (Lausanne, [1865] 1888), p. 84.
16. H. Trabaud, 'Un auteur vaudois – Alfred Ceresole' in *Revue de Belles-Lettres* (1885) 14, 1, p. 3.
17. Philippe Godet, *Histoire littéraire de la Suisse française* (Neuchâtel, Paris, 1890) and Virgile Rossel, *Histoire littéraire de la Suisse romande: des origines à nos jours* (Neuchâtel, [1889–91] new edn, 1903).
18. E. Rambert, 'La Flore Suisse – et ses origines' published in 1880 and reprinted in *Etudes d'histoire naturelle* (Lausanne, 1888), pp. 225–7; Rambert, 'Les plantes alpines', published in 1865, republished in his *Etudes d'histoire naturelle*, pp. 42–4.
19. Cf. Henri Bordeaux, preface to Emile Javelle, *Souvenirs d'un Alpiniste* (Lausanne, Paris, 1920), pp. 26–7. In the summer of 1859 alone, climbers reached the summit of Mont Blanc sixteen times and it took them less than thirty years to conquer the remaining peaks.
20. On these ambivalences, see Rambert, *Etudes d'histoire naturelle*, pp. 84, 87, 123, and his essay 'Le chevrier de Praz-de-Fort' (1865) in his *Récits et Croquis* (Lausanne, 1889); Javelle, *Souvenirs d'un Alpiniste*, pp. 30, 42; Olivier, *Canton de Vaud*, p. 34.
21. Olivier, *Canton de Vaud*, pp. 14, 24, 34.
22. Rambert, *Etudes d'histoire naturelle*, p. 117; René Descartes cited in D. W. Cohen, *The French Encounter with Africa* (Bloomington, IN, 1980), p. 77; Talleyrand cited in Lucien Febvre, 'Civilization: evolution of a word and a group of ideas' in Peter Burke (ed.), *A New Kind of History: from the writings of Lucien Febvre* (London,

1973), p. 238.
23 Javelle, *Souvenirs d'un Alpiniste*, p. 258.
24 Rambert, 'Les plantes alpines', p. 87.
25 Cited by Rossel, *Histoire littéraire*, pp. 653, 655. See especially Rambert, 'Le Brisenstock' and Javelle, 'Salvan: un village valaisan' in Javelle, *Souvenirs d'un Alpiniste*.
26 Javelle, *Souvenirs d'un Alpiniste*, p. 295. See also Benjamin Grivel, 'Alpinisme et Romantisme: le gout de la montagne' in D. Baud-Bovy et al. (eds), *La Vie romantique au pays romand* (Lausanne, 1930), pp. 180ff.
27 R. Murchison, 'On the antiquity of the physical geography of inner Africa', *Journal of the Royal Geographic Society* (1864) p. 34; R. Stafford, *Sir Roderick Murchison: Scientific Exploration and Victorian Imperialism* (Cambridge, 1989); R. Stafford 'Annexing the landscapes of the past: British imperial geology in the nineteenth century' in J. M. MacKenzie (ed.), *Imperialism and the Natural World* (Manchester, 1990), pp. 83–4; S. Dubow, 'Earth history, Natural history, and Prehistory at the Cape, 1860–1875', *Comparative Studies in Society and History* (2004), pp. 115–22. See also Nicolaas A. Rupke, *Richard Owen: Victorian Naturalist* (New Haven, CT, and London, 1994), pp. 84–5.
28 J. Bryce, *Impressions of South Africa* (London, 1899, 3rd edn), pp. 7, 29.
29 Arnold Guyot, *Creation; or, the Biblical Cosmogony in the Light of Modern Science* (New York, 1884), pp. 4, 7, 29. For a comparative example, see R. Bedell, *The Anatomy of Nature: Geology and American landscape painting, 1825–1875* (Princeton, NJ, 2001); Barbara Novak, *Nature and Culture: American Landscape Painting, 1825–1875* (New York, 1995).
30 Anon., 'Exploration de M. H. Berthoud entre les Spelonken et Lorenzo Marques', in *l'Afrique explorée et civilisée* (1886), p. 303; H. Berthoud, 'Deux problèmes hydrographiques du pays de Gaza', *Bulletin de la société neuchâteloise de géographie (BSNG)* (1904) 15, p. 14.
31 Berthoud, 'Deux problèmes hydrographiques', p. 15. See also Junod, *Zidji: Etude de moeurs sud-africaines* (St. Blaise, 1911), p. 26, for the same imagery.
32 Junod, 'Correspondences', Rikatla 23 November 1891, *BSNG* (1892–93) VII. Oswald Heer's *Die Urwelt der Schweiz* was translated by James Heywood (ed.), *The Primeval World of Switzerland* (London, 1876). See also p. 128 below.
33 Cf. P. Knox-Shaw, *Explorers in English Fiction* (New York, 1986), p. 145; Stafford, 'Annexing the landscapes of the past', p. 84; R. Stafford, 'Scientific Exploration and Empire' in A. Porter (ed.), *The Oxford History of the British Empire: The Nineteenth Century* (Oxford, 1999), pp. 313, 317.
34 Bryce, *Impressions of South Africa*, pp. 55–6.
35 Junod, 'Les Ba-Ronga. Etude ethnographique sur les indigènes de la baie de Delagoa', *Bulletin de la société neuchâteloise de géographie* (1998) X, p. 147; Junod, *Life of a South African Tribe (LSAT)* (1912–13, London, 1927) II, p. 633.
36 W. C. H. Malton, *The Story of the Diocese of Lebombo* (London, 1912), p. 76; Junod, *LSAT* II, pp. 5–7. Sandra Greene contrasts European ways of seeing landscape, born of the Enlightenment, with Anlo ways of infusing landscape with spirituality. See her *Sacred Sites and the Colonial Encounter: A history of meaning and memory in Ghana* (Bloomington, IN, 2002).
37 Junod, *LSAT*, II, pp. 376–84.
38 H. Berthoud, 'Deux problèmes hydrographiques', p. 7.
39 Junod, *LSAT*, II, pp. 78–9, 368, 374.
40 On the preponderance among Swiss peasants of utilitarian rather than scenic interpretations of landscape, see R. C. Germond, *Chronicles of Basutoland* (Morija, 1967), p. 526; David Ambrose and Albert Brutsch (eds), *Thomas Arbousset, Missionary excursion into the blue mountains in the year 1840* (Morija, 1991), pp. 51, 146.
41 Alphonse Mabille, quoted in Germond, *Chronicles of Basutoland*, pp. 417–18.
42 R. C. Germond, *Chronicles of Basutoland*, p. 526, cited in Terence Ranger 'New approaches to African landscape' (MS 1997).
43 Edouard Jacottet, 'Le bassin du Haut-Orange et de ses affluents' in *l'Afrique explorée et civilisée* (1885), pp. 30, 34.
44 O. Zimmer, 'In Search of Natural Identity: Alpine landscape and the reconstruction of the Swiss nation', *Comparative Studies in Society and History* (1998), p. 639, n. 4; Linda Colley, *Britons: Forging the Nation, 1707–1837* (London, 1992), pp. 173–4.
45 J. M. Coetzee, 'The picturesque and the South African landscape' in his *White Writing: On the Culture of Letters in South Africa* (New Haven, CT, 1988).
46 Eugènie Berthoud, letter from Morija, 16 November, 1874 in Paul Berthoud, *Lettres missionnaires: 1873–1879 de M. et Mme Berthoud* (Lausanne, 1900), p. 204.
47 P. Berthoud to Rev'd J. Favre, 7 September 1874 in *Lettres missionnaires*, p. 188. For a similarly evocative representation of the Maluti mountains, see Eugène Casalis, *Les Bassoutos* (Paris, 1859), pp. 148, 150.
48 P. Berthoud to Commission des Missions, 6 July 1874 in *Lettres missionnaires*, p. 179.
49 Junod, *Zidji: Etude des moeurs sud-africaines* (St Blaise, 1911), pp. 26, 69, 203.
50 Eugenie Berthoud, 29 December 1872 and 11 January 1873 in *Lettres missionnaires*, pp. 28–9, 35. See also

Jeanne Jacot to her family, 16 March 1884 in *Nouvelles de nos missionnaires* (1884) 6, 5, p. 12.
51 E. Berthoud, 30 January 1873 in *Lettres missionnaires*, p. 49.
52 Jeanne Jacot to her family, 16 March 1884 in *Nouvelles de nos missionnaires* (1884) 6, 5, p. 12.
53 P. Berthoud to his family, n. d. August 1873 and E. Berthoud, 27 June 1875 in *Lettres missionnaires*, pp. 123, 244; Ruth Berthoud-Junod, 9 November 1884 in *Nouvelles de nos missionnaires* (1885) 7, 6, p. 87; Arthur Grandjean, *La Mission romande* (Lausanne, 1917), p. 88.
54 R. Berthoud-Junod, *Du Transvaal à Lourenço Marques: lettres de Mme R. Berthoud-Junod* (Lausanne, 1904), pp. 56, 84.
55 *BMR* (1876) 19, p. 36; *BMR* (1876) 20, July, p. 44; *Nouvelles de nos missionnaires* (1886) 8, 4, p. 58.
56 E. Berthoud, 11 June 1873 in *Lettres missionnaires*, p. 94.
57 Jacottet in Germond, *Chronicles of Basutoland*, p. 423.
58 R. Berthoud-Junod, letter written 25 August 1887, in *Du Transvaal à Lourenço Marques*, p. 200.
59 Letter of 11 January 1873 in *Lettres missionnaires*, p. 35.
60 To his family, 8 June 1873 in *Lettres missionnaires*, p. 83.
61 Letter of 6 May 1884 in *Nouvelles de nos missionnaires* (1884) 7, 2, p. 24.
62 R. Berthoud-Junod, *Du Transvaal à Lourenço Marques*, p. 74.
63 *Nouvelles de nos missionnaires* (1887) 10, 1, p. 6.
64 Mr Jeanmairet to Mr and Mrs C. , Pretoria, 6 February 1884 in *Nouvelles de nos missionnaires* (1884) 6, 4, p. 12.
65 See his numerous poems and essays in the student periodical, *Revue de Belles-Lettres*.
66 Junod, 'Jules Gerster' in *Revue de Belles-Lettres* (1884) 13, 1, p. 12; Junod, 'Noel à Berlin', *Revue de Belles-Lettres* (1885) 13, 3, p. 90; Junod, 'Hommes et Bêtes', *Revue de Belles-Lettres* (1885) 13, 7, p. 215.
67 Junod, 'Etude sur Racan', *Revue de Belles-Lettres* (1881) 9, 7, pp. 193–212.
68 Junod, 'Correspondences: de Rikatla à Marakouène', *BSNG* (1891) 6, pp. 319, 321–2.
69 Bryce, *Impressions of South Africa*, pp. 27, 29, 50–1, 55–6.
70 Ibid., pp. 56–7.
71 *Nouvelles de nos missionnaires* (1887) 10, 1, p. 8. The Comaroffs develop the notion of 'moral geography' in *Of Revelation and Revolution, Christianity, Colonialism and Consciousness in South Africa* (Chicago, 1991) I, pp. 95ff.
72 Junod, 'Le climat de la baie de Delagoa', *Bulletin de la société des sciences naturelles de Neuchâtel* (1896–7) 25, pp. 77–8.
73 P. Berthoud, *Les Nègres gouamba* (Lausanne, 1896), p. 148; Grandjean in *Nouvelles de nos missionnaires* (1889) 12, 2, p. 43; Swiss Mission Archive (SMA), Lausanne 1255/B Henri Berthoud, Rapport sur la visite fait à Goungounyana en juillet 1892.
74 Grandjean, letter of 25 June 1890, in *Nouvelles de nos missionnaires* (1890) 2, 13.
75 UNISA. Junod Collection. 6. Conférences: à Neuchâtel, 1897.
76 Junod, 'Les Ba-Ronga', pp. 384, 389; Junod, *LSAT*, I, p. 9.
77 Junod, 'Les Ba-Ronga', p. 248.
78 This is particularly clear in Junod's novel, *Zidji*, in which the eponymous hero is tempted, seduced and finally destroyed by a dissolute townswoman.
79 Junod, 'Les Ba-Ronga', p. 245.
80 Cf. J. Povey, 'Landscape in Early South African Poetry' in M. van Wyk Smith and D. McLennan (eds), *Olive Schreiner and After* (Cape Town, 1983); D. Kenton, 'Landscape painting and the search for an indigenous ethos in South Africa' (PhD., University of Natal, Pietermaritzburg, 1989); I. Hofmeyr, 'Building a nation from words: Afrikaans language, literature and ethnic identity' in S. Marks and S. Trapido (eds), *The Politics of Race, Class and Nationalism in Twentieth Century South Africa* (London, 1987).
81 Junod, 'Correspondences: de Rikatla à Marakouène', *Bulletin de la sociètè neuchâteloise de géographie* (1891) 6, p. 321.
82 28 August 1889 in *Nouvelles de nos missionnaires* (1889) 12, 1; *Nouvelles de nos missionnaires* (1890) 3, 13, p. 44.
83 Junod, *BMR* (1889) 7, p. 86.
84 Letter from Rikatla, n. d. in *Nouvelles de nos missionnaires* (1890) 3, 13, p. 44. A similar description is in Junod, 'Correspondences: de Rikatla à Marakouène', pp. 321–2.
85 A. Grandjean, 'Un vivant parmi les morts' in *Chez les Gouamba: glanures dans le champ de la Mission romande* (Lausanne, 1893), p. 15; E. Berthoud, letter written June 1875 near Marabastad, in *Lettres missionnaires*, p. 242.
86 *Nouvelles de nos missionnaires* (1893) 16, 2, pp. 28–9.
87 *Nouvelles de nos missionnaires* (1885) 7, 4, p. 64.
88 The seizure and sale of slaves had, until recently, been a fairly common practice in this region. Cf. Transvaal *Staats Courant*, 15 November 1867, 'Rapport omtrent de zaak van Zoutpansberg'. Transvaal Archives, Pretoria. State Secretary's file, SS110 R365 Albasini to State President; SS55 R210/64 Verklaring van Monene, 11 April 1864. J. B. De Vaal, 'Die rol van Joao Albasini in die geskiedenis van dis Transvaal', *South African Archives Yearbook*, (Pretoria) 1953, I, p. 82. Jan Boeyens, '"Black Ivory": The indenture system and

slavery in Zoutpansberg, 1848–1867', in E. Eldredge and F. Morton (eds), *Slavery in South Africa: Captive Labour on the Dutch Frontier* (Boulder, CO, 1994).

89 SMA 8.10.B, Paul Berthoud to mission council, 28 December 1876 and 22 December 1877; *Nouvelles de nos missionnaires* (1887) 10, 1, p. 8; Berthoud-Junod, *Du Transvaal à Lourenço Marques*, p. 47. See also *Bulletin de la Mission vaudoise* (*BMV*) (1875) 5, p. 73. Arthur Grandjean would refer to Albasini as an 'Africanized Portuguese', in 'L'Invasion des Zoulous dans le Sud-est Africain', *Le Globe* (1897) 36, p. 20.

90 *Nouvelles de nos missionnaires* (1887) 10, 1, p. 8. The British colonial state on the Cape's eastern frontier prosecuted farmers who turned to African diviners for protection against witchcraft, cf. *South African Commercial Advertizer*, 21 October 1843, pp. 163–4. The notion of Boer degeneracy propagated by travellers like Lichtenstein and Barrow, and more popular writers like Livingstone and Bryce, is reflected in later works such as J. Agar-Hamilton, *The Native Policy of the Voortrekkers* (Cape Town, 1927), p. 66; W. M. Macmillan, *Africa Emergent* (London, 1937, new edn, 1949), p. 21. On the general precariousness of life on this frontier, cf. P. Berthoud, *Les Nègres gouamba*, p. 20.

91 *BMV* (1876) 18, March, p. 17; *BMV* (1876) 19, April, p. 17; P. Berthoud, *Les Nègres gouamba*, pp. 86–7; Arthur Grandjean, *Labours, semailles, et moissons dans le champ de la Mission romande* (Lausanne, 1898), p. 13.

92 *BMV* (1889) 85, 7; SMA 503, Junod to Paul Leresche, 22 August 1889; Berthoud, *Les Nègres gouamba*, p. 157. Junod, 'Les Ba-Ronga', p. 482; Botanical Conservatory Genève (BCG) Junod to W. Barbey, 30 October 1889.

93 Junod, *Grammaire ronga suivie d'un manuel de conversation* (Lausanne, 1896), p. 23.

94 Gaston de la Rive, Introduction to Ruth Berthoud-Junod, *Du Transvaal à Lourenço Marques*, p. 4; Grandjean, *La Mission romande*, pp. 119–21.

95 R. Berthoud-Junod in *Nouvelles de nos missionnaires* (1884) 6, 5, p. 28; Junod, 'Quelques contes africains', *Bibliothèque universelle et revue suisse* (1897) VII, pp. 514–15.

96 P. Berthoud to mission council, 22 December 1877 in *BMV* (1877) 24, pp. 129–30; Schlaefli in *Nouvelles de nos missionnaires* (1893) 15, 4, p. 49; Junod, 'Les Ba-Ronga' p. 390; Junod, *LSAT* II, p. 383.

97 SMA 8.27.T, Eugène Thomas to mission council, 17 May 1885.

98 Junod, 'Les Ba-Ronga', pp. 413–16; Anon., 'Le nouveau-né chez les Gouambas' in *La Messagère du monde païen* (1895), p. 8; Anon., 'L'infanticide en Afrique', *La Messagère du monde païen* (1893), p. 76.

99 Anon., 'La pluie chez les Gouambas', *La Messagère du monde païen* (1890), pp. 98–9.

100 *BMR* (1889) 7, 87, p. 352.

101 P. Berthoud, *Les Nègres gouamba*, p. 115.

102 'Véra, la jeune esclave' in Anon., *Chez les Gouamba* (Lausanne, c. 1893), pp. 34–40; Berthoud-Junod, *Du Transvaal à Lourenço Marques*, p. 232–3, 264.

103 P. Berthoud, *Les Nègres gouamba*, pp. 52–4; Grandjean, *Labours, semailles*, p. 27.

104 On these customs, see pp. 229–31.

105 Cited by Arthur Grandjean, *La Mission romande*, p. 98.

106 SMA 1255B, Berthoud, 'Rapport sur l'expedition à Magud,' presented to the Mission Conference, 6 October 1885.

107 P. Berthoud, *Les Nègres gouamba*, p. 74. See also letter from A. Grandjean, 14 November 1889 in *Nouvelles de nos missionnaires* (1890) 4, 12, p. 52; and Junod in *Nouvelles de nos Missionnaires* (1890) 3, 13, p. 44; Junod, 'Les Ba-Ronga', p. 12.

108 Eugenie Berthoud in *BMV* (1874) 10, 7 March, p. 156; Ernest Creux in *BMV* (1875) 3. See also Berthoud-Junod, *Du Transvaal à Lourenço Marques*, pp. 105–6.

109 *BMR* (1889) 7, 83, p. 212; P. Berthoud, *Les Nègres gouamba*, p. 74.

110 *BMV* (1876) 20, 39, 44; Berthoud-Junod, *Du Transvaal à Lourenço Marques*, p. 214.

111 On Antioka, see A. Grandjean in *Nouvelles de nos missionnaires* (1892) 15, 1, p. 21.

112 Berthoud-Junod, *Du Transvaal à Lourenço Marques*, p. 214.

113 Junod, 'Observations météorologiques faites à Rikatla', *Boletim da Sociedade de Geografia de Lisboa* (1891) 10, 1; BCG.HB, 'A propos de l'herbier de Shilouvane, rapporté en 1893 par Henri-Alexandre Junod'; Junod, 'Le climat de la baie de Delagoa' *BSNG* (1897) XXV; P. Berthoud, 'Tableaux comparatifs. Résultats des observations météorologiques faites resp. à la station missionnaire de Lourenço Marques à 53 mètres d'altitude, et de l'Observatoire de Tananarive, à 1400 mètres d'altitude', *BSNG* (1901) XII, pp. 153–7; Anon., 'Travaux scientifiques des missionnaires', *BMR* (1905) 18, July–August, pp. 225, 232–3.

114 R. Berthoud-Junod, 11 April 1886 in *NM* (1886) 1, 9, 16; Cantonal and University Library of Neuchâtel. Archives of the Geographical Society of Neuchâtel (GSN), Dr. Georges Liengme to Prof. C. Knapp, 8 February, 1893; P. Berthoud to Knapp, 10 June 1899 and 25 January 1900.

115 E. Renevier, 'Renseignements géographiques et géologiques sur le sud de l'Afrique, extraits des lettres du missionnaire P. Berthoud', *Bulletin de la société vaudoise des sciences naturelles* (1873) xiii, pp. 385–7. See Berthoud's 'Carte de la partie orientale de l'Afrique du Sud' in *BMV* (1874) 10, February. The standard map of the period, by F. Jeppe and A. Merensky, was published in 1868 by A. Petermann in Berlin.

116 P. Berthoud, 'Carte des Spelonken avec la Mission vaudoise de Valdézia' in *BMV* (1880) 39. Reprinted in

117 *l'Afrique explorée et civilisée* (1880–1881), p. 168.
117 Council of the Romande Mission, 'Route map of the Gaza country by St. Vincent Erskine with adjunctions on the north–west corner'. Copies of this map are held in a box labelled Cartes 12.10 'Géographie – continent Afrique – Afrique du Sud' in the SMA. See also Jane Carruthers, 'Friedrich Jeppe: Mapping the Transvaal c. 1850–1899', *Journal of Southern African Studies* (2003) 29, 4.
118 These maps are held in a box labelled 'Cartes de Géographie', No. 1–35 in SMA.
119 Richards in *Missionary Herald* (1885) March. When Richards visited Umzila in 1881, he travelled with an aneroid barometer, a thermometer (with which he took temperature readings three times a day) and a pedometer. Anon., *The Mission to Umzila's Kingdom* (Boston, MA, 1882), p. 21.
120 H. Berthoud, 'Carte du district du Zoutpansberg et littoral de la baie de Delagoa' in *BMR* (1885) 82.
121 Anon., 'Exploration de M. H. Berthoud entre les Spelonken et Lorenzo Marquez', *l'Afrique explorée et civilisée* (1886), pp. 301–2.
122 E. H. Schlaefli-Glardon, 'De Valdezia à Lourenço Marques', *BSNG* (1892–93) vii, pp. 157, 162. The maps are situated between pp. 132 and 133 and 172 and 173. On Berthoud's achievements, see the obituary, 'Henri Berthoud, 1855–1904', *BMR* (1905) 18, 228, March, pp. 69–76.
123 Many of Grandjean's readings were confirmed by those taken at various places along the Nkomati by Capt. Freire de Andrade, at that time an engineer in the Portuguese army. P. Berthoud, 16 November 1891, *l'Afrique explorée et civilisée* (1892), pp. 22–3.
124 A. Grandjean, 'Notice relative à la carte du Nkomati inférieur et du district portugais de Lourenço Marques' *BSNG* (1892–93) VII, pp. 113–121; Junod, 'Une course au Tembé' in *BSNG* (1894), p. 112.
125 P. Berthoud, 11 July 1890 in *l'Afrique explorée et civilisée* (1890), p. 325; J. van Butselaar, *Africains, missionnaires et colonialistes: Les origines de L'église presbyterienne du Mozambique (Mission Suisse) 1880–96* (Leiden, 1984), pp. 116–7.
126 Grandjean, 'La côte orientale de l'Afrique', *BSNG* (1894–95) VIII, pp. 80–99; Grandjean, 'Le Bassin du Nkomati et sa communication avec celui du Limpopo', *BSNG* (1900) XII, pp. 306–15; Grandjean, 'Cartographie de la Province de Lourenço Marques', ibid., pp. 316–41.
127 H. Berthoud, 'Deux problèmes hydrographiques', p. 25n. 1.
128 The map was engraved by H. Kümmerley and Frey in Bern.
129 H. Berthoud, 'Deux problèmes hydrographiques', p. 7.
130 P. Berthoud, *Les Nègres gouamba*, p. 19; Grandjean, *La Mission romande*, p. 87.
131 In *Nouvelles de nos missionnaires* (1889), p. 43; GSN. A. Grandjean to C. Knapp, 22 November 1892; Junod, 'Une course au Tembé', 1895, p. 115; H. Berthoud, 'Deux problèmes hydrographiques', p. 27. On the notion of cartographic subversion, see P. Carter, *The Road to Botany Bay: An Exploration of Landscape and History* (New York, 1988).
132 P. Berthoud, 12 December 1885 in *l'Afrique explorée et civilisée* 1886, p. 94.
133 Ibid., pp. 92–4.
134 Anon., 'Exploration de M. H. Berthoud entre les Spelonken et Lorenzo Marquez' in *l'Afrique explorée et civilisée* 1886, p. 300–4.
135 *Nouvelles de nos missionnaires* (1885) 3, 8, p. 41 and ibid. (1892) 14, 6, p. 94.
136 SMA 8.27.T, Eugène Thomas to mission council, 4 June 1884; *Nouvelles de nos missionnaires* (1890) 3, 13, p. 44.
137 R. Berthoud-Junod, December 1887 in *Du Transvaal à Lourenço Marques*, p. 270.
138 '… et la reconnaissance remplissait nos coeurs à tous. ' *NM* (1891) 2, 14; Grandjean, *La Mission romande*, p. 91.
139 SMA 8.27.T, Eugène Thomas to mission council, 4 June 1884; SMA 836 R. Berthoud-Junod 27 May 1884 (unpubl. MS); P. Berthoud, *La Mission romande et la baie de Delagoa*, p. 14; C. Vulliemin (ed.), *Recueil de chants de la section vaudoise de la société de Zofingue* (Lausanne, 1856), pp. 60–2.
140 Berthoud-Junod, *Du Transvaal à Lourenço Marques*, pp. 252, 267.
141 Junod, *LSAT* I, p. 537.
142 Berthoud-Junod, *Du Transvaal à Lourenço Marques*, p. 214.
143 Junod, *LSAT* II, pp. 96–97; Grandjean, *Mission romande*, p. 85.
144 Berthoud-Junod, *Du Transvaal à Lourenço Marques*, p. 214; P. Berthoud, *Les Nègres gouamba* p. 107; *Nouvelles de nos missionnaires* (1885) 3, 8 p. 43 and ibid. (1894) 16, 5, p. 74.
145 Berthoud-Junod, *Du Transvaal à Lourenço Marques*, pp. 275–6.
146 Junod, *LSAT*, II, pp. 535–6; R. Berthoud-Junod, *Nouvelles de nos missionnaires* (1886) 8, 4, p. 95; Berthoud-Junod, *Du Transvaal à Lourenço Marques*, pp. 180, 252–3.
147 Junod, 'Quelques contes africains', *Bibliothèque universelle et revue suisse* (1897) VII, pp. 515–16.
148 The *nyaka* is the dark, fertile soil found in the coastal areas, see p. 102 above. Junod, 'Les Ba-Ronga' p. 185.
149 Junod, 'Les Ba-Ronga', pp. 231–7; Junod, 'Some remarks on the folklore of the Ba-Thonga' in *Folk-lore* (1903) XIV, 2, June, p. 116; Junod, *LSAT* II, p. 595.

5
Natural Sciences

And out of the ground the Lord God formed every living beast of the field, and every fowl of the air; and brought them unto Adam to see what he would call them: and whatsoever Adam called every living creature, that was the name thereof.
(Genesis 2:19)

When Henri-Alexandre Junod left Southampton for Lourenço Marques on 16 June 1889, his mind was occupied by thoughts of his first posting as a missionary. His excitement rose noticeably as he neared Africa. When the 'Tartar' docked at Lisbon, the exotic plants found in the city's botanical gardens captivated him.[1] Three weeks later the ship stopped at Durban for two days where he greatly appreciated the 'luxuriant winter vegetation'. It 'would be impossible to describe', he exclaimed, 'the pleasure we experienced in the presence of this new nature: flowers, butterflies, all unknown until that moment!'[2] Three months after his arrival in Mozambique Junod had to reassure the mission council in Lausanne that the passion with which he pursued natural history in his spare time had not dented his evangelical zeal. The biological and theological sciences were organically tied, he reminded his superiors, for 'nature is the work of God and merits attention and calls for study'.[3]

The glorification of God through the examination of his handiwork was only one of the reasons for Junod's interest in the natural sciences. By ordering the world of plants and animals, Junod seemed to bring an element of domestication to the amorphous and chaotic world that surrounded the mission. Through his entomological and botanical studies, he was able to explain the local environment in terms of a system of understanding that he and others qualified as universal. But this understanding was built on a hierarchy of knowledge that, as this chapter will reveal, created and encouraged imperialism. Local people were excellent observers and collectors of data, had their own ideas about classification and contributed in important ways to 'scientific' knowledge; but ultimately Junod felt that they were unaware of the true system underlying the organization and understanding of nature.

This chapter suggests that the division of scientific knowledge into racial categories helped portray the seizure of other peoples' lands as a natural process, even a benevolent duty. In this chapter I attempt to show how research in the natural sciences rested on an unequal encounter between different ways of naming, organizing and understanding nature. The racialized concept of 'science', I believe, accompanied and informed the deliberate, rational decisions, taken on the basis of political and economic criteria that informed the logic of imperialism. But science also supplied individuals such as Junod with the methodology needed to study society and, at the same time, provided indigenous scholars with some of the intellectual capital needed to secure their position as a political élite.

Collecting in Switzerland

The role of churchmen as agents of Christianity and civilization has a long history in Switzerland. In the late eighteenth century roving evangelists and educated clergymen stranded in rural outposts found in the study of nature both an intellectual challenge and a diversion from a humdrum existence.[4] Sharp differences of soil, temperature, rainfall, vegetation and animal life, often on the same mountain, provided the collector in Switzerland with a rich environment in which to practise his pastime. Pastors confined by their profession to one small district gained national renown by supplying urban experts with a range of rare specimens. They formed the backbone of the learned associations that provided a forum for discussion cutting across regional, linguistic and religious differences.[5] Stern Calvinist ministers promulgated the disciplined collecting of plants, insects and rocks as an edifying way of displacing frivolous, even pagan village pastimes. Collecting also took the pastor into the fields where his knowledge of science allowed him to act as the secular as well as spiritual advisor to his parishioners. But the overriding reason for this clerical enthusiasm for collecting and classifying was the glorification of God's handiwork: the demonstration that the rich diversity of nature could be reduced to visible patterns and systems that could only be explained in terms of divine inspiration. In this sense, collecting was like poetry or painting, a means of celebrating both the landscape and its maker.[6]

By uncovering the natural order of the earth and the living objects that inhabited it, learned individuals were able to exercise a symbolic dominance over the environment. They (re)ordered the perception of nature in a way that made it entirely familiar to their generation. By cataloguing and classifying plants, animals and minerals according to 'modern' criteria, or by collecting meteorological statistics, they convinced themselves of their ability to understand their world and exercise some control over its development. This confidence was supported by the many learned societies, established in the early nineteenth century, that gave a new professionalism to the study of nature. These popularized findings through small and large meetings as well as through the media of scientific journals and monographs, museum exhibitions, botanical gardens and herbaria.[7] Members of learned societies in Switzerland constructed scientific truth when they tested their findings in open debate and corroborated their evidence by drawing on the work of colleagues elsewhere. For the Swiss, these societies stressed the regional or federal basis of intellectual life in the country, and they provided an important forum in which men of ability could advertise talents appreciated by the growing commercial and industrial bourgeoisie. This activity gave men of science and letters a new source of intellectual and social capital and a very personal stake in the identification of science with progress.[8]

The intellectual filing system developed by men of science and letters tamed the chaos of the world and reduced the terror of the unknown. This heroic role was one of the principal attractions of natural science. While botanizing in the High Alps, Jean-Jacques Rousseau thought himself 'almost another Columbus'.[9] Other collectors were perhaps more modest in their musings, but they shared with Rousseau the self-imagery of the intrepid explorer as they 'discovered' and 'penetrated' 'lost valleys' and 'new worlds'.[10] Romanticism compounded the heroic imagery of these explorers who, like Alexander von Humboldt, tested their vigour and masculinity in the Alps before journeying to unexplored parts of the world. In the mid-nineteenth century, a climber such as Emile Javelle imagined the conquest of an alpine peak to be the equivalent of crossing an unexplored Australian desert.[11] The peasants in this wilderness were as ignorant as they were close to God.[12] The locals might be naturally hospitable, but they were still *hommes sauvages*, 'children burned by the sun' whose ideas showed a 'mixture of reason and superstition'.[13] They were good observers of nature but were unable to classify or explain the data they collected with such vigour.[14]

Men of science and letters took their idea of knowledge into the Alps with missionary zeal, for they believed their studies would lead the popular classes from the bondage of ignorance into a universal, objective and egalitarian system of understanding. In the nineteenth century, the light of civilization brought by books and libraries to dark mountain huts and villages became an important literary motif in Switzerland.[15] This new way of thinking relegated local ideas to the position of 'folk beliefs' that would disappear under the swell of modernity, together with linguistic dialects and pagan customs. Men of science and letters substituted the tyranny of knowledge for the tyranny of superstition in Switzerland, and in less than a generation, they would take these ideas and practices to Africa.

Science in Support of Religion

Henri-Alexandre Junod was raised in this intellectual climate. When his father Henri left the small village of Lignières to study in Neuchâtel, the cantonal capital had developed into an international centre of scientific research. The polymath Frédéric de Rougemont was one of the earliest to return from the Prussian capital where he had studied under the geographer Karl Ritter. But most famous was Louis Agassiz who, after his move to the newly-established Neuchâtel Academy in 1832, became the moving force behind the recently formed natural history society. He quickly provided this institution with its own scientific journal and turned the town's museum into one of the best regional repositories of natural history specimens in Europe. Grants from the Prussian king and local wealthy amateurs paid for these and other institutions in Neuchâtel; their generosity also funded field expeditions that allowed Agassiz to send Johan von Tschudi to Peru in the footsteps of von Humboldt in 1838.

During his stay in Neuchâtel, Agassiz built up an internationally renowned research team. Its members included Arnold Guyot, who had studied under Ritter and von Humboldt in Berlin. In 1848 Guyot would follow Agassiz to the United States where he started a long and distinguished career six years later, as professor of physical geography and geology at Princeton, then called the College of New Jersey.[16] Carl Vogt would become a well-known figure in political and scientific life in Germany and Switzerland. After leaving Neuchâtel, he became a leading materialist thinker, a member of the cantonal and federal parliaments and rector of the University of Geneva towards the end of his life. Like Vogt, Edouard Desor was a political refugee from Giessen in the Grand Duchy of Hesse. He was the only member of Agassiz's team to remain in Neuchâtel, where he became professor of geology at the Academy and a leading intellectual and political figure in the canton.[17] In 1846 Agassiz moved to the United States where, in the words of Stephan Jay Gould, he became 'the most powerful and imperious biologist' in the country. 'Without doubt,' writes Gould (who admittedly stood in Agassiz's line of descent at Harvard), he was 'the greatest and most influential naturalist of nineteenth-century America.'[18] It should be stressed that, on his departure from Switzerland, Agassiz endowed his small town with an important physical and intellectual heritage that served as an inspiration to later generations of aspirant natural scientists in Neuchâtel.

Part of the renown of Agassiz and his colleagues came from their willingness to spend extended periods of time in the Alps where they recovered the fossil remains of marine and other animals, and measured the structure and movement of glaciers. Through his field studies, Agassiz came to punctuate the long history of the world with a series of catastrophes followed by distinct, special creations. At least partly for religious reasons, Agassiz refused to recognize any connection between these 'epochs of creation'. Like Cuvier, he refuted Lamarck's explanation of the resemblance between the fossilized plants and animals found in different geological strata: that living organisms were able to adapt themselves physically, over generations, to their changing environment. Instead, Agassiz saw the will of God behind the evolution of life on earth. His findings and those of his colleagues pushed back the age of the world and filled it with a startling diversity. But they quickly divided into two schools. While Guyot and de Rougemont reassessed the Biblical narrative of Creation in the light of recent geological discoveries, Vogt developed a purely materialist approach to the subject.[19] Agassiz's work said little about the origins of humanity, which he left dangling on the edge of a monstrous gap bordered on the one side by the act of creation and on the other by Biblical and classical scholarship. To fill this void, Desor and Frédéric de Rougement threw themselves into the study of primitive societies.[20]

During the 1850s interest in this work increased palpably as engineers cut the first railways through the mountains of Switzerland. When they drilled through different geological strata, they uncovered a series of fossils that allowed a far closer reading of the prehistoric past. At the same time, the discovery of Stone Age villages along the shores of several Swiss lakes merely heightened the passion with which people searched for their origins. Henri Junod's generation obsessively gathered evidence on the beginnings and development of the physical world and the place occupied by humanity in its long history. This deep concern with the relationship between geology, society and history was transmitted to his son's generation, many of whom, as missionary explorers trained in Greek and Latin, would see in Africa a reflection of Europe's prehistory and, more distantly, the primitive origins of humanity.

While pastor of Chezard-Saint-Martin, Henri Junod taught natural history, particularly geology and ornithology, in the village school. One of the young people who fell under the spell of this charismatic clergyman was a young primary school teacher named Fritz Tripet. Self-taught and from a humble background, Tripet, with Junod and others, became in 1873 a founder member of the Independent Church of

Neuchâtel. A decade later, equally under the influence of Junod, he was appointed the professor of botany at the town academy.[21]

When Henri Junod and his family moved to the cantonal capital in 1867, he introduced his children to the botanical diversity found in the Collégiale's garden and encouraged them to collect and classify plants. This led Henri-Alexandre to assemble his first formal register of dried plants with the help of his elder sister Elizabeth.[22] The boy's love for natural history blossomed when he entered Neuchâtel's classical *collège latin*, a building housing the town's library and the outstanding natural history museum built up by Agassiz and his colleagues. The school's teaching staff included Paul Godet (1836-1911), a Berlin-trained expert in the taxonomy of regional molluscs, a field that lent itself both to the collection of fossils and the careful observation of minute detail. Paul formed part of the intellectual aristocracy of the town. His father, Charles-Henri Godet (1797-1879), was an internationally-renowned botanist whose friends and acquaintances stretched from Alexandre von Humboldt to Agassiz, Shuttleworth and Jacob Burckhardt (who lodged with the family as a young man).[23] Paul's uncles, Frédéric and Georges Godet, were the town's two outstanding theologians and his cousin Philippe Godet was an important literary and intellectual figure who later became an influential Liberal politician and eventually rector of the university. Henri-Alexandre Junod would later remark on the profound impact on his life of this family of eminent humanists.[24]

While at school in Neuchâtel, Henri-Alexandre Junod also benefited from the patronage of Fritz Tripet, at this time secretary of the natural history society founded by Agassiz. As the editor of its journal for almost 30 years and professor of botany at the academy, he was a locally influential figure. Throughout his long career, Tripet organized outings aimed at introducing students to the glorious detail of uncorrupted nature, and encouraged his charges to find a patriotic pride in the discovery of plants which he duly named and classified. In general, Tripet emphasized what we might today call 'fieldwork' over and above the more abstract questions raised by plant anatomy.[25] He also managed to publish the work of promising young scientists; in the late 1870s–80s, he was able to place Henri-Alexandre Junod's first articles on zoological and botanical topics in *Le Rameau de Sapin*, the journal of the junior branch of the canton's natural history society.[26]

At college Junod was strongly influenced by Paul Godet's uncle Georges, the professor of theology who introduced him to the work of Kant. He particularly fell under the spell of Georges' brother Frédéric, the professor of exegesis and criticism who, through his lectures, tutorials and publications, kept before his students the unique elements of Christianity: Christ's virgin birth, the incarnation of God in man, the crucifixion and resurrection. In an intellectual climate shaken by the recent discoveries of Darwin and others, these pious Calvinists and their *émigré* friends in America and elsewhere battled against conservatives who saw science solely as a breeding-ground for the scepticism and rationalism undermining Biblical revelation. The contemplation of nature embraced by the Godets and their friends provided hope to lives weighed down by original sin and the fear evoked by the doctrine of predestination. Their faith was confirmed rather than shaken by the extended size of the heavens discovered by astronomers, the wealth of detail revealed by the microscope and, particularly in Neuchâtel, the series of preordained, divine creations uncovered by geology and palaeontology. God's power and benevolence were visible to them in the intricate design and wonderful harmony of nature. For these deeply religious men, Psalm 104 rang with new meaning as they read it in the light of scientific discovery: 'How manifold are thy works, O Lord! In wisdom hast thou made them all!' Rather than undermine belief, science served to increase the patent glory of God.

From America, their friend Louis Agassiz saw the diversity in the natural world as the product of a 'superior intelligence' that was also responsible for the physical resemblances between species of different epochs. The species 'manifested in the animal and vegetable kingdoms', he wrote, were produced by 'the thoughts of the Creator of the Universe'.[27] But Agassiz left the Biblical tradition when he abandoned the Mosaic version of creation and refuted the idea that species originated in single pairs. Instead, he ascribed life on earth to a series of special creations when he asserted that, after the destruction of species during catastrophes, they were repeatedly created again in new forms and in large numbers, in habitats intended for them by God.[28]

The influential works of Arnold Guyot and his close friend Frédéric Godet conformed more closely to the Biblical narrative. Like Buffon and Cuvier, they reinterpreted the seven days of Biblical creation as seven stages or geological epochs in the cosmic history of the world.[29] Like Schleiermacher, they believed human reason as much as personal revelation demonstrated the existence of God. For Godet, science was 'a sister, a powerful ally of faith'.[30] 'The light of religious revelation and science shines from different origins', he wrote in the manner of Francis Bacon, 'one comes from the sky and the other from the earth, but in meeting they combine to produce perfect clarity.'[31] For Guyot, 'the book of Nature' was as much the work of God as the Bible: both were a source of divine knowledge. 'Coming from the same Author, [they] complement one another, forming together the whole revelation of God to man.' By revealing nature's intricacy of design, its regularities and laws, scholars provided 'innumerable proofs of the almighty power and wisdom of its author'.[32] The glimpse of the 'Celestial Pilot' provided by nature was even clearer when viewed from the pulpit. There, Henri-Alexandre's father thundered against 'the obscurantists, the stiflers, the gagging priesthood', who questioned the material and social benefits brought by science. Like his friends Frédéric Godet and Arnold Guyot, Henri believed that a thorough knowledge of science would reinforce the doctrines of Christianity and draw to it 'the noblest of thirsting souls'.[33]

These Christians found their religious beliefs confirmed as they came to view the act of creation as less the product of a single divine *fiat* somewhere in a remote past and more as an ongoing process, linking the past with the present and the future. In this way God was not, as St Augustine had first speculated, a transcendental figure beyond the stars who had created the world and then left it to its own devices; nor was he a watchmaker who had merely set the mechanism ticking. God was rather an all-pervading presence whose immanence and omniscience could be read in the series of creations that constituted the world in both time and space. This way of perceiving nature, as the harmonious handiwork of God, infused earnestly severe men like Henri Junod and Frédéric Godet with a sensibility that could move them to tears when reading a weighty scientific tome such as Oswald Heer's *The Primeval World of Switzerland*. In the canton of Vaud, it led pastor Henri Berthoud to write a treatise on the relationship between the science of geology and the Biblical notion of creation.[34] The dogged earnestness of the collector appealed strongly to the evangelical temperament, as did the wondrous detail produced by God's creative powers through time and space. For this reason, many eminent Christians in the Swiss Romande, particularly those associated with the missionary movement, devoted themselves to collecting and systematizing elements of nature that revealed the existence of a benevolent creator.[35]

For these men the study of nature was associated with the thrill of discovery, conquest and pride, but it was also a mark of virtue and good taste, a source of consolation for those weighed down by the consequences of sin and an emotional release from an otherwise rigorous lifestyle. The naturalist drew his energy in different measure from this stew of concerns, a situation quickly reflected in the divisions within natural theology. Not all evangelicals ranked reason above mystery or valued logic more than emotion. Many pietists continued to follow the Biblical narrative of creation, and criticized the attempts of Agassiz and others to establish natural laws that were not the direct product of divine ordination.[36]

In Neuchâtel this perspective produced the sort of natural history undertaken by Samuel Robert (1853–1934) who saw lepidoptera purely as an expression and proof of God's glory. Through purchase and exchange, Robert assembled a magnificent collection of 23,000 butterfly species from all over the world. But while Robert was only interested in the remarkable beauty and diversity of these insects, a collector such as Frédéric de Rougemont's son Frédéric (a pastor in the Independent Church) sought to discern the divine laws behind the ordering of the diversity of nature. To achieve this, he hunted and raised butterflies, investigated their habitats, and attempted, within the narrow confines of one specific region, to uncover a classificatory 'system' based on the Linnaean model.[37] He also sought to infuse the young with his enthusiasm. When his brother, the professor of natural history at the academy, died unexpectedly, de Rougemont and Tripet arranged for Henri-Alexandre to continue his research into microlepidoptera. In 1884 the twenty-one-year-old Junod published his findings on the anatomy, habitat and customs of a tiny butterfly in the scientific journal founded by Louis Agassiz some forty years earlier.[38]

During his first year at college, Henri-Alexandre joined the Société de Belles-Lettres, the intellectually and socially important student association presided over by Edouard Jacottet, future missionary-linguist in Lesotho. In the close world of the faculty of theology Junod counted Henry Appia, the son of one of the founders of the Red Cross, among his closest friends.[39] Junod finished his four years at university as head student of the faculty and president of the local chapter of the Société de Belles-Lettres. In the society's *Revue* he published poetry and articles on regional history and literature from a romantic perspective. But as a student he was particularly renowned for natural history essays, strongly derivative of Lamartine, that personified nature. Through a combination of sentimentality, information and moral philosophy, these works spoke of a lofty spirituality in God's handiwork. His readings could hold an auditorium of *belletriens* spellbound. An admirer wrote of a young man

> whose gaze knows how to penetrate the mysteries of nature and discover movement and life where the greatest scientists have seen only inertia and immobility, Junod, who recognizes a soul under the icy exterior of a drop of frozen rain and who believes he is able to perceive religious and moral instincts in the soul of a small tree frog and a yearning for perfectibility.[40]

Inevitably, Agassiz stood out as an exemplary figure for the young theology student who, as president of the society, commissioned a bust of the great man. On his return from his studies in Berlin in 1885, Junod took up the position of pastor at Môtiers, a small town in the Val-de-Travers from which, exactly 120 years earlier, Jean-Jacques Rousseau had been expelled by the local clergyman and his followers after a stay of two years. The botanizing philosopher had then moved to the neighbouring village of Couvet, where he was fêted as a hero, before moving to a safer abode on a small island in the nearby Lake Bienne. In 1885 Rousseau's spirit and his reflections on the plants and people of the upper stretches of the Val-de-Travers, were still felt in Couvet, the seat of the Dubieds, Henri-Alexandre's mother's family, and in Môtiers, the site of his church. At the foot of the valley the spirit of Agassiz was recalled when the bust of the great man, ordered by Junod and his friends, was eventually unveiled in the Neuchâtel Academy in 1887.[41]

When Junod left for Lourenço Marques in 1889, he carried with him a love of the natural and theological sciences typical of the dominant male figures in his life. He saw the post to which he had been sent by his vocation as not only an opportunity to convert the heathen and revivify his church at home but a chance to uncover new botanical and zoological species.[42] This was a good time for an energetic young man to seek his fortune overseas, for there was little left to discover in Switzerland; collectors had been reduced to discovering sub-species or at best filling in gaps in previous studies.

Perhaps Junod was aware that, as early as the middle of the century, an ambitious botanist such as Pierre-Edmond Boissier (1810–85) had been obliged to look to Spain, then later the Middle East and the edges of India, to discover new plants. Boissier's willingness to move to the edges of Europe and beyond had paid handsomely. In a manner that set a shining example for younger botanists, he had described (alone or with the aid of collaborators) a phenomenal 131 new genera of plants and 5,990 new species. William Barbey (1842–1914) continued this tradition when he established the Boissier Herbarium in Geneva in honour of his father-in-law. This institution pursued a policy of purchasing botanical collections, sponsoring expeditions, and publishing the findings of men on the spot worldwide.[43] The long depression at the end of the nineteenth century restricted costly periods of fieldwork or extended them into a permanent expatriation, causing several naturalists from the Swiss Romande to became pioneering figures in the fields of entomology and botany in places as far removed as Russia, Cuba, Costa Rica and Venezuela.[44] Perhaps most importantly for Henri-Alexandre Junod, Paul Berthoud had sent several new species of ants from the Transvaal; and when his sister married the widowed missionary, she too started to send insects back to Neuchâtel. Her packages included a particularly large and rare collection of butterflies that arrived on Godet's desk at the museum just as Junod discovered that his microlepidoptera did not represent a new species.[45] As Junod left Switzerland, it seemed fame could only be won by collectors in those rare parts of the world little touched by European enterprise.

The natural sciences were also being rapidly transformed at the end of the nineteenth century. For decades the *homme de cabinet* or armchair expert and the amateur collector in the field had existed in an easy symbiosis. In Neuchâtel the growth of the Natural History Museum had traditionally depended on the generosity of the town's many traders, missionaries, soldiers and travellers living abroad. In a way that reinforced their ties with home, these men sent 'curiosities' to their compatriots in the museum. But the gap between the collector and the classifier widened into something of a generational gap following the spectacular achievements of Darwin, when botanical and zoological excursions lost ground to theory and the rise of the 'new biology' in the German universities. In the last third of the century, innovators in the field shifted from collecting and documenting the majestic diversity of nature to revealing its causes and consequences. In England this tension was captured by George Eliot in *Middlemarch*, where the old order of science and the new are represented by the figures of Mr. Farebrother and Lydgate: the one concerned with collecting and systematizing, the other with embryology and connective tissues.

Technological developments also encouraged the move from the field to the laboratory as increasingly powerful microscopes allowed professionals to pierce below the surface and specialize in morphology, embryology and physiology. In some cases this led them to reclassify plants and insects according to minutiae previously not visible to the human eye. The sheer volume of species discovered rendered the old, encyclopedic museum collections impracticable and forced experts to specialize in narrow fields. As prestige and status passed to the professional scientist, the thrill of discovery shifted away from the painstaking but plodding 'antiquarian' work of collectors such as Tripet and de Rougement.[46] Even Boissier, an internationally renowned botanist, came under fire for his unwillingness to ask more general and abstract questions of his material.[47]

Religion underlay much of this shift in thinking. If conservatives had seen the work of Agassiz and his colleagues as leading towards an unsavoury deism, the direction taken by science at the end of the nineteenth century pointed towards a far less savoury atheism. The social and economic instability accompanying industrialization was compounded as biologists and geologists reformulated species and dissolved the clear distinctions between the sexes, the animal and plant kingdoms and even the existence of humanity as a separate species. For many Darwinians, evolutionism publicized the arbitrary nature of classification by contradicting the idea that anatomical characteristics of living organisms were fixed and constant through time. As science challenged established ideas on the fixity of species and the place of humanity in the universe, it inevitably cast doubt on the story of creation and even the existence of God. It promoted the secularization of science as clergymen lost their leading role in the study of nature.[48] As a believer by temperament and an amateur with a broad appreciation of the natural sciences, Junod was better suited to be in the field in Africa than in the laboratory in Europe.

African Adventures in Taxonomy

For many years only the most intrepid naturalists had visited Lourenço Marques, a backward corner of a shabby colony.[49] But when Junod arrived, the town was entering a period of sudden and unprecedented prosperity. As the natural port for the newly discovered Witwatersrand gold fields, it attracted a diverse, cosmopolitan population – figures such as Rose Monteiro, who earned an income by selling zoological and botanical specimens to collectors in Europe, or the young soldier, Captain Freire de Andrade, who produced a valuable book on the tree flowers of Mozambique.[50] Junod arrived in Africa from a country where nature was being divided, demarcated and domesticated, where wild animals lived increasingly on sufferance. At Rikatla he felt that he had been transported into 'an entirely new world' where nature was in an almost pristine condition.[51]

Three months after coming to Rikatla, Junod wrote to William Barbey for the first time. Although he specialized in the Near and Middle East, Barbey had purchased several important southern African herbaria and was prepared to subsidize the work of collectors living on the edges of the European world.[52] He was keen to expand his institute's African holdings and viewed missionary societies as a means of achieving this end.[53]

In October 1889 Junod offered to send Barbey both dried plants and the seeds of species suitable for cultivation in hot houses or gardens where they would 'flourish ... beneath the sky of the fatherland'.[54] Ambitious and energetic, he took just sixteen months to gather over 300 different plant species. Starting from the hill above Lourenço Marques, he explored the 23-kilometre stretch of land between the town and Rikatla, to the north. He spent his spare time from his mission investigating the groves of palm trees and marshy hollows lying behind the coastal dunes. There, he found new plants soon to be named *Striga junodii* Schinz and *Triumfetta junodii* Schinz (see plate 5). Evangelical itineration allowed him to scour the plant life of five distinct geographical areas. These included the Manununu forest covering the bend in the Nkomati valley, the sandy dunes along the coast, the wet depressions behind the coastal hills, the clayey patches of black, *nyaka* soil and the rocky Libombo mountains on the border with the Transvaal.[55] In the Makororo forest on the route from Rikatla to Antioka, he discovered the *Empogona junodii* Schinz. However, it was the Morakwene forest that received his full attention, an area covering the south bank of the Nkomati estuary from the coast to the drift, as well as two small islands in the river. With its dense underbrush and thick creepers, this impenetrable forest was an 'eldorado' for the naturalist. Junod was particularly attracted by the striking burgundy-coloured flowers that appeared after the first summer rains on a tree orchid and he quickly gave his name to this plant, *Monodora junodii* (family name Annonaceae). The Makandja forest on the left bank of the Nkomati estuary also impressed him, with its rich and varied flora supported by a dark clay soil.[56]

One of Junod's first steps at his mission station was to establish what he called, with a touch of irony, 'a museum'. In this centre he dried plants that he dispatched for the first time, in January 1891, to Geneva, where Barbey undertook to have them named, classified and described in an article tentatively called 'Plantae Junodiae'.[57] The missionary was 'very proud' when told that his first consignment contained at least one unknown species that would thenceforth bear the name *Melhania junodii* Schinz.[58] As further encouragement Barbey supplied Junod with the equipment needed to establish a herbarium, with information on how to dry plants, particularly during the sub-tropical wet season, and how to ensure their safe delivery to Europe.[59] He also offered to act as an agent for the sale to museums and collectors in Europe of any of Junod's plants not required by his herbarium. In response, Junod assembled collections holding 100 different species of lichen, fruit, flowers and roots. With the money earned from the sale of these plants he offered sixpence to guides to take him into inaccessible swamplands where rare plants were to be found, and hired the services of others prepared to journey up the Nkomati river in search of other plantlife. He also trained and employed an assistant to dry and press specimens and prepare them for dispatch to Europe.[60] When Junod left Mozambique for Switzerland in 1896 he had inscribed 500 different plant species in his botanical register.

Three years later he returned to Africa to take up a post at the school for evangelists at Shiluvane in the Eastern Transvaal. The flora of the Delagoa Bay area paled in comparison with that of Junod's new home.[61] Shiluvane was at the heart of a rich botanical area encompassing the Drakensberg and adjoining plateau, the thick forests on the eastern slope of the mountain, the foothills in which the mission was situated and the hot Lowveld folding into the coastal plain. Shiluvane occupied a central position in the Swiss mission field and on his various trips to Pietersburg, via the Woodbush and Haenertsberg, and to the Spelonken and Komatipoort, Junod was able to enlarge and diversify his botanical collection. At the height of the malarial summer, he and his family spent several weeks every year in the highlands, at Howick in Natal or in Lesotho. In 1903 alone, he gathered over 200 plant species while holidaying in the mountainous terrain of Witzieshoek and Thababosigo. As he combed the area around the Paris mission stations with his friend Edouard Jacottet, he looked with envy at the unexplored flora of the Maluti mountains. By the time Junod left Shiluvane for Rikatla in 1906, he had added over 2300 plant species to the original 500 in his collection.[62]

During the ten years that Junod had spent in Switzerland and the Transvaal, the Delagoa Bay region had been thoroughly botanized. The Portuguese had sent an official to collect plants, and a renowned collector and future professor of botany in Berlin, Rudolf Schlechter, had also spent four months scouring the area.[63] Sadly for botany but happily for anthropology, this competition encouraged Junod to specialize in the study of human beings. Over the next decade, he inscribed fewer than 100 plants in his register. But once he had established his reputation in the field of anthropology, he returned with relish to botanize in his free time. In the three years before Junod returned definitively to Switzerland in 1920, he collected examples of 1,550 different plant species drawn from many parts of southern Mozambique as well as the Zoutpansberg, the Spelonken, Johannesburg, Witzieshoek, and Pinetown in Natal.[64]

Henri-Alexandre Junod discovered many new plants during his years in Southern Africa and is today recognized as one of the pioneer botanical explorers of the region. Apart from Barbey, he corresponded with various botanists to whom he sent material. These included John Briquet, the director of the Delessert Conservatory in Geneva, a botanical institute housing numerous South African collections;[65] Fritz Tripet and Paul Godet in Neuchâtel; J. M. Wood, the director of the botanical gardens in Durban; Joseph Burtt Davy, the government botanist in Pretoria; and Thomas Durand, the director of the botanical gardens in Brussels.[66] The plants he gathered in the Delagoa Bay region were described in 1899 in two articles co-authored with Hans Schinz.[67] The celebrated Swiss botanist continued to publish articles on Junod's collection over the next thirty years and, with perhaps some exaggeration, placed him amongst the greatest collectors of African flora of his generation.[68] Junod's memory was perpetuated by the genus *Junodia paxis* of the family Euphorbiaceae (later synonymized with *Epinetrum delagoense*) and by some thirty different plant species, including the *Gladiolus junodi* pictured on plate 4. Today his plant specimens are housed in herbaria throughout the world.[69]

Despite this success in the field of botany, Junod found the Delagoa Bay region a richer field for entomology and it was in this area that he initially invested most of his energy.[70] Although Lourenço Marques lay on the edge of the tropics, the hill above the town was arid and the meagre vegetation produced few flowers. But on this bush, he wrote with pleasure in 1891, 'live an astonishing and surprising collection of fauna', particularly the caterpillars that serve as the larval form of several species of butterflies and moths.[71] At Rikatla he found it more difficult to trace rare species;

*5.1 Henri-Alexandre Junod hunting butterflies on the escarpment near Shiluvane.
(© Swiss Mission Archive, Lausanne)*

but within two years he had trained 'intelligent natives' to recognize exotic insects and uncover their habitat. In the Morakwene forest he found rare caterpillars and large numbers of wood-boring beetles called longicorns or Cerambycidae. The wide diversity of trees and bushes in the forest provided a home for a large range of *Papilio* in spring and summer and several varieties of African *Charaxes* in autumn and winter. In a field of cashew trees hosting rare bushes and tropical vines lived a world of exotic Swallowtail, Swordtail and Dawn butterflies.

Junod sometimes raised butterflies and moths from their form as caterpillars, but more frequently he resorted to employing assistants to chase these insects from their habitat by beating the bush at specific times of day or night. His assiduousness brought quick results. In November 1890 he discovered a butterfly (*Teracolus calais*) in the Lower Nkomati valley that had only been associated with tropical areas previously. In the same year he found a new species of wattle bagworm, the larval form of the moth *Acanthopsyche junodi*, now *Kotochalia (Chaliopsis) junodi* (Heylaerts), at Howick in Natal, as well as five examples of the lovely *Precis cuama*. Later, he discovered the first example of this species in the Delagoa Bay area. In 1891 one of his assistants brought him a magnificent butterfly belonging to the large, fast-flying *Papilio* group, a genus first established by Linneaus in 1758. The man had caught the butterfly in the Morakwene forest and Junod quickly sent it for identification to Roland Trimen, the entomologist who served as director of the South African Museum in Cape Town.

In 1893 Trimen described the butterfly, pictured in plate 6, as a new species and gave it the name *Papilio junodi*, commonly known today as 'Junod's swordtail'. It took Junod just seven years to assemble some 200 different species of moths and 184 species of butterfly. This came close to half the butterflies thought to exist in the entire subcontinent at that time.[72]

From his 'museum', Junod tirelessly sought out and studied crickets, grasshoppers, ants, spiders, wasps, bees, moths, molluscs, lizards, frogs and especially caterpillars, beetles, bugs and butterflies. He sold rare butterflies to the museum in Neuchâtel and to collectors such as Roland Trimen.[73] He also sold entomological collections, including a wide spectrum of Coleoptera (beetles) from Shiluvane, to the newly opened Rothschild Museum of natural history in Tring, England.[74] He later assembled a beautiful collection of butterflies and coleoptera for the natural history museum in Lourenço Marques.[75] His 'baboon' spider, or tarantula, remains a prize for any arachnophile (see plate 8).[76] In an attempt to identify and name his specimens Junod corresponded with experts in Lausanne, Geneva, Zurich, Berlin, Bucharest, Turin, Paris, Caen, London and Cape Town. Lepidoptera (butterflies and moths) were sent to Frédéric de Rougemont, Trimen, and A. G. Butler at the British Museum. In Lourenço Marques he met and later corresponded with the distinguished entomologist, W. L. Distant. Coleoptera went to Dr Bugnion in Lausanne and especially Louis Péringuey at the museum in Cape Town; Tenebrionidae (darkling beetles) to Mr Fairmaire in Paris; Orthoptera (crickets, grasshoppers and cockroaches) and Hymenoptera (wasps, bees and ants) to Dr von Schulthess-Rechberg in Zurich (where some were classified by Auguste Forel); Hemiptera (including the bugs of which he was particularly fond) were sent to Prof. Montandon in Bucharest; and caterpillars to Mr Heylaerts, a Dutch specialist.[77]

Henri-Alexandre Junod won an international reputation as an entomologist. Like Roger Hamley in Elizabeth Gaskell's *Wives and Daughters* (1866), who was received as a 'fashionable lion' after his return home following a tour of exploration sponsored by the Geographical Society, Junod was admired for his scientific achievements. During his first furlough in Switzerland (1896–9) he worked through his collections and co-authored a series of articles with European experts. In a work on the beetles of the Delagoa Bay region, written with Bugnion, he listed 479 species, including eight new species of darkling beetles (amongst which a 'toktokkie' beetle, *Psammodes junodi*), about 80 species of long-horned, wood-boring beetles (Cerambycidae), as well as seven new species of locusts and mantids (together with a new genus, *Junodia amoena*). This led Bugnion to compare the wealth of beetles to be found in the Delagoa Bay area with the vaunted fields of Brazil and India.[78] In other articles published in 1899 Junod noted hundreds of different species of Orthoptera, Hemiptera and Hymenoptera, of which several dozen were new discoveries.[79] His collection of Hydrophilidae was analysed and described in articles by Dr Achille Griffini of Turin and Dr Maurice Regimbart of Evreux.[80] In 1904, W. F. Purcell published an article on the numerous scorpions and spiders found by Junod at Shiluvane, and Forel determined the ants found by the industrious missionary and his colleagues Paul Berthoud and Georges Liengme. Louis Péringuey was full of praise for Junod's work on Coleoptera, especially those found around Rikatla, and also published an article on the missionary's findings at Shiluvane.[81] Junod hoped that his many scientific articles would one day be assembled in a single volume, tentatively entitled *The Natural History of Delagoa* or *The Flora and Entomological Fauna of Delagoa* and, as late as 1914, he displayed his rich botanical and zoological collections at the Swiss National Exhibition.[82]

5.2 *African collectors provided Junod with a range of plants and insects. In this photograph a 'botanist' and a 'coleopterist', both unnamed, flank Spoon Libombo, Junod's butterfly collector and one of his major informants in the field of ethnography. All three men hold the equipment needed to undertake their various tasks.*
(© *Swiss Mission Archive, Lausanne*)

Although Junod's interest in natural science was overtaken by his new passion for anthropology, he left an indelible mark on the entomological map of south-east Africa. Scores of insects and plants today bear his name, or that of his wife, or the many stations of the Swiss Mission.[83] The missionary doctor Georges Liengme also scoured nature for new species and passed his name to beetles, and like Paul Berthoud, to ants found in Gazaland.[84] This system of naming, using Latin binomials, was an integral part of the process of taking hold of the land, for it embraced and assimilated the local in a way that made the foreign familiar and domesticated the disorderly for the European scientist.

Throughout his stay in Southern Africa Junod supplied the Natural History Museum in Neuchâtel with a wide range of animals and insects. The museum supplied him with flasks, dissecting cases, cyanide and nets and frequently paid for the items collected or for their delivery. This policy paid handsome dividends. The Museum register records receiving from Junod in 1911 'a precious collection' of Hemiptera and in 1912, 187 Orthoptera and Hymenoptera. His molluscs were also considered 'extremely interesting' and were accompanied by a steady stream of sea shells, bird skins, eggs and nests, sea urchins, snakes and lizards, several frogs, a crocodile and various (unidentified) mammals.[85] By appealing to men on the spot such as Junod, as well as to other Neuchâtelois resident overseas, the museum built up a mass of objects that could later be sifted through by the experts.[86] Junod concurred with this ethos. 'In collecting all these facts,' he remarked, 'we accomplish a sort of highly dignified ministry and, perhaps, we furnish those who will systematize them one day with the key to many problems.'[87]

Just as biology and theology overlapped, botany and zoology frequently imbricated. This happened when Junod stumbled upon a little-known bush housing several new species of longicornes or when he found an unusual caterpillar lodged on the underleaves of a plant that he was drying for his herbarium. Biology and sociology met up when Junod used his considerable linguistic skills to question informants about local plants and animals. His strong interest in landsnails, for example, moved in an ethnographic direction when informants told him that they used the animals' shells as containers in which to deposit money earned in South Africa. The uninspiring moth *Acanthopsyche junodi* (Heylaerts) took on a new allure when it was noted that its larval form (as the wattle bagworm) produced a cocoon, often found hanging on thorn trees, that proved useful as a penis-sheath. He developed a deep respect for indigenous powers of observation and an admiration for the indigenous system of classification. He also had a high regard for the way in which local people exploited plants for qualities that were at once medicinal, magical, sartorial and nutritional in edible or liquid form. He was intrigued by the way trees were associated with deities and spirits, and plants and animals were employed in rituals as talismans, objects of taboo, or as a means of divination.[88]

At a time when biologists seldom mentioned the names and achievements of their native assistants, Junod made a point of drawing attention to the work of these individuals and on one occasion he photographed his three major collectors.[89] Elias Libombo or 'Spoon', a local diviner who sold thatching grass, and whose wife had joined the mission, proved a particularly adept butterfly collector. As a young boy looking after his father's goats, 'Spoon' had chased after birds, mice, lizards and rabbits and he had observed the habits and movements of a wide range of animals. This proved a useful training for a naturalist and contributed to Spoon's skill as a butterfly collector.

To succeed in this field, a collector has to be aware of the short life span of the butterfly, its selective feeding habits and its sensitivity to ecological and climatological change. An expert like Elias Libombo had to catch the high-flying, swooping charaxes as well as skippers flitting from plant to plant. He needed to recognize the larval host plants of different species of butterfly and he had to know where on these plants the female would lay her eggs. He needed to identify when, and for how long, adults would emerge and fly, the places favoured by males searching for mates, and the kind of food preferred by both male and female adults. To achieve these ends he had to be able to distinguish in particular the coloration, shape and design according to which butterflies were situated in genera, species and varieties. Because of his abilities as a collector, Junod entrusted Spoon with a net, bottles, ether, and numerous paper cones in which to capture, kill and store his specimens. He was frequently sent on expeditions to the butterfly collectors' 'Eldorado' on the lower Nkomati. On at least one occasion Junod sent Spoon on an extended trip of several days to the *terra incognita* on the bend in the Nkomati.[90]

It did not take long before the missionary's attention was drawn to the way in which locals made sense of their environment. He was intrigued by the names often given by children to beetles because of their shape, colour, taste or design; or because certain species, like the weevil (*Curculionidae Brachycerus*), were considered a sign of good fortune. Perhaps most importantly, he discerned a 'notion of *order*' in the natives' classification of Mammalia.[91] Although the locals did not group animals into large classes resembling genera and species, they placed animals in small groups, if only because some were considered taboo or physically disgusting.[92] They also speculated on the place of humanity in this system of classification when they saw apes as a degenerate form of humankind.[93] More broadly, he noted that the Thonga had a 'rather pantheistic notion' of creation that they shared with 'many very educated scientists of our age'.[94]

Junod was particularly impressed by the locals' ability to name plants and situate them in groups that broadly resembled genera and even species. Natives recognized the visible relationship between various forms of Lobeliae that they grouped together under the term *Shilawana*. The same sense of classification caused them to give the name *Shitshinyambita* to all the Strigae, a genus of the Scrophulariaceae family. Ferns were also placed in a common 'genus' when they were labelled *Tsuna*. Locals not only distinguished between different genera; they also broke these large categories into 'species' through the use of diminutive terms or by attaching the generic name of a plant to the habitat in which it was found. So the *Muhlu* (a tree of the Asclepiadaceae family) was called a *Muhlu wa ntlhaba* when found in dry bushland, and a *Muhlutjobo* when located in the wet marshlands along the coast. In a similar way, the *Ntjhesi* (*Hibiscus*) was divided into the *Ntjhesi* of the *ntlhaba* (*Hibiscus surratensis*, etc.), the *Ntjhesi* of the *nyaka* (dark soil), and the little *Ntjhesi* of the *ntlhaba* (the *shitjhesi sha ntlhaba* or *Sida cordifolia* of the *Hibiscus* genus of the Malvaceae family). Natives also sometimes distinguished male and female forms within their plant categories. In this way the 'genus' *Munywane* was divided into male and female forms that European scientists would recognize as *Epaltes gariepina* and *Blumea aurita*.[95]

Junod came to realize that the botanical knowledge of the natives was the product of 'a true and, in a certain sense, scientific observation on their part'. It was certainly 'more general' than that of the European peasantry, he speculated, perhaps comparable to 'that of our forefathers of two or three hundred years ago, before Botany became a true science'. Even children, he observed, could point out roots used for medicinal purposes.[96] This practical outcome was fortunate, for he was coming under increasing pressure from the mission to demonstrate the utility, explanatory value and didactic benefits of his entomological and botanical studies.[97]

Junod found the indigenous people had a great deal to teach European scientists about the utility of plants. On several occasions he invited natives to his museum where they supplied him with the local names and uses of plants in exchange for a shilling. He never seemed to consider that this source of commercial gain might inspire informants to exaggerate or embellish their accounts. Junod recognized that diviners (who predicted the future) and *gobelas* (skilled in exorcizing unwelcome spirits) possessed an intricate knowledge of the animals and plants used in the pursuance of their professions. He particularly admired old women and *nangas*, or specialist medicine-men, whose knowledge of the medicinal, nutritional and magic properties of plants constituted a rough form of classification. The *nanga* were familiar with 'real, powerful drugs' which they administered in conjunction with therapeutic practices.[98] In a way that indicates a genuine desire to coax medicinal cures from local plants, Junod assembled a 'Ronga pharmacopoeia' in the ethnographic museum in Neuchâtel and sent plants to Geneva for analysis.[99] He also attempted, with little success it seems, to commercialize the pith of a local palm (probably *Corchons junodi*)

5.3 *Butterfly and insect trays. Insect collections captured the intricacy and beauty of God's world. But they also encouraged missionary entomologists to study the reproduction of species and to confront the process of natural selection.*
(© *Swiss Mission Archive, Lausanne*)

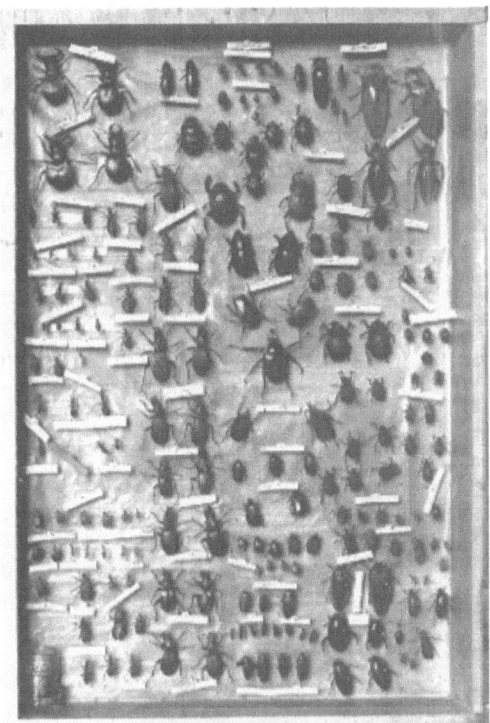

as a substitute for cork. In general, Junod valued the religious utility of the study of nature over and above the commercial benefits to which it could be applied.[100]

In 1893 Junod saw 'God's infinite wisdom' behind the diversity of nature. 'Nature is a book, in Africa as in Europe', he wrote, and a means of praising 'the beauty and power of the Creator'.[101] Four years later he drew the attention of an audience in Neuchâtel to natural history as a means 'to admire the magnificent work of the Creator on the marvellous planet that we inhabit'.[102] In his retirement he carved this belief on the two large cupboards, filled with butterflies and beetles, that occupied a central place in his home in Geneva. 'The earth is full of Your riches' read the inscription, from the Psalms.[103] Junod was thrilled by the discovery of new animal and plant species and delighted in their infinite range of detail, colour, shape, design and texture. The blue and green *Chrysomilidae* shone 'like saphyrs and emeralds', while the ground beetle of this family, called *Euschizomerus junodi* (Pér), was 'a charming little insect with a triangular thorax'. He thought the *Amaurodes passerini* Westwood a 'magnificent species' of the scarab group (of dung beetles).[104] He was also enthralled by the way in which insects communicated with one another, protected themselves against predators and reproduced their species. Very quickly, he came to tie the classification of insects to customs and habits that were shaped by environmental factors rather than divine design. By emphasizing natural processes as well as taxonomic structures, Junod gave more immediate agency to nature and history than to God. This meant that, as the missionary-scientist reiterated his belief in the powers of the creator, he was also disengaging the hand of God from the order of nature.

Social Evolution and Natural Imperialism

By the end of the century Junod stressed (if only to scientists) that as a collector he was no longer just concerned with classification and anatomy. His major interest had become the place of plants and animals in the human and natural environment. This shift in interest was largely motivated by his growing engagement with the theory of evolution through natural selection.[105] In Cape Town Roland Trimen was at the centre of a circle of collectors who sought to explain the existence and reproduction of animal and plant species in terms of natural selection. He quickly introduced Junod to the works of evolutionists such as A. R. Wallace and H. W. Bates. Another important influence at this time was James Bryce, who Junod met in Lourenço Marques in 1895 and with whom he shared an interest in botany. Bryce portrayed Africa as both a menagerie for fauna extinct elsewhere in the world and as an endlessly sprawling, unkempt botanical garden. He attributed this abundance of nature to 'the fact that the country was occupied only by savages, who did little or nothing to extinguish any species nature had planted'. He went on to speculate that this 'may have caused many weak species to survive when equally weak ones were perishing in Asia at the hands of more advanced races of humankind'.[106]

For Bryce and many other Europeans, Africa was a privileged site from which to view the process of natural selection: what had transformed Europe during prehistoric times was taking place before their eyes. The Cape lion had been exterminated in the mid-1860s, the last quagga had died in the Amsterdam zoo in 1883 and the white rhinoceros teetered on the brink of extinction. By the end of the century, the last remnants of vast herds of migrating springbok, gnu and hartebeest were being gathered into game reserves.[107]

Africa's early stage of evolution was particularly visible to entomologists. In many parts of Europe, they watched nervously as the butterflies' original floral habitat was replaced by commercial crops, plantations and forests, or by the new and hardy plant species that followed in the wake of population movements. In sharp contrast, the natural vegetation of Africa and the fauna it hosted seemed to have undergone little change. W.L. Distant believed that, because the vegetation of south-east Africa had been little disturbed by human agency, it harboured species of butterfly that had been destroyed by more industrious races elsewhere in the world. Hence more species of butterfly were found in Southern Africa than in the entire European continent; Britain's sixty-six species were the meagre vestiges of a far richer age. Distant believed that lepidoptery would provide, like paleontology or philology, a window into prehistoric times. 'These pleasant Durban glades were no longer only emporiums to supply museum drawers with specimens, but were full of nature's record of the past – like hieroglyphic writings, but unlike them, most at present we cannot read.' Similarly, a cabinet of butterflies 'now not only exhibits what used simply to be called the "works of nature", but absolutely in many cases shows how nature works'.[108]

Under the influence of Trimen, Distant, Bryce and others, Junod soon started to see natural selection at work, particularly in the fields of Lepidoptera and Hemiptera. In order to distinguish and classify butterflies more clearly, he focused on the reproductive cycle of the insects, particularly the various stages of their metamorphosis. He quickly noted the relationship between insects and a changing rather than pristine environment. In many areas the butterfly *Papilio corinneus* had been decimated because the bush on which it laid its eggs was an important source of indigenous medicines. But the same butterfly proliferated in the Morakwene forest where the underbrush proved impenetrable to human agency. He noted that only the fittest butterflies and moths survived, as spiders, birds, rodents, mantises, lizards and frogs preyed upon them incessantly. Their caterpillars were parasitized by wasps and flies or eaten by human beings.[109] Junod realized that, in order to preserve themselves in such a way as to reproduce their species, insects had evolved various protective mechanisms. To repel their enemies, insects would sting and bite, adopt threatening postures, or emit discharges that were venomous, painful, irritating or malodorous. They had also developed camouflage into a fine art. This was clearly visible when the immature larval form of the Swallowtail butterfly curled itself in such a way as to resemble the droppings of a bird, or when the wattle bagworm hid itself in a sheath of twigs or leaves.

Most startling was the mimicry practised by butterflies and moths. Junod came to see that the survival of egg-laying female butterflies depended on how closely their coloration and design conformed to butterflies considered by predators to be malodorous, bitter-tasting or even toxic. Through this natural selection the animals seemed to practise an involuntary form of deceptive mimicry. Other butterflies developed a protective camouflage when the only survivors over generations were those whose design and colour conformed to elements of the local environment. Through a close comparison of the spectrum of variation in a species, Junod was able to document the degree to which these insects adapted physically to changing floral and faunal kingdoms. When a species of butterfly left its home area and moved to an area to which it was not adapted, he noticed that the butterflies declined in number, strength and size, or were made extinct. He saw how in one area a female butterfly would 'mimic' the colour of a local, poisonous butterfly in such a way as to protect itself against predatory birds. Yet in a neighbouring area, where the birds did not exist, members of this species of butterfly would keep their original colouring and design as they had no need to participate in this 'mimicry'. The same process was observable when the clearing of vegetation caused a poisonous or malodorous butterfly to emigrate or die and render the mimicking species unprotected. Similarly, when a change in climate caused the dark lichen on the pale bark of a tree to die, dark butterflies lost their 'natural' camouflage and became an easy prey to predators.

Through these entomological observations Junod noted the effect of rapid changes in the physical world upon the involuntary mutation, or evolution, of what he started to call 'Darwinian species'. He came to recognize that the process of 'natural selection' in the animal world was the product of many centuries of 'pitiless' struggle.[110] While he could accept Darwinian ideas about the evolution of plants and animals, Junod was, perhaps understandably, only able to apply these ideas to humankind in a selective manner.

For Mary Barber, one of Trimen's circle, the theory of natural selection had fundamentally challenged the idea of divine providence, the Christian tenets of humility, love and compassion and the special place of humanity in the order of the world.[111] For Darwin, natural selection was a purely mechanical phenomenon; devoid of all purpose, it was marked by callous indifference to the human condition. These were the starkly materialist ideas that Carl Vogt had carried to Neuchâtel in the winter of 1862-63 and that Agassiz, Godet and Guyot had so stridently opposed. Agassiz had hammered away at the rivets of Biblical truth that no longer seemed plausible in the light of scientific explanation. But like the geologists who had peopled the Alps with dragons a generation earlier, he refused to remove those rivets and combined his strictly scientific work with an unshakable belief in God's plan. For example, Agassiz's careful observation of the movement of glaciers led him to discover the ice age, but it also led him to see these huge blocks of frozen water functioning as God's ploughs in prehistoric times. In a similar way, he thought God's creation of each individual species of flora and fauna served to magnify his majesty through deep time.[112]

Junod had been raised with this conception of the world. But the view of his father's generation, that the organic world was the product of successive divine creations, was challenged by Junod's entomological observations in Africa and by a new intellectual climate. Within the space of twenty years, the young student who had erected the bust to Agassiz at the Academy in Neuchâtel had come to adopt Darwin's ideas on the dominant role of the environment in natural selection.[113] But although Junod could accept the random and 'pitiless' way in which natural selection affected the animal and plant kingdoms, he found it far more difficult to apply these ideas to laws of human development. If eternal salvation was the aim of life on earth, the process of evolution had to be influenced by individual choice, reason and morality – ultimately by order, progress, and divine purpose. Under the influence of the popular Free Church of Scotland natural scientist and African traveller, Henry Drummond, Junod focused on God's role as an 'Invisible' or 'Spiritual' Environment that encompassed the evolution of organic material. The comparative study of humanity in Africa and Europe showed how mankind had evolved with God's help from a primitive stage, still visible in Africa, to a more advanced phase in Europe. The path of progress was far from smooth but it gave a purpose to the present and instilled the future with the prospect of perfectibility.[114] Through this compromise with Darwinism, Junod was able to retain both his belief in the basic tenets of Christian humanism and his faith in science.

Over time, Junod came to view Africa's isolation from the centres of world enlightenment as both the cause of the continent's retarded material development and its means of protection from the vices of industrial civilization. At the end of the nineteenth century these vices threatened to engulf Africans who, unlike butterflies or beetles, had not been hardened by an extended struggle against invasive marauders. The indigenous Bushmen, Hottentots and Vaalpens were clearly dying out.[115] In a way that echoed Darwin's views in *The Descent of Man*, Junod feared that the black man 'has not been moulded by a civilization where the struggle for survival is pursued without truce or respite'.[116] This was a defenceless world into which a corrupt European civilization had suddenly inserted slavery, alcoholism and greed. Gonorrhea, syphilis, TB, as well as the acquired habits of prostitution, homosexuality and onanism, threatened to curtail the reproduction of indigenous society. Money was eating at the ligaments of tribal controls. Without the ability to defend itself, primitive society was increasingly threatened by a retrograde movement in the process of evolution toward simplification, degeneration and, finally, extinction, like certain entomological and botanical species.[117] In 1898 Junod still vacillated about the physical threat to native peoples brought by the vices of industrialization.[118] As medical evidence pointed towards the possibility of racial extinction, he wrote in 1912 that the situation in South Africa was 'very serious'. Fifteen years later he thought 'the extinction of the race is possible in the long run'.[119]

This threat of extinction was particularly visible to Junod (as it was to Darwin) when 'primitive people' were removed from their natural homes to industrial cities. As an entomologist interested in the geographical distribution of forms, Junod had supplied de Rougement with butterflies for comparison with members of the same species found in Switzerland. Just as the small size of the African variants indicated an incomplete adaptation to the local environment, the physical infirmities of tribesmen in the towns and their degenerate and imitative culture underlined the unnatural nature of this urbanization.[120] In the insalubrious, impersonal environment of the towns, primitive people were exposed to all the vices of European civilization and could deteriorate in strength or even suffer extinction, like the humble butterfly.[121]

Many Social Darwinists regarded this environmental threat to humanity as a natural process, even a form of progress, through which society purified and strengthened itself. For the distinguished hunter and naturalist, F. C. Selous, the unequal 'struggle for survival' between indolent natives and vigorous Europeans seemed to legitimate the seizure of a continent.[122] For men like A. R. Wallace and particularly Ernst Haeckel, civilization seemed to stand in the way of the progress accompanying natural selection. They believed that the extinction of weaker races was inevitable and that the process of natural selection, if left to its true course, would bring about an improvement in the racial stock of humankind.[123] By the end of the century Auguste Forel started to advocate chilling ways of intervening in what Herbert Spencer had called 'the natural process of elimination by which society continually purifies itself'. Forel came to believe that the composition of humanity could be improved by a 'rational selection' and 'a bit by bit ... elimination ... of those who were of limited use to the development of humanity'.[124] In South Africa, the anthropologist Dudley Kidd became an early and influential proponent of eugenics.

Junod refused to explain society in these strictly materialist terms. In a way that conformed more closely to Lamarck's notion of evolution, he believed that a weak or inferior society could change, adapt and fortify itself through rivalry and competition. Like Henry Drummond, Junod was convinced that human beings, particularly missionaries, had a moral duty to intervene on the side of the weak in the unequal struggle for survival. By exercising their superior qualities of compassion and self-sacrifice, human beings could shape and direct the course of evolution in a way that converged with Christian principles. Junod argued that the onus on society to defend the weak was imperative, even in terms of natural selection, because the weak provided the strong with the continuing competition that ultimately ensured their strength and the reproduction of the species.[125]

Slipping again from Darwin's notion of natural selection to Lamarck's concept of adapted evolution, Junod believed that Africans could fortify themselves as a race if they adopted the work habits of their white employers and, particularly, if they took on the beliefs and practices of Christianity.[126] But they needed equally to adopt the scientific rationality and logic brought to Africa by Europeans.[127] The eradication of superstition 'will only be possible under a twofold influence, the increase of the scientific spirit, which will conquer and destroy the absurdities of the animistic magical conceptions involved in these practices, and the Christian Religion'.[128] For Junod, as for a scientist like Edward O. Wilson today, the idea of science divided the world into two unequal camps. 'The fundamental difference between the European and the Bantu mind' was that Europeans have the *'scientific spirit* and the Bantus the *magic conception of Nature'*.[129] For the natives, nature was not governed by impersonal forces that could be observed in an objective and scientific manner; nature was rather linked to spiritual forces that had continually to be propitiated. From this perspective, science and enlightenment were ranged on the side of Europe against the superstition and darkness that pervaded life in Africa.

In the final sermon delivered to his congregation in Môtiers before leaving for Edinburgh and Africa, Junod referred to Immanuel Kant as 'the greatest philosopher of our time'.[130] In a famous essay on the Enlightenment, still the starting point for any university option on the subject, Kant described how society emancipated itself from an immature stage of ignorance and error through the attainment of Reason.[131] This way of thinking was rooted in the ideas of Diderot and Condorcet who equated reason with truth and saw in the Enlightenment a superior stage in the development of humanity. For these *esprits de lumière*, the movement of humanity towards a common, enlightened adulthood held out the possibility of universal equality; but in the process they also tied social difference to distinct, hierarchical stages in the evolution of civilization.[132] Many of these ideas took a racial hue that became stronger as the nineteenth century advanced. In some circles they still hold currency today.[133]

Junod ascribed to this view of science as a touchstone of civilization for, although the natives' concept of science was 'extremely interesting', in the final instance they exhibited 'the want of an enlightened botanical sense'. This was partly because their botanical knowledge was overly utilitarian. In practice, unless related species served as food or medicine, or were known to attract good fortune or ward off evil, they were given only the most generic titles.[134] Thus while Junod was able to distinguish between over twenty types of lichen, the locals merely called these *bulele*. They used the same generic classification when they referred to all ferns indiscriminately as *tsonna*, while Junod assiduously detailed and sorted this order of Filicopsida into different species.[135] Perhaps most importantly, the natives grouped plants according to their external characteristics alone. Because they had never dissected a flower and showed no interest in the morphology of plants or how they lived and reproduced, locals were unable to see or explain the respiratory function of leaves or generalize about the male and female characteristics of plants. This meant that they were unable 'correctly and universally' to recognize the relationship between species and that their broad categorization of plants seldom conformed to the genera defined by 'modern science'. For example, three different kinds of Vernonia were given different names under the local system of classification, although belonging to the same genus, that is, *Ntshontshongori* (*V. cinerea*), *Nkukulashibuya* (*V. perotteti*) and *Hlunguhlungu* (*V. tigna*). On the other hand, plants belonging to entirely different genera could be grouped together in local categories. Hence the *Ndjiba* (*Apalatoa delagoensis*) was grouped with the little Ndjiba, or *Shindjibana*, in a way that obscured its membership (as *Synaptolepis oliveriana* Thymeleaceae) of a completely different plant family.[136]

The zoological knowledge of the indigenous people was, Junod believed, still at a 'very primitive stage'. It was perhaps equal to that of Leviticus, the Old Testament figure associated with taboos.[137] As most insects were not eaten, they were called by only the most general names. All butterflies bore the title *phaphalati* and all the black beetles living in sandy areas were named *shifoufounounou*. Although women of the Nkuna clan distinguished between animals with hoofs and those with paws, they did so merely because the latter were wild beasts whose meat was fit only for men. While it was rare to find a native who could trace a species of moth or butterfly to a particular type of pupa or chrysalis, insect pests or those associated with local 'superstitions' were named, as were all edible insects.[138] Wizards could introduce copridae beetles (*gadlen*) into the bodies of their victims. The long-legged *shitshinyariendo* bird foretold misfortune on the road. The *buwumati* snake and the *nkangu* bird also served to warn of danger. Owls were seen as dangerous familiars, the agents used by witches in the pursuit of evil. Witches employed a range of animal familiars; apparently sent to harm individuals and their families, locals regarded such creatures with a level of suspicion that amounted to a rudimentary form of classification.[139]

Junod believed that the natives' knowledge of botany and zoology exhibited an appreciation of systematics and logic and that it showed a capacity for improvement. But their naming practices differed from one area to another, changed over time and their meaning was infused with superstition and magic. The universal principles of description and organization brought to Africa by Europe were clearly superior to a vision of the environment still dominated by despotic chiefs and mindless customs. Natural selection would run its course as the 'strange, unscientific ideas' of the natives locked in an unequal struggle with the 'scientific knowledge' of the Europeans.[140] 'Let the great modern principle of experimental science be instilled into their minds', advised Junod, 'and all that scaffolding of superstitions, which appear to them most reasonable now, will tumble down at once.'[141] He believed that these 'superstitions will not withstand the test of science and will pass away'.[142]

Imperialism had a strong effect on this binary, hierarchical and racialised arrangement of knowledge. During a furlough in Switzerland in January 1897, Junod presented a paper on 'The Climate of Delagoa Bay' before the Natural History Society of Neuchâtel.[143] The paper was an interesting mixture of themes reminiscent of his student essays. In a way that combined scientific observation with morality and meteorological statistics with political commentary, he spoke of the tripartite conquest that formed the essence of colonialism. The first was the military conquest of Africa. Speaking in the aftermath of the Luso-Gaza war of 1894–95 that had resulted in the burning of Rikatla and his removal from the Portuguese colony, Junod expressed bitterness at the way imperial armies ignored the social and spiritual well-being of indigenous peoples and trampled on their rights. Small wars brought in their wake the unrestricted sale of alcohol and the social degradation of the population. Fortunately, evangelical Christianity counter-balanced the wars of conquest with its 'second crusade'. 'But there is a third conquest that is taking place today from one end of the world to the other':

> it is that of science, that goes out across the continents, gathering its rich harvest of facts, studying geographical and climatic phenomena, collecting new animal forms, observing the customs and languages of primitive races, all in order to one day reconstruct the admirable set of facts, to understand if not the reason behind, at least the way in which humans and things are arranged on our marvelous planet.[144]

This portrayed science as a closed system of knowledge capable of transforming the world into a single, ordered and comprehensible universe dominated by Europe. Mary-Louise Pratt has remarked that taking possession of the world in this manner, without violence and destruction, was part of the utopian, innocent vision of European global authority.[145] It rested on the enlightened reformers' notion of rational knowledge as a liberating, politically neutral force, a way of understanding the world that was as noble, but ultimately as authoritarian, as religion. There was a closed finality in the faith Junod attached to both creeds, ranging light against darkness and reason against ignorance. The contribution of his representation of science to the constitution of power became clear when he described the 'temple of science' as the home to the 'scientific truth' that 'rules the whole of the civilized world'.[146] Or when he wrote that 'the light of knowledge will certainly, in the course of a long time, dissipate all those shadows of animism from the native soul'.[147] In an age preceding mechanized and atomic warfare, industrial genocide, HIV/AIDS and the destruction of the environment, Junod felt that 'to work for science is noble, science has never opposed the betterment and ennoblement of humanity'.[148] At times, he personified science as a living thing.[149] Junod's faith in science led him to believe, like Buxton and Livingstone, that enlightened thought and religion were the keys to progress and the means to regenerate Africa's 'intellectual energies and inventive faculties'.[150]

This path had been visibly trodden in Europe where the remnants of pagan practices provided tangible proof of the need for men of science and letters to complete the modernization of society. 'In all civilized countries, the peasantry or the less cultivated portion of the town population' still adhered to the vestiges of an age of magic and animism.[151] The culture of reason and religion carried by 'the enlightened classes' had yet to conquer the final redoubts of ignorance in Switzerland.[152] Junod saw the incomplete nature of this struggle in the botanical knowledge of European peasants, which he considered less thorough than that of Thonga tribesmen.[153] Even in places like La Chaux-de-Fonds, one of the industrial centres of modern Switzerland, witchcraft was still to be found. In this watchmaking centre in the canton of Neuchâtel, Junod had seen the heart of a goat or sheep pierced by a woman with at least fifty big pins in an attempt to injure her enemy.[154] Animistic beliefs were still current in other parts of western Switzerland where peasants talked to their bees in the same manner as Thonga tribesmen talked to their pigeons.[155] In both Africa and the Alps progress was held in check by customs that few dared to challenge for fear of disturbing the equilibrium of small, isolated communities.[156]

Junod found a common humanity when he compared 'the popular ideas, the superstitions of the less educated classes of our own countries with those of the black Africans'. But there was little equality in his vision of the struggle between a popular culture, based on superstition and mindless custom, and an elite culture built on the body of knowledge associated with modern science and enlightened religion. These 'superstitions' and 'animistic conceptions' were the product of inviolable customs 'transmitted from prehistoric times'. In those parts of Europe 'where education is thinly spread ... they still form the very basis of the mentality'.[157] The form of enlightenment pursued by church and school was based on a combination of religion and science, spirituality and materialism. With the help of this blend of reason and religion, the ruling class had delivered most of Europe from the tutelage of superstition and magic. In Africa, it promised to do the same.[158]

Many Africans must have been perplexed by the manner Junod learned from their ways of examining and organizing nature, and yet dismissed them as 'superstitions'. At the same time his ranking of animals into a hierarchy of species seemed to undermine their utility. By distinguishing between higher and lower species, he found the small animals, such as caterpillars, coleoptera, larvae, termites and locusts 'hideous' and 'nauseating' while locals considered them tasty and nutritious.[159] The obsession with which Junod gathered individual plants and insects must have seemed particularly frivolous to people pitted against nature and concerned to draw from it a raw practicality. They could neither understand his disdain for the prophetic significance of certain animals and plants, nor his reckless insouciance in the face of their supernatural powers.

It did not take much ingenuity to see that the story of creation featured in Junod's textbook on elementary science, published in Thonga in 1904, contradicted that found in the entire existing repertoire of literature in that language. In *Butibi*, Junod sought to provide Thonga scholars with a scientific understanding of the world, but his chapters on geological history and palaeontology inevitably recast as 'superstition' the Mosaic interpretation of creation found in the *buku* and Old Testament publications in Thonga.[160] Despite these contradictions, some young people started to see Junod's way of making sense of nature as a source of power to be harnessed. In 1909 one of Mozambique's earliest nationalist figures, Francisco Albasini's son João, publicly repudiated the old Gaza king Gungunyana and advocated rule by 'the civilized, serious, thoughtful men who truly possess scientific knowledge'.[161] An influential *assimilado* like Raúl Honwana thought his teacher Henri-Alexandre Junod 'a great man of learning' with an impressive 'science laboratory in his house'. In the same way as his teacher, or Albasini and many others like him, Honwana built the fortunes of his powerful family on the enlightenment of science and the revelation of religion.[162]

This notion of science as a closed system of knowledge regulated by precise rules, gave little recognition to the collection of data by Africans and ignored the systems and arrangements through which they ordered knowledge and infused it with meaning. In the process it portrayed modern science as the product of a civilization diffused from Europe to a grateful world. Yet, as I have tried to show in this chapter, one root of modern science has to be located in the messy, everyday encounters between men on the spot such as missionaries, diviners, *nangas*, *gobelas*, rain-makers and Christian converts. Like similar processes in many corners of a world increasingly dominated by

Europe, these African encounters contributed to the triumph of the Linnean model as a 'universal' way of understanding nature. At the same time, this way of seeing contributed to the authority of a 'modern' elite equipped with the skills and energy needed to push both metropole and colony in new and exciting directions.

A web of intellectual, social and institutional forces associated with Western learning and literacy held this idea of 'progress' in place. But in the 1890s the community of readers fed by the Swiss mission was limited in size. The following two chapters examine the historical role of the missionaries in the transcription of the local language and in the spread of literacy. Reading and writing were closely associated with the dissemination of science and Christianity, but the role of literacy was contested and (re)constituted, as was the meaning attributed to these ideas and practices.

Notes

1. *Bulletin de la Mission romande* (*BMR*) (1889) 85,7, August, p. 285.
2. Swiss Mission Archives (SMA), Lausanne. 503. Junod to mission council, 5 July 1889.
3. SMA 503. Junod to mission council, 30 October 1889.
4. As did doctors obliged to live in rural villages by their calling or by their interest in the healing properties of plants. C. Secrétan, 'Savants et chercheurs' in Daniel Baud-Bovy, Paul Bessire, Charly Clerc (eds), *La Vie Romantique au Pays Romand* (Lausanne, 1930), pp. 199, 200; Marc Weidemann, 'Un pasteur-naturaliste du XVIIIe siècle: Elie Bertrand (1713–1797), *Revue Historique Vaudoise* (1986), pp. 63–108. For the same process in Britain, cf. Charles J. Withers, 'Geography, Natural History and the Eighteenth-century Enlightenment: putting the world in place', *History Workshop Journal* (1995) no. 39, spring, p. 154.
5. L. Vulliemin, *Le Doyen Bridel: essai biographique* (Lausanne, 1855), pp. 120–3. On these learned associations, see note 7, below.
6. Benjamin Grivel, 'Alpinisme et Romantisme: le goût de la montagne' in Baud-Bovy et al., *La Vie Romantique*, p. 181.
7. The Société helvétique was founded in 1767 and the Société helvétique de sciences naturelles in 1815. In western Switzerland, the Société de physique et d'histoire naturelle was founded in Geneva in 1790 and the Conservatoire botanique in 1824. In Lausanne, the Société vaudoise de sciences naturelles was established in 1815 as a section of the Société helvétique. A natural history museum was built in 1817 and a scientific journal established in 1841.
8. Eugène Rambert, *La Société vaudoise des sciences naturelles: sa fondation et son développement* (Lausanne, 1876), pp. 8–9.
9. J-J. Rousseau, *Rêveries du promeneur solitaire* (Paris, [1782] 1933), p. 725.
10. Charles Secrétan, 'Albert de Haller' in *Galerie Suisse: Biographies Nationales* (Lausanne, 1876), p. 604; M. Murith, *Le guide du botaniste qui voyage dans le Valais* (Lausanne, 1810), p. 31; Marc Théodore Bourrit (1776) cited in C. Reichler and R. Ruffieux (eds), *Le Voyage en Suisse: anthologie des voyageurs français et européens de la Renaissance au XXe siècle* (Paris, 1998), p. 284. See also 'Introduction,' p. 8.
11. Emile Javelle, *Souvenirs d'un alpiniste* (Lausanne, Paris, [1886] 1920), p. 295.
12. On these ambivalences, see Eugène Rambert, 'Les plantes alpines' (pp. 84, 87, 123) and 'Le chevrier de Praz-de-Fort' [1865] in his *Récits et Croquis* (Lausanne, 1889); Javelle, *Souvenirs d'un alpiniste*, pp. 30, 42; Juste Olivier, *Le Canton de Vaud* (Lausanne, 1837) 1, p. 34.
13. André Bordier, *Voyage pitoresque aux glacières de Savoye* (Geneva, 1773) cited in Reichler and Rufieux, *Le Voyage en Suisse*, p. 342; Horace-Benedicte de Saussure, *Premières ascensions au Mont-Blanc* (Geneva, 1834), p. 129; Rambert, 'Les plantes alpines' pp. 84, 87.
14. For an expansion of these ideas, and much of this section, see P. Harries, 'From the Alps to Africa: Swiss missionaries and the rise of anthropology' in Hellen Tilley and Robert Gordon (eds), *Anthropology, European Imperialism, and the Ordering of Africa* (Manchester, 2007).
15. Marc Théodore Bourrit (1776) cited in *Le Voyage en Suisse*, p. 333; Vuillemin, *Doyen Bridel*, p. 198; Secrétan, 'Savants et Chercheurs' in Baud-Bovy et al. (eds), *La Vie Romantique*, p. 200; Rambert, 'Une bibliothèque à la montagne' in *Récits et Croquis*.
16. Guyot remained at Princeton until his death in 1884. See L. C. Jones, *Arnold Guyot et Princeton* (Neuchâtel, 1929). For Guyot's ideas on Creation, see Ronald L. Numbers, *Creation by Natural Law: Laplace's Nebular Hypothesis in American Thought* (Seattle, WA, and London, 1977), pp. 91–100; David N. Livingstone, *Darwin's Forgotten Defenders: The Encounter between Evangelical Theology and Evolutionary Thought* (Edinburgh, 1987),

pp. 2–23, 77–80.
17 Vogt remained with Agassiz from 1839 to 1844. He then mixed with radical figures in Paris and Geneva before returning to Giessen. The political upheavals of 1848 in Germany caused him to return to Switzerland where he became professor of geology and paleontology in Geneva in 1853 and of comparative anatomy in 1872. See F. Gregory, *Scientific Materialism in Nineteenth Century Germany* (Dordrecht and Boston, MA, 1977), pp. 51–79, 175–8, 197–204. On Desor, see Karl Vogt, *Eduard Desor. Lebensbild eines Naturforschers* (Breslau, 1883); Marc-Antoine Kaeser, *L'Univers du Préhistorien: science, foi et politique dans l'oeuvre et la vie d'Edouard Desor (1811–1882)* (Paris, 2004)
18 S. J. Gould, *Bully for Brontosaurus* (London, 1991), p. 312; Gould, *Hen's Teeth and Horses' Toes* (London, [1983] 1990), p. 108; R. L. Numbers, *The Creationists* (New York, 1992), p. 7. But note that Adam Kuper refers to Agassiz as 'the eccentric Lamarckian biologist of Harvard' in his *The Invention of Primitive Society* (London, 1988), p. 44. Another member of Agassiz's team, the botanist Léo Lesquereux, also moved to an important career in the United States.
19 Frédéric de Rougemont published his lectures on this theme, given at the Neuchâtel Academy in the winter of 1841, as *Fragments d'une histoire de la terre, d'après la Bible, les traditions païennes et la géologie* (Neuchâtel, 1841). See also his *Histoire de la terre d'après la Bible et la géologie* (Paris, 1856). On Guyot, see p. 128 above. Vogt translated Robert Chambers' *Vestiges of Creation* and, following the publication of *The Origin of Species*, became a vigorous Darwinian propagandist, see p. 24 above.
20 Cf. Frédéric de Rougemont, *Le Peuple primitif: sa religion, son histoire et sa civilisation* (Geneva and Paris, 1855–57) 3 vols; also his *L'Homme primitif* (Neuchâtel, 1870). On Desor, see Kaeser, *L'Univers du Préhistorien*, pp. 265–356.
21 M. de Tribolet 'Fritz Tripet: professeur de botanique à l'académie: 1843–1907' in *Bulletin de la société neuchâteloise des sciences naturelles (BSNSN)* (1909), pp. 35, 92, 99; Henri Junod [père], *Sermons* (Neuchâtel, 1884), p. ix.
22 Botanical Conservatory, Geneva; Boissier Herbarium (henceforth BCG. BH), Junod to W. Barbey, 2 January 1892.
23 Charles–Henri Godet collected twelve thousand plant species and in 1852 published the classic *Flore du Jura*, a work supplemented by new findings in 1869. Lionel Gossman, *Basel in the Age of Burckhardt: A Study in Unseasonable Ideas* (Chicago, 2000), pp. 207–8.
24 In a letter to the secretary of the Swiss Mission, dated 30 October 1889, Junod recalled Paul Godet's profound influence on him as both collector and teacher (SMA 503). In a later letter to Philippe Godet, dated 15 October 1912, he mentioned Frédéric, Georges and Philippe as the greatest influences on his life, apart from his father. University and Cantonal Library of Neuchâtel, Philippe Godet papers MS 3164.131. On Paul Godet, see G. Dubois, *Naturalistes Neuchâtelois du XXe siècle* (Neuchâtel, 1976), pp. 49–51. Paul Godet's most famous doctoral student was Jean Piaget, an expert in molluscs who would go on to revolutionize the world of child psychology, see J.-M. Barrelet and A.-N. Perret-Clermont (eds), *Jean Piaget et Neuchâtel: l'apprentie et le savant* (Lausanne, 1996), pp. 35, 57, 97–9; F. Vidal, *Piaget before Piaget* (Cambridge, MA, 1994), pp. 23–33, 116. The role of the Godets in the intellectual life of fin-de-siècle Neuchâtel is remembered in Guy de Pourtalès, *Chaque mouche a son ombre 1881–1919* (Paris, 1980) vol. I, pp. 70–8. In the context of this tightly-woven intellectual world, it is interesting to note that Jean Piaget's father, the historian Arthur Piaget, was a contemporary of Henri-Alexandre Junod and that the two families mixed socially. Jean's parish pastor was Henri-Alexandre's brother, the amateur palaentologist and temperance activist, Charles-Daniel Junod. Archives of the Société de Belles-Lettres, Neuchâtel, Henri-Philippe Junod to Comité des anciens Belletriens, 23 February 1982.
25 The stress on direct observation as a method of teaching went back to Rousseau and the Vaudois pedagogue, H. Pestalozzi. De Tribolet, 'Fritz Tripet,' p. 94. See also the narrative of Louis Favre's popular novel, *Robinson de la Tène* (Neuchâtel, 1875) in which he combined instructive tours through the countryside with lessons on geography, natural history and prehistory.
26 H.-A. Junod, 'Le triton lobé' in *Le Rameau de Sapin* (1879) 13, August, pp. 31–2, 35–6; 'L'Erythronium dens canis. Linné' in *Le Rameau de Sapin* (1882) 16, November, pp. 41–2.
27 Elizabeth Cory Agassiz, *Louis Agassiz: his Life & Correspondence* (Boston, MA, 1885) vol. I, p. 244; L. Agassiz, *Contributions to the Natural History of the United States of America* (1859) vol. I, p. 135, cited in Ernst Mayr, *Evolution and the Diversity of Life* (Cambridge, MA, 1976), p. 256.
28 Ronald L. Numbers, 'Creating Creationism: Meanings and Uses since the Age of Agassiz' in D. N. Livingstone, D. G. Hart and M. A. Noll (eds), *Evangelicals and Science in Historical Perspective* (New York, 1999), p. 235. E. Lurie, 'Louis Agassiz and the idea of evolution', *Victorian Studies* (1959) 3.
29 Frédéric Godet, 'Les six jours de la création' in his *Etudes bibliques* (Neuchâtel and Paris, 1889); Guyot's ideas on Creation are treated in Numbers, *Creation by Natural Law*, note 16 above. One of the pioneers of this 'day-age theory' was Hugh Miller (1802–56) of the Free Church of Scotland, an institution with close links to evangelicals in western Switzerland. See his *The Two Records: Mosaic and Geological* (n. p. , 1854) and *The Testimony of the Rocks* (Edinburgh, 1857). On the tenacity of the 'day-age' theory of Creation, see Numbers, *The Creationists*, pp. 7, 9, 12, 67, 107.

30 V. Rossel, *Histoire littéraire de la Suisse romande* (Neuchâtel, 1903), p. 606.
31 Godet, 'Les six jours', p. 88.
32 Arnold Guyot, *Creation, or, the Biblical Cosmogony in the Light of Modern Science* (New York, 1884), pp. 3–4, 7.
33 'Les obscurantistes, les éteignoirs, la prêtraille,' in H. Junod, *Du manque de pasteurs et des moyens d'y remédier* (Neuchâtel, 1864), pp. 17, 23–4, 29, 40. See also Junod, *Sermons*, p. 186, and Jones, *Arnold Guyot et Princeton*, p. 92 and passim.
34 Junod, *Sermons*, p. ix. See also P. Godet, *Frédéric Godet: 1812–1900* (Neuchâtel, 1913), pp. 82, 334. Henri Berthoud (sen.), *Etude sur les rapports de la cosmogonie mosaïque avec la géologie: précédée de quelques considérations générales sur la Bible et les sciences* (Lausanne, 1859).
35 These included the professor of geology at the Lausanne Academy, Eugène Renevier, who served on the major governing bodies of the mission for almost forty years, and as its president from 1883 to 1906; the naturalist and former missionary in India, Auguste Glardon (a member of the mission council, 1869–73 and 1881–89) and the famous botanist William Barbey (council member from 1891 to 1908). Henri-Alexandre's brother, the future pastor Charles-Daniel Junod, would in his turn become a noteworthy palaeontologist. A. Grandjean, *La Mission romande* (Lausanne, 1917), pp. 268–9, 311–12; Dubois, *Naturalistes Neuchâtelois*, p. 108. For a parallel situation with comparable outcomes, see J. Clifford, *Person and Myth: Maurice Leenhardt in the Melanesian World* (Berkeley and Los Angeles, 1982), pp. 13–15.
36 Cf. Jules Marcou, *Life, Letters and Works of Louis Agassiz* (New York, 1896), pp. 192–3, 218. Numbers distinguishes between 'progressive creationists' and 'strict creationists', see his 'The Creationists' in David N. Lindberg and Ronald L. Numbers (eds), *God and Nature: Historical Essays on the encounter between Christianity and Science* (Berkeley and Los Angeles, 1984), pp. 391–3. See also J. R. Topham, 'Science, natural theology and evangelicalism in early nineteenth century Scotland' in David. N. Livingstone, D. G. Hart and M. A. Noll (eds), *Evangelicals and Science in Historical Perspective*, (New York, 1999), pp. 142–3.
37 C. Dufour and J-P. Haenni, *Musée d'histoire naturelle de Neuchâtel* (Hauterive, Neuchâtel, 1985), p. 46; Dubois, *Naturalistes Neuchâtelois*, p. 51.
38 H–A. Junod (étudiant) 'Les états de larve et de nymphe de l'hyponomeuta stannellus (Thunberg)' in *BSNSN* (1884) 14, pp. 1–9.
39 Cf. Anon., *Henry Appia: sa jeunesse – son activité: souvenirs receuillis* (Geneva, 1905), p. 118. This work provides a sympathetic picture of student life in Neuchâtel's Faculty of Theology in the early 1880s.
40 The essays were published between 1880 and 1887. The praise came from 'J. C. ' [James Chepard], 'Chronique de Neuchâtel' in *Revue de Belles-Lettres* (1883) 11:6, p. 219.
41 See the *Souvenir de l'inauguration du buste élevé à L. Agassiz par la Société de Belles-Lettres dans le bâtiment académique de Neuchâtel, le 12 mai 1887* (Neuchâtel, 1887).
42 Junod, 'Sur quelques larves inédites de Rhopalocères', *BSNSN* (1891–92) 20, p. 18; Junod, 'La faune entomologique de Delagoa – Lèpidoptères', *BSNSN* (1898–99) 27, p. 10; Junod, 'La faune entomologique du Delagoa – coléoptères' *Bulletin de la société vaudoise des sciences naturelles* (henceforth *BSVSN*) (1899) 35, p. 162.
43 Jacques Naef, 'La botanique' in J. Trembley (ed.), *Les savants genevois dans l'Europe intellectuelle: du XVIIe au milieu du XIXe siècle* (Geneva, 1987), pp. 360–7. New plants were still discovered in the Alps de Bex and the Pays d'Enhaut in the early 1880s, see T. Durand and H. Pittier, *Catalogue de la flore vaudoise* (Lausanne, 1882), p. 395. Entomologists like Auguste Forel were also obliged to look beyond Switzerland in their search for new species. Cf. A. Forel, *Mémoires* (Neuchâtel, 1941), pp. 63, 164, 183ff.
44 Cf. P. L. Gorchakovsky, C. Favarger and P. Küpfer, 'Onésime Clerc (1845–1920), naturaliste: un Neuchâtelois en Russie', *Bulletin de la société neuchâteloise des sciences naturelles* (1995), p. 118; Jordí Martí-Henneberg and Anne Radeff, *Henri-François Pittier, 1857–1950* (Lausanne, 1986); Paul Biolley, *Costa Rica et son avenir* (Paris, 1889).
45 Cf. *Formica Berthoudi, Camponotus Eugeniae* and *C. Valdeziae*. Auguste Forel, 'Etudes Myrmécologiques en 1875', *BSVSN* (1876) 14, pp. 33–8; 'Etudes Myrmécologiques en 1879', *BSVSN* (1879) 16, pp. 108–10. Museum of Natural History, Neuchâtel, annual reports for 1884, 1886, 1889; *Nouvelles de nos missionnaires* (1886) 1:9, 9.
46 Rambert, *La Société vaudoise*, pp. 25–6. See also W.-L. Distant, *A Naturalist in the Transvaal* (London, 1892), p. 124; D. E. Allen, *The Naturalist in Britain: a Social History* (London, 1976), pp. 179–93.
47 Naef, 'La botanique', p. 364.
48 J. H. Brooke, *Science and Religion: some historical perspectives* (London, 1991), p. 50.
49 G. Bertoloni, 'Illustratio rerum naturalium Mozambici' in *Novi Commentarii Academiae Scientiarum Instituti Bononiensis* (Bologna) (1849) X; W. C. H. Peters, *Naturwissenchaftliche Reise nach Mossambique in den Jahre 1842–1848* (Berlin, 1861, 1864, 1868), 3 vols.
50 Rose Monteiro had lived and worked with her husband in west-central Africa. See Joachim John Monteiro, *Angola and the River Congo* (London, [1875] new edn 1968). She helped Joachim send dried plants collected in the Lourenço Marques area to Kew Gardens in 1876–78 when he served as the Cape's labour agent in the town. She returned in the late 1880s to Lourenço Marques where she lived on the Polana bluffs, to complete

her husband's work and collect saleable insects. Junod felt that her *Delagoa Bay, its Natives and Natural History* (London, 1891) contained 'much interesting information', although 'without claiming any great scientific accuracy', see *Life of a South African Tribe* (London, 1927) (*LSAT*) II, pp. 147–8, n1. He was more critical of her work in a private letter to Eugène Autran, the conservator of the Boissier Herbarium, 19 May 1892 in BCG.BH. On Rose Monteiro, see Jeanne Penvenne, *African Workers and Colonial Racism: Mozambican Strategies and Struggles in Lourenço Marques, 1877–1962* (Portsmouth, NH, London, 1995), pp. 58–9. On Freire de Andrade as botanist, see Henri-Philippe Junod, *Henri-A. Junod: Missionnaire et Savant, 1863–1934* (Lausanne, 1934), p. 43.

51 See chapter four, p. 107.
52 These included the collections of Boivin, Gueinzius and Krauss, as well as the herbarium of Pierre Verreaux (1807–1873). An associate of Andrew Smith at the Cape, Verreaux became a celebrated dealer in natural history specimens on his return to Paris. H. M. Burdet and A. Chapin, 'Les herbiers de Genève', *Webbia* (1993) 48, pp. 238–9.
53 Cf. his letter to Harry Bolus, February 1890 in University of Cape Town, Bolus Collection, p. 234. Barbey had asked Paul Berthoud to collect plants in the Northern Transvaal just as the region was being scoured by the German botanist R. Rehmann. See his *Polypetalae Rehmannianae* (1887–8).
54 BCG.BH, Junod to Barbey, 30 October 1889; SMA 503 Junod to secretary, 30 October 1889.
55 SMA 503, Junod to secretary, mission council, 30 October, 1889; Junod, 'Correspondences: de Rikatla à Marakouène' *BSNG* (1891) 6, p. 320; Hans Schinz and H.-A. Junod, 'Zur Kenntnis der Pflanzenwelt der Delago-Bay' in *Bulletin de l'Herbier Boissier* (1899) 7, 2. BCG.BH, 'A propos de l'herbier de Shiluvane, apporté en 1893 [sic. 1903] par Mr Henri-Alexandre Junod. '
56 Junod, 'La faune entomologique du Delagoa – lepidoptères', *BSNSN* (1898–99) 27, pp. 186, 189; *Nouvelles de nos missionnaires* (1892) 15,1, p. 11.
57 BCG.BH, Junod to Barbey, 1 September 1891; *Nouvelles de nos missionnaires* (1892) 15,1.
58 BCG.BH, Junod to Barbey, 25 July and 4 October 1891. I have been unable to find this species as it does not conform to the rules of the International Code for Botanical Nomenclature.
59 BCG.BH, Junod to E. Autran, 15 February and 5 September 1892. Junod had in fact learned to press and dry plants from a Paris Geographical Society publication for travellers.
60 Junod, 'Correspondances', Rikatla, 23 November 1891, *BSNG* (1892–93) vii, p. 531; BCG.BH, Junod to Autran 19 May and 5 September 1892; note entitled 'Collections Junod à vendre', 15 March 1904.
61 BCG.BH, Junod, 'A propos de l'herbier de Shilouvâne'; Junod, *LSAT*, II, p. 238.
62 BCG.BH, Junod to Barbey, 15 January 1903 and 24 May 1906; Junod to Schinz, 20 October 1903; Junod to Beauverd, 2 March 1910.
63 BCG.BH, Junod to Barbey, 25 February 1898. In 1891 F. R. R. Schlechter (1872–1925) embarked on extensive botanical voyages in Southern Africa, including Mozambique. F. A. Mendonça, 'Botanical collectors in Mozambique' in A. Fernandes (ed.), *Comptes rendus de la IVe réunion plénière de l'association pour l'étude taxonomique de la flore d'Afrique tropicale à Lisbone et Coimbra* (Lisbon, 1962).
64 BCG.BH, Junod to Maurice Barbey, 25 April 1919; CBG.HB, 'Compte des plantes de l'herbier sudafricain de H. A. Junod expédié à l'herbier Boissier', annexure III attached to Junod to Prof. Chodat, 3 January 1921. See also Junod's original botanical register, lodged in the Boissier Herbarium.
65 Cf. J. Thunberg and N. L. Burman, Allioni, Houttuyn, Van Royen and others.
66 Junod, *LSAT* II, p. 147 n. 1.
67 Schinz and Junod, 'Zur Kenntnis der Pflanzenwelt', continued in *Mémoire de l'herbier Boissier* (1900) 10.
68 Cf. Hans Schinz, 'Beiträge zur Kenntnis der Afrikanischen Flora', *Bulletin de l'herbier Boissier* (1896) 4; (1896) 5 and (1899) 7. J. Burtt-Davy was less glowing in his praise. Although he recognized the pioneering work of Junod around Shiluvane, Burtt-Davy found his plant specimens 'often scrappy and unfit for determination'. J. Burtt-Davy, 'First annotated catalogue of the vascular plants of the Transvaal and Swaziland' in *Report of South African Association for the Advancement of Science* (*RSAAAS*) (1908), p. 232.
69 See the *Index Kewensis*. Also the entry on Junod in M. Gunn and L. E. Codd (eds), *Botanical Exploration of Southern Africa: an Illustrated History* (Cape Town, 1981), p. 203.
70 Junod, *LSAT* I, p. 1.
71 Junod, 'Correspondence: de Rikatla à Marakouène', p. 322.
72 Trimen described *Papilio junodi* in the *Transactions of the Entomological Society of London* (1893), p. 138. The genus was later changed from *Papilio* to *Graphium* and the butterfly is now known as *Graphium junodi*, a Swordtail (Trimen, 1893). Junod, 'La faune entomologique – lèpidoptères', pp. 180, 184, 200, 219, 224, 240. E. L. L. Pringle, G. A. Hening and J. B. Ball (eds), *Pennington's Butterflies of Southern Africa* (Cape Town, 1978, 2nd edn, 1994), pp. 301, 306.
73 In December 1891 Junod claimed to have amassed a collection of beetles and butterflies worth almost £200, CBG. HB, Junod to Barbey, 2 December 1891. On his sales to Trimen, see South African Museum, Trimen letterbooks, 31 July 1890 to 17 February 1892. Junod's gifts and sales of butterflies were noted in the Annual Reports of the Natural History Museum, Neuchâtel for 1892, 1894 (SF50 for 'insects') and 1911. Anon., *Le musée d'histoire naturelle* (Neuchâtel, 1899), p. 40, mentions receiving a 'rich collection' of butterflies from Junod at Rikatla.

74 This collection was bought by the Hon. Walter Rothschild who opened the museum in 1889. Today it is in the Natural History Museum, London. W.-L. Distant, *Insecta Transvaaliensia: a contribution to the entomology of South Africa* (London, 1924), p. 99 and plate xvi.
75 SMA 303/11C, P. Loze to mission secretary, 5 June 1934.
76 In 2002 Richard Gallon discerned a new tarantula genus, *Harpactirinae*, in which he grouped the species *Augacephalus junodi*. This species had earlier been named *Pterinochilus junodi* (Simon 1904). *Bulletin of the British Arachanological Society* (2002) 12, 5.
77 Junod, 'La faune entomologique – coléoptères', pp. 132, 163, 177; Junod, 'Rikatla à Marakouène', p. 323.
78 E. Bugnion, 'Remarques supplémentaires' following Junod, 'La faune entomologique – coléoptères,' p. 189.
79 Junod and O. de Schulthess-Schindler, 'La faune entomologique du Delagoa – *orthoptères*', *BSVSN* (1899) 132; Junod and A. L. Montandon, 'La faune entomologique du Delagoa – *hémiptères*', *BSVSN* (1899) 132; Junod and A. de Schulthess-Schindler, 'La faune entomologique du Delagoa – *hyménoptères*', *BSVSN* (1899) 133.
80 Dr Griffini, 'Sui Cybiser raccolti dal Rev. Junod a Delagoa', *Boll. dei Musei di Turino* XIII (1898) N° 325; Dr Regimbart, 'Monogr. Gyrinidae', *Ann. Soc. Entomologique de France* (1893); Regimbart, *Dytiscidae et Gyrinidae d'Afrique et de Madagascar* (Brussels, 1895).
81 L. Péringuey, 'A descriptive catalogue of the coleoptera of South Africa. Pt II', *Transactions of the South African Philosophical Society* (henceforth *TSAPS*) (1896) 7, pp. 113–480; Péringuey, 'Descriptive catalogue of the coleoptera of South Africa – part III', *TSAPS* (1897) 10, 1, p. 23; Péringuey, 'Fourth contribution to the South African coleopterous fauna,' *TSAPS* (1892) 6, 2, pp. 95–6. Péringuey, 'Some new coleoptera collected by Rev Henri A. Junod at Shiluvane, near Leydsdorp, in the Transvaal', in *Trans. Novitat Zoologicae* (1904) 11, pp. 448–50. W. F. Purcell, 'On the scorpions, Solifugae and a trapdoor spider collected by the Rev. Henry A. Junod at Shiluvane near Leydsdorp in the Transvaal', *Trans. Novitat Zoologicae* (1903) 10, 2. For the ants, cf. *Carebara junodi* Forel (1904) and *Monomorium junodi* Forel (1910). In 1894 Forel determined *Monomorium delagoense*, *Tetramorium delagoense*, *Camponotus delagoensis*, *Crematogaster transvaalensis*, *Crematogaster delagoensis* and *Opthalmopone Berthoudi*.
82 He envisaged reworking published articles into chapters on the region's climate, flora, butterflies, coleoptera, orthoptera and hemiptera. CBG.HB, Junod to Autran, 19 February 1900. On the National exhibition, see H. Büchler, *Drei Schweizerische Landesausstellungen: Zurich 1883, Genf 1896, Bern 1914* (Zurich, 1970).
83 The beetles included *Eudema Rikatlense* (found in the small lake behind the hill on which the mission was built) and *Graphopterus antiokanus*. The butterflies, *Papilio junodi* (Trimen), *Paralethe dendrophilus junodi* (Van Son), *Acrae nohara junodi* (Oberthür). He raised an emperor moth, *Gonimbrasia belina junodi* (Oberthür), from the *mopane* worm; another moth, *Eumeta Junodi*, from the larval form while on holiday at Howick. He named another moth after his wife Emilie (*Chalia Emiliae*). E. L. L. Pringle, G. A. Henning and J. B. Ball (eds), *Pennington's Butterflies of Southern Africa* (2nd edn, Cape Town, 1994) p. 33. E. C. G. Pinhay, *Moths of Southern Africa* (Cape Town, 1975), pp. 39, 114. For some of the other insects, including ants, rove beetles, assassin bugs and owlflies, see *Bulletin of the American Museum of Natural History* (1921–2) XLV; Péringuey, 'Fifth contribution to the South African coleopterous fauna', *TSAPS* (1892) 6:2, pp. 248, 326–7, 479; Distant, 'Descriptions of new species of Hemiptera-Heteroptera' *Annals and Magazine of Natural History* (1898) 2; Junod, 'La faune entomologique – lépidoptères', p. 233.
84 *Crematogaster liengmei, Pheidole liengmei* and *Tetraponera liengmei*. Peringuey gave the name *Bostrichophorus liengmei* Pér. to a beetle found by Liengme on the banks of the Limpopo. Junod, 'La faune entomologique – coléoptères', p. 165.
85 The molluscs were mainly giant land snails (Achatina). See also the species *Lentorbis junodi* (Connolly, 1922), *Ferrissia junodi* (Connolly, 1925), *Hippeutis junodi* (Connolly, 1922) and *Haloschizopera junodi* (Monard, 1935).
86 In this way, for instance, it was discovered that two of the reptiles sent from Lesotho in 1907 by Mlle Jacot represented new species.
87 Junod, 'Le climat de la baie', p. 78. He was correct here, for scientists are turning increasingly to old museum collections to study the variation in species and to gauge historical changes in the ecological balance. See also the reference to Mlle Jacot in the previous footnote.
88 Junod, *LSAT* I, pp. 65–6; II, p. 332.
89 Steven Shapin, 'The invisible technician' in *American Scientist* (1989) 77, November-December.
90 University of South Africa (UNISA), Junod Collection (JC) 3. 3 'Elias, un ancien de l'église africaine'; Junod, 'La faune entomologique – lèpidoptères', pp. 179, 223.
91 Emphasis in the original. Junod, 'Les Ba-Ronga: étude ethnographique sur les indigènes de la baie de Delagoa', *BSNG* (1898) 10, 21, p. 419; Junod, 'La faune entomologique – coleoptères', pp. 170, 176, 177, 184; Junod, *LSAT* II, pp. 344–45.
92 Junod, *LSAT* II, pp. 81–3, 344.
93 Junod, *LSAT* II, p. 344.
94 Junod, *LSAT* II, p. 302.
95 Junod, *LSAT* II, pp. 329–30. This form of classification is still employed today, see C. A. Liengme, 'Plants

used by the Tsonga people of Gazankulu' in *Bothalia* (1981) 13, 3 and 4, pp. 513–14.
96 Junod, 'Rikatla à Marakouène,' p. 320; Junod, *LSAT* II, pp. 332, 345, 589; Junod, 'Les Ba-Ronga', p. 22. For a good introduction to the disordered history of European plant taxonomy, see Anna Pavord, *The Naming of Names: The Search for Order in the World of Plants* (London, 2005).
97 BCG.BH, Junod to Barbey, 2 January 1892.
98 BCG.BH, 'Botanique indigène', attached to Junod to Barbey, 16 October 1891. Junod, *LSAT* II, pp. 328, 435ff, 482, 657; Junod, 'The best means of preserving the traditions and customs of the various SA native races', *Report of the South Africa Association for the Advancement of Science* (1907), p. 149.
99 BCG.BH, Junod to Autran, 1 December 1896. He sent plants known to supply antidotes against migraines, gonorrhoea and other maladies to Mr Chodat in Geneva for medical analysis. See the archives of the Ethnographic Museum of Neuchâtel for lists of plants making up the 'pharmacy of the Ba-Ronga' and a 'collection of native medicinal roots'.
100 Junod declined, for instance, to take up Barbey's suggestion that coffee could be established as a cash crop in the Delagoa Bay area, see BCG.BH, Junod to Barbey, 5 July 1893.
101 Junod, 'Une promenade aux environs de Rikatla' in Anon., *Chez les Gouamba: glanures dans le champ de la Mission romande* (Lausanne, n.d., approx 1893), p. 11.
102 UNISA.JC: 6. Conférences: à Neuchâtel, 1897.
103 Henri-Philippe Junod, *Henri-A Junod: Missionnaire et Savant 1863–1934* (Lausanne, 1934), p. 64.
104 Junod, 'La faune entomologique – coleoptères', pp. 172, 175, 186.
105 Ibid., p. 178.
106 J. Bryce, *Impressions of South Africa* (3rd edn, London, 1899), p. 17.
107 Cf. A. H. Keane's entry on 'South Africa' in the *Encyclopaedia Britannica* (1902) XXXII, p. 711.
108 Distant, *Naturalist in the Transvaal*, pp. 41, 124–5.
109 Junod 'La faune entomologique – lèpidoptères', pp. 228, 242; Junod, *LSAT* II, pp. 80–1; Junod, 'Promenade aux environs de Rikatla'.
110 Junod, 'La faune entomologique – lèpidoptères', p. 232; Junod, *LSAT* I, p. 65.
111 Compare M. E. Barber on 'a divine guardianship, a Protecting Power, which cares and provides for all' in her 'On the structure and fertilization of Liaris Bowkeri', *Journal of the Linnean Society* (1869), 5, pp. 470–1, with her starkly Darwinian approach in 'On the peculiar colours of animals in relation to habits of life', *Transactions of the South African Philosophical Association* (1877–78), 1:4, pp. 27ff. On Barber, see William Beinart, 'Men, Science, Travel and Nature in the Eighteenth and Nineteenth-century Cape,' *Journal of Southern African Studies* (1998) 24, 4, pp. 792–9.
112 S. J. Gould, *Hen's Teeth*, p. 81.
113 Agassiz held these views until his death in 1873. In 1908, on receipt of Mrs Barbey's translation of a work by A. R. Wallace, Junod acknowledged that he found the theory of evolution to be 'true and fruitful' ('juste et féconde'). BCG.BH, Junod to Barbey, 9 October 1908.
114 Junod, 'God's Ways in the Bantu Soul', *International Review of Missions* (1914) 111, pp. 96–7. On Henry Drummond's fusion of science and religion, see James R. Moore, 'Evangelicals and Evolution', *Scottish Journal of Theology* (1985) 38. Drummond's most influential work, which sold 70,000 copies in five years and was published in multiple editions, was *Natural Law in the Spiritual World* (London, [1883] 29th edn, 1890).
115 On the extinction of the Bushmen and the Vaalpens, see A. C. Haddon, Presidential address to Section H – Anthropology – of the British Association for the Advancement of Science, *Report of the 75th meeting*, 1905, pp. 521, 525.
116 Junod, 'Les Ba-Ronga', p. 114. See the section of chapter seven entitled 'On the extinction of the races of men' in Darwin, *The Descent of Man* (London, 1874). These ideas anteceded Darwin, cf. A. M. Kass and E. H. Kass, *Perfecting the World: The life and times of Dr. Thomas Hodgkin, 1798–1866* (New York, 1988), p. 392. In 1865 Tiyo Soga criticized the notion of social and physical degeneration in 'What is the destiny of the Kaffir race?' in D. Williams (ed.), *The Journal and Selected Writings of the Rev. Tiyo Soga* (Cape Town, 1983), p. 178.
117 Junod, *LSAT* I, p. 10; Junod, *LSAT* II, pp. 96–7, 111, 166.
118 See the contradictory passages in 'Les Ba-Ronga,' pp. 7 and 486.
119 Junod, *LSAT* II, pp. 541, 629–30. On the medical evidence, see J. Bruce-Bays, 'The injurious effects of civilisation upon the physical condition of the native races of South Africa' and J. A. Mitchell, 'The growth of the native races of the Cape Colony and some factors affecting it', both in *Report of the South African Association for the Advancement of Science* (1908). Junod was a vice–president of section F of this association.
120 F. de Rougemont, 'Catalogue des lépidoptères du Jura neuchâtelois' in *BSNSN* (1900–1901) 29, pp. 291, 307.
121 Junod, *LSAT* I, p. 10.
122 F. C. Selous, *Sunshine and Storm in Rhodesia* (New York, [1896] 1969), p. 67, cited in Brooke, *Science and Religion*, p. 295.
123 Jacques Roger, 'L'Eugénisme, 1850–1950' in his *Pour une histoire des sciences à part entière* (Paris, 1995), pp. 411–12.

124 Auguste Forel, *Mémoires* (Neuchâtel, 1941), p. 167. The quote from Spencer is in Karl Degler, *In Search of Human Nature: the decline and revival of Darwinism in American social thought* (New York, 1991), p. 11. Until recently, August Forel was regarded as a sufficiently neutral public figure for the SF1000 note to carry his image.
125 Junod, 'Les Ba-Ronga', p. 116; Junod, *LSAT* I, p. 11; *LSAT* II, p. 632. For Henry Drummond's views on this issue, see his *The Ascent of Man* (London, 1894) and Brooke, *Science and Religion*, pp. 16–17, 311.
126 See p. 82.
127 Junod, 'Les Ba-Ronga', pp. 115–16.
128 Junod, *LSAT* II, p. 536.
129 Junod, 'The Magic conception of nature amongst Bantus', *South African Journal of Science* (1920) 17, p. 79. Italics in the original.
130 UNISA. Junod Collection. Seven Sermons. Sermon given at Môtiers, 1 January 1887 and Couvet, 25 January 1887. See also Cantonal and Public Library, Neuchâtel, Philippe Godet Collection MS 3164.131, Junod to P. Godet, 15 October 1912. On the wider influence of Kant's teachings on aspirant missionaries in Neuchâtel, see H. Perregaux, *Edmond Perregaux missionnaire: d'après sa correspondence 1868–1905* (Neuchâtel, 1906), p. 70.
131 Immanuel Kant, 'What is Enlightenment?' in Peter Gay (ed.), *The Enlightenment: A Comprehensive Anthology* (New York, 1973), p. 385. On the racial tenor of Kant's approach, see Wolbert Schmidt, *Afrika im Schatten der Aufklärung. Das Afrikabild bei Immanuel Kant und Gottfried Herder* (Bonn, 2000).
132 Jacques Roger, 'La lumière et les lumières' in his *Pour une histoire des sciences*.
133 Cf. David Elliston Allen, who writes, 'a taste for nature, in fact, seems to arise of its own accord at a certain point in the maturing of civilizations'. *The Naturalist in Britain: a Social History* (London, 1976), p. 27.
134 Cf. Junod, 'Les Ba-Ronga', p. 16; BCG.BH, Junod, 'Botanique indigène'.
135 Junod, 'Rikatla à Marakouène', p. 320; BCG.BH, Junod, 'Botanique indigène'; Schinz and Junod, 'Zur Kenntnis der Pflanzenwelt', p. 888.
136 Cf. Junod, *LSAT* II, pp. 328–32.
137 Junod, *LSAT* II pp. 344–5.
138 Junod, 'La Faune entomologique – coléoptères', p. 184; Junod, 'Les Ba-Ronga', pp. 419–20; Junod, *LSAT* I, p. 65; Junod, *LSAT* II, pp. 80, 83, 341–2.
139 Junod, *LSAT* II, pp. 336, 512, 515.
140 Junod, *LSAT* I, pp. 9, 166, 521..
141 Junod, 'The best means', p. 143.
142 Junod, *LSAT* I, pp. 9, 521.
143 Later published as Junod, 'Le climat de la baie de Delagoa', *BSNSN* (1896–97) 25.
144 'Le climat de la baie de Delagoa', p. 77. See also LSAT I, pp. 541–2.
145 Mary Louise Pratt, *Imperial Eyes: travel writing and transculturation* (London, 1992), pp. 39, 57.
146 Junod, 'The best means of preserving', p. 142; Junod, 'La faune entomologique' *BSNSN* p. 178; Junod, *LSAT* I, p. 7.
147 Junod, 'The best means of preserving', p. 143.
148 Junod, *LSAT* I, pp. 10–11.
149 Junod, *LSAT* II, p. 301.
150 Junod, 'Les Ba-Ronga', p. 248. See also J. M. MacKenzie (ed.), *Imperialism and the Natural World* (Manchester, 1990), pp. 6–7.
151 Junod, 'Best means of preserving', p. 143.
152 Junod, 'Sorcellerie d'Afrique et sorcellerie d'Europe: étude d'ethnographie comparée', *Foi et Vie* (1910) 13, p. 622.
153 Junod, *LSAT* II, p. 332.
154 Junod, 'The Magic conception of nature', p. 84.
155 Junod, *LSAT* II, pp. 336n1, 345–6n1.
156 Junod, 'Les Ba-Ronga,' p. 246; Junod, *LSAT* II, p. 150.
157 Junod, 'Les Ba-Ronga,' p. 246; Junod, 'Sorcellerie d'Afrique', p. 622.
158 Junod, 'The Magic conception of nature', p. 84.
159 Junod, *LSAT* I, p. 65; *LSAT* II, pp. 80–2.
160 H. A. Junod, *Butibi: Notions of Elementar[y] Science; Noçoes de Sciencia Elementár* (Lausanne, 1904). An enlarged edition appeared in Ronga in 1928, *Vutivi: Notions of Elementary Science* (Lausanne, 1928). The New Testament was translated into Gwamba in 1894 and the full Bible into Thonga in 1907.
161 João Albasini, editorial in *O Africano*, 22 May 1909, cited by J. Penvenne, 'Principles and passions: capturing the legacy of João dos Santos Albasini', paper presented to the African Studies Centre, Boston University, 1991.
162 Allen Isaacman (ed.), *The Life History of Raúl Honwana: an inside view of Mozambique from colonialism to independence, 1905–1975* (Boulder, CO and London, 1988), p. 58.

6
Language

And the whole earth was of one language, and of one speech.
(Genesis 11:1)

The Mission of the Free Church of the Canton of Vaud entered the northern Transvaal along a linguistic corridor linking Sotho-speaking communities in the Caledon river valley and Drakensburg mountains with those in the north. In the 1860s Adolphe Mabille believed that linguistic forms related to Sotho, the language transcribed by the PEMS, were spoken 'from Lesotho to the sources of the Nile'.[1] When he and Paul Berthoud eventually arrived in the Spelonken foothills of the Zoutpansberg in 1873 they thought they were entering an area in which people spoke Sotho – or at least Pedi, a related language form.

As described in chapter three, the Spelonken hills had been settled over the previous forty years by immigrants from the coastal plain. Initially trickling eastwards as traders operating from the vicinity of Lourenço Marques and Inhambane, these people had been pursued into the Transvaal by the triad of war, famine and disease. Many of them settled under local chiefs in the Transvaal and gradually adopted the language and culture of their hosts. But several thousand maintained an independent existence by occupying the low-lying areas made insalubrious by malarial mosquitoes and tste-tse fly. In these areas they gathered in scattered settlements under their own small chiefs. Those who placed themselves under João Albasini were able to move to the healthier hill country of the Spelonken where they either lived on his sprawling estate at Goedewensch or in its vicinity.

The Berlin and Dutch Reformed missionaries working in the region had not extended their work to these outsiders, partly because they spoke what a Cape missionary referred to as 'Cafre ... an extremely difficult language'.[2] The Swiss missionaries at first thought the local language a mixture of 'cafre' and 'séchuana' but believed the immigrants could understand South Sotho.[3] Because of this, when Mabille and Berthoud returned to Lesotho, they left the new mission field in the hands of Asser Segagabane, Eliakim Matlanyane and Josias Molepo. These Basotho evangelists had been educated in the language employed by the PEMS and their training in South Sotho strongly influenced the linguistic policy of the Swiss mission in its early years.

On their return to Basutoland, Mabille and Berthoud advised the PEMS to take over the new mission field which, they envisaged, 'in all forms, language, literature, native workers to train, would always more or less depend on the Lesotho mission'.[4] But the establishment of a separate Vaudois mission and the fractious relations between the French missionaries and the Boers caused the PEMS to hand over the new mission field to the Swiss. Berthoud asserted that his mission would have little difficulty in preaching and teaching in South Sotho and he envisaged that it would become 'a sort of linguistic province of the Lesotho mission'.[5] He was particularly anxious that the Swiss would not have to invest both time and money in linguistic work that could more profitably be used in spreading the gospel. He also believed that by using South Sotho as a *lingua franca*, the mission would be able to operate in areas south of the Spelonken where people spoke a related language.

Berthoud could only imagine the linguistic condition of his mission field. When he and Creux moved to the Spelonken in mid-1875 they discovered that the rudimentary taxonomy used by philologists in South Africa belied the linguistic complexity of the situation.[6] They came to realize that the immigrants in the Spelonken could not be slotted into the existing framework of linguistic studies. The community in which they found themselves was made up of a *pot pourri* of refugees drawn from the length and breadth of coastal south-east Africa. These people shared no common language and lived in scattered villages independent of one another. They had few important chiefs and no concept of themselves as a community. Nevertheless, the indigenous peoples of the area defined these newly arrived immigrants as a group. By applying to them a number of generic terms, the local people attempted to exclude, as foreigners, those immigrants who had refused to join their ranks. Sotho-speakers called them 'MaKoapa', the Boers referred to them as 'knobnoses', while others named the immigrants 'MaGwamba' after an eighteenth-century chief who had lived on the east coast near Inhambane.[7]

Separated from the signs, symbols and imagery that had structured their lives in Europe, the missionaries built on some of the translations undertaken by the Basotho evangelists. With the help of his 'Makoapa' domestics and Eliakim Matlanyane, Paul Berthoud translated into 'sekoapa' both the Lord's Prayer and the first of a series of hymns.[8] The missionaries soon came to see that *Koapa* was a Sotho term applied to the immigrants arriving from the east and they adopted what they saw as the more authentic term for these people and their language: 'Gwamba'.[9]

Within weeks of her arrival, Eugénie Berthoud, Paul's wife, wrote that the local language was 'Shigwamba ... [of which] ... we cannot understand a single word ... [as it] ... is completely different from seSotho'. Clinging to the missionaries' desire for a vehicular language and trapped within the bounds of existing linguistic taxonomy, she speculated that Shigwamba was 'more related to the Zulu of Natal' than to the South Sotho of Basutoland.[10] But within three months it became clear to the missionaries that Shigwamba did not fit into the known schema of African languages. Paul Berthoud informed his church headquarters that 'we speak Sesotho but no-one understands us. We must learn [what in South Sotho is called] Sekoapa', the language of the Gwambas.[11]

Well over a year after his arrival Paul Berthoud was still evangelizing in South Sotho and using an interpreter when addressing an audience.[12] In July 1877 when François Coillard passed through Valdezia, he remarked that people spoke 'sessouto', sang the hymns of his Paris Missionary Society and that the evangelists had named their village 'Lesotho'. Berthoud and Creux were fully occupied with the establishment of their station and only gradually became aware of the linguistic complexity of their situation. In February 1877 Creux wrote that he 'had been able to spend more time in studying ChiGwamba. It is very difficult to learn a language whose grammar one has gropingly to create. And it would be even more laborious if we did not know Sesotho.'[13] Disheartened by the difficulties presented by this new language, Berthoud wrote almost a year later that 'Sigwamba is neither Cafre nor Setchwana, it is a cousin, perhaps a brother of Zulu' and he suggested replacing the Paris Evangelical Missionary Society's South Sotho as the basic reference for Shigwamba with the Zulu drawn up by the American Board missionaries in Natal.[14] Nevertheless, by May 1878 Berthoud reported that he and Creux had produced some hymns and a few translations, and were about to start a book in Shigwamba.

Despite these small beginnings of a distinctly local, written language, the mission continued to operate largely in South Sotho. There were several reasons for this. The proliferation of phonetic systems and mission orthographies presented a major obstacle to the recording of a new language. There was no single method of representing the individual sounds that constituted local speech forms in the characters of the Latin alphabet. The alphabet with which the missionaries were familiar is made up of twenty-six letters (or signs), each of which constitutes one basic sound (or phoneme) in a language. The problem was that Gwamba, like all languages, had more phonemes than letters in this alphabet. The English language, with which we are familiar, transcribes about 40 phonemes with only 26 letters. This means that the same sign carries different phonemes (cat, precise), different signs might bear the same phoneme (cat, key), or a combination of signs might be used to create phonemes (chicken). At the same time, the inflection given to a combination of signs might change the meaning of a written word (to read or have read; to desert, a desert, his just desert). Rules determine the vowel length or stress in a word (desert, dessert). Ascribing a sign to a phoneme is therefore not just a case of putting sounds to paper or, as is popularly thought, transcribing or 'recording' a language. Merely in terms of phonology and orthography, transcribing a language requires the taking of a number of decisions and a good deal of common agreement.[15] This became apparent to the Swiss as they discovered the complexity of the linguistic situation in the Spelonken. But as they and other missions advanced into new areas, individuals and stations developed a stake in specific language forms; the transcription of phonemes and grammatical rules became a source of friction as linguistic decisions had clear political consequences.

Defining a Written Language

Most immediately, the linguistic problems facing the Swiss in the Spelonken were compounded by the composition of the mission party. About twenty PEMS Christians, born and educated in Lesotho, had accompanied Creux and Berthoud. These people acted as a link between the missionaries and the local population and, although they undertook a few translations, taught their congregants to read in South Sotho. In consequence, a small number of literate Gwamba converts had a stake in the preservation of South Sotho, as did local minorities such as the Lemba and 'Pedi,' or those who had learned the language during their travels. The Swiss had also grown fond of South Sotho, a language Berthoud considered 'elegant and harmonious' in comparison with the 'much poorer, more nasal, heavier' Gwamba language. Abandoning South Sotho, Berthoud thought, was 'almost heart-breaking'.[16]

The Swiss were also extremely loath to abandon the Sotho literature on which the Paris Mission had been working for almost forty years. The long investment of their colleagues and compatriots in Lesotho was about to bear fruit as, in the space of six years (1876–81), they would produce a vocabulary, two grammars and the entire Bible in South Sotho. But the inability of the missionaries to converse with the inhabitants of the Spelonken in their own language hampered evangelical work. This was poignantly expressed by a Gwamba woman, addressing Eugénie Berthoud, who complained that 'I do not know how to pray. If God were able to understand Shigwamba I would try, for I cannot speak to him in Sesotho.'[17] The missionary's wife, who seemed unaware of the political implications of this statement, merely encouraged the woman to improve her Sotho.

Paul Berthoud was more aware of the danger of creating a written language used only by the mission. South Sotho would serve as a *lingua franca* for the church, and as a source of power for the literate elite but, like Latin in medieval Europe or French in Norman England, it would separate the mission and its converts from the vast majority of the local population. With their time consumed by the physical establishment of the mission station, Berthoud and Creux had to rely on the Gwamba linguistic skills of their Basotho evangelists, Asser Segagabane and Eliakim Matlanyane. As Berthoud came to grips with the local language, he saw that Matlanyane was 'massacring the language in an unimaginable way', and he turned increasingly for help to Spelonken converts who had become proficient in South Sotho. As most of these men were immigrants from the coastal plain, the speech forms of that region exerted a strong influence on the written language of the Spelonken. Mbizana (soon to become Gideon Mpapele) particularly helped Paul Berthoud with his sermons and translations. His home language, the Hlengwe spoken in the coastal areas to the north of the Limpopo, inevitably influenced Berthoud's linguistic work.[18] Ernest Creux, on the other hand, came to rely increasingly on Yosefa and Yacob Mhalamhala who spoke the language form called Djonga, used by the Khosa chiefdom on the northern bend in the Inkomati river.[19]

From their base in the Spelonken, Berthoud and Creux gradually became aware, through information brought to them by hunters, traders and migrant workers, of the existence in the Transvaal of other immigrant communities from the east coast. These lived in independent chiefdoms strung out along the Levubu river as well as to the south of the Spelonken where communities had settled under Modjadji and other *Pedi* chiefs. The Swiss missionaries rapidly laid claim to this entire linguistic diaspora. Their desire to evangelize these people, whom they referred to increasingly as 'Gwamba', was encouraged by the willingness of the Berlin missionaries to take charge of those people living on Swiss mission stations who did not speak Gwamba – what Paul Berthoud referred to as the *bismarkism* of his German neighbours. This occurred as Venda- and North Sotho-speakers left to join the Lutheran and Dutch Reformed missionaries who had a greater experience of working with their linguistic communities. In 1879 the Swiss and Berlin Mission Societies formally recognized this situation when they divided the mission field along linguistic lines: the Berliners would work with Venda- and North Sotho-speakers and the Swiss would confine their activities to those who spoke Gwamba.[20]

This linguistic separation of the Christian community became more pronounced in December 1883, when the Sotho-speaking evangelists employed by the Swiss returned to Basutoland and their place was taken by Gwambas trained at Morija by the PEMS. As the Gwamba language came to dominate the outstations of the Swiss Mission, increasing numbers of North Sotho- and Venda-speakers left the mission to join neighbouring communities run by the Berlin and Dutch Reformed Missions.[21] This process, whereby the Swiss Mission became a *de facto* national church, confirmed the belief of several of the missionaries that they had been ordained by God to save the Gwamba. The Gwamba were 'the race that God had prepared for us,' wrote Arthur Grandjean. As the Swiss Mission 'dedicated itself uniquely to the Gwambas', he continued, it 'had to create a literature in that language'.[22] The definition of the Gwamba mission field was tied to the delineation of the language, and language work took a leap forward when Paul Berthoud returned to Switzerland in 1881. While Paul worked on the Gwamba language in Lausanne, his brother Henri replaced him in the field. The work of these two men would lay the foundations of Gwamba as a written language, provide the mission field with new and ambitious frontiers, and create an imagined community that would one day mobilize itself as a political entity.

Henri Berthoud immediately linked the development of a written Gwamba language to the work of the mission. Unlike his elder brother and Ernest Creux, he had no ties of loyalty to Sotho and devoted each afternoon to the study of the language he regarded as essential for evangelical work: Gwamba. By June 1882 Henri Berthoud and a Christian assistant, probably Timothee Mandlati (Zambiki), were busy at Valdezia translating parts of the Old Testament from South Sotho into Gwamba. But without a Gwamba grammar, dictionary or even a reader, translation was slow, often erroneous and the missionaries had still to rely on the Sotho publications of the PEMS.[23] Three months later, Henri started gathering material for a vocabulary and engaged himself in what he referred to as 'a task of systematizing' Shigwamba. By April 1883 he was teaching the Ten Commandments in Gwamba rather than Sotho and had handwritten a rudimentary grammar and vocabulary.

His brother Paul played a major role in the establishment of the written language later that year, when in Switzerland, following the death of his wife and children, he oversaw the production of the *buku*, the first book in the Gwamba language. This 150-page work consisted of fifty-seven hymns, the Ten Commandments, early passages from Genesis, and a Harmony of the Gospels. This was followed by translations of the Gospel of St Luke and the Acts of the Apostles. These simple texts, published by the British and Foreign Bible Society, provided an impartial record in Gwamba of Jesus' life and ministry and of his disciples' attempts to spread the Gospel beyond the Roman province of Palestine. At the same time, Paul corresponded with Lepsius in order to standardize the phonology and orthography of Gwamba. The courses he gave in the language, while in Lausanne, were published in a 46-page, lithographed booklet entitled *Leçons de Shigwamba* (Shigwamba Lessons).[24] In 1884 he added an elementary school reader or ABC to this Gwamba literature. Then, at the request of Robert Cust, a leading missionary activist and scholar of the languages of the British Empire, Paul Berthoud published a thirty-page article for the Royal Asiatic Society in London on the Gwamba tribe and the structure of their language.[25] Support came from a new direction when Eugène Thomas arrived at Elim, where he quickly set to work with Yacob Mhalamhala on the translation of the New Testament.[26]

South Sotho had made an indelible mark on the written Gwamba language but, as the new church literature appeared, it lost its dominance within the mission field.²⁷ The 'task of systematizing' Gwamba as the written *lingua franca* of the mission had yet to be achieved. The Spelonken population was composed of refugees or immigrants drawn to the area from throughout southern Mozambique. Gwamba thus provided a vehicular language for people whose linguistic differences, as Henri Berthoud remarked, reflected their origins in 'all parts of Gaza and the south'. He described Gwamba as 'a fruit-salad of Hlengwe, of Djonga, of Boer, of English, of Nwaloungou, of Hlavi, of Venda, of Sotho'.²⁸ Many of the forms of speech current amongst the refugees in the Spelonken were barely mutually comprehensible. Some six months after his arrival in the area, Henri Berthoud wrote despondently:

> Despite my utmost I cannot yet preach in Sigwamba; I can make myself understood depending on the intelligence and goodwill of those listening to me. As far as understanding the natives, it is altogether another thing; each one has his own particular dialect and often I cannot understand a word of what they are saying. That is what slows down the understanding of the language, that one has to learn numerous different dialects before understanding a conversation.²⁹

Nor did the people on the coastal plain share a single, stable language. In the south, west and north, the Zulu, Swazi and Gaza had exercised a fluctuating influence on the local linguistic forms. Because of the political cleavages and low degree of social and economic intercourse between the chiefdoms, these people had never needed a common, unifying language. Indeed, the different chiefdoms stressed their independence of one another by magnifying their linguistic differences. Junod was later to remark, 'The Natives take an immense delight in making fun of what they esteem an erroneous pronunciation, each clan laughing at the other for peculiarities of dialect'.³⁰ Consequently when people from the coastal area entered the Transvaal, they brought with them a number of speech forms and these changed and developed as they came into contact with local languages.

As the Swiss missionaries became aware of the extent of the Gwamba settlements, Gideon Mpapele's far-off Hlengwe dialect was seen to be less important than the more central and widespread Djonga form spoken by the Khosa on the coastal plain, and by the Nkuna who had settled at Shiluvane in the eastern Transvaal. This led Henri Berthoud and Timothee Mandlati at Valdezia to begin a process of 'correcting' the Gwamba found in Paul Berthoud's *buku*.³¹ Eugène Thomas believed that Yacob Mhalamhala's 'very pure version of his language' and 'his way of pronouncing' was 'the rule' at the Elim mission station.³² On the coast, Paul Berthoud soon came to depend on the language skills of Yosefa Mhalamhala.³³ Mandlati and the Mhalamhala brothers would have a lasting influence on the development of the written language as they brought their Djonga linguistic skills to bear on the (re)formulation of Gwamba.

This new direction in the development of the language, like the earlier influence of Hlengwe, had nothing to do with linguistic science. The new importance given to the Djonga linguistic form was a purely pragmatic, political decision taken by the Swiss. This began in April 1882 when Yosefa Mhalamhala established the branch of the Spelonken mission at Magude's and his sister and her husband settled at Rikatla. At the same time, Creux undertook small expeditions to assess the extent of immigration from the east coast, particularly in the area to the south of the Spelonken where many refugees had settled near or under the control of Modjadji.³⁴ During the winter of 1883 Henri Berthoud mounted the first of his voyages of discovery aimed at gaining familiarity with the peoples and geography of the area between the

Zoutpansberg and the sea. This expedition confirmed that immigrants from the east coast had settled all along the Levubu river from its confluence with the Limpopo to the Spelonken, and attested to the presence of Gwamba communities in the Haernertsberg and areas as far south as Sekukuniland. A second expedition two years later led Berthoud to estimate the size of the 'Gwamba nation' as three to four million. It also confirmed his earlier hypotheses that the heartland of the Gwamba lay in the area stretching from the Zulu border to the Zambezi river.[35] On his 1886 map of the area from the Zoutpansberg to Lourenço Marques, Berthoud drew a line marking the western extent of Gwamba-speaking settlement. This stretched up the Levubu from its confluence with the Limpopo before sweeping eastwards to the Lebombo mountains. The Gwamba-speaking communities in the Spelonken and the smaller Nkuna group further south were both separated from their coastal 'homeland' by the dry, malarial, and largely uninhabited Lowveld.[36]

The missionaries claimed the Gwamba as their natural mission field and only gradually became aware of the extensive divisions within what they defined as a common language group. When Paul Berthoud returned to the Transvaal in 1884, he wrote that 'several dialects are to be found in the Gwamba language, and their variations are sometimes very remarkable'.[37] The following year Henri divided the language into eight branches, each of which possessed 'its own territory and particular dialect'. He stressed that these 'dialects' were 'sufficiently different from one another to need an interpreter' and recommended that the mission concentrate its energies on the area between the Nkomati and Limpopo rivers. This was where Yosefa Mhalamhala had established his mission; it was, equally importantly, the area where people spoke Djonga, the language form that had strongly influenced Ernest Creux's work on the Gwamba language in the Spelonken. Henri Berthoud then classified the language to the south of the Nkomati as Ronga, a dialect of the Gwamba language. He believed that Ronga was sufficiently close to Gwamba to allow evangelical work to begin in the area to the west and north of Lourenço Marques. But Gwamba could not be employed in the Tembe and Maputo chiefdoms, to the south of the Portuguese settlement, as people spoke a markedly different linguistic form in this area. He remarked that the term Gwamba itself was only used in the Spelonken, where people employed it as a means of distinguishing themselves from immigrants whose origins lay in the east. As the term Gwamba had no ethnic precision and was seldom used in the coastal areas, Henri Berthoud recommended that it be replaced by the widely accepted genericism, Tonga or Thonga. This word had acquired a derogatory connotation in the south where it was used by the Zulu, but elsewhere on the coast, the term 'Thonga' carried the inoffensive meaning of 'easterners'.[38]

In the meantime the syncretic excesses of the religious revival on the coast had led Paul Berthoud in July 1887 to take charge of the mission in that region. Chapter three described how this division of the mission field into coastal and Spelonken sections, divided by the wide, arid Lowveld and an international border, had caused political tensions within the church. The institutional separation of the mission field also led to a serious questioning of the hegemonic role of the language defined and recorded by the missionaries and their assistants in the Spelonken.

Henri Berthoud's final expedition, undertaken in 1891, anticipated the mission's expansion into a third region, the Gaza empire north of the Limpopo. After visiting the Gaza king, Gungunyana, at Mandlakazi on the lower Limpopo, Berthoud readjusted his earlier speculative classification of the language groups north of the Limpopo. This led him to divide the Gwamba (or Thonga) language into eight sub-groups.[39] As Berthoud was the first to admit, his linguistic taxonomy was far from scientifically watertight.

Adapting Borders: Classification

The parameters of Henri Berthoud's linguistic classification were not altogether new. At the end of the eighteenth century William White had compiled a list of 140 words used by the inhabitants of Delagoa Bay. Heinrich Lichtenstein had included some of these in his list comparing words and sentences drawn from several indigenous southern African languages.[40] In 1835 Sebastião Botelho published a vocabulary collected in the Delagoa Bay area, and a few years later the German naturalist, W. C. H. Peters, drew up another list of words gathered in the same region, alongside plant and animal species.[41] Wilhelm Bleek praised the legibility and accuracy of this list that Peters, with the help of 'the son of an Italian born at Lourenço Marques' (presumably João Albasini), drew up in the columns of a blank copy of the Vocabulary printed by the Niger Expedition of 1842.

Before placing his considerable talents at the disposal of Bishop Colenso, Bleek had served as a linguist on Baikie's 1854 Niger expedition. He continued to exercise these skills in Natal where he heard Zulus refer to 'the slaughter' of the language, called 'Kutugeza', spoken by the people living north of Zululand. This led him to include 500 'Tekeza' words in a comparative dictionary compiled for the use of the anti-slavery squadron patrolling off the East African Coast. Published by the Foreign Office, this work was based on both Peters' wordlist and on information gathered from liberated slaves employed in the Cape Town dockyards.[42] Two years later Bleek divided what he now called the Bántu 'family of languages' of southern Africa into three 'species' and divided the north-eastern branch, Tekeza, into three distinct dialects: Ma-ncolosi, Ma-tonga and Mahloenga.[43] Gustave Fritsch employed this classification of the Bantu languages in his *Die Eingeborenen Sud-afrika's* (1872), the first major anthropological work on the peoples of southern Africa.[44] But when Robert Cust produced his *Sketch of the Modern Languages of Africa* in 1883, he chose to draw on Berthoud's outline of the Gwamba language rather than the German philologist's Tekeza. Cust divided Gwamba into two branches separated by the Limpopo river, Hlengwe in the north and Gwamba in the south, and classed the language as an Nguni dialect.[45] Although the word Tekeza continued to be used in some circles well into the twentieth century, it never achieved general acceptance, probably because of its origins as a term of exclusion used by the Zulu to distinguish themselves from those they wished to maintain as outsiders.[46] Whatever the reason, linguists soon replaced the word Tekeza with the newer, more acceptable term, 'Thonga'.

Another Zulu term of social exclusion was used by the British diplomat and explorer of the Limpopo, Frederick Elton, when he claimed that the entire area stretching north of Zululand to the Busi river was occupied by the *amatonga* who 'resemble each other in manners and custom [and] variation in dialect'.[47] St Vincent Erskine, the great explorer of southern Mozambique, immediately criticized these attempts 'to define the limits of the Amatongas, Butongas, Tongas etc. These are not tribal appellations', he objected, adding that Elton 'might as well try to define the limits of the "Kafirs". Tonga simply means something which is not Zulu.' Erskine believed that the 'tribes or nations' of southern Mozambique 'were at one time and in fact are now as distant from each other as the English and French and can understand each other's language as little as those European nations can'.[48]

Henri Berthoud never claimed that his linguistic divisions were scientifically defined. The Ronga in the south, he believed, 'properly speaking do not form a specific tribe, and their name is a geographical designation rather than an ethnographic one. They could be considered a transition between the Thonga to the north of Lourenço Marques and the [southern] tribes of Tembe and Mapouta.' The Hlanganou linguistic form, spoken around Lydenburg in the Transvaal, and Tswa in the area to the west of Inhambane, were sufficiently distinct to be classified as dialects. Berthoud considered Gwamba a special case as it had developed into the vehicular language of a heterogeneous group of refugees. But he claimed 'all the other Thonga', although exhibiting regional differences, 'speak a language sufficiently homogeneous that our books can be read and understood from the Sabi to Lourenço Marques'. Berthoud stressed the mobility of oral linguistic forms and opposed the view, prevalent in the rising tide of late nineteenth-century European nationalism, that language mirrored the soul or spirit of a social, and latent political, community. 'The Baloyi clan can serve as new proof of the falseness of the system that determines race according to language [for it was] a Tshwana tribe that transformed itself into a Thonga one and today speaks Gwamba.'[49]

American Board missionaries had for some years remarked on this phenomenon in some parts of the Gaza empire where children of Nguni-speaking immigrants sometimes adopted the Tswa language of the local people, as in the coastal areas north of the Limpopo. But in other areas of Gazaland, where the Nguni-speaking population was especially well represented and powerful, local men adopted the language of their Nguni betters. Women, on the other hand, clung to their language, presumably because it reinforced ties with blood kin who provided them with material and social security in their marital homesteads. In many parts of Gazaland, this confined the reproduction of Tswa as a living language to the privacy of the domestic unit where it was spoken largely by women.[50]

Benjamin Ousley, the American Board linguist at Inhambane, commented on the same shifting, historical relationship between language and identity. In this area, communities speaking Tswa, Tonga and Lenge mixed and overlapped in such a way that it was impossible to ascribe one tract of territory to a single language.[51] In 1886 Erwin Richards described a similar situation to the south of Inhambane where there was no geographical border separating people who spoke Tswa, Tonga and Chopi, 'and it sometimes happens that there is a babel of tongues in a single kraal'.[52] Almost fifty years later, Dora Earthy saw the same process in operation near Inhambane where the younger Valenge spoke 'Thonga-Shangaan' while their elders conversed in Chopi. 'Where the Thonga are concerned', she wrote, 'the linguistic definition of a tribe as a people speaking a common language breaks down at the outset.'[53] Anthropologists would later remark on this process when they commented on the facility with which members of Chopi, Zulu and Ngoni groups abandoned the language of their parents and adopted that of locally-dominant Tsonga-speakers.[54] In the area to the south and west of Delagoa Bay language practices became gender issues as men learned the prestige language forms of their Zulu and Swazi overlords and women instructed their children in the local Thonga language. This led to a high degree of bilingualism among men that continues to this day in the southern part of Maputoland.[55]

Henri Berthoud could not, of course, have anticipated this weight of opinion. His information about the languages of the coastal plain came from hearsay, as he was unable to travel north of the Limpopo or south of Lourenço Marques; he had little contact with the American missionaries at Inhambane. Furthermore, the nomenclature he used to distinguish the Thonga linguistic sub-groups indicates a false degree of separation and cohesion, for most were merely terms of exclusion used in a generic way by people who wished to distinguish themselves from their neighbours. Like the Zulu term Tekeza, adopted by Bleek, the names employed by Berthoud did not refer to categories of linguistic inclusion. Berthoud probably derived these terms from his Nkuna assistant, Timothee Mandlati, whose linguistic home lay on the Limpopo-Olifants confluence, for they referred to Rongas (easterners), Nwalungus (northerners) and Djongas (southerners).[56] It is obvious that Berthoud's dialect zones were not defined according to linguistic criteria. They were delineated in a subjective manner and their borders were a social construct, like those of the Gwamba language itself.

Henri Berthoud's explorations opened a Pandora's box for his mission. His response to this new linguistic disarray had been to create order and logic by classifying as dialects or patois the coastal conglomerate of languages enclosed within the linguistic borders defined by the American Board missionaries (Zulu in the south, Tswa in the north, Tonga at Inhambane), and the Berlin missionaries (North Sotho and Venda in the west). The uniformity and standardization of Gwamba was then defined in opposition to Zulu, Venda, Pedi and Tswa, as well as oral 'dialects' and 'patois' such as Ronga, Hlanganou and ChiNgoni, the 'Zulu dialect' employed by the Gaza aristocracy to the north of the Limpopo.[57] Having determined the boundaries of the language, the missionaries sought to reinforce their spatial classification by tracing the historical roots of the Gwamba/Thonga language. But without historical records, they could only base their suppositions on conjecture. Because the missionaries believed the African societies around them to be at an early stage of human evolution, it was self-evident and in the natural order of things that they would exhibit the same structures as their early European counterparts. Hence they applied the political term 'tribe', derived from the classics, to a linguistically-defined community. They then divided the 'tribe', again on linguistic grounds, into a series of units that they called 'clans', confusingly for us. The word is drawn from the terminology of kinship. What lay behind this curious muddle of political and linguistic terms, of course, was the understanding that the Thonga language had evolved so slowly that it was still spoken by an extended family divided into different 'clan' groups. This belief led the missionaries to explain the various linguistic forms of the Thonga language as the product of outside influence, in the shape of a series of foreign invasions in the fifteenth and sixteenth centuries, rather than the result of a historical dynamic internal to the language itself.[58] This understanding of the tribe as a biological unit was reflected and propagated in the everyday language of the missionaries, most notably in the way Junod anthropomorphized the tribe in the title of his celebrated monograph.

The missionaries' faith in the links between identity and language, culture and biology, was reinforced as they clothed *their* people in familiar stereotypes. The Berliners believed the Gwamba and Basuetla (Venda) possessed the same characteristics as the French and Germans; to the Swiss the two 'races' were comparable to the Athenians and Spartans. When Creux and Berthoud arrived in the Spelonken, the Berlin missionaries had told them that the Gwamba were a 'miserable race'; liars and thieves, they were 'mischievous, proud and cruel'. Berthoud believed that the Germans looked down on the weak Gwamba communities in the Spelonken and admired the authority and despotism of the Basuetla/Venda. He considered the Gwamba, on the other hand, to be natural businessmen, 'proud, obstinate like the Zulu but very anxious to acquire an education'.[59] Paul's brother Henri went so far as to describe 'the Venda' as 'an inhospitable, fierce race that turns to cannibalism in times of war and resists the Gospel'.[60]

It is from within this conception of the world that one has to understand how a fine scholar like Paul Berthoud came to describe Shigwamba in 1883 as 'the language of the Magwamba, kaffir tribe of South Africa'. The following year he was more explicit about the relationship between tribal identity and language. 'As a rule', he wrote

> A large tribe has not, as such, any proper and general name. But the tribe being divided into a certain number of clans, each one of these smaller communities goes by its proper name; where it is incumbent on the foreigner, either black or white, to apply a generic name to all the people and clans which belong to the same tribe. The propriety then, of such a generic name, lies in its being related to the special character of the tribe, and in its being taken from the tribe's own language. This is the case with the name 'Ma-Gwamba'.[61]

Three years later this perspective was developed further in an anonymous article, probably authored by Paul Berthoud, in *l'Afrique explorée et civilisée*. As the author assumed Africans to be at a primitive stage of evolution, he considered the extended family, or clan, to be the seat of both political power and language. Each clan constituted a separate linguistic group and it was these linguistically-related clans that made up the tribe.[62]

Once the missionaries had defined the borders of the Gwamba language, they entered into a discourse on the 'standardization', 'systemization' and 'purification' of the language. This reflected their belief that the various dialects of Gwamba could be reduced to a single, written form, perhaps based on an older, prestige variety of the language. In practice, this 'codification' and 'standardization' lifted a missionary *lingua franca* into the position of a written 'national' or 'tribal' language. In putting an oral linguistic form to paper, the missionaries' methods were based on their concept of linguistics as a science. But the consequences of their work on the Gwamba language were highly political.

Language and Structures of Power

An ability to read the Scriptures was a cornerstone of the Swiss missionaries' Protestantism. Literacy allowed a personal interpretation of the Bible without the mediation of a caste of clergymen.[63] This reinforced the Presbyterian view of conversion as a spontaneous, emotional and individual act and stimulated the growth of a self-governing, self-propagating, indigenous church. In addition to its utility as a means of communication, writing soon acquired a political significance for the Swiss. Their monopoly of the Thonga language became increasingly important as other missionary societies entered the Delagoa Bay area, anxious to follow their converts home from the mines.[64]

The Bible reader of the Swiss, the *buku*, was both 'the book of God' and a powerful instrument of evangelization. It contained the first four chapters of Genesis and a harmony of gospels that recounted the life, death and resurrection of Christ. This synopsis of Christian belief was supported by a collection of hymns that spread the articles of faith to those both familiar and unfamiliar with reading. The status of the *buku* was also enhanced by its position as the only example of local vernacular literature. It was, after all, the only book available to those who had acquired a modicum of literacy in Gwamba. When Paul Berthoud returned to Lourenço Marques on the *SS Dunkeld* with his new wife, Ruth Junod, in early 1884, he showed the first example of the *buku* to a group of labourers who had spent several years working in Cape Town. Ruth informed her mother that the twenty-five men were 'delighted' to find their language transcribed and one of their number carried a draft copy to Yosefa Mhalamahala at his mission on the bend in the Nkomati.[65] Spread in this way, the *buku* planted the seed of conversion without the presence or cost of a white missionary. The written texts and sung hymns found in 'the book of God' also served to reinforce and sustain the religious beliefs of many Christians living in isolated villages, particularly those who had converted while working in South Africa.[66]

As a form of oral reading, hymn-singing was especially important, for it introduced illiterate people to the Swiss Mission and the language that unified their field of operation. The production of grammars formed an integral part of this process. As the rules of language were codified and fixed, European missionaries and their converts became the guardians of the written language. Linguistic correctness was divorced from the speakers of the Thonga language and came to rely on written rules rather than on negotiated practice, the consent of listeners, or the wisdom of an historical figure. Once grammars had been constituted, their man-made origins were forgotten and they were perceived as givens operating according to natural laws of science. Henri Junod was particularly impressed by the Thonga *bukhaneli*, what he referred to as 'the grammar of their own language'.[67] Yet he had himself invented the term *bukhaneli*, derived from the word *ku-khanela* (to speak) and, as we shall see, he played a crucial role in determining the grammatical rules of the language through the elimination of inconsistencies. In a way that further served to separate these rules from the traditional practices they purported to describe, the missionary linguists froze them in time by fixing them on paper. They attempted to standardize their orthographic practices by turning to Lepsius' *Standard Alphabet* (1863). But the reduction of local speech sounds to an alphabet of twenty-nine written signs imposed rather than reflected a phonetic orthodoxy and logic. The missionaries also tried to impress a new order on the Thonga language through bilingual dictionaries that served to isolate words from their social contexts and imposed new meanings upon them. A new vocabulary provided people with the means to express not only Biblical, educational and liturgical ideas, but also sweeping new concepts such as scientific truth and error. As we have seen, in this process, words like Gwamba, Thonga and Ronga were changed from expressions of exclusion to terms of social inclusion that had never existed in the mental lexicon of the people to whom they were applied.

The written Thonga language was not only controlled by the missionaries but, in a manner that combined endearment, loyalty and possession, they almost owned it. Gwamba was 'our' language with 'our' orthography.[68] The missionaries saw the language as an instrument of modernization, firmly tied to Christianity and progress. Ideas or events recorded on paper in the Thonga language escaped the social controls exerted by the 'pagan' community over oral 'dialects' and 'patois'. The missionaries believed that 'their' written language would civilize and modernize the native population in the same way that Latin had domesticated the early tribes of Switzerland and France.[69] While Thonga was the product of the mission, the subordinate dialects and patois were linked to the chiefs and headmen who, with few exceptions, presented a major barrier to evangelization. The Thonga print language provided the missionaries with a means of subverting the cultural dominance of the old order. The grammar and orthography of a written language provided the reader with a stable and enduring cultural marker, and the printed word took on the power of non-perishable truth. Importantly, this written language provided people with a new means of communication and expression, just as capitalism expanded their economic and social horizons.

On the ground, this difference remained the distinction between inclusion and exclusion. The missionaries believed that for the members of a backward, oral society to become civilized, they had to become literate in Thonga. The acquisition of this language entailed a restructured perception of the world and a shift of political loyalty away from the chief to the mission and, in the long term, to those people who shared a common constant, the written Thonga language. This transformation was linked firmly to modernization or to the process that determined that the benefits of speaking the language surpassed those of speaking the dialect/patois. Thus the division or cut-off point between a language and a dialect/patois was defined socially rather than scientifically. However, these man-made linguistic borders were considered politically neutral because they were the product of a science whose objective criteria, the laws of grammar and orthography, had been located in much the same way as botanical or entomological species. It was again their search for a world held in place by God and by science that led the missionaries to believe, not that they had created a linguistic category, but that they had 'recognized the Thonga as a tribe' and that they had 'discovered the Thonga language' in the same way as they had 'discovered' (rather than assembled) species of plants and animals.[70]

The monopoly held by the Swiss mission over the written language was further tightened by the requirement that all books be published in Lausanne. In this way, mission headquarters could prevent disputes within the church by strictly controlling what Africans read. A very different policy was pursued by the inter-denominational PEMS in Lesotho, where its presses started to roll in 1841. *Leselinyana*, the newspaper first edited by Mabille, burst with secular contributions from its Sotho readership. After their arrival in July 1883, the American missionaries at Inhambane took only two years to establish a printing press. They trained Tizora Neves as a compositor who was able to set a page of type a day within a few weeks. By September 1885 the Americans had assembled wordlists containing over 1,600 items in both Tonga and Tswa and a short catechism of seventy questions and answers.[71] In June 1886 Erwin Richards printed the first Christian reader in Tonga, made up of the Sermon on the Mount, a catechism of 125 questions, the nineteenth, twenty-third and fifty-first Psalms, and more than a dozen hymns. The American missionaries on the spot determined the content of this very particular reading of the Christian message. They viewed their Tonga reader as an arm in the struggle against darkness and disbelief. It was the 'sword of the spirit' and 'the shoeing of our feet'. By early 1888 their four printers were churning out 2000 pages of text per day and they had succeeded in printing the Gospels of Mark and Matthew in Tonga.[72] A reading primer in Tswa was also produced, as was a catechism with hymns, and a 'Story of the Gospels'.[73] The American Board also ingratiated itself with the colonial authorities by using its printers to produce several hundred passports and contracts for labourers, shipped from Inhambane to Durban, as well as a printed compendium of native laws in Portuguese.[74]

In contrast, the absence of a press on the Swiss stations led to interminable printing delays and a good deal of dissatisfaction amongst the missionaries. Paul Berthoud had applied to headquarters in Lausanne as early as 1876 for a printer with which to publish his first manuscripts.[75] When his application was effectively turned down, the decision over what to print was left securely in the hands of the mission council in Switzerland. This policy could at times act as an effective form of censorship. In 1904 Henri Berthoud's request for the mission to produce a *Life of Jesus* was refused because headquarters thought the Bible a sufficient literature for the Thonga.[76] Ronga literature also emerged slowly. Pierre Loze published a Biblical history of the Old Testament in 1901 in the language, and a translation of *The Pilgrim's Progress* eventually appeared in 1928.[77] However, it would take another decade before non-missionaries started to publish in Thonga and, even then, their works were essentially moral and didactic, dominated by a Christian ethos that marginalized the humour, anarchy and pathos found in great literature.

Although missionary newspapers such as *Nyeleti Ya Mixo* (founded 1921) and the *Valdezia Bulletin* (1931) came to provide a limited outlet for secular writings, the mission exercised a strict control over published works in the Thonga language. This led G. P. Lestrade to note, as late as 1933, that 'everything Thonga, except the language, seems to have been carefully banned' from the Swiss Mission's school readers.[78] Through their control of dictionaries, grammars, vernacular literature and primary school education, the missionaries were able to recuperate in Africa the enormous power over the conceptual world that they had lost to the forces of secularism in Switzerland.[79]

As mentioned earlier, the missionaries saw the distinction between written and oral linguistic forms in hierarchical terms. This ranking of (written) languages above (oral) dialects is still a common practice today.[80] A dictionary defines *dialect* as 'a regional, social or subordinate variety of a language, usually differing distinctly from the standard or original language'. The missionary linguists also viewed a 'standard' language as a synonym for an 'original' language. This practice, common in much of South Africa at the time, was built on the frequent use of the terms 'standardization' and 'purification' to explain what was in effect the elevation of one language form to a dominant status. The early linguists were, therefore, the ones who chose the markers that produced simultaneously both a standard language and its subordinate dialects.[81] This linguistic hierarchy was imbued with a spatial political identity as Thonga was conceived of as the ethnic or, as they called it, the 'tribal' or 'national' language. Under the influence of contemporary philology and nationalism, linguists believed that it was possible to purify the language by ridding it of its foreign influences. Once the language was reduced to its original state, the identity of the tribe/nation would reawaken and re-emerge from the unconscious. In this way linguistic differences took on a core–periphery relationship. Henri Berthoud knew that the 'dialects would be forced *ipso facto* into the position of patois destined to disappear with time'.[82] While oral languages were highly mobile and dynamic, and observed no frontiers in space or time, a written language was bound by rules that delineated it spatially and fixed it temporally.

Adapting Borders: the Ronga Language

By the early 1890s, under the auspices of the Swiss missionaries, Thonga was gradually emerging as the literary language of north-eastern Transvaal and southern Mozambique. But the process of transcription was accompanied by innumerable frustrations and delays. Although the mission had adopted Lepsius' system of transcribing sounds into letters, translations were only sent to Switzerland for publication once their orthography had been accepted by both the Spelonken and Coastal mission councils. As no single spoken language linked the different mission stations, linguistic problems had often to be referred to mission headquarters in Lausanne, or even to experts in Berlin and Geneva. In the Spelonken, Henri Berthoud was charged with the task of correcting the language of the *buku* produced in 1883, which had been strongly influenced by South Sotho and Hlengwe. But he became increasingly impatient as he saw the publication of his precious translations impeded by disputes pitting the linguistic conventions of one language form against another. He watched with concern as his manuscripts disappeared into an opaque, administrative fog.[83]

Matters came to an uncertain head when Paul Berthoud at Lourenço Marques started to realize that there were considerable differences between the Gwamba language spoken in the Transvaal and the Gwamba employed on the coast, particularly to the south of the Portuguese town. At first he had been unaware of these differences. The Mhalamhalas and other Gwamba-speaking evangelists who accompanied him to the coast had little sympathy for the contortions of their language found at Rikatla, Lourenço Marques and in Tembeland. Besides, people on the coast willingly spoke Gwamba as they considered it the language of the *buku* and the *lingua franca* of their church. When Ruth Berthoud-Junod arrived on the coast in the winter of 1887 with her husband, she had noted that people in her new mission field did not recognize themselves as Gwambas. But although they used other terms of political self-identification, 'their language (was) the same as Gwamba'. She did remark, however, that there were quite strong differences of intonation between the Gwamba of the Spelonken and the language spoken on the coast. She also found that the coastal peoples did not employ the Dutch words commonly used in Gwamba and that, because of a few sound shifts, the language on the coast was closer to Zulu. Ruth Berthoud-Junod found the novel aspects of the language disconcerting but attributed her inability to master its finer points to her limited linguistic skills.[84] In the meantime, work on the Gwamba language advanced with the arrival of Arthur Grandjean at Rikatla in July 1888. Calvin Matsivi Mapopé introduced the new missionary to the intricacies of his language and within six weeks Grandjean claimed to have understood the fundamentals of Gwamba and to have drawn up a 1000-word dictionary. In January 1889 he gave his first sermon in Gwamba and started work on a translation of the Psalms.[85]

Despite Grandjean's contribution to the standardization of the Gwamba language, questions were raised about the versions of the language spoken on the coast and in the interior. The extent of the differences within the language became clearer in late 1889 with the circulation of the draft versions of Henri Berthoud's 'corrected' Gwamba translations. His elder brother Paul, who had been responsible for the Gwamba of the *buku*, started to find numerous inconsistencies between the corrected, written language used in the Transvaal and the oral medium used on the coast. He particularly noted that the fricative *v* of the Gwamba in the Spelonken became an explosive *b* in the mouths of people on the coast and he advised that mission texts should incorporate this difference. This issue quickly became an embarrassment to the mission council in Lausanne, for it again brought the rivalry between the Berthouds into the public arena. It threatened to overturn confidence in more than twenty years' linguistic work.[86]

Most importantly, the production of reading primers and religious works was held back by these uncertainties over the definition of the standard, written language of the mission. This both hampered the missionaries' ability to bring about conversions and reduced their competitiveness in an increasingly crowded evangelical field. Henri Berthoud complained volubly that the American missionaries at Inhambane, who had their own printers and the assistance of their country's Bible Society, were moving far faster with their translations than the Swiss. While the Swiss were delayed by endless debates and disputes, the American missionaries (who had initially based much of their linguistic work on Paul Berthoud's early Gwamba literature) defined and transcribed their own, separate Tswa language.[87] Benjamin Ousley had translated the synoptical gospels and the book of Acts into Tswa, and the American Bible Society successfully printed this 372-page work in August 1891.[88]

The language policy of the Swiss Mission took a firmer direction after Grandjean moved to Antioka on the bend in the Nkomati where the linguistic form was closer to the Gwamba of the Spelonken. While Grandjean worked on translations in this northern section of the mission field, Henri-Alexandre Junod replaced him at Rikatla. Like Grandjean, Junod threw himself into the study of the Gwamba language and was able to undertake translations within weeks with the assistance of the irrepressible Matsivi. In February 1890 he presented his first sermon in Gwamba and shortly thereafter wrote an article on this language. Defined and transcribed by the mission in the Transvaal, it was a rich and expressive language and, most importantly, a gateway to the 'soul' of the Gwamba people.[89] Junod brought his unbending confidence in science to his linguistic work. He wrote that Matsivi 'knows his language, but has no idea of the rules he observes so well. Ignorant as I was about Gwamba, I was nonetheless able to teach Matsivi a good few things about his own language.'[90]

Junod also felt able to teach the mission's pioneers in linguistics a few things about the Gwamba language. A major dispute started to brew as the New Testament was prepared for publication in Gwamba and Henri Berthoud's reading primer arrived on the coast. At first the missionaries there accepted the ABC with reservations, but as they measured the differences between this written language and the oral linguistic forms employed by their congregants, they rejected the work. They repudiated what they called the Gwamba 'dialect' and called for the establishment of a separate Ronga language that would make up the Thonga language cluster with Tswa and Gwamba. Junod was at the centre of this secessionist action. Originally, his language work at Rikatla had led him to believe that the dialect of the north and that of the south were different, 'even very different'. But both languages shared a sufficient number of common expressions for books, 're-edited with the addition of local words', to be understood in the areas to the north and south of the Nkomati river. However, in early 1893 he changed his mind and a few months later admitted:

> I do not think it possible nor desirable to proceed with a single book i.e. that of shigwamba. The two dialects are so essentially different that I am of the opinion that our mission in the Ronga

country will not be able to develop in a normal manner until it possesses its own books, books in shi-ronga.[91]

There were good, practical reasons for this decision. The work of the Swiss Mission was at a low ebb throughout south-east Africa in the early 1890s. The number of conversions in the Transvaal had stagnated and, although they increased at Lourenço Marques, also dwindled to a trickle at Antioka and Rikatla. As this study has argued, the mission's depressing situation was the result of the suppression of the revivalist movement and its African leadership a few years earlier.[92] But Junod ascribed the setback purely to the linguistic situation, for the language of the *buku* was being rejected as a foreign dialect. The Tembe chief had even referred to the *buku* contemptuously as 'this book that comes from the north'.[93]

Most seriously, Catholics, Anglicans and Methodists had penetrated the mission field conferred on the Swiss by God. While the Anglicans largely confined their work to Chopi refugees at Lourenço Marques, the Catholics attracted a Thonga following by teaching Portuguese and by exercising a more accommodating attitude towards local customs. The major source of competition for the Swiss came from the Methodists. Instead of looking to what the Swiss missionaries saw as the 'national church' of the Gwambas, local people tended to join Robert Mashaba's Methodist community. Mashaba had been born in Tembeland and spoke the local linguistic form as his first language. He had worked in Natal and the Cape, where he had attended Lovedale college; he spoke English fluently, writing the language with a firm hand. With these skills, Mashaba had helped the British consul E. W. Smith at Lourenço Marques assemble the first wordlist in Ronga, a *Shironga Vocabulary*. With the help of the Lovedale Press, he went on to produce a *First* and then a *Second Thonga Reader* and a collection of hymns in Ronga.[94]

Junod was critical of Mashaba's untrained linguistic approach, but he was also well aware that the Methodist minister's vocabulary was far richer than the utilitarian set of words and expressions employed by the Swiss. The mission used a limited number of terms to get its message across and, as some of these developed their own meanings, it produced a 'special dialect'. The problem was compounded as converts adopted this 'impoverished and mutilated' language and very quickly associated it with the mission.[95] Mashaba's richer and more expressive language appealed to local sentiments, and won converts in much the same way as the Swiss missionaries' *buku* only a few years earlier. Robert Mashaba 'produces for them a pure sironga', Junod wrote ruefully in 1893. He 'tries hard to present himself as the true missionary of the country, speaking to people in their language, while we are *Bakalanga*, or foreigners from the north'. The Thonga words of the *buku* were viewed in the area around Lourenço Marques as 'a special Christian language', and local people made fun of the foreign accent, expressions and words employed by the missionaries and their evangelists. 'They are not from this country!' the pagans fulminated. 'These people from the north should go home; we don't want them here!'[96]

Junod was alarmed by the inability of his mission to compete with the Methodists and feared the Swiss would lose their position as the *de facto* national church in the region south of the Nkomati river. He claimed that Paul Berthoud had not realized the extent of the difference between the Thonga and Ronga languages, because he had initially worked at Rikatla, where most people spoke Djonga, and had later been surrounded at Lourenço Marques by evangelists drawn from the Transvaal and the north. At Rikatla, Gwamba/Thonga had become the language of the mission, while at Lourenço Marques people had found it considerate to use this language form when addressing the missionaries. This had isolated the mission from the Ronga-speaking community and had caused people not fully to understand their prayers.[97]

Junod carried the coastal mission with him and in 1893 they decided to create a literature in what they referred to as the Ronga *idiom*.[98] Later that year, Junod was able to devote more time to the study of the language when a skilled artisan arrived from Switzerland to take charge of the physical maintenance of the mission station. Freed from the duties concerned with the upkeep and physical extension of the mission, Junod threw himself into the difficult task of 'deciphering and writing' the Ronga language. In preparing a reading primer in that language, he turned for assistance from Calvin Mapope to a Ronga-speaker who, because he had lived in the Spelonken, was 'attentive to the differences between the two languages'.[99] Junod then drew up an ABC in 'the Ronga of the Church'. As he was anxious to avoid time-consuming debate over the structure of the language, he published this work in 1894 at his own expense.[100] In this reading primer, he referred to Ronga as a dialect. Two years later, with the aid of the Portuguese government, he produced a Ronga grammar that included a conversation manual, a short collection of folklore (or oral literature) and an elementary vocabulary.[101] In this book he referred to Ronga interchangeably as a 'dialect' or 'language'. Junod's delineation of a language separate from Thonga was strengthened when he published a substantial collection of Ronga folktales in the same year and, in 1898, a long anthropological monograph on the Ronga in French.[102] Junod had never travelled north of the Nkomati and hence made only a few changes to Berthoud's linguistic classification of that region. The area he knew best was Lourenço Marques and it is the debate over the status of Ronga that best shows the subjective nature of linguistic classification.[103]

Henri Berthoud saw Ronga as a transitional linguistic form with numerous variations, midway between Djonga on the Nkomati river in the north and Maputo on the southern border of Mozambique. Junod saw a division in the region between the 'real Ronga' spoken by the clans around Lourenço Marques, and the mixture of Ronga and Zulu, spoken by followers of chief Manaba in the extreme south. He believed that Thonga and Ronga were 'varieties' of the same language rather than different 'species', but that they were too different to share the same books. The translation of the Ten Commandments from Thonga to Ronga required changes to between 130 and 150 of the 400 words. Of 150 pronominal forms, 70 changed entirely from Thonga to Ronga. The Portuguese were also aware of the linguistic differences in the Lourenço Marques area, and used a shibboleth to distinguish between friendly and foreign Africans who were picked up on the streets of Lourenço Marques and press-ganged into their colonial army.[104] Junod agreed that terms like 'Thonga' and 'Ronga' were merely externally defined geographical labels that said nothing about the ethnographic makeup of a community.[105] But in 1896 this did not stop him from portraying the 'Ba-Ronga' as a 'clan' of the Thonga 'tribe'. Two years later he extended this image when he referred to the 'Ba-Ronga' in his monograph as a culturally-defined group distinguishable from the Djonga, Hlengwe and other language groups that he called 'clans'. By 1903 Junod was referring to the Ronga as a 'tribe', by which he meant not a political unit but a *volk*, or people, who were not necessarily conscious of their common identity.[106]

Berthoud rejected the closed nature of this cultural classification. It became obvious in the ensuing debate that the division erected between Ronga and Gwamba/Thonga was at least partly the product of the rivalry between the Spelonken and coastal branches of the Swiss Mission. But it was also the product of conflicting interpretations over the relationship between language and society. Junod was influenced by the Romantic tradition going back to Herder, Fichte and von Humbold and reflected through Juste Olivier, believing that the linguistic relationship between the speakers of Ronga and Gwamba/Thonga caused them to share a deep-rooted and emotional understanding of the world. Their language was the single, shared cultural form defining what he variously called a tribe, people or nation. Referring to the linguistic sub-groups delineated by Berthoud, Junod wrote:

> The Ronga of Delagoa Bay do not believe that they are any more related to the Khosa of the Nkomati and the Hlengwe of the Limpopo than to the Zulu or the Sotho, and on closer examination one quickly notices that all the clans forming the Thonga people have in common only a few customs tending to disappear. The only thing that they possess in common is a language that is distinctive, old and rich. The unity of this tribe is very much more linguistic than national.[107]

Like Herder, Junod believed that a common language imbued a 'people' or 'nation' with a *Geist* or 'soul'. 'Beneath the manifold manifestations of the Life of the Tribe', Junod maintained, the ethnographer tries to 'penetrate into the soul of the tribe', tries to 'discover its soul'. At the basis of this search was 'the language of a nation' which is 'one of the most trustworthy and complete manifestations of its mind'.[108]

When Junod sought to delineate the language of what he called the 'real Ronga,' he felt he was peeling away the linguistic accretions of time to discover the essence or 'soul' of a people. Through linguistic work that he often compared to palaeontology or geology, Junod hoped to restore the authentic or 'real' character of Ronga. This unravelling of linguistic miscegenation was part of Junod's broad strategy aimed at yoking the creativity of a primitive people while tying their language to the benefits of writing at the same time.[109] The (oral) dialects were a natural casualty of this process as their linguistic 'impurity' and 'backwardness' represented an earlier stage of development that impeded the progress of the Ronga people.[110] Junod employed the weight of science to support his perspective. He believed that an 'almost mathematical' relationship existed between the different 'branches of the African linguistic tree' and that linguistics was a branch of science in much the same way as geology or palaeontology.[111] Linguistic research particularly 'resembled that of the palaeontologist', he ventured, for 'man's history, his migrations, is revealed to he who investigates the languages and traditions of primitive people'.[112] In essence, Junod saw the tribe as a Kulturvolk and located its unity in a common set of social practices and beliefs – joined by language – rather than in the politics that divided and weakened it.

Henri Berthoud, on the other hand, saw no primordial connection between language and identity. A native of the Francophile canton of Vaud, Berthoud's understanding of this issue followed the path established by Ernest Renan: the nation was less the natural product of a common language than a voluntary act, 'an everyday plebiscite' through which people expressed their desire to form a nation. From this perspective, people constructed their language in much the same way as they crafted the history and invented the tradition on which they based their identity. As discussed earlier, this led Berthoud to stress that individuals were at liberty to choose and change both the language they spoke and the group to which they belonged. In many areas, a his-

6.1 Henri-Alexandre Junod and Henri Berthoud. Junod's work on a separate Ronga language undermined the unity of the Thonga language delineated by Berthoud. The two missionaries represented different approaches to the study of African languages. (© Swiss mission Archive, Lausanne)

tory of conquest and migration had introduced a marked linguistic fluidity.[113] Had he known, Berthoud might have added that the American Board missionaries' decision to distinguish between Tswa and Gwamba as written languages was as much a political decision, taken for pragmatic reasons, as was Junod's decision to separate Ronga from Thonga.[114] But Junod and Berthoud were little concerned with these theoretical niceties. At the root of the linguistic debate was the very specific problem faced by the coastal mission, for without using the local speech form, their evangelical work could not progress or compete with the Methodists, and nor could they match the achievements of their colleagues in the Spelonken.

Henri Berthoud pointed out the practical consequences of Junod's formulation of a separate Ronga language. The New Testament had been published in Gwamba/Thonga in 1894 and a double literature would dramatically increase the costs of printing. It would divert to translating and editing the time and energy that missionaries should invest in evangelical work. A double literature would lead to a 'schism' in the mission by driving a wedge between the African congregations in the Spelonken and those on the coast. Left unsaid was the fact that Ronga's challenge to Gwamba was synonymous with the coastal mission's challenge to the dominance of the parent mission in the Spelonken. Also left unsaid was the way the simmering rivalry between Paul Berthoud and his younger brother Henri tended to polarize the interests of the Spelonken and coastal missions. The uneasy relationship between these siblings had bubbled to the surface during the dispute over the nature of the revival on the coast and more generally, over the direction to be taken by the native church. It re-emerged when Paul and Henri argued over the renaming of Gwamba. Paul opted for the widely used term for an easterner, Tonga, while Henri felt this unsuitable, as the word had taken on a derogatory meaning in the mouths of the Zulu. He preferred the word Thonga (with an aspirated 'h'), employed by members of the Khosa chiefdom on the Nkomati bend.[115] All this highlights the importance of social criteria in the classification of languages. Berthoud believed that Junod's linguistic constructs were as artificial as those that defined the Thonga/Gwamba language. There were no objectively scientific grounds for the creation of a separate written language. If each mission station were to devise its own written dialect, the mission field would become irretrievably fragmented. Thonga/Gwamba was similar to the language spoken sixty kilometres north of Lourenço Marques. Its similarities with Ronga and the other dialects of the Thonga cluster were sufficient for it to be accepted as the language of unity for the church through its role as the medium of schooling and literacy.

Although Berthoud's primary concern was the future unity of the church, he was also aware of the implications for the local people of a double literature. It was one thing for missionaries like Junod to publish scientific linguistic studies on a language that had no documents, but it was another thing

> from a missionary point of view to turn this language into a language with a right to survive, to exaggerate its importance and create a split within the nation and the church ... 'Linguistic knowledge' and science, do they have the right to cheapen the spiritual condition of the natives for whose soul we work? What are our rights and duties towards the different dialects of one language and the natives who speak it? What will be the results of one or other decision on the future of these people and the mission work that is undertaken amongst them? Because they had not considered these questions the missionaries of South Africa, to mention them alone, have taken several wrong turnings and have slowed down, without a doubt, the advance of God's kingdom and the unification of Christian missions. There has been too much personal chauvinism and the wish to see one's own particular dialect triumph.[116]

Berthoud recalled that the Paris Missionary Society's South Sotho literature had played a central role in unifying the Basotho nation, 'a nation that was far from possessing the homogeneity that it has since acquired'. In the eastern Transvaal the Berlin Mission Society had abandoned the use of (South) Sotho, and the language of 'the Pedi of Lydenburg' had been accepted as the standard written language over a wide area that was rich in particularistic dialects. This successful imposition of one literature could be contrasted with the situation in the Zoutpansberg. There, the Berlin Missionary Society complained of the disunity resulting from the existence of two separate elementary readers, compiled by the early missionaries, and from the limited but successful implantation of Pedi.

Henri Berthoud's view of the future was further influenced and shaped by the European experience where standard, written languages had played a central role in fuelling national consciousness in Europe. To underline the importance of a single literature and the validity of historical comparison, Berthoud recounted an anecdote told to him by a plaintive Berlin missionary. 'One day', Mr Gottscheling had said, 'five of us German missionaries from different provinces met, and each told a story in his [German] dialect; we did not understand each other, but despite that we have only one Bible, that of Luther, for all of Germany.'[117] In a similar vein Berthoud warned that as the Swiss Mission expanded its work north of Lourenço Marques using Thonga as its linguistic medium, Ronga would be reduced to the status of Basque in France: an isolated, 'foreign language spoken by an antagonistic ethnic minority'.[118] He felt that the only positive result stemming from the linguistic split between Ronga and

Thonga was that it brought to a halt the interminable debates between the Spelonken and coastal mission fields.

In January 1898 Henri Berthoud attempted to reach a compromise with Junod and his supporters. In this he had the backing of the Spelonken mission and the three Gwamba-speaking evangelists who had helped establish the mission on the coast. He proposed that the Djonga dialect of the Nkomati-Limpopo area of southern Mozambique which constituted the basis of Gwamba/Thonga, be accepted as the national language and that the mission abandon both the Ronga and the Gwamba literatures. But by then, in the wake of the Luso-Gaza war, the coastal mission had outgrown its elder sibling in the Spelonken and its members replied that if one literature were needed, it should be Ronga. They considered Berthoud's notion of a central, unifying language 'utopian' and repeated that to abandon the local Ronga dialect would set their church at a competitive disadvantage that would restrict the rate at which they achieved conversions.[119] The secession of Ronga from Thonga was confirmed when Paul Berthoud gave his support to the new language. But he entirely lacked his brother's foresight when he wrote that the double literature would not create a schism between the two mission fields and that 'perhaps one day when the tribe is unified [as in Lesotho at present], that is to say, a long time from now, we might be able to abandon one of the two literatures'.[120]

The debate over the two literatures ended suddenly when Henri Berthoud contracted yellow fever and died in 1904. By this time Junod had lived for several years at Shiluvane in the Transvaal where he had spent much of his time studying the language of the Nkuna. This chiefdom had moved into the area from the bend in the Nkomati river in the mid-nineteenth century and its members spoke the Djonga language form that lay at the core of the original Gwamba language defined by the Swiss. In 1907 Junod published part of this linguistic work in his *Elementary Grammar of the Thonga/Shangaan language,* a book that applied to the central Tsonga linguistic group the terminology suggested by Henri Berthoud during the last years of his life. Two years later Junod added this short grammar to the dictionary edited by Charles Chatelain that had consumed much of Berthoud's remaining time on earth.[121] This splendidly Swiss piece of consensual politics was rounded off the following year when Berthoud's supporters edited and published his posthumous *Shangaan Grammar*. These two works marked the final displacement of the word 'Gwamba' by the term 'Thonga/Shangaan'. Within a few years distinct Ronga, Thonga/Shangaan and Tswa languages were established within the Tsonga language cluster on the basis of separate grammars and orthographies.[122] Importantly, these languages were supplied with foundational literatures. In 1907 Eugène Thomas brought together various passages translated into Thonga by missionaries from the Vulgate, Hebrew, Greek or French. He then corrected their grammar and spelling and unified their style to produce the full Bible in Thonga. Three years later American missionaries produced a version in Tswa and in 1923 Pierre Loze oversaw the production of the Bible in Ronga.[123]

With its establishment as an independent language, Ronga no longer competed with Thonga/Shangaan for the attention of the mission's linguists. But another threat to the Ronga language was soon to emerge from a new quarter. The Roman Catholic Church, colonial administrators and the assimilationist African politicians grouped around the newspaper *Brado Africano* encouraged the adoption of Portuguese as the *lingua franca* of the colony of Mozambique. They saw the European language as a means of social integration and political upliftment and discouraged the use of Ronga in schools.[124] For many, the decrees passed in 1907, aimed at restricting the proliferation of Protestant schools and teaching in vernacular languages, were part of a wider process of natural selection that would ultimately see the Bantu languages replaced by the unifying language of the colonizer.[125] Junod opposed the 'stupidity and short-term utilitarianism' of this policy. By this time he believed that African languages had to be encouraged because they reflected the creative energy of the tribe. This would allow the Thonga to make a special contribution to the development of humankind and to fortify themselves against the social degeneration induced by the vices of European civilization.[126]

Henri Berthoud and Henri-Alexandre Junod used entirely pragmatic criteria to define the borders of the Thonga and Ronga languages at the turn of the century. I like to think they would have found the social and political consequences of this linguistic work both unexpected and unsavoury in the form of tribal antipathies and, later, segregation and apartheid. But their linguistic work was part of a wide policy of social engineering that inevitably had political consequences. The inability of the missionaries to control the uses to which their work was put is perhaps most evident when we turn to examine the consequences of literacy in the following chapter.

Notes

[1] *Rapport adressé au synode par la commission des missions de l'église évangélique libre du canton de Vaud 1869–70*, p. 36.
[2] Junod, *Ernest Creux et Paul Berthoud: Les fondateurs de la mission suisse en Afrique du Sud* (Lausanne, 1933), p. 40.
[3] Swiss Mission Archive, Lausanne (SMA) 8.10.B, Paul Berthoud to mission council, 18 September 1873; *Bulletin de la Mission vaudoise* (*BMV*) (1874) 10, March, p. 158; Paul Berthoud, *Lettres missionnaires: 1873–1879 de M. et Mme Paul Berthoud* (Lausanne, 1900), p. 118.
[4] Junod, *Ernest Creux et Paul Berthoud*, p. 42.
[5] H.-P. Junod, *Henri-Alexandre Junod: missionnaire et savant 1863–1934* (Lausanne, 1934), p. 81.
[6] For a chronological treatment of the establishment of written African languages in South Africa, see C. M. Doke and D. J. Cole, *Contribution to the History of Bantu Linguistics* (Johannesburg, 1961).
[7] H.-A. Junod, 'The Ba-Thonga of the Transvaal', *Addresses and Papers of the South African Association for the Advancement of Science* (1905) III, pp. 222–3. For other names generally used as terms of exclusion, see P. Harries, 'Exclusion, classification and internal colonialism: the emergence of ethnicity among the Tsonga-speakers of South Africa' in Leroy Vail (ed.), *The Creation of Tribalism in Southern Africa* (London and Los Angeles, 1989), pp. 85–6, 111–12, notes 13–17.
[8] *BMV* 18, March 1876, p. 9.
[9] *BMV* 20, 25 July 1876, p. 49.
[10] Berthoud, *Lettres missionnaires*, p. 246. Victor Sampson classed the 'Makwapa' as a 'Zulu tribe' in his 'Our relations and responsibilities to the Native races', *Cape Monthly Magazine* (1877) 92, December, p. 330.
[11] SMA 8.10.B, Paul Berthoud to council, 30 September 1875.
[12] Berthoud, *Lettres missionnaires*, p. 334.
[13] Ibid., p. 81; F. Coillard, *Sur le Haut-Zambèze: Voyages et Travaux de Mission* (Paris, 1899), p. 15.
[14] SMA 8.10.B, Paul Berthoud to council, 14 March 1878.
[15] For the Gwamba (or Tsonga) case, see Mary C. Bill, 'Berthoud's *Leçons de Shigwamba* (1883): the first Tsonga grammar' in A. Traill, R. Vossen, M. Biesele (eds), *The Complete Linguist* (Cologne, 1995) esp. p. 499.
[16] P. Berthoud, *Les Nègres gouamba* (Lausanne, 1896), p. 32.
[17] Berthoud, *Lettres missionnaires*, p. 259.
[18] SMA 8.10.B, Paul Berthoud to mission council, 6 June 1889; Paul Berthoud, *Les Nègres gouamba*, p. 34.
[19] SMA 8.10.B, H. Berthoud to mission council, 6 June 1889.
[20] SMA 8.11.C, A. Creux to Leresche, 24 July 1880; C. Knothe, 'Ein Rekognoszierungsreise', *Berliner Missions-Berichte* (1879) 3/4, p. 53; Grandjean, *La Mission romande* (Lausanne, 1917), p. 107. Jonas Mapopé (Chihoçi) continued to work for many years among the Pedi-speaking Khaha near Shiluvane.
[21] Grandjean, *Mission romande*, pp. 87–9, 101, 108; Junod, *Ernest Creux et Paul Berthoud*, p. 81.

22 A. Grandjean, *Labours, semailles et moissons dans le champ de la Mission romande* (Lausanne, 1898), p. 11; Grandjean, *La Race thonga et la Suisse romande* (Lausanne, 1921), p. 3; Paul Berthoud, *Considérations sur la constitution des églises indigènes dans la mission romande* (Neuchâtel, 1912), p. 33; SMA 8.11.B, Paul Berthoud to council, 2 September 1886; Junod, *Ernest Creux et Paul Berthoud*, p. 55.

23 SMA 8.10.B, Henri Berthoud to council, 17 May 1882.

24 The full title is *Leçons de shigwamba: langage des Magwamba, tribu cafre du Sud de l'Afrique*. This work, of which the original is in the Archives of the Swiss Mission (SMA) in Lausanne, was lithographed from a copy of the hand–written notes taken by one of Berthoud's students. Mary Bill provides a careful analysis of this work in 'Berthoud's *Leçons de shigwamba* (1883). See also Anon., *Notice sur la Mission vaudoise chez les Magwamba au sud-est de l'Afrique – souvenir de l'exposition nationale suisse de Zürich, 1883* (n.d., n.p.), p. 14.

25 Paul Berthoud, 'Grammatical note on the Gwamba language in South Africa', *Journal of the Royal Asiatic Society*, (1884) 16. Junod, *Ernest Creux et Paul Berthoud*, pp. 118–20.

26 SMA 8.27.T, E. Thomas to mission council, 18 December 1885.

27 SMA 8.27.T, E. Thomas to mission council, 9 March 1885. On the influence of South Sotho on the *buku* and its lasting influence on Gwamba more generally, see Samuel Tinyiko Maluleke, '"A Morula Tree Between Two Fields": The Commentary of Selected Tsonga Writers on Mission Christianity' (Unpublished PhD., University of South Africa, 1995), p. 31n. 29.

28 Henri Berthoud, 'Quelques remarques sur la famille des langues bantou et sur la langue tzonga en particulier', in Xe *Congrès International des Orientalistes, 1894* (Leiden, 1896), p. 173.

29 SMA 8.10.B, Henri Berthoud to mission council, 25 February 1882.

30 H.-A. Junod, *Life of a South African Tribe (LSAT)* (London, 1927) II, p. 262; P. Berthoud, *Les Nègres gouamba*, p. 34.

31 SMA 1255B, H. Berthoud, 'Rapport sur l'expédition à Magude,' 6 October 1885.

32 SMA 8.27.T, Thomas to mission council, 17 June 1884.

33 SMA 834, Ruth Berthoud-Junod, July 1887 in the manuscript version of her *Du Transvaal à Lourenço Marques: lettres de Mme Ruth Berthoud-Junod* (Lausanne, 1904).

34 SMA 8.11.C, Ernest Creux to mission council, 20 January 1880.

35 SMA 1255/B, 'Rapport sur l'expédition chez Magud', 6 October 1885.

36 SMA 8.10.B, Henri Berthoud to council, 9 October 1883.

37 Paul Berthoud, 'Grammatical note on the Gwamba language in South Africa', p. 47.

38 On Tonga as a derogatory term used by the Zulu, see Junod, *Grammaire ronga. Suivie d'un manuel de conversation et d'un vocabulaire ronga-portugais-français-anglais, pour exposer et illustrer les lois du ronga, langage parlé par les indigènes du district de Lourenço Marques* (Lausanne, 1896), p. 3. Henri Berthoud's eight linguistic zones consisted of Maputo to the south of Delagoa Bay; Ronga to the west and north of the Bay; Djonga in the area between the Nkomati and Olifants rivers; Nwalungu between the Olifants and Limpopo rivers; Hlangano straddling both sides of the Lebombos; Makwakwa along the coast north of Limpopo and Hlengwe to the west and north. SMA 1255/B, Berthoud 'Rapport sur l'expedition chez Magud', 6 October 1885. On the present-day Tsonga dialects, see E. J. M. Baumbach, *Introduction to the Speech Sounds and Speech Sound Changes of Tsonga* (Pretoria, 1974).

39 In 1891 Berthoud reclassified Makwakwa as Nwanati, which he then linked to the Maluleke dialect in the Transvaal. He also reclassified Hlengwe as Tswa, as this term was more acceptable to the people north of the Limpopo. He also defined a new dialect (Hlavi) just north of the confluence of the Limpopo and Shangane rivers. SMA 1255/B, 'Rapport sur l'expédition à Gungunyana', 27 October 1891. In *LSAT* I, pp. 16–19, H.-A. Junod incorporated Maputo into Ronga, Hlavi into Djonga, Nwanati into Hlengwe and carved out a Bila linguistic group on the Lower Limpopo.

40 William White, *Journal of a Voyage from Madras to Columbo, and Delagoa Bay* (London, 1800); W. H. C. von Lichtenstein, *Allgemeines Archiv für Ethnographie und Linguistik* (Weimar, 1808).

41 Sebatião Botelho, *Memoria estatistica sobre os dominios portuguezes na Africa oriental* (Lisbon, 1835). Eugène Casalis placed these words under the simple heading 'Delagoa' in his *Les Bassoutos* (Paris, 1859), p. 387.

42 Wilhelm Bleek, *The Languages of Mozambique. Vocabularies of the dialects of Lourenço Marques, Inhambane etc. drawn up from the manuscript of Dr. W. Peters … and from other materials* (London, 1856). The fuller manuscript version of this work is in the South African Public Library, Cape Town, MSB71. See also O. Spohr (ed.), *The Natal Diaries of W. H. I. Bleek* (Cape Town, 1965), p. 76, and Robert Thornton, 'The Discovery of Southern African Literatures: the works of W. H. I. Bleek', Paper presented to the Centre for African Studies, University of Cape Town, September 1983, p. 23.

43 Wilhelm Bleek, 'South African languages and books', *Cape Monthly Magazine* (1858) 3, p. 325. Bleek employed this classification of the Bantu languages in his *Comparative Grammar of South African Languages* (London, 1862) I and (1869) II.

44 Gustave Fritsch, *Die Eingeborenen Sud-afrika's* (Breslau, 1872), pp. 246–8. See also Anon., 'Les langues de l'Afrique' in *l'Afrique explorée et civilisée* (1881–1882), pp. 34–5.

45 R. Cust, *A Sketch of the Modern Languages of Africa* (London, 1883) II, pp. 302–4.

46 William Holden, *The Past and Future of the Kaffir Races* (London, 1866), p. 354; W. Hammond-Tooke, 'Uncivilised man south of the Zambesi' in W. Flint and J. D. F. Gilchrist (eds), *Science in South Africa: a Handbook and Review* (Cape Town, Pretoria and Bulawayo, 1905), p. 88. C. M. Doke still used the classificatory label 'Gwamba' in his *The Southern Bantu Languages* (London, 1954).
47 *Natal Mercury*, 10 October 1871. American missionaries at Inhambane initially adopted this Zulu usage and called Gwamba-speakers *amatongas*. Cust, *A Sketch*, II, p. 304.
48 St V. Erskine, 'Journal of a Voyage to Umzila; king of Gaza, 1871–72', *Journal of the Royal Geographical Society*, (1875) 45, p. 259.
49 SMA. 548/D, Henri Berthoud to mission secretary, 14 December 1899.
50 Bleek thought the Gaza, a branch of the Mtetwa, spoke the Tefula dialect of Zulu. Spohr, *The Natal Diaries of W. H. I. Bleek*, p. 77. In 1882 Richards commented on the disappearance of the Zulu 'court language' of the 'Amanguni' when he visited Umzila on the upper Sabi river, *Missionary Herald* (1882) April, p. 141. Three years later Erwin Richards found that 'nearly every man' understood Zulu in Bilene on the Lower Limpopo, but few women or children. *Missionary Herald* (1885) September, p. 359. See also H.-A. Junod, *Grammaire ronga* (Lausanne, 1896), p. 22; *Missionary Herald* (1885) March, pp. 97–8. In 1888 Francis Bates travelled to the capital of Umzila's son, Gungunyana, on the headwaters of the Buzi, where he thought Gungunyana was enforcing 'Zulu' as the spoken language of his kingdom, *Missionary Herald* (1888) December, p. 558. Anthropologists have commented on a similar situation found amongst Tsonga-speakers (the 'Tembe-Thonga') in present-day northern KwaZulu-Natal. Robert K. Herbert, 'The political economy of language shift: language and gendered ethnicity in a Thonga community' in R. Mesthrie (ed.), *Language in South Africa* (Cambridge, 2000); David Webster, '*Abafazi bathonga bafihlakala*: ethnicity and gender in a KwaZulu border community' in A. D. Spiegel and P. A. McAllister (eds), *Tradition and Transition in Southern Africa* (Johannesburg, 1989). See note 54 below.
51 Ousley in *Missionary Herald* (1888) June, p. 256.
52 Richards in *Missionary Herald* (1887) January, p. 5.
53 Dora Earthy, *Valenge Women: The Social and Economic Life of the Valenge Women of Portuguese East Africa* (London, 1933), pp. 9, 281.
54 N. J. van Warmelo related that members of the Tsonga-speaking Ngomane group near Barberton claimed their ancestors had once spoken only North Sotho. He added that the Nkuna of the Shiluvane area in Mpumalanga were once Zulu-speaking. This process of adopting a new language is most visibly displayed by the descendants of the Gaza refugees who fled Mozambique in 1895–97. These Ngoni-speakers quickly adopted the Tsonga language of the people amongst whom they settled in the Bushbuckridge area. N. J. Van Warmelo, 'The classification of cultural groups' in W. Hammond-Tooke (ed.), *The Bantu Speaking Peoples of Southern Africa* (London, 1974), pp. 70–1.
55 Particularly in the Tembe-Thonga area allocated to Britain when the southern border of Mozambique was fixed in 1875. The Tsonga-speaking population of this region was later incorporated into the Kwazulu bantustan. It today falls within the Zulu-dominated province of KwaZulu-Natal. See note 50 above.
56 SMA 543/F, P. Loze to mission council, 2 May 1900. The term Hlengwe was used by Lourenço Marques traders and not by the people to whom it was applied.
57 On ChiNgoni, see SMA 1255/B, Georges Liengme, 'Report on the visit to Gungunyane', July 1892; SMA 1254/B, Liengme, 'Report on the expedition and stay at Mandlakazi, May–September 1893'; SMA 436/A, Liengme to mission council, 18 November 1893.
58 Paul Berthoud, 'Grammatical note on the Gwamba language' p. 47; Junod, *Grammaire ronga*, pp. 11–15.
59 SMA 8.11.B, Paul Berthoud to mission council, 7 April 1878, 24 July 1880, 5 August 1888; P. Berthoud, 'Les Spelonken' in *l'Afrique explorée et civilisée* (1880–81), p. 163; Junod, *Creux et Berthoud*, p. 55; Berthoud, *Lettres missionnaires*, pp. 396, 422; Berthoud, *Les Nègres gouamba*, p. 41; Grandjean, *La Mission romande*, p. 59.
60 SMA: 10.B, HB to council, 5 August 1888.
61 P. Berthoud, 'Grammatical note on the Gwamba language', p. 47.
62 Anon., 'Exploration de M. H. Berthoud entre les Spelonken et Lorenzo Marques' in *Afrique explorée et civilisée* (1886) pp. 308–9.
63 Literacy is dealt with in detail in the next chapter.
64 SMA 8.10.B, Henri Berthoud to council, 22 April 1890, 10 January 1892.
65 *Nouvelles de nos missionnaires* (1884) 6, 5, pp. 23–5.
66 P. Harries, *Work, Culture, and Identity: Migrant Laborers in Mozambique and South Africa, c. 1860–1910* (London, 1994), pp. 106, 160–62, 177.
67 Junod, *LSAT*, II, pp. 154–62; R. de Sa Nogueira, *Dicionário Ronga-Português* (Lisbon, 1960).
68 SMA 548/D, H. Berthoud to council, 14 December 1899.
69 This idea lay behind much of the insistence with which Junod compared contemporary Africa with prehistoric Europe. The association of the French language with modernity and the dialects with backwardness was a common theme in French and Swiss linguistic and historical studies. Cf. Juste Olivier, *Le Canton de Vaud* (Lausanne, 1837), I, pp. 219, 277; Virgile Rossel, *Histoire littéraire de la Suisse romande: des origines à nos jours*

(Neuchâtel, [1889–91] 1903), p. 647.
70. Grandjean, *La Mission romande*, p. 232; Berthoud, *Les Nègres gouamba*, pp. 31, 34–5. The first quote is from Junod, 'The Ba-Thonga of the Transvaal', p. 229.
71. William Wilcox in *Missionary Herald* (1886) January, p. 20; ibid. (1886) September, p. 346.
72. *Missionary Herald* (1887) January, p. 5; ibid. (1888) August, p. 352; ibid., September, p. 374.
73. *Missionary Herald* (1891), p. 314. On the American Board literature in Tswa and Tonga.
74. SMA 6007D, E. Richards – a short biography, pp. 18–9, 34, 41; E. Richards in *Missionary Herald* (1888) November, p. 502. On the emigration of labour from Inhambane at this time, see Harries, *Work, Culture and Identity*, pp. 46, 108.
75. SMA 8.10.B, P. Berthoud to mission council, 13 August 1877.
76. SMA 548/D, H. Berthoud to mission council, 14 March 1904.
77. Pierre Loze, *Katekisma da Tinhaka ta testament da Khale – Catéchisme d'histoire biblique de l'ancien testament en langue ronga* (Lausanne, 1901). Students read *The Pilgrim's Progress* in Portuguese before Charles Bourquin translated the work into Ronga in 1916. It took another twelve years to appear in print. *BMR* (1914) 27, p. 15.
78. Cited in C. M. Doke, 'Preliminary investigation into the state of the native languages of South Africa', *Bantu Studies* (1933) 7, p. 92. On the early literature of the mission, see Grandjean, *Mission romande*, pp. 232–6; Mary C. Bill, *Tsonga Bibliography 1883–1983* (Johannesburg, 1983) esp. pp. 14, 17, 20–1.
79. *Zoutpansberg Review* (1906) 8 June; Lemana Training Institute Brochure (1936); C. M. Doke, 'Vernacular textbooks in South African Native Schools', *Africa* (1935), 8, p. 190.
80. Cf. Ronald Wardhaugh, *An Introduction to Sociolinguistics* (Oxford, 1992), pp. 19–30.
81. I draw attention to this practice in early KwaZulu-Natal in Harries, 'Imagery, Symbolism and Tradition in a South African Bantustan: Mangosuthu Buthelezi, Inkatha, and Zulu History', *History and Theory* (1993) 2, 4, p. 109.
82. SMA 548/D, Henri Berthoud to council, 14 December 1899.
83. SMA 1255/B, Henri Berthoud, 'Rapport sur l'expédition à Magude 1885'; SMA 8.10.B, Henri Berthoud to council, 22 April 1890.
84. R. Berthoud-Junod, 9 July 1887 in *BMR* (1887), pp. 325–6.
85. The translation of the Psalms took him eighteen months to complete. Jean Rambert, *Arthur Grandjean* (Lausanne, n.d., 1931?), pp. 16–17.
86. SMA 8.10.B, Henri Berthoud to mission council, 1 October 1889; H.-A. Junod, *Ernest Creux et Paul Berthoud*, p. 156.
87. SMA 8.10.B, Henri Berthoud to mission council, 10 January 1892. See also note 115 below.
88. *Missionary Herald* (1891) August, p. 314.
89. Junod, 'Pays des Gouambas: difficultés de la langue', *Revue des missions contemporaines* (1890) II, August.
90. Junod, letter of 30 October 1889 in *BMR* (1889) 7, 87, pp. 350–51; UNISA.JC. Sermons, 2 February 1890. Grandjean also commented on Matsivi's intelligence and remarked that he 'would not be out of place in Europe'. At Antioka, Grandjean continued to produce Bible translations in Gwamba. Rambert, *Arthur Grandjean*, pp. 16, 22.
91. SMA 1254/B, Junod, 'Etude comparative', Resumé in 'Thonga, Gouamba, Djonga, Ronga', *BMR* (1894) 114, April 1894; Junod, *Grammaire ronga*, pp. 41–4, 78–82. Junod first established this criticism in March, 1893, see untitled report in UNISA.JC.9.1.
92. See chapter three, pp. 79–80, 84–5.
93. *BMR* (1887) 6, 71, p. 210.
94. E. W. Smith-Delacour, *Shironga Vocabulary* (London, 1893). Junod, *Grammaire ronga*, pp. 24–5. On Mashaba, see Harries, *Work, Culture and Identity*, pp. 34, 105–6, 160.
95. Junod, 'A propos de la traduction de la Bible en thonga' in *Liberté Chrétienne* (1898) 15 December, p. 598.
96. UNISA.JC.9.1. Junod's untitled report, March 1893. See also SMA 840, Liengme to council, 3 January 1896.
97. UNISA.JC.9.1. Junod's untitled report, March 1893.
98. SMA 1254/A, 'Rapport de la Conférence du Littoral'; *Nouvelles des nos missionnaires* (1893) 15, 6.
99. Junod, letter from Rikatla, 29 Aug 1893, in *Nouvelles de nos missionnaires* (1893) 16, 3, p. 37. At this time, Junod referred to his dependence on native speakers in letters to William Barbey. Cf. CBG. Boissier herbarium: Junod to Barbey, 1 February 1894, 27 January 1897.
100. Junod, *Sipele sa Sironga: abecedaire et livre de lecture en dialecte ronga parlé aux environs de la baie de Delagoa* (Lausanne, 1894).
101. Junod, *Grammaire ronga*.
102. Junod, *Grammaire ronga*; *Les chants et les contes des Ba-Ronga* (Lausanne, 1897); 'Les Baronga: étude ethnographique sur les indigènes de la baie de Delagoa,' *Bulletin de la société neuchâteloise de géographie* (1898) 10, pp. 1–517. On other early translations, see Grandjean, *La Mission romande*, p. 234.
103. For this debate, see SMA 1254/B, Junod, 'Etude comparative'; Junod, *Grammaire ronga*; H. Berthoud, 'Quelques remarques sur la famille des langues Bantou'; SMA 543/F, P. Loze, 'Au sujet de la double littérature'.

104 UNISA, JC. Junod, 'Les Causes de la Rébellion', letter to Virgile Rossel, 1895.
105 Junod, *LSAT* II, p. 625n1.
106 Junod, *Grammaire ronga*, pp. 5–6. In 'Some remarks on the folklore of the Ba-Thonga' he wrote of 'the tribe of Delagoa Bay which calls itself the Ba-Ronga'. *Folk-lore* (1903) XIV, 2, June, p. 116.
107 Junod, *Grammaire ronga*, pp. 5, 15. He repeated this point in *LSAT*, I, pp. 14–15. See Olivier's strong statements on this issue in his *Canton de Vaud*, I, pp. 216–19.
108 Junod, *LSAT*, I, pp. 9, 32–3; ibid., II, p. 153.
109 This return to the source through philology, particularly the Sanskrit and Indo-Germanic languages, was part of a wider movement built on the Gothic revival, archaeology, palaeontology and anthropology, see chapter 2 pp. 44–5 above.
110 These were common ideas at the time, see Nélia Dias, 'Langues inférieures, langues supérieures' in *Des Sciences contre l'homme, I, classer, hiérarchiser, exclure* (Paris, 1993).
111 Junod, *Grammaire ronga*, dedication and p. 41.
112 Junod, *Grammaire ronga*, p. 2.
113 See note 54 above.
114 In May 1885 William Wilcox thought Shitswa to be 'only a slight variation of Gwamba ... the language which is spoken, with some variations, from Delagoa Bay to the Sabi river.' *Missionary Herald* (1885) November, p. 467. In September that year Wilcox made no distinction between 'Shitswa or Gwamba as the Swiss Mission call it'. *Missionary Herald* (1886) January, p. 20.
115 P. Berthoud, *Les Nègres gouamba*, p. 34; P. Berthoud, letter of 1 November 1890 in *l'Afrique explorée et civilisée* (1890), p. 26. In 1896 Junod supported the adoption of the term 'Thonga' for the cluster of related languages called Ronga, Thonga and Tswa. *Grammaire ronga*, pp. 3–4.
116 SMA 548/D, Henri Berthoud, 'Réponse à la note de M. Junod sur la question de la double littérature'.
117 SMA 8.10.B, Henri Berthoud to Secretary, 22 February 1898.
118 SMA 548/D, Henri Berthoud to council, 14 December 1899.
119 SMA 584/D, Henri Junod, 'La question de la double littérature', 5 April 1898; 543/F, P. Loze to Secretary, 2 May 1900.
120 SMA 543/F, Paul Berthoud, appendix to P. Loze to mission secretary, 2 May 1900.
121 Ch. W. Chatelain and H.-A. Junod, *A Pocket Dictionary, Thonga (Shangaan)-English; English-Thonga (Shangaan) preceded by an Elementary Grammar* (Lausanne, 1909). In South Africa, men from the east coast working in the diamond and gold mines had for many years been called 'Shangaans,' after Shoshangaan or Munukosi, the first Gaza king. Cf. Junod, 'The Ba-Thonga', p. 222.
122 Junod, *Bukhaneli bya Xirjonga* (Lausanne, 1903); W. Benoit, *Gramatica Portuguesa em Lingua Ronga* (Lausanne, 1914, 2nd edn); Antonio Lourenço Farinha, *Elementos de Grammaire ronga* (Lausanne, 1920). It is of some interest to note that Lestrade (Appendix J of Doke, 'Preliminary investigations', p. 90) found Berthoud's *Shangaan Grammar* to be 'much superior to Junod's work'. M. Bill also finds it 'a much clearer exposition of the verbal system of the Shangaan (Tsonga) language,' see Bill, 'Berthoud's *Leçons de Sigwamba* (1883)', p. 500.
123 René Cuenod, 'Les langues africaines et la traduction de la Bible', *Revue missionnaire* (1928) 20, December, p. 100.
124 Valdemir Zamparoni, 'As "escravoas perpétuas" e o "ensino pratico": raça, gênero e educaçao no Moçambique Colonial, 1910–1930', *Estudos Afro-Asiaticos* (2002) 24, 3, p. 465.
125 This belief was particularly strong in South Africa, see Bryce, *Impressions of South Africa*, pp. 366, 464; W. A. Norton, 'African life and language', *Bantu Studies* (1950) 9 (1), p. 1; Junod, 'The Native Languages and Native education', *Journal of the Royal African Society* (1905) XVII, October, p. 10; E. Jacottet, 'Introduction' to E. Jacottet and Z. Magoaela, *A Grammar of the Sesuto Language*, (ed.), C. M. Doke, (Johannesburg, 1927), p. v.; C. M. Doke, 'The linguistic situation in South Africa', *Africa* (1928) 1, 4, p. 483. This view was still being expressed in the mid-1940s, see William Plomer, *Electric Delights* (ed.), R. Hart-Davis (Boston, MA, 1978), p. 18.
126 SMA 597/A, Junod to council, 11 November 1914; Junod, 'The Native Languages and Native Education'; Junod, *LSAT*, II, pp. 613–22.

7
Literacy

Are my words not like fire? saith the Lord; and like a hammer that breaketh the rocks in pieces!
(Jeremiah 23:29)

This chapter looks at the ways in which the missionaries spread Thonga and Ronga as standard written languages throughout their field of operations in the northern Transvaal and southern Mozambique. First, it examines how the context in which literacy was acquired in Switzerland led the missionaries to conceive of reading and writing as revolutionary tools for the transformation of society. Second, the very different contexts in which Swiss and African readers acquired the skills of literacy are examined and how these influenced the ways in which they read. In the fourth and longest section, these ways of reading are tied to the interpretation of texts and to the construction and maintenance of local networks of power.

Reading in Western Switzerland

For the missionaries of the Free Churches in Switzerland, reading was both an agent of modernization and an integral part of their history and religion. By the early nineteenth century, French-speaking, republican Switzerland had developed into a major centre for the distribution of the printed word. Protestant literature in the vernacular had been sent across the border for many years alongside streams of works stretching from the philosophical to the pornographic, proscribed in Catholic, monarchical France. Radical politicians who seized power in Switzerland in the mid-nineteenth century underlined the importance of reading. For these harbingers of secularism and progress, literacy was the key to knowledge, reason and logic; it was the foundation of civic culture. In a canton such as Neuchâtel, education for all children between the ages of seven and sixteen was made obligatory in 1850, fees were suppressed in 1861 and the school system was secularized in 1872. Two years later the rest of the Confederation adopted this form of education.[1] At the same time, politicians seeking to break the church's hold on education supported the construction of school buildings, libraries and reading rooms. In Neuchâtel in 1889, an obligatory year of pre-school was introduced and the number of pupils per class was limited to fifty. The following year the state started to supply pupils with books and other learning materials. This investment in education and the institutions that supported it produced a population of readers who in turn created a healthy market for an extremely wide range of journals and publications.[2]

The origins of the remarkable degree of literacy in Switzerland may be traced to the Calvinist insistence on reading as a skill encouraging inner reflection and meditation upon sin and the consequent need for contrition, conversion and personal salvation. A church stripped of the paintings and sculptures that had once moved religious belief looked to the textual message carried by the printed word to inspire faith. The development of the printing industry and the fall in the price of paper aided this movement as the cost of the Bible dropped precipitously and colporteurs carried hand-held copies to even the poorest homes.[3] From early childhood, Christians in western Switzerland were taught to read in ways that evoked deep emotions. Instead of having texts explained by a priestly elite, they saw reading in the vernacular as a personal, interpretive act through which they formed their own judgments and opinions on the word of God and his disciples. For the Free Church Calvinists, reading was the foundation of their faith: the rock upon which they built a Church that was at once independent of government, democratic in its composition and unencumbered by cramping dogma. Under the influence of the revival, evangelists took this active form of reading into isolated areas where they linked a belief in the God of the Protestants to the ability to read. Protestant villagers read the Bible aloud at home in a ponderous, measured way that distinguished them from Catholic neighbours over time. Placed in a corner of the communal living space once occupied by a Catholic crucifix, heavy family Bibles represented a link with the past, a marker of identity and a source of knowledge.[4]

During the third quarter of the century, literacy increased markedly as the radicals wrestled with the church and its liberal allies to control local institutions of knowledge. As we saw in chapter one, the struggle between church and state to control education and other aspects of life eventually led evangelicals to break from the established churches. The Free Church of the canton of Vaud and the Independent Churches of Neuchâtel and Geneva sought to maintain their control over the morality of the population by establishing their own publishers, libraries and reading rooms, Bible study groups and, particularly, a vibrant Sunday school movement. While liberals abhorred the intervention of the state in education, evangelicals believed that the secularization accompanying this development would further advance the immorality of an industrial age; they fought this secularization with a flood of religious material produced by Bible and Tract societies, Christian associations and especially the Sunday schools.[5] By the late 1860s–70s, the practice of reading in western Switzerland was deeply anchored in a wide range of institutions extending from publishing houses, through public, church and Sunday schools, to a network of libraries for young people and workers.

Perhaps most importantly, literacy both strengthened and spread the evangelical message. From his rocky village in the High Alps of France, Félix Neff ruminated on the importance of literacy as a proselytizing agent. 'Allow me to suppose a case', he wrote in the 1820s, that

> an inhabitant of central Africa finds a copy of the Bible in his own language; he reads it, believes it, and acknowledges its truth; invokes the name of Jesus, and finds in him that peace, which

in spite of all the vendors of indulgences, Christ alone can, and does, give to whom he will. Converted by the study of this book, our Neophyte renounces his idols, proclaims the glad tidings to his brethren, and assembles around him a little church.[6]

In the final quarter of the nineteenth century, Neff's wishful thinking became a vivid aspect of the Christian experience in south-east Africa.

The Transformative Powers of the Word

By the early 1870s the rise of commercial farming, plantation agriculture and mining was generating a massive movement of men across the landscape of southern Africa. Some of these men tramped home with devotional works in their baggage, literature with which they spread the seed of belief and provided guidance for people living far from centres of Christianity. In Lesotho, Paul Berthoud was impressed by the heavy demand for books at the Morija printing works and by the large number of New Testaments in South Sotho sold to Pedi migrants returning home from the Cape Colony. When Berthoud travelled northwards to the Pedi homeland with Adolphe Mabille in the winter of 1873, scattered groups of Christians frequently asked him for reading material. In response to this demand, he developed the practice of preaching from his wagon. Once a good crowd had assembled Berthoud would hand out books and reading primers in South Sotho to his audience.[7] On one occasion, at a village near Albasini's home at Goedewensch, Berthoud considered that every one of the seventy listeners assembled to hear Mabille preach 'would like to learn to read'.[8]

The Swiss built their mission in the northern Transvaal on the labours of migrants who had come into contact with reading while working in the British colonies. These individuals welcomed the mission as a conveyer of both Christianity and the writing with which it was associated. John Songele had travelled several times to the diamond fields where he had encountered Christianity and converted. On his return from Kimberley in 1873-74, he found the Sotho evangelists near his home and was taught to read in Sotho by Eliakim Matlanyane. In his passion to read, Songele had committed the entire South Sotho ABC to memory. The desire to read was so strong, François Coillard felt when he passed through Valdezia in 1877, that he could have sold three wagons packed with religious works, particularly the New Testament in 'sessouto'.[9]

Soon after their arrival, the missionaries became aware that a foundation for their evangelical work had been prepared by anonymous migrant workers who returned home with the Christian message, sometimes in written form, from their places of employment in the south. However, once cut off from the literate world of the mine or the mission, many of these men soon relinquished both the habit of reading and with it the central tenets of Christianity. For this reason, the evangelists who first reconnoitred the coastal plain in the winter of 1881 carried with them writing materials and introduced local people to the Sotho readers still in use at Valdezia. With these instruments, the evangelists established a native church on the coast and quickly turned Rikatla into a centre for the diffusion of Christianity and literacy.[10] When the newly-converted returned home from this 'centre of pilgrimage' with these skills, they stoked the embers of faith and encouraged the religiosity of readers whose isolated villages became 'homes of light and life in pagan darkness'.[11] Yet others found religious inspiration – even a cause for conversion – when presented with devotional texts printed in a language with which they were familiar.[12] 'In this way,' Paul Berhoud wrote in 1888, 'the *buku* was itself a powerful means of evangelization.'[13]

The missionaries valued literacy as a cheap and effective means of spreading the gospel and with it the possibility of salvation. They saw God's guiding hand behind their discovery of the vast mission field occupied by the Gwamba-speaking people in Mozambique and the Transvaal. But for some missionaries, as for some modern historians, literacy was also tied to ways of thinking that were a synonym for progress. For these men, reading was an essential part of the modernity that had brought wealth to regions of Switzerland known only for producing mercenaries, emigrant teachers and American colonists. But although literacy had contributed to the construction of a reasoning, responsible and diligent workforce, the secularization of education had stripped away the morality they needed to cope with an alienating, industrial age. Many missionaries in Africa believed that, through their control of literacy, they could exert a strong influence on the forces of social change. Through their actual control of the language, from translation work to the printing and dissemination of texts, they would shape readers' perceptions and cultural practices. Literacy would revolutionize the natives' intellectual habits and ways of thinking. Almost a century before Jack Goody launched an examination of the topic, or Elizabeth Eisenstein explored the social effects of print, several Swiss missionaries had clearly identified the cognitive consequences of literacy.[14] Vernacular literacy would create nothing less than a 'new society in the heart of the tribal bantu', as Henri-Alexandre Junod wrote. His colleague Henri Berthoud concurred: 'the printing of the word of God' would lead to 'a new people emerging from darkness'.[15]

Junod traced the achievements of the 'Indo-European peoples' to their historical ties with the forms of writing developed in ancient Mesopotamia and Egypt. He considered the skills of reading and writing to be universal rather than narrowly racial, as they were the historical product of the accumulated talents of a wide range of peoples. Junod believed that Africa's isolation from this world of reading was one of the major reasons for the continent's material backwardness. Only writing could transfer to Africa the ideas and experiences needed to engage Africa's potential. Junod felt that deciphering the characters printed on a page not only concentrated the mind and encouraged reflection, it also constituted a marker of intellectual evolution. For Junod, a language was an evolving organism, and a language that was 'still living and creating new expressions, enriching itself by means of vocables invented on all sides' was both a source of capricious inventiveness and an indication of an early 'phase of human development'.[16] Nevertheless, Junod's study of the language led him to admire the richness of Thonga, particularly the 'power of classification' and its 'mechanism of reasoning'.[17] His research led him to believe that the Bantu languages

> have reached a high degree of development; they reveal the existence of intellectual powers not essentially different from those of civilized races. They certainly constitute the greatest achievement of Bantu mental activity and the most precious treasure inherited by the Bantus of today from their forefathers.[18]

Such ideas, that might seem merely idle musings to today's reader, carried an important political message in the late nineteenth century. For at that time many philologists believed that through the study of languages they could situate communities on a ladder of evolution in a way that would indicate how they should be governed.[19]

These theories on the hierarchy of languages and peoples affected philology in South Africa in various ways. Wilhelm Bleek, for instance, viewed the Kaffir branch of what he called south-eastern Bantu as akin to Sanskrit and Gothic. He initially thought Tekeza 'broad and soft' in comparison with Zulu and Kaffir but he eventually came to see Kaffir as the richest, fullest and most melodious of the south-eastern Bantu languages.[20] For Ernst Haeckel, the linguistic work of his cousin Wilhelm Bleek served to prove that the 'languages of the lower races of men' were closer to those of 'the gorilla and the chimpanzee' than to those 'of Kant or Goethe'.[21] Others saw African languages as degenerate remnants of a primeval monotheistic stage of development or viewed them as 'childish' and 'weak' in ways that reinforced earlier descriptions of the ties between African languages and racial inferiority.[22]

Junod preferred to draw on a tradition running from Sigismund Koëlle in West Africa to Eugène Casalis in Lesotho and Max Müller in Oxford, that found an ordered structure and a deep humanity reflected in African languages.[23] He was particularly pleased to detect in the Thonga language the same care for classification and systematics that he had discovered in the zoology, and particularly the botany, of local people. Through their classification of prefixes and nouns, the Thonga showed a clear ability to systematize language in a way that was perhaps even superior to the Indo-Germans. On the other hand, because their language was still at an oral stage, Thonga-speakers were able to create idioms not matched by Europeans. For the same reason, their 'descriptive adverbs' were deeply felt, almost instinctual, expressions that were 'far superior' to those of Europeans. Junod believed, in general, the study of Bantu languages showed Africans' intellectual powers to be little different from those of Europeans.[24]

Junod was convinced that once an ordered grammar and a regular orthography had disciplined the capriciousness of the rich Ronga and Thonga languages, the missionaries could raise their charges to think in the manner of enlightened Europeans. Language was the single most important expression of the Bantu peoples. However, the full genius of the language could only be captured when it was harnessed by the skills of literacy. Once it had been fixed on paper, the Thonga language would 'train the (Bantu) mind to understand the process of thought'. Part of this task included sentence parsing, an occupation he considered particularly useful for people to accustom their minds to the rigours of analysis and classification.[25] Literacy would allow 'great minds' to spread their ideas and transfer them to the next generation. This circulation of ideas through time and space would liberate individuals from the constricting conservatism of community control. Ideas would become rules, laws and moral principles fixed in writing and hence no longer subject to the will of the strongest and often the most brutal members of the community. By inscribing these principles on paper, the 'Bantu mind' would be freed from its 'capriciousness' and acquire the discipline needed to inspire progress. Literacy would ensure that written rules and precedent rather than changing human relations or physical force would determine the morality of society. Order, rigour and self-control would replace the flexibility, impermanence and instability associated with orality.

Literacy was intimately linked to the regeneration of society. As it replaced a 'capricious existence' with 'an orderly life', blacks would learn to embrace 'the gospel of work'.[26] Writing would also stimulate the memory, and fix images in the imagination and the sentiments. 'Writing is the mother of history', declared Junod, who clearly believed that a fixed past would place precedent in the hands of science and justice rather than in the service of sectional interests.[27] Perhaps most importantly, writing would provide Africans with a sense of morality that was not restricted to the kinship group or the chiefdom. Without this notion of right and wrong, African society would not withstand the trauma of industrialization and would lose the possibility of entering the kingdom of heaven. For Africans 'emerging from the state of collectivism', morality did not depend on 'clearly conceived' laws but on 'the will of the community (as) the feeling of being right or wrong is above all determined by the attitude of the group'. They 'readily submit to the will of the superior', irrespective of the 'real moral value' of a decision, Junod noted ruefully.[28] Political despotism was another cause of Africa's backwardness, as it restricted the emergence of a personal religion and limited the development of individual talent. The result was a society dominated by custom in which individuals performed rituals as though 'hypnotised' or 'in a mesmeric sleep'.

> You see them carrying out the act, constrained by a mysterious necessity and without knowing why they do so. The hypnotising factor here is the weight of heredity, of all this hoary antiquity, which belongs indeed to the past, but still influences the subliminal life of the tribe...[29]

Junod believed reading as a silent, private practice would bring Africans to think about personal choice and individual responsibility. However, in the process, it was important to avoid the anarchy, greed and breakdown of moral structures that industrialism and the rise of the individual had brought to Europe; hence the need to subject the natives' reading habits and material to a strict stewardship. A new Christian literature would produce a community of readers who shared common expressions, ideas and principles, and it would extend their moral community from the kin-based clan to a 'tribe' or 'nation' defined by a fixed, written language. Gradually the tribe's sense of morality would become universal as its members attached themselves to a transcendental yet personal God.[30] In this way, writing would aid the intellect, reason and logic to triumph over brute physical power. It would unleash Africa's potential and provide the continent with a shared Christian morality.

Of course, there are other ways of looking at the consequences of literacy. Johann Michaelis, for instance, wrote in the eighteenth century that 'language is a democracy where use or custom is decided by the majority'.[31] However, Junod chose to stress the link between 'great minds', implicitly associated with the mission and its converts, and a written language. Underlying this notion was the desire for a very specific shift in political power as the chiefs lost control over words and their meaning to the new, educated, Christian elite.[32] Also implicit in Junod's ideas was a fear of the way in which individuals in Europe had interiorized many of the ideas and images carried by the written word. Rationalism, materialism and revolution were the offspring of writings that had subverted the church and ruptured her hold over social life. The missionaries believed that ideas carried in written texts could transform society, but they equally believed that this transformation had to be controlled by the church. Control should extend over the spiritual and the secular content of written works but it should equally govern the disciplined grammar and orthography of the language.

As discussed in the previous chapter, the mission's control of the language was first challenged in 1893 when Robert Mashaba fixed his mother tongue on paper. Junod criticized Mashaba's unusual approach to the Ronga language, particularly his unorthodox orthography and the oral forms of expression that structured his written work.[33] Junod considered a disciplined vernacular grammar, dictionary and a strict orthography the fundamental tools needed to encourage both abstract and ordered thinking. While they fixed words and their meanings in time, these manuals uncovered the order and regularity of language. In this sense, Junod and others saw what I would call 'oral writing' to be the product of individuals like Mashaba who were unqualified to discipline and train the 'Bantu mind'. This form of writing was ultimately a threat to the fundamental task of literacy: the fostering of both Christianity and scientific knowledge.[34]

The shape and content of the vernacular language was of such importance that, for many years, mission headquarters in Lausanne jealously guarded its control. Writing in Ronga and Gwamba (or Thonga), and, indeed, almost controlling the development of these languages, the missionaries and their converts would direct the upward evolution of 'the Bantu race'. Literacy would aid them to combat alcoholism and avarice as effectively as the devil and disbelief. The historical experience of the missionaries in Switzerland had taught them to link economic and social progress, but just as importantly, moral upliftment to the ability to read and write.

They were determined to make literacy the driving force behind a massive plan of social engineering in Africa. Literacy would domesticate the savage mind by providing knowledge, the analytical skills of grammar, and the power of exegesis. 'This alphabet', Junod wrote,

> [will] give a fresh aspect to things in general. These twenty or thirty letters of which the Blacks had not the slightest notion, these signs, thanks to which wood and paper have been made to speak, will henceforward allow great minds to transmit their thoughts direct to their fellow-men. The knowledge of one epoch will then be passed on intact to following generations, whilst, formerly, ideas were frequently lost or distorted by popular tradition; progression will henceforth be not merely *arithmetical* but *geometrical*. The *book* will be the accumulator in which the intellectual strength of the race will be stored for future transmission, without wastage, prolific of light and stimulus to every sphere of human activity. Printing will increase its operations a hundredfold.[35]

Free Church evangelicals charged literacy with an enormous symbolism as it was the foundation upon which humankind would be born again in Africa. Literacy was associated with the cognitive conversion needed to save both the spirit and the flesh. The printed word carried not only the redemptive message of the gospel, it also promised a physical and moral rebirth by propagating the idea of a virtuous, hard-working society freed of sin, drunkenness and debauchery. For the Swiss missionaries, literacy rang with the sound of regeneration.

This view of literacy as a revolutionary tool for the transformation of society was the product of the missionaries' specific experience, but it was also created by the way in which they defined reading in stark opposition to orality. Junod noted that the absence of reading marked an early stage of human evolution when the mind was dominated by irregular and inconsistent thoughts. He saw literacy and orality locked in a ruthless struggle. 'The book will conquer, it will kill ignorance, superstition, useless conservatism and intellectual laziness.'[36] He was supported in this contention by the secretary-general of the mission who held literacy to be engaged in a combat against 'ignorance and superstition'.[37] Elsewhere Junod continued with this martial imagery when he compared African society to a 'wild buffalo' with the 'yoke' of literacy and education 'placed on its neck'. He remarked confidently that 'the savage mind of the Bantu is now being trained to civilized methods, and the Elementary School gathers in the goatherds of the bush.' Literacy, he warned darkly, was the only way in which 'the Black race' could adapt itself to the requirements of modern society.[38]

Literacy as a Local Skill

The missionaries' view of the revolutionary potential of literacy took little account of the African context in which the skill was imparted and acquired. Switzerland was awash with literacy. The missionaries came from a country where durable and powerful institutions taught individuals to read and write in a particular way, filled their lives with printed documents and signs and with texts calculated to appeal to a wide range of interests. With the suppression of plagiarism and the piracy of ideas, books had become sources of authoritative knowledge. The skills of literacy had an everyday utility for the Swiss who considered them a marker of identity and achievement, almost a rite of passage to adulthood. But in Africa the mission had little control over the spread of literacy. It had neither the institutional strength to implement the type of reading conceptualized by Junod and his colleagues, nor the means to maintain the level of literacy it required.

As a skill based on the need to transfer knowledge and information, literacy was particularly useful in towns. Paul Berthoud had remarked on this as early as 1873 when he considered the Kimberley diamond fields a centre for the diffusion of books, reading skills and Christian knowledge.[39] Fifteen years later, when the Congregationalists thought the diamond fields 'the most important missionary centre in South Africa', Berthoud's brother Henri commented that mineworkers were starting to write to each other and to their families at home.[40] A brisk trade in books printed in African and European languages was conducted at Kimberley and, once gold was discovered in 1886, soon spread to the Witwatersrand. By the turn of the century tens of thousands of migrant workers came into contact with religious literature on the mines of South Africa every year.[41]

These men learned to read at the mines in various ways. It is these 'ways of reading' that should alert us to the dangers of interpreting 'literacy' as simply the opposite of 'orality'. The context in which reading was acquired and the manner and reasons for its acquisition could be very different. On Sundays, noisy crowds of Christians intruded into the mineworker's world. For many of them, bands of evangelizing Christians provided a source of entertainment and a welcome relief from their grinding, dangerous work, interspersed by long spells of boredom in the compounds. Even those who preferred other diversions could hardly escape the Christians' rumbustious singing, accompanied by a harmonium or brass band, their cajoling of sinners and their lively sermons. On such occasions men came into contact with reading for the first time as evangelists brandished their Bibles and read and sang aloud from books and hymnals. For some, an introduction to reading went no further, and they sought other forms of entertainment and instruction during their leisure hours. But others grew uneasy before the missionaries' threats of eternal damnation and, perhaps because they lived in a world filled with death, looked anxiously for the means to secure eternal salvation. Some accepted the illustrated religious cards inscribed with short Biblical texts proffered by missionaries or watched their lantern slide shows. Those men who wished to extend their brush with reading into something more substantial could attend the church services, prayer meetings and Bible readings that took place in Christian dormitories in the compound or in the small evangelical halls built on and around mine property.[42]

Other miners perhaps found a purely secular utility in writing. They were all aware of the printed words on their passes, contracts and work tickets and they found posters and signposts on mine property and in the towns clustered around the diggings, often inscribed with illustrations and texts. In this way, men who had not learned to read developed an everyday familiarity with the printed word. Letter writing brought the migrant and his home into a single geographical space.[43] On the Witwatersrand the imagined community created by the standard vernacular literatures of the rural missionaries was made tangible: confronted by competing ethnic groups, membership of a bounded linguistic community became a cornerstone of the worker's sense of security, mobility and belonging. An ability to read in the vernacular, particularly in English, gave the miner access to both spiritual and secular worlds, while a familiarity with the symbols and codes of whites allowed him a certain upward mobility. The literate worker could become a dormitory scribe, writing dictated letters for one shilling, or move into domestic service, clerical posts or other positions in the service sector of the economy.[44] The reading time available to workers increased when the length of the underground shift was reduced, artificial lighting introduced to the dormitories and optical aids made available.

It is instructive to look at the way these men learned to read. Early in the twentieth century an average of about forty men attended the night classes held six days a week at the compound mission school on the Crown Reef mine. Between 7.00 and 8.00 p.m., novices learned to read the alphabet while the more advanced students practised their writing. For the next half-hour, beginners scratched letters and words on slates, the seniors read the Bible aloud and posed questions. During the final fifteen minutes they recalled the power of literacy by singing hymns, praying and reading the roll-call.[45] We can only speculate on how these men deciphered the printed word. Social relations exercised a crucial influence on the way texts were read, as did the size and cost of the book. Reading aloud or collectively was a social act far removed from the silent, private, sustained and reflective practice envisaged by Junod. The use of a single and familiar text sometimes resulted in rote memorization and the recital rather than reading of passages from the Bible. Memorized verses from the Bible served as a sign of belonging, a form of exhortation and a subject of serious conversation.[46] The study of the Bible in this focused situation probably encouraged an 'intensive' form of reading that left little intellectual space for the exercise of great minds. The verbal commentaries on the Good Book produced by this tight gathering were probably more about explanation than exegesis.[47] The Bible, like the *buku*, was ideal for the ruptured reading of neophytes as it consists of short passages suitable for discussion and reflection. But we can only guess how these migrants made sense of what they read, as they worked their way between narrow rural societies and a cosmopolitan industrial world. It is almost certain that their interpretation of the texts set before them would be foreign to us.

As a skill, reading requires an active engagement with its raw material. It is not a neutral practice that engraves textual images on the mind passively like print upon a page. Reading is an interpretive act, a way of constructing meaning that is crucially shaped by the experience, situation and needs of the reader.[48] People who were born and raised in an oral culture read in a very different way from those raised in a culture saturated with the practice and means of reading, like that of the Swiss.

This situation was visible in the 1880s at Rikatla where Loïs Xintomane and Eliachib Mandlakusasa developed the mission into a centre of pilgrimage. Their daughter Ruth had been taught to read in South Sotho by evangelists of the PEMS employed by the Swiss in the Transvaal; her readings from the New Testament were initially translated by Loïs. Local Christians learned to read in the courtyard at Rikatla and were often provided with a copy of the *buku* on their return home. Ruth Berthoud-Junod was 'astonished how well' people read at Rikatla, for 'everyone goes to school'.[49] As the object of these lessons was to impart to students the edifying knowledge contained in the Bible, little attention was paid to the mechanism of reading and no attempt was made to teach the alphabet or to discern the structure of words or sentences on a page. Older people who had been raised and nurtured in an oral culture found it impossible to read in an active way. Some might even have believed that an ability to recite the Bible was an indispensable aspect of conversion to Christianity.[50]

'They would read page after page, perhaps twenty', wrote Junod, 'ready to stop at the twenty-first saying: "From here I don't know any more..." They had quite simply learned all these pages by heart!'[51] Junod recalled the way in which Martha, the cook at Rikatla (the woman who was described as being accused of witchcraft in chapter three) read with zeal. 'Never having learned to read in the normal way, she would decipher the New Testament nicely, half remembered, half guessed, and knew admirably well how to recite her passage from the catechism.'[52] For generally middle-aged or elderly women whose society placed a high premium on oratorical skills, 'reading' meant the memorization and recitation of long Biblical passages. Texts were 'read' in entirely oral ways. Indeed, the missionaries recognized the importance of oral linguistic expressions and even commented favourably on the natives' 'wonderful' ability to memorize and on the 'sanctity' with which they imbued the spoken word.[53] Junod even expressed the fear that 'books and book language will destroy this most interesting mode of speech', employed 'by those natives who are true Bantus'. 'The genius of the race will certainly suffer from this loss.'[54] But in the final instance Junod and his colleagues condemned oral culture. They were concerned when an evangelist such as Diamane, who had been converted on the mines by A. W. Baker's Compound Mission, returned to Khosen to 'read' the two pages of his open Bible that he knew by heart.[55] Recitation led to a 'tendency to imitation' and it encouraged a passive approach to knowledge. 'Native children (and often teachers) are perfectly satisfied with a parrot-like learning of words and sounds which they do not understand. They commit to memory entire books in a purely mechanical manner, without bothering at all about the meaning of the words.'[56] The missionaries would sometimes only detect those people who had learned to recite their readers by heart when the errant pupil was seen reading a book upside down.[57]

The missionaries' literate or documentary view of the world disqualified forms of reading that bridged the gulf between the written and the spoken. For incorrigibly literate individuals such as Junod, orality appropriated all ways of reading that did not conform to his ideal of reading as a silent, private practice. Yet many individuals read in ways that cannot be classed as either literate or illiterate.

While adult readers associated knowledge with the ability to express oneself orally, the more politically marginalized seem to have found a source of power in reading. Even within Christian families, a range of reading abilities emerged when parents sent their children to Rikatla to acquire a functional literacy. On their return home the children read aloud to adults who would frequently learn the written passages by heart.[58] This caused the family gathering to become the milieu for diverse reading habits, as in Protestant Switzerland. It also caused literacy to penetrate the African equivalent of the Swiss *veillées*, gatherings where family and friends met around a fire at night-time to share knowledge and build up an orally-based culture. On these occasions collective readings formed a sort of acculturation to the printed text as children introduced the wonders of the written word to their grown-up listeners.[59]

We can only guess at the way the Rikatla evangelists taught children to read to their families. However, men returning from the mines, together with those who attended the classes already established in the country, invariably learned to read in other ways. Some no doubt faltered and stumbled as they worked their way through a page, but others were probably sufficiently versed in the world of print to read silently to themselves. There were a few who escaped the control of the mission by reading aloud in Zulu, English and Dutch from works acquired in South Africa. Others even learned both to read and to write. A small number left the mines and ports, acquired a formal education in South Africa and returned home to spread their new skills. The point is that the ability to read covered a wide spectrum, from those who merely listened to the printed word to those who read fluently and in private.

Print came in many forms. Printed cards, engravings and lantern slides provided a colourful medium through which viewers 'saw' Biblical characters and events.[60] When Paul Berthoud received his first collection of one hundred lantern slides, an 'enormous crowd' gathered to watch the projection. Viewers invested the pictures with emotions that became inflamed when they started to sing hymns. When images of the crucifixion appeared on the screen, one old woman broke down and started to sob in a way that became almost a tradition as years went by.[61] As mnemonic devices, such images and hymns probably moved viewers more than their hesitant and distracted reading of texts. Hymns required other forms of reading. Written or printed, they were easily memorized when divided into verses, packed with slogans and locked into tunes that stirred memory and emotion. One of Junod's enduring memories was of Elias 'Spoon' Libombo (the diviner who became his major source of information in the fields of entomology, botany and ethnography) singing hymns from an open New Testament, without knowing how to read.[62] The hymns published in the *buku* constituted a form of 'sung reading' that appealed to people with little knowledge of Christianity or literacy. Together with the Christian message, it was passed over long distances to places such as the capital of the Gaza empire, viewed by the missionaries as one of many centres of pagan darkness.[63] Deciphering this form of 'text' required very different skills from those needed to 'read' a lantern slide or an illustrated Bible card in Thonga or equally those needed to make sense of a novel in English.

That context should have exercised such an impact on the way in which readers practised their skills might not seem unexpected. What was startling, at least for Junod and his colleagues, was the many ways in which locals made sense of the texts coming into their lives. For missionaries trained to see literacy as an element of European culture, the product of the natives' reading was at various times amusing, bewildering and edifying. It was the very different ways in which printed texts could be read that made it so difficult for the missionaries to direct and control the social consequences of literacy. No common or universal message was inherent in the words scratched or printed across a page; reading was frequently put to uses very different from those envisaged by the missionaries. Far from literacy domesticating the savage mind, in many cases its power was appropriated, harnessed and yoked by indigenous enterprise.

Ways of Reading

Literacy often served to reinforce local beliefs rather than to challenge or transform them. Instead of spreading light and learning, a letter from the mines could be used to invoke protection against supernatural forces. Even the image of an individual projected by a magic lantern or contained in a photograph was at times interpreted as the product of a maleficent act that had captured the shade or essence of that person.[64] Isabel Hofmeyr has recently shown the very different ways in which it was possible to read *The Pilgrim's Progress*.[65] In south-east Africa the Swiss missionaries and some of their followers produced equally divergent readings of the Bible.

Georges Liengme's patients at Antioka found a comfortable familiarity in the missionary doctor's story of Jesus chasing out demons, for they recognized in this passage from the New Testament a reflection of Christianity's understanding of the problems associated with spirit possession. Its practitioners, like the *gobela*, had the skills to expel these 'demons'.[66] Such a reading of the Bible dismayed Junod. He was particularly discomfited when converts found in the passage on 'sorcerers' in Revelation (XXII:15) a Biblical confirmation of their belief in witchcraft; or when (Matt. X:28) they identified the *baloyi* in the injunction to 'fear not them which kill the body, but are not able to kill the soul'.[67] Junod might have added that a careful reader would find in the Bible a swift solution to the problem of witchcraft. In Exodus (XXII:18) the faithful are told clearly: 'thou shalt not suffer a witch to live'. Utilitarian readings of the Bible counteracted missionary attempts to discredit witchcraft. Converts both mobilized the considerable weight of Holy Scripture behind the belief in witches and found in the missionaries' religious manual the best methods to resist its practice.

The Bible likewise confirmed the belief in dreams as a vehicle of divine communication. Just as the wise men who were warned in a dream not to return to Herod or report the whereabouts of the Christ child, local people looked to their dreams for advice. Most disquietingly for the missionaries, local Christians, as did Abraham in Genesis (XIII:7), reported frequent contacts with God. Here again, converts and pagans alike found confirmation in the Bible of their conviction that dreams were a source of divinatory power to be harnessed by ordinary men and women. As we saw in chapter three, belief in the power of dreams led some converts at one stage to regard contact with God through this medium as a *sine qua non* for membership of the church.[68] The converts of the Swiss Mission read the Bible aggressively. Like Zulu converts in Natal or Mormons in Utah, they found God's approval for polygamy in the marriage practices of some Old Testament prophets. In general, by drawing new and original meanings from the word of God, they reworked the missionaries' stories into their own cosmos.[69]

The migrant workers frequenting South African towns were familiar with printed texts and the utility of reading. However, once they returned home the purpose of reading took new forms, for documents were as rare in the rural areas as the economic opportunities attached to reading.[70] People on the coast obviously valued literacy as the medium for the transmission of a new religious message. But it was not just religious specialists who read: many of the prestigious *gayisa* returned from the mines with this skill and it was a practice frequently exercised by powerful European traders and soldiers. For many rural villagers, these people derived much of their power from the rituals attached to literacy. While the missionaries tied the power of reading to the acquisition of knowledge, many local people saw reading as a performance that carried with it new sources of power and authority. From this perspective, learning to read had little to do with deciphering or comprehending a written message; it was not a skill to be acquired but rather a ritual to be harnessed. Viewed in this light, 'reading' was a source of power that could be appropriated to serve very different ends from those envisaged by missionary teachers.

Jim Ximungana was one of the leading converts of the Swiss Mission. Although he had learned to read in Natal, his commercial activities initially kept him from attending classes at Rikatla on a regular basis and prevented him from acquiring any formal religious training. At first the missionaries saw in Ximungana's ignorance of Calvinist liturgy and his limited knowledge of the Bible, the innocence and authenticity of the primitive church. Ximungana had invested a considerable part of his fortune in the purchase of land on the Lourenço Marques hill where he kept cattle, ploughed his fields and built twenty huts on either side of a straight road. He had then spent seven pounds on a small building to serve as a church for the town.[71] However, as he came to occupy a position of authority, Ximungana's lack of religious training was a source of concern for the missionaries, particularly when he engaged Francisco João Albasini to run the church in his absence. Ximungana was frequently called away by his commercial interests and he found it natural to entrust his congregants to a local notable. Francisco was a son of João Albasini, the warlord and former Portuguese vice-consul in the Transvaal, and was born of an African mother. His wife was the grand-daughter of the head of the Maxaquene chiefdom, whose lands occupied the centre of Lourenço Marques. Through his connections, capital and knowledge, Francisco established an important political and cultural mixed-race dynasty in the town. But he had been educated and baptized as a Roman Catholic, and his principal reason for attending the Calvinist church was to read the *buku*, a devotional work published in a linguistic medium of which he approved. To add to the consternation of the missionaries, Ximungana's other choice as preacher in Lourenço Marques was a young man who did not believe in God.[72] What was important to Ximungana was that this man was able to read, like Francisco Albasini. This associated the Church with power in the eyes of congregants who viewed reading as a source of authority and influence. They were people who were perhaps more concerned to profit from this 'ritual' than to understand the message it conveyed.

Jim Ximungana's actions in Tembeland to the south of Lourenço Marques gave the missionaries further cause for concern, for when he left his village on business he arranged for a young slave girl to read the church lessons. Ximungana's primary concern was once again that his preacher should be able to read, and in this way convey the power of the gospel, without (it should perhaps be added) possessing kinship ties that could be exploited for secular ends. The Swiss were concerned by the girl's lowly status and particularly by the fact that she was unbaptized and had little knowledge of the gospel. 'He who knows how to read takes charge of the service', wrote Paul Berthoud despairingly. 'Here it's a young girl, there a woman, elsewhere a young boy and so on and so forth.'[73] As shown in chapter three, Berthoud's solution to this problem was to take direct control of the mission field rather than leave its outposts in the hands of agnostics, the ignorant, and the Church of Rome.

The written word was not only a source of ritual authority, it was also often imbued with totemic power. For many villagers, writing incarnated a guardian spirit or hosted some kind of powerful essence. Printed or written words were not just ink on a page; they were evidence that a spirit or force inhabited that piece of paper. Probably the most celebrated example of this view is that provided by the West African freed slave, Olaudah Equiano. In his biography, published in 1789, Equiano described how, when confronted by reading for the first time, he attempted to listen to the voice in his master's book, addressed it and, in turn, expected it to reply.[74] Arthur Grandjean enjoyed employing this belief in an attempt to amplify the awe with which local people regarded him. He would tell some of these 'innocents' that he needed something from home and then send them with a written message, 'the paper that speaks', instructing his wife to supply the bearer with the desired object. 'Their astonishment will be complete', continued the mischievous missionary,

> when having arrived at the mission station and having said nothing, they will see my wife take a hook and give it to the messenger, just as I promised him. It is thanks to facts of this nature that a legend has spread through the country according to which he who becomes master of the difficult art of writing will lack nothing because he will receive for free all that he will demand by letter from any white.[75]

Henri-Alexandre Junod also remarked on this belief in the power locked within writing. When one of his neighbours prepared to embark on a journey, the missionary was requested to provide him with a written message. Junod was intrigued that the subject of the message was of no importance; its function lay merely in its utility as a sign of authority that would frighten his neighbour's debtors into repaying their loans.[76] Some travellers also employed the practice when they carried sheets of printed paper in an attempt to protect themselves from bandits.[77]

This particular belief in the power of print was expressed in other ways, such as when an old Nkuna diviner, Maselesele, compared the Bible's capacity to reveal the truth with that of divinatory bones, or when an old woman described the words scattered on the page of a book as the equivalent of the bones thrown by a diviner. For such an individual, print had to be read in the same ideographic way as the bones. Anyone could read a diviner's bones but only a practitioner who had undergone the long and expensive training in the art knew how to interpret them correctly. His or her reading of the bones required both a high level of skill and the support of an ancestor who had once been a diviner in turn. In this sense, God bore the same responsibility for the alphabetic writing on the page of the Bible as did the ancestor-diviner for the message conveyed by the bones. Reading these alphabetic and ideographic texts required both skill and divine intercession.[78] Junod frequently commented on the extensive training required to decipher the messages carried by the diviner's bones and the evangelist's print, and he associated both forms of reading with sacred knowledge and power. Yet he also stressed that literacy freed the individual from the dark world of the diviner and that it, alone, gave the reader access to the field of enlightenment formed by Christianity and science.[79]

Skilled readers did not always share this opinion. It was common for them to attribute totemic powers to the printed word. Zakaria, one of the African evangelists employed by the Swiss, sought to harness the power of writing when he covered a local waterhole with a sheet of newsprint. He believed this action would scare off unsanitary pagans and maintain the cleanliness of the water supply.[80] This view of writing as talisman or charm imbued with magical powers was again suggested by the experience of a man known to us only as Motsikéri. On his conversion, Motsikéri secured the only book he was able to find, a Dutch reading primer that 'he believed to be the Lord's Book', according to Paul Berthoud. His desire to be 'a disciple of the book' led him into conflict with his chief, who eventually stripped him of his cattle, fields, grain and even his wife. Paul Berthoud took Motsekéri's actions to be reflective of the 'simple and living faith' of converts dwelling in the land of pagan darkness.[81] But a more sceptical view might raise the observation that this man valued the book less for its message, with which he seemed unconcerned, than for the abstract and independent force that dwelt within its pages. Without the intercession of the chief or the diviners, the meanest tribesman could harness this force.

To read 'the power of the book' in this way perhaps explains why many converts considered owning a Bible to be both a sign and an instance of faith.[82] It would also explain why evangelists were so eager to display a book, held in the hand or discreetly tucked into a pocket, in official photographs.[83] But it was not only Christians who bought books. In the late 1880s the library of a man by the name of Pakoule, a retired civil servant and practising agnostic living in Lourenço Marques, consisted of only one book: an illustrated Bible history (probably in Portuguese).[84] Pakoule was typical of the many readers who possessed a copy of works like the *buku* without adhering to its message.[85] Another indication of the importance attached to owning and displaying the written word rather than deciphering its contents may be gained from the voracious demand for books that far outstripped the size of the 'reading public'. When the first shipment of 1,400 *bukus* and ABCs arrived at Elim in 1884, Eugène Thomas was unsure of his ability to sell works that cost about one-tenth of an evangelist's monthly salary (2s 6d each). There was little money in circulation and although many people paid cash for their *bukus*, they paid the equivalent of sixpence in labour for their ABCs. Yet eight years later, the demand for the *buku* had far outstripped supply. The last of the 5,000 copies in print would soon be sold, wrote Henri Berthoud in 1892, for 'all those who can read will want a copy, if only to keep up their reading skills'. Berthoud believed that the absence of a written literature in Thonga was holding back the work of conversion in the Transvaal.[86]

The sale of Thonga and Ronga books in Johannesburg, the northern Transvaal and Mozambique far exceeded the number of individuals who had passed through even a cursory education.[87] For those who owned the word, books were probably a sign of status as well as a marker of loyalty and identity. Possibly, they were also a source of totemic and ritual magic that elided with the power stemming from the knowledge contained in the book. This view associates power with literacy in a way that was essentially foreign to the missionaries. It leads to the suggestion that, far from revolutionizing society, the skill of reading often served to invigorate the very beliefs and practices that it aimed to demolish.

For Henri-Alexandre Junod these reading practices were a sign of backwardness. Rather than legitimately different ways of reading, they were the cause of mistakes that had to be corrected. Sadly, Junod did not extend his criticisms of local reading habits to Europeans who invested the Bible with supernatural powers when taking an oath, or who read the Good Book as divine revelation or self-evident truth. He seemed unaware that many evangelicals, after a literal reading of Jonah (I:7), Numbers (XXVII:21) and Acts (I:26) followed St Augustine's example and used the Bible as a tool of divination. Members of the North German Missionary Society practised *Däumeln*, opening the Bible arbitrarily and pointing to verses, or *Bibellose*, a lottery with verses, both ways of entering into direct contact with God through his sacred word.[88] It was only in the 1870s that the Moravians formally stopped the practice of opening the Bible in a random manner in search of passages providing them with God's guidance for the church and the lives of its members.[89] As Keith Thomas has shown, this form of *sortilège* was widespread and lasted well into the nineteenth century in Europe.[90] Nor did Junod's understanding of literacy take account of the way in which Europeans often collected books not for the information and ideas they contained but in order to present a show of knowledge, wealth, aesthetic taste or intellectual persuasion.[91]

Junod seemed unaware of the different ways in which print was used, nor was he conscious of the social and symbolic capital with which it was associated even within his own society. He viewed literacy solely as a sign of modernity and social evolution. From this perspective, the acquisition of literacy required more than just a functional ability to read a simple text and write one's name. Reading as an individual, private act, was fundamentally opposed to the mechanisms of a society 'still plunged in the dim notions of collective morality'.[92] Cheaply produced, small, hand-held books encouraged individuals to read in a way that contradicted the social expressions of orality, gesture and performance. At the same time, private reading challenged a collective morality that condoned or encouraged 'barbaric customs' as long as they were considered to be in the interests of the community. Junod believed that a social environment dominated by orality produced immutable institutions and mindless practices that crushed free will.[93] Literacy had the potential to free human beings to think for themselves and to take charge of their lives in a way that would encourage a controlled modernization and 'elevate and purify the social and family system of the tribe'. Collectivism was not only old-fashioned; it 'belongs to another age', Junod asserted. 'The opposition between the collectivist and the Western conception is absolute', he warned and prophesied a campaign during which 'individualism will kill primitive collectivism and all its rites'.[94]

Mission schools were in the front line of this combat as they spread the ability to read and write in Ronga and in Thonga, linguistic forms that many referred to as *Xineri*, the language of the missionaries or *muneri*.[95] So, too, were the annual church synods in which (after 1903 on the coast, and 1905 in the Spelonken) elected representatives gathered to discuss their affairs in the language of the church.[96] The imagined community created by two standard written languages soon influenced the identity of this church elite. The early convert and Morija graduate, Samuel Malalé, expressed himself publicly on this issue in 1904 at the burial of Henri Berthoud with whom he had collaborated at Valdezia. On this emotional occasion Malalé spoke for the first time of 'we the baThonga' and outlined the borders of 'the country inhabited by the baThonga'.[97] A year earlier, Junod had also referred to this new tribal consciousness when he wrote of 'the tribe ... which calls itself the Ba-Ronga'.[98] In a short space of time, literacy had encouraged readers and their listeners to start seeing themselves as members of tribal or ethnic communities that cut across many historic divisions in south-east Africa.

It should come as no surprise that the missionaries' view of the consequences of literacy provoked ambivalent reactions from those who were the chief object of its attentions. 'Aha! this is the book they spoke about!' Chief Mapounga in Nondwane exclaimed when first shown the missionaries' Bible reader, 'thus are we conquered by this book alone!'[99] The Tembe Chief Mabaï, who had been openly critical of the *buku* – 'this book that comes from the north' – fined Jim Ximungana two head of cattle and £1 for bringing it into his territory.[100] One of chief Magude's elders, Shongi, feared that words he had seen written in his presence would later alter themselves of their own accord. 'It will not stay in the form that it has been written down', he told Grandjean. 'When we transact business we say things in front of witnesses and the word remains.' 'And it's true, the word is sacred for a black', Grandjean wrote.[101] This ambivalent attitude to the written word perhaps explains why the schoolteacher's house, the mission at Rikatla and the collection of books at the Tembe Mission were destroyed at the start of the Luso-Gaza war in 1894, and why Ruth Holene, the pioneer reader and itinerant evangelist, was killed during this conflict.[102]

Although chiefs regarded the social changes provoked by literacy with suspicion, they initially sought to assimilate what Mapounga called its 'magic power' into their battery of resources by employing professional secretaries or by sending children, slaves or women to learn to read.[103]. It was hoped that such a strategy would restrict the malevolent effects of literacy by attaching its skills to people on the edge of society who were less able to misuse its powers.

Missionaries attempted to counteract local ambivalences towards literacy by accommodating their teaching to the demands of an oral, visual culture. In Europe, their revivalist cousins had developed various strategies to spread the gospel beyond the confines of a church-going, literate public. Many of these were adopted by itinerant evangelists in Africa who carried a noisy, tub-thumping Christianity into public spaces. Evangelists also brought these performances into mine compounds or rural villages where the word of God became a familiar spectacle. In these areas the 'heathen' were introduced to the short vernacular texts carried on engravings, illustrated Bible cards and the images produced by the magic lantern.[104]

Hymns became an important oral medium for the transmission of written messages. In Switzerland the revival had added boisterous and emotional hymn-singing, often accompanied by the harmonium, to the dour psalmodizing of the early Reformed Church. Even the elegant but staid Methodist compositions were infused with new meaning by those eager to manifest and spread their reinvigorated faith. Hymns provided severe Christians with an emotional outlet and, like prayer, a direct link with God. Their popular melodies, simple texts and raw emotions were often derided by the middle class, but drew many Swiss to the church.[105]

In Africa, hymns took both writing and the Christian ethic far beyond Dominical services. 'Some travel a long way', Ernest Creux wrote of these hymns in 1878. 'I sometimes hear them in villages where an evangelist has never put his foot.' The pivotal role of hymns in the revival of the Reformed Church in Switzerland encouraged him to recognize the evangelical appeal of music that touched local emotions, as well as lyrics that reflected the everyday concerns of indigenous people. 'I am sure that the pagans would be much better instructed, attracted, charmed by the Truth, if we could give them popular hymns recounting the story of Jesus and the main aspects of sacred history, together with a music appropriate to their national character.'[106] By the mid-1890s, the singing of religious texts had even brought the Christian message into the Gaza king's *shigodlo* where Georges Liengme liked to sing hymns with Gungunyana's wives. Hymns such as 'Hallelujah! He has risen!' carried aspects of the

7.1 Jim, Paulus and Philemon Ximungana. Literacy created a new élite in south-east Africa. Books featured prominently, as symbols of knowledge and power, in the photographs of Christian converts. See also the photograph of Yosefa Mhalamhala on p. 72. (© Swiss Mission Archive, Lausanne)

gospel, in this instance the resurrection, into the darkest recesses of Gazaland. Even the early Gwamba hymn called 'Work!' served to spread new ideas about the links between religiosity and labour.[107] When performed in accompaniment with important figures, such as the king's father's brother, Nkouyou, who was also a general in the Gaza army, these hymns became a vital means of spreading the Christian message.[108] But hymns not only carried the Christian message in a sung form; in some cases they also served as a devotional 'literature' for Christians living far from centres of missionary enterprise.[109]

Within five years of their arrival in the Transvaal, the missionaries had published 57 hymns in the *buku*. They produced two new printed collections in the early 1890s and followed these with hymnals including music.[110] This form of printed text proved extremely popular. Creux, Junod, the Berthouds and other missionaries set new lyrics to the founding hymns of the Free Church, but, although these spoke to the personal world of congregants and bound them as a community, the music was too sombre and restrained for local tastes. Converts felt uneasy with the grim morality and resignation reverberating in tunes inspired by the recognition of sin and the need for contrition. They sought rather to express spontaneity and joy in their religious singing. Swiss Mission converts favoured the lively, repetitive refrains in the American gospel hymns of Dwight Moody and Ira Sankey; or they adapted imported music to conform to local tonality.[111] The strength of oral culture also pushed the mission to encourage reading aloud and to advocate a more festive religiosity. Through exuberant outdoor rituals of welcome and departure and through the celebration of church festivals filled with colour, song and movement, the mission inevitably added to its austere liturgy the emotion, spectacle and performance associated with orality.[112]

It is clear that the strength of orality in local culture restricted the spread of reading and writing. But it should not be forgotten that material conditions were equally responsible for the hesitant and spasmodic way in which people embraced the written word. The spread of literacy in the rural areas was most hindered by the paucity of teachers and schools, by the restricted circulation of reading material and by the limited appeal of didactic and edifying religious works. The seasonal nature of agriculture also inhibited the spread of literacy as parents pulled young children out of school to plant or harvest crops. When the crops failed, these children were sent to look for roots and fruits or were conscripted into communal fishing expeditions, while older boys departed for the mines in South Africa. The missionaries complained of the continual pressure on school-going children to abandon their studies, for, once they had acquired some knowledge of reading and writing, they frequently left home and school to earn money in the towns. In the Transvaal, the initiation lodges of the Pedi were another source of concern for the Swiss as they both drew young men away from the mission schools and provided them with alternative knowledge and values.[113]

Perhaps most importantly, if individuals were unable to attach themselves to a reading community with access to written material, they lost their literate skills very quickly. It is also important to note that orality did not domesticate literacy everywhere and always. Literacy lost much of its association with the marginalized when the Portuguese seized control of Southern Mozambique in 1895. The number of converts soared and children started to attend school in greater numbers. At the same time, political disturbances in South Africa pushed home tens of thousands of Mozambican miners, almost all of whom had come into contact with reading. Well before the turn of the century, a small number of men had succeeded in acquiring an education in South Africa. Foremost amongst these was the Lovedale graduate, pioneer linguist and Methodist clergyman, Robert Mashaba. Another was Jim Ximungana's younger brother Philemon who returned home from Lovedale in 1893. Philemon included in his library books in English, works on arithmetic and grammar, several dictionaries and a Bible, and he furnished his home with chairs, a mirror and other signs of his new status.[114] Ceteway Goba, another Lovedale graduate, was employed by the American Board Mission near Inhambane; Muti Sikobele, who worked for the Methodist Episcopalians, was a graduate of Adam's College in Natal; and John Matthews Nyoko, the Chopi linguist, had attended an Anglican school in South Africa.[115]

Literacy and Politics

The growth of a literate, black Christian elite transformed the ability to read into a major political issue in both Mozambique and South Africa. In the Cape Colony a new literacy qualification introduced in 1892 excluded any man unable to write his name, address and occupation from the common voters' roll. In Mozambique Francisco Albasini's son, the journalist João Albasini, stridently called for government funds to be invested in education. Many whites came to see literacy as a political litmus test of civilization, a way of distinguishing civilized citizens with national rights from native subjects whose rights should be confined to the 'tribe' and 'clan'. For Junod, the ability to sign one's name and read with facility were not sufficient reasons to allow an uncontrolled assimilation into the 'depraved and unscrupulous civilization' of Europe.[116] Although he did not favour formal segregation, Junod admired many pre-industrial, rural values and he advocated their protection by the Christian chief, native commissioner and missionary. Although he encouraged the participation of the black elite in national affairs, he was suspicious of the 'hundreds of thousands of superficially educated Natives' who called for the extension of the Cape franchise to other parts of South Africa, on the eve of Union.

> They know more or less how to read and write, but are absolutely unable to understand the tenth part of what is published in the *Star* or the *Argus*, because their horizon is totally different from that of the white man, although they are perhaps not much inferior in intelligence to many European voters. To be able to write one's own name is not a sufficient qualification for taking part in the politics of the South African Union.[117]

Twenty years later he would change his mind on this issue. In the meantime he continued to see reading as an intensive, silent act, closely tied to his vision of progress and modernity.

Junod combined an intensive study of oral literature or folklore with his investigation of the language. He first published a collection of folktales in 1896 as an appendage to his *Grammaire ronga*. The following year he produced a full volume of folktales and a year later a smaller collection.[118] Junod's examination of the extraordinarily rich oral literature of the Thonga led him to criticize the idea that African folklore had experienced a degeneration. It also strengthened his belief that Africans formed part of a common humanity and that they proved themselves to have the same mental capacity as Europeans through the inventiveness of their literature.[119] Junod felt that the study of language and literature gave him access to the system of thought of local people and allowed him to penetrate their 'ancient history'.[120] He would later consider their folklore 'a monument upon which the soul of the race has recorded, unconsciously perhaps, its ideas and its inspirations.'[121] The study of language and folklore led Junod to appreciate the creative impulses of local society; anthropology would provide him with the means to understand it.

Notes

[1] Anne-Françoise Jeanneret, 'Le développement de l'instruction' in *Histoire du pays de Neuchâtel* (Neuchâtel, 1993), pp. 258–9.
[2] D. Maggetti, *L'Invention de la littérature romande, 1830–1910* (Lausanne, 1995), pp. 162–8.
[3] In 1904 the full vernacular Bible sold for less than a shilling and, thanks to the British and Foreign Bible Society, the New Testament could be bought for a few pence. The first industrially produced vernacular Bible, the Osterwald version, had cost 8s when introduced in 1797. In 1805 the Bible of the Company of Genevan Pastors sold for 15s. Anon., 'La Bible dans le monde', *La messagère du monde païen* (1904), p. 70.
[4] A. Niederer, 'Mentalités et sensibilités' in P. Guichonnet (ed.), *Histoire et civilisation des alpes* II *Destin Humain* (Toulouse and Lausanne, 1980), pp. 128–9. See also Eugène Rambert, 'Une bibliothèque à la montagne' in his *Récits et Croquis* (Lausanne, 1889).
[5] Cf. P. Harries, 'Missionary endeavour and the politics of identity in Switzerland' in *Le Fait Missionnaire* (1998), No. 6, September.
[6] Ami Bost, *Letters and Biography of Félix Neff, Protestant Missionary in Switzerland, the department of Isère and the High Alps* (trans. Margaret Anne Wyatt, London, 1843), p. 235. On reading in these areas, see also pp. 147, 192, 215, 229.
[7] Swiss Mission Archives, Lausanne (SMA): 8. 10. B, P. Berthoud to council, 25 March 1885; P. Berthoud in *Lettres missionnaires: 1873–1879 de M. et Mme P. Berthoud* (Lausanne, 1900), pp. 84, 104, 118, 131; Grandjean, *La Mission romande: ses racines dans le sol Suisse romande* (Lausanne, 1917), p. 48.

8 Grandjean, *La Mission*, p. 48.
9 *Bulletin de la mission vaudoise* (BMV) (1876) 21, 30 September, p. 65; F. Coillard, *Sur le Haut-Zambèze: Voyages et Travaux de Mission* (Paris, 1899).
10 Jan van Butselaar, *Africains, missionnaires et colonialistes: les origines de L'église Presbytérienne du Mozambique (Mission Suisse), 1880–1896* (Leiden, 1984), pp. 27, 29–39.
11 P. Berthoud, *Les Nègres gouamba ou les vingt premières années de la Mission romande* (Lausanne, 1900), p. 107; P. Berthoud, *La Mission romande à la baie de Delagoa* (Lausanne, 1888), pp. 16–17; R. Berthoud-Junod, *Du Transvaal à Lourenço Marques: lettres de Mme R. Berthoud-Junod* (Lausanne, 1896), p. 114.
12 Cf. Berthoud-Junod, *Du Transvaal à Lourenço Marques*, pp. 88, 211.
13 Berthoud, *La Mission romande à la baie de Delagoa*, p. 17.
14 J. Goody and I. Watt, 'The consequences of literacy' in J. Goody (ed.), *Literacy in Traditional Societies* (Cambridge, 1968). J. Goody, *The Domestication of the Savage Mind* (Cambridge, 1977). For a critical approach to Goody's thesis see R. Finnegan, *Literacy and Orality: studies in the technology of communication* (Oxford, 1988).
15 H.-A. Junod, *The Life of a South African Tribe (LSAT)* (London, 1927), II, pp. 617–18; H.-P. Junod, *Henri-Alexandre Junod, missionnaire et savant* (Lausanne, 1934), p. 84; SMA 8.10.B, H. Berthoud to mission council, 21 December 1893.
16 Junod, *LSAT*, II, pp. 155–160, 166, 627; Junod, 'Les Ba-Ronga – Etude enthnographique sur les indigènes de la baie Delagoa', *Bulletin de la société neuchâteloise de géographie* (1898) X, p. 248.
17 Junod, 'Les Ba-Ronga', p. 403.
18 Junod, *LSAT* II, p. 175.
19 T. R. Metcalfe, 'Language, race and history' in his *Ideologies of the Raj* (Cambridge, 1995), pp. 80–92. T. R. Traitmann, *Aryans and British India* (Berkeley, CA, 1997).
20 Wilhelm Bleek, 'South African languages and books', *Cape Monthly Magazine* (1858) 3, p. 325; Bleek, *A Comparative Grammar of South African Languages* (Cape Town, 1862–69), p. 5. This view was repeated by William Holden, *The Past and Future of the Kaffir Races* (London, 1866), p. 354. The comparative philology pursued by Bleek arose out of William Jones' discovery in the late eighteenth century of the relationship between Sanskrit and German, Latin and other European languages.
21 Ernst Haeckel, preface to Wilhelm Bleek, *On the Origins of Language* (New York, 1869), p. v. On this approach, linking language to a racial hierarchy, see Arthur de Gobineau, *Essai sur l'inégalité des races humaines* (Paris, 1884) I, p. 213, cited in P. Curtin, *The Image of Africa. British Ideas and Action, 1780–1859* (Madison, WI, 1964), pp. 395–6; C. L. Miller, *Blank Darkness: Africanist Discourse in French* (Chicago, IL, 1985), pp. 15, 122; Thomas F. Gossett, *Race: The History of an Idea in America* (New York, 1963), pp. 124–5.
22 For African languages as degenerate, see J. Bryant, 'The Zulu Language', *Journal of the American Oriental Society*, (1849), p. 395; J. W. Appleyard, *The Kafir Language* (Kingwilliam's Town, 1850), pp. 7–8. As childish, see Henri Perregaux, *Edmond Perregaux missionnaire: d'après sa correspondance 1868–1905* (Neuchâtel, 1906), p. 108. More generally, see L. Gerhardt, 'Afrikanische Sprache im gelehrte deutschen Urteil' in R. Nestvogel (ed.), *Afrika und Deutsche Kolonialismus* (Hamburg, 1987).
23 For Koëlle on language and society, see Jon Miller, *The Social Control of Zeal: a Study of Organizational Contradictions* (New Brunswick, NJ, 1994), p. 206n2. Casalis admired the richness of the Sotho language although, like Boyce and Appleyard, he thought it had degenerated from a previous, more evolved stage of existence. *Les Bassoutos ou vingt-trois années d'études et d'observations au sud de l'Afrique* (Paris [1859] 1933), p. 387. Müller found that all languages exhibited 'order and wisdom'. See his *Einleitung in die vergleichende Religionswissenschaft* (Strasburg, 1874), p. 240, cited in Ulrich Berner, 'Africa and the Origin of the Science of Religion. Max Müller (1823–1900) and James George Frazer (1854–1941) on African Religions' in Ludwig Frieder and Afe Adogame (eds), *European Traditions in the Study of Religion in Africa* (Wiesbaden, 2004).
24 Junod, *LSAT* II, p. 155, 158–64, 175. Junod, *Le problème indigène dans l'Union sud-africaine* (Lausanne, 1931), p. 13.
25 Junod, 'Les Ba-Ronga', p. 248; Junod, *LSAT* II, pp. 151, 154–62, 618.
26 SMA 517/B, Junod to Renevier, 10 October 1895; Junod, 'Les Ba-Ronga', p. 116.
27 Junod, *Grammaire ronga* (Lausanne, 1896), p. 7.
28 Junod, *LSAT* II, pp. 582–3.
29 Junod, *LSAT* I, p. 271.
30 Junod, *LSAT* II, pp. 581n1, 582–3.
31 Cited in R. J. W. Evans, *The Language of History and the History of Language: an inaugural lecture delivered before the University of Oxford on 11 May 1998* (Oxford, 1998), p. 18.
32 This is a common aspect of language politics, cf. J. Tollefson, *Moving Language, Planning Inequality and Language Politics in the Community* (London, 1991), p. 13.
33 Junod, *Grammaire ronga suivie d'un manuel de conversation et d'un vocabulaire ronga-portugais-français-anglais* (Lisbon, 1896), pp. 24–5. See also chapter six, pp. 171–2 above.
34 Junod was equally critical of this process on Zulu mission stations in Natal. Junod, 'The Native Language and

Native Education', *Journal of the Royal African Society* XVII (1905), October, pp. 4–5, 12–13. See also René Cuenod, 'Les langues sud-africaines et la traduction de la Bible', *Revue missionnaire* (1928) 20, December, pp. 98–9.
35 Junod, 'Les Ba-Ronga', p. 248. This was reprinted almost unchanged in *LSAT* II, pp. 151–2.
36 Junod, 'Les Ba-Ronga', p. 248; *LSAT* II, p. 151.
37 Grandjean, *Mission romande*, pp. 46, 223.
38 Junod, *LSAT* II, p. 613.
39 Berthoud, 13 September 1873 to mission council in *Lettres missionnaires*, p. 131.
40 SMA 8.10.B Henri Berthoud to mission council, 4 May 1888.
41 P. Harries, *Work, Culture and Identity: Migrant Labourers in Mozambique and South Africa, c. 1860–1910* (London, 1994), pp. 76–7, 216.
42 Cf. H. Bennet, *Romance and Reality: The Story of a Missionary on the Rand* (Leeds, 1912), pp. 30–31, 57, 89; A. W. Baker, *Grace Triumphant* (Glasgow, 1939), p. 104; *Bulletin de la Mission romande (BMR)* (1913), p. 34. Archives of the Swiss Mission in the Gubbins Library, University of the Witwatersrand: Annual Reports of the Johannesburg Presbytery, 1907–10, 1915–16.
43 Jaas, a Shangaan informant (native no. 627) before the (South African) *Native Grievances Commission, 1913–14*.
44 Junod, *Zidji: Etude de moeurs sud-africaines* (St. Blaise, 1911), pp. 242, 298.
45 Harries, *Work, Culture and Identity*, p. 217.
46 P. Berthoud, *Les Nègres gouamba*, p. 138; Ruth Berthoud-Junod, *Du Transvaal à Lourenço Marques*, p. 228.
47 On the notion of intensive reading, see Robert Darnton, 'History of Reading' in Peter Burke (ed.), *New Perspectives on Historical Writing* (Cambridge, 1991), pp. 148–9; Darnton, *The Great Cat Massacre* (New York, 1985), p. 249; J. S. Allen, *In the Public Eye: A History of Reading in Modern France, 1800–1940* (Princeton, NJ, 1991), p. 62.
48 R. Darnton, 'Readers respond to Rousseau: the fabrication of romantic sensitivity' in his *The Great Cat Massacre*, p. 215; Darnton, 'History of Reading', p. 152
49 Berthoud-Junod, *Du Transvaal à Lourenço Marques*, p. 145.
50 As had been rumoured at Valdezia. Cf. *BMV* (1876) 21, p. 66.
51 H.-A. Junod, *Ernest Creux et Paul Berthoud: Les fondateurs de la Mission Suisse en Afrique du Sud* (Lausanne, 1933), p. 143; P. Berthoud, *La Mission romande*, pp. 16–17; Berthoud, *Les Nègres gouamba*, p. 107.
52 Junod, *Domesticité africaine* (Lausanne, 1923), p. 9.
53 Junod, *LSAT*, II, p. 619; G. Liengme, letter of 28 August 1891 in *Nouvelles de nos missions* (1891) 3, 14, p. 46.
54 Junod, *LSAT*, II, p. 166.
55 Junod, *BMR* (1902) 15, 190, June, p. 10.
56 Junod, *LSAT*, II, p. 619.
57 Junod in *Causeries sur l'Afrique à l'usage des cercles d'étude missionnaire pour enfants, des écoles de dimanche, des unions cadettes et des familles* (Lausanne, 1922), p. 8.
58 P. Berthoud, *La Mission romande*, pp. 16–17; Berthoud-Junod, *Du Transvaal à Lourenço Marques*, p. 229; P. Loze, letter of 16 November 1893 in *Nouvelles de nos missionnaires* (1894) 16, 5, p. 77.
59 R. Chartier, 'Culture as Appropriation: Popular Cultural Uses in Early Modern France' in S. Kaplan (ed.), *Understanding Popular Culture: Europe from the Middle Ages to the Nineteenth Century* (New York, 1984), pp. 242–3.
60 Paul Berthoud, *Les Nègres gouamba*, pp. 23, 192.
61 Letter from Ruth Berthoud-Junod, dated 25 November 1885 in *Nouvelles de nos missionnaires* (1886) 8, 4, p. 73; ibid., letter of 11 April 1886 in (1886) 1, 9, pp. 39–40; ibid., letter of 14 May 1890 in (1890) 1, 13, p. 12.
62 Junod, 'La biographie d'Elias Libombo, jadis connu sous le nom de Spoon' in *Causeries sur l'Afrique*, p. 12.
63 SMA 438/A, G. Liengme to mission council, 9 August 1895; *Missionary Herald* (1892) July, p. 295. See also note 65 below. On the notion of 'sung reading', see M. Ducreux, 'Reading unto Death: Books and Readers in eighteenth century Bohemia' in R. Chartier (ed.), *The Culture of Print: Power and the Uses of Print in Early Modern Europe* (Oxford, 1989), pp. 217–19.
64 Junod, *LSAT* II, pp. 363, 535–6n1.
65 I. Hofmeyr, *The Portable Bunyan: A Transnational History of The Pilgrim's Progress* (Princeton, NJ, 2004), especially chapters 4, 5 and 6. Roger Chartier has similarly pointed out that, during the revolution, Louis XVI and his *sansculottes* subjects read Voltaire and Montesquieu in radically different ways. R. Chartier, *Les origines culturelles de la révolution française* (Paris, 1990), pp. 105–7.
66 Georges Liengme at Antioka, 12 February 1893 in *Nouvelles de nos missionnaires* (1896) 15, 6, p. 87.
67 In Junod, *LSAT* II, p. 535n1. Note that witchcraft is prohibited in Deuteronomy XVIII:10–11.
68 Berthoud-Junod, *Du Transvaal à Lourenço Marques*, pp. 241–2.
69 N. Etherington, 'Kingdoms of this World and the Next: Christian beginnings among Zulu and Swazi' in R. Elphick and R. Davenport (eds), *Christianity in South Africa: A Political, Social and Cultural History* (Oxford, 1997), p. 101. See also Junod, *LSAT* II, p. 352; M. Wilson et al., *Keiskammahoek Rural Survey*, III. *Social*

Structure (Pietermaritzburg, 1952), p. 191. G. West, 'Africa and the Bible' in J. Rogerson (ed), *The Oxford Illustrated History of the Bible* (Oxford, 2001), pp. 330–6.

70 This statement is open to correction. There is some evidence that, at least as early as the first decade of the twentieth century, migrant workers sent home fairly substantial numbers of letters, cf. Keith Breckenridge, 'Love letters and Amanuenses: Beginning the cultural history of the working class private sphere in southern Africa, 1900–1933', *Journal of Southern African Studies* (2000) 26, 2, p. 341. Junod believed that, because of unschooled handwriting, few of these letters reached their destination. Junod, *Zidji*, p. 274.

71 P. Loze, letter of November 1893 in *Nouvelles de nos missionnaires* (1894) 16, 5, p. 74; Junod, 'Une course au Tembé', *BSNG* (1894), p. 122.

72 Paul Berthoud referred to Francisco as Djiouaoua (Jiwawa), his father's name. P. Berthoud, *La Mission romande*, p. 19; Berthoud-Junod, *Du Transvaal à Lourenço Marques*, pp. 168, 211; Jeanne Marie Penvenne, 'João dos Santos Albasini (1876–1922): The contradictions of politics and identity in colonial Mozambique', *Journal of African History* (1996) 37, 3, pp. 429–32.

73 Berthoud-Junod, *Du Transvaal à Lourenço Marques*, p. 176; Berthoud, *La Mission romande*, p. 19.

74 Paul Edwards (ed.), *The Life of Olaudah Equiano* ([1789] Harlow, 1988), pp. 34–5.

75 SMA 513, Grandjean to mission council, 11 December 1893.

76 Junod, *LSAT* I, p. 339n1.

77 SMA 1255/B, Liengme to mission council, July 1892. Almost fifty years later, Jomo Kenyatta related that young Kikuyu saw 'reading and writing' as 'the white man's magic', a source of 'new magical power'. Kenyatta, *Facing Mount Kenya* (London, 1938), p. 272.

78 Junod, *LSAT* II, p. 541; A. Grandjean, *La race thonga et la Suisse romande* (Lausanne, 1921), p. 47; *BMR* (1902) 15, 196, July, p. 191. For similar observations elsewhere, see Walter Elmslie, *Among the Wild Ngoni* (London, 1899), p. 169; J. and J. Comaroff, *Of Revelation and Revolution* (Chicago, Il, 1991), I, p. 229; D. Chidester, *Savage Systems: Colonialism and comparative religion in southern Africa* (Cape Town, 1996), pp. 231–2.

79 Junod, 'The best means of preserving the traditions and customs of the various South African native races – in a form available for future Scientific Research' in *South African Association for the Advancement of Science* (1907), p. 143; Junod, 'The Magic conception of nature amongst Bantus', *South African Journal of Science* (1920) 17, p. 83; Junod, *LSAT* II, pp. 385, 541, 564–70.

80 Berthoud-Junod, *Du Transvaal à Lourenço Marques*, p. 137. Grandjean also referred to a local description of writing as 'the medicine of knowledge'. SMA 467. Grandjean diary, 1890, p. 7. In other parts of southern Africa, treating the body with script and newsprint became a regular part of healing rites. Jean Comaroff, *Body of Power, Spirit of Resistance* (Chicago, IL, 1985), pp. 203, 250. See also I. Dinesen, *Shadows on the Grass* (New York, [c. 1960], 1974), pp. 54–8.

81 P. Berthoud in *Lettres missionnaires*, p. 104.

82 *Berliner Missionsberichte* (1876) 23, 24, p. 400.

83 Cf. the photographs on pp. 72, 199.

84 Berthoud-Junod, *Du Transvaal à Lourenço Marques*, p. 215. Pakoule's wife was a leading member of the Swiss Mission, to which he later gave his adherence, see Van Butselaar, *Africains, missionnaires et colonialistes*, p. 194.

85 SMA 8.10.B, H. Berthoud to mission council, 10 January, 1892.

86 SMA 8.27.T, E. Thomas to mission council, 26 November 1884; SMA 8.10.B, Henri Berthoud to council, 10 January 1892.

87 For information on print runs and new editions, see SMA 8.10.B, Henri Berthoud to mission council, 10 January 1892; and the annual reports of the Council of the Swiss Romande Mission. For this phenomenon elsewhere in Africa, see I. Hofmeyr, *'We Spend our Years as a Tale that is Told,' Oral Historical Narrative in a South African Chiefdom* (London, 1994), p. 51; and F. Raison-Jourde, *Bible et pouvoir à Madagascar au XIXe siècle* (Paris, 1991), pp. 502–3.

88 Birgit Meyer, *Translating the Devil: Religion and Modernity Among the Ewe in Ghana* (Edinburgh, 1999), p. 38.

89 B. Krüger, *The Pear Tree Blossoms: A History of the Moravian Mission Station in South Africa, 1737–1869* (Genadendal, 1966), pp. 14, 21, 107, 172, 182–3, 209–10, 248, 265, 288.

90 K. Thomas, *Religion and the Decline of Magic* (London, [1971] 1997), p. 118.

91 At the height of the Art Nouveau movement, Oscar Wilde's Dorian Gray possessed nine copies of his favourite book. Each was bound in a different colour and style, in a way calculated to appeal to his changing moods. Asa Briggs, 'Changing values in art and society' in Briggs (ed.), *The Nineteenth Century* (London, 1970), p. 19.

92 Junod, *LSAT* I, p. 152.

93 See p. 186 above.

94 Junod, *LSAT* I, pp. 525–6.

95 Mary Bill, *Tsonga Bibliography 1883–1983* (Morija, Lesotho, 1983), p. 18.

96 Anon., 'Le pastorat Indigène' in *BMR* (1906) 19, September, pp. 214–23.

97 *BMR* (1905) 18, February, p. 50.
98 Junod, 'Some remarks on the folklore of the Ba-Thonga', *Folk–lore* (1903) 14, 2, p. 116.
99 Berthoud-Junod, *Du Transvaal à Lourenço Marques*, p. 18; SMA 8.10.B, P. Berthoud to mission council, 2 September 1886.
100 Henri Berthoud, letter of 20 January 1887 in *BMR* (1887) 71, p. 210. See also Berthoud-Junod, *Du Transvaal à Lourenço Marques*, pp. 115–16.
101 G. Liengme, letter of 28 August 1891 in *Nouvelles de nos missionnaires* (1891) 3, 14, p. 46.
102 Berthoud, *Les Nègres gouamba*, pp. 201–2.
103 Cf. SMA 840, Liengme to Rossel, 31 January, 1896; Berthoud, *Les Nègres gouamba*, p. 195.
104 Berthoud, *Nègres gouamba*, pp. 23, 192; Letter from R. Berthoud-Junod in *Nouvelles de nos missionnaires* (1886) 8, 4, p. 73; Liengme letter of 13 May in *Nouvelles de nos missionnaires* (1893) 16, 2, p. 29.
105 G. Chamorel in A. Laufer (ed.), *Psaumes et cantiques: hymnes de la chrétienté protestante* (Lausanne, 1926), pp. i, iii, viii, ix, xiii.
106 Cited in Junod, *Ernest Creux and Paul Berthoud*, pp. 82–3.
107 Junod, *Ernest Creux et Paul Berthoud*, p. 83; P. Berthoud in *BMV* (1876) 18, March, p. 9.
108 Foundation for the study of the Swiss overseas, Geneva. Liengme diary, entries for July and August, 1895; SMA 438/A, Liengme to mission council, 9 August 1895.
109 Mme P. Berthoud in *BMR* (1886) 6, p. 173.
110 Twelve new hymns appeared in the 24-page *Supplement ya Buku* of 1891. The *Buku ya tinsimo* (*The Book of Hymns*, 1893) was a more substantial work of 72 pages. The *Buku ya tinsimu* of 1909 contained music and hymns for schoolchildren. Reprinted six times in the next six years, 20,000 copies of this work were produced in 1929 on the occasion of its eighth reprinting. See Bill, *Tsonga Bibliography*, pp. 13, 157–58; *Rapport annuel de la Misson suisse romande*, 1929, p. 14.
111 Junod, letter written August 1889 in *BMR* (1889) 7; Ruth Berthoud-Junod, letter of 7 July 1887 in *BMR* (1887) 72, p. 322; Berthoud-Junod, *Du Transvaal à Lourenço Marques*, pp. 252, 267. On local tonality, see Junod, *LSAT* II, pp. 294ff.
112 These festivals were also an occasion for conversion, cf. R. Berthoud-Junod in *Nouvelles de nos missionnaires* (1887) 9, 6, p. 93.
113 SMA 834, Ruth Berthoud-Junod, note made in August 1887; Berthoud, *La Mission romande*, p. 17; Berthoud-Junod, *Du Transvaal à Lourenço Marques*, p. 229; Grandjean, *La Mission romande*, p. 229; *Rapport annuel de la mission suisse romande*, 1918, p. 37; Junod, *LSAT* I, pp. 522–3.
114 P. Loze, letter dated November 1893, 'Séjour à Tembé' in *Nouvelles de nos missionnaires* (1894) 16, 5, p. 74. On Mashaba, see Harries, *Work, Culture and Identity*, pp. 34, 105–6, 160; and Harries, 'Christianity in Black and White: the establishment of Protestant Churches in Southern Mozambique' in *Lusotopie* (1998).
115 Harries, ibid., pp. 331–2.
116 Junod, *LSAT* I, p. 19.
117 Junod, *LSAT* I, pp. 545, 548–9. Most historians agree that an ability to sign one's name is evidence of fluency in reading. Cf. Roger Schoefield, 'Dimensions of illiteracy, 1770–1850', *Explorations in Economic History* (1973) 10, pp. 437–54; David Levine, 'Illiteracy and family life during the first industrial revolution' in Peter N. Stearns (ed.), *Expanding the Past* (New York, 1988), pp. 36–7.
118 Junod, *Les Chants et contes des Ba-Ronga* (Lausanne, 1897); Junod, *Nouveaux contes ronga* (Neuchâtel, 1898).
119 Junod, 'Les Ba-Ronga,' pp. 252, 278; *LSAT*, II, pp. 222, 628.
120 Junod, 'Les Ba-Ronga,' p. 278.
121 Junod, *LSAT* II, p. 222.

8
Anthropology

> The acid test of the investigator's understanding of the primitive people he studies is whether or not he makes sense of what appears to the ordinary observer as a mass of vices, follies, and superstitions. Field-Marshal J. C. Smuts[1]

Social anthropology became of concern to the citizenry of Neuchâtel in the 1850s with the discovery of the prehistoric lacustrine villages of Switzerland. The interest in far-off primitive peoples grew as missionaries like Samuel Gobat reported from Ethiopia, the Ramseyers from the Gold Coast or Frederic Ellenberger from Lesotho.[2] It was at this time that Frederick de Rougement and Edouard Desor expressed a growing interest in the customs and habits of primitive humanity, and in America their émigré colleague, Louis Agassiz, speculated on the origins and destiny of separate races, when he was confronted by the problem of slavery. This interest took a new turn in the 1870s when Europe slid into a long depression and the Swiss looked to Africa as a potential market for their goods, particularly cottons. Without a merchant navy, colonies or even spheres of influence in Africa, trading houses in Switzerland were at a distinct disadvantage. Businessmen sought to publicize knowledge about Africa and its economic opportunities by supporting a range of activities stretching from exploratory expeditions to museum exhibitions. At the same time, they encouraged the work of missionary societies and supported the publication of information about Africa in geographical and other journals.[3]

New Knowledge

Geographical societies assembled businessmen and intellectuals in a common patriotic effort to explore the unknown and open new markets for Swiss products during the depression. Like the natural history museums and the herbaria, the geographical societies depended in large measure on Swiss living overseas for the information needed to fill the pages of their journals. In Neuchâtel, Charles Knapp established a Geographical Society in 1885. Within twenty years, this institution had assembled a library of over 15,000 books in 23 languages, 550 periodicals, 4,000 maps and 1,600 photographs.[4] Knapp also encouraged missionaries and others to send ethnographic artifacts to the town's Natural History museum. This collection had been founded on the ethnographic curiosities sent home by General Charles-Daniel de Meuron from the Cape and other areas of the late eighteenth-century world. It was built on by future generations of Neuchâtelois *emigrés* who provided the funds needed to establish an imposing Ethnographic Museum in 1904, to which missionaries and other expatriates sent examples of exotic material culture. The Geographical Society's journal was particularly devoted to discovery and exploration overseas and provided missionaries with an outlet for writings considered too secular for inclusion in their societies' bulletins or other religious publications.

In the 1880s Vaudois missionaries contributed articles on their travels and observations in south-east Africa to the Geneva Geographical Society's *Le Globe* and the ancillary *L'Afrique explorée et civilisée*. The missionaries from Neuchâtel tended to publish in the journal of their canton's Geographical Society.[5] At times these articles could contain remarkably enlightened passages on African customs. In a description of his trip from Valdezia to Lourenço Marques in 1892, E.H. Schlaefli-Glardon gave a sympathetic account of the attempts by women in a village on the Olifants river to space the births of their children. When this failed and a woman accidentally became pregnant, it was normal for her to resort to abortion or infanticide to protect the well-being of her older children. Far from condemning these practices as diabolical acts, Schlaefli-Glardon expressed an understanding of their causes and even provided his readers with the name of the root used to terminate what he called a 'premature child'.[6] Auguste Jaques was able to discuss cannibalism in an equally composed manner. 'The eating of people should not be attributed to a revolting taste for the flesh of warriors', he assured the readers of the mission bulletin in 1887. 'It is just that there exists amongst many Africans the inveterate belief that whoever tastes human flesh is invulnerable in battle. Of all the medicines, this one is the most effective to repel the blows of the enemy and to give victory.'[7] A few years later Ernest Creux published a report in the same journal on witchcraft trials and their function within native communities. This was followed by a long article published in the bulletin of the Geographical Society by Grandjean's young assistant at Antioka on the Nkomati. In this work, Philippe Jeanneret showed a deep appreciation of the customs and material culture of the people he defined as 'the Ma-Khosa'. He used the language of Rousseau when he described them as 'eminently perfectible', with 'a future, let's hope, a good future'.[8] Henri Berthoud was the mission's recognized expert on native life. His tours of exploration had made him particularly knowledgeable about the Gwamba communities living between the coast and the Highveld, and in a series of articles the younger Berthoud had displayed his skills in the fields of cartography, linguistics and ethnography.[9]

Henri-Alexandre Junod's interest in anthropology emerged within the context of this intellectual tradition – and fed off its energy and excitement. Although his interests initially focused on the natural sciences, he moved in a world eager to draw knowledge about itself from the study of primitive people. After four years at the Academy of Neuchâtel, he spent the winter semester of 1884–85 at the university of Basel. When Junod arrived in the city, physical and social anthropology were divided into two separate streams led by Julius Kollmann, whose student Carl Passavant had just published a book on the craniology of African peoples, and Johann Bachofen, whose ideas were influenced by a correspondence with Lewis Morgan and Adolph Bastian and by a wide reading on Africa and other areas of the world.[10] Bachofen was concerned to unveil the early origins and universal nature of religion and – particularly through a study of mythology and funerary symbolism – the ways in which primitive peoples had expressed this fundamental idea. In *Das Mutterrecht* (1861), Bachofen had first mixed ancient Europe texts with the writings of missionaries, travellers and others, to present a history of the family as a social institution. In his work, Bachofen was particularly concerned to investigate figures such as the mother's brother, for he believed this figure to be a remnant or vestige of an earlier, matriarchal phase in the development of the family in some societies. The rise of political radicalism in Switzerland, and the growing threat of militarized nationalism on the country's borders, fired Bachofen's determination to salvage the earliest phases of a world in a spiral of decline. An investigation of the structure of modern social institutions and practices, he came to believe, could be pushed further back through time by the study of primitive cultures in Africa and elsewhere in the world.

Bachofen was an armchair anthropologist who never travelled to Africa, or, as he wryly remarked, only in his slippers. But he took a serious and pioneering interest in the customs of the people of that continent.[11] Like Bachofen, Junod remained sceptical throughout his life of the materialist approach underlying the physical anthropologists' study of humanity. Bachofen's ideas spoke of the importance of religion and the perfectibility of humanity. Junod might only have encountered this approach to the study of society as a fleeting and youthful enthusiasm, but it was an experience that would be of some consequence to his development as an anthropologist.

In the summer of 1885 Junod moved to Berlin to complete his degree. When he arrived in the Prussian capital, the city was being transformed into the cultural and intellectual centre of the new German empire. The young student from Neuchâtel could hardly have remained insensitive to the way in which Germany was building a new sense of patriotism and power on excavations in the ancient world. These resulted in the assemblage in Berlin of monumental edifices like the Great Altar of Pergamon and the Processional Way in Babylon. The three natural history museums attached to the university were also being rehoused in an impressive new structure on the Invalidenstrasse. This building would hold the newly-discovered remains of Archaeopteryx lithographica, an animal that combined the characteristics of both reptiles and birds and provided strong evidence in support of the theory of evolution. The museum also displayed more recent victims of natural selection, such as a Mauritian dodo and a South African quagga. Agassiz's reconstruction of extinct species of fish, his illustrations of the ice age, or the restoration of the Collégiale in Neuchâtel to its Romano-Gothic origins, brought ancient times alive in tangible and visible ways. Perhaps it was their example that reinforced the young Junod's view that equally ancient times could be recaptured through the study of primitive populations in Africa.

During his stay in Berlin, Junod developed his interests in Kant, natural history and the social geography practised by Karl Ritter's disciples. Franz Boas, who had recently returned from Baffin Island, also moved in these intellectual circles.[12] In the same semester that Boas finished his habilitation and prepared to embark on a career as an anthropologist in North America, Junod returned home to complete his degree. Both men would move from Berlin to new lands where, as outsiders, they developed an appreciation of cultural relativism.

In late 1885 Junod arrived back in Neuchâtel to graduate from the university and take up the position of pastor of the Independent Church in Môtiers, Rousseau's old refuge in the Val-de-Travers. He was accepted as a missionary in June 1886 and, after several months in Edinburgh where he perfected his English and acquired a knowledge of medicine, he finally left for Africa in the summer of 1889. At Rikatla, as we have seen, his thoughts were taken up by his evangelical work, his deep interest in entomology and botany, and by a pragmatic concern with the transcription of the Ronga language. From his base at the mission station he was concerned to encourage the glimmer of light he discerned in the natives' dark practices. As shown in chapters three and four, he initially viewed those practices as obstacles to the spread of Christianity and invested little time in their observation. However, he started to see their world from a new perspective as the focus of his interest moved from natural history to linguistics and oral literature, and finally to primitive peoples' ways of doing things.[13]

Junod's first sermon in Gwamba, given a few months after his arrival at Rikatla, drew on the most ethnographic of the Old Testament books, in which the tribes of Israel labour against the forces of darkness in the land of Canaan, guided by their Judges.[14] In 1893 he sent his first ethnographic article to the *Revue des missions contemporaines*. Edited in Neuchâtel for the Basel Mission, this journal published articles on African customs and politics, and seemed the right place for a paper on spirit possession amongst the natives living to the north of Delagoa Bay. Yet in this piece Junod showed little sympathy for exorcism ceremonies that he compared to (witches) Sabbaths. They presented the viewer with 'infernal scenes' that were associated with the 'activities of the kingdom of darkness'. He believed that exorcism exhibited 'the satanic power in paganism through which the prince of darkness holds captive these poor, unhappy souls'.[15]

After this unpromising start, Junod was fortunate enough to meet James Bryce, the former Oxford classicist who, like Bachofen, had extended his search for primal cultures from Rome to Africa. The two men met when Bryce passed through Lourenço Marques in 1895. Both shared a passion for botany, but Bryce was particularly captivated by the indigenous population on the coast in which he saw the outlines of the pre-Roman tribes of Europe.[16] He thought that missionaries who served as advisers to native chiefs were like bishops in ancient Gaul; African converts reminded him of Frankish warriors who adopted Christianity in the wake of Clovis' conversion.[17]

In later life Junod would ascribe his Pauline conversion to anthropology to Bryce's remarks on the similarity between the populations of ancient Europe and modern Africa. Junod would have Bryce recount in 1912: 'How thankful should we be, we men of the nineteenth century, if a Roman had taken the trouble fully to investigate the habits of our Celtic forefathers! This work has not been done, and we shall always remain ignorant of things which would have interested us so much!'[18] This statement on anthropology's sacred role in recording cultures threatened by extinction would serve as a rallying-call for later generations of anthropologists.[19] But in 1898 Bryce was still an anonymous, although 'charming and perceptive', 'conversationalist' in Junod's *oeuvre*. It seems unlikely that Bryce's comments were the cause of the missionary-biologist's switch to anthropology.[20]

As outlined in this chapter, Junod's secular conversion was rather the product of a drawn-out dialogue with his African informants in the fields of entomology, botany, and especially linguistics and folklore. By the time Bryce arrived in Lourenço Marques, Junod had produced his ungainly essay on spirit possession and exorcism. He was busy drawing up a short ethnographic introduction on 'the Thonga' that he would append the following year to both his Ronga grammar and a small collection of folklore that he had gathered over the previous two to three years. In this short introduction to 'the tribe' he acknowledged his debt to Georges Liengme and especially to Henri Berthoud. At the same time, he added, prophetically rather than with any substance, that 'the natives' were his real informants and teachers.[21] When Bryce passed through Lourenço Marques, Junod was also preparing two other long ethnographic articles, with the support of Philippe Godet in Neuchâtel, for publication in the *Bibliothèque universelle*, Switzerland's most celebrated intellectual review.[22] Junod's recognition of Bryce's influence came much later and then only when the French-speaking missionary needed a powerful patron to break into the world of British imperial anthropology.

Junod only produced his ethnographic description of the 'Ba-Ronga' once he had familiarized himself with the landscape of south-east Africa and could visualize its occupants. Equally importantly, by this time his anthropological studies were of growing appeal to Swiss readers anxious to find the origins of their own world in the beliefs and practices of primitive societies.[23] But it was the changing political situation in southern Mozambique that had the most immediate influence on the content of Junod's first monograph. For several years, the Portuguese had regarded Gungunyana as a subject chief and consequently interpreted his participation in the war of 1894–95 as a rebellion. Yet at the outbreak of war, Gungunyana controlled the areas in which the Swiss ran their mission stations at Mandlakazi and Antioka, while Rikatla operated in a frontier zone dominated by no single source of legitimate authority. At the end of the war the Portuguese attributed the origins of the conflict to the machinations of Protestant missionaries living in these rebel areas. Although the actions of Junod and his colleague Georges Liengme came under critical investigation, the state concentrated its energies on Robert Mashaba. Without powerful patrons to protect him, the Methodist minister was summarily arrested, convicted of treason, and dispatched to the Cape Verde Islands under a life sentence. Serious accusations were also levelled against Junod and Liengme. In an attempt to prevent the closure of their Mission in Mozambique, the Swiss hastily withdrew the two men from the Portuguese colony.

This unexpected furlough in Switzerland allowed Junod to organize and put to paper the data he had gathered from informants in his mission field. It also allowed him to see the African polities of southern Mozambique in a new light. The defeat of the Gaza king and his allies had placed the entire coastal mission under the protection of the Portuguese, and a rush of conversions along the coast followed the destruction of the power of the chiefs. This new situation transformed the missionaries' relations with local African communities. No longer subjected to the whims of Gungunyana and local potentates, they saw themselves increasingly as mediators between the Portuguese and the local population. It was this role, inevitably controversial during the war, that had brought the two missionaries into conflict with the Portuguese. The closing of the frontier and the subjugation of the African chiefdoms in the months after the war gave Junod the freedom to infuse sombre practices with meaning and menacing beliefs with understanding. Once European hegemony had been established, the natives' customs were threatened with extinction. Under these circumstances, the missionary could look more favourably on indigenous cultural practices and, through their collection, seek to understand and even protect them. In the process, Junod moved from the view of the brash young missionary, confronted in 1889 by the 'most hideous noises of which the human throat is capable', to that of a seasoned anthropologist, nine years later, who found in this music both a recognizable scale and the uplifting ring of the new.[24]

The Geographical Society of Neuchâtel published 'Les Ba-Ronga' in 1898 as volume ten in its bulletin series.[25] This 500-page work stood out in two specific ways. First, it extolled the role of direct observation while at the same time stressing the need to provide the natives' perspective through an understanding of their language. This focus on the field study of one group provided anthropology with an alternative methodology to that of the seasoned traveller, whose accounts depended on hearsay or a brief encounter with the subject of study. It also produced an implicit, gentle critique of the stress on theory developed by armchair experts in the metropole. Second, Junod's monograph bore the influence of a long sociological tradition in France, for it treated the Ba-Ronga as a biological organism made up of various functioning parts. This approach appealed to the editors of *L'Année Sociologique*, a new journal largely devoted to analyzing field studies from various parts of the world. But Emile Durkheim's review also criticized Junod's ignorance of comparative ethnography, for this caused the missionary to pay too much attention to detail and not enough to explanation. In a separate review, Marcel Mauss welcomed Junod's monograph but thought the Ba-Ronga of little interest as they did not display the elementary forms of social life, for they were too caught up in the forces of change.[26] In London the work gathered a more appreciative reception from James Bryce who had become a parliamentary expert on the subcontinent after the publication of his *Impressions of South Africa*. In sharp contrast to Mauss, who saw only vestiges of primal life in Junod's account of the Ba-Ronga, Bryce valued the book for its record of a 'savage' people whose primitive customs were threatened with extinction.[27]

The development of Junod's interest in anthropology was advanced by personal tragedy. On the eve of the South African war he left Switzerland to establish a school for the training of evangelists at Shiluvane in the Transvaal. A few months later the South African war broke out and in February 1901 his sister Ruth died of dysentery in war-ravaged Durban. In July Emilie Junod contracted malaria at Shiluvane during a pregnancy. When her child died in the womb, Georges Liengme was called to remove the foetus. The operation was performed without chloroform and Emilie died on the surgeon's table, exhausted by the ordeal. The Junods had lost two infant children a few years earlier and after this new tragedy, the widowed missionary decided to send his four-year-old son, Henri-Philippe, back to Neuchâtel. Perhaps as a way of overcoming his grief, Junod threw himself into the question of native education. In mid-1902 he received a copy of Booker T. Washington's autobiography, *Up from Slavery*, from William Barbey in Geneva and started to implement the American educator's ideas at Shiluvane, convinced by the Tuskegee model.[28] In February 1903, eight months after the end of the war, Junod left Shiluvane on furlough. A month later, he was in London where, presumably through an introduction from Bryce, he presented a paper on the 'Thonga' before the Folklore Society. He then left for Couvet, the seat of the Dubied family in the Val-de-Travers, from where his mother's brothers watched over the fortunes of the family. In this tranquil setting he read widely in anthropology and, towards the end of his furlough, married Helène Kern who had worked as a missionary assistant in the Congo.

In June 1904 Junod returned to the British colony of the Transvaal where the newly-founded Department of Education had started to subsidize the schooling of black children. A few weeks after his return he presented an outline of the Tuskegee system before the first general assembly of the South African Missionary Association. As the government looked to missionaries to educate the black population of the colony, this was a particularly august body. Junod's address on racially adapted education, stressing industrial training and the importance of the vernacular, was acclaimed by these representatives of the missionary movement. Soon, he published influential essays on this subject in the *Christian Express* and the *Journal of the Royal African Society*.[29] His anthropological work also found a new audience as professionals in Britain attempted to harness their discipline to the task of governing the native peoples of the former Boer republics.[30] In 1905 Junod had the opportunity to present his research around Shiluvane on the 'Ba-Thonga of the Transvaal', to another august gathering when the British Association for the Advancement of Science toured the colonies of south Africa. The president of section H, the Cambridge anthropologist A. C. Haddon, used this occasion to support the work of men in the field like Junod when he praised the 'scientific thoroughness' of 'Les Ba-Ronga'. The great man stated that Junod's monograph was 'the best piece of work on any single tribe'.[31]

As anthropology started to attract the attention of British administrators and others engaged in redrawing the indigenous societies of south Africa, Junod wrote increasingly in English. He sought to influence native commissioners, liberal colonists and missionaries, as well as imperial anthropologists, rather than the intellectual 'specialists' and practical 'friends of mission work' who had been the target of his French monograph.[32] In 1907 his essay on 'The best means of preserving the traditions and customs of the various South African native races' won a prize from the South African Association for the Advancement of Science when it called for a comprehensive study of each tribal group in the country.[33] Junod's achievements led to a vice-presidency of Section F of the Association and membership of its standing committee on anthropology. This group of senior administrators and 'native experts' called on the governments of the South African states to preserve the observations made by missionaries and others before 'the advance of civilization began to obscure and even obliterate all true traditions, customs and habits of the South African peoples'. These would soon be 'irrevocably lost', the committee warned in its annual report for 1908. It added its voice to the growing calls for the establishment of a central ethnographical bureau to undertake a survey of the native peoples of the British colonies of south Africa.[34] In the meantime, Junod set about reworking his French monograph into a two-volume English edition. Bryce, who was by this stage British ambassador in Washington, put Junod in touch with Sir James Frazer, who came to see 'Les Ba-Ronga' as 'one of the best accounts that has ever been published of an African tribe'. This appreciation of Junod's work led Frazer to introduce the Swiss missionary to his editors at Macmillan, the leading publisher of anthropological work.[35]

Junod spent the years between 1904 and 1906 at Shiluvane where he produced text books on science for his students and extended his research among the Nkuna. By this time the border between Mozambique and South Africa and the implementation of divergent policies in the two countries had effectively divided the mission's field of operations. When the Transvaal government increased the subsidy provided for the education of black children in 1907, the mission established a secondary school closer to its major establishments at Lemana in the north, and moved the school for evangelists from Shiluvane to Rikatla. When Junod returned to Rikatla to take charge of the school he found there was little left to discover in the fields of entomology and botany, because natural scientists had combed the coastal area for new species. In Mozambique his interest in native education found little echo in the corridors of power, so he threw himself with vigour into the study of anthropology. By combining his material on the Nkuna chiefdom, the original homeland of which lay between the Inkomati and the Limpopo, with that of 'the Ronga', he was able to extend his study to include the entire 'Thonga tribe'. At this period, he entered into correspondence with E. S. Hartland, a vice-president of the Folk-lore Society, who alerted him to ways in which the theory of evolution could help explain his field data.

Although the publishers Macmillan declined the new monograph, the International Missionary Conference held in Edinburgh in 1910 strongly supported Junod's ethnographic work. At this historic meeting, representatives of the major missionary movements in the world supported the need to respect the cultures of indigenous peoples and called on missionaries to enter into serious study of the communities occupying their fields of operation. With this backing and the support of Bryce, Frazer and J. H. Oldham (the influential secretary of the International Missionary Conference), Junod succeeded in raising the several hundred subscribers needed to produce his study of the 'Thonga tribe'.[36]

Another furlough in Neuchâtel (1909–13) gave Junod the opportunity to rework 'Les Ba-Ronga' into a longer English text. It also allowed him to form close ties with Arnold van Gennep who expounded on the critical importance of language and fieldwork to the evolving methodology of anthropology in the columns of his *Revue des études ethnographiques et sociologiques*. Junod reiterated his support for this approach when he wrote in Van Gennep's journal of the 'profundity and complexity' of the rites of 'so-called savages'. The anthropologist could only understand these 'strange customs', he declared, if he abandoned his prejudices and 'immersed' himself in the natives' point of view.[37] Junod had been advancing these ideas for a decade but his association with Van Gennep's multi-national, polyglot circle provided a new, influential and supportive audience for his views.[38]

In 1912–13 Junod's old classmate, Gustave Attinger, published *The Life of a South African Tribe* in Neuchâtel. The two-volume work was dedicated to Lord Bryce and contained an effusive reference to his influence. In the monograph Junod applied a far more sophisticated evolutionist approach to his material. He showed a new familiarity with recent theories in French anthropology such as those of Van Gennep on rites of passage and Durkheim on primitive forms of classification. Perhaps most importantly, he 'uncovered' systems of thought and practice that showed the Thonga to be little different from Europeans in their conceptualization of the world.[39] By adopting these innovations, Junod brought *The Life of a South African Tribe* into the mainstream of modern anthropology. Further, his fieldwork observations gave full substance to the promise first made twelve years earlier in his short introduction to the Thonga, for the natives' voice suffused the work. Charles Seligman of the London School of Economics immediately recognized his text as 'the most important account yet given of any South African tribe'. William Rivers considered it 'of extraordinary merit', Father Wilhelm Schmidt praised it in *Anthropos*, and H. E. Rawson devoted an entire article to Junod's 'classic' work in the *Journal of the Royal African Society*.[40]

During his furlough in Neuchâtel, the town's geographical society asked Junod to present a course on anthropology at the university, into which the Academy had been transformed a few years earlier. He was also included in the governing body of the ethnographic museum and in a committee dedicated to raising funds for a university chair in 'anthropology and the history of comparative civilizations'. Junod's cousin and former classmate, Arthur Dubied, was a central figure in these deliberations as he served as both secretary of the geographical society and registrar of the university. In October 1912 the university elected Arnold van Gennep to the post, the first professorship in social anthropology in Switzerland. The new incumbent quickly set about organizing the First International Congress of Ethnology and Anthropology. Held on the eve of the First World War, this meeting drew a large number of participants to Neuchâtel from a wide range of countries. It aimed to establish a professional basis for social anthropology by freeing the discipline from the dominance of physical anthropology and archaeology (or prehistory). In Switzerland this meant separating physical anthropology under Eugène Pittard at Geneva, from social anthropology under Van Gennep at Neuchâtel. More ambitiously, it aimed to establish social anthropology as a distinct discipline with its own institutional base and methodology. This pitted Van Gennep in an unequal struggle against the Durkheimian sociologists who dominated an integrated *science de l'homme*, situated in Paris, made up of philosophers, historians, economists, linguists and physical anthropologists. Van Gennep was determined to free social anthropology from this group. Practised largely by former colonial officials and missionaries, the discipline occupied an undistinguished and marginal position in France. As Switzerland's leading social anthropologist, Junod was to play an unenviable and possibly unconscious role in this academic tussle.[41]

In a paper read at the conference in his absence, on 'Ancestral religion in South Africa', Junod used Durkheim's ideas on ritual and taboo to examine the function of ancestor worship as a coherent religion. But in the same breath he criticized the sociologist's view of religion as 'no more than a social phenomenon'. A few months earlier, Marcel Mauss had employed Junod's *The Life of a South African Tribe* as the central text in his course at the Ecole pratique des hautes études in Paris. He loudly praised the detail and diligence of Junod's work in his presentation to the Neuchâtel conference on 'The BaRonga taboo of the mother-in-law'; but he was more critical of the missionary's explanation of the practice. Junod ascribed his understanding of the taboo to indigenous authority, for Viguet had told him at Shiluvane that a man avoided his mother-in-law because he was not permitted to have sexual relations with her. Mauss's interpretation of the taboo drew on an earlier debate at the French Anthropological Institute, a Durkheimian bastion in Paris, where the ritual had been viewed as a means of joining two exogamous clans linked by marriage.[42]

This was a pioneering discussion on the role of kinship as a social system. But it also marked a point of tension at the conference, for it divided participants into amateur men-on-the-spot, who turned to native informants for an understanding of the evidence they gathered in the field, and the university professionals who devised their own theories, sorting through huge amounts of field data. This division of labour tended to be reinforced by divergent secular and religious approaches to the study of humankind and by a call for the discipline to be more objective and professional. It particularly resurfaced when missionary Georges de Tribolet's paper called on the Portuguese colonial state to protect Ronga customs from degeneration, provoked by the consumption of great quantities of alcohol imported through Lourenço Marques. Discussants remarked on the unprofessional, moralistic tone of the paper and criticized its call for Europeans to intervene in the life of the tribe. Despite its appeal for social anthropology to be more sovereign and professional, the conference was ultimately a disappointment; it failed to break the supremacy of anatomy in the field of anthropology and it left unchallenged the Durkheimians' dominance of the humanities. This furthered the isolation of Van Gennep from the scholars gathered around *L'Année sociologique*, few of whom had more than a passing interest in Africa. Later, it helped to push Junod closer to British social anthropology.[43]

The tensions raised at Van Gennep's conference were clearly visible in Junod's work. He had inherited an anthropology informed by the thrill of exploration and the struggle against slavery. The new challenge was to influence colonial policy in such a way as to make its effects on native peoples both serviceable and enlightened. This concern with the role of knowledge in improving the lives of tribespeople in Africa led him to play a leading role in the establishment and running of the International Organisation for the Defence of Natives in Geneva.

Junod arrived in the city in 1920, three years after the death at Rikatla of his second wife, to supervise the schooling of his children and represent the interests of the mission. Geneva had become the home of the new League of Nations, an organization committed through its charter to the belief that 'the wellbeing and development of peoples not yet able to stand by themselves, form a sacred Trust of Civilization'. Junod quickly joined the International Organisation for the Defence of Native Peoples and started to rework *The Life of a South African Tribe* in such a way as to render it more scientific and professional. In the process, he replied to Durkheim's criticism by extending the sections on totemism and by including important comparative material on the North Sotho or Pedi (largely the Khaha neighbours of the Nkuna) and the Venda (living in the vicinity of Elim and Valdezia).[44] Macmillan eventually published this work in London in 1927. Junod's sturdy empiricism found an appreciative readership in Britain and the second edition of *The Life of a South African Tribe* very quickly became a classic in the field. It was 'the finest monograph written on any African tribe', wrote the missionary anthropologist E. W. Smith.[45] Bronislaw Malinowski thought it 'unique', 'the only satisfactory synthesis that embraces every aspect of tribal life'.[46] Writing in 1934, Isaac Schapera called it 'one of the greatest monographs on the ethnography of Africa ... one of the most exhaustive treatises we have on any African people'.[47] In the new anthropology departments opening in South African universities, the second edition of Junod's monograph quickly became a foundational text.[48]

The work was less well received in the Francophone world. This was partly because the Durkheimian sociologists continued to believe that Africa's troubled history with the world made the continent an unsuitable place to study primitive society. But they had also nudged Arnold van Gennep, Junod's major ally in the field of French academic anthropology, into a reclusive semi-retirement.[49] With Van Gennep out of the way, social anthropology in Switzerland slid back into its position as the junior partner in a field dominated by anatomy and anthropometry. Perhaps most harmfully, Lucien Lévy-Bruhl in France harnessed Junod's overemphasis on the succession of ceremonies and rituals through which Thongas gave spiritual meaning to their lives, to generalize about a primitive 'pre-logical' mechanism of reasoning. The missionary quietly sought to distance himself from Lévy-Bruhl's opinions as he thought there was 'no great difference' between the minds of African and European peoples. However, there was little Junod could do to prevent his name from being associated with the contentious, even racist, ideas of the philosopher.[50] His *The Life of a South African Tribe* eventually appeared in a French translation in 1936 as *Moeurs et coutumes des Bantous*. Beyond the field of anthropology, Junod's books were read and cited by authors as varied as Blaise Cendrars and Sigmund Freud.[51] By this time Junod had received various honours in recognition of his scholarship. These included fellowships from the geographical societies of Lisbon and Neuchâtel, an honorary doctorate from the University of Lausanne and an honorary fellowship from the Royal Anthropological Institute in 1928.[52]

Anthropology and the Scientific Method

Junod built his anthropology on the methodology employed in his entomological and botanical studies. He carried into his ethnographic writing the impersonal, authoritative style of the scientific genre. In the preface to his monograph he was careful to draw attention to his linguistic competence, the skills of his informants and the reasons for producing what he described as 'a collection of biological phenomena which must be described objectively'.[53] But his disengaged, scientific style inevitably came into conflict with his religious views and his deep concern for the welfare of the local population. 'An African tribe is not just an object of study like the birds, animals or insects displayed in the windows of our museums and dissected by diligent scientists,' he wrote, straining against the conventions of the scientific genre, 'a tribe is a living thing.'[54] To resolve the contradiction between the humane missionary and the detached scientist, the compassionate romantic and the objective scholar, Junod took the subjective commentaries, scattered throughout 'Les Ba-Ronga', and placed them in passages 'carefully separated from the scientific treatise' in *The Life of a South African Tribe*. It was 'out of respect for science' that he relegated discussions on the changing culture of the Thonga to the appendices of the monograph.[55] In the text he focused on the detail of customs and material objects that he could observe directly and classify into discrete categories. He confined his discussion of the problems raised by social change to the appendices of the monograph and particularly to a rich correspondence made up of private letters, public conferences, reports and popular essays.

Added to these non-academic texts, Junod wrote a novel, an extended short story and a handful of stage plays in which he highlighted the effects of social change on the Thonga.[56] However, his scientific work was concerned with the species and its reproduction. Junod's basic unit of study was the tribe, which he often called a 'nation' or a 'people' and sometimes a 'race'. He defined the Thonga as a *Kulturvolk* marked by tribal practices and beliefs that depended on language for their coherence and unity. 'The Thonga language ought to be considered as the oldest element in the life of the tribe, and we can then understand how it has given it its unity.'[57] Like Herder and Wilhelm von Humboldt, Junod believed that language served as 'the mirror of the soul of a people'.[58] Not all the missionaries found the same positive image in the reflection of the soul cast by language.[59] But for Junod, again anthropomorphizing the tribe, its language was proof of a developed and sophisticated 'mind'.[60]

Language constituted a natural form of ethnic taxonomy that grouped together even those who, unaware of their membership of a common linguistic community, had no shared name for themselves as a group.[61] This made language and culture far stronger markers of identity than political unity, common historical experience or, especially, physical type. Junod's view of the tribe as a primordial unit of identity and belonging provoked the criticisms of Henri Berthoud examined in chapter six.

It would also lead Swiss physical anthropologists, who measured population groups according to anatomical differences, to criticize the 'artificial' manner in which he determined the outlines of the tribe.[62] In the meantime, following the tradition established by Max Müller, Junod conflated linguistic and social categories. Linguistic categories that started off as concepts, such as Bantu, Ronga and Thonga, were very soon reified into social groups that were equipped with their own intellectual strength, civilization, mind and soul, like the Aryans and the Germans. Ultimately, they were as distinguishable as visible species of plants or beetles.[63]

Junod and his missionary colleagues had little trouble in determining the linguistic content and borders of a tribe. But the creative process involved in the delineation, construction and assemblage of a written standard was obscured when they claimed to have 'discovered' languages in the same way as naturalists were thought to have uncovered species of beetles and plants. Junod was aware of the variation in the cultural practices of the people he classified as 'Thongas'. He particularly saw the Nkomati river as the border dividing 'the Ronga' (the subject of his 1898 monograph) from 'the northern clans'. He supported this geographical division between the language groups with biological data; for while he traced the Ronga origins to Likalahumba and Nsilambowa, the 'northern clans' regarded Gwambe and Dzabana as their founding ancestors.[64] Despite these and other social divisions, Junod portrayed the Thonga tribe as an organic unit whose customs and level of evolution were defined by him increasingly through comparison with those of other tribes.

Junod not only wrote about the Thonga as a tribe. He also advised that artifacts be arranged in museum displays according to tribal origin rather than evolutionary typology, race or region. He particularly favoured the adoption of dioramas that had proved so successful in exhibiting biological specimens in their natural habitat. 'An ethnographical sample without the knowledge of its origin is no more use than a fossil without the indication of the locality or the geological stratum from which it comes.' By embedding artifacts in their cultural settings, Junod hoped to provide museum visitors with realistic displays. The power of museum exhibitions could produce 'at a short glance, more comprehension of the Kafir life than many descriptions in ethnographical books.'[65] In Neuchâtel, the Ethnographic Museum initially assembled a Khosa domestic scene out of a number of artifacts brought home by Philip Jeanneret. This display later evolved into a small 'Ronga hut' accompanied by a window filled with Ronga objects in the African section of the museum. By arranging artifacts in this realistic mode and by separating them into discrete tribal categories, the museum introduced an ethnic taxonomy that presaged or accompanied developments in museums elsewhere in the world. This manner of arranging exhibitions created a 'pure' culture only by ignoring the powers of individual creativity, as well as the human capacity for imitation and borrowing. In the process, it turned the museum into a time capsule that carried the visitor into a past stripped of change or history. A careful choice of material objects created this portrayal of a clearly defined, primitive culture. Junod contributed to this process when he assembled a display of Ronga culture that included only 'authentic' tribal artifacts. This strategy prevented him from including articles of daily consumption, such as balls of string, iron wire and locks, as well as packets of biscuits and tins of sardines, that were freely available at the local trading store. By ignoring the extent to which the Ronga had adopted these items of modern consumption, Junod created a picture of a primitive society that no longer existed. These ethnographic displays, based on the natural science model, facilitated the exhibition of a rich variety of indigenous handiwork. But they also had the pernicious effect of creating a striking representation, at once visible and tangible, of Africans as naturally tribal peoples fixed at an inferior level of evolution.[66]

Photographs were also used to create an image of tribal verisimilitude. Junod seemed unaware of how photographs were infused with meaning through their composition and selection or when they were provided with captions or even tampered with. Instead, he considered them 'a faithful, unprejudiced witness' which he used liberally to illustrate his writings.[67] Photographs of 'native salt manufacture' or natives 'consulting the bones', contributed to his picture of reality by representing individual behaviour as general, often tribal, practice. This image of the tribe was reproduced and reinforced when photographs of individuals were inscribed with the adjective 'Thonga,' despite the fact that the people depicted were probably unaware of this externally imposed identity. The dominance of the tribe was such that the voices of individual informants were sometimes submerged in the text by faceless 'Thongas', all experts on aspects of tribal culture.[68]

Cartography also helped create a vision of the tribe as a 'natural' community. It inscribed the tribe on the map and broke it into various dialect zones. Fusing language and primitive politics, Junod gave the kinship term 'clans' to these 'groups'. He suggested that the clans were 'a natural extension of the patriarchal family', and their several hundred or thousand members shared a common patronym or *shibongo*.[69] On the 'map of the Thonga tribe' in his monograph (see plate 2), these 'clans' were presented as clearly defined tribal segments highlighted by sharp lines and primary colours. The tribe was ultimately as homogeneous as the genera of plants or insects that filled the biologists' distribution maps. Just as species of related plants or animals constituted a genus, these linguistic groups or 'clans', based on shared physical descent, made up the tribe. This perspective allowed Junod to apply fieldwork observations recorded in only one restricted area to a large number of people, occupying a wide locality. In this way he transformed individual creations, such as huts, carvings, calabashes, basketwork, kitchenware, weapons, villages or people into standard 'Thonga' types. For instance, he had no difficulty in naming a drawing of a clutch of spears and other weapons in 1898 as 'Ba-Ronga weapons' and then renaming the exact same drawing 'Thonga weapons' fourteen years later.[70]

In contrast to Dudley Kidd, the arch lumper whose *The Essential Kaffir* was filled with imprecisions, Junod was a splitter who saw the tribe, like the species, as the correct level for investigation. 'The essential Kafir will not be known till a scientific and thorough study of all the tribes has been completed.'[71] In his prize-winning essay of 1907, Junod raised the benefits of establishing an Anthropological Commission to collate and compare ethnographic material collected in the field by different missionary societies.[72] By applying the taxonomic approach of the natural sciences to the collection and comparison of ethnographic data, Junod ranged African societies according to a hierarchy of evolution that would indicate how best they should be ruled. At the same time, he hoped to make the Thonga more visible to his readers and to instil in them an appreciation of the rich diversity of African cultures. This section has shown how Junod's narrative strategy, and particularly his choice of categories, shaped the 'understanding' of African society that Field Marshal Smuts referred to at the start of this chapter. The following section underlines how Junod's temporal understanding of the tribe reinforced its spatial outlines.

Salvage Anthropology

As an organic unit, Junod's tribe had a physical presence and soul, a life of its own and a capacity to reproduce itself. It was around this concept of the tribe as a unit capable of reproduction that Junod constructed chapters on 'the evolution of the man,' and 'the life-cycle of the woman'. By tracing the individual's passage from birth through childhood, maturity and death, even the narrative structure of the first volume of his *Life of a South African Tribe* drew on the analogy of the evolution of species. The second volume began with a description of the natural environment and its influence on what Adolf Bastian called the 'psychic' or mental life of the tribe.[73] The tribe was certainly the main character in an ethnographic plot that dissolved other actors into roles and types that made up the overall anatomy of the institution, each with its appropriate function, like distinct organs.

Junod subjected the tribe to the insights of direct observation, the methodological convention used to describe zoological and botanical species. In these fields, this way of seeing created a stark dichotomy between the viewer and the object of interest. However, when applied to the study of humans, this form of observation gave the impression that Junod was divorced from his informants' community, that his sometimes disturbing questions did not contribute to the changing scene he was busy observing. His vision of an organically stable tribal society was reinforced when Junod presented his evidence in the present tense, concerned only with the moment of observation. At the same time, his experience in the domains of entomology and botany led him to apply the broader skills of the field naturalist's world to the study of humanity.

Fieldwork was a cornerstone of this scientific methodology. Junod stressed his linguistic competence and gathered evidence from a wide cross-section of informants. Although his family duties and missionary vocation precluded long spells away from home, he gathered information on the verandah, as well as during evangelical itineraries and summer breaks. In the various areas he visited, he was able to observe cultural practices at first hand and gather information from individuals who still adhered to the old ways. Two Ronga-speaking individuals provided most of his initial information. Spoon Libombo lived near Rikatla and, as we saw in chapter five, had distinguished himself as Junod's butterfly collector. Tobane came from the nearby Mfumo chiefdom displaced by the building of Lourenço Marques. This meant that Junod's two primary informants were drawn from a narrow patch of land on the coast where the Portuguese had a long presence. Both men converted to Christianity after the Portuguese conquered the area, as did Mboza, a third, new informant who also lived near Rikatla. As such, the three men were hardly representative of the 'Ronga' who, following Junod's definition, stretched south of Lourenço Marques into northern Zululand. In the Transvaal, Junod relied on two major informants: a member of the Nkuna royal family named Mankhelu and a Christian called Viguet. These men supplied him with information on the sprawling 'northern clans' living between the Nkomati and Save Rivers (as well as isolated immigrant settlements in the Transvaal). As time went by, Junod attempted to make his survey more representative of 'the tribe' by interviewing more informants.[74] But he interviewed few members of the 'clans' living north of the Nkomati River and never conducted fieldwork in that vast area. This was a serious omission for a work on the 'Thonga tribe': over half its population lived on the coastal plain between the Nkomati and Save rivers. Furthermore, the Gaza Ngoni had ruled the entire region north of the Nkomati-Limpopo rivers for seventy years until their defeat at the hands of the Portuguese in 1895 and, inevitably, they had exercised a major influence on its population.[75]

In the field, Junod collected folktales from men and women of all ages, although he found adult women, who often dictated the stories directly to him, to be his best informants. He also persuaded his students at Rikatla to write essays on such topics as polygamy and included a verbatim account of one of these, 'The life of a Ronga woman', in his monograph.[76] When gathering information on social life, however, he interviewed few women and fewer young boys and girls. As the twentieth century advanced, his patriarchal view was increasingly filtered through the accounts of recent converts. He generally took care to name, and even provide photographs of, his informants; but at times he fell back on information provided by unnamed representatives of specific communities, age groups or occupations. Most surprisingly, Junod was sometimes a fairly insensitive interviewer. He seemed unconscious of the problems associated with students providing information to their teacher or Christians to their missionary. On a trip to England in 1909 he was pleased to find a delegation from the newly formed South African Native Congress on board ship. John Dube, Walter Rubusana and D. Dwanya were on their way with W. P. Schreiner to protest against the colour bar clause in the South Africa Act. Junod ignored this aspect of their voyage and merely valued these three 'Zulus' for the valuable comparative information they could provide on tribal customs. The missionary seemed genuinely taken aback when the 'Christian chief' (presumably Dwanye) 'for some obscure reason' declined to provide him with information on witchcraft, and his disappointment grew further when Dube turned the discussion into an assessment of the witchcraft and mesmerism practised by Europeans![77]

Junod believed that the information given by indigenous informants provided a true picture of native life. It was the task of the anthropologist in the field to gather this material in an objective and scientific manner. The role of the professional at home, on the other hand, was to compare, classify and systematize findings from all over the world, and to devise theories that would explain their existence.[78] Ethnographic work could 'be done only by the co-operation of two different agencies, those who are to collect the materials, and those who are to work them out'. In the manner of the entomologist in the field, the 'man on the spot' was to observe the object of study in its natural surroundings and his job was simply 'to note the facts carefully and to describe them accurately'.[79]

Junod liked to cast himself in the role of the sturdy fieldworker gathering the information from which metropolitan experts developed explanatory theories. This separated him from professionals like Durkheim and Mauss, but it did not relegate him to the role of a credulous collector of data for, by subjecting his material to comparison and analysis, he succeeded in turning information into knowledge.[80] His work was marked by a strict pragmatism: he wanted to supply magistrates, missionaries and others with the native logic and indigenous understanding underlying local customs and beliefs. It was for this reason that his work became more confident as (perhaps rather gullibly) he turned increasingly to locally knowledgeable people for explanations.[81] As a former diviner, Elias Libombo did not simply supply Junod with information on his erstwhile occupation; he also explained how divining operated, and made clear why people believed implicitly in its powers. Junod's respect for local knowledge increased as he deepened his familiarity with the language, extended his fieldwork and grasped the different systems that underlay indigenous understandings of botany, zoology or linguistics. He stressed the need 'to enter into the mind of these primitive men', and he tried to capture the meaning of their words through a liberal use of vernacular terms in his ethnography.[82]

The imposition of Portuguese colonial rule made Junod's portrayal of the Thonga as a people scarcely influenced by European contact, less tenable. But as the Portuguese entrenched their hegemony, Swiss missionaries came under both personal and political pressure to filter out the destructive consequences of European rule from their work. Junod was perfectly aware that Christianity would transform local beliefs and cultural practices. It would 'put the axe at the root of an immense tree, and sooner or later the tree will fall'.[83] He regretted this consequence of his evangelical duty and, as early as 1898, called for the protection and preservation of African customs that would contribute to the development of humanity. He opposed a mindless assimilation that would destroy the genius of the African people and advised that the natives should be protected from 'useless luxury, servile imitation, dangerous and deleterious borrowings'. They should 'keep all that is possible of their simplicity and their primitive good nature, while at the same time enriching their lives with new knowledge and the discipline of regular work'.[84] He particularly stressed the importance of the chief in the structure of local society. 'Let us retain all that is pleasing and moral in the picturesque circle of huts, the respect for elders, the sense of family unity, the habit of mutual help, the readiness to share food with others.'[85] Sorting cultural practices in this way required a thorough knowledge of what should be kept – or salvaged – and what should be abandoned.

Politics also exercised a growing influence on Junod's representation of Thonga society. In a long report to his Missionary Society on the causes of the Luso-Gaza war of 1894–95, Junod had pointed to the devastating impact of forced labour or *xibalo* on the lives of the people in the Crown Lands around Lourenço Marques. When he returned to Rikatla in 1907, forced labour had become a daily institution that invaded individuals' homes and forced them to hide in the bush for extended periods. As the practice grew in Mozambique, several missionaries called on their society to denounce *xibalo* publicly.[86] This led to an impassioned debate within the mission as, in what was almost a replay of the moral issues it faced during the Luso-Gaza war of 1894–95, the institution was forced to choose between its spiritual role, the dissemination of the gospel, and its social task, to protect and guide its real and potential congregants. By this time, Junod had established a working relationship with important members of the Portuguese colonial administration, particularly the governor, Freire d'Andrade, to whom he had dedicated his *Grammaire ronga* when a young captain. When Junod prepared *The Life of a South African Tribe* for publication in 1912, Andrade subscribed to the purchase of 100 copies, almost a quarter of the edition. Later, he supported the translation of the work into Portuguese and its publication by the Imprensa Nacional.[87] In this situation, there seemed little reason for Junod to mention *xibalo*, the conditions of migrant labour or the system of land alienation and racism experienced by Africans under colonialism.

The question of how to respond to the contravention of human rights in Mozambique proved a divisive issue for the mission. A quarter century earlier Georges

Liengme had remarked that missionaries could not comment openly on the violence of colonial rule. 'He has a gag over his mouth', he had written bitterly at the time, 'he has to hide part of the truth and, if he divulges it, it is scrupulously classified with the secret papers' of the mission.[88] The question of forced labour again revealed the mission's compromised position as a foreign institution working in a Portuguese colony. In January 1921 the Portuguese ambassador in Switzerland gave a lecture in Neuchâtel before Henri-Alexandre Junod and other church dignitaries, in which he praised the contribution of the Swiss to Portugal's civilizing mission, particularly their role in the fight against alcoholism and forced labour. The speech provoked a heated correspondence in the columns of the newspaper *La Suisse libérale* when Henri Guye, with the full support of the mission in Mozambique, reported publicly on the growth of *xibalo* in the colony. Junod and others, fearful of the Portuguese reaction, called for moderation.[89] Guye reported that growing numbers of women were being conscripted into the forced labour gangs and he watched with dismay as private employers started to use *xibalo*. Prompted by the coastal mission, he first asked mission headquarters in Lausanne to raise the matter with the Portuguese, but when this failed to elicit a clear response, he entered into correspondence with J. H. Oldham, a voluble critic of forced labour in British East Africa. In a reply to a circular from the great man, Guye described how Mozambicans were hunted down for *xibalo*, even in their homes, and sometimes attached by a cord around the neck, in the manner of slaves. *Xibalo* undermined the family, disrupted the church and made education difficult when pressgangs invaded the schools and seized the older boys.[90]

The matter arose again after the League of Nations turned to eradicate the last vestiges of slavery. Edward Ross, a sociologist at the University of Wisconsin, published a report in 1925 on forced labour in Portugal's African colonies. Ross revealed that he had gathered important information from Swiss missionaries in the field. This placed Junod in a difficult position for, as vice-president of the International Organisation for the Defence of Native People in Geneva, he was in direct contact with the Slavery Commission of the League of Nations whose Portuguese representative was none other than Freire de Andrade. In response to Junod's queries, Guye produced a long letter supporting Ross' claims. He provided details of government complicity in forced labour for private and public works, commented on the growing demands for *xibalo* caused by intensive road-building in Gaza province and drew attention to the inability of government to stop the imposition of forced labour on women and children. Guye particularly pointed out that Junod must be aware of the widespread nature of forced labour because his eldest son, Henri-Philippe, was a missionary in one of the worst affected areas.[91] It had become impossible to visit some out-stations as their members were hiding in the bush from the *xibalo* gangs. The mission's schools provided children, who were routinely abducted, with only a modicum of protection. One man had earned only £6 after labouring on public works for a year and another had earned only £4 when pressed into the service of a private individual for six months.[92] Junod responded to this and other reports by calling on the missionaries to refrain from embarrassing the Portuguese in public and he advised that the question of forced labour be left in the hands of the League of Nations. In the event Freire d'Andrade succeeded in pushing the governor of Mozambique to issue a decree in November 1926 outlawing the use of *xibalo* by private individuals.[93]

As the second edition of Junod's monograph went to press, missionaries continued to report on the disturbing prevalence of forced labour in southern Mozambique.[94]

But the missionary-anthropologist, although a severe and vociferous opponent of forced labour in other parts of Africa, was less willing to criticize the practice in his own mission field.[95] He later came to admit that the Mozambican government had never implemented its restrictions on forced labour, and that there was nothing the mission could do to stop the practice. Although *xibalo* had become an everyday custom in Mozambique, he refused to bring this grim source of change into his 'scientific' anthropology of African life.[96] Besides, by this time European poets, painters and photographers, eager to break from their artistic conventions, had found inspiration in the picture of Africans living in harmony with nature. Politicians in South Africa had also started to use the salvage anthropology of Junod and others, at last, to construct a coherent answer to 'the native question'. In the event, Junod only mentioned forced labour in one prosaic footnote in the 1927 edition of his monograph. He left the destructive effects of colonialism and capitalism to the appendices of his study.[97]

It was only after the South African war that Junod applied himself to the field of British anthropology. Swept up by the political events of the period, the author of 'Les Ba-Ronga' read Edward Tylor on 'survivals' and animism and W. H. R. Rivers on diffusionism. At the same time, he familiarized himself with the arguments of South African writers like Bishops Callaway and Colenso, W. C. Willoughby and, later, Winifred Hoernlé and E. W. Smith.[98] He particularly employed van Gennep's ideas to organize and explain the detail gathered in *The Life of a South African Tribe*. Using the notion of rites of passage, Junod described Thonga practices as a series of movements in space and time that were marked by ritual and taboo and represented new stages in the evolution of the individual. Marriage, for instance, passed through three stages: betrothal, the passage of the *lobolo* and the ceremony taking the bride to her new home. Circumcision marked the movement of a boy or girl from childhood to adulthood, and a woman giving birth for the first time passed from the status of woman to mother. Junod's study of the intricate taboos and customs that signified and protected these role changes helped raise his work from run-of-the-mill description to detailed, scientific explanation.[99]

In 1909 E. S. Hartland sent Junod Sir James Frazer's list of questions on 'the customs and rites of savage people'. In a letter to Frazer, seeking the anthropologist's help in the publication of his book, Junod claimed that the questions opened 'many new subjects', encouraged him to speak to more 'trustworthy natives' and in general produced a lot of new material, particularly on the significance of taboos and aspects of sexual life. Nevertheless, he only devoted a small part of his book to answering Frazer's famous questions for the man in the field.[100]

Evolutionist ideas were already present in 'Les Ba-Ronga' where Junod expressed the belief that Europeans could recapture their lost prehistory by examining African peoples and their customs in the way that palaeontologists studied an assemblage of bones. The idea that Africans represented an early stage in the evolution of humanity was also written into his texts in hidden ways when he frequently compared the peoples of modern Africa with those of European antiquity.[101] By comparing Africans with ancient Hebrews and Greeks or the prehistoric lacustrians of Switzerland, Junod attempted to create understanding through analogy. But by drawing his examples from the Old Testament or ancient Europe, his language constructed a picture of Africans as primitive people. As shown in chapter five, this view was confirmed by his representation of the undisturbed vegetation and primal animal life of south-east Africa. In this supposedly 'pristine' natural environment he had discovered a new world of plants and animals, and he believed he could in the same way discover a 'pure' population marked by simple virtues and uncorrupted values. Hence Africa was an exemplary location in which to apply the methodology of the field naturalist to the study of humankind in its most primitive state.

Junod was not alone in this view. In the early part of the twentieth century, many anthropologists saw the object of their discipline as the recording of primitive customs before the spread of modernity destroyed all trace of their specific contribution to the development of humanity.[102] Some believed Junod's study of the Thonga had come too late, as the tribe had been exposed to European influences for too long.[103] Several of Junod's most learned missionary colleagues were also of this opinion. Arthur Grandjean thought the 'real Africans' lived in the interior, for those on the coast had been too influenced by European civilization.[104] 'The natives of the south have been bastardised and demoralised by the influence of an unhealthy civilization, whereas those of the north, further removed from the seaport, have been more sheltered from the deleterious influences that have gradually annihilated their brothers.'[105] Georges Liengme was particularly lyrical about the people he found at Antioka in the interior. 'I love this country,' he wrote of the bend in the Nkomati in 1891,

> because it is the real Africa, with its rich nature, its immense plains, its far-off horizons lit morning and evening by a fiery sun. The natives, too, are real Africans; they have not yet been bastardized by contact with our civilized whites. There is an enormous difference between them and the blacks on the coast who, in many respects, are less interesting.[106]

The imprint of Europe's lost innocence found in Africa's present had a strong impact on Junod's conceptualization of the discipline of anthropology. It confirmed his evolutionist ideas and these, in turn, endorsed the need to salvage a picture of the 'real' customs of Africa before they suffered a corrupting evolution and were lost to scholarship.[107] In capturing on paper a civilization on the verge of extinction, Junod was motived by the wish to preserve for posterity an image of lost prehistoric Europe as much as precolonial Africa. Yet, just as his transcription of the language endangered the creative freedom and flexibility of the oral medium, so too did his evangelical work threaten to destroy the fresh and original aspects of 'authentic' African cultural practices.

Salvage anthropology was a compromise that kept the old values on paper in a way that provided Europe with a picture of its early beginnings while at the same time offering no resistance to a controlled modernization. Like Joseph Conrad's narrator Marlow, Junod saw the dark heart of his own civilization in Africa; vices of materialism and greed and various unspeakable rites banished to the appendices of his monograph.[108] From his vantage point at Mandlakazi during the last years of independence, Georges Liengme looked with growing horror at the stream of concession-seekers trading alcohol, guns and political influence at the Gaza capital. He compared the unsavoury morality of these hollow men with that of the noble Gaza Nguni unfavorably.[109] For men like Junod and Liengme, the primitive simplicity of Africa threw into relief the corruption brought to society by the materialism and greed of an industrial age. Ethnography gave them a new means of criticizing the vices and corruption of a continent that had rejected the guiding hand of the Christian Church. The picture of African innocence threw into relief many of Europe's growing and increasing failures, and through its representation of a people such as the Thonga, it held out the living example of a society in which enchantment, creativity and emotion had not yet been extinguished by dry rationalism and stifling rules.[110]

Junod viewed the African tribe from his place in a society shaken by waves of industrialism, secularism, materialism and new concepts of deep time. In the search for an ontology more adapted to their age, intellectuals in Europe had peeled away the layers of time and drawn inspiration and understanding from their primitive origins. When renovators in Neuchâtel stripped away the fifteenth-century wooden gallery of the Collégiale to reveal and restore its Romano-Gothic structure, they uncovered the purest and most authentic expression of ancestral creativity. In much the same way, Junod's ethnography stripped away the layers of change brought on by culture contact that hid the original, real examples of mankind.

Just as the physical restoration of buildings required an inventive reconstruction, so too did that of salvage anthropology. By the time Junod published 'Les Ba-Ronga' in 1898, Mozambican workers had been tramping to the colonies of South Africa for almost fifty years. They played a major part in the development of the sugar plantations in Natal, the diamond fields at Kimberley and the gold mines of the eastern Transvaal, and they helped build the ports and railways in the Cape that provided the subcontinent with a modern economic infrastructure. After the discovery of gold on the Witwatersrand, Mozambicans became the primary source of labour for the outcrop and deep level mines.[111] Although almost 100,000 workers drawn from southern Mozambique were employed in South Africa by the turn of the century, Junod chose not to mention these men in 'Les Ba-Ronga'. In the extended English editions of this work, the only major reference to migrant workers was placed in an appendix on homosexuality in the compounds, a practice Junod viewed as a threat to the continued reproduction of the tribe. Nor did the well established system of labour tenancy in the Transvaal appear in any of his monographs. These absences are clearly visible in Junod's choice and arrangement of photographs. Junod generally situated human subjects in bucolic, primitive surroundings and almost never in urban settings. When an urban environment was chosen (the shabby, smoke-filled, 'Native tin town near Pretoria station'), it was juxtaposed with an arcadian image ('the Thonga hut') in such a way as to reinforce textual statements on the relationship between environment and social evolution.[112] Through the use of photographs, first taken in the early 1890s and republished unchanged as late as 1936 (and even in the unauthorized 1969 edition), Junod and his editors froze this rural environment into a simple, secure and seemingly immutable primitivism.

Junod's desire to salvage a vision of Thonga society before it was transformed by capitalism and colonialism also led him to leave out of his picture of native weapons examples of the tens of thousands of guns that became an integral part of indigenous weaponry during the last quarter of the nineteenth century.[113] Nor did he feature the ubiquitous tin spoons, enamel cups, heavy iron pots, padlocks and other imported goods commonly used in the area. Perhaps most notably omitted from the anthropological picture were the labour recruiters, Portuguese officials and colonists who had become a daily part of many Africans' lives well before the 1890s. Also excluded were the pictures of missionaries and converts, so filled with the potential of change and racial integration, that dominated missionary propaganda as a literary genre.

In some cases Junod's desire to capture primitiveness before it disappeared led him to tamper with the photographic evidence. This could mean an innocent but strategic choice of photographs, such as the picture of the diviner, Hokoza, and his retinue

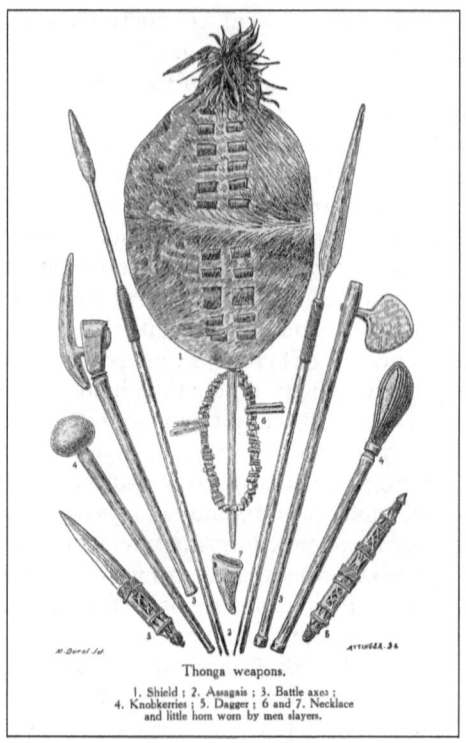

Thonga weapons.
1. Shield ; 2. Assagais ; 3. Battle axes ;
4. Knobkerries ; 5. Dagger ; 6 and 7. Necklace
and little horn worn by men slayers.

8.1 Left out of this illustration of 'Thonga weapons' is the most common weapon of all by the 1890s: the second-hand or remaindered European gun. By excluding imported guns from this illustration in his monograph, Junod sought to represent the Thonga as an exotic and primitive people. Through this form of careful omission he developed a powerful genre of 'salvage' anthropology.
(Junod, The Life of a South African Tribe *(London, 1927) I, p. 453)*

8.2 (a & b) Junod chose to include this picture of the diviner Hokoza and his assistants in his The Life of a South African Tribe. *If instead he had chosen the photograph of Hokoza, his wife, Mrs Benoit, and their children (as featured on the cover of this book), or the picture of the diviner and his Swiss visitors, the impression on the reader would have been very different. Junod chose photographs as carefully as the facts he decided to display in his monograph. In this way he constituted the picture of a primitive society that conformed to the expectations of the ethnographic genre at the turn of the century. This picture of an unchanging African society contributed to the development of segregationist policies. In the late 1920s it was subjected to a growing criticism from a new generation of university-trained anthropologists.*
(© Swiss Mission Archive, Lausanne)

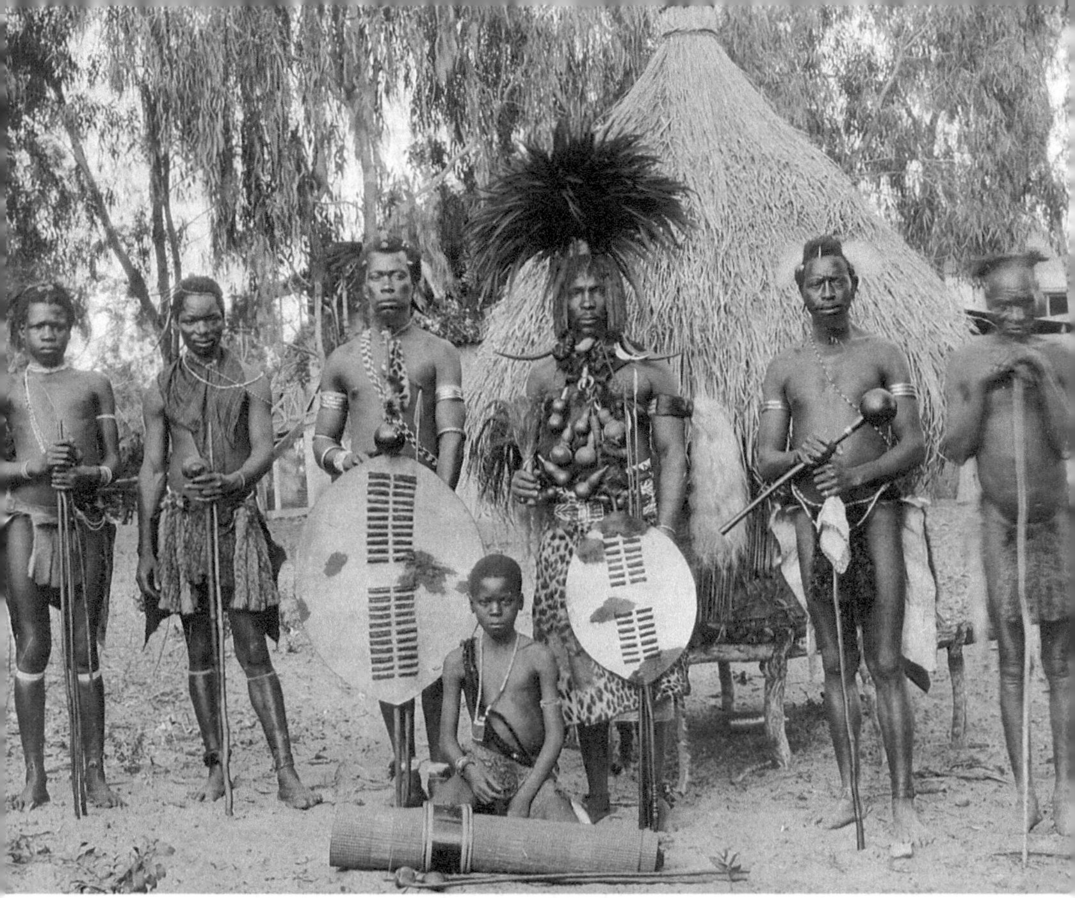

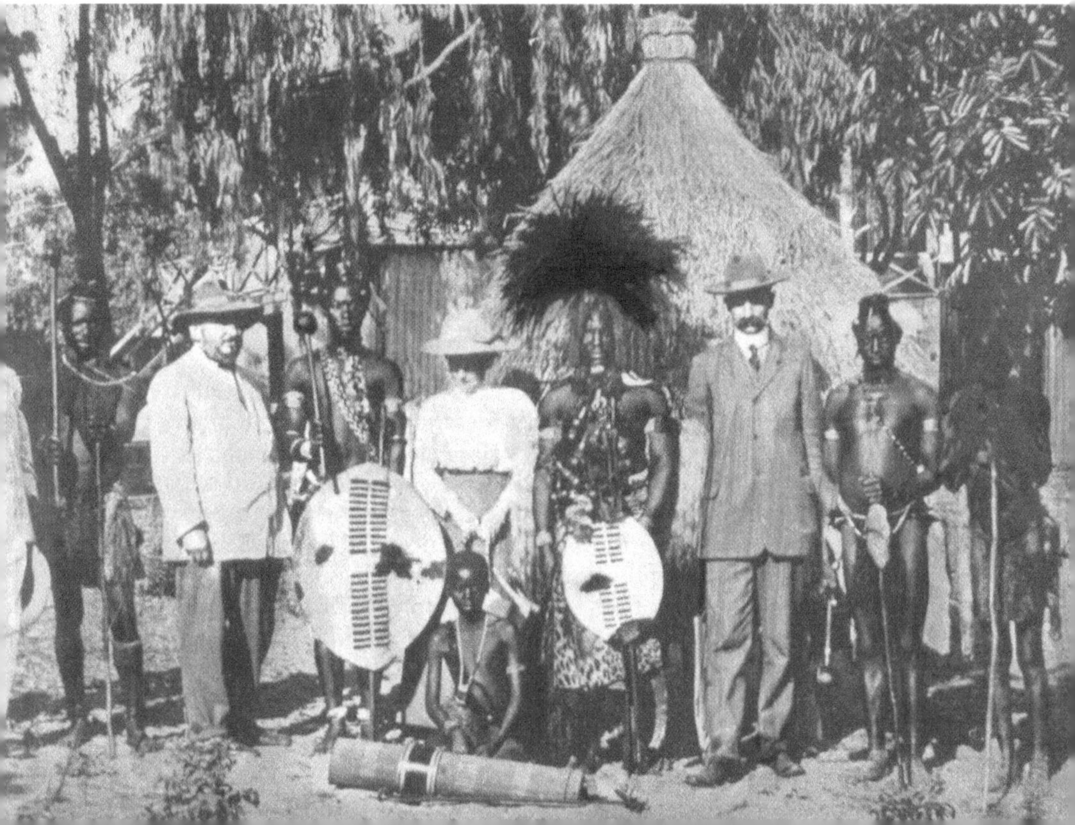

used to illustrate *The Life of a South African Tribe*.[114] This photograph was taken in Tembeland in 1912 by William Benoit on a visit to the area led by Arthur Grandjean (secretary general of the mission at that time). Benoit took several photographs of Hokoza during the visit, including a picture of the diviner and the missionaries (Grandjean, Bonnard, Mr and Mrs Benoit) and another featuring Hokoza, his wife and Mrs Benoit. By choosing to include the one photograph that excluded all missionaries, Junod presented Hokoza in his monograph as though he came from a pre-contact society; and in this way the photograph helped construct the image of a pure and original Thonga community. The problems with the methodology employed by Junod to construct his view of an authentic African society is most vivid when we turn to the illustration of chief Ntchoungi used in his first monograph (and reproduced on page 229). In the drawing, the Khosa sub-chief living near Antioka is presented as a *Khela*, an adult man permitted to wear the wax crown called *ngiyana* in Ronga and *shidlodlo* in Djonga. He holds a stick surmounted by a carved figure, wears an ebony snuffbox on his chest and a wildcat skin around his waist. But a quick comparison with the original photograph shows that a chair of European manufacture, a prominent feature in the original photograph, has been omitted from the drawing. Although Junod must have been aware that chairs had become a symbol of royal power in the region, he chose to exclude this piece from the drawing as it conflicted with his idea of what constituted an authentic African chief.[115]

This use of photographs to illustrate textual information extended to the construction of mock scenes. In one instance a passage on the ruthlessness with which local soldiers dealt with their captives was underscored by a photograph of men pretending to spear an individual lying on his back.[116] This unabashed manipulation of images in salvaging the past seems to us a rather unethical practice. But it was, I think, little different from Agassiz's reconstruction of prehistoric fish out of a few fossilized bones, or Viollet-le-Duc's restoration of medieval buildings on the basis of equal measures of ingenuity and comparative probability. Nor was Junod's attempt to salvage a picture of pre-contact African society much different from that of novelists and playwrights who sought an authentic Ireland or England in isolated rural communities. For the salvage anthropologist Africans remained 'real' only as long as they remained 'other' and it was in the real customs and traditions of a people that its genius could be found and preserved.

Evolutionism

The evolutionist hypothesis helped Junod explain his picture of a primitive Thonga society. Although he had used Darwinian ideas to explain his entomological work, he only developed a concerted evolutionist approach to his anthropological material after the publication of 'Les Ba-Ronga'. Under the influence of E. S. Hartland, Junod sought to explain many of his observations, particularly in the field of kinship, by searching for the origins of institutions and practices and by tracing their evolution over time. Evolution did not provide an absolute chronology, but it did impose historical order on an otherwise confusing and undifferentiated mass of information. If the origins of the Thonga family were to be found in a primitive promiscuity, he wrote, it was no longer possible to find vestiges of this stage of evolution in the customs he

8.3 (a) In this photograph Ntchoungi, a Khosa sub-chief, leans against a chair of European manufacture. (b) In the illustration taken from the photograph, and included by Junod in his first monograph, the chair has been removed. Rather than portray Ntchoungi as a chief grappling with the changes brought by capitalism and colonialism, Junod sought to represent him as the ruler of a primitive tribe. In this case, Junod could only salvage the image of a pre-colonial African chief by actively erasing an aspect of the photograph.
(© Swiss Mission Archive, Lausanne)

was able to observe. However, relics of the next stage, when groups were formed and all the women of one group married the men of another group, could be found in the rights and preferences of a Thonga man to marry certain women in his wife's family, particularly her younger sisters and her brothers' daughters.[117] It was also perhaps possible to find a remnant of this group stage in the names given to kinsmen. So when Thongas called all their father's wives and all their mother's sisters 'mothers' – and all their father's brothers 'fathers' – they were perhaps employing a naming practice that had once existed in a lost past where all the men of the group stood in relation to ego as 'fathers' and all the women as 'mothers'.[118] In modern Thonga practices, he was able to observe clearer remnants of the next stage of evolution, when the family constituted itself around the mother as the owner of the children and as the individual through whom they traced descent. During this 'matriarchal' phase, when marriage was unknown and the father's role was confined to the act of reproduction, the boy's closest male relative was his mother's brother. This man officiated over the worship of her ancestors and left his inheritance to his sisters' sons when he died.[119]

In the final phase of the evolution of the Thonga family, the emergence of private property caused men to become the dominant figures through whom kinspeople (including the father) traced their ancestry.[120] Junod believed the Thonga he studied were at an early phase of this agnatic, patriarchal stage of development and consequently displayed several vestiges of the earlier, matriarchal phase. When he published 'Les Ba-Ronga' in 1898, he had thought the special, warm relationship between the *malume* and the *mupsyana* (Ronga) was caused by the latter's ability to inherit his mother's brother's wife (a woman with whom his father was strictly prohibited from having sex).He, the young uterine nephew, was her closest marriageable relative. This was one aspect of the logic of kinship; another helped explain why a man preferred to marry his wife's younger sisters or her brother's daughters, following the passage of the *lobolo*.[121] A decade later Junod started to apply a more thoroughly evolutionist approach to his ethnographic data. He had used these ideas in his entomological work and had probably come across them in Bachofen's writings, but Hartland drew his attention to the ways in which the theory of evolution could explain ethnographic data.[122] Once he turned to study 'the northern clans', this led Junod to see the importance of the *malume* as a vestige of what had once been a lively Thonga cultural practice during the earlier 'matriarchal stage'. Remnants of this ancient custom could be seen at a man's funeral when his *ntukulu* (Thonga: uterine nephew) made noisy claims to his material goods, at the time his inheritance was distributed to his sons. The vestige of the *ntukulu's* former role as the rightful heir to his *malume's* possessions was publicly recognized when he received a small, symbolic assegai from his maternal kinsmen.[123]

Through the study of the stringent rules and regulations governing kinship, Junod showed the strict system of marriage, and series of classificatory roles within the 'family' or group, developed by the Thonga. The transfer of brideprice, he argued, should not be equated with the purchase of a woman. It functioned rather to compensate a group for the loss of a female member. Once understood in this way, the passage of the brideprice served to explain the logic behind a series of complicated marriage preferences and avoidances.[124] The study of kinship not only showed that Africans were able to order their lives and infuse them with reason; it also provided Europeans with a glimpse of their lost past – and helped them locate the tribe on the ladder of evolution.[125] This was of great practical value as the level of evolution attained by a tribe or nation indicated how its members should be governed, what sort of education they should receive, or whether they were fit to assume the responsibilities of democracy.

Junod's interest in the origins of polygamy also had practical consequences. He speculated that it could have emerged under slavery, or when there were insufficient husbands for the womenfolk due to the high mortality of men in warfare. As a practice, polygamy could also be read as a remnant of the 'old system of group marriage' when men and women formed polygamous and polyandrous unions.[126] 'Marriage in primitive or semi-civilized tribes', he stated categorically, 'is not an individual affair as it has become with us. It is an affair of the community. It is a kind of contract between two groups, the husband's family and the wife's family.'[127] This led him to believe that it was wrong to see *lobolo* as a contract between two families aimed at securing the fair treatment of a wife, nor was it a pledge or security claimed by the wife's parents as protection for their daughter. 'The lobolo is a compensation given by one group to another group in order to restore the equilibrium', he wrote. When the one group acquired a new member, the second felt itself diminished in numbers and claimed a *lobolo* so as to acquire another woman. This made the wife the property of the family that acquired her – and not the individual property of one man. His colleagues went too far when they judged a wife the slave of her husband; yet, as the rights of the individual were not recognized in this situation, she could not be protected against maltreatment. In addition to this reason for opposing polygamy, Junod felt the practice inflamed sexual passions and that bridewealth debts led to eternal disputes between families. However, over time his condemnation of these customs became less severe. He came to believe that polygamists should not be expelled from the mission but rather kept on trial, and he advised the state to discourage rather than outlaw polygamy by registering only one wife and then taxing all subsequent marriages.[128]

Evolutionism led Junod to re-evaluate the religious beliefs and practices of the Thonga. In 1898 he stated categorically that 'the Gwamba' worshipped their male ancestors, had no idea of 'a unique and supreme God' and that their religion had most probably experienced a form of degeneration. As he read the work of the evolutionist anthropologists and came to realize the importance of cultural understanding to the spread of the Gospel, he broadened his concept of religion and started to discern a system in the way the Thonga related to the spiritual world.[129] He came to believe that, like religious communities anywhere in the world, the Thonga depended on 'higher, supranatural powers' to help them in times of distress. However, as 'no Native philosopher or theologian (had) ever classified this somewhat confused mass of religious ideas', he set about the task with zeal. Using the comparative method, he tried to 'bring some order' to the religious ideas of the Thonga – in much the same way as he had ordered their ideas on botany, entomology, language, kinship or music by uncovering the 'system' that linked and explained these practices.[130]

Elias 'Spoon' Libombo helped Junod to see many of the 'superstitions' of the Thonga as legitimate expressions of a religious belief that, in the end, was advancing slowly towards the same objective as Christianity. Nathan Söderblum, the professor of Missiology at Uppsala in Sweden, convinced Junod that God used various religious practices to attract non-Christians to him. Through this thesis on the polygenic origins of religion, Junod combined his belief in God with his evolutionist approach to the development of society. Over time, he found in Thonga practices both 'the religious instinct' and a hesitant advance towards monotheism. This led him to conjecture that the Thonga had developed a dualistic religion, combining a belief in personal spirits (ancestor-gods) with the worship of a transcendental Supreme Being who, around 1500, took on the outlines of God. This religion degenerated after about 1820 when this overarching God-like figure lost ground to the self-serving ancestors (presumably due to the Gaza invasion and, later, the vices brought by Europeans). What remained of the earlier monotheism of the Thonga was a vague belief in a Supreme Being recalled by the word *Tilo*. Junod thought this word was probably a 'disfigured remnant' of the term for God used by Thonga-speakers during their early, partly monotheistic, stage of evolution. This was what 'intelligent elderly natives' seemed to imply when they used the word or spoke of the belief in a Supreme Being having once been much stronger. For Junod, the word *Tilo* clearly represented 'an embryonic state' of monotheism.[131] However, in less guarded moments he called *Tilo* 'the Ba-Ronga name for God', adding, however, that the 'ancestors are the real object of worship'.[132]

Junod came to attribute the evolution of his ideas about native religion to Elias Libombo. But the evolution of his approach was also strongly influenced by the work of metropolitan intellectuals looking for the origins and function of religion, as well as by the findings of a growing number of missionary activists searching for an indigenous root on which to graft Christianity. Many found this in the local belief in a Supreme Being, perhaps only a vestige, or even a dim memory, of His presence; or the ease with which people adopted an imported word for God.[133] Others discerned the outlines of local social beliefs and practices that could be regarded as religious in nature.[134] Junod's description of totemic practices, and especially of Thonga ancestrolatry as a religion, particularly bears the (unacknowledged) imprint of Emile Durkheim. Thonga ancestor worship was 'essentially *ritualistic*', and left 'very little place for true religious feeling'. However, drawing on his criticism of Durkheim at Van Gennep's conference in Neuchâtel, he added that 'elements of *personal religion* are not altogether wanting'.[135] Ancestrolatry was spiritualistic and, in general, exhibited the elementary forms of the religious life. It was 'a clear, well-defined religion, with its theology, its sacrifices, and its prayers'.[136] Although the natives had no visible churches, priests or services, he came to believe that they were religious and that their religion had the capacity to evolve. This was clearly expressed in central-southern Mozambique during the First World War when priests representing the High God Murimi arrived from Rhodesia (where the god was known as Mwari), with a potion capable of finding witches. For Junod, this movement represented a higher stage of religious practice as it drew followers from a wide range of clans and chiefdoms. In this way, Murimi introduced a transcendental morality into the lives of people who, when they expressed the belief that he was the son of God, inched towards an indigenous monotheism.[137] By this time, Junod had even come to regard the coastal revival that he, Paul Berthoud and Arthur Grandjean had suppressed so effectively at the turn of the 1880s–90s, as an example of the way a folk religion could evolve towards monotheism.[138]

Informants ranging from Elias Libombo to Emile Durkheim inspired Junod to uncover a strongly religious element in the spirituality of the Thonga. Junod's view of a 'primitive religion' was also constructed through the discursive strategies of translation and analogy. The way that the Thonga regarded the afterlife, particularly their idea of *Tilo*, was not far different from that of the ancient Greeks. Their funerary rites bore comparison with those of early Europeans and their baptism by smoke exhibited close parallels with the Christian rite. Junod assured his readers that even Thonga bone-throwing had once been practised by both ancient Greeks and prehistoric, lacustrian communities in Switzerland.[139]

Junod's conceptualization of Thonga religion had important consequences for the nature of mission work. As a young missionary, he had condemned Thonga cultural practices such as spirit possession as the work of the devil, and shortly after his arrival he had imposed a heavy hand on native expressions of Christianity. Junod's anthropological work led him to differentiate between Thonga cultural practices and to hold out the prospect of a Christianity built on local foundations. Because people like the Thonga were imbued with a remarkably spiritual temperament, he even argued that they presented a more fertile field for Christianity than his European compatriots.[140] Yet many of his colleagues disputed the idea that natives were able to adopt Christianity so easily, almost without the tutelage of missionaries. Some saw little sign of evolution in the hesitant response of the Thonga to the Christian message and they continued to attribute the slow pace of conversion to a social degeneration initiated by original sin and accelerated by imported European vices.[141] Others joined the chorus of criticism directed against words like *Tilo* which, they claimed, meant only 'sky' or, at best, 'heaven'.[142] Others searched in vain for the sign of light observed by Junod in pagan initiation ceremonies and found only darkness and diabolical agency behind acts of sacrifice, totemism and ancestor worship.[143]

Junod did not portray the evolution of society in an entirely unilinear way, for, as we have seen, he saw some elements of Thonga culture as decidedly more advanced than others. He believed the evolution of various beliefs and practices could be traced to the diffusion of outside influences rather than internal dynamics. Indeed, African customs indicated 'a slow progress, generally due to outside influences.'[144] It was the natural scientist and perhaps the Berlin geographer in Junod who thought 'the centuries-old stagnation' of the Thonga could be attributed to environment. This was not so much a harsh, exacting environment as an environment that isolated the Thonga from ideas and advances elsewhere in the world.[145] Despotic chiefs and communal values compounded the inability of society to change from within. Africa was a languid and lethargic continent, weighed down by customs 'transmitted from prehistoric times'.[146]

From this perspective, the creative energies of the Thonga had only been stirred once they came into contact with outsiders. These included Arabs, Lemba and, of course, Europeans, but they also included a mysterious group of Iron Age immigrants. Junod believed that the absence of Stone Age tools indicated that the Thonga had passed from the age of wood to the Iron Age without passing through the Bronze Age and that by implication they had received the knowledge of iron-working from an in-migrating group.[147] These diffusionist ideas fed into a stream of concepts that would marginalize Africans in the history of South Africa and, in the wider context, would underplay African agency in the history of the continent well into the 1960s.[148]

As an evolutionist, Junod speculated about origins and sweeping changes, but he showed little concern for the sequence of events or for the causes of change. His main concern was to document the rules, regulations and rituals that filled a specific phase of tribal development. The uniformity of these tribal practices was rarely broken by different environmental conditions, varied historical experiences or individual enterprise. There was no place in his ethnographic text for the unconventional, the non-conformist or the dissident that historians situate at the heart of change. Nor was the Thonga agriculturalist's harmonious relationship with nature disturbed by the frightening, cyclical droughts and famines that afflicted south-east Africa and brought starvation, war, disease and migration in their wake.

Junod's frequent references to the weight of mindless custom, held in place by the despotism of chief and community, served to remind his readers of the link between progress, individual enterprise and accountability. But in the process of depicting a social order bound by unmoving traditions, he portrayed intelligence as a collective act concerned with the wellbeing and, ultimately, the reproduction of the community. In *The Life of a South African Tribe*, individuals perform specific functions, live and die, replace and renew, as if driven by instinct and habit rather than by will, reason, or God. Only on very few occasions do they exercise the power of thought or the ability to act in innovative ways. Junod's training in the narrative traditions of the natural sciences led him to portray 'Thongas' less as individuals with their own sense of volition than as specimens concerned with bringing about the reproduction of the larger group: the tribe.

Junod's presumptions and presuppositions led him to choose his subjects for discussion as carefully as he edited his photographs. Here I can take only two examples.

In his monograph, Junod described the ideal 'Thonga village' as a collection of about a dozen huts, built in a circle around the cattle kraal. This homestead was a 'social organism ... regulated by strict laws ... [that] ... presents a remarkable uniformity all through the tribe'. Yet we know from other sources that the hut tax caused some polygamous men to reduce the number of huts within the homestead. 'In one village I found only two huts', wrote Junod's colleague Paul Rosset in 1900 from the north-eastern corner of the Transvaal. 'One was occupied by the chief, his four wives and the girls, the other by four boys and two unmarried young men. This is merely one example amongst many others.' As a description of the homestead, Rosset's image contradicted Junod's picture of the unchanging, 'traditional' village.[149]

Junod's treatment of slavery provides another example of the way in which he airbrushed from the ethnographic record any evidence that did not conform to the pattern he had established or 'uncovered'. This institution was particularly important in the area north of the Inkomati-Limpopo rivers where the Gaza Ngoni exercised a strong influence on local cultural practices. In this area, slavery created ties of kinship when youths were integrated into their captor's family. Young men who grew up together in a single family came to call each other 'brother', despite their different biological origins and their unequal status. Yet Junod viewed this form of kinship in the same way as the Portuguese: as an artificial construct that had no legal basis or place within his monograph.[150]

Race and Politics

If the broad sweep of evolutionism took little account of historical detail, it did reinforce arguments about the monogenic origins of humanity. At the end of the nineteenth century, Switzerland had still to be conquered by a belief in the common unity of humankind. Louis Agassiz had little trouble in ascribing a common origin to mankind, but he thought that as communities spread into different parts of the world, they became so acclimatized to their environment as to form races that had all the attributes of different species.[151] He believed that, as the single ancestral population fragmented geographically, a process of (what we would call) speciation set in. Through their isolation in Africa, black people came to constitute a separate and inferior race. Agassiz believed that this race had its own special characteristics and destiny and could be improved if these were recognized. This made him a strong opponent of racial mixing, for he believed that, because the fate of each race was intimately tied to its environment, miscegenation served to produce degenerate and weak populations, frequently unable to reproduce themselves.[152]

In Geneva, Agassiz's old colleague, Carl Vogt, combined Darwinian evolutionism with polygenism in such a way as to trace racial origins back to different species of hominids. In one of his famously incautious statements, Vogt expressed the belief that it was better to be 'a perfected ape than a degenerate Adam'. His anthropometric studies told him that Africans, particularly women, were physically primitive and their brains undeveloped. As 'ideas come from the brain like bile from the liver and urine from the kidneys', this meant that Africans had produced only primitive ideas.[153] At the same time, he applied to Africans the theory of recapitulation, according to which there is a physical correspondence between the young members of an animal species and their primitive adult ancestors.[154] This led him to believe that African children grew at the same mental pace as European children, but that at the age of puberty they suffered an 'arrested development' that halted the growth of their mental capacity.[155] African adults shared with European children the ability to imitate, as well as a high degree of sensuality and capriciousness, but they marked an early phase of human development and were physically incapable of evolving into the mature species of humankind represented by adult, male Europeans.[156] Vogt was not alone in these ideas but he expressed them in a particularly brutal and uncompromising manner. 'The [African] race has never, neither in the past nor in the present, accomplished anything useful to the course of human development, certainly nothing worthy of being conserved.'[157]

The evocation of these grim and sordid ideas serves to remind us of the many cul-de-sacs in the history of the natural sciences. But it also underlines that a country like Switzerland, without colonies and without a black population, was an important centre of scientific work on the racial question. Agassiz was the most famous biologist in America until his death in 1873. Vogt exerted a strong influence on several founders of anthropology, from Charles Darwin and James Hunt in England to Paul Broca in Paris.[158] He also served as the rector of the University of Geneva, and gave his name to one of the principal boulevards in the city. Vogt's most racist work, *Lessons on Man* (1863), was translated into eight European languages, by which time he was sufficiently famous to appear in one of Dostoyevsky's novels.[159] Nor were these celebrated intellectuals alone in their views on race; many of Switzerland's leading intellectuals at the time, from Carl Passavant to Jacob Burckhardt, saw Africans as either racially different or as a *Naturvolk* living at an early stage of evolution.[160]

In South Africa the population of European descent tended to share Carl Vogt's ideas on the arrested mental development of Africans.[161] Junod forcefully rejected these ideas but he did tentatively accept the notion that Africans could be intellectually precocious as children and then experience a 'decrease' in cerebral activity at puberty. 'It may be said that the vivacity of mind, the rapidity of comprehension, which is sometimes wonderful amongst the younger boys, decreases when they reach the age of fifteen or sixteen.'[162] However, unlike Vogt and his followers, Junod stressed that this form of arrested development could be reversed, for it was the product of Africa's environmental isolation rather than the result of a racial, specifically African, physical condition. Writing with Gobineau and Vogt in mind, he stated that 'many casual observers [believe that] the Bantu races are incapable of progress. They are condemned, by reason of their mental and spiritual constitution, to vegetate in perpetual barbarism or to make themselves ridiculous by a servile imitation of the superior races.'[163] Junod was led to reject this physical determinism by his early training at the hands of Karl Ritter's disciples, by his close observation of nature and perhaps by his religious convictions. He firmly believed that the influence of the environment was of far greater importance to human development than the physical constitution of individuals or types. In America, Franz Boas' pursuit of these ideas eventually undermined and shattered the very notion of race as a physical category.[164]

In an intellectual environment dominated by the polygenic ideas of Agassiz and Vogt, Junod found it necessary to state that all humankind had one, single origin. In the early 1930s he still felt compelled to write: 'the African is a man, as much a variety of *homo sapiens* as the European or the Asiatic. We find in him all the essential elements of human nature.'[165] Henri-Alexandre Junod's work in the natural sciences, linguistics and oral literature challenged the racial findings of the Swiss physical anthropologists. Yet for this disciple of Immanuel Kant and Jacob Burckhardt, Africans had yet to leave the torpor and ignorance of childhood and enter into the light of mature understanding. 'The African tribe is like a child who has hardly entered conscious life', Junod wrote in 1898.[166] Thirty years later, Africans were still visibly children, 'younger brothers' who constituted a 'weak', 'indolent', 'primitive, childish race', an 'inferior race made to serve'.[167] Through this familial metaphor, Junod portrayed Africans as junior members of the human race who would one day reach senior status, but only under careful parental guidance and tuition.

At the end of the nineteenth century, many Europeans still believed in the capricious and unstable nature of Africans (an idea picked up and propagated by Linnaeus) or their disregard for the law (a positive attribute in the eyes of Rousseau and his antimodernist followers). Junod made a point of showing that the Thonga were governed, like Europeans, by rules and systems of thought stretching from matrimony to music and from polygamy to politics. The contribution of the Thonga to the development of humanity could be found in various areas, extending from the ways in which they classified and explained nature to the manner in which they organized and regulated kinship. This led him to recognize Africans as members of a common humanity and to reject Lucien Lévy-Bruhl's concept of a pre-logical or primitive way of thinking different from that of modern Europeans. Jacob Burckhardt's model of the evolution of civilization influenced Junod to assign a heroic role to missionaries. For by liberating the individual's powers of creativity, missionaries would both bring about a controlled cultural Renaissance in Africa and take the fruits of this Renaissance to the attention of the world.

These ideas had a direct influence on Junod's notion of the place to be occupied by the African population in a common South African society. While at Shiluvane, he wrote of the need for a 'special native curriculum', based on vernacular education in the early years, that would prevent the 'denationalization of African children' and build on their 'special wants or gifts'.[168] Life at the evangelist's school at Shiluvane was soon 'entirely based' on this attempt through education (inspired by Washington's Tuskegee) to bring about 'a gradual emancipation of the black race'.[169] These ideas received the support of a wide range of interests, from the South African General Mission Council to South African politicians leaning towards segregation. In the 1920s they were incorporated into the findings of the Phelps-Stokes Commission and pursued in areas of British colonial education by the founders of the International Institute of African Languages and Cultures, Lord Lugard, Hanns Vischer, J. H. Oldham and E. W. Smith.[170]

Junod's wish to protect 'the black race' from the vices of European civilization led him to portray 'true Bantus' as naturally rural people who, like butterflies in an inappropriate environment, were out of place in the city. Tribespeople suffered social degeneration and were even faced with physical extinction, when they moved out of the environment that had shaped their *Volksgeist*.[171] These ideas led him to favour the pass laws as a means of reducing uncontrolled urbanization.[172] At the same time, he criticized developments in the Cape Colony where the education system produced 'black English Christians' and the qualified franchise led to an over-hasty political assimilation.[173] Instead, he called for government to strengthen the powers of the chief and to extend the district councils of the Transkeian territories to the other Bantu reserves of South Africa. These district councils were advisory bodies through which Africans engaged in the democratic process without challenging the dominance of white electors in the national parliament. While the Christian chief, the native commissioner and the missionary nurtured and protected the interests of the tribe, and the district councils provided it with a voice, a small, educated and Christianized elite should have the right to participate in national politics. 'Could not the Bantu then evolve into some new, original, and interesting political organism', Junod speculated, 'in which the evils of heathenism would have disappeared and a healthy national life would prevail?'[174] Through this process the population in the reserves would dispense with the need for separate political representation and eventually achieve political equality with those whites and blacks who qualified to vote for the national parliament. But he estimated that full social and political integration could only be accomplished after one or two hundred years.

As we all know, authors are not owners of their ideas. Junod's categories of race and tribe and the meanings he gave to these terms were used in various ways. Stevenson-Hamilton read his hypothesis on arrested development as proof of the racial superiority of whites.[175] Smuts was impressed by his scientific approach and supported his idea that Africans should be subjected to European tutelage, although without noting when this would end.[176] Others found in Junod's work scientific evidence in support of a racial segregation that would both protect blacks from the aggressive materialism of an industrial age and allocate to whites the economic heartland of South Africa. Much of the segregationist legislation passed in the 1920s sought to answer the native question by salvaging the African tribe as the natural home for the black population of South Africa.

By the mid-1920s, when Junod was preparing the second edition of his *Life of a South African Tribe* for publication, the world that he had observed thirty years earlier was undergoing a rapid transformation. For a growing number of critics, his monograph had created a model of tribal life that no longer accorded with the facts. Some suspected that his picturesque view of tribal life in the north-eastern Transvaal had never existed or that it was inapplicable to other parts of South Africa. In some areas such as the Ciskei, chiefs did not exist or had to be created by the Native Administration. Communal tenure of land no longer existed in some reserves and in many areas extensive land alienation had created reserves unable to support their populations without the assistance of wages repatriated by migrant workers. Junod's anthropology hid the large-scale movement (both migratory and permanent) of African men and women to the cities. It failed to take account of the far-reaching changes brought to rural society by the labour recruiter, the trader and missionary, and it ignored the large African population living outside the reserves on white-owned farms and in the cities. Most especially, Junod's account of tribal life disregarded the economic ties that bound whites and blacks into a common South African society. By this time anthropology had emerged as a university discipline in South Africa and criticisms of Junod's ideas soon came from this quarter.

Notes

[1] Foreword to E. J. Krige and J. D. Krige, *The Realm of a Rain-Queen: A Study of the Pattern of Lovedu Society* (Oxford, 1943).

[2] I look at the rise and fall of missionary anthropology in P. Harries, 'Anthropology' in Norman Etherington

(ed.), *The Oxford History of the British Empire*. Companion volume on missionaries (Oxford, 2005).
3. Anon., 'La part des Suisses dans l'exploration et la civilisation de l'Afrique', *L'Afrique explorée et civilisée* (1883), p. 215; Anon., 'Le commerce de la Suisse avec l'Afrique', *L'Afrique explorée et civilisée* (1889), pp. 55–60.
4. 'Neuchâtel' in *Dictionnaire géographique de la Suisse* (Neuchâtel, 1905) vol. III, p. 502.
5. Cf. H. Berthoud, 'Exploration de H. Berthoud entre le Spelonken et Lourenço Marques', *L'Afrique explorée et civilisée* (1886) 7; Junod, 'Correspondences: de Rikatla à Marakouène' in *Bulletin de la société neuchâteloise de géographie (BSNG)* (1891) 6, pp. 318–26; 'Correspondence de Rikatla', *BSNG* (1892–93) 7.
6. He explained that children should ideally be spaced at two–year intervals. A child born too soon after its sibling brought shame on the mother as it was likely that she would have insufficient milk to support two children. Medicine taken from the root of the lowveld croton (*xunguxungu* or *croton megalobotrys*) was used to abort this unwanted pregnancy. Schlaefli-Glardon also noted that pregnancy resulting from an adulterous union was terminated in the same manner. E. H. Schlaefli-Glardon, 'De Valdezia à Lourenço Marques', *BSNG* (1892–93) vii, p. 152.
7. A. Jaques, 'Craintes de guerre', *Bulletin de la mission romande (BMR)* (1887) 6, 73, pp. 281–2. These ideas were later adopted by Junod, *Life of a South Africa Tribe (LSAT)* (London, 1926–7) 2 vols, I, p. 477; II, pp. 90n1, 506, 535.
8. E. Creux, 'Elim. Etat du pays', *BMR* (1891) 8, 98, pp. 292–5; Philippe Jeanneret, 'Les Ma-Khoça', *BSNG* (1894) especially pp. 130, 137, 153. Others would go on to write on the history and ethnography of the Gaza. Cf. A. Grandjean, 'L'invasion des Zulu dans le sud-est africain', *BSNG* (1899) 11; G. Liengme, 'Goungounyana et son régne', *BSNG* 13, 1901.
9. Junod, *Ernest Creux and Paul Berthoud: Les fondateurs de la Mission Suisse en Afrique du Sud* (Lausanne, 1933), p. 131. In 1899 Henri Berthoud became a corresponding member of the Geographical Society of Neuchâtel. He was honoured with a diploma from the Society in the same year; H. Berthoud to C. Knapp, 13 July 1899 in Archives of the SNG, Cantonal and University Library, Neuchâtel.
10. Julius Kollmann divided Europeans into various races on the basis of anatomical differences. Cf. Kollmann, *Craniologische Gräbefunde in der Schweiz* (Basel, 1885). Carl Passavant extended his ideas to Africans, see Christoph Keller, 'Sieben Schädel und eine Theorie: Die anthropologischen Forschungen Carl Passavants' in Jürg Schneider, Ute Röschenthaler and Bernard Gardi (eds), *Fotofieber: Bilder aus West- und Zentralafrika. Die Reisen von Carl Passavant 1883–1885* (Basel, 2005). See also Passavant, *Craniologische Untersuchung der Neger und der Negervölker* (Basel, 1884). For Bachofen's work at this time, see his *Antiquarische Briefe* (Strasburg, 1880, 1886).
11. L. Gossman, *Basel in the Age of Burckhardt: a study in unseasonable ideas* (Chicago, IL, 2000), pp. 140–1, 495n. 11. Morgan, McLennan and Engels developed the notion of matriarchy and introduced it into the world of Anglo-American anthropology.
12. Adam Kuper, 'Project of a cosmopolitan anthropology' in his *Among the Anthropologists: History and Context in Anthropology* (London, 1999), p. 39; George Stocking, 'From Physics to Ethnology' in his *Race Culture and Evolution* (Chicago, IL, 1982 edn).
13. In mid-1893 he considered their customs to be 'overflowing with the picturesque'. University and Cantonal Library, Neuchâtel. Philippe Godet collection. Junod to Godet, 28 June 1893.
14. See his 'Impressions à l'auditoire du cours de Théologie biblique du Nouveau Testament à l'université de Berlin par le professeur Pfleiderer', April 1885. The sermon, given in Gwamba (Thonga) in February 1890, was based on the book of Judges. Both documents are in the UNISA. JC.
15. Junod, 'La possession chez les indigènes de Delagoa Bay', *Revue des missions contemporaines* (1893) V, 18, pp. 17–18.
16. Bryce considered 'the Tongas of the east coast' to be 'complete savages'. Bryce, *Impressions of South Africa* (3rd edn, London, 1899), p. 361.
17. Bryce, *Impressions of South Africa*, pp. 373, 376.
18. Junod, *LSAT*, I, p. 1.
19. Evans-Pritchard repeated it, almost word for word, in his *Social Anthropology* (London, 1951), pp. 122–3. See also W. D. Hammond-Tooke, *The Roots of Black South Africa* (Johannesburg, 1993), p. 7; George Stocking, *After Tylor: British Social Anthropology, 1888–1951* (London, 1995), p. 335.
20. In Junod's first monograph, the statement was shorter and merely attributed to 'a very distinguished traveller. ' 'Les Ba-Ronga'. 'Etude ethnographique sur les indigènes de la baie de Delagoa', *Bulletin de la societé neuchâteloise de géographie* (1898) X, pp. 7–8. Fifteen years later, for reasons outlined below, Junod increased his tribute to Bryce by dedicating to him the first edition of *The Life of a South African Tribe* and by attributing to him the genesis of the work.
21. Junod, *Grammaire ronga suivie d'un manuel de conversation et d'un vocabulaire ronga-portugais-français-anglais* (Lausanne, 1896), p. 5. n2; Junod, *La tribu et la langue thonga: avec quelques échantillons du folklore thonga* (Lausanne, 1896).
22. Junod mentioned these two articles, and his work on folklore, in a letter to Philippe Godet dated 23 June

1893. University and Cantonal Library, Neuchâtel, Godet Collection: MS 3164.131. The articles appeared as 'Galagala: tableaux de moeurs de la tribu des Rongas' and 'Quelques contes africains' in *Bibliothèque universelle et revue suisse* (1896) II and (1897) VII. See also Henri-Alexandre Junod, 'L'art divinatoire ou la science des osselets chez les Rongas de la baie de Delagoa', *Bulletin de la société neuchâteloise de géographie* (1896–97) 9.

23   I trace these themes in chapters two, four and five.
24   Junod, 'Quelques contes africains', *Bibliothèque universelle et revue suisse* (1897) VII, p. 515–16; 'Les Ba-Ronga,' p. 265. See also *LSAT* II, p. 282. Compare these positive views of African singing with those in chapter four, pp. 96–7.
25   E. Jacottet, 'Moeurs, coutumes et superstitions des Ba-Souto', *BSNG* (1897) IX, pp. 107–51; Junod, 'Les Ba-Ronga', *BSNG* (1898) X, pp. 1–503.
26   See the reviews of 'Les Ba-Ronga' in *L'Année Sociologique* (1898–99) 3, by Mauss (pp. 220–2) and Durkheim (pp. 370–2). Mauss' review is republished in *Oeuvres 3. Cohésion sociale et divisions de la sociologie* (Paris, 1969), pp. 126–8.
27   In *The Speaker* (London), 5 November 1898. See also the favourable, anonymous review in the *Bibliothèque universelle* (1898) 12, 4, pp. 205–7.
28   Botanical Conservatory Geneva: Boissier Herbarium. Junod to Barbey, 23 October 1902.
29   Henri-Philippe Junod, *Henri-A. Junod: missionnaire et savant, 1863–1934* (Lausanne, 1934), pp. 38–9. *BMR* (1904) August, 17, 221; *BMR* (1904) October 17, 223, p. 269. James Stewart, the founder-editor of the *Christian Express*, presided over the 1904 conference. His ideas on native education were close to those of Junod. Junod, 'The Native languages and Native education', *Journal of the Royal African Society* (1905) XVII, October. See also the appendices to *LSAT* II, pp. 613–19, on 'The Problem of Native Education', 'The Necessity of a special Native Curriculum' and 'The Place of the Vernacular in Native Education'.
30   C. H. Read, 'Presidential address to Section H – anthrop', *Nature* (1899) 60, pp. 554–7; A. C. Haddon, 'A plea for the study of native races in South Africa', *Nature* (1900) 63; Sydney Hartland, 'On the Imperfections of our Knowledge of the Black Races of the Transvaal and Orange River Colony', *Journal of the Royal Anthropological Institute* (1900) 29–30, pp. 22–4; Anon., 'A plea for the scientific study of the native laws and customs of the natives of South Africa', *Man* (1903) 3, pp. 70–4.
31   A. C. Haddon's Presidential address to Section H – Anthropology – of the British Association for the Advancement of Science, *Report of the 75th Meeting*, 1905, p. 525. Junod's address was published as a long paper, 'The Ba-Thonga of the Transvaal', *Addresses and Papers of the South Africa Association for the Advancement of Science* (1905) 3. See also Junod, 'The theory of witchcraft amongst South African natives', *Report of the South African Association for the Advancement of Science* (1905/6), p. 230.
32   Compare 'Les Ba-Ronga', pp. 12 and 439 with *LSAT*, I, p. 1.
33   Junod, 'The best means of preserving the traditions and customs of the various South African native races', *Report of the South African Association for the Advancement of Science (Natal)*, 1907, pp. 141–59.
34   A. C. Haddon, 'An Imperial Bureau of Anthropology', *Nature* (1909) 80. Robert Gordon, 'Early Social Anthropology in South Africa', *African Studies* (1990) 49, 1, pp. 17, 40n.2.
35   Wren Library, Trinity College, Cambridge University, Frazer papers (CU.FP). Junod to Frazer, 9 July 1910; Ts attached to Junod to Frazer, 14 October 1910.
36   Swiss Mission Archive, Lausanne (SMA) 518/C, Junod to mission council, 29 August, 1910; CU.FP. Junod to Frazer, 16 May 1910. J. Stanley Friesen, *Missionary Responses to Tribal Religions at Edinburgh, 1910* (New York, 1996).
37   Junod, 'Les conceptions physiologiques des bantous Sud-Africains et leurs tabous', *Revue des études ethnographiques et sociologiques*, (1910), p. 126.
38   Emmanuelle Sibeud, *Une science impériale pour l'Afrique? La constitution des savoirs africanistes en France 1878–1930* (Paris, 2002), pp. 164–7.
39   Arnold van Gennep, *Les Rites de Passage* (Paris, 1909). Junod did not mention the influence of Durkheim and Mauss, but his monograph bears the imprint of Durkheim on totemism ('La prohibition de l'inceste et ses origins', *L'Année sociologique* (1896–97) 1) and particularly, Durkheim and Mauss on primitive forms of classification ('De quelques formes primitives de classification', *L'Année sociologique* (1901–2) 6.
40   C. G. Seligman, *Man* (1913) review 24; William Halse Rivers, *Report upon the present condition and future needs of the science of anthropology; presented to the Carnegie Institution of Washington, DC* (Washington, 1913), p. 16; W. Schmidt, 'Henri A. Junod of the Swiss Romande Mission: The Life of a South African Tribe', *Anthropos* (1913) VIII, pp. 903–5; H. E. Rawson, 'The Life of a South African Tribe', *Journal of the Royal African Society* (1913) 13, xlix, pp. 1–13. See also the more critical review by W. C. Willoughby in the *International Review of Missions* (1913), pp. 588–91.
41   A. van Gennep, 'La signification du 1er Congrès d'ethnographie', *Mercure de France*, 16 August 1914; Sibeud, *Une science impériale pour l'Afrique?* Chapter 6. Van Gennep dedicated the fifth volume of his *Religions, moeurs et légendes* (Paris, 1914) to Henri-Alexandre Junod.
42   Cf. Marcel Mauss, *Oeuvres 3*, pp. 104–107, 111, 124–5. For Junod's perspective, see *LSAT* I, pp. 238–41.
43   Musée Ethnographique, Neuchâtel. Archives of the Congrès internationale d'anthropologie et d'ethnographie,

1–5 June 1914. Pierre Centlivres, 'Le rendez–vous manqué: Van Gennep et la première chaire d'ethnologie de Neuchâtel (1912–1915) in M. Gonseth, J. Hainard, R. Kaehr (eds), *Cent ans d'ethnographie sur la colline de Saint-Nicolas 1904–2004* (Neuchâtel, 2005), p. 147. Wendy James points out that Africa occupies little place in the work of the Durkheimians. This was because they thought international commerce, the slave trade and colonial conquest had brought too much change to the continent for it to harbour archaic, pristine forms of social life. Wendy James, 'The African ethnography in 'L'Année sociologique", *L'Année sociologique* (1998) 4, 1, pp. 195–6, 199. See also note 26 above.

44 These concerns were expressed earlier in Junod, 'Le totemisme chez les Thongas. Les Pedis et les Vendas', *Globe* (1924) 63,pp. 1–22.

45 E. W. Smith in *Africa* (1929) 1, p. 391. See also Smith's glowing review in the *International Review of Missions* (1928) 17, pp. 381–3.

46 Bronislaw Malinowski, 'The Anthropology of Africa', *Nature* (1931) 127; H. Powdermaker, *Stranger and Friend* (London, 1966), p. 43; H.-P. Junod, *Henri-Alexandre Junod: missionnaire et savant, 1863–1934* (Lausanne, 1934), pp. 70–1. For Malinowski's critique of missionaries and 'antiquated anthropology', see his *A Diary in the Strict Sense of the Term* (London, 1967), pp. 31, 42; and his 'The life of culture' in G. B. Smith et al., *Culture: the diffusion controversy* (New York, 1928), pp. 26–46.

47 Isaac Schapera, 'The present state and future development of ethnographical research in South Africa', *Bantu Studies* (1934) 8, pp. 253, 339.

48 Hilda Kuper, 'Function, History, Biography: reflections on fifty years in the British anthropological tradition' in George W. Stocking (ed.), *Functionalism Historicized: Essays on British social anthropology* (Madison, WI, 1984), p. 195; W. D. Hammond-Tooke, *Imperfect Interpreters: South Africa's Anthropologists 1920–1990* (Johannesburg, 1997), pp. 60, 199n. 32; A. T. Bryant, *The Zulu People: as they were before the white man came* (Pietermaritzburg, 1949), p. 1. On his appointment as professor of anthropology in the School of African Life and Languages at the University of Cape Town, A. R. Radcliffe-Brown set Junod's *The Life of a South African Tribe* and Smith and Dale's *The Ila-speaking People* (London, 1920) as the two text books for second year students. *University of Cape Town, General prospectus, Faculty of Arts and Faculty of Science*, 1921 (Cape Town, 1921), p. 57; *UCT, General prospectus, Faculty of Arts and Faculty of Science*, 1922, p. 47.

49 Van Gennep was expelled from Switzerland in 1915 because of his public support for France during the war. He was replaced by the ubiquitous Charles Knapp, by that stage professor of geography, director of the museum and editor of the *Dictionnaire géographique de la Suisse* (1902–10). Jean Gabus, *175 ans d'ethnographie à Neuchâtel* (Neuchâtel, 1967), p. 27; P. Centlivres and P. Vaucher, 'Les tribulations d'un ethnographe en Suisse: Arnold van Gennep à Neuchâtel (1912–1915)', *Gradhiva* (1994) 15.

50 Junod, *LSAT*, II, p. 159; H.-P. Junod, *Henri-A. Junod: missionnaire et savant*, p. 67. However, Junod did sometimes write of 'the Bantu mind' in the same way as Lévy-Bruhl, cf. chapter five, p 144. Lévy-Bruhl, *Les Fonctions mentales dans les sociétés inférieures* (Paris, 1910) and *La Mentalité primitive* (Paris, 1922). During the last years of his life Lévy-Bruhl privately admitted that the difference between people is based not on the way they think but on their access to different forms of knowledge. Alan Barnard, *History and Theory in Anthropology* (Cambridge, 2000), p. 107.

51 Gérald Berthoud, 'Entre l'anthropologue et le missionnaire: la contribution d'Henri-Alexandre Junod (1863–1934)' in *Réseaux* (1985) 8, 220; S. Freud, *Totem et Tabou: interprétation par la psychanalyse de la vie sociale des peuples primitifs* (Paris, 1980 edn), p. 21; Alfred Berchtold, *La Suisse romande au cap du vingtième siècle* (Lausanne, 1966), p. 851.

52 *Société de Belles-Lettres de Neuchâtel: Livre d'or 1832–1960* (Neuchâtel, 1962).

53 Junod, *LSAT* I, p. 7.

54 Junod, 'Les Ba-Ronga,' p. 481.

55 These included such topics as 'alcoholism and the South African tribe' and 'the place of the vernacular in native education', Junod, *LSAT* I, p. 11; ibid., II, pp. 609, 616.

56 'Fazana' in *La Semaine littéraire* (1910) November and December 110, pp. 536–64. The hero of this short story lived near Shiluvane. Her death from malaria deprived her brother Zidji of the bridewealth needed to acquire a wife, which caused him to leave home and seek his fortune. Junod traced the battering received by Zidji in the white man's world in his novel, *Zidji* (St Blaise, 1911). Junod informed his mission council that parts of *Zidji* were published by Arnold van Gennep in *Le mercure de France*. SMA 518/C, 29 August 1910.

57 Junod, *LSAT* I, p. 32. See also chapter six, p. 173 above.

58 Junod, *Grammaire ronga*, p. 99; Junod, *LSAT* I, p. 9; ibid., vol. II, p. 153.

59 Arthur Grandjean also believed language to be 'the mirror of the soul of a race'. But he saw only sin and immorality in the grammar and syntax of the language. A. Grandjean, 'Le vieil évangile a-t-il fait son temps?' (a long pamphlet written approximately 1898 and published in 1907 by the Société de traités religieux).

60 Junod, *LSAT* II, p. 153.

61 Junot, *LSAT* I, pp. 14–15.

62 Junod, *Grammaire ronga*, p. 5. Cf. E. Pittard, 'Contribution à l'étude anthropologique des Ba-Ronga' in *Bulletin de la Société neuchâteloise de géographie* (1917) 26, p. 159. This article was based on Junod's measurement of

22 Rikatla students. Junod arranged for Calvin Mapopé to be measured, probably by Eugène Pittard, when he visited Geneva. Although he suggested employing mine personnel to take the scientific measurements of African workers, he showed no sustained interest in Physical Anthropology. See Junod, 'The best means of preserving', p. 151. Pittard and other university-based academics were engaged in an attempt to read the prehistory of Switzerland from the physical remains of its population. Cf. Pittard, 'Anthropologie', in *Dictionnaire historique et biographique de la Suisse* (Neuchâtel, 1921); T. Studer, 'Recherches anthropologiques' in *La Suisse au XIXme Siècle* (Lausanne, 1900).

63 Junod, 'Les Ba-Ronga' p. 245, 248; *LSAT*, I, pp. 152, 157, 166; 'The Magic conception of nature amongst Bantus' in *South African Journal of Science* (1920) 17, pp. 76, 84. See also Grandjean, *La Mission romande*, chapter 3. Note that these plant and animal species were themselves analytical categories whose borders were just as constructed as were those employed by linguists, see Lionel G. Higgins, *The Classification of European Butterflies* (London, 1975), p. 10. See also chapter five, pp. 131, 138, 140.

64 Junod, *LSAT* II, pp. 302, 348–50. See also Grandjean, *La Mission romande*, p. 121.

65 Junod, 'The best means to preserve', pp. 151–2.

66 Junod, 'Les Ba-Ronga', p. 244n. 1; *LSAT* II, p. 146n. 1. I stress the role of the museum as a time machine representing the tribe as a community stuck in a primitive stage of evolution in Harries, 'Primitivisme au Musée: la récolte des missionnaires en Afrique australe' in Marc-Olivier Gonseth, Jacques Hainard and Roland Kaehr (eds), *Cents ans d'ethnographie sur la colline de Saint-Nicolas, 1904–2004* (Neuchâtel, 2005).

67 Junod 'The best means to preserve', p. 153. P. Harries, 'Terrible Truths: Swiss missionaries and the role of photography in the early ethnographic monograph', paper presented to the conference 'Encounters with Photography', Cape Town, July 1999.

68 Junod, *LSAT* I, p. 221. Typical examples are 'the Khosa native who gave me information' (ibid., p. 240); 'From a Thonga of the Maputju country I once heard' (*LSAT* I, p. 251); 'A Venda who is one of the best informants I ever had' (ibid., p. 303); or merely 'a Thonga' or 'a native' who gives his (rather than her) opinion. Unnamed representatives from different tribes provided information (ibid., p. 240), as did anonymous pupils at Rikatla (most of whom were adults) (ibid., pp. 287–8), as well as 'men and women of all ages.' (Junod, *LSAT* II, pp. 211, 215).

69 Junod, *Le problème indigène dans l'Union sud-africaine* (Lausanne, 1931, p. 13.

70 Compare Junod, 'Les Ba-Ronga,' p. 164 with Junod, *LSAT* I, p. 453.

71 Junod, *LSAT* I, p. 7.

72 Junod, 'The best means of preserving', p. 157.

73 Junod devoted the second volume of the first edition of *LSAT* (1913) to the 'Psychic Life' of the tribe. In the second edition (1927) he anglicized this term into 'Mental Life'.

74 Junod, *LSAT* I, p. 3. These included 'an old Thonga', Abraham Mabanyisis, Simeon Gana, a 'very good and clear-headed informant' on marriage ceremonies of the northern clans and an 'old Ronga heathen' named Magingi who reported on the differences between wives (ibid., pp. 116, 250, 284). Viguet reported on kinship, Mboza provided the nomenclature of his wife's relatives and Gidhlana Ngwetsa reported on bridewealth practices (ibid., pp. 237, 506–10).

75 Alexandre A. Jaques raised these criticisms of Junod's fieldwork in his 'Terms of kinship and corresponding patterns of behaviour among the Thonga', *Bantus Studies* (1929) 3.

76 Junod, *LSAT* I, pp. 169–72, 288. *LSAT* II, pp. 211, 215.

77 Junod, *LSAT* I, p. 2.

78 Junod, 'The best means of preserving,' p. 153; Junod, *LSAT* I, p. 1. Sir James Frazer, Marcel Mauss and Lucien Lévy-Bruhl performed this function for Junod.

79 Junod, *LSAT* I, p. 11.

80 His modesty was at least partly inspired by his need to solicit the patronage required to break into the world of 'Anglo-Saxon' anthropology. Lord James Bryce fulfilled this role for Junod.

81 Junod, *LSAT* I, pp. 8–9. A point stressed by Serge Reubi, in 'Aider l'Afrique et servir la science: Henri-Alexandre Junod, missionnaire et ethnographe (1863–1934)', *Revue historique neuchâteloise: Musée neuchâtelois* (2004) 4, p. 207.

82 Junod, 'Some remarks on the folklore of the Ba-Thonga' in *Folk-lore* (1903) 14:2, pp. 121, 123; *LSAT* II, p. 329.

83 Junod, 'The best means of preserving', p. 142.

84 Junod, 'Les Ba-Ronga', pp. 115–16.

85 Junod, *LSAT*, I, p. 539.

86 Cf. SMA 9/114F, L. Perrin, 'Rapport sur la station du Tembe, 1911–12'; SMA 9/196 H. L. Berthoud, 'Rapport d'Antioka' 1915. For the earlier years, see Harries, *Work, Culture and Identity*, pp. 167–70.

87 UNISA.JC 5.1., Junod to Alfreido Freire de Andrade, 3 December 1912; Director-General, Ministry of Colonies to Junod, 15 April 1913; Junod to Encarregado do Governo, 10 September 1918. The translation was undertaken by the Geographical Society of Lisbon and published as *Usos e Costumes dos Bantu. A vida duma tribo do sul de Africa* 1917–18.

88 SMA 437, Berthoud to mission secretary, 20 November 1894, cited in Jan van Butselaar, 'The gospel and

culture in nineteenth-century Mozambique', *Missiology* (1988) 16, 1, p. 52.
89 SMA 8/100C, Procès-verbal de la conférence du littoral, March 1921. *La Suisse libérale* 28 January, 10 April, 19 April, 1921.
90 SMA 397D, Rapport de H. P. Guye sur des 'Relations du missionnaire avec le gouvernement colonial. Etat social et politique des indigènes'. 20 December 1921; Réponse au questionnaire de M. J. H. Oldham du 16 November 1922 par H. P. Guye, 10 January 1923. See also SMA 14/172B and F, Guye, Rapport sur la station de Rikatla, 1920–21, 1924. Oldham visited the coastal Mission in March 1926. Keith Clements, *Faith on the Frontier: A Life of J. H. Oldham* (Geneva, 1999), p. 235.
91 SMA 417D/4, Guye to Junod, 10 February 1925.
92 SMA 172F, Guye, Rapport de Rikatla, October 1924; SMA 3/30 H P. Loze, Rapport de Lourenço Marques, 15 October 1926; SMA 3/30 B, B. Terrisse, Rapport de la station de Chikhombane, 6 October 1926; SMA 3/30I Ant. Aubert, Rapport de la station de Mathouthouene, 1925–26, October 1926.
93 SMA 127B, H.-A. Junod, 'Le travail forcé devant la Société des Nations', October 1925.
94 SMA 3/25K, C. Perrier-Peney, Rapport sur la station de Manjakaze pour 1927–28; SMA 3/25H, A. Aubert, Rapport annuel de la station de Matoutouene, 23 October 1928.
95 Particularly in Liberia and, following the publication of André Gide's *Voyage au Congo*, the French Congo (Brazzaville). H.-A. Junod, 'Le Mécontentement au colonies', *Christianisme Social* (1928) 3, April–May; ibid., 'Une Question de Moral Coloniale', *Stockholm International Review for the Social Activities of the Churches* (1929) 3; ibid., 'La supplique du Liberia', *Bureau International pour la défense des indigènes*, October 1931.
96 Junod, 'Le travail forcé va-t-il être aboli?', *BMSAS* 37, September–October 1929; Henri-Philippe Junod, 'L'Exploitation coloniale en Afrique du Sud', *Le Christianisme Social* (1930) 5, July, pp. 20–2.
97 Junod, *LSAT* I, p. 538n1.
98 Ibid., pp. 240, 251, 272, 532.
99 Cf. ibid., pp. 121, 278, 552–3.
100 UC.FC. Junod to Fraser 9 July, 1910. Junod, *LSAT* I, p. 125.
101 Junod, *Grammaire ronga*, p. 18; 'Les Ba-Ronga', pp. 7–8, 245, 247; Junod, *LSAT* I, p. 249. See also chapter 2 notes 80 and 81.
102 H. L. Jameson, 'An Ethnographic bureau for South Africa', *Report of the South African Association for the Advancement of Science* (1907), p. 161.
103 Cf. John Roscoe, *Man* (1914), pp. 118–19; see also Mauss in note 26 above.
104 SMA 435F, Grandjean to council, 16 October 1891.
105 A. Grandjean, 'Notice relative à la carte du Nkomati inférieur et du district portugais de Lourenço Marques', *BSNG* (1892–93) vii, p. 121.
106 Liengme, cited in E. Krieg, *Nos missionnaires*, p. 502.
107 He never abandoned his belief that the evolutionist hypothesis was 'the best solution to many problems'. See Junod, *Moeurs et Coutumes des Bantous* (Paris, 1936) I, p. 256; Junod, *Le Noir Africain. Comment faut-il le juger?* (Lausanne, 1931), pp. 5, 18–19.
108 As a young man, Junod had indicted the materialism of his age in strident poems and essays. See particularly 'Hommes et bêtes' (Men and Animals), a virulent critique of the Berlin stock exchange printed in *Revue de Belles-Lettres* (1884), pp. 209–16.
109 Fondation pour l'histoire des Suisses à l'étranger, Geneva. Liengme diary. Cf. Entries for 23 June, 3 July 1893, 29 September 1893.
110 See chapter two, pp. 47–9.
111 See P. Harries, *Work, Culture and Identity: Migrant workers in Mozambique and South Africa, c. 1860–1910* (Portsmouth, NH, 1994).
112 Junod, *LSAT* II, pp. 109, 110.
113 Junod, *LSAT* I, p. 453. Compare this with a contemporaneous photograph (taken by H. W. D. Longden) of soldiers armed with rifles in the Delagoa Bay area in 1894. Longden, *Red Buffalo: the Story of Will Longden, pioneer, friend and emissary of Rhodes* (Cape Town, 1950), p. 102.
114 Junod, *LSAT* II, p. 490.
115 Junod, 'Les Ba-Ronga,' p. 44. On the political symbolism of chairs at this time, cf. Grandjean in *Nouvelles de nos missionnaires* (1890) 2, 13, pp. 31–2; Jean Rambert, *Arthur Grandjean* (Lausanne, n. d. , 1931?), p. 18. In one of the only two photographs of Gungunyana (taken by his friend Georges Liengme), the Gaza king is seated on a similar chair to that held by Ntchongui in the photograph.
116 Junod, *LSAT* I, p. 515.
117 Ibid., pp. 264–7. Following his reading of W. H. R. Rivers, Junod doubted that a promiscuous stage had ever existed.
118 Junod, *LSAT* I, p. 236. But note that, thirty pages later, Junod thought marrying a wife's sister might function as the logical thing to do when the first marriage had worked well.
119 In 1910 Junod believed implacably that the Thonga had passed through a matriarchal phase. In 1927 he seemed less sure, considering it merely a hypothesis. Compare his 'Deux enterrements à 20,000 ans de distance',

Anthropos (1910) v, p. 968 with *LSAT* I, pp. 220, 274. But see also *LSAT* II, pp. 623–4.
[120] Junod, *LSAT* I, p. 272.
[121] Junod, 'Les Ba-Ronga', pp. 73, 77, 122.
[122] Bachofen had first discussed the role of the *umäluma* (*malume*) in southern Africa in 'Die Genealogie ab avunculo Vorbereitende Zusammenstellungen' in *Bachofens Gesammelte Werke* 8 (Basel, 1966).
[123] Junod, *LSAT* I, pp. 270–1. In 1908 Junod was still not convinced by the evolutionist hypothesis. Six years later, he thought that 'the theory of evolution has completely transformed our point of view'. Compare Junod, 'The fate of the widows amongst the Ba-Ronga', *Report of the South African Association for the Advancement of Science 1908* p. 372n2 with Junod, 'God's ways in the Bantu soul', *International Review of Missions* (1914) 3, p. 96. In 1927 he thought 'the evolutionist theory to be the best solution of many problems', although it was a 'hypothesis' and not a 'dogma', Junod, *LSAT* II, p. 301.
[124] Cf. Junod, *LSAT* I, pp. 204n1, 240–3, 261–3.
[125] Junod, 'Deux enterrements à 20,000 ans de distance', p. 968; Junod, *LSAT* I, pp. 122, 220, 310.
[126] Junod, *LSAT* I, p. 283.
[127] Junod, *LSAT* I, pp. 120, 252.
[128] Junod, *LSAT* I, pp. 119–20, 278–82, 285, 531–3. See also chapter three, p. 80.
[129] Compare Junod's comments in 'Les Ba-Ronga', pp. 56–60, 381n. 1, 403 with *LSAT* I, 9; ibid., II, p. 595. See also William Rivers, 'Anthropology and the Missionary', *Church Missionary Review* (1920) 71.
[130] Junod, *LSAT* II, 372–3.
[131] Junod, *LSAT* II, p. 429. See also pp. 303, 372, 431, 446–50. Nathan Söderblum, *Das Werden des Gottesglaubens: Untersuchungen über die Anfänge der Religion* (Leipzig, 1917).
[132] Junod, *Causeries sur l'Afrique à l'usage des cercles d'étude missionnaire pour enfants, des écoles du dimanche, des unions cadettes et des familles* (Lausanne, 1922), p. 6.
[133] In the early nineteenth century Johannes van der Kemp and other missionaries in the Cape and Natal translated the word *uThixo* as 'God'. In southern Mozambique, Erwin Richards reported in 1881 that the Gaza called their Supreme Being *Nkulunkulu*; Anon., *The Mission to Umzila's Kingdom* (Boston, MA, 1881), p. 22. His American missionary colleagues around Inhambane used this 'Zulu' word when translating the Scriptures into Tswa and (Inhambane) Tonga and the word was sometimes employed further south in the Delagoa Bay hinterland. B. Ousley in *Missionary Herald* (1886), p. 62; Junod, 'Les Ba-Ronga', p. 381n. 1; E. W. Smith, *African Ideas of God* (London, 1950), p. 116.
[134] The Anglican missionary bishop Henry Callaway was particularly important. See his *The Religious System of the Amazulu. Izinyanga Zokubula; Or Divination, as Existing Among the Amazulu. In their own words, with a translation into English* (London, 1870). See also James MacDonald, 'Manners, Customs, Superstitions, and Religions of South African Tribes', *The Journal of the Anthropological Institute of Great Britain and Ireland* (1890) 19. Max Müller, *Anthropological Religion* (London, 1892), p. 287.
[135] Junod, *LSAT* II, pp. 427–8; Junod, 'La divination au moyen de tablettes d'ivoire chez les Pedis' in *Bulletin de la société neuchâtelois de géographie* (1925) 34, p. 56. See also 'Les Ba-Ronga', pp. 245–6, 483–4. Durkheim, *Les formes élémentaires de la vie religieuse: le système totémique en Australie* (Paris, 1912).
[136] Junod, *LSAT* II, pp. 427–8; Junod, 'Bantu heathen prayers', *International Review of Missions* (1922) 11, p. 44; 'Le sacrifice dans l'ancestrolatrie sud-africaine', *Archives de Psychologie* (1932) 23, 92, pp. 305–35.
[137] Junod, 'Le mouvement de Mourimi: un réveil au sein de l'animisme thonga' in *Journal de Psychologie Normale et Pathologique* (1924) December; Junod, *LSAT* II, p. 598. On the belief that Murimi was the son of God, see SMA 556/A, Junod to mission council, 13 June 1916; SMA 558/A, Guye to mission council, 10 January 1919. See also *Africa's Golden Harvest*, February (1915).
[138] See his *Ernest Creux et Paul Berthoud: Les fondateurs de la Mission Suisse en Afrique du Sud* (Lausanne, 1933), p. 145 and 'Le Mouvement de Mourimi'. The religious movement is discussed in chapter three, pp. 73–9.
[139] Junod, 'Deux enterrements à 20,000 ans de distance', *Anthropos* (1910) v, p. 968; *LSAT* I, p. 522; *LSAT* II, pp. 364, 571n1; 'Les Ba-Ronga', pp. 408–9.
[140] Junod, 'The Magic conception of nature amongst Bantus', in *SAJS* (1920) 17, November, p. 76.
[141] Junod, *LSAT* II, p. 628; P. Berthoud, *Les Nègres gouamba*, pp. 49, 75–6.
[142] Paul Berthoud was an early critic of *Tilo* as a word for God. See his *La Mission romande et la baie de Delagoa* (Lausanne, 1888), p. 54. Dorothy Earthy thought it referred to a 'vague power' but not 'God'; see her *Valenge Women: The Social and Economic Life of the Valenge Women of Portuguese East Africa* (London, 1933), p. 182. In Sà Nogueira's *Dicionario Ronga-Português* (1960) it is translated as 'sky' and 'heaven'. In R. Cuenod's *Tsonga-English Dictionary* (Braamfontein, 1967) it is merely 'sky'.
[143] Junod, *LSAT* I, p. 523. Arther Grandjean, when secretary-general of the mission, explicitly saw no evolution in a culture that he qualified as 'barbarousness, savagery in its raw form'. See 'Le vieil évangile a-t-il fait son temps?'.
[144] Junod, *LSAT*, II, p. 629.
[145] Junod, 'Les Ba-Ronga', pp. 248, 151; Junod, *LSAT*, II, p. 629.
[146] Junod, 'Les Ba-Ronga', pp. 150, 246, 486; Junod, *LSAT* I, p. 271.

[147] These were perhaps the same people who had brought sophisticated iron smelting technologies to the neighbouring North Sotho and Venda peoples. Junod, 'Les Ba-Ronga' p. 238; *Zidji*, pp. 30–2.

[148] In 1937 G. P. Lestrade attributed the gold-working at Mapungubwe to the Lemba, while a number of physical anthropologists gathered around Raymond Dart held that an ancient (pre-Bantu) race of Bush-Boskop people was responsible for this and other 'advanced' cultural achievements, Saul Dubow, *Illicit Union: Scientific Racism in Modern South Africa* (Johannesburg, 1995), pp. 47, 96–101. In 1962 Schapera could still consider 'the most convenient method of investigating and answering problems of both uniformity and variation is by comparisons of *social change under European influence*.' Schapera, 'Should anthropologists be historians?', *Journal of the Royal Anthropological Institute of Great Britain and Ireland* (1962) 92,5, p. 151. My italics.

[149] UW.SMA, Paul Rosset, 'Rapport sur la paroisse de Paul Rosset à Mhinga', 8 October, 1900. Compare with Junod, *LSAT* I pp. 310–18.

[150] SMA 558/A, Henri Guye to AG, 21.01.1916.

[151] These ideas went back to an article by Agassiz published in 1845 in the *Revue Suisse*. After his arrival in the United States, he reworked them in his 'Sketch of the Natural Provinces of the animal world and their relation to the different types of man' in J. C. Nott and George Gliddon (eds), *Types of Mankind* (Philadelphia, PA, 1854). In the same volume (pp. 182–90), Nott and Gliddon placed African peoples on a scale starting with Bushmen and Hottentots (Khoisan), who were little different from orang-utangs, with Bantu-speakers in the middle and Nubians and Ehiopians at the top.

[152] Elizabeth Cory Agassiz, *Louis Agassiz: his Life and Correspondence* (Boston, MA, 1885) vol. II, pp. 497–8, 598. L. Agassiz, 'The diversity of the human races' in *Christian Examiner* (1850) 49; Agassiz, 'Sketch of the natural provinces of the animal world'; Gossett, *Race: The History of an Idea*, pp. 59–60, 242.

[153] Phrase taken from his *Physiologische Briefe* (1847) and cited in Owen Chadwick, *The Secularisation of the European Mind in the Nineteenth Century* (Cambridge, 1975), p. 166.

[154] On the theory of recapitulation, see John R. Baker, *Race* (Oxford, 1974), pp. 129–32; Peter J. Bowler, *Evolution: the history of an idea* (London, 3rd edn, 2003), pp. 191, 228, 294.

[155] 'As soon as they reach the fatal period of puberty', Vogt wrote, 'the intellectual faculties become stationary and the individual becomes incapable of progress, as does the entire race.' Carl Vogt, *Leçons sur l'homme, sa place dans la création et dans l'histoire de la terre* (Paris, [1863] 1865), p. 251.

[156] Vogt, *Leçons sur l'homme*, especially 'leçon sept'. On Vogt, cf. William Vogt, *La vie d'un homme: Carl Vogt* (Paris and Stuttgart, 1896) and Johannes Jung, *Karl Vogts Weltanschauung* (Paderborn, 1915). In France, the influential anthropologist Armand de Quatrefages employed these ideas to delineate the most primitive races of humanity as 'living fossils'. He estimated that the cephalic index of Africans was about equal to that of a Parisian child. He also held that the cerebral development of Africans stopped once they reached the age of European teenagers. For both Quatrefages and Vogt, Africans were physically overgrown children. William B. Cohen, *The French Encounter with Africans* (Bloomington, IN, 1980), p. 243. On the cephalic index, see note 164 below.

[157] Vogt, *Leçons sur l'homme*, p. 252.

[158] Hunt, the president of the Anthropological Society of London, translated Vogt's *Lessons on Man* into English in 1863. Darwin's most anthropological work, *The Descent of Man*, appeared in 1871, a year that saw the publication of the early classics in the field by Lewis Morgan and Edward Tylor. Darwin cited Vogt extensively throughout *The Descent of Man* and at times reproduced his racist ideas (cf. pp. 200–201). Although Vogt wrote the preface to the French edition, *La descendance de l'homme* (Paris, 1873), Darwin opposed Vogt's appointment as the translator of either *The Variation and Domestication of Animals and Plants under Domestication* (1867) or *The Descent of Man*. See Aidrian Desmond and James Moore, *Darwin* (London, 1991), pp. 543, 573.

[159] In Dostoyevsky's *The Possessed*, lieutenant Erkel replaces religious images with the works of Vogt and other materialists, see Chadwick, *The Secularisation of the European Mind*, p. 181.

[160] Carl Passavant, *Craniologische Untersuchung der Neger*; Aram Mattioli, *Jacob Burckhardt und die Grenzen der Humanität* (Vienna, 2001), pp. 17–21.

[161] Perhaps most notably, the missionary anthropologist Dudley Kidd and the educationist C. T. Loram. Cf. Kidd, *Essential Kaffir*, pp. 277ff. and Loram, *The Education of the South African Native* (London, 1917), p. 225. See also South Africa's leading historian at the time, G. M. Theal, *The Ethnography and Condition of South Africa before A. D. 1505* (London, [1912], 1922), p. 310; J. Stevenson-Hamilton (director of the Kruger National Park), *The Low-Veld: Its Wild life and its People* (London, [1929] 1934), pp. 196–7. Monica Wilson commented on the strength of this belief as late as the 1920s in her introduction to *Freedom for My People: the autobiography of Z. K. Matthews* (London, 1981), p. 217.

[162] Junod, *LSAT* I p. 99.

[163] Junod, *LSAT* II, p. 148. Junod lifted this entire sentence, word for word, from Vogt, *Leçons sur l'homme*, p. 251. Junod suggested that Gobineau might have changed his racist ideas had he known that Africans share the dolichocephalic characteristic with the 'noble Aryan'. See *Le Noir africain: comment faut-il le juger?* (Lausanne, 1931), p. 4.

[164] See particularly Boas' seminal 'The Cephalic Index', *American Anthropologist* (1899) July. See also note 43 above.

165 Junod, 'Le Noir Africain', p. 18.
166 Junod, 'Les Ba-Ronga', p. 481.
167 Junod, 'Les Ba-Ronga', pp. 481–2, 486. These were common views, cf. SMA 514 Grandjean to council, 7 July 1895. In 1927 Junod still thought Africans to be 'indolent', 'weak', and an 'inferior race'. Junod, *LSAT*, I, p. 11; *LSAT*, II, pp. 136, 166, 609–11, 621, 633. They lived at 'a stage of development through which whites have also passed, many centuries ago'. Junod, 'Les coutumes matrimoniales des Thonga', *BMR* (1926) 36, p. 135. He also considered the Thonga to be at a less advanced 'stage of evolution' than the centralized Baganda. Junod, *LSAT* II, pp. 409, 593–4.
168 His ideas on education were printed in the *Reports* of the South African General Missionary Conference 1904 and 1909 and in 'The Native language and native education', *Journal of the Royal African Society* (1905) October. Junod also included them in an appendix to *LSAT*, II ('On the problem of Native Education'), pp. 613–21.
169 M. D. Lenoir, Shiluvane, 26 November, 1902 in *BMR* (1903) 16, February, p. 23. Washington's *Up From Slavery: An Autobiography* was published in New York in 1901.
170 See the reports of the Phelps-Stokes Commission, *Education in Africa* (New York, 1922) and *Education in East Africa* (New York, 1925). More generally, see Reginald Coupland, 'The native problem in Africa', *International Review of Missions* (1929) 18, p. 143; Clements, *Faith on the Frontier*, chapter 10.
171 See chapter 5. These ideas were accepted and propagated by the British Association for the Advancement of Science during its visit to South Africa in 1905. See *Report of the South African Association for the Advancement of Science* 1908, p. xxiv.
172 In his novel, written in 1911, Junod had his missionary explain that the pass laws were needed to maintain public order because of 'the state of savagery in which the [African] race was still plunged'. Junod, *Zidji*, p. 276. He still supported passes in 1931 although he criticized their proliferation. Junod, *Le problème indigène*, p. 22.
173 Here Junod's views coincided with those of Dudley Kidd, *Kaffir Socialism and the Dawn of Individualism* (London, 1908), p. 115.
174 *LSAT*, I, pp. 546, 548. On the history of the district system in the Transkei, see W. D. Hammond-Tooke, *Command or Consensus: the Development of Transkeian Local Government* (Cape Town, 1975) chapter 5; Ifor Evans, *Native Policy in Southern Africa* (Cambridge, 1934), pp. 52–60.
175 Stevenson-Hamilton, *The Low-Veld: Its Wild Life and its People* (London, [1929], 1934), pp. 196–7.
176 Cf. Jan Smuts, 'Foreword' to Monica Hunter, *Reaction to Conquest: Effects of contact with Europeans on the Pondo of South Africa* (1936 London, 1961), p. vii and passim. See also his Introduction to Stevenson-Hamilton, *The Low-Veld: Its Wild Life and its People*.

9
Politics

Review the past for me, let us argue the matter together; state the case for your innocence.
(Isaiah 43:26)

The Swiss Romande Mission grew strongly during the first quarter of the twentieth century. The pressure to appoint converts to positions of authority became more pressing as members contributed to the financial prosperity of the mission and found a voice in the consistories and synods established at the start of the century. On every mission station elders were chosen and, together with nominated members, evangelists and missionaries, they formed the station's consistory. These bodies sent delegates to the annual synods that discussed the policies and practices of the two native churches in the Transvaal and Mozambique. In both regions an Assembly of Pastors served to prevent this rush of democracy from extending Christian practices in directions unacceptable to the church in Switzerland. Much like the old 'venerable class' of pastors in early nineteenth-century Vaud and Neuchâtel, this body acted as the supreme executive of the two churches.[1]

There was good reason for this ecclesiastical caution: as the gold mines grew, thousands of men returned from South Africa with an uncertain knowledge of Christianity. In 1904 Henri Guye marvelled at 'the almost continual procession' of migrants returning from the mines, many of whom 'have converted to Christianity and wish to practise it here'.[2] Three years later Mozambicans on the Witwatersrand created a provident society to assist the evangelization of their home areas by Christians converted on the mines.[3] The enterprise of the individuals behind this proliferation of independent churches accounted for much of the success of the mission during this period. The case of Levi Magwebu, who left Johannesburg in 1908 to found a school at Manyiça on the Inkomati, is particularly noteworthy. When the number of children attending his school grew to over one hundred, this migrant worker turned to the Swiss for assistance and his establishment was incorporated into the Rikatla mission as a distant outstation. By 1913 the number of children attending the school had doubled and the outstation counted well over one hundred members. To the northeast of Lourenço Marques another migrant, known to us only as Tchem, established a series of Christian settlements that were soon brought into the fold of the Romande Mission.[4]

The Portuguese attempted to control these schools, many of which operated in English and Zulu, by obliging teachers to work in Portuguese. This led the coastal synod to decide in 1907 to send Calvin Mapopé, his brother Jonas Mapopé (the former Chihoçi) and Samuel Malalé to Morija in Lesotho to be trained for the ministry by Edouard Jacottet. On their return all three were ordained as pastors and put in charge of mission stations. But as Morija operated in South Sotho and English, the coastal synod expanded the school for evangelists at Rikatla into a theological college that produced its first five graduates in mid-1920, a few months before Junod's departure.

By 1925 the mission included nine black pastors, who ran seven of its twenty mission stations, and 209 black evangelists who directed its 159 outstations. Almost 7,000 students attended the mission's primary schools and 1,580 adults frequented the night schools run by its establishments in Pretoria (founded in 1898) and in Johannesburg (1904). Over 8,000 full and on-trial members of the Native Evangelical Reformed Church contributed almost £3,200 to the running of their church and its mission.[5] In the same year the Swiss Romande Mission celebrated its fiftieth anniversary by inviting Calvin Mapopé to Switzerland. Over the previous half-century the mission had influenced the church in many ways. It had drawn increasing numbers of women into the organizational structure of the institution at home, and through their voting power women exercised a growing influence in the consistories, although they could not stand for public office. They also became more visible within the mission: after the establishment of the Romande Mission in 1883, unmarried women were allowed to serve in Africa as missionaries. The mission's experience of adult baptisms in Africa also influenced the church at home to accept the practice of baptizing children once they had reached adolescence and were conscious of the meaning of this fundamental Christian rite. When Arthur Grandjean returned home in 1896 to become secretary-general of the mission, he stressed the need for clergymen to be trained in Hebrew and Greek, Ecclesiastics, Dogmatics and Philosophy. The experience of the mission in Africa had shown that the church could not be built on zeal alone.

Calvin Mapopé's visit tightened the bonds between church and mission. His speeches drew 2,000 listeners to the Temple du Bar in Neuchâtel, packed the cathedral in Lausanne, and filled the Reformation Hall in Geneva where, only a few years earlier, the League of Nations had held its first meeting. Over 30,000 heard Mapopé speak during his tour, and the sale of some 24,000 picture postcards bearing his image paid for the anniversary celebrations.[6] Mapopé served as the *vox populi* of the mission in Switzerland. He spoke in glowing terms of the Swiss as a people chosen by God to take his message to the Thonga as a *Gemeinschaft*. 'Other tribes look towards other European people', he declared. 'We, the Thongas, look towards Switzerland, to Switzerland alone.' He spoke clearly of his confidence in the church's ability to sift from European civilization only its most positive elements.[7]

Another friend of the mission, Edgar Brookes, a professor of political science at the Transvaal University College (soon to be the University of Pretoria), expressed many of the same ideas in his *History of Native Policy in South Africa*.[8] The work was published in 1924 with financial assistance from the Prime Minister, J. B. M. Hertzog, and clearly supported segregation. In the book he called for the value of African cultural practices to be recognized and for the bad to be filtered from the good in such a way as to encourage 'a proper race-pride'. This would stop the 'educated Native' from aspiring to be an 'imitation European' and lead him to 'take his rightful place as the natural

9.1 *Calvin Matsivi Mapopé and Henri-Alexandre Junod. This photograph, taken in 1925 during Mapopé's visit to Switzerland, was widely used in missionary propaganda to advertise the Mission's policy of racial partnership. The photograph was never used in Junod's ethnographic publications, however, as the picture of a European would have spoiled his depiction of a primitive tribe at (what some anthropologists would later call) the 'zero point of change'.*
(© Swiss Mission Archive, Lausanne)

leader of his own people'. The other leader was the chief, 'the embodiment of the tribe, the head and centre of the whole fabric', wrote Brookes. 'If we are to develop the Bantu along their own lines,' he continued, 'we must have the monarchical element'.[9]

Anthropology and Social Change

In the early 1920s, anthropology was almost a missionary science.[10] Through its near monopoly of this branch of knowledge, the church had been able to reoccupy in many parts of Africa the leading position in society that it had only recently lost in Europe. Through a range of institutions and their publications, missionaries informed lawmakers, government officials, politicians and the general public on the needs of the African population. Pastors of the Free Churches in Switzerland who had lost the struggle against the townhall in their homeland saw the church, its hall and bell, occupy a central place in the new social communities emerging in Africa. Through their leading role in the system of education developed in the Transvaal, and a more limited role in Catholic Mozambique, they were able to re-establish in Africa their lost role as tutors of the youth. In general the Church and its clergy regained in Africa much of the venerable authority that it had relinquished in Europe.

In the early part of the twentieth century the ecumenical missionary movement rooted in the 1910 Edinburgh conference, the *International Review of Missions* and the International Institute of African Languages, came to view Indirect Rule as a means of protecting African peoples and their cultures. The leaders of the movement believed that this could be achieved while fostering the educational, moral and material progress of indigenous peoples. In South Africa, however, this cheap form of 'trusteeship' tended to support the ideals of segregation. This became increasingly obvious in 1920 when the Smuts government passed a Native Affairs Act that extended the system of segregationist district councils, advocated by Junod and others, to the rural reserves of South Africa. Seven years later another Act reinforced the powers of the chiefs and confirmed the extension of segregation to the reserves. In this same year, just as Junod's second edition emerged from the press, the Hertzog government started the process that would extend within a decade the size of the rural reserves, while depriving Africans in the Cape of their limited rights to vote for the national parliament.

Metropolitan anthropologists had at first achieved little success in selling their professional skills to the rulers of the new South African state. When Junod served as president of Section E of the SAAAS in 1920, missionaries and clergymen still made up over half his committee; and his inaugural lecture showed little concern for the theories of metropolitan professionals. However, under the premiership of the intellectual Jan Smuts local lobbyists acquired sufficient government funding to establish a chair in anthropology in 1920 in the newly-created School of African Life and Languages at the University of Cape Town. At the same time, they succeeded in appointing A. R. Radcliffe-Brown to the curatorship of ethnology at the Transvaal Museum in Pretoria. Eight months later this Cambridge graduate moved to Cape Town when the university post finally materialized in August 1921.

As the first professor of social anthropology in the British empire, Radcliffe-Brown set about defining the professional frontiers of his discipline in a way that would leave little place for amateurs. Rather than focus his criticism on the work of his patrons at home, Radcliffe-Brown turned on the missionary rivals with whom he competed for funding and university posts in the colonial context. In a seminal article published in 1923 in the mouthpiece of the South African Association for the Advancement of Science, he relegated all studies of culture and society employing an evolutionist approach to the category of 'ethnology'. This he distinguished from 'social anthropology' which was concerned with 'the application of certain logical methods' and 'certain general laws'.[11] The following year he stridently promoted the practical value of anthropology when he warned missionaries that 'a knowledge of social anthropology' could not be acquired by 'living amongst a native people' and 'reading a few books'. Without 'systematic scientific study', their attempts to 'control or modify' native customs would, he warned, have 'evil results'. It was particularly important for missionaries to realize this, as the changes they brought to native societies were not restricted to the field of religion. They were deeply involved in native education; when teaching about the miracles recounted in the Bible, they could inadvertently strengthen the natives' belief in magic. Missionary criticism of ancestor worship merely served to undermine the stability of a society ruled by male elders. He announced that it was also 'a complete misunderstanding' to see *lobolo* as a dowry, and the view that a wife became the 'property' of her husband through the bridewealth transaction was one 'of complete ignorance'.[12]

Radcliffe-Brown then published another combative article in which he raised important criticisms of the methodology and findings of Henri-Alexandre Junod, the flag-bearer of missionary anthropology. In the article he took scant notice of Junod's linguistic abilities or his extensive fieldwork experience. Although he praised the missionary's attempt to explain the function of the *lobolo* as a compensation payment to the bride's father, he focused his criticism on Junod's application of a pseudo or conjectural history to understand the natives' marriage strategies. He particularly drew attention to the evolutionist approach used by Junod to explain the special relationship in Thonga society between the son and his mother's brother. The close bond between these two men, Radcliffe-Brown argued, was not a vestige of a matriarchal past but rather a function of the warm relationship between the son and his mother and, by extension, his mother's kin. The relationship with the mother's brother was especially close because in the absence of the mother's father, the *malume* was the senior male relative able to communicate with his maternal ancestors.[13]

Junod answered this criticism with two essays and a passage in the new edition of his monograph. In his essay on the Murimi phenomenon in southern Mozambique during the First World War, he showed a new sensitivity to social change. In this analysis of a very modern witchcraft eradication movement, he underlined ways in which Africans changed and adapted their cultural practices (although he effectively excluded this approach from the subject of anthropology when he relegated it to the appendices of his monograph).[14] In a very different article on the marriage customs of the Thonga in the bulletin of his missionary society, he restated his view that the relationship between the son and his mother's brother was a 'survival' of a previously matriarchal stage. It was one of the 'relics of the past that project their shadow onto the present'.[15] The following year, in the new edition of his monograph, he challenged Radcliffe-Brown's view of the *ntukulu's* actions as the product of natural feelings of tenderness extended to the *malume*. Instead, Junod drew attention to the symbolic inheritance that was left by the *malume* to his *ntukulu*, and underlined the importance of the mother's family in a system of patrilineal descent. He concluded that an evolutionist hypothesis was 'probably' the best means of understanding this practice.[16] However, he abandoned this approach without scruple when he found other forms of analysis more useful to understanding language, religion or art.

Junod's anthropology was not only challenged by a growing number of university professionals. Radcliffe-Brown had singled out Edwin Smith as a missionary prepared to use the skills of anthropology to develop a more liberal approach to native customs. Smith's perspective came to dominate the ecumenical missionary conference held in 1926 at Le Zoute in Belgium. One of the Swiss missionary delegates at the conference reported that participants had stressed 'the need to conserve the African heritage as far as is possible' and that they believed 'only the radically bad customs should be condemned'.[17] This conformed to Smith's belief that, through the 'retention and sublimation' of indigenous cultural practices, missionaries could construct a form of Christianity adapted to the needs of African peoples. The support for this view by Oldham and others stemmed from a sea change in the perspective on human rights that developed at the end of the Great War. Oldham's liberalism also grew out of a fear that the rise of nationalist movements in countries like India and Egypt could be blamed on Christian insensitivity to the ways of indigenous peoples. Others worried that, through the creation of 'black Englishmen', missionaries obliterated the genius of African peoples and reduced their novel contribution to the growth and development of humanity.[18] A growing swell of missionary opinion came to see the heathen practices studied by anthropologists as far from uniformly evil. For example, Christians could retain the educative aspects of initiation practices while suppressing explicit references to sex and deeply painful forms of excision.[19] This perspective lay behind the new emphasis on developing a form of education adapted to local aptitudes and conditions, and calling for new strategies of conversion.

An earlier generation of missionaries had equated the transfer of bridewealth with the purchase of a wife but, on closer inspection, some came to see the *lobolo* as a source of dignity for the woman and as a guarantee of fair treatment by her in-laws. Sharp differences of opinion arose as missionaries came to believe that they should build Christianity on the basis of indigenous beliefs and practices rather than undermine the finely-balanced texture of primitive societies. Lectures at Le Zoute by Lord Lugard and W. T. Welsh, the Chief Magistrate of the Transkeian Territories, extolled indirect rule as a means of containing and protecting African Christianity. For the missionary committed to the construction of an indigenous Christianity, social anthropology was a key tool.[20]

Junod was not entirely comfortable with the new direction taken by missionary anthropology. He had been unable to attend the Le Zoute conference and addressed its concerns in the article containing his reply to Radcliffe-Brown. He applauded missionaries for the careful way in which they studied native customs that were both 'picturesque' and useful. Through their detailed field studies, missionaries could indeed assess which aspects of native practices to retain or sublimate. He agreed with the need to create a 'real, authentic ... African Christianity' that was not merely 'a servile imitation' of 'European Christianity'. But he advocated evolutionism as a means to achieve this objective and gave little weight to the functionalist analysis that had dominated much of the discussion at Le Zoute.

Junod suggested that anthropologists could discern the authenticity of native practices by analyzing the cultural survivals of an earlier age, in this case marriage practices. This led him to argue that brides who affected a ritual hesitation when moving to the homes of their new husbands or who publicly 'fled ' from their new situation were unconsciously expressing their opposition to the authoritarian control to which they would be subjected by their affines. These expressions of ritual opposition were a reflection of the dim memory held by women of the superior position they had once held in former, matriarchal times. Their oppression could be related to the passage of the *lobolo*, a practice that had emerged during the patriarchal phase of evolution as a means of compensation for the family's loss of a woman. The *lobolo* served to guarantee the good treatment of a wife only if she could return to her father's family when maltreated. But in reality this was almost impossible because her father needed her bridewealth to secure the marriages of her brothers and other male agnates. The passage of the *lobolo* led to a great deal of mistrust between families. If the marriage failed, or if the woman remained childless or died and her family had no other daughter to replace her, the *lobolo* would have to be returned. In consequence, several marriages would be threatened. Through this application of an evolutionist analysis to marriage practices, Junod hoped to convince younger missionaries that bridewealth exchange was unacceptable to the church.

E. W. Smith gently chided Junod when he wrote that Christianity needed a more flexibile approach to rites of initiation. These were often painful and immoral but they taught boys the virtues of endurance, discipline, obedience and manliness. By filtering out the obscene and the brutal and by retaining the positive in these practices, the church could build an African Christianity on authentic foundations.[21] In his articles and in book reviews, Junod continued to stress the continuing importance of 'salvage' or 'reconstructive' anthropology. The 'conflict of cultures' could only be understood once missionaries had a good grasp of the meaning of original, primitive practices. He worried that the teachings of the New Testament could not accommodate too much native custom, but on the other hand he felt that if the beatings and circumcision associated with initiation as a rite of passage were removed, or if the songs and dances were cleansed of their indecent expressions, the rite would no longer be authentic or acceptable. Ultimately, the pursuit of what Junod called 'pure anthropology' turned around the documentation of *bona fide* customs, not the description of new and improved ones. 'I am one of those who regrets change', he wrote as late as 1929, 'and wish to see the tribes conserve their originality and keep those of their customs that are compatible with a healthy civilization and a comprehensive and spiritual Christianity.'[22]

At the University of Cape Town Radcliffe-Brown was, in practice, unable to implement a clear distinction between the work of amateurs and professionals. This was partly because he had to rely on the data in missionary monographs for teaching purposes and partly because, in the process of establishing the utility of anthropology, he ran lively diploma courses at the University for missionaries and civil servants.[23] But as anthropology gained a disciplinary confidence, the professionals increasingly distanced themselves from the missionaries.

Isaac Schapera followed Radcliffe-Brown's lectures at the University of Cape Town on 'the historical study of the native problem'. In the mid-1920s, when Schapera graduated and Radcliffe-Brown left South Africa, the native problem was distinctly different from the one faced by Junod in southern Mozambique and in the Transvaal at the turn of the century. Large numbers of Africans were moving to the mines and cities, where their competition with South Africans of European descent threatened to provoke political instability. At the same time, the destruction of native cultures in the reserves threatened to transform aboriginal peoples into dangerous proletarians, no longer subject to the social and political controls of their leaders. To understand this new development in the ongoing native problem, Schapera claimed, anthropologists had to turn their gaze from the stable African tribe and focus on 'transitional figures', such as migrant labourers, as well as on the dislocating forces of 'culture contact' and change. Furthermore, as segregation was clearly impossible to achieve in the context of a common economy, anthropologists should include in their studies of African populations such individuals as the missionary, the native commissioner and the labour recruiter.[24] Schapera's perspective transformed the missionary as empathetic observer, committed to solving 'the native problem', into a major source of the upheaval that had caused the problem in the first place. This seemed clear to most academic anthropologists working in the field, particularly those who, like Malinowski and his students, aimed to provide the profession with a rigorous methodology.[25] This injurious turn of opinion would soon be adopted by a broad spectrum of political thought in South Africa.[26] Such criticism quickly served to marginalize missionaries in the world of anthropology.

The anthropologists' critique of missionary interference in the lives of native peoples was not entirely misplaced. The Romande Mission had acquired several sprawling farms, ostensibly to protect its members and potential converts from the government's land-grabbing policies. The Hertzog Bills aimed to expel black sharecroppers and rent-paying tenants from white-owned land or transform them into wage workers, or into tenants engaged to white farmers for six months every year without being paid. The threat posed by this sudden change to the lives of African tenants in the northeastern Transvaal prompted large numbers of people to move to the reserves or to seek protection on the private estates owned by the Swiss Romande Mission. This brought various tensions to the surface as the mission welcomed these people as rent-paying tenants, but in the process, it became a 'kaffir farming' institution. By concentrating African 'squatters' on its land, it sheltered them from the labour demands of white farmers. There was little to distinguish the mission farms, which extracted rents in the form of cash, labour and kind, from the white-owned farms on which Africans 'squatted'. In this sense the crisis occasioned by the Hertzog Bills, which had aimed to outlaw any form of 'squatting' that deprived white farmers of black labour, impacted directly on the mission and drew from it an impassioned response.[27]

In 1925 the mission started to encourage the formation of a class of black landowners by selling plots to its members around Valdezia.[28] At the same time, Junod denounced the government's attempts to force African tenants to pay farm-owners 180 days' labour every year for the right to squat on their land. Junod declared that this system was close to slavery, certainly 'no less than serfdom'. He rejected the discriminatory aspects of Hertzog's segregationist solution to the native problem, but continued to advocate a racial 'differentiation' based on Edgar Brookes' idealization of the District Councils in the Transkei and the Shepstonian system in Natal. The latter had allowed 'each race to develop in conformity with its nature', for Shepstone 'did not want to make the Bantu a second-class European, but a first-class Bantu'.[29] Junod's concern to defend the interests of Africans as a race eventually led him to view the Independent (or Ethiopian) churches with some sympathy.[30] Perhaps Henri-Philippe Junod best caught the ambiguity in his father's politics when he wrote, a few years later that

Henri Junod wanted the collaboration and not the fusion of races. As a true anthropologist, he saw only the disadvantages of the fusion of blacks and whites, and he knew that the deep intuition of the former, as much as that of the latter, hardened against that mixture. But he knew that the only path is that of collaboration, of mutual comprehension and reciprocal respect.[31]

In 1930 Henri-Philippe advocated segregation as a middle way between the extremes of repressive exploitation and mindless assimilation. By protecting native rights, segregation prevented Africans from becoming 'caricatures of the English, failed French or half-Portuguese'. 'A missionary can only support the methods of segregation as it regards the development of the Bantus on their soil and in their milieu.' Echoing Edgar Brookes, he counterpoised this form of 'differential' or 'parallel' development with an unacceptable 'artificial segregation' that failed to recognize the equality of man or gain the approbation of the black population.[32] His missionary colleague, Charles Bourquin, Brookes' father-in-law, supported this form of soft segregation. Like the Junods, he looked to the southern states of America where Booker T. Washington advocated a form of separate development and industrial education that aimed to reduce racial competition and conflict.[33]

While these Swiss missionaries accepted the protectionist aspects of segregation, they opposed its discriminatory features. They found the recommendations on land reform from the Beaumont Commission pusillanimous, and they publicly condemned the passages on job reservation in the 1926 Colour Bar Bill.[34] Their opposition to the discrimination suffered by the black population was driven by a respect for human rights but it was also propelled by the fear that discrimination fed the fires of African nationalism and 'Bolshevism'. They believed that the answer to the native question lay in increased communication between the races, through bodies such as the Joint Councils and ultimately through the moral rejuvenation of the white population.[35]

By this time Henri-Alexandre Junod had been suffering from multiple sclerosis for some years and his death in March 1934 came as no surprise. During the funeral in Geneva the (physical) anthropologist, Eugène Pittard, praised his contribution to the discipline, describing *The Life of a South African Tribe* as a 'catechism for all the universities of southern Africa'.[36] In his will, Junod asked for his ashes to be sent to Rikatla where they were buried later that year in the graveyard of the mission station holding the remains of his first son, Henri-Alexis, his second wife, Helen Kern, and his old friend, Paul Berthoud.

Bantu Heritage and History

Junod's death coincided with a major outburst of energy in South African anthropology. In 1934 Schapera published an important collection of essays, *Western Civilization and the Natives of South Africa*, in which contributors examined the effects of social change on the black population of the country. The book strongly criticized those who saw segregation as a compromise situated between the extremes of repression and assimilation. But it also caught the ambivalent attitude of anthropologists to the 'problem' of social change. Despite his criticisms of missionary anthropology, Schapera seemed to think it possible and worthwhile to salvage a picture of tribal society before the fall initiated by social change. Echoing Junod, he wrote, 'In order to appreciate [the effects of change] correctly it is necessary first to have some idea of Bantu culture as it flourished in its purely native state.' He introduced this idea by writing two contrasting chapters: one on a timeless 'Old Bantu Culture' and the other on the changing 'Present-day Life in the Reserves'.[37] More unexpectedly, the volume contained two essays by economists who warned that reinforcing and bolstering 'decaying remnants of tribalism' would have dark consequences. H. M. Robertson wrote that the proponents of these ideas were 'false friends to native welfare'. He and his colleague W. H. Hutt felt that attempts to protect the reserves from the social upheaval produced by capitalism merely caused these areas of the country to stagnate economically. Hutt was particularly critical of those who saw change in the reserves as merely 'the disturbance of the calm equanimity of primitive existence'. He believed that individualism, leasehold tenure and education should replace communal rights.[38]

In the same year, another critique of the political consequences of focusing on the 'old Bantu culture' came from Edgar Brookes. As segregation became more discriminatory, Brookes abandoned his earlier belief in the separation of races and now blamed 'the older anthropological school' for having 'supplied the segregationists with a badly-needed philosophy'.[39] By dividing society into 'civilized' and 'primitive' categories, anthropologists treated the African as 'something of a museum specimen'. By regarding 'tribal natives' as the only phenomenon of study, they had created the impression that all natives belonged in reserves. Those who lived outside tribal structures were an embarrassment, as they refused to live 'on their own lines', as the anthropologists felt they should. The old anthropology treated Africans as an almost homogenous category of people living in rural reserves, who needed a form of tribal government and an education adapted to their special needs. Through this native policy, Brookes now believed that the development of the African population was held back and the contribution to the country of Africans in the city was ignored. Artists reinforced this picture by focusing on traditional clothing and beehive huts in their work rather than on the tin shanties and forms of European clothing that were the reality of life for a large part of the population. Representing Africans as members of a uniformly primitive society created a picturesque image but it was as far from the truth as a picture of Europeans living in the age of the stagecoach and the ox-wagon.

Debates over the contribution of anthropology to the solution of the political crisis took place in many circles. In July 1934 Bronislaw Malinowski, Winifred Hoernlé, W. M. Eiselen, Monica Hunter and Isaac Schapera all addressed a New Education Fellowship Conference in Johannesburg. Henri-Philippe Junod attended the symposium, departing with the feeling that missionaries and their anthropology (perhaps particularly that of his father), had been unfairly criticized by these 'scientists' for wanting to change native customs to make them acceptable to imported, Christian mores. In a combative article published the following year in the *International Review of Missions*, Junod *fils* defended the rights of missionaries to protect the interests of their communicants by filtering out, amending or prohibiting unacceptable cultural practices. He conceded that the payment of bridewealth for a wife was understandable but not the rights of possession that went with the *lobolo* and that condemned a wife to be inherited by one of her deceased husband's male relatives. He rejected what he considered obscene aspects of initiation but praised their educative elements. He also stressed the importance of Wayfarers' and Pathfinders' associations in educating young people. Henri-Philippe drew attention to the importance of religion and spirituality in the missionary anthropologists' work, for it combated the sterile materialism that was the real cause of the destruction of native customs. In a final crescendo, Henri-Philippe Junod decried the detachment of professional anthropologists from their object of study and their tendency 'to preserve native custom as a curio for some African museum'.[40]

Three years later Henri-Philippe Junod mounted another reply to the criticism of those anthropologists who were more 'concerned with culture contact than with the permanent elements of Bantu heritage':

> The true meaning of culture contact, with regard to the Bantu, is not found in the transitory forms of hybrid features of life, but in the manner in which Bantu heritage helps us to create a new era, a new Bantu society, where the positive elements of Bantu social and tribal life, where the spiritual forces of the Bantu past will become part and parcel of a solid Bantu civilization.[41]

In some areas, the debate over the task of anthropology took on overtly political tones. The professor of history at the University of the Witwatersrand, W. M. Macmillan, had addressed the Le Zoute conference and was aware of the debates within missionary anthropology. An active Presbyterian, Macmillan counted anthropologists like Edwin Smith, Donald Fraser and Merle Davis among his friends. He admired the direction in which these Christians, and J. H. Oldham, were pushing the ecumenical missionary movement. At the same time he found himself marginalized within his university as anthropologists came to occupy the ground of African Studies and to monopolize the considerable funding mobilized by Oldham and his associates. Historians were not asked to play a role in the International Institute of African Languages and Cultures and, despite their titles, journals like *Africa* and *Bantu Studies* failed to carry articles by historians. Nor were historians invited to join bodies such as the School of African Life and Languages at U.C.T. or the Department of Bantu Studies at Wits. Just as importantly, they were excluded from the (South African) Inter-University Committee for African Studies that was affiliated to the International Institute of African Languages and Cultures in London and guarded access to wealthy American foundations. As the anthropologists became the recognized experts in the field, they began to influence government policy and, especially, native education.[42]

Macmillan was critical of the anthropologists' concern with 'data collection' and 'social change', as it ignored the root causes of poverty. He aimed his strongest criticism at the old anthropology that colluded with segregation and at the 'scientists' who were responsible for 'the break away from the ideal of common citizenship' by protesting against Europe's 'perverting influence' on 'pure African culture'. By contrasting 'a highly idealized African rusticity' with 'diabolical slums', the anthropologists represented the rural reserves as the natural home of the African population. 'The facts of Africa as we begin to know them', he continued, 'make nonsense of the dream that tribal life is a state of idyllic peace and contentment marred only when civilization interferes.' These rural societies were dominated by hunger and disease, witchcraft and superstition, and they lacked freedom and democracy.

Macmillan found large shards of the old anthropology in the work of the new generation. These were particularly visible in N. J. van Warmelo's influential *Preliminary Survey of the Bantu Tribes of South Africa*. Published by the Native Affairs Department in 1935, this work employed population distribution maps to divide the African people of south Africa into linguistic categories that van Warmelo called 'tribes'. Perhaps more surprisingly, the influence of the *Kulturvolk* approach used by Junod and others dominated a seminal collection of essays sponsored in 1937 by the Interuniversity Committee for African Studies, *The Bantu-Speaking Tribes of South Africa*. Although the book claimed to be 'a manual of South African ethnography', Isaac Schapera noted in the introduction that its greater part was devoted to 'an account of the Bantu as they were before being affected by the intrusion of white civilization'. Museum collections were also reordered at this time to conform with, and contribute to, the picture of Africans as members of distinct tribal groups. Visitors to natural history museums saw Africans ranged into tribes made tangible and visible in attractive ethnographic displays. This perspective gave little space to social change and Macmillan felt that by stressing the importance of 'decaying native customs', anthropologists exaggerated the role of ethnic differences in the country.

By treating the tribe as the classic unit of study for Africans, anthropologists racialized the study of society and gave body to the myth that South Africa contained discrete cultures and peoples that could be segregated and, equally importantly, treated as distinct political communities. Macmillan believed that the anthropologists' approach contributed to the 'absurdity' of 'two civilizations'. It portrayed the black population as an 'inferior category' in a racial hierarchy that contradicted the quest for a common society. Indeed, this approach served the cause of segregation, for it separated the white population, treated as a national force, from a fractured and fragmented patchwork of tribes – what Margery Perham would go on to call a 'multicellular tissue of tribalism'.[43] The anthropologists' concern with race relations also seemed to undermine the notion of a common society.

In sum, Macmillan saw anthropology as a reformist discipline with monopolistic designs. The investigations undertaken by anthropologists of social change in the cities and the reserves offered only an ameliorative form of social work as a solution to the native problem.[44] Perhaps most seriously, many functionalist anthropologists continued to view social change as an unsolicited source of disruption to life in the tribal village. From this perspective, Junod's salvage anthropology confected a picture of tribal equilibrium at the moment, just before European intrusion, that Lucy Mair would call the 'zero point of change'. For critics like Macmillan, this perspective portrayed change as a source of trouble and confusion rather than a font of innovation and progress. It trapped Africans in a primitive world incapable of responding to the challenges of a new age.[45]

Notes

[1] Arthur Grandjean, *La Mission romande* (Lausanne, 1917), pp. 128–9.
[2] Swiss Mission Archive, Lausanne (SMA) 547/A, H. Guye to mission council, 25 July 1904.
[3] See, for example, *Africa's Golden Harvest* (1907) October, p. 2.
[4] Grandjean, *La Mission romande*, pp. 187, 193–4. For the wider context of independent evangelical movements in southern Mozambique, see Carlos Serra and David Hedges, *Historia de Moçambique*, II (Maputo, 1999), pp. 18–20 ; Valdemir Zamparoni, 'Deus branco, almas negras: colonialismo, educação, religião e racismo em Moçambique, 1910–1940', unpublished paper presented to Conference *Lusofonia em Africa: Historia, Democraçia e Integraçao Africana*, Universidade Eduardo Mondlane, Maputo, May 2005.
[5] Henri-Alexandre Junod, *Le Pasteur Calvin Mapopé* (Lausanne, 1925), pp. 3–4, 24–5, 29; *Rapport annuel de la Mission suisse romande*, 1925, p. 10.
[6] Edouard Vautier, *La Maison des Cèdres* (Lausanne, 1935), pp. 88–9. A. Amiet, 'La Mission suisse romande', *Revue missionnaire* (1925) 5, pp. 5–7.
[7] Junod, *Pasteur Calvin Mapopé*, p. 35. C. Mapopé, 'Comment les peuples africains pourront-ils trouver le

salut?' *Revue missionnaire* (1925) 5, April.

8   See also Brookes, 'The South African Race problem', *International Review of Missions* (1927) 16. Brookes married Swiss missionary Charles Bourquin's daughter Heidi in 1925. He wrote *A Retrospect and a Forecast: Fifty Years of Missionary Work in South Africa 1875–1925. Swiss Mission to Shangaan Tribes* (Lausanne, c. 1925). In 1929 he served as South African representative to the League of Nations in Geneva and visited Tuskegee two years later.

9   Brookes, *The History of Native Policy in South Africa from 1830 to the Present Day* (Cape Town, 1925), pp. 156, 175, 462–3.

10 W. C. Willoughby, book review in the *International Review of Missions (IRM)* (1913), p. 588; E. W. Smith, 'Social Anthropology and Mission work', *IRM* (1924) 13, p. 518.

11 'Methods of ethnology and social anthropology', *South African Journal of Science* (1923) 20. More generally, see Radcliffe-Brown, 'The present position of anthropological studies' (1931) in a collection of his essays, M. N. Srinivas (ed.), *Method in Social Anthropology; Selected Essays* (Chicago, IL, 1958), p. 144.

12 *Cape Times*, 9 January 1924. In this article Radcliffe-Brown praised Edwin Smith's attempts to push missionary anthropology in the direction of 'science' or 'knowledge systematised'.

13 Radcliffe-Brown, 'The mother's brother in South Africa', *South African Journal of Science* (1924) 21.

14 Junod, 'Le mouvement de Mourimi: un réveil au sein de l'animisme thonga' in *Journal de Psychologie Normale et Pathologique* (1924) December; Junod, *The Life of a South African Tribe (LSAT)* (London, 1926–7, 2nd edn) II, p. 597–602. See also chapter 8, p. 232.

15 Junod, 'Les coutumes matrimoniales des Thonga', *Bulletin de la mission romande (BMR)* (1926) 36, pp. 195–97. See also Junod, 'Les rites défensifs et les rites d'évitement dans les coutumes matrimoniales des Bantous Sudafricains', *Bulletin der Schweizerischen Gesellschaft für Anthropologie und Ethnologie* (1926/27) 3, 4. pp. 6–7.

16 Junod, *LSAT* II, pp. 272–4, 301. The complexity of the debate generated by this issue is well caught in Adam Kuper, 'Radcliffe-Brown, Junod and the Mother's Brother in South Africa', *Man* (1976) 11, 1. See also Mauss' 1925 review of Radcliffe-Brown's article, published for the first time in *L'Année sociologique* (2004) 54, 1, pp. 220–1 and his 'Parentés et plaisanteries' (1928) in Mauss, *Oeuvres 3* (Paris, 1928), pp. 112–13. The notion of an evolution from matriarchal to patriarchal stages somewhere in a lost past was thought quite plausible by Thomas Hodgkin, *Nigerian Perspectives: An Historical Anthology* (London, 1960), p. 20.

17 Abel de Meuron, *Revue missionnaire* (1926) 12, December, p. 71. Smith edited and provided a long introduction to the report on the Le Zoute conference. See his *The Christian Mission in Africa* (London, 1926).

18 Cf. Diedrich Westermann, 'The value of the African's past', *International Review of Missions (IRM)* (1926) 15, p. 429.

19 Cf. E. W. Smith, 'The Sublimation of Bantu life and thought', *IRM* (1922) 11; Dora Earthy, 'The customs of Gazaland women in relation to the African Church', *IRM* (1926) 15; W. Vincent Lucas, 'The educational value of initiatory rites' and J. Raum, 'Christianity and African puberty rites', *IRM* (1927) 16. More broadly, see W. C. Willoughby, 'Building the African Church', *IRM* (1926) 15.

20 Cf. the classic statement by E. W. Smith on 'Christianity in Africa' in his *The Golden Stool* (London, 1926). See also his 'The Sublimation of Bantu life', pp. 83–4. This approach led Smith to criticize the Phelps-Stokes Commission's failure to build on African institutions and practices. Smith, 'Indigenous education in Africa' in E. E. Evans-Pritchard et al., *Essays presented to C. G. Seligman* (London, 1934). For Junod's view of the Phelps-Stokes Commission on education, see his 'L'education en Afrique', *Revue internationale de la Croix-Rouge* (1923) 53.

21 Smith, 'The Sublimation of Bantu life', p. 89.

22 Junod, 'Les coutumes matrimoniales', pp. 135–41, 192–97; Junod, Review of E. W. Smith, *The Golden Stool* in *IRM* (1926) 15, pp. 607–9; Junod, 'La seconde école de circoncision chez les Ba-Khaha du Nord du Transvaal', *Journal of the Royal Anthropological Institute* (1929) 59, pp. 145–7.

23 The courses were attended by missionary anthropologists such as Dora Earthy and Tom Brown, together with others, such as D. D. T. Jabavu and Z. K. Matthews, who would publish anthropological work in mission journals. It is perhaps noteworthy that E. W. Smith served in 1929 as the external examiner of Isaac Schapera's PhD at the London School of Economics: W. John Young, *Quiet Wise Spirit, Edwin D. Smith 1876–1957 and Africa* (Peterborough, 2002), p. 143.

24 Schapera, 'Economic changes in South African Native life', *Africa* (1928) 1; Schapera, 'The Present state and future development of Ethnographic research in South Africa', *Bantu Studies* (1934) 8, p. 244. More broadly, see Adam Kuper, *Anthropology and Anthropologists: The British School* (London, 1973), p. 71.

25 Malinowski harboured an acquired antipathy toward missionaries who, he considered, interfered unnecessarily in the lives of native peoples, but he limited any public expression of this opinion to a short caricature in the introduction to *Argonauts of the Western Pacific* (London, 1922). Malinowski famously called on the anthropologist to relinquish the comfort of the long chair on the verandah of the missionary compound. Yet at the same time, he heaped public praise on the work of missionary anthropologists, at least partly because his relationship with J. H. Oldham gave him access to the financial support of international foundations.

Malinowski, *A Diary in the Strict Sense of the Term* (London, 1967), pp. 31, 42. Hortense Powdermaker remarked that Malinowski thought missionaries 'were an enemy, except Edwin Smith and H.-A. Junod, who apparently were more interested in learning about tribal peoples than in converting them.' Powdermaker, *Stranger and Friend* (London, 1966), p. 43. Winifried Hoernlé, the influential head of anthropology at the University of the Witwatersrand (1923–37), had also complained of missionary interference during her fieldwork in Namaqualand in 1912. Deborah Gaitskell, 'Religion embracing science? Female missionary ventures in southern African anthropology: Dora Earthy and Mozambique, 1917–1933', Basel Afrika Bibliographien, 1998, working paper no. 5, p. 5.

26 On Jan Smuts' views on the disruptive effects brought by missionary teaching to primitive African communities, see his 'Foreword' to Monica Hunter, *Reaction to Conquest: Effects of Contact with Europeans on the Pondo of South Africa* (London, [1936] 1961), p. vii–viii. Jomo Kenyatta expressed the same views in stronger terms in his *Facing Mount Kenya* (London, 1938), pp. 165, 271–2. They were soon picked up by Africa nationalists and communists in South Africa and elsewhere. Cf. R. Sobukwe, 'Address on behalf of the Graduating Class at Fort Hare, October 1949' in T. Karis and G. Carter (eds), *From Protest to Challenge*, II (Stanford, CA, 1973), p. 335. See also N. Majeke, *The Role of the Missionaries in Conquest* (Johannesburg, 1953, new edn, Cape Town, 1986). On Hastings Banda's more moderate criticisms, see Peter G. Forster, *T. Cullen Young: Missionary and Anthropologist* (Hull, 1989), pp. 62–3, 155–9.

27 Caroline Jeannerat, Eric Morier-Genoud, Didier Péclard, 'Swiss Churches, Apartheid and South Africa: The Case of the Swiss Mission in South Africa' (Report to the National Research Programme 42+ of the Swiss National Science Foundation, 2004), pp. 32–8.

28 The Mission eventually sold about half of Klipfontein farm. However, most 'farmers' found it more profitable to rent their land to waves of squatters expelled from white farms. P. Harries, 'Exclusion, Classification and Internal Colonialism: the emergence of ethnicity among the Tsonga-speakers of South Africa' in Leroy Vail (ed.), *The Creation of Tribalism in Southern Africa* (London and Los Angeles, 1989), pp. 92–5.

29 Junod, *Le Problème indigène dans l'union sud-africaine* (Lausanne, 1931), pp. 17, 28. See also Anon., 'La lutte anti-esclavagiste et ses tâches actuelles', *Revue missionnaire* (1928) 17, p. 17.

30 He blamed racial discrimination for the proliferation of Ethiopian churches and supported the independence of African clergymen as long as their beliefs and practices did not move too far from the central tenets of the mission churches. Junod, 'L'église éthiopienne', *Revue missionnaire* (1924) 1, p. 6.

31 Henri-Philippe Junod, *Henri-A. Junod: Missionnaire et Savant, 1863–1934* (Lausanne, 1934), p. 69.

32 H.-P. Junod, 'L'exploitation coloniale en Afrique du Sud', *Le Christianisme Social* (1930) 5, July, pp. 22–3, 26–7.

33 Charles Bourquin, 'Le problème sud-africain', *Revue missionnaire* (1926) 11. For the equivocation of the Le Zoute conference on the question of segregation in South Africa, see de Meron, *Revue missionnaire* (1926) 12, pp. 75.

34 *BMR* (1926) 36, November; H.-A. Junod, *Le Problème indigène*, p. 30; H.-P. Junod, 'L'exploitation coloniale', p. 28.

35 H.-A. Junod, '*Le Problème indigène*', p. 31; H.-P. Junod, 'L'exploitation coloniale', pp. 13–15, 29–30.

36 Eugène Pittard, 'Nécrologie: Henri A. Junod', *Archives suisses d'anthropologie* (1935–39) 7, 8, p. 92; Edwin Smith, 'Obituary: Henri-Alexandre Junod', *Man* (1934) July, p. 111; Abel de Meuron, *Revue missionnaire* (1934) 42.

37 Isaac Schapera (ed.), *Western Civilization and the Natives of South Africa* (London, 1934), p. 3.

38 H. M. Robertson, 'The economic condition of the rural natives' and W. H. Hutt, 'The economic position of the Bantu in South Africa' both in I. Schapera (ed.), *Western Civilization and the Natives of South*, pp. 150, 155, 209.

39 Edgar Brookes, *The Colour Problems of South Africa* (London, 1934), p. 145. The following paragraph is drawn from chapter four, 'The Anthropological Approach: its value and its dangers'.

40 H.-P. Junod, 'Anthropology and Missionary Education', *IRM* (1935); H.-P. Junod, *Henri-A. Junod: Missionnaire et savant*, p. 72. For Henri-Philippe's suggestions on how to modify brideprice exchange, see his 'Le marriage par achat ou "lobolo" et L'église indigène naissante', *Revue missionnaire* (1930) 25.

41 Henri-Philippe Junod, *Bantu Heritage* (Johannesburg, 1938), pp. 139–40.

42 W. M. Macmillan, *My South African Years: An Autobiography* (Cape Town, 1975), pp. 197–8, 214–16, 219; W. D. Hammond-Tooke, *Imperfect Interpreters: South Africa's Anthropologists 1920–1990* (Johannesburg, 1997), pp. 45–57.

43 Margery Perham, 'The British problem in Africa', *Foreign Affairs* (1951) 29, 4, p. 638.

44 C. C. Saunders, *The Making of the South African Past* (Cape Town, 1988), p. 56. Macmillan, *Africa Emergent* (Harmondsworth, [1938] 1949), pp. 12, 70, 228; Bruce Murray, *Wits: the Early Years* (Johannesburg, 1982), pp. 129–31.

45 A view captured in the title of Monica Wilson (née Hunter)'s *Reaction to Conquest: Effects of Contact with Europeans on the Pondo of South Africa*. More generally, see Malinowski, 'The value of history and its limitations: the search for the zero point of change' in his *The Dynamics of Change* (New Haven, CT, and London, 1945). For Schapera's view in 1962, see chapter 8, p. 244n148. In 1975 Lucy Mair saw the 'disruption to village life' as the major consequence of migrant labour. Mair, 'Anthropologists and Colonial Policy', *African Affairs* (1975)

74, no. 295. See also Jan Vansina's experiences amongst the functionalists in the anthropology department of University College, London in the early 1950s. Vansina, *Living With Africa* (Madison, WI, 1994), pp. 10–11. The functionalist view that change had a negative effect on tribal communities also influenced the few historians prepared to broach this topic, cf. C. W. de Kiewiet, 'Social and economic developments in native tribal life' in *Cambridge History of the British Empire* (Cambridge, 1936), vol. 8, pp. 821–2; De Kiewiet, *A History of South Africa* (London, 1941), p. 242.

Conclusion

W. M. Macmillan resigned from the University of the Witwatersrand in 1932. Four years later, as I pointed out in the Introduction to this book, Max Gluckman made his way up the Lebombos from where he saluted the memory of Henri-Alexandre Junod. Although Gluckman bore the imprint of Macmillan, and his advocacy of a single society in South Africa would soon attract the disapproval of authority, he represented a new generation. Anthropology in South Africa had secured its hold over a field of African Studies that encompassed Bantu philology and archaeology, and the young Gluckman could look to a bright future. He had received a thorough training in the discipline at the University of the Witwatersrand where he had access to first-rate libraries, excellent professors, an international network of scholars, and the research funding needed to produce original work.

The emergence of anthropology as a university-based discipline had pushed missionaries from the field in South Africa. But the contribution of missionaries to the production of knowledge in other fields had also declined. Botanists and zoologists now required specialized training as well as costly laboratories and equipment. Professionals manned government departments of trigonometry and meteorology where they centralized the business of map-making and the collection of statistics on climate. University graduates moved into departments of veterinary science and agriculture and worked with collectors at museums and herbaria, as well as with academics, to bring a professional order to the study of the environment and its uses. Although missionaries continued to exercise an influence in site-specific practical fields, such as native education, rural medicine and philology, their amateur status and approach barred them from leading roles within professional institutions of learning. Soon, only the new discipline of Missiology could provide missionaries with a secure niche in a secular world concerned with the accumulation and preservation of knowledge about Africa.[1]

The indigenization of missionary societies and the withdrawal of foreign personnel accompanied this process. The Europe that greeted Macmillan was caught up in a far more violent struggle over blood and soil than the one he had quit in South Africa. As the old continent hurtled towards the tragedy of World War Two, public enthusiasm for missionary causes took a back seat. The task of the missionary had also changed, for he no longer explored a dark continent or engaged in titanic struggles with slavery, forced labour and other immoral practices. Instead, he was caught up increasingly in administrative duties and cultural compromises that failed to catch the imagination of a European public. In a secularizing Switzerland more concerned after the war with human rights and self-determination than with culpability and conversion, popular support for the missionary movement plummeted. At the same time, the concentration of knowledge about Africa in Europe shifted from amateur bodies like the missionary society and the learned association to the new and expanding universities. Caught up in the adventure and excitement of decolonization, redbrick and ivy league universities established new disciplines, departments, journals and publishing houses in a way that raised the level of scholarly attention focused on Africa. At the same time they supplied the continent with scholars who professionalized the world of knowledge and left little room for the amateurs situated in remote mission stations.[2]

In a post-war climate of regained liberties and exaggerated economic expectations, some black politicians in South Africa read the salvage anthropology of Junod's generation as the story of a golden age destroyed by capitalism and colonialism, and found in this work both a description of cultural authenticity and yet another reason to mobilize as a race in opposition to white supremacy.[3] On the other hand, for many Afrikaner nationalists, Junod's model of a *Kulturvolk* seemed to justify an increasingly strict segregation or apartheid. At the liberal, English-speaking universities, Junod's attempt to retrieve the genius of a people by salvaging a picture of their premodern customs seemed out of step with the times. Instead of stimulating a cultural rebirth, the portrayal of Africans as primitive tribesmen had helped place rural communities under the command of conservative chiefs and their political allies. This placed individuals in the rural reserves or bantustans more firmly under communitarian controls and restricted the development of both a modern economy and a single nation. Confronted by the results of state-driven social engineering, liberal anthropologists looked increasingly to History rather than Heritage to understand the dynamics of indigenous communities in South Africa.

As the professional anthropologists working at the liberal universities grappled with the ominous social changes enveloping South Africa, they distanced themselves from the second generation of Swiss missionary-anthropologists. Henri-Philippe Junod and Alexandre Jaques had written promising articles on deep rural communities for anthropological reviews in the 1920s–30s. However, as the focus of anthropology changed and the command of the discipline moved from the missionary societies to the universities, both men turned to other fields.[4] Jaques devoted himself to education while the young Junod became chaplain to the condemned at Pretoria Central prison. During a career stretching from 1931 to 1960, he accompanied over 800 men to the gallows. From this vantage point in the judicial system the Junods' interpretation of 'authentic' African perspectives on customary law, at 'zero-point change', attracted the attention of lawmakers. During these years, Henri-Philippe fought courageously for penal reform and human rights but never extended this criticism of South African society into an unambiguous rejection of segregation. When apartheid Africanized his post in 1960 he left for Geneva where, the following year, he became the first director of the Africa Institute (today the Institut universitaire d'études du développement) and the co-founder of the journal *Genève-Afrique*. His belief that apartheid could be 'fair and honest' if stripped of its discriminatory aspects, and his misgivings about African nationalism, brought him into conflict with the Third World supporters in the city and finally influenced his resignation. In his last years he returned to

South Africa where he wrote a history of the Tsonga-speaking people, supported the government of the Gazankulu bantustan and approved of the political reforms introduced by P.W. Botha. He died believing in the possibility of an apartheid without discrimination.[5]

The decline of missionary anthropology in the post-war years was accompanied by a more critical view of missionary activity in the country. The clash between rival nationalisms in South Africa, and the stranglehold of the fascist *Estado Novo* in Mozambique, deprived missionaries of the space they had once occupied in politics. The new missionaries still contributed to the constitution of knowledge about Africa, but they formulated their ideas in reaction to political changes and their debates were confined to narrow circles. Most were unwilling to embroil themselves in the politics associated with anthropology and turned to the more neutral study of the Tsonga language or devoted themselves to rural healthcare, education or conservation issues. At this time, members of the church produced a rapidly expanding range of publications that raised and debated issues of concern to the 'Tsonga people'.[6] As command of the church passed to the Transvaal synod and an indigenous pastorate, the need for foreign supervision quickly fell away. In 1962 the indigenous arm of the mission in South Africa became fully independent as the Tsonga Presbyterian Church. Many in the TPC supported apartheid's politicization of ethnicity as this gave the 'Tsonga people' their own 'homeland', the bantustan of Gazankulu. When in 1982 the church renamed itself the Evangelical Presbyterian Church of South Africa, it was severely divided by the responses of its members to the politics of apartheid. For while some members of the church were exiled, persecuted and imprisoned by apartheid, the head of the church ran the homeland with the support of a large part of the EPCSA.[7] These painful divisions raised a lively debate when, as the transfer of power to the African National Congress took place in the mid-1990s, church circles reassessed the nature of the cautious and controlled indigenization of the mission engineered by the EPCSA and the parent body in Lausanne.[8]

If the cultural politics of the mission could be appropriated to serve segregationist policies in South Africa, in Mozambique the same policies provided a space for opponents of the Portuguese regime. Portuguese attempts to halt the 'denationalization' of southern Mozambique peaked in 1929 with the passage of two decrees aimed at controlling the proliferation of Protestant schools teaching in Ronga and Thonga. The new laws prohibited the use of the vernacular in schools, banned books in Bantu languages from the schools (including the Bible), required schools to be constructed of masonry, closed down schools with less than 25 scholars and set 14 years as the maximum age for attendance at primary school. Schools had to be authorized by the state and all teachers had to acquire a primary school certificate. These state controls severely restricted the growth of Protestant schools and vernacular literacy.[9] But they could not prevent the formation of a church élite, educated in Portuguese, that was singularly respectful of indigenous languages and cultures.

Robert Mashaba had become a symbol for many members of this community when in 1902 the Methodists secured his release from jail. During Mashaba's exile in the Transvaal and Swaziland his portrait hung in the offices of the Gremio Africano, a largely *mestizo* organization calling for political reform in Mozambique. Members of this organization and their urban, intellectual friends celebrated Mashaba's return to his birthplace on his retirement in 1934 and remembered his achievements long after his death five years later.[10] In the meantime the synods, consistories and youth groups of the Swiss Mission spread a knowledge of the Ronga and Thonga languages that Mashaba and others had done so much to define. Although some regretted the continued division of the Tsonga language into separate Ronga and Thonga wings, most saw these linguistic forms as vital carriers of the ethnic customs and values that supported an indigenized Christianity.[11] This process bounded forward in 1948 when the mission became the Presbyterian Church of Mozambique. By this time African clergymen were beginning to dominate the hierarchy of the church and congregants were largely responsible for its administration. For many, the policies of the church created a space into which they could retreat from the politics of assimilation practised by the Portuguese. Wittingly or not, the Presbyterian Church of Mozambique became a centre of resistance to Portuguese colonialism.[12]

The ideas about Africa developed by the first generation of Swiss missionaries deeply informed the history of the Evangelical Presbyterian Church of South Africa and the Presbyterian Church of Mozambique as they negotiated their way through the final, perilous decades of the twentieth century. In this book I have looked at the birth and development of these ideas in Switzerland and south-east Africa during the nineteenth and early twentieth centuries. It is my contention that they are still important to an understanding of Africa today.

Notes

[1] Elsewhere missionary anthropology proved more tenacious. Maurice Leenhardt moved to the Ecole Pratique des Hautes Etudes in 1932 and eventually occupied the chair established by Marcel Mauss. Karl Laman's *The Kongo* appeared in four volumes (between 1953 and 1968) and Father Schmidt's *Anthropos* remained an important anthropological review. James Clifford, *Person and Myth: Maurice Leenhardt in the Melanesian World* (Berkeley, CA, and London, 1982).

[2] On the amateurs, see Ruth Finnegan (ed.), *Participating in the Knowledge Society: Researchers Beyond the University Walls* (Basingstoke, 2005).

[3] Cf. Anton Lembede whose strict Linnaean racial taxonomy closely resembled that of Junod. A. M. Lembede, 'Some Principles of African Nationalism', February 1945 in T. Karis and G. Carter (eds), *From Protest to Challenge* (Stanford, CA, 1973) II, p. 315. See also Nelson Mandela's 'admiration of the structure and organization of early African societies' in South Africa where 'there were no rich and poor and there was no exploitation'. Rivonia Trial Statement in Karis and Carter, *From Protest to Challenge*, p. 303.

[4] Cf. Alexandre A. Jaques, 'Terms of kinship and corresponding patterns of behaviour among the Thonga', *Bantus Studies* (1929) 3; Jaques, 'A Survey of Shangana-Tsonga, Ronga and Tswa literature', *Bantu Studies* (1940) 14, 3; Henri-Philippe Junod, 'Some notes on Tshopi origins', *Bantu Studies* (1927) 3, 1; H.-P. Junod, 'Les VaNdau de l'Afrique orientale portugaise', *Bulletin de la société neuchâteloise de géographie* (1935) 44, 1; H.-P. Junod, 'Les cas de possession et l'exorcisme chez les Vandau', *Africa* (1935) 8, 3; H.-P. Junod and A. A. Jaques, *Vulthari bya vatonga (matshangana): the Wisdom of the Thonga-Shangaan people* (Pretoria, 1936). The fate of these two men bears comparison with that of the Anglican missionary-anthropologist in southern Mozambique, Dora Earthy. See Deborah Gaitskell's poignant account in 'Religion embracing science? Female missionary ventures in southern African anthropology: Dora Earthy and Mozambique, 1917–1933' Basel Afrika Bibliographien (1998), working paper no. 5.

[5] Cf. Robert Turrell, *White Mercy: A Study of the Death Penalty in South Africa* (London, 2004), pp. 20–1, 180–1, 196n20. As chaplain to the condemned, Henri-Philippe Junod took up the work first started by Ernest Creux and Charles Bourquin. My thanks to Eric Morier-Genoud for this information and for directing me to Junod's article on 'Les différents visages de l'apartheid en Afrique du Sud', *Tribune de Genève*, 10 February 1965. See also H.-P. Junod, 'Farewell to South Africa!', *Penal Reform News* (1961) 55, April. On the history, see his *Matimu Ya Vatsonga 1498–1650* (Braamfontein, 1977) and Mandla Mathebula, *800 Years of Tsonga History (1200–2000)* (Polokwane, 2002).

[6] The newspaper *Nyeleti Ya Miso* appeared in Ronga and Thonga in the second half of 1920 when it sold 1,600 copies in Johannesburg alone. A decade later the Valdezia community produced the *Valdezia Bulletin* in Thonga and English. *Bulletin de la mission suisse romande* (*BMSR*) (1921), pp. 15–16; *BMSR* (1922), pp. 17–18; *BMSR* (1929), p. 15. See also note 8 below.

Conclusion

7   Nicolas Monnier, 'De la bière dans les théières: Essai sur les fondements et l'avenir du partenariat missionnaire Afrique du Sud-Suisse', *Le Fait Missionnaire* (1999) 8; C. Jeannerat, E. Morier-Genoud and D. Péclard, 'Swiss Churches, Apartheid and South Africa: The case of the Swiss Mission in South Africa' (Report to the National Research Programme 42+ of the Swiss National Science Foundation on 'Relations between Switzerland and South Africa', 2004).
8   Tinyiko Maluleke, 'Mission, ethnicity and homeland – the case of the EPCSA', *Missionalia* (1993) 21, 3; Klauspeter Bläser et al., 'The ambivalence of ethnic identity: A response to T. S. Maluleke', *Missionalia* (1994) 22, 3; Maluleke, 'North-South Partnerships – The Evangelical Presbyterian Church in South Africa and the Département missionnaire in Lausanne', *International Review of Mission* (1994) 83, 328, January; Maluleke, 'Some legacies of 19th century mission: the Swiss Mission in South Africa', *Missionalia* (1995) 23, 1; Maluleke, 'The Valdezia Mission station, then and now', *Missionalia* (2003) 31, 1.
9   A. Grandjean, 'Situation inquiétante des missions dans la colonie de Moçambique', *Bulletin de la mission suisse en Afrique du Sud* (1929) 37, p. 423. In 1928 the mission sold 15,889 publications in the Transvaal and 4000 in Mozambique. *BMSAS* (1929), p. 15.
10 'Robert Mashaba' in *Encyclopedia of World Methodism* (Nashville, TN, 1974) vol. II, pp. 1530–31; Eduardo Moreira, *Portuguese East Africa: A Study of its Religious Needs* (New York, 1936), p. 24; Raúl Honwana, *The Life History of Raúl Honwana* (Boulder, CO, and London, 1988) edited by Allen Isaacman, pp. 103–4. Muti Sikobele left the Methodist Episcopal Mission in 1918 to establish the Luso-African Church Association that would, in its turn, spawn a number of other Independent Churches. Tizora Neves took a more political direction when he founded a branch in Inhambane of *O Congresso Nacional Africano*. Alf Helgesson, *Church, State and People in Mozambique* (Uppsala, 1994), pp. 201–8, 244–7, 290–2.
11 Henri-Philippe Junod, *Henri-A. Junod: Missionnaire et Savant, 1863–1934* (Lausanne, 1934), p. 20. See also the correspondence between Professor Lestrade and the Swiss Mission on the orthographic and general linguistic unification of Thonga, Ronga, and Tswa, University of Cape Town, MSS and Archives, Bc255, A1.84–A1.98; and *Rapport annuel de la mission suisse romande, 1922*: p. 18. R. H. W. Shepherd felt the existence of three print languages within the Thonga group was unjustified. See his 'African literature' in E. Hellmann (ed.), *Handbook of Race Relations in South Africa* (Cape Town, 1949), pp. 602, 608. More generally, see G. P. Lestrade, 'European influences on the development of Bantu languages and literature' in I. Schapera (ed.), *Western Civilization and the Natives of South Africa: Studies in Culture Contact* (London, 1934), pp. 108–9.
12 Teresa Cruz e Silva, *Protestant Churches and the Formation of Political Consciousness in Southern Mozambique (1930–1974)* (Basel, 2001), ed. Didier Péclard; Cruz e Silva, 'Identity and Political Consciousness in southern Mozambique, 1930–1974: Two Presbyterian Biographies Contextualised', *Journal of Southern African Studies* (1998), 24, 1; Nadja Manghezi, *O meu coraçao esta nas maos de um negro. Uma historia da vida de Janet Mondlane* (Maputo, 1999), chapter three; Charles Biber, *Cent ans au Mozambique: Le parcours d'une minorité* (Lausanne, 1987), chapters 8, 11, 12; Severinho Ngoenha, *Estatuto e Axiologia de Educaçao: o Paradigmatico Questionamento de Missao Suiça* (Maputo, 2000); Neil Faris, 'A Changing Paradigm of Mission in the Protestant Churches of Mozambique: A Case Study of Eduardo Mondlane' (Unpublished PhD, University of Cape Town, 2007). On the difficult relations between the church and Frelimo in the early years of independence, see Claudine Roulet, *Petite chronique mozambicaine* (Geneva, 1987) and the correspondence of M. Vonnez from Beira, 1974–75, in the Swiss Mission Archive, Lausanne, 3056.

Bibliography

Archives

South Africa
Pretoria: University of South Africa (UNISA),
   Junod Collection, two boxes
Johannesburg: University of the Witwatersrand, William Cullen Library:
   A.179 American Zulu Mission
   Archives of the Swiss Mission in South Africa (UW.SMA)
Cape Town: University of Cape Town (UCT), manuscripts division:
   Papers of James Stewart (SP), correspondence with Robert Mashaba
   Bolus Collection
Cape Town: South African Museum
   Letterbooks of Roland Trimen
Pietermaritzburg: KwaZuluNatal Archives
   Secretary for Native Affairs (SNA)

United Kingdom:
Cambridge: Wren Library, Trinity College, University of Cambridge: Papers of Sir James Frazer, correspondence with H-A.Junod. (CU.FP)
Oxford: Rhodes House: Papers of the United Society for the Propagation of the Gospel
London: National Archives:
   Foreign Office (FO), British Consul in Lourenço Marques

Switzerland
Lausanne: Département Missionnaire: Archives of the Swiss Mission in South Africa (SMA)
   Various boxes
Geneva: Botanical Conservatory. Boissier Herbarium (BCG:BH) Barbey Collection
Geneva: Cantonal and University Library: Papers of René Claparèdes. Correspondence with H-A.Junod
Geneva: Musée ethnologique: Papers of Prof. Pittard: correspondence with H-A.Junod
Geneva: Fondation pour l'histoire des Suisses à l'étranger: correspondence, cuttings, private diary of Georges Liengme
Neuchâtel: University and Cantonal Library:
   Papers of Philippe Godet (MS 3164)
   Archives of the Geographical Society of Neuchâtel: correspondence with H-A.Junod and G. Liengme (SGN)
Neuchâtel: City Archives: Papers of the Société de Belles-Lettres
Neuchâtel Ethnographic Museum: Archives of the Congrès internationale d'anthropologie et d'ethnographie, 1-5 juin 1914
   Correspondence concerning artifacts

United States
New Haven, CT: Harvard University, Archives of the American Board Mission (ABM)

Journals

L'Afrique explorée et civilisée (Geneva)
Bulletin de la mission vaudoise (*BMV*)
Bulletin de la mission romande (*BMR*)
Bulletin de la mission Suisse (*BMS*)
Bulletin de la société neuchâteloise de géographie (*BSNG*)
Bulletin de la société des sciences naturelles de Neuchâtel (*BSNN*)
Bulletin de la société vaudoise des sciences naturelles (*BSVSN*)
Cape Monthly Magazine (*CMM*)
L'Education chrétienne (Lausanne)
Le Globe (Geographical Society, Geneva)
International Review of Missions (*IMR*)
Liberté Chrétienne
La Messagère du monde païen (*MMP*)
Missionary Herald (Boston, MA)
Musée neuchâtelois (*MN*)
Nouvelles de nos missionnaires (Neuchâtel) (*NM*)
Le Rameau de sapin (Neuchâtel)
Revue de Belles-Lettres (Neuchâtel)
Revue missionnaire (Lausanne)

Selected Books and Articles

Ade Ajayi, J.F. *Christian Missions in Nigeria, 1841-1891: the Making of a New Elite* (Evanston, IL, 1965).
Agassiz, Louis 'The diversity of the human races' in *Christian Examiner* (1850) 49.
— 'Sketch of the Natural Provinces of the animal world and their relation to the different types of man' in J. C. Nott and George Gliddon (eds) *Types of Mankind* (Philadelphia, PA, 1854).
Agassiz, Elizabeth Cory *Louis Agassiz: his Life and Correspondence* (Boston, MA, 1885).
Anon., *The Mission to Umzila's Kingdom* (Boston, MA, 1882).
Anon., *Chez les Gouamba: glanures dans le champ de la mission romande* (Lausanne, n.d., c. 1893).
Anon., *Evangélisation des Païens au sud-est de l'Afrique par les églises libres de la Suisse romande* (exposition Nationale Suisse, Genève, 1896).
Arlettaz, Gérald et al., *Les Suisses dans le miroir: les expositions nationales suisses* (Lausanne, 1991).
Aston, Nigel *Christianity and Revolutionary Europe, c.1750–1830* (Cambridge, 2002).
Ayandele, E.A. *The Missionary Impact on Modern Nigeria, 1842–1914* (London, 1966).
Bank, Andrew *Bushmen in a Victorian World: the Remarkable Story of the Bleek-Lloyd Collection of Bushman Folklore* (Cape Town, 2006).
Barkan, Elazar and Ronald Bush (eds), *Prehistories of the Future: The Primitivist Project and the Culture of Modernism* (Stanford, CA, 1995).
Barnard, Alan, *History and Theory in Anthropology* (Cambridge, 2000).
Baud-Bovy, Daniel, Paul Bessire, Charly Clerk (eds), *La Vie romantique au pays romand* (Lausanne, 1930).
Bayly, C.A. *The Birth of the Modern World 1780–1914* (Oxford, 2004).
Beinart, William 'Men, Science, Travel and Nature in the Eighteenth and Nineteenth-century Cape', *Journal of Southern African Studies* (1998) 24, 4.
Berchtold, Alfred *La Suisse romande au Cap du vingtième siècle* (Lausanne, 1966).
Berthoud, Gérald 'Entre l'anthropologue et le missionnaire: la contribution d'Henri-Alexandre Junod (1863–1934)' in *Réseaux* (1985) 8.
Berthoud, Henri *La Question ecclésiastique du Canton de Vaud* (Lausanne, 1845).
— 'Quelques remarques sur la famille des langues bantous et sur la langue tzonga en particulier', in Xe *Congrès International des Orientalistes, 1894* (Leiden, 1896).

— 'Deux problèmes hydrographiques du pays de Gaza', *Bulletin de la société neuchâteloise de géographie* (1904) 15.
Berthoud, Paul 'Grammatical note on the Gwamba language in South Africa', *Journal of the Royal Asiatic Society*, (1884) 16.
— *La Mission romande et la baie de Delagoa* (Lausanne, 1888).
— *Les Nègres gouamba ou les vingt premières années de la mission romande* (Lausanne, 1896).
— 'Tableaux comparatifs. Résultats des observations météorologiques faites resp. à la station missionnaire de Lourenço Marques à 53 mètres d'altitude, et de l'Observatoire de Tananarive, à 1400 mètres d'altitude', *Bulletin de la société neuchâteloise de géographie* (1901) XII.
— *Considérations sur la Constitution des églises indigènes dans la mission romande* (Neuchâtel, 1912).
Berthoud, Paul and Eugènie, *Lettres missionnaires: 1873–1879 de M. et Mmme Paul Berthoud* (Lausanne, 1900), with an introduction and notes by Arthur Grandjean.
Berthoud-Junod, Ruth *Du Transvaal à Lourenço Marques: lettres de Mme Ruth Berthoud-Junod* (Lausanne, 1904).
Bill, Mary C. *Tsonga Bibliography 1883–1983* (Johannesburg, 1983).
— 'Berthoud's *Leçons de shigwamba* (1883): the first Tsonga grammar' in A. Traill, R. Vossen, M. Biesele (eds) *The Complete Linguist* (Cologne, 1995).
— 'Tsonga literatures: the future of a memory', *Le Fait Missionnaire* (2000) 9, June.
Bleek, Wilhelm *The Languages of Mozambique. Vocabularies of the dialects of Lourenço Marques, Inhambane etc drawn up from the manuscript of Dr. W. Peters ... and from other materials* (London, 1856).
— 'South African languages and books', *Cape Monthly Magazine* (1858) 3.
— *A Comparative Grammar of South African Languages* (Cape Town, 1862–69).
— *On the Origins of Language* (New York, 1869).
Boeyens, Jan "Black Ivory': The indenture system and slavery in Zoutpansberg, 1848–1867' in E. Eldredge and F. Morton (eds), *Slavery in South Africa: Captive Labour on the Dutch Frontier* (Boulder, CO, 1994).
Bordeaux, H. 1920. Preface to Emile Javelle, *Souvenirs d'un Alpiniste* (1920).
Bost, Ami *Letters and Biography of Félix Neff, Protestant Missionary in Switzerland, the department of Isère and the High Alps* (trans. Margaret Anne Wyatt) (London, 1843).
— *Visite dans la portion des Hautes-Alpes de France qui fut le champ des travaux de Félix Neff* (Geneva, 1841).
Bourdieu, Pierre 'Participant Objectivation', *Journal of the Royal Anthropological Institute* (2003) 9.
Bowler, Peter J. *The Environmental Sciences* (London, 1992).
— *Evolution: the history of an idea* (London, 3rd edn, 2003).
Breckenridge, Keith 'Love letters and Amanuenses: Beginning the cultural history of the working class private sphere in southern Africa, 1900–1933', *Journal of Southern African Studies*, (2000) 26, 2.
Bridel, E. *Résumé de l'histoire des écoles du dimanche dans le canton de Vaud* (Lausanne, 1927).
Bridel, Philippe 'Théologiens, moralistes et philosophes' in Baud-Bovy et al. (eds), *La Vie romantique* (op. cit.).
Bridel, Yves and Roger Francillon, *La 'Bibliothèque universelle' (1815–1924): Miroir de la sensibilité romande au XIXe siècle* (Lausanne, 1998).
Brooke, J. H. *Science and Religion: some historical perspectives* (London, 1991).
Brown, Stewart J. and Michael Fry (eds), *Scotland in the Age of Disruption* (Edinburgh, 1993).
Bryce, James *Impressions of South Africa* (3rd edn, London, 1899).
Bullard, Alice *Exile to Paradise: Savagery and Civilization in Paris and the South Pacific, 1790-1900* (Stanford, CA, 2000).
Burckhardt, J. 'Society & Festivals' in *The Civilization of the Renaissance in Italy* (Leipzig, n.d.).
Burrow, J. W. *The Crisis of Reason: European Thought, 1848–1914* (New Haven, CT, and London, 2000).
Caldas Xavier, A.A. 'Reconhecimento do Limpopo: os territorios ao sul do Save e os Vatuas' in *Boletim da Sociedade de Geografia de Lisboa* (1894) 3.
Carruthers, Jane 'Friedrich Jeppe: Mapping the Transvaal c.1850–1899', *Journal of Southern African Studies* (2003) 29, 4.

Cart, Jacques *Histoire du mouvement religieux et ecclésiastique dans le canton de Vaud pendant la première moitié du XIXième siècle* (Lausanne, 1870–80), 6 vols.
Carter, P. *The Road to Botany Bay: An Exploration of Landscape and History* (New York, 1988).
Casalis, Eugène *Les Bassoutos ou vingt-trois années d'études et d'observations au sud de l'Afrique* (Paris, 1859).
Cell, John *The Highest Stage of White Supremacy: the Origins of Segregation in South Africa and in the American South* (New York, 1982).
Centlivres, Pierre 'Le rendez-vous manqué: Van Gennep et la première chaire d'ethnologie de Neuchâtel (1912–1915)' in M. Gonseth, J. Hainard, R. Kaehr (eds), *Cent ans d'ethnographie sur la colline de Saint-Nicolas 1904–2004* (Neuchâtel, 2005).
Centlivres, P. and M. Fleury, *De l'église d'état à l'église nationale (1839–1863)* (Lausanne, 1963).
Centlivres, R. and H. Meylan (eds), *L'église vaudoise dans la tempête: lettres choisies de Samson Vuilleumier 1843–1846* (Lausanne, 1947).
Centlivres P. and P. Vaucher, 'Les tribulations d'un ethnographe en Suisse: Arnold van Gennep à Neuchâtel (1912–1915)', *Gradhiva* (1994) 15.
Chatelain, Ch. W. and H.-A. Junod, *A Pocket Dictionary, Thonga (Shangaan) -English; English-Thonga (Shangaan) preceded by an Elementary Grammar* (Lausanne, 1909).
Chidester, David *Savage Systems: Colonialism and Comparative Religion in Southern Africa* (Charlottesville, VA, 1996).
Clements, Keith *Faith on the Frontier: A Life of J. H. Oldham* (Geneva, 1999).
Clifford, James *Person and Myth: Maurice Leenhardt in the Melanesian World* (Berkeley, CA and Los Angeles, 1982).
Coetzee, J. M. *White Writing: On the Culture of Letters in South Africa* (New Haven, CT, 1988).
Cohen, W. B. *The French Encounter with Africans* (Bloomington, IN, and London, 1980).
Cohn, Bernard S. *An Anthropologist among the Historians and Other Essays* (Oxford, 1987).
— *Colonialism and its Forms of Knowledge: the British in India* (Princeton, NJ, 1996).
Comaroff, Jean *Body of Power, Spirit of Resistance* (Chicago, IL, 1985).
Comaroff, John and Jean *Ethnography and the Historical Imagination* (Boulder, CO, 1992).
— *Of Revelation and Revolution* I *Christianity, Colonialism and Consciousness in South Africa* (Chicago, IL, 1991); II, *The Dialectics of Modernity on a South African Frontier* (Chicago, IL, 1997).
Coombes, Annie *Reinventing Africa: Museums, Material Culture and Popular Imagination* (New Haven, CT, 1994).
Cooper, Frederick and Anne Stoler (eds), *Tensions of Empire: Colonial cultures in a Bourgeois World* (Berkeley, CA, 1997).
Couzens, Tim *Murder at Morija* (Johannesburg, 2003).
Cruz e Silva, Teresa *Protestant Churches and the Formation of Political Consciousness in Southern Mozambique (1930–1974)* (Basel, 2001), ed. Didier Péclard.
Cust, Robert *A Sketch of the Modern Languages of Africa* (London, 1883), 2 vols.
Darnton, Robert *The Great Cat Massacre* (New York, 1985).
— 'History of Reading' in Peter Burke (ed.), *New Perspectives on Historical Writing* (Polity Press, Cambridge, 1991).
Delmont, E. and J. Dubow 'Thinking through landscape: colonial spaces and legacies' in the exhibition catalogue *Panoramas of Passage: changing landscapes of South Africa* (Johannesburg and Washington, D.C., 1995).
Desmond, Aidrian and James Moore, *Darwin* (London, 1991).
Detraz, C., Crettaz, B. and E. DaLan, *Suisse, mon beau village: regards sur l'exposition nationale de 1896* (Geneva, 1983).
De Vaal, J. B. 'Die rol van João Albasini in die geskiedenis van dis Transvaal', *South African Archives Yearbook* (Pretoria) 1953, I.
Dias, Nélia 'Langues inférieures, langues supérieures' in Claude Blanckaert (ed.) *Des Sciences contre l'homme*, I, *Classer, hiérarchiser, exclure* (Paris 1993).
Distant, W-L. *A Naturalist in the Transvaal* (London, 1892).
Dubow, Saul *Illicit Union: Scientific Racism in Modern South Africa* (Johannesburg, 1995),.
— 'Earth history, Natural history, and Prehistory at the Cape, 1860–1875', *Comparative Studies in Society and History* (2004).

— (ed.) *Science and Society in Southern Africa* (Manchester, 2000).
Ducreux, M. 'Reading unto Death: Books and Readers in eighteenth century Bohemia' in R. Chartier (ed.), *The Culture of Print: Power and the Uses of Print in Early Modern Europe* (Oxford, 1989).
Dufour, Christophe and J-P. Haenni, *Musée d'histoire naturelle de Neuchâtel* (Hauterive, Neuchâtel, 1985).
Earthy, Dorothy *Valenge Women: The Social and Economic Life of the Valenge Women of Portuguese East Africa* (London, 1933).
Elbourne, Elizabeth 'Words made flesh: Christianity, Modernity, and Cultural colonialism in the work of Jean and John Comaroff', *American Historical Review* (2003) 108, 2.
Elphick, Rick and Rodney Davenport (eds), *Christianity in South Africa: A Political, Social and Cultural History* (Oxford, 1997).
Etherington, Norman *Preachers, Peasants and Politics in Southeast Africa, 1835–80* (London, 1978).
— 'Missionaries and the intellectual history of Africa', *Itinerario* (1983) 7, 2.
— 'Kingdoms of this World and the Next: Christian beginnings among Zulu and Swazi' in R. Elphick and R. Davenport (eds), *Christianity in South Africa* (op. cit.).
— 'Recent trends in the Historiography of Christianity in Southern Africa', *Journal of Southern African Studies* (1996) 22, 2.
Fabian, Johannes *Time and the Other: How Anthropology Makes its Object* (New York, 1983).
— 'Hindsight: Thoughts on Anthropology upon reading Francis Galton's Narrative of an Explorer in tropical South Africa (1853)' *Critique of Anthropology* (1987) 7, 2.
— *Language and Colonial Power: the Appropriation of Swahili in the Former Belgian Congo, 1880–1938* (Cambridge, [1986], 1991).
— *Out of Our Minds: Reason and Madness in the Exploration of Central Africa* (Berkeley, Los Angeles, CA, and London, 2000).
Favre, Edouard *François Coillard: missionnaire au Lessouto* (Paris, 1912).
— *Notice sur la mission vaudoise chez les Magwamba* (Lausanne, 1883).
Finnegan, Ruth *Literacy and Orality: studies in the technology of communication* (Oxford, 1988).
Forel, A. *Mémoires* (Neuchâtel, 1941).
Forster, Peter G. *T. Cullen Young: Missionary and Anthropologist* (Hull, 1989).
Freire d'Andrade, A and J. Serrano 'Exploraçoes Portugueses em Lourenco Marques e Inhambane', *Boletim da Sociedade de Geógrafia de Lisboa* (1894) 5, 13.
Frieder, Ludwig and Afe Adogame (eds), *European Traditions in the Study of Religion in Africa* (Wiesbaden, 2004).
Friesen, J. Stanley *Missionary Responses to Tribal Religions at Edinburgh, 1910* (New York, 1996).
Fritsch, Gustave *Die Eingeborenen Süd-Afrika's* (Breslau, 1872).
Gaitskell, Deborah 'Religion embracing science? Female missionary ventures in southern African anthropology: Dora Earthy and Mozambique, 1917–1933' Basel Afrika Bibliographien (1998) working paper no. 5.
Gay, Peter *Pleasure Wars* (New York, 1999).
Godet, Frédéric 'Les six jours de la création' in his *Etudes bibliques* (Neuchâtel and Paris, 1889).
Godet, Philippe *Frédéric Godet: 1812–1900* (Neuchâtel, 1913).
Goody, Jack *The Domestication of the Savage Mind* (Cambridge, 1977).
Goody, Jack and Ian Watt 'The consequences of literacy' in Goody (ed.), *Literacy in Traditional Societies* (Cambridge, 1968).
Gordon, Robert 'Early Social Anthropology in South Africa' *African Studies* (1990) 49, 1.
Gossman, Lionel *Basel in the Age of Burckhardt: A Study in Unseasonable Ideas* (Chicago, IL, 2000).
Grandjean, Arthur 'Notice relative à la carte du Nkomati inférieur et du district portugais de Lourenço Marques', *Bulletin de la société neuchâteloise de géographie* (1892–93) vii.
— (ed.) *Chez les Gouamba: glanures dans le champ de la mission romande* (Lausanne, 1893).
— 'Le vieil évangile a-t-il fait son temps?' (c.1898, Société de traités religieux, 1907).
— *Labours, semailles, et moissons dans le champ de la mission romande* (Lausanne, 1898).
— *L'Union chrétienne et la Mission* (Lausanne, 1899).
— 'L'invasion des Zulu dans le sud-est africain', *Bulletin de la société géographique de Neuchâtel*

(1899) 11.
— *La Mission romande: ses racines dans le sol suisse romand. Son épanouissement dans la race thonga* (Lausanne, 1917).
— *La Race thonga et la Suisse romande* (Lausanne, 1921).
Greene, Sandra *Sacred Sites and the Colonial Encounter: A history of meaning and memory in Ghana* (Bloomington, IN, 2002).
Guichonnet, P. 'L'Homme devant les Alpes' in Guichonnet (ed.), *Histoire et civilisation des Alpes* II, *Destin humain* (Toulouse and Lausanne, 1980).
Guy, Jeff *The Heretic: A study of the life of John William Colenso, 1814–1883* (Pietermaritzburg, 1983).
— 'Class, Imperialism and Literary Criticism: William Ngidi, John Colenso and Matthew Arnold', *Journal of Southern African Studies* (1997) 23, 2.
Guyot, Arnold *Creation or the Biblical cosmogony in the light of modern science* (New York, 1884).
Hall, Catherine *Civilizing Subjects: metropole and colony in the English imagination, 1830–1867* (Cambridge, 2002).
Hammann, Gottfried 'L'église réformée et les communautés protestantes' in Jean-Marc Barrelet (ed.) *Histoire du pays de Neuchâtel*, Vol III: *de 1815 à nos jours* (Hauterive, Neuchâtel, 1993).
Hammond-Took, W. D. *Imperfect Interpreters: South Africa's Anthropologists 1920–1990* (Johannesburg, 1997).
Harries, Patrick 'Exclusion, Classification and Internal Colonialism: the emergence of ethnicity among the Tsonga-speakers of South Africa' in Leroy Vail (ed.), *The Creation of Tribalism in Southern Africa* (London and Los Angeles, CA, 1989).
— *Work, Culture and Identity: Migrant Labourers in Mozambique and South Africa, c.1860–1910* (London, Portsmouth, NH, Johannesburg, 1994).
— 'Missionaries, Marxists and Magic: Power and the Politics of Literacy in South-East Africa', *Journal of Southern African Studies* (2001) 27, 3.
— 'Dompter les sauvages domestiques: le rôle de l'Afrique dans les écoles du dimanche en Suisse romande, 1860–1920' in Sandra Bott et al. (eds), *Suisse-Afrique (18e–20e siècles): De la traite des Noirs à la fin du régime de l'apartheid* (Berlin, 2005).
— 'Primitivisme au musée: la récolte des missionnaires' in Marc-Olivier Gonseth, Jacques Hainard and Roland Kaehr (eds), *Cent ans d'ethnographie sur la colline de Saint-Nicolas, 1904–2004* (Neuchâtel, 2005).
— 'Anthropology' in Norman Etherington (ed.), *Missions and Empire*, Oxford History of the British Empire. Companion series (Oxford, 2005).
— 'From the Alps to Africa: Swiss missionaries and the rise of anthropology' in Hellen Tilley and Robert Gordon (eds), *Anthropology, European Imperialism, and the Ordering of Africa* (Manchester, 2007).
Hastings, Adrian *The Church in Africa, 1450–1950* (Oxford, 1994).
Hawkins, Sean *Writing and Colonialism in Northern Ghana: the Encounter Between the LoDagaa and 'the Word on Paper'* (Toronto and London, 2002).
Hedges, David (ed.), *Historia de Moçambique* II (Maputo, 1999).
Heintze, Beatrix *Ethnographische Aneignungen: Deutsche Forschungsreisende in Angola* (Frankfurt-am-Main, 1999).
Helgesson, Alf *Church, State and People in Mozambique: an historical study with special emphasis on Methodist developments in the Inhambane Region* (Uppsala, 1994).
Herbert, Robert K. 'The political economy of language shift: language and gendered ethnicity in a Thonga community' in Raj Mesthrie (ed.), *Language in South Africa* (Cambridge, 2000).
Heusch, Luc de 'The Debt of the Maternal Uncle: Contribution to the Study of Complex Structures of Kinship', *Man* (1974) 9, 4.
— 'Heat, Physiology and Cosmogony: rites de passage among the Thonga' in I. Karp and C. S. Bird (eds), *Explorations in African Systems of Thought* (Bloomington, IN, 1979).
— *Sacrifice in Africa: a structuralist approach* (Manchester, 1985).
Hofmeyr, Isabel 'Building a nation from words: Afrikaans language, literature and ethnic identity' in S. Marks and S. Trapido (eds), *The Politics of Race, Class and Nationalism in Twentieth Century South Africa* (London, 1987).

— 'We Spend our Years as a Tale that is Told', Oral Historical Narrative in a South African Chiefdom (London, 1994).
— The Portable Bunyan: A Transnational History of The Pilgrim's Progress (Princeton, NJ, 2004).
Isaacman, Allen (ed.), The Life History of Raúl Honwana: an inside view of Mozambique from colonialism to independence, 1905–1975 (Boulder, CO and London, 1988).
Jacobs, Nancy J. 'The intimate politics of ornithology in colonial Africa', Comparative Studies in Society and History (2006) 48.
Jacottet, Edouard 'Moeurs, coutumes et superstitions des Ba-Souto', Bulletin de la société neuchâteloise de géographie (1897) IX.
Jacottet, Edouard with Z. Magoaela, A Grammar of the Sesuto Language (Johannesburg, 1927) (ed.) C. M. Doke.
James, Wendy 'The African ethnography in l'Année sociologique', L'Année sociologique (1998) 4, 1.
Jaques, Alexandre A. 'Terms of kinship and corresponding patterns of behaviour among the Thonga', Bantus Studies (1929) 3.
— 'A Survey of Shangana-Tsonga, Ronga and Tswa literature', Bantu Studies (1940) 14, 3.
Javelle, E. Souvenirs d'un Alpiniste (Lausanne and Paris, First edn, 1886, this edition 1920).
Jeanneret, Anne-Françoise 'Le développement de l'instruction' in Histoire du pays de Neuchâtel, III, (Neuchâtel, 1993).
Jeanneret, Philippe 'Les Ma-Khoça', Bulletin de la société neuchâteloise de géographie (1894).
Jequier, François 'Une Entreprise horlogère du Val-de-Travers: Fleurier Watch Co SA. De l'atelier familial du XIXe aux concentrations du XXe siècle' (Neuchâtel, 1972).
— 'Fondements ethiques et réalisations pratiques de patrons paternalistes en Suisse romande, XIXe-XXe siècles' in E. Aerts, C Beaud and J. Stenges (eds), Liberalism and Paternalism in the 19th Century (Brussels, 1990).
Joseph, J. Les écoles du dimanche de la Suisse romande (Lausanne, 1896).
Junod Henri (Sen.) 'Un récit neuchâtelois de la 2ième bataille de Vilmergue', Musée neuchâtelois, 1865.
— Du manque de pasteurs et des moyens d'y remédier (Neuchâtel, 1864).
— Guillaume Farel (Tonneins, 1872).
— Sermons (Neuchâtel, 1884).
— and A. Bouchardat (eds) L'Eau de vie, ses dangers (Paris, 1863).
Junod, Henri-Alexandre 'Le triton lobé' in Le Rameau de sapin (1879) 13, August.
— 'L'Erythronium dens canis.Linné' in Le Rameau de sapin (1882) 16, November.
— (étudiant) 'Les états de larve et de nymphe de l'hyponomeuta stannellus (Thunberg)' in Bulletin de la société neuchâteloise des sciences naturelles (1884) 14.
— 'Un très vieux livre neuchâtelois', Musée neuchâtelois (1889).
— 'Une moralité du XVIième siècle', Musée neuchâtelois (1889).
— 'Pays des Gouambas: difficultés de la langue', Revue des missions contemporaines (1890) II, août.
— 'Correspondances: de Rikatla à Marakouène', Bulletin de la société neuchâteloise de géographie (1891) 6.
— 'Observations métérologiques faites à Rikatla', Boletim da Sociedade de Geografia de Lisboa (1891) 10, 1.
— 'Sur quelques larves inédites de Rhopalocères', Bulletin de la société neuchâteloise des sciences naturelles (1891–92) 20.
— 'Correspondances de Rikatla', 23 November 1891, Bulletin de la société neuchâteloise de géographie (1892–93) vii.
— 'La possession chez les indigènes de Delagoa Bay' in Revue des missions contemporaines (1893) V, 18.
— Sipele sa Sironga: abecedaire et livre de lecture en dialecte ronga parlé aux environs de la baie de Delagoa (Lausanne, 1894).
— Grammaire ronga suivie d'un manuel de conversation et d'un vocabulaire ronga-portugais-français-anglais, pour exposer et illustrer les lois du ronga, langage parlé par les indigènes du district de Lourenço Marques (Lausanne, 1896).
— La tribu et la langue thonga: avec quelques échantillons du folklore thonga (Lausanne, 1896).
— 'Galagala: tableaux de moeurs de la tribu des Rongas', Bibliothèque universelle et revue suisse (1896) II.

- 'Le climat de la baie de Delagoa', *Bulletin de la société des sciences naturelles de Neuchâtel* (1896–7) 25.
- 'L'art divinatoire ou la science des osselets chez les Rongas de la baie de Delagoa', *Bulletin de la société neuchâteloise de géographie* (1896–7) 9.
- 'Quelques contes africains', *Bibliothèque universelle et revue suisse* (1897) VII.
- *Les Chants et les contes des Ba-Ronga de la baie de Delagoa* (Lausanne, 1897).
- *Nouveaux contes ronga* (Neuchâtel, 1898).
- 'Les Ba-Ronga. Etude ethnographique sur les indigènes de la baie de Delagoa', *Bulletin de la société neuchâteloise de geographie* (1898) X.
- 'Quelques lettres d'Alphonse Bourquin à Fritz Courvoisier: à propos des événements de 1831', *Musée neuchâtelois* (1898).
- 'A propos de la traduction de la Bible en thonga', *La Liberté chrétienne* (1898) pp.579-95, 598-607.
- 'La faune entomologique de Delagoa – *Lépidoptères*', *Bulletin de la société neuchâteloise des sciences naturelles* (1898-99) 27.
- 'La faune entomologique du Delagoa – *Coléoptères*', *Bulletin de la société vaudoise des sciences naturelles* (1899) 35.
- 'Some remarks on the folklore of the Ba-Thonga', *Folk-lore* (1903) 14, 2, June.
- *Bukhaneli bya Xirjonga* (Lausanne, 1903).
- *Butibi: Notions of Elementar[y] Science; Noções de Sciencia Elementár* (Lausanne, 1904).
- 'The Native languages and Native education', *Journal of the Royal African Society* (1905) XVII, October.
- 'The Ba-Thonga of the Transvaal', *Addresses and Papers of the South African Association for the Advancement of Science*, 1905.
- 'The theory of witchcraft amongst South African natives', *Report of the South African Association for the Advancement of Science* 1905/6.
- 'Sécheresse et costumes païenes', *Bulletin de la mission romande* (1906) 19, 238.
- 'The best means of preserving the traditions and customs of the various SA native races', *Report of the South Africa Association for the Advancement of Science* 1907.
- 'The fate of the widows amongst the Ba-Ronga', *Report of the South African Association for the Advancement of Science* (1908).
- 'Les conceptions physiologiques des Bantous sud-africains et leurs tabous', *Revue des études ethnographiques et sociologiques* (1910).
- 'Sorcellerie d'Afrique et sorcellerie d'Europe: étude d'ethnographie comparée', *Foi et Vie* (1910) 13.
- 'Deux enterrements à 20,000 ans de distance', *Anthropos*, (1910) v.
- *Les Perplexités du vieux Nkolélé* (Lausanne, 1910).
- *L'homme au grand coutelas* (Lausanne, 1910).
- 'Fazana. Scènes de moeurs sud-africaines', *La Semaine littéraire* (1910) pp. 536-64.
- *Zidji: Etude de moeurs sud-africaines* (St. Blaise, 1911).
- 'Fritz Courvoisier et sa famille en 1831', *Musée neuchâtelois* (1912).
- *The Life of a South African Tribe* (Neuchâtel, 1st edn, 1912–13), 2 vols.
- 'The conditions of the Natives of South-East Africa in the sixteenth century according to the early Portuguese documents', *South African Association for the Advancement of Science* (1913) 10.
- 'God's ways in the Bantu soul', *International Review of Missions* (1914) 3.
- 'Native Customs in relation to small-pox amongst the Ba-Ronga', *South African Association for the Advancement of Science* (1918) 15.
- 'The Magic conception of nature amongst Bantus', *South African Journal of Science* (1920) 17, November.
- 'Some features of the religion of the Ba-Venda', *South African Association for the Advancement of Science* (1921) 17, 2.
- *Causeries sur l'Afrique à l'usage des cercles d'étude missionnaire pour enfants, des écoles de dimanche, des Unions Cadettes et des familles* (Lausanne, [1917], 1922).
- 'Bantu Heathen Prayers' *International Review of Missions* (1922) 11, 44.

— 'L'éducation en Afrique', *Revue internationale de la Croix-Rouge* (1923) May.
— *Domesticité africaine* (Lausanne, 1923).
— *La jeteuse de sorts* (Lausanne, 1923).
— 'L'education en Afrique', *Revue internationale de la Croix-Rouge* (1923) 53.
— 'Le totemisme chez les Thongas, les Pedis et les Vendas', *Le Globe* (1924) 63.
— 'La religion des primitifs' in *La valeur universelle du christianisme*: travaux présentés à la Conférence de Genève, 1923 de l'Association chrétienne d'étudiants de la Suisse romande (Lausanne, 1924).
— 'Le mouvement de Mourimi: un réveil au sein de l'animisme thonga', *Journal de Psychologie Normale et Pathologique* (1924) December.
— 'La divination au moyen de tablettes d'ivoire chez les Pedis', *Bulletin de la société neuchâtelois de géographie* (1924) 34.
— 'La religion des primitifs', *Christianisme social* (1924) 6.
— 'L'église ethiopienne', *Revue missionnaire* (1924) 1.
— 'La genèse des contes africains: ou comme quoi les Noirs inventent des contes sans le savoir', *Folk-lore* (1924) 35.
— *Le Pasteur Calvin Mapopé* (Lausanne, 1925).
— 'Les coutumes matrimoniales des Thonga', *Bulletin de la mission romande* (1926) 36.
— *The Life of a South African Tribe* (2nd edn, London, 1926–27), 2 vols.
— 'Moral sense among the Bantu', *International Review of Missions* (1927) 16, 61.
— *Theatre africain* (Lausanne, 1928).
— 'Le mécontentement aux colonies', *Christianisme social* (1928) 3, April-May.
— 'Grundlagen für die Missionsarbeit in Südafrika' in H.-A. Junod et al. *Fünfzig Jahre Schweizer Mission in Südafrika* (Zürich, 1928).
— 'Une question de morale coloniale', *Stockholm International Review for the Social Activities of the Churches* (1929) 3.
— 'La seconde école de circoncision des Ba-Khaha du nord du Transvaal', *Journal of the Royal Anthropological Institute* (1929) 59.
— 'L'alcoolisme chez les Noirs africains', *Bibliothèque universelle et revue de Genève* (1930) September.
— 'La supplique du Liberia', *Bureau international pour la défense des indigènes* (1931) October.
— *L'année de la famine* (Lausanne, 1930).
— 'Comment juger le Noir africain?', *Africa* (1931) 4, 3.
— *Le Noir africain. Comment faut-il le juger?* (Lausanne, 1931).
— *Le problème indigène dans l'union sud-africaine* (Lausanne, 1931).
— 'Le sacrifice dans l'ancestrolâtrie sud-africaine', *Archives de psychologie* (1932) 23.
— *Ernest Creux et Paul Berthoud: Les fondateurs de la mission suisse en Afrique du Sud* (Lausanne, 1933).
Junod, Henri-Alexandre and Hans Schinz 'Zur Kenntnis der Pflanzenwelt der Delago-Bay', *Bulletin de l'Herbier Boissier* (1899) 7, 2.
Junod, Henri-Alexandre and O. de Schulthess-Schindler 'La faune entomologique du Delagoa. Orthoptères', *Bulletin de la société vaudoise des sciences naturelles* (1899) 132.
Junod, Henri-Alexandre and A. L. Montandon 'La faune entomologique du Delagoa. Hémiptères', *Bulletin de la société vaudoise des sciences naturelles* (1899) 132.
Junod, Henri-Alexandre and A. de Schulthess-Schindler 'La faune entomologique du Delagoa. Hyménopteres', *Bulletin de la société vaudoise des sciences naturelles* (1899) 133.
Junod, Henri-Philippe 'L'Exploitation coloniale en Afrique du Sud', *Le Christianisme Social* (1930) 5, juillet.
— *Henri-A.Junod: missionnaire et savant, 1863–1934* (Lausanne, 1934).
— 'Les VaNdu de l'Afrique orientale portugaise', *Bulletin de la société neuchâteloise de géographie* (1935) 4, 1.
— 'Les cas de possession et l'exorcisme chez les Vandau', *Africa* (1935) 8, 3.
— 'Henri-Alexandre Junod (1863–1934): Bibliographie de ses ouvrages', *Acta Africana* (1965) 4, 2.
— *Matimu Ya Vatsonga 1498–1650* (Braamfontein, 1977).
Junod, Henri-Philippe and Alexandre A. Jaques, *Vulthari bya vatonga (matshangana): the Wisdom of the Thonga-Shangaan people* (Pretoria, 1936).

Junod, Violaine 'H-A.Junod' in *International Encyclopaedia of the Social Sciences* (1968) vol 8.
Kaehr, Roland 'Léopard dévorant ... un Anglais', *Bibliothèque et Musées* (Neuchâtel, 1990).
Kaeser, Marc-Antoine *L'Univers du préhistorien: science, foi et politique dans l'oeuvre et la vie d'Edouard Desor (1811–1882)* (Paris, 2004).
Knox-Shaw, Peter *Explorers in English Fiction* (New York, 1986).
Koelle, Sigismund *Polyglotta Africana* ((London, 1854).
Kuklick, Henrika *The Savage Within: The Social History of British Anthropology, 1885–1945* (Cambridge, 1991).
Kuper, Adam *Anthropologists and Anthropology: The British School 1922–72* (1973, London, 1976).
— *The Invention of Primitive Society* (London, 1988).
— 'Project of a cosmopolitan anthropology' in *Among the Anthropologists: History and Context in Anthropology* (London, 1999).
— 'South African Anthropology: An Inside Job', *Paideuma* (1999) 45.
Landau, Paul *The Realm of the Word: Language, Gender and Christianity in a Southern African Kingdom* (Portsmouth NH, 1995).
— 'Hegemony and History in J. and J. L. Comaroff's *Of Revelation and Revolution*' *Africa* (2000) 70, 3.
Lejeune, Dominique *Les Sociétés de géographies en France* (Paris, 1993).
Liengme, Georges 'Notice de géographie médicale: quelques observations sur les maladies des indigènes des provinces de Lourenço Marques et Gaza', *Bulletin de la société neuchâteloise de géographie* (1894–95) VIII.
— 'Un potentat Africain: Goungounyana et son regne', *Bulletin de la société neuchâteloise de géographie* (1901) 13.
Liesegang, Gerhard 'Notes on the internal structure of the Gaza kingdom of Southern Mozambique, 1840–1895' in J. Peires (ed.), *Before and After Shaka* (Grahamstown, 1981).
Lindberg, D. C. and Ronald L. Numbers (eds), *God and Nature: Historical essays on the encounter between Christianity and science* (Berkeley and Los Angeles, CA, 1984).
Livingstone, David N. *Darwin's Forgotten Defenders: The Encounter between Evangelical Theology and Evolutionary Thought* (Edinburgh, 1987).
Livingstone, David N., D. G. Hart and M. A. Noll, *Evangelicals and Science in Historical Perspective* (New York, 1999).
Longden, W. H. C. *Red Buffalo: The Story of Will Longden* (Cape Town, 1950).
MacCulloch, Diarmaid *Reformation: Europe's House Divided 1490–1700* (London, 2003).
MacKenzie, John M. (ed.), *Imperialism and Popular Culture* (Manchester, 1986).
— *Imperialism and the Natural World* (Manchester, 1990).
— 'Empire and Metropolitan Cultures' in Andrew Porter (ed.), *The Oxford History of the British Empire, III, The Nineteenth Century* (Oxford, 1999).
MacLeod, Roy and Philip F. Rehbock (eds), *Darwin's Laboratory: Evolutionary Theory and Natural History in the Pacific* (Honolulu, 1994).
Macmillan, W. M. *Africa Emergent* (London, [1937], 1949.
Maggetti, Daniel *L'Invention de la littérature romande, 1830–1910* (Lausanne, 1995).
Mitchell, W. T. J. (ed.), *Landscape and Power* (Chicago, IL, 1994).
Malton, W. C. H. *The Story of the Diocese of Lebombo* (London, 1912).
Mapopé, Calvin 'Comment les peuples africains pourront-ils trouver le salut?', *Revue missionnaire* (1925) 5, April.
Martins, Rocha *Historia das Colonias Portuguesas* (Lisbon, 1933).
Mathebula, Mandla *800 Years of Tsonga History (1200–2000)* (Polokwane, 2002).
Mauss, Marcel *Oeuvres 3. Cohésion sociale et divisions de la sociologie* (Paris, 1969).
Mayr, Ernst 'Agassiz, Darwin and Evolution' in Mayr, *Evolution and the Diversity of Life* (Cambridge, MA, 1976).
Means, John O. *Umzila's Kingdom: A Field for Christian Missions* (Boston, MA, 1880).
Menoud, Philippe H. 'L'église réformée neuchâteloise il y a cent ans', *Musée neuchâtelois* (1973) 10.
Meyer, Birgit *Translating the Devil: Religion and Modernity Among the Ewe in Ghana* (Edinburgh, 1999).

Miller, David Philip and Peter Hans Reill (eds), *Visions of Empire: Voyages, Botany and Representations of Nature* (Cambridge, 1996).

Miller, Jon *The Social Control of Religious Zeal: A Study of Organizational Contradictions* (New Brunswick, NJ, [1994], 2004).

Monnier, Nicolas 'Stratégie missionnaire et tactiques d'appropriation indigènes: La Mission romande au Mozambique 1888–1896' in *Le Fait Missionnaire* (1995) 2, December.

— 'De la bière dans les théières: Essai sur les fondements et l'avenir du partenariat missionnaire Afrique du Sud-Suisse', *Le Fait Missionnaire* (1999) 8.

Monteiro, Rose *Delagoa Bay, its Natives and Natural History* (London, 1891).

Monvert, C. *Histoire de la fondation de l'église évangélique neuchâteloise indépendente de l'état* (Neuchâtel, 1896).

Moorhead, Caroline *Dunant's Dream: War, Switzerland and the History of the Red Cross* (London, 1998).

Mudimbe, V. Y. *The Invention of Africa* (Bloomington, IN, 1988).

Murchison, R. 'On the antiquity of the physical geography of inner Africa', *Journal of the Royal Geographic Society* (1864) 34.

Ngoenha, Severinho *Estatuto e Axiologia de Educaçao: o Paradigma tico Questionamento de Missao Suiça* (Maputo, 2000).

Niederer, A 'Mentalités et sensibilités' in Guichonnet ed., *Histoire et Civilisation des Alpes* (op. cit.).

Niehaus, Isak 'Ethnicity and the boundaries of belonging: reconfiguring Shangaan identity in the South African lowveld', *African Affairs* (2002) 101.

Nora, Pierre (ed.), *Les lieux de mémoire* (Paris, 1997), 3 vols.

Noronho, Eduardo *O districto de Lourenço Marques e a Africa do Sul* (Lisbon, 1895).

Nott, J. C. and George Gliddon (eds), *Types of Mankind* (Philadelphia, PA, 1854) .

Numbers, Ronald L. *Creation by Natural Law: Laplace's Nebular Hypothesis in American Thought* (Seattle and London, 1977).

— *The Creationists* (New York, 1992).

— 'Creating Creationism: Meanings and Uses since the Age of Agassiz' in D. N. Livingstone et al., *Evangelicals and Science in Historical Perspective* (op. cit.).

Numbers, Ronald L. and John Stenhouse (eds), *Disseminating Darwinism: The Role of Place, Race, Religion, and Gender* (Cambridge, 1999).

Olivier, Juste *Le canton de Vaud* (Lausanne, 1837), 2 vols.

Pavord, Anna *The Naming of Names: The Search for Order in the World of Plants* (London, 2005).

Peel, J. D. Y. *Religious Encounter and the Making of the Yoruba* (Bloomington, IN, 2000).

Pélissier, René *Naissance du Mozambique: résistances et révoltes anti-coloniales (1854-1918)* (Orgeval, 1984), 2 vols.

Pels, Peter 'Anthropology and Mission: towards a historical analysis of professional identity' in R. Bonsen, H. Marks, J. Miedema (eds), *The Ambiguity of Rapprochement: Reflections of anthropologists on their controversial relationship with missionaries* (Amsterdam, 1990).

— *A Politics of Presence: contacts between missionaries and Waluguru in late colonial Tanganyika* (Amsterdam, 1999).

Penvenne, Jeanne Marie 'João dos Santos Albasini (1876–1922): the contradictions of politics and identity in colonial Mozambique', *Journal of African History* (1996) 37, 3.

— *African Workers and Colonial Racism: Mozambican Strategies and struggles in Lourenço Marques, 1877–1962* (Portsmouth, NH, and London, 1995).

Perregaux, H. *Edmond Perregaux Missionnaire: d'après sa correspondance 1868–1905* (Neuchâtel, 1906).

Perrenoud, Marc 'Economie et société' in Jean-Marc Barrelet (ed)., *Histoire du Pays de Neuchâtel* III (Neuchâtel, 1993).

Pestre, Dominique 'Pour une histoire culturelle des sciences. Nouvelles définitions, nouveaux objets, nouvelles pratiques', *Annales*, HSS 1995.

Peters, W. C .H. *Naturwissenschaftliche Reise nach Mossambique in den Jahre 1842–1848 ausgeführt* (Berlin, 1861, 1864, 1868).

Peterson, Derek *Creative Writing: Translation, Bookkeeping, and the Work of Imagination in Colonial Kenya* (Portsmouth, NH, 2004).

Peterson, Derek and Jean Allman 'Introduction: New Directions in the History of Missions in Africa', *The Journal of Religious History* (1999) 23, 1.
Pitt, Alan 'The cultural impact of science in France: Ernest Renan and the vie de Jésus', *The Historical Journal* (2000) 43, 1.
Pittard, Eugène 'Contribution à l'étude anthropologique des BaRonga', *Bulletin de la société neuchâteloise de géographie* (1917) 26.
Porter, Andrew *Religion versus Empire? British Protestant missionaries and overseas expansion, 1700-1914* (Manchester, 2004).
— '"Cultural Imperialism" and Protestant Missionary enterprise, 1780–1914', *Journal of Imperial and Commonwealth History* (1997) 25, 3.
Porter, Roy and Miklaus Teich (eds), *The Enlightenment in National Context* (Cambridge, 1981).
Povey, J. 'Landscape in Early South African Poetry' in M. van Wyk Smith and D. McLennan (eds) *Olive Schreiner and After* (Cape Town, 1983).
Pratt, Mary Louise *Imperial Eyes: travel writing and transculturation* (London, 1992).
Pringle, E. L. L., G. A. Hening and J. B. Ball (eds), *Pennington's Butterflies of Southern Africa* (2nd edn, Cape Town, 1994).
Raison-Jourde, Françoise *Bible et Pouvoir à Madagascar au XIXe siècle: Invention d'une identité chrétienne et construction de l'état* (Paris, 1991).
Rambert, Eugène 'Le chevrier de Praz-de-Fort' in Rambert *Récits et Croquis* (Lausanne, [1865], 1889).
— *La Société vaudoise des science naturelles: sa fondation et son développement* (Lausanne, 1876).
— *Etudes d'histoire naturelle* (Lausanne, 1888).
— *Les Alpes suisses: études de littérature alpestre* (Lausanne, 1889).
— 'La Suisse romande' in Rambert *Poésies* (Lausanne, 3rd edn, 1895).
Rambert, Jean *Arthur Grandjean* (Lausanne, n.d., 1931?).
Ranger, Terence 'Missionaries, migrants and the Manyika: the invention of ethnicity in Zimbabwe' in Leroy Vail (ed.) *The Creation of Tribalism in Southern Africa* (Berkeley, CA, 1989).
— 'The local and the global in Southern African religious history' in Robert Hefner (ed.) *Conversion to Christianity: Historical and Anthropological Perspectives on a Great Transformation* (Los Angeles, CA, 1993).
— 'African views of the land: a research agenda', *Transformation* (2000) 44.
Reubi, Serge 'Aider l'Afrique et servir la science: Henri-Alexandre Junod, missionnaire et ethnographe (1863–1934)', *Revue historique neuchâteloise: musée neuchâtelois* (2004) 4.
De Reynold, Gonzague 'Notre Romantisme' in Daniel Baud-Bovy et al. (eds), *La Vie romantique* (op. cit.).
Reynolds, Pamela '"Not Known Because Not Looked For": Ethnographers listening to the young in Southern Africa', *Ethnos* (1995) 60, 3-4.
Ricard, Alan *The Languages and Literatures of Africa* (Oxford, 2004).
Rich, Paul 'The Appeal of Tuskegee: James Henderson, Lovedale, and the Fortunes of South African Liberalism, 1906–1930', *International Journal of African Historical Studies* (1987) 20.
de la Rive, G. (ed.), *Lettres missionnaires de M & Mme Paul Berthoud* (Lausanne, 1900).
Robert, Daniel *Les églises réformées en France 1800–1830* (Paris, 1961).
Roney, J. B. and M. I. Klause *The Identity of Geneva: the Christian Commonwealth, 1564–1864* (London, 1998).
Rossel, Virgile *Histoire littéraire de la Suisse romande* (Neuchâtel, 1903).
Rupke, Nicolaas A. *Richard Owen: Victorian Naturalist* (New Haven and London, 1994).
Said, Edward *Orientalism* (London, [1978], 1985).
Sales, Richard 'The Work of the American Board Mission in Inhambane' in Steve de Gruchy (ed.) *Changing Frontiers. The Mission Story of the UCCSA* (Gaberone, 1999).
Sanneh, Lamin *Translating the Message: The Missionary Impact on Culture* (Maryknoll, NY, 1989).
De Saussure, Horace-Benedict *Voyages dans les Alpes* (Geneva, [1834], 2002).
Schaetti, Eduard *Henry-A.Junod (1863–1934), Ein grosser Freund der Afrikaner* (Zürich, 1942).
Schama, Simon *Landscape and Memory* (London, 1995).
Schapera, Isaac 'The present state and future development of ethnographical research in South Africa', *Bantu Studies* (1934) 8.

— *The Bantu Tribes of South Africa* (London and Johannesburg, 1937).
Schaufelbuehl, Janick 'L'anti-esclavagisme suisse sous l'emprise du Réveil' in O. Pétré-Grenouilleau (ed.), *Abolitionnisme et Société: France, Portugal et Suisse, XVIIIe–XIXe siècles* (Paris, 2005).
Schinz, Hans and H.-A. Junod 'Zur Kenntnis der Pflanzenwelt der Delagoa-Bay' in *Mémoire de l'Herbier Boissier* (1900) 10.
Schlaefli-Glardon, E. 'De Valdezia à Lourenço Marques', *Bulletin de la société neuchâteloise de géographie* (1893) VII.
Schneider, Jürg and Ute Röschenthaler, Bernhard Gardi (eds), *Fotofieber: Bilder aus West- und Zentralafrika. Die Reisen von Carl Passavant 1883–1885* (Basel, 2005).
Sibeud, Emmanuelle *Une science impériale pour l'Afrique? La constitution des savoirs africanistes en France 1878-1930* (Paris, 2002).
Smith, Edwin W. *African Ideas of God* (London, 1950).
South African Native Races Committee (eds), *The Natives of South Africa* (London, 1901).
Stafford, Roderick *Sir Roderick Murchison: Scientific Exploration and Victorian Imperialism* (Cambridge, 1989).
— 'Annexing the landscapes of the past: British imperial geology in the nineteenth century' in J. M. MacKenzie (ed.), *Imperialism and the Natural World* (op. cit.).
— 'Scientific Exploration and Empire' in Andrew Porter (ed.), *The Oxford History of the British Empire: The Nineteenth Century* (Oxford, 1999).
Stepan, Nancy Leys 'Race and gender: the role of analogy in science' in David Theo Goldberg (ed.), *Anatomy of Racism* (Minneapolis, MN, 1990).
Stevenson-Hamilton, J. *The Low-Veld: Its Wild Life and its People* (London, [1929], 1934).
Stocking, George 'From Physics to Ethnology' in Stocking (ed.) *Race Culture and Evolution* (Chicago, IL, 1982 edn).
— *Victorian Anthropology* (New York, 1987).
— *After Tylor: British Social Anthropology, 1888–1951* (London, 1995).
Street, Brian *Cross-Cultural Approaches to Literacy* (Cambridge, 1993).
Stunt, Timothy C. F. 'Diversity and early strivings for unity in the early Swiss Réveil' in R. N. Swanston (ed.) *Studies in Church History* (1996) 32.
— *From Awakening to Secession: Radical Evangelicals in Switzerland and Britain, 1815–35* (Edinburgh, 2000).
Sundkler, Bengt and C. Steed, *A History of the Church in Africa* (Cambridge, 2000).
Sweet, James *Recreating Africa: Culture, kinship, and religion in the African-Portuguese World, 1441–1770* (Chapel Hill, NC, 2003).
Temperley, Howard *White Dreams, Black Africa: the Antislavery Expedition to the River Niger, 1841–1842* (New Haven, CT, and London, 1991).
Thorne, Susan *Congregational Missions and the Making of an Imperial Culture in Nineteenth-century England* (Stanford, CA 1999).
Thornton, John *The Kongolese Saint Anthony: Donna Beatrix Kimpa Vita and the Antonian Movement (1684–1706)* (Cambridge, 1998).
— *Africans and the Atlantic World, 1400–1800* (Cambridge, 1998).
Trivier, Paul *Album de la Mission romande: mission des églises libres de la Suisse romande* (Lausanne, [1888], 1889).
Vail, Leroy and Landeg White, *Power and the Praise Poem: Southern African Voices in History* (Charlottesville, VA, and London, 1991).
Van Butselaar, Jan *Africains, missionnaires et colonialistes: Les origines de l'église presbytérienne du Mozambique (Mission Suisse), 1880–1896* (Leiden, 1984).
— 'The gospel and culture in nineteenth-century Mozambique', *Missiology* (1988) 16, 1.
Van Gennep, Arnold *Les Rites de Passages* (Paris, 1909).
Vautier, Edouard *La Maison des Cèdres* (Lausanne, 1948).
Vidler, Alec R. *The Church in an Age of Revolution* (Harmondsworth, 1972).
Vinet, Alexandre *Questions Ecclésiastiques* (Lausanne, 1946), preface and commentary by E. Vautier.
Vischer, Lucas et al. (eds) *Histoire du Christianisme en Suisse* (Genève, Fribourg, 1995).
Vogt, Carl *Leçons sur l'homme, sa place dans la création et dans l'histoire de la terre* (Paris, [1863], 1865).

Warhurst, Philip *Anglo-Portuguese Relations in South-Central Africa 1890–1900* (London, 1962).
Whiteside, J. *A History of the Wesleyan Methodist Church of South Africa* (London, 1906).
Warnery, H. 'Chronique romand' in *Au Foyer Romand* (Lausanne, 1895).
Webster, David *'Abafazi bathonga bafihlakala*: ethnicity and gender in a KwaZulu border community' in A. D. Spiegel and P. A. McAllister (eds), *Tradition and Transition in Southern Africa* (Johannesburg, 1989).
West, G. 'Africa and the Bible' in J. Rogerson (ed.), *The Oxford Illustrated History of the Bible* (Oxford, 2001).
Withers, Charles J. 'Geography, Natural History & the Eighteenth-Century Enlightenment: putting the world in place', *History Workshop Journal* (1995) 39, spring.
Young, Robert J. C. *Colonial Desire: Hybridity in Theory, Culture and Race* (London, 1995).
Zahan, Dominique P. Erny and M.-L. Witt, *Le feu en Afrique et thèmes annexés. Variations autour de l'oeuvre du H.A. Junod* (Paris, 1995).
Zamparoni, Valdemir 'As 'escravoas perpétuas' e o 'ensino pratico': raça, gênero e educação no Moçambique Colonial, 1910–1930', *Estudos Afro-Asiaticos* 24, 3, 2002.
Zimmer, Oliver 'In search of natural identity: alpine landscape and the econstruction of the Swiss past', *Comparative Studies in Society and History* (1998) 40.
— *A Contested Nation: History, Memory and Nationalism in Switzerland, 1761–1891* (Cambridge, 2003).
Zorn, J-F., *Le Grand siècle d'une mission protestante: la mission de Paris de 1822 à 1914* (Paris, 1993).

Unpublished Theses, Reports & Papers

Harries, Patrick 'Labour migration from Mozambique to South Africa: with special reference to the Delagoa Bay hinterland, c.1862 to 1897' (PhD., School of Oriental and African Studies, University of London, 1983).
Jeannerat, Caroline, Eric Morier-Genoud and Didier Péclard, 'Swiss Churches, Apartheid and South Africa: The Case of the Swiss Mission in South Africa' (Report to the National Research Programme 42+ of the Swiss National Science Foundation on 'Relations between Switzerland and South Africa', 2004).
Kenton, D. 'Landscape painting and the search for an indigenous ethos in South Africa' (PhD, University of Natal, Pietermaritzburg, 1989).
Krüger, Gesine 'Die Verbreitung der Schrift in Südafrika: Zur Praxis des Schreibens in alltags- und sozialgeschichtlicher Perspektive, 1830–1930' (unpublished Habilitation, University of Hanover, 2002).
Liengme, Georges 'Contribution à l'étude de l'hypnotisme et de la suggestion thérapeutique' (doctoral thesis, University of Geneva, 1890).
Liesegang, Gerhard 'Beiträge zur Geschichte des Reiches der Gaza Nguni im südlichen Moçambique, 1820-1895' (PhD, University of Cologne, 1967).
Michler, Bronwyn 'A Biographical Study of H.-A. Junod: The Fictional Dimension' (M.A., University of Pretoria, 2003).
Pienaar, Claudia 'Missionary Education in the Northern Transvaal: The Swiss Mission and Lemana, 1906–1948' (B.A. Hons thesis, University of Cape Town, 1990).
Ranger, Terence 'New approaches to African landscape' (MS 1997).
Rennie, J. K. 'Christianity, colonialism and the origins of nationalism among the Ndau of southern Rhodesia, 1890–1935' (PhD, Northwestern University, 1973).
Rich, Paul B. 'Landscape, social Darwinism and the cultural roots of South African racial ideology' (unpublished paper presented to the Centre for African Studies, University of Cape Town, 1983).
Rohrbasser, Charles 'L'oeuvre sociale de la mission suisse au Mozambique' (Mémoire de licence, faculté des lettres, université de Lausanne, 1991).
Spicher, Ariane 'La Ligue suisse pour la défense des indigènes et le nouvel esclavage (1908–1940)' (Mémoire de licence, faculté des lettres, université de Fribourg, 1990).

Index

abortion 207, 238n6
Academies, Lausanne 15, 17; Neuchâtel 22, 25-6, 126-7, 129-30, 149n19, 207, 214
Agassiz, Louis 44, 57, 125-8, 130, 142, 153n113, 234
Albasini, João (snr) 110, 121n89, 155, 162, 184; João (jnr) 200; Francisco João 147, 194, 204n72
alcohol 82, 109-10, 143, 240n55; absinthe 27, 49
Alps 10, 26, 50, 61, 97-101, 118n19, 124, 147, 183
amaTonga 162
American Board of Commissioners for Foreign Missions 87-8, 157, 163, 167, 176, 122n123, 131, 221-2
Andrade, Freire de 122n123, 131, 221-2
Anglican Church 86ff, 171, 200
anthropology 6, 206ff, 214, 249ff; evolution 208, 223, 228-32, 238n11, 242n107, 243n120, 243n123, 245n167, see also Hartland; kinship 228-30, 250-2, see *malume*; method 46, 216-19, 241n65, 241n74, see also Libombo, Viguet; physical 207-8, 214, 216-17, 236, 238n10, 240n62, see also Pittard; salvage 212, 217-28, 252, 255-7, 262; and social change 221, 250-7, 259n45, see also 'pass laws'; religion 231-2, see *Tilo*
Antioka 73, 75, 85, 90, 114-15, 171, 193, 207, 210, 224, 228
ants, see entomology
anti-slavery 19, 40-1
apartheid 262-3
Appia, Henry 129, 243n143; Louis 19
art xv, 4, 52-3, 65n106
Aryans 44
Attinger brothers 29

Bachofen, Johann 207-8, 243n122
Baker, A. W. 191
baloyi, see witchcraft

Barbey, William xv, 30n15, 130, 132, 150n35, 151n53, 153n113, 211
Barber, Mary 142, 153n111
Barroso, Antonio 89
Berlin Missionary Society 68-9, 155, 158
Basel Mission 21, 61n3, 62n21
Bastian, Adolphe 207, 219
Benoit, William 228
Berthoud, Eugènie 69, 104-5, 150n45, 156
Berthoud, Henri (snr) 21, 31n39, 32n57
Berthoud, Henri (jnr) 3, 21, 52, 69, 73, 75, 78, 101-2, 197, 207, 210, 238n9; as explorer and cartographer 71, 114-15; on language 159-64, 168-77, *174*, 178n38, 178n39, 185
Berthoud, Paul 1, 21-2, 68-70, 73-80, 84-5, 104, 113-14, 184-5, 196, 207, 254; as biologist 130, 136, 151n53; as linguist 156, 158-71, 174
Berthoud-Junod, Ruth 50, 115, 111, 130, 166, 169, 191
Bible 11, 13-14, 19, 23, 38, 113, 115, 128, 158, 165-6, 167-8, 170, 175-6, 183, 193, 201n3, 209, 238n14. See also *buku*
Biolley, Alexis 27; Emilie 1, 27, 36, 111, 211
Bleek, Wilhelm 47, 162, 179n50, 186
Boissier Herbarium xv, 130
Boissier, Pierre-Edmond 130-1
Boissier, Valérie 30n15
Boas, Franz 208, 235
Bost, Ami 10-12
botany xvi, xvii, 3, 5, 55, 98, 123-33, 137-40, 144-5, 209, 261
Bourquin, Charles 254, 258n8
Breckenridge, Keith 204n70
Bridel family 29
British and Foreign Bible Society 13, 30n14
Brookes, Edgar 247-48, 253, 255, 258n8

280

Bryce, James 101-2, 106, 140, 209-12, 238n20, 241n80
Bugnion, E. 135
buku 71, 91n11, 159-60, 165-6, 171, 178n27, 198
Buisson, Ferdinand 25, 33n71
Burtt-Davy, J. 151n68
Burckhardt, Jakob 51, 236
butterflies, see entomology
Buys, Coenrad de 110

Callaway, Henry 64n68, 223, 243n134
Calvin 11-12, 79, 183
Calvinism 11-13, 79
cannibalism 42, 63n42, 111, 207
cartography xvi, 56, 71, 113ff, 218
Casalis, Eugène 31n43, 50, 53, 202n23
Cendrars, Blaise, 52, 215
Chambers, Robert 24
charivari 16
Chatelain, Henri 3, 29, 52, 65n103
Chopi 80, 87, 111, 163; language 94n109
Christian Union 27-8
Christianity 4-5, 11-13, 19, 21, 25, 44, 49, 51, 67-91, 98, 101, 112, 123, 127-9, 144, 146, 148, 166, 184, 191-3, 221, 231-2, 246, 251-2
Church of Scotland 16, 142, 149n29
civilization: primitive 45-6, 48-9, 58, 63n65, 96-9, 100, 109-12, 125; mission and, 90, 113, 116-17; science and 144-6; unhealthy 81-2, 143, 146
clan 172, 218
Coetzee, J. M. 103
Coillard, François 18, 42, 62n21, 68, 156
Colenso, William 86, 162, 223
collections 4-5, 47, 52, 54-5, 65n103, 124-5, 130-5, 148n7, 166, 171-2, 192, 201, 206-7, 210, 214, 216, 218. See also Neuchâtel, ethnographic museum
Congo scandal 58
Conrad, Joseph 47-8, 96, 102, 224
conversion 74-7, 83-5, 92n42, 183-4, 210
Courvoisier, Fritz 27

Creationism 24, 128-9, see also Agassiz, Guyot, Darwin
Creux, Ernest 21-2, 69, 93n65, 104, 198, 207
Cust, Robert 159, 162
Cuvier, Georges 44, 126, 128

Darwin, Charles 24, 33n67, 44, 65n126, 127, 130, 140-4, 147, 152n111
Davel, Major 15, 38
Desor, Edouard 126, 206
diseases 81, 110-11, 143
Distant, W. L. 135, 141
diviners 76-7, 83, 115, 121n90, 147, 228. See also Hokoza and Libombo.
Djonga 158, 160-1, 164, 170, 176, 178n38
dreams 74, 92n43, 193
Droz, Numa 25
Druey, Henri 17
Drummond, Henry 142, 144, 153n114, 154n125
Dube, John 220
Dubied, Arthur 214; Edouard 27; Gustave 27; Marie 26-7, 211
Dunant, Henri 19
Durand, Thomas 133
Durkheim, Emile 211, 214, 220, 232, 239n39, 240n43
Du Pasquier, James 23, 26
Dutch Reformed Missionary Society 68, 155, 158
Duvoisin, Louis 18, 32n44

Earthy, Dora 163, 243n142, 258n23, 264n4
Edinburgh Missionary Conference, (1910) 213, 249
education, colonial 211-12, 236-7, 239n29, 246, 249
Eisenstein, Elizabeth 185
Elim 70, 115, 196
Ellenberger, Frédéric 3, 18, 31n43, 206
Elton, Frederick 162
Ennes, Antonio 89
entomology xvii, 55, 130-1, 133ff, 141ff, 151n72, 151n73, 209
Erskine, St. Vincent 162

eugenics 143
evolution 24, 47-8, 92n27, 126,
  131, 140-4, 153n113, 164-5, 185,
  208, 213, 217-19, 223-5, 228-35,
  242n107, 243n123, 245n167, 249,
  250-2
exhibitions 54-5, 65n117, 65n118, 217-
  18, 257

Farel, Guillaume 12
folklore 4, 47, 52, 64n68, 172, 201,
  209, 220
Forel, Auguste 31n37, 135, 139, 143,
  150n43, 154n124
forced labour 221-3, 242n95, 262
forests 107, 132, 134
Free Church of the Canton of Vaud 4,
  16-21, 29, 31notes32, 37, 38 and 39,
  247
Frazer, James 48, 212-13, 223
Freud, Sigmund 48, 215

Gaugin, Paul 53
Gaza kingdom, 80, 85, 87-8, 90, 141,
  163-4. For ChiNgoni see Ngoni,
  language
Gebuza, Thomas 90-1, 95n138
gender 13, 56-7, 76, 79, 82, 107, 220,
  234-5
Geneva 11ff
Geographical Societies 32n48, 206-
  7; of Bern 19, Geneva 19, 32n48;
  Lisbon 216; Neuchâtel 19, 206-7,
  211, 213-14, 216
geology 3, 101-2, 126-9, 150n35
Germond, Paul 18, 32n44, 103
Glardon, Auguste 18, 39, 150n35
Gluckman, Max 1-2, 261
Goba, Cetewayo 87, 200
Gobat, Samuel 23, 32n61, 37, 206
Godet, Charles-Henri 127, 149n23;
  Frédéric 23, 25, 33n71, 44, 49,
  127-8, 149n24; Georges 127, 130,
  149n24; Paul 127, 133, 149n24;
  Philippe 127, 149n24, 210
Gonin, Henri 18, 32n44
Goody, Jack 185
Gould, Stephan Jay 126
Grandjean, Arthur 27-8, 54, 79-80, 83-
  4, 114, 169, 224, 240, 240n59
Greene, Sandra 119n36
Gungunyana 71, 87-9, 147, 179n50,
  198, 210, 242n115
guns 224-6, 242n113
Guye , Henri 222, 246
Guyot, Arnold 44, 125-8, 148n16
Gwamba 5-6, 71-2, 91, 156-9, 161-5,
  172, 174, 176, 179n46, 181n114

Haddon, A. C. 53, 212
Hammond-Tooke, W. D. 2
Haekel, Ernst 143, 186
Haller, Albrecht von 98
Hanyane, 71
Hartland, E. S. 213, 223, 228
Heer, Oswald 102, 128
Hertzog, J. B. M. 247, 253
Hlengwe 158, 160, 162, 169, 178n39,
  179n56
Hofmeyr, Isabel 193
Hodler, Ferdinand 101
Hoernlé, Winifred 223, 255
Hokoza 225-9, *227*
Holene, Ruth 69, 79, 198
Hongwana, Andreas 82
Honwana, Raul 147
human sacrifice 42, 111
Humboldt, Alexandre von 44
Hunter, Monica 255
Hutt, W. H. 255

identity: Christian 82; Thonga 2, 5-
  6, 117-18, 197, 247, 256, see also
  language and identity; Swiss 97ff,
  see also Switzerland, patriotism
immorality 42-3, 47-8, 53, 57
Independent Church of Neuchâtel 22-
  7, 29, 126
Indirect Rule 223, 236-7, 249, 251, 253
infanticide 42, 111, 207
Inhambane 87-9
International Institute of African
  Languages and Cultures 236, 256
International Organisation for the
  Defence of Natives 58, 60, 215, 222
International Red Cross 19, 60

Jacottet, Edouard 3, 52, 64n68,

65n103, 103
Jacottet, Henri 26, 33n76
Jaques, Alexandre 262; Auguste 207
Javelle, Emile 50
Jeanneret, Philippe 207
Junod, Charles-Daniel 149n24, 150n35
Junod, Henri (snr) 26-7, 63n60
Junod, Henri-Alexandre *iii*, 27, 36, 49-53, 57-8, 63n60, 79-80, 83, 96-7, 102, *248*, 261; on natural history 123ff, *134*; on languages 160, 166, 170-7, *174*, 181n115, 185, 187-9, 191, 195; on anthropology 1-2, 207ff, 249-54; on polygamy 80, 231, 242n118, 251-2
Junod, Henri-Philippe 211, 222, 253-6, 259n40, 262-264n5

Kant, Immanuel 23, 127, 144, 154n130, 186, 236
Kern, Helen 1, 211, 254
Knapp, Charles 206, 240n49
knowledge: local 103, 115, 137-8, 144-5, 147, see also diviners, *nanga;* Swiss peasants 103, 138, 146-7
Koelle, Sigismund 88, 186, 202n23
Kuper, Adam 2, 149n18, 258n16

Lacroix, Alphonse-François 23, 32n61, 37
Lamarck Jean-Baptiste 126
landscape, of Switzerland 97-101; of Africa 5, 101ff, 210; views held by indigenous people 102-3, 119n36; views held by Swiss peasants 103, 119n40
language: corridor 68, 155; history 44-5, 47, 173, 179n50, 179n54, 179n69; and identity xvi, 155-6, 160, 171-3, 175-6, 190, 197, 216, 264; translation and transcription 5, 55, 87-8, 90-1, 94n109, 154n160, 156ff, 177, 178n24, 185, 216-17; language forms 44-5, 167-8, 178n38, 178n39; oral 64n73, 64n79, 166, 168, 179n69, 198-200, see also folklore and Gwamba, Hlengwe, Ngoni, Ronga, Thonga, Tonga, Tsonga; German 175; Portuguese 171, 176-7, 247, 263
Leenhardt, Maurice 64n85, 264n1
Liengme, Georges 28-9, 90, 136, 152n84, 193, 198, 210, 222, 224
Lemana college 115, 212
Lesotho 4, 14, 18, 104-6, 133, 156, 184, 247
Lesquereux, Leo 149n15
Lestrade, G.P. 168, 265n11
Lévy-Bruhl, Lucien 215, 236, 240n50,
Le Zoute, ecumenical mission conference, (1926) 251, 256, 258n17, 259n33
Liberals 15-16
Liberal Christianity 21, 25-6
Libombo, Elias Spoon 136-7, 192, 219-21, 231-2
Lovedale college 87, 90, 104, 171, 200
literacy 69, 110, 184ff; and Bible 165; in Switzerland 182-4, 189; ways of reading 190-7, 204n77; and politics 200-1

Mabille, Adolphe 3, 18, 22, 31n43, 57, 68, 103, 155, 167, 184
Machado, Joachim 114
MacMahon Award 94n102, 94n105
Macmillan, W. M. 256-7, 261
Macmillan publishers 212, 215,
Magude 69-71, 115-16, 160
Mair, Lucy 257, 259n45
Maitin, Joseph 14, 18, 31n22, 32n44
MaKoapa 156, 177n10
Makhunye, Yonas 85
Malalé, Samuel 69, 197, 247
Malan, César 12, 30n8; Major Charles 87
Malinowski, Bronislaw 215, 240n46, 253, 255, 258n25
malume, 230, 243n122, 250-1, see also anthropology, kinship
Mandela, Nelson 264n3
Mandlakazi 210
Mandlakusasa, Eliachib 69-70, 85, 191
Mandlati, Timothy 159, 160,
Mapopé, Calvin *59*, 69, 79-80, 169, 172, 241n62, 247, *248*
Mapopé, Jonas (Chihoçi) 69, 177n20, 247

283

maps 122n119, 122n123
Maputoland 82, 95n138, 137-8, 163
Mashaba, Robert Ndevu 90, 171-2, 187-8, 263-4
massinguita (revelations) 77-8
Matlanyane, Eliakim 155-6, 158, 184
Mauss, Marcel 211, 214, 220, 258n16, 264n1
Mavabaze 71
Mavilo, Isaac 82
Mbenyane, Zebedee *72*
Mbizana, Jacob 69
McKenzie, Douglas 86
meteorology 113-14, 145-6
Methodists 15, 88, 90, 171, 198, 200
Meuron, Charles-Daniel de 207
Mhalamhala, Yacob 68-71, 85, 158, 160, 169; Yosefa 68-70, *72*, 75, 77-8, 85, 158, 160-1, 169
Michaelis, Johann 187
migrant labour 68, 86, 194, 225, 237; and spread of Christianity 4-5, 82-3, 86ff, 246
mineral revolution 67-8, 86, 184
Mission (Vaudoise to 1883; Romande to 1927; then Swiss Mission) 4, 7n10, 12-14, 18, 20-2, 29, 49, 54-7, 62n21, 67-70, 73ff, 91n1. Evangelical Missionary Society of Lausanne 14; of Neuchâtel 23. Financial base 35-6, 39, 61n31, 41n4, 62n15, 63n45, 70, 91n8, 261-2; social base 4, 11ff, 27, 36; church government 12, 22, 197, 246-7, 263-4; native church 4, 73, 247, 263; hymns and songs 37, 54, 60, 63n18, 113, 116-17, 166, 189, 192, 198-9, 205n11; iconography xv, 38, 40-4, 56, 58-9, 62n15; literature 37-41, 120n78, 187, 189, 196; and primitive church 13, 73. As source of liberty 67, 81-2; wages of evangelists 84-5
Mizeki, Bernard 86
Molepo, Josias 155,
Monteiro, Rose 131, 150n50
moral reform 13, 35, 43-4, 54, 62n16, 85. See also anti-slavery, Christian Union, international organizations,
Sunday observance, Sunday schools, temperance, World Alliance of Young Men's Christian Associations
Motsikéri 196,
Mpapele, Gideon 158, 160,
Muller, Max 186
Murimi 232, 243n137, 250
music 3-4, 52, 65n101, 77, 96-7, 116-18, 210-11, 239n24. See also Mission, hymns and songs

naming practices 79, 85, 98, 103, 115-16, 123-4, 136, 153n96, 156, 177n7, 220, 229,
nanga (herbalist) 83, 138, 140, 147
natural selection, see Darwin
Neff, Felix 10, 12, 183
Neuchâtel 13, 22-9, 44-5. See also Independent Church of Neuchâtel
Neuchâtel Ethnographic Museum 52-3, 55, 61n1, 153n99, 207, 217, 241n66
Neuchâtel, Natural History Museum 127, 130, 135-7, 207
Neves, Tizora 167, 265n10
Ngoni language, ChiNgoni 163-4, 179notes50, 54 and 57, 234
Njakanjaka 70
Nkuna 160-1
Ntchoungi 228, *229*
nyaka (dark, fertile soil) 102, 118, 138
Nyam-Nyam 42, 63n42
Nyeleti Ya Mixo 168, 264n6
Nyoko, James M 87, 200

Oldham, J. H. 213, 222, 236, 251, 256, 258n25
Olivier, Juste 45, 99
ornithology 126
Ousley, Benjamin 87, 163
Overbeck, Franz 25

Pakoule 196, 204n84
palaeontology 3, 44, 47, 127-8, 173
Paris Evangelical Missionary Society (PEMS) 14, 18, 21-2, 29, 32n58, 61n3, 68, 105, 155-9, 167, 191
pass laws 236, 245n172
paternalism 19, 74, 81

Pedi 68, 155, 160-1, 164, 177n20, 184
Péringuey, Louis 135, 152n81
Perregaux, Edmond 29; Henri 3
Peters, W. C. H. 78, 162
Phelps-Stokes Commission 236, 258n20
Philafricaine Mission 29
photography 60, 108-9, 112, 218, 228-9
Piaget, Jean 149n24
Pictet, Adolphe 44
pietism 11, 24, 62n21, 127
Pilgrim's Progress 168, 193
Pittard, Eugène 214, 241n62, 254
Plakkerswet (anti-squatter law) 81, 90
Pohleni, John 87
Poungana 76
Pratt, Mary-Louise 146
Price, Sally 53
Prussia 22-3, 208

race 5, 57, 79, 81, 97, 144-5, 234-7, 245n167, 252-4, 259n30
Radcliffe-Brown, A. R. 240n48, 249-52, 258n16
rainmaking 83, 111, 147
Rambert, Eugène 50, 99
Ramseyer, Fritz 28-9, 41, 62n30, 206
Religious Tract Society of Great Britain 13, 30n14
Renan, Ernest 24, 173
revival, Christian, in Switzerland 3-4, 11, 13-15, 49, 64n84, 183; in Mozambique 4, 73-9, 88, 171; in south Africa 92n20
revival, Gothic 45, 208, 225
reverse colonization 110, 121n90
Richards, Erwin 87-9, 114, 122n119, 167, 179n50
Rikatla 70-1, 73-9, 102, 171, 184, 191, 212, 247
Ritter, Karl 125, 208, 235
Rivers, William 213, 223, 228
Robert, Samuel 129
Robertson, H. M. 255
Roman Catholic Church 89
Romanticism 3, 10, 100, 106, 125, 173, 216
Ronga 6, 7, 90, 161, 164, 169-77, 178n38, 180n99, 186, 197

Ross, Edward 222
Rougemont, Frédéric de 26, 44, 126, 131, 135
Rousseau, Jean-Jacques 50, 98, 125, 130, 149n25, 207-8, 236
Royal Anthropological Institute 216,
Rubusana, Walter 220

Saint-Imier 26, 44
Sanscrit 186
Schinz, Hans xvi, 132-3
Schlaefli-Glardon, Honoré 89, 105, 107, 114, 207
Schleiermacher, Friederich 23, 128
Seligman, Charles 213
Schapera, Isaac 215, 252-5, 257, 258n23, 259n45
Schlechter, Rudolf 133, 151n63
science and Christianity 3, 124-9, 144, 188
Schreiner, W.P. 220
Segagabane, Asser 155, 158
segregation 6, 201, 233, 237, 247-9, 253-7, 259n33, 262-3. See also Indirect Rule
sex 48, 111-12, 143, 229-31
Shangaan 181n121
Shiluvane 84, 114, 132-5, 151n68, 211-12, 236
Sikobela, Muti 89, 200, 265n10
Sioux 14
slaves and slavery 41, 71, 80, 111, 120n88, 194, 234, 262; liberated slaves 86, 88, 162; marriage as slavery 54, 81
Smith, Edwin W. 215, 223, 236, 240n45, 251-2, 256, 258notes12, 17, 20, 23, 259n25
Smuts, Jan 206, 218, 237 259n25
Smyth, Edmund 86-7
Söderblum, Nathan 231
Sonderbund 16, 20
Songele, John 68, 184
South African Association for the Advancement of Science (SAAAS) 212, 249
South Sotho 7, 156-60, 175, 178n27, 184, 191, 247
spirit possession 42, 112, 209

Stanley, H. M. 63n40
Stocking, George 63n48
Strauss, David 24
Sue, Eugène 58
Sunday schools 4, 8n15, 13, 19-20, 27-8, 30n15, 38-44, 53-4, 60, 61n1, 62n21, 62n31, 63n45, 63n47, 183
Sunday observance 19, 26
Sundkler, Bengt 56, 74
Swazi 71, 160, 163
Swiss Confederation, history of 12, 20, 22, 58, 60, 183; and image of Africa 35, 46, 48-58, 60-1; and image of past 44-7, 60-1, 247; and patriotism 20, 38, 99, 100, 132

Tekeza 162-3
Tembe-Thonga 90-1, 95n138, 179n50, 179n55
temperance 19. See also alcohol
theatrical sketches 62n16
theology 78-9, 84, 189; natural theology 124, 140
Thomas, Samuel 14, 31n39
Thomas, Eugène 71, 160, 176, 196
Thonga 6, 161-3, 166-7, 169, 172, 175-6, 181n115, 186, 197, 209-10, 211, 247
Tilo 78-80, 232-3, 243n133, 243n142
timetravel 100-102
Tlakula, Hlakamula 68-9
Tonga 88, 167, 174, 178n38, 179n47
Trimen, Roland 140-1
Tribolet, Georges de 214
Tripet, Fritz 126, 129, 131, 133
Tsonga 170, 176, 264
Tswa 6, 87, 163-4, 167, 170, 174, 176, 178n39,180n73, 181n114, 243n133, 265n11
Tuskegee system 211-12
Tylor, Edward 223

Umzila 71, 87
universities, as sources of knowledge 1, 237, 262; University of Basel 15; Cape Town 249, 252, 256; Geneva 235; Lausanne 216; Neuchâtel 214, 181n114; Witwatersrand 256, 261. Institut universitaire d'études du développement 262. See also 'academies'
Valdezia 22, 69-70, 75, 112, 114-15, 150n45, 156, 159, 203n50, 253, 259n28; *Valdezia Bulletin* 168, 264n6
Van Gennep, Arnold 214-15, 223, 239n41, 240n49
Van Warmelo, N. J. 179n54, 256
Venda 164-65
Verraux, Pierre 151n52
Viguet 214, 219
Vinet, Alexandre 15, 20-1
Viret, Pierre 12, 20
Vogt, Carl 24, 44, 57, 125, 149n17, 149n19, 234-5, 244n163
Vuilleumier, Samson 17
Voltaire 30n5

Wallace, A. R. 140, 143, 153n113
Washington, Booker T. 211
watch-making 26-8
Wilcox, William 87-8, 181n114
Willoughby, W. C. 223, 239n40
witchcraft 40, 42, 59, 83, 111, 207, 220, 250; *baloyi* (witches) 83
Wood, J. M. 133
World Alliance of Young Men's Christian Associations 19, 32n45, 60

Ximungana, Jim 71, 73, 79-80, 82, 93n54, 194, 198-9, *199*; Philemon *199*-200; Paulus *199*

Zambiki 68
Zidji 120n78, 216, 240n56, 245n172
Zionism 74, 92n27
Zola, Emile 58
zombies 83
zoology 5, 98, 145, 261
Zulu 163, 192-3

www.ingramcontent.com/pod-product-compliance
Lightning Source LLC
Chambersburg PA
CBHW031234290426

44109CB00012B/293